Microsoft Win32

Programmer's Reference

VOLUME 1

Window
Management and
Graphics Device
Interface

PUBLISHED BY
Microsoft Press
A Division of Microsoft Corporation
One Microsoft Way
Redmond, Washington 98052-6399

Library of Congress Cataloging-in-Publication Data
Microsoft Win32 programmer's reference / Microsoft Corporation.
      p.   cm.
   Includes indexes.
   Contents: v.   1. Window management and graphics device interface --
v.   2. System services, multimedia, extensions, and application
notes -- v.   3. Functions, A–G -- v.   4. Functions, H–Z -- v.
5. Messages, structures, and macros. ISBN 1-55615-515-8 (v. 1) --
ISBN 1-55615-516-6 (v. 2) -- ISBN 1-55615-517-4 (v. 3) --
ISBN 1-55615-518-2 (v. 4) -- ISBN 1-55615-519-0 (v. 5)
   1. Windows NT.   2. Computer software--Development.   3. Microsoft
Win 32.   I. Microsoft Corporation.
QA76.76.O63M524   1993
005.4'469--dc20   93-15990
                                                       CIP

Printed and bound in the United States of America.

1 2 3 4 5 6 7 8 9 AG-M 8 7 6 5 4 3

Distributed to the book trade in Canada by Macmillan of Canada, a division of Canada Publishing Corporation.

Distributed to the book trade outside the United States and Canada by Penguin Books Ltd.

Penguin Books Ltd., Harmondsworth, Middlesex, England
Penguin Books Australia Ltd., Ringwood, Victoria, Australia
Penguin Books N.Z. Ltd., 182-190 Wairau Road, Auckland 10, New Zealand

British Cataloging-in-Publication Data available.

U.S. Patent No. 4974159

Document No. PC52820-0593

Contents

Part 1   Window Management

Part 2   Graphics Device Interface

Introduction

The Microsoft ® Win32 ™ application programming interface (API) allows applications to exploit the power of 32-bits on the Microsoft® Windows™ family of operating systems. Applications written to the Win32 API are scalable on single and multiprocessor systems, and portable to RISC architectures. These manuals document the complete Win32 API including window management, graphics, file I/O, threading, memory management, security and networking.

Organization of this Manual

Following are brief descriptions of the main parts of this manual.

Part 1, "Window Management," describes the portion of the Win32 API that applications use to create and manage windows. The chapters in this part provide detailed information about windows, messages, message queues, controls, dialog boxes, and other window-management topics.

Part 2, "Graphics Device Interface," describes the portion of the Win32 API that applications use for device-independent graphics. The chapters in this part provide detailed information about device contexts, transformations, metafiles, graphics primitives, bitmaps, and other graphics-related topics.

This manual is intended to describe the purpose of the Win32 API and to explain the operating system concepts behind the API. It also shows how the Win32 functions work together to carry out specific tasks. It does not show how to write, compile, and link programs containing these functions.

About the Microsoft Win32 Programmer's Reference

The *Microsoft Win32 Programmer's Reference*, a set of five volumes, fully describes the Win32 API, including functions and related data types, macros, structures, and messages. The *Programmer's Reference* is the source for specific information about programming for Windows.

Volumes 1 and *2* describe the purpose of the functions in the Win32 API and explains the concepts and principles behind the functions. These volumes are intended for programmers who are new to Windows or who are learning parts of it for the first time. These two volumes provide the basic information needed for an understanding of Windows programming.

Volumes 3 and *4* consist of an alphabetical listing of the Win32 functions. These volumes define the details of the syntax, parameters, and return values of each function. *Volume 5* contains alphabetical listings of the Win32 data types, macros, messages, and structures. *Volumes 3* through *5* are intended for programmers already acquainted with Windows programming and who need only specifics of particular functions.

Microsoft Windows and the C Programming Language

The C programming language is the preferred development language for Windows-based applications. Many of the programming features of Windows were designed with C in mind. Windows-based applications can also be developed in other languages, but C is the most straightforward and easiest language to use to access Windows functions. For this reason, all syntax and program samples are written in the C programming language.

The Win32 API uses many types, macros, and structures that are not part of standard C language. These types, macros, and structures have been defined to make the task of creating Windows-based applications simpler and to make application sources clearer and easier to understand. All types, macros, and structures discussed in this manual are defined in the Win32 C-language header files.

Many chapters in *Volumes 1* and *2* include code examples. These examples show how to use Win32 functions to accomplish tasks. In nearly all cases, the examples are code fragments, not complete programs. Each example is intended to show the context in which a function can be used; often, an example presumes that variables, structures, and constants used in the example have been defined or initialized, or both. An example may also use comments to describe a task, without presenting the appropriate statements.

Although the examples are not complete, you can use them in your applications by taking the following steps:

- Include the WINDOWS.H file in your program.
- Define the appropriate include constants for the functions, structures, and constants used in the example.
- Define and initialize all variables.
- Replace comments that represent tasks with appropriate statements.
- Check return values for errors and take appropriate actions.

Some examples in this manual combine both Win32 and C run-time functions to carry out their tasks.

Document Conventions

The following conventions are used throughout this manual to define syntax.

Convention	Meaning
Bold text	Denotes a term or character to be typed literally, such as a predefined data type or function name (**HWND** or **CreateWindowEx**), a command, or a command-line option (**/x**). You must type these terms exactly as shown.
Italic text	Denotes a placeholder or variable: You must provide the actual value. For example, the statement **SetCursorPos**(*X, Y*) requires you to substitute values for the *X* and *Y* parameters.
[ ]	Enclose optional parameters.
I	Separates an either/or choice.
...	Specifies that the preceding item may be repeated.
.	Represents an omitted portion of a sample application.
.	
.	

In addition, certain text conventions are used to help you understand this material.

Convention	Meaning
SMALL CAPITALS	Indicate the names of keys, key sequences, and key combinations—for example, ALT+SPACEBAR.
FULL CAPITALS	Indicate filenames and paths, most type and structure names (which are also bold), and constants.
monospace	Sets off code examples and shows syntax spacing.

PART 1

Window Management

C H A P T E R   1

Windows

1.1 About Windows

A window in an application written for Microsoft ® Windows ™ is a rectangular area of the screen where the application displays output and receives input from the user. A window shares the screen with other windows, including those from other applications. Only one window at a time can receive input from the user. The user can use the mouse, keyboard, or other input device to interact with this window and the application that owns it.

Windows are the only means a Windows-based application has to interact with the user and accomplish tasks, so one of the first tasks of a Windows-based application is to create a window. This chapter describes the application programming interface (API) elements of Windows that applications use to create and use windows; manage relationships between windows; and size, move, and display windows.

1.1.1 Desktop Window

When Windows starts, it automatically creates the desktop window. The *desktop window* is a system-defined window that paints the background of the screen and serves as the base for all windows displayed by all Windows-based applications.

The desktop window uses a bitmap stored in a bitmap file (with the .BMP filename extension) to paint the background of the screen. The pattern created by the bitmap is called the *desktop wallpaper*. By default, the desktop window uses the bitmap from the file specified in the following key of the registry as the desktop wallpaper:

HKEY_CURRENT_USER\Control Panel\Desktop\Wallpaper

A system configuration application, such as Windows Control Panel, can change the desktop wallpaper by using the **SetDeskWallpaper** function to specify a different bitmap filename. **SetDeskWallpaper** loads the bitmap from the specified file, uses the bitmap to paint the background of the screen, and enters the new filename in the **Wallpaper** key of the registry. For more information about bitmaps, see Chapter 29, "Bitmaps." For more information about the registry, see Chapter 52, "Registry and Initialization Files."

1.1.2 Application Windows

Every Windows-based application creates at least one window, called the *main window* that serves as the main window for the application. This window, serves as the primary interface between the user and the application. Most applications also create many other windows, either directly or indirectly, to carry out tasks related to the main window. Each window plays a part in displaying output and receiving input from the user.

1.1.2.1 Components of an Application Window

An application window can include a title bar, a menu bar, a System menu (also called the Control menu), a minimize box, a maximize box, a sizing border, a client area, a horizontal scroll bar, and a vertical scroll bar. An application's main window typically includes all of these components. The following illustration shows these components in a typical main window.

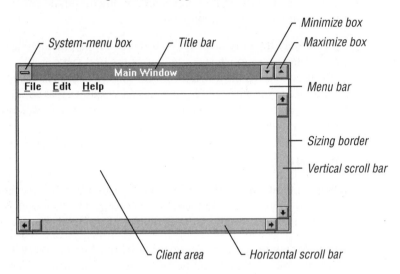

The *title bar* displays an application-defined line of text; typically, the text specifies the name of the application or indicates the purpose of the window. An application specifies the text when creating the window. The title bar also makes it possible for the user to move the window by using a mouse or other pointing device.

Most applications include a menu that lists the commands supported by the application. Items in the menu bar represent the main categories of commands. Choosing an item from the menu bar typically opens a pop-up menu whose items correspond to the tasks within a given category. By selecting a command, the user directs the application to carry out a task.

The System-menu box is a bitmap that, when clicked, displays the System menu. The System menu is a menu created and managed by Windows. It contains a standard set of menu items that, when chosen by the user, set a window's size or position, close the application, or open the Windows Task List. For more information about menus and the System menu, see Chapter 16, "Menus."

The maximize and minimize boxes are bitmaps that, when clicked, affect a window's size and position. When the user clicks the *maximize box*, Windows enlarges the window to the size of the screen and positions the window, so it covers the entire screen. At the same time, Windows replaces the maximize box with the restore box. The *restore box* is a bitmap that, when clicked, restores the window to its previous size and position.

When the user clicks the *minimize box*, Windows reduces the window to the size of an icon, positions the window at the bottom of the screen, and displays the window's icon at the position of the window. An icon is a 32- by 32-pixel bitmap that represents a window. For more information about icons, see Chapter 23, "Icons."

The *sizing border* is an area around the perimeter of the window that enables the user to size the window by using a mouse or other pointing device.

The *client area* is the part of a window where the application displays output, such as text or graphics. For example, a desktop publishing application displays the current page of a document in the client area. The application must provide a function, called a window procedure, to process input to the window and display output in the client area. For more information about window procedures, see Chapter 4, "Window Procedures."

The horizontal and vertical scroll bars convert mouse or keyboard input into values that an application uses to shift the contents of the client area either horizontally or vertically. For example, a word processing application that displays a lengthy document typically provides a vertical scroll bar to enable the user to page up and down through the document.

The title bar, menu bar, System menu, minimize and maximize boxes, sizing border, and scroll bars are referred to collectively as the window's *nonclient area*. Windows manages most aspects of the nonclient area; the application manages everything else about the window. In particular, the application manages the appearance and behavior of the client area.

1.1.2.2 Controls, Dialog Boxes, and Message Boxes

An application uses several types of windows in addition to its main window, including controls, dialog boxes, and message boxes.

A control is a window that an application uses to obtain a specific piece of information from the user, such as the name of a file to open or the desired point size of a text selection. Applications also use controls to obtain information needed to control a particular feature of an application. For example, a word processing application typically provides a control to let the user turn wordwrapping on and off. For more information about controls, see Chapter 9, "Controls," through Chapter 15, "Static Controls."

Controls are always used in conjunction with another window—typically, a dialog box. A dialog box is a window that contains one or more controls. An application uses a dialog box to prompt the user for input needed to complete a command. For example, an application that includes a command to open a file would display a dialog box that includes controls in which the user specifies a path and filename. The following illustration shows the Open dialog box and its associated controls file.

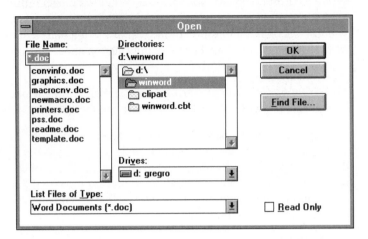

A message box is a window that displays a note, caution, or warning to the user. For example, a message box can inform the user of a problem the application has encountered while carrying out a task. The following illustration shows a message box that explains why the application, Microsoft ® Word for Windows ™ cannot complete a file-save operation.

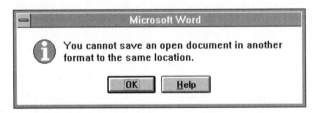

Dialog boxes and message boxes do not typically use the same set of window components as does a main window. Most have a title bar, a System menu, a border (non-sizing), and a client area, but they typically do not have a menu bar, minimize and maximize buttons, or scroll bars. For more information about dialog boxes and message boxes, see Chapter 18, "Dialog Boxes."

1.1.3 Window Creation

An application creates it main window by using the **CreateWindow** or **CreateWindowEx** function and providing information Windows needs to define the attributes of the window. The **CreateWindowEx** function has a parameter, *dwExStyle*, that the **CreateWindow** function does not have; otherwise, the functions are identical. In fact, **CreateWindow** simply calls **CreateWindowEx**, setting the *dwExStyle* parameter to zero. For this reason, the remainder of this chapter refers only to the **CreateWindowEx** function.

Windows provides additional functions—including **DialogBox**, **CreateDialog**, and **MessageBox**—for creating special-purpose windows such as dialog boxes and message boxes. For more information about these functions, see Chapter 18, "Dialog Boxes."

1.1.3.1 Window Attributes

An application must provide the following information when creating a window:

- Window class
- Window name
- Window style
- Parent or owner window
- Size
- Location
- Position
- Child-window identifier or menu handle
- Instance handle
- Creation data

These attributes are described in the following sections.

Window Class

Every window belongs to a window class. An application must register a window class before creating any windows of that class. The window class defines most aspects of a window's appearance and behavior. The chief component of a window class is the window procedure, a function that receives and processes all input and requests sent to the window. Windows provides the input and requests in the form of messages. For more information about window classes, window procedures, or messages, see Chapter 3, "Window Classes," Chapter 4, "Window Procedures," or Chapter 2, "Messages and Message Queues."

Window Name

A window can have a name. A *window name* (also called *window text*) is a text string that identifies a window for the user. A main window, dialog box, or message box typically displays its window name in its title bar, if present. For a control, the appearance of the window name depends on the control's class. A button, edit control, or static control displays its window name within the rectangle occupied by the control. A list box, combo box, or static control does not display its window name.

An application uses the **SetWindowText** function to change the window name after creating the window. It uses the **GetWindowTextLength** and **GetWindowText** functions to retrieve the current window-name text from a window.

Window Style

Every window has one or more window styles. A *window style* is a named constant that defines an aspect of the window's appearance and behavior that is not specified by the window's class. For example, the SCROLLBAR class creates a scroll bar control, but the SBS_HORZ and SBS_VERT styles determine whether a horizontal or vertical scroll bar control is created. A few window styles apply to all windows, but most apply to windows of specific window classes. Windows and, to some extent, the window procedure for the class, interpret the styles.

Parent or Owner Window

A window can have a parent window. A window that has a parent is called a *child window*. The *parent window* provides the coordinate system used for positioning a child window. Having a parent window affects aspects of a window's appearance; for example, a child window is clipped so that no part of the child window can appear outside the borders of its parent window. A window that has no parent, or whose parent is the desktop window, is called a *top-level window*. An application uses the **EnumWindows** function to obtain the handle of each of its top-level windows. **EnumWindows** passes the handle of each top-level window, in turn, to an application-defined callback function (a function called by Windows).

A window can own, or be owned by, another window. An *owned window* always appears in front of its *owner window*, is hidden when its owner window is minimized, and is destroyed when its owner window is destroyed.

Location, Size, and Position in the Z Order

Every window has a location, size, and position in the Z order. The location is the coordinates of the window's upper-left corner, relative to the upper-left corner of the screen or, in the case of a child window, the upper-left corner of the parent's client area. A window's size is its width and height measured in pixels. A window's position in the *Z order* is the position of the window in a stack of overlapping windows.

Child-Window Identifier or Menu Handle

A child window can have a *child-window identifier*, a unique application-defined value associated with the child window. Child-window identifiers are especially useful in applications that create multiple child windows. When creating a child window, an application specifies the identifier of the child window. After creating the window, the application can change the window's identifier by using the

SetWindowLong function, or it can retrieve the identifier by using the **GetWindowLong** function.

Every window, except a child window, can have a menu. An application can include a menu by providing a menu handle either when registering the window's class or when creating the window.

Instance Handle

Every Windows-based application has an instance handle associated with it. Windows provides the instance handle to an application when the application starts. Because it can run multiple copies of the same application, Windows uses instance handles internally to distinguish one instance of an application from another. The application must specify the instance handle in many different windows, including those that create windows.

Creation Data

Every window can have application-defined creation data associated with it. When the window is first created, Windows passes a pointer to the data on to the window procedure of the window being created. The window procedure uses the data to initialize application-defined variables.

1.1.3.2 Main Window Creation

Every Windows-based application must have a **WinMain** function as its entry point. The **WinMain** function performs a number of tasks, including registering the window class for the main window and creating the main window. **WinMain** registers the main window class by calling the **RegisterClass** function, and it creates the main window by calling the **CreateWindowEx** function.

Portability Issue In Windows NT, the entry point can have a name other than **WinMain**. In Windows version 3.*x*, the entry point must be named **WinMain**.

Windows does not automatically display the main window after creating it; the application must use the **ShowWindow** function to display the main window. Typically, the application's **WinMain** function calls **ShowWindow** immediately after creating the main window. **WinMain** passes two parameters to **ShowWindow**: the handle of the main window and a flag specifying whether the main window should be minimized or maximized when it is first displayed. Normally, the flag can be set to any of the constants beginning with the SW_ prefix that are defined in the Windows header files. However, when **ShowWindow** is called to display the application's main window, the flag must be set to SW_SHOWDEFAULT. This flag tells Windows to display the window as directed by the program that launched the application.

1.1.3.3 Window-Creation Messages

When creating any window, Windows sends messages to the window procedure for the window. Windows sends the WM_NCCREATE message after creating the window's nonclient area and the WM_CREATE message after creating the client area. The window procedure receives both messages before Windows displays the window. Both messages include a pointer to a **CREATESTRUCT** structure that contains all the information specified in the **CreateWindowEx** function. Typically, the window procedure performs initialization tasks upon receiving these messages.

When creating a child window, Windows sends the WM_PARENTNOTIFY message to the parent window after sending the WM_NCCREATE and WM_CREATE messages. It also sends other messages while creating a window. The number and order of these messages depend on the window class and style and on the function used to create the window. These messages are described in the remaining sections of this chapter and in other chapters of this book.

1.1.3.4 Multithread Applications

A Windows NT application can have multiple threads of execution, and each thread can create windows. An application can use the **EnumThreadWindows** function to enumerate the windows created by a particular thread. This function passes the handle of each thread window, in turn, to an application-defined callback function. The **GetWindowThreadProcessId** function returns the identifier of the thread that created a particular window.

1.1.4 Window Handles

After creating a window, the creation function returns a *window handle* that uniquely identifies the window. An application uses this handle in other functions to direct their actions to the window. A window handle has the **HWND** data type; an application must use this type when declaring a variable that holds a window handle.

Windows includes several special constants that can replace a window handle in certain functions. These constants begin with the HWND_ prefix. For example, an application can use the HWND_TOP or HWND_BOTTOM constant in the **SetWindowPos** function to move a window to the top or bottom of the Z order.

Although the NULL constant is not a window handle, an application can use it in some functions to specify that no window is affected. For example, specifying NULL for the **CreateWindowEx** function's *hwndParent* parameter creates a window that has no parent or owner. Some functions may return NULL instead of a handle, indicating that the given action applies to no window.

An application can use the **FindWindow** function to discover whether a window with the specified class name or window name exists in the system. If such a window exists, **FindWindow** returns the handle of the window. The **IsWindow** function determines whether a window handle identifies a valid, existing window.

1.1.5 Window Styles

Windows provides general window styles and class-specific window styles. The general windows styles are constants that begin with the WS_ prefix; they can be combined to form different types of windows, including main windows, dialog boxes, and child windows. The class-specific window styles define the appearance and behavior of windows belonging to the predefined control classes such as edit controls and list boxes. This section describes the general window styles. For information about class-specific window styles, see Chapter 10, "Buttons," through Chapter 15, "Static Controls."

An application usually sets a window's styles when creating the window. It can also set the styles after creating the window by using the **SetWindowLong** function.

1.1.5.1 Overlapped Window

An *overlapped window* is a top-level window that has a title bar, border, and client area; it is meant to serve as an application's main window. It can also have a System menu, minimize and maximize boxes, and scroll bars. An overlapped window used as a main window typically includes all of these components.

An application creates an overlapped window by specifying the WS_OVERLAPPED or WS_OVERLAPPEDWINDOW style in the **CreateWindowEx** function. An overlapped window created with the WS_OVERLAPPED style has a title bar and border. The WS_OVERLAPPEDWINDOW style creates an overlapped window with a title bar, sizing border, System menu, and minimize and maximize boxes.

1.1.5.2 Pop-up Window

A *pop-up window* is a special type of overlapped window typically used for dialog boxes, message boxes, and other temporary windows that appear outside an application's main window. A title bar is optional for a pop-up window; otherwise, a pop-up window is the same as an overlapped window created with the WS_OVERLAPPED style.

An application creates a pop-up window by specifying the WS_POPUP style in the **CreateWindowEx** function. To include a title bar, the WS_CAPTION style must also be specified. An application can use the WS_POPUPWINDOW style to create a pop-up window that has a border and a System menu. The

WS_CAPTION style must be combined with the WS_POPUPWINDOW style to make the System menu visible.

1.1.5.3 Child Window

A child window has the WS_CHILD style and is confined to the client area of its parent window. An application typically uses child windows to divide the client area of a parent window into functional areas. An application creates a child window by specifying the WS_CHILD style in the **CreateWindowEx** function.

A child window must have a parent window. The parent window can be an overlapped window, a pop-up window, or even another child window. An application specifies the parent window when it calls the **CreateWindowEx** function. If the application specifies the WS_CHILD style in the **CreateWindowEx** function but does not specify a parent window, Windows does not create the window.

A child window has a client area, but it does not have any other features unless they are explicitly requested. An application can request a title bar, a System menu, minimize and maximize boxes, a border, and scroll bars for a child window, but a child window cannot have a menu. If the application specifies a menu handle, either when it registers the child's window class or creates the child window, the menu handle is ignored.

Positioning

Windows always positions the child window relative to the upper-left corner of the parent window's client area. No part of a child window ever appears outside the borders of its parent window. If an application creates a child window that is larger than the parent window or positions a child window so that some or all of the child window extends beyond the borders of the parent, Windows clips the child window; that is, the portion outside the parent window's client area is not displayed. Actions that affect the parent window can also affect the child window, as follows.

Parent window	Child window
Destroyed	Destroyed before the parent window is destroyed.
Hidden	Hidden before the parent window is hidden. A child window is visible only when the parent window is visible.
Moved	Moved with the parent window's client area. The child window is responsible for painting its client area after the move.
Shown	Shown after the parent window is shown.

Clipping

Windows does not automatically clip a child window from the parent window's client area. This means the parent window draws over the child window if it carries out any drawing in the same location as the child window. Windows does, however, clip the child window from the parent window's client area if the parent window has the WS_CLIPCHILDREN style. If the child window is clipped, the parent window cannot draw over it.

A child window can overlap other child windows in the same client area. A child window that shares the same parent window as one or more other child windows is called a *sibling window*. Sibling windows can draw in each other's client area, unless one of the child windows has the WS_CLIPSIBLINGS style. If the application specifies this style for a child window, any portion of the child's sibling window that lies within this window is clipped.

If a window has either the WS_CLIPCHILDREN or WS_CLIPSIBLINGS style, a slight loss in performance occurs. Each window takes up system resources, so an application should not use child windows indiscriminately. For optimum performance, an application that needs to logically divide its main window should do so in the window procedure of the main window rather than by using child windows.

Relationship to Parent Window

An application can change the parent window of an existing child window by calling the **SetParent** function. In this case, Windows removes the child window from the client area of the old parent window and moves it to the client area of the new parent window. If **SetParent** specifies a NULL handle, the desktop window becomes the new parent window. In this case, the child window is drawn on the desktop, outside the borders of any other window. The **GetParent** function retrieves the handle of a child window's parent window.

The parent window relinquishes a portion of its client area to a child window, and the child window receives all input from this area. The window class need not be the same for each of the child windows of the parent window. This means that an application can fill a parent window with child windows that look different and carry out different tasks. For example, a dialog box can contain many types of controls; each control is a child window that accepts a different type of data from the user.

A child window has only one parent window, but a parent can have any number of child windows. Each child window, in turn, can have child windows. In this chain of windows, each child window is called a descendant window of the original parent window. An application uses the **IsChild** function to discover whether a given window is a child window or a descendant window of a given parent window.

The **EnumChildWindows** function enumerates the child windows of a parent window. Then **EnumChildWindows** passes the handle of each child window to an application-defined callback function. Descendant windows of the given parent window are also enumerated.

Messages

Windows passes a child window's input messages directly to the child window; the messages are not passed through the parent window. The only exception is if the child window has been disabled by the **EnableWindow** function. In this case, Windows passes any input messages that would have gone to the child window to the parent window instead. This permits the parent window to examine the input messages and enable the child window, if necessary.

A child window can have a unique integer identifier. Child window identifiers are important when working with control windows. An application directs a control's activity by sending it messages. The application uses the control's child window identifier to direct the messages to the control. In addition, a control sends notification messages to its parent window. A notification message includes the control's child window identifier, the parent window used by to identify the source of the message. An application specifies the child-window identifier for other types of child windows by setting the *hmenu* parameter of the **CreateWindowEx** function to a value rather than a menu handle.

1.1.5.4 Window Border

Windows provides the following border style.

Style	Description
WS_BORDER	Creates a window with a thin-line border.
WS_DLGFRAME	Creates a window with a double border, a style typically used with dialog boxes. A window with this style cannot have a title bar.
WS_EX_DLGMODALFRAME	Creates a window with a double border. Unlike the WS_DLGFRAME style, an application can also specify the WS_CAPTION style to create a title bar for the window.
WS_THICKFRAME	Creates a window with a sizing border.

A window with the WS_OVERLAPPED or WS_POPUPWINDOW style has the WS_BORDER style by default. One of the other border styles must be combined with the WS_OVERLAPPED or WS_POPUPWINDOW style to give an overlapped window a different border style.

If no border style is specified for a window with the WS_POPUP or WS_CHILD style, the system creates a borderless window. An application can use borderless child windows to divide the parent window's client area while keeping the divisions invisible to the user.

1.1.5.5 Nonclient-Area Components

The nonclient area of a window can include a title bar, System menu, minimize and maximize boxes, sizing border, and horizontal and vertical scroll bars. An application can create a window with one or more of these components by specifying the following styles in the **CreateWindowEx** function.

Style	Description
WS_CAPTION	Creates a window that has a title bar (includes the WS_BORDER style).
WS_HSCROLL	Creates a window that has a horizontal scroll bar.
WS_MAXIMIZEBOX	Creates a window that has a maximize box.
WS_MINIMIZEBOX	Creates a window that has a minimize box.
WS_SYSMENU	Creates a window that has a System-menu box in its title bar. The WS_CAPTION style must also be specified.
WS_VSCROLL	Creates a window that has a vertical scroll bar.

1.1.5.6 Initial State

The following styles determine whether a window is enabled or disabled, visible or invisible, and minimized or maximized.

Style	Description
WS_DISABLED	Creates a window that is initially disabled. A disabled window cannot receive input from the user.
WS_MAXIMIZE	Creates a window that is initially maximized.
WS_MINIMIZE	Creates a window that is initially minimized.
WS_VISIBLE	Creates a window that is initially visible.

1.1.5.7 Parent and Child Styles

The following styles affect the clipping relationship between a parent window and its child windows and between a child window and its sibling windows.

Style	Description
WS_CLIPCHILDREN	Excludes the area occupied by child windows when drawing within the parent window. Use this style when creating the parent window.

| WS_CLIPSIBLINGS | Clips child windows relative to each other; that is, when a particular child window receives a WM_PAINT message, the WS_CLIPSIBLINGS style clips all other overlapping child windows out of the region of the child window to be updated. If WS_CLIPSIBLINGS is not specified and child windows overlap, it is possible, when drawing within the client area of one child window, to draw within the client area of another neighboring child window. Use this style with the WS_CHILD style only. |

1.1.5.8 Dialog Box Styles

A dialog box includes a built-in keyboard interface that processes the direction and TAB keys. The user can use these keys instead of the mouse to navigate among the controls in the dialog box. The following styles affect how the built-in keyboard interface processes the direction and TAB keys.

Style	Description
WS_GROUP	Specifies the first control of a group of controls. The user can change the keyboard focus from one control in the group to the next by using the direction keys. All controls defined with the WS_GROUP style after the first control belong to the same group. The next control with the WS_GROUP style ends the group and starts the next group.
WS_TABSTOP	Specifies a control that can receive the keyboard focus when the user presses the TAB key. Pressing the TAB key changes the keyboard focus to the next control that has the WS_TABSTOP style.

1.1.5.9 Extended Styles

The following styles can be specified in the *dwExStyle* parameter of the **CreateWindowEx** function.

Style	Description
WS_EX_ACCEPTFILES	Specifies that a window created with this style accepts drag-drop files. For more information about drag-drop files, see Chapter 78, "Shell Library."
WS_EX_DLGMODALFRAME	Creates a window with a double border. Unlike the WS_DLGFRAME style, an application can also specify the WS_CAPTION style to create a title bar for the window.
WS_EX_NOPARENTNOTIFY	Specifies that a child window created with this style will not send the WM_PARENTNOTIFY message to its parent window when either created or destroyed.

WS_EX_TOPMOST   Specifies that a window created with this style should be placed above all non-topmost windows and stay above them even when the window is deactivated.

1.1.6 Owned Windows

An overlapped or pop-up window can be owned by another overlapped or pop-up window. Being owned places several constraints on a window.

- An owned window is always above its owner in the Z order.
- Windows automatically destroys an owned window when its owner is destroyed.
- An owned window is hidden when its owner is minimized.

Only an overlapped or pop-up window can be an owner window; a child window cannot be one. An application creates an owned window by specifying the owner's window handle as the *hwndParent* parameter of the **CreateWindowEx** function when it creates a window with the WS_OVERLAPPED or WS_POPUP style. The *hwndParent* parameter must identify an overlapped or pop-up window. If *hwndParent* identifies a child window, Windows assigns ownership to the top-level parent window of the child window. After creating an owned window, an application cannot transfer ownership of the window to another window.

Dialog boxes and message boxes are owned windows by default. An application specifies the owner window when calling a function that creates a dialog box or message box.

An application can use the **GetWindow** function with the GW_OWNER flag to retrieve the handle of a window's owner.

1.1.7 Disabled Windows

A window can be disabled. A *disabled window* receives no keyboard or mouse input, but it can receive messages from other windows, from other applications, and from Windows. An application typically disables a window to prevent the user from using the window. For example, an application may disable a push button in a dialog box to prevent the user from choosing it. An application can enable a disabled window at any time; enabling a window restores normal input.

By default, a window is enabled when created. An application can specify the WS_DISABLED style, however, to disable a new window. An application enables or disables an existing window by using the **EnableWindow** function. Windows sends a WM_ENABLE message to a window when its enabled state is about to change. An application can determine whether a window is enabled by using the **IsWindowEnabled** function.

When a child window is disabled, Windows passes the child's mouse input messages to the parent window. The parent uses the messages to determine whether to enable the child window. For more information about mouse input, see Chapter 6, "Mouse Input."

Only one window at a time can receive keyboard input; that window is said to have the keyboard focus. If an application uses the **EnableWindow** function to disable a keyboard-focus window, the window loses the keyboard focus in addition to being disabled. **EnableWindow** then sets the keyboard focus to NULL, meaning no window has the focus. If a child window or other descendant window has the keyboard focus, the descendant window loses the focus when the parent window is disabled. For more information about the keyboard focus, see Chapter 5, "Keyboard Input."

1.1.8 Foreground and Background Windows

In Windows NT, each process can have multiple threads of execution, and each thread can create windows. The thread that created the window with which the user is currently working is called the foreground thread, and the window is called the *foreground window*. All other threads are background threads, and the windows created by background threads are called *background windows*.

Each thread has a priority level that determines the amount of CPU time the thread receives. Although an application can set the priority level of its threads, normally the foreground thread has a slightly higher priority level than the background threads. Because it has a higher priority, the foreground thread receives more CPU time than the background threads. The foreground thread has a normal base priority of 9; a background thread has a normal base priority of 7.

The user sets the foreground window by clicking a window or by using the ALT+TAB or ALT+ESC key combination. An application sets the foreground window by using the **SetForegroundWindow** function. If the new foreground window is a top-level window, Windows activates it; otherwise, Windows activates the associated top-level window. An application retrieves the handle of the foreground window by using the **GetForegroundWindow** function.

1.1.9 Show State

At any one given time, a window may be active or inactive; hidden or visible; and minimized, maximized, or restored. These qualities are referred to collectively as the window's *show state*.

1.1.9.1 Active Window

An *active window* is the top-level window of the application with which the user is currently working. To allow the user to easily identify the active window, Windows places it at the top of the Z order and changes the color of its title bar and border to the system-defined active window colors. Only a top-level window can be an active window. When the user is working with a child window, Windows activates the top-level parent window associated with the child window.

Only one top-level window in the system is active at any particular time. The user activates a top-level window by clicking it (or one of its child windows) or by using the ALT+ESC or ALT+TAB key combination. An application activates a top-level window by calling the **SetActiveWindow** function. A number of other functions can cause Windows to activate a different top-level window, including **SetWindowPos**, **DeferWindowPos**, **SetWindowPlacement**, and **DestroyWindow**. Although an application can activate a different top-level window at any time, to avoid confusing the user, it should do so only in response to a user action. An application uses the **GetActiveWindow** function to retrieve the handle of the active window.

When the activation changes from a top-level window of one application to the top-level window of another, Windows sends both applications the WM_ACTIVATEAPP message notifying them of the change. When the activation changes to a different top-level window in the same application, Windows sends the WM_ACTIVE message to both windows.

1.1.9.2 Visibility

A window can be either visible or hidden. Windows displays a *visible window* on the screen. It hides a *hidden window* by not drawing it. If a window is visible, the user can supply input to the window and view the window's output. If a window is hidden, it is effectively disabled. A hidden window can process messages from Windows or from other windows, but it cannot process input from the user or display output. An application sets a window's visibility state when creating the window. Later, the application can change the visibility state.

A window is visible when the WS_VISIBLE style is set for the window. By default, the **CreateWindowEx** function creates a hidden window unless the application specifies the WS_VISIBLE style. Typically, an application sets the WS_VISIBLE style after it has created a window to keep details of the creation process hidden from the user. For example, an application may keep a new window hidden while it customizes the window's appearance. If the WS_VISIBLE style is specified in the **CreateWindowEx** function, Windows sends the WM_SHOWWINDOW message to the window after creating the window, but before displaying it.

An application can determine whether a window is visible by using the **IsWindowVisible** function. An application can show (make visible) or hide a window by using the **ShowWindow**, **SetWindowPos**, **DeferWindowPos**, or **SetWindowPosition** function. These functions show or hide a window by setting or removing the WS_VISIBLE style for the window. They also send the WM_SHOWWINDOW message to the window before showing or hiding it.

When an owner window is minimized, Windows automatically hides the associated owned windows. Likewise, when an owner window is restored, Window automatically shows the associated owned windows. In both cases, Windows sends the WM_SHOWWINDOW message to the owned windows before hiding or showing them. Occasionally, an application may need to hide the owned windows without having to minimize or hide the owner. In this case, the application uses the **ShowOwnedPopups** function. This function sets or removes the WS_VISIBLE style for all owned windows and sends the WM_SHOWWINDOW message to the owned windows before hiding or showing them. Hiding an owner window has no effect on the visibility state of the owned windows.

When a parent window is visible, its associated child windows are also visible. Likewise, when the parent window is hidden, its child windows are also hidden. Minimizing the parent window has no effect on the visibility state of the child windows; that is, the child windows are minimized along with the parent, but the WS_VISIBLE style is not changed.

Even if a window has the WS_VISIBLE style, the user may not be able to see the window on the screen; other windows may completely overlap it or it may have been moved beyond the edge of the screen. Also, a visible child window is subject to the clipping rules established by its parent-child relationship. If the window's parent window is not visible, it will also not be visible. Because a child window is drawn relative to the parent's upper-left corner, if the parent window moves beyond the edge of the screen, the child window also moves. For example, a user may move the parent window containing the child window far enough off the edge of the screen that the user may not be able to see the child window, even though the child window and its parent window both have the WS_VISIBLE style.

1.1.9.3 Minimized, Maximized, and Restored Windows

A *maximized window* is a window that has the WS_MAXIMIZED style. By default, Windows enlarges a maximized window so that it fills the screen or, in the case of a child window, the parent window's client area. Although a window's size can be set to the same size of a maximized window, a maximized window is slightly different. Windows automatically moves the window's title bar to the top of the screen or to the top of the parent window's client area. Also, Windows disables the window's sizing border and the window-positioning capability of the title bar (so that the user can not move the window by dragging the title bar).

A *minimized window* is a window that has the WS_MINIMIZED style. By default, Windows reduces a minimized window to the size of an icon and moves the minimized window to the lower part of the screen or the lower part of the parent window's client area. The lower part of the screen or client area is sometimes called the icon area. Windows moves a minimized window into the first available position in the icon area, unless the application specifies another position. A *restored window* is a window that has been returned to its pre-minimized or pre-maximized size and position.

If an application specifies the WS_MAXIMIZED or WS_MINIMIZED style in the **CreateWindowEx** function, the window is initially maximized or minimized. After creating a window, an application can use the **CloseWindow** function to minimize the window. The **ArrangeIconicWindows** function arranges the application's minimized top-level windows along the bottom of the screen, or it arranges a parent window's minimized child windows along the bottom of the parent window.

The **ShowWindow** function can minimize, maximize, or restore a window. At the same time it can set the window's visibility and activation states. The **SetWindowPlacement** function includes the same functionality as **ShowWindow**, but it can also override the window's default minimized, maximized, and restored positions.

The **IsZoomed** function determines whether a given window is maximized, and the **IsIconic** function determines whether a given window is minimized. The **GetWindowPlacement** function retrieves the minimized, maximized, and restored positions for the window, and it also determines the window's show state.

When Windows receives a command to maximize or restore a minimized window, Windows sends the window a WM_QUERYOPEN message. If the window procedure returns FALSE, Windows ignores the maximize or restore command.

Windows automatically sets the size and position of a maximized window to the system-defined defaults for a maximized window. An application can override these defaults by using the **SetWindowPlacement** function or by processing the WM_GETMINMAXINFO message that is received by a window when Windows is about to maximize the window. The message includes a pointer to a **MINMAXINFO** structure containing values Windows uses to set the maximized size and position. Replacing these values overrides the defaults.

1.1.10 Size and Position

A window's size and position are expressed as a bounding rectangle, given in coordinates relative to the screen or the parent window. The coordinates of a top-level window are relative to the upper-left corner of the screen; the coordinates of a child window are relative to the upper-left corner of the parent window. An application specifies a window's initial size and position when it creates the window, but it can change the window's size and position at any time.

1.1.10.1 Size

A window's size (width and height) is given in pixels. A window can have zero width or height. If an application sets a window's width and height to zero, Windows sets the size to the default minimum window size. To discover the default minimum window size, an application uses the **GetSystemMetrics** function with the SM_CXMIN and SM_CYMIN flags.

An application may need to create a window with a client area of a particular size. The **AdjustWindowRect** and **AdjustWindowRectEx** functions calculate the required size of a window based on the desired size of the client area. The application can pass the resulting size values to the **CreateWindowEx** function.

An application can size a window so that it is extremely large; however, it should not size a window so that it is larger than the screen. Before setting a window's size, the application should check the width and height of the screen by using the **GetSystemMetrics** function with the SM_CXSCREEN and SM_CYSCREEN flags.

1.1.10.2 Position

A window's position is defined as the coordinates of its upper-left corner. These coordinates, sometimes called window coordinates, are always relative to the upper-left corner of the screen or, for a child window, the upper-left corner of the parent window's client area. For example, a top-level window having the coordinates (10,10) is placed 10 pixels to the right of the upper-left corner of the screen and 10 pixels down from it. A child window having the coordinates (10,10) is placed 10 pixels to the right of the upper-left corner of its parent window's client area and 10 pixels down from it.

The **WindowFromPoint** function retrieves the handle of the window occupying a particular point on the screen. The **ChildWindowFromPoint** function retrieves the handle of the child window occupying a particular point in the parent window's client area.

1.1.10.3 Default Size and Position

An application can allow Windows to calculate the initial size or position of a top-level window by specifying the CW_USEDEFAULT constant in the **CreateWindowEx** function. If the application sets the window's coordinates to CW_USEDEFAULT and the application has created no other top-level windows, Windows sets the new window's position relative to the upper-left corner of the screen; otherwise, Windows sets the position relative to the position of the top-level window that the application created most recently. Similarly, if the width and height parameters are set to CW_USEDEFAULT, Windows calculates the size of the new window. If the application has created other top-level windows, Windows bases the size of the new window on the size of the application's most recently created top-level window. Specifying CW_USEDEFAULT when creating a child or pop-up window causes Windows to set the window's size to the default minimum window size.

1.1.10.4 Tracking Size

Windows maintains a minimum and maximum tracking size for a window of the WS_THICKFRAME style; a window with this style has a sizing border. The *minimum tracking size* is the smallest window size the user can produce by dragging the window's sizing border. Likewise, the *maximum tracking size* is the largest window size the user can produce by dragging the sizing border.

A window's minimum and maximum tracking sizes are set to system-defined default values when Windows creates the window. An application can discover the defaults and override them by processing the WM_GETMINMAXINFO message. For more information about this message, see Section 1.1.10.8, "Size and Position Messages."

1.1.10.5 System Commands

An application that has a window with a System menu can change the size and position of that window by sending system commands. System commands are generated when the user chooses commands from the System menu. An application can emulate the user action by sending a WM_SYSCOMMAND message to the window. The following system commands affect the size and position of a window.

Command	Description
SC_CLOSE	Closes the window. This command sends a WM_CLOSE message to the window. The window carries out any steps needed to clean up and destroy itself.
SC_MAXIMIZE	Maximizes the window.
SC_MINIMIZE	Minimizes the window.
SC_RESTORE	Restores a minimized or maximized window to its previous size and position.
SC_SIZE	Starts a size command. The user can change the size of the window by using the mouse or keyboard.

1.1.10.6 Z Order

The Z order of a window indicates the window's position in a stack of overlapping windows. This window stack is oriented along an imaginary axis, the z-axis, extending outward from the screen. The window at the top of the Z order overlaps all other windows. The window at the bottom of the Z order is overlapped by all other windows. An application sets a window's position in the Z order by placing it behind a given window, or at the top or bottom of the stack.

Windows maintains three separate Z orders—one for top-level windows, one for sibling windows, and one for topmost windows. A *topmost window* overlaps all other non-topmost windows, regardless of whether it is the active or foreground window. An application creates a topmost window by assigning it the WS_EX_TOPMOST style.

By default, Windows puts a window at the top of the Z order when creating the window. The user changes the Z order by activating a different window; Windows always positions the active window at the top of the Z order. An application uses the **BringWindowToTop** function to bring a window to the top of the Z order. It can rearrange the Z order by using the **SetWindowPos** or **DeferWindowPos** function.

1.1.10.7 Size and Position Functions

After creating a window, an application can set the window's size or position by calling one of a several different functions, including **MoveWindow**, **SetWindowPos**, **DeferWindowPos**, and **SetWindowPlacement**. The **MoveWindow** and **SetWindowPos** functions are similar; both set the size or position of a single application window. The **SetWindowPos** function includes a set of flags that affect the window's show state; **MoveWindow** does not include these flags. The **BeginDeferWindowPos**, **DeferWindowPos**, and **EndDeferWindowPos** functions are used together to set the size, position, position in the Z order, and show state of a number of windows simultaneously. The **SetWindowPlacement** function sets a window's minimized position, maximized position, restored size and position, and show state.

An application can retrieve the coordinates of a window's bounding rectangle by using the **GetWindowRect** function. **GetWindowRect** fills a **RECT** structure with the coordinates of the window's upper-left and lower-right corners. The coordinates are relative to the upper-left corner of the screen, even for a child window. The **ScreenToClient** or **MapWindowPoints** function maps the screen coordinates of a child window's bounding rectangle to coordinates relative to the parent window's client area.

The **GetClientRect** function retrieves the coordinates of a window's client area. **GetClientRect** fills a **RECT** structure with the coordinates of the upper-left and lower-right corners of the client area, but the coordinates are relative to the client area itself. This means the coordinates of a client area's upper-left corner are always (0,0), and the coordinates of the lower-right corner are the width and height of the client area.

1.1.10.8 Size and Position Messages

Windows sends the WM_GETMINMAXINFO message to a window whose size or position is about to change. For example, WM_GETMINMAXINFO is sent when the user chooses the Move or Size command from the System menu or

clicks the sizing border or title bar, or when an application calls the
SetWindowPos function to move or size the window. The
WM_GETMINMAXINFO message includes a pointer to a **MINMAXINFO**
structure containing the default maximized size and position for the window, and
the default minimum and maximum tracking sizes for the window. An application
can override these defaults by processing the WM_GETMINMAX message and
setting the appropriate members of the **MINMAXINFO** structure. A window
must have the WS_THICKFRAME or WS_CAPTION style to receive the
WM_GETMINMAXINFO message. A window with the WS_THICKFRAME
style receives this message during the window-creation process, as well as when it
is being moved or sized.

Windows sends the WM_WINDOWPOSCHANGING message to a window
whose size, position, position in the Z order, or show state is about to change.
This message includes a pointer to a **WINDOWPOS** structure that specifies the
window's new size, position, position in the Z order, and show state. By setting
the members of the **WINDOWPOS** structure, an application can affect the
window's new size, position, and appearance.

After changing a window's size, position, position in the Z order, or show state,
Windows sends the WM_WINDOWPOSCHANGED message to the window.
This message includes a pointer to a **WINDOWPOS** structure that informs the
window of its new size, position, position in the Z order, and show state. Setting
the members of the **WINDOWPOS** structure that is passed with the
WM_WINDOWPOSCHANGED message has no effect on the window. A
window that must process WM_SIZE and WM_MOVE messages must pass the
WM_WINDOWPOSCHANGED message to the **DefWindowProc** function;
otherwise, Windows does not send WM_SIZE and WM_MOVE messages to the
window.

Windows sends the WM_NCCALCSIZE message to a window when the window
is created or sized. Windows uses the message to calculate the size of a window's
client area and the position of the client area relative to the upper-left corner of
the window. A window typically passes this message to the default window
procedure; however, this message can be useful in applications that customize a
window's nonclient area or preserve portions of the client area when the window
is sized. For more information, see Chapter 20, "Painting and Drawing."

1.1.11 Window Destruction

In general, an application must destroy all the windows it creates. It does this by
using the **DestroyWindow** function. When a window is destroyed, the system
hides the window, if it is visible, and then it removes any internal data associated
with the window. This invalidates the window handle; it can no longer be used by
the application.

An application destroys many of the windows it creates soon after creating them. For example, an application usually destroys a dialog box window as soon as the application has sufficient input from the user to continue its task. An application eventually destroys the main window of the application (before terminating).

Before destroying a window, an application should save or remove any data associated with the window, and it should release any system resources allocated for the window. If the application does not release the resources, Windows will free any resources not freed by the application.

Destroying a window does not affect the window class from which the window is created. New windows can still be created using that class, and any existing windows of that class continue to operate.

Destroying a window also destroys the window's descendant windows. The **DestroyWindow** function sends a WM_DESTROY message first to the window, then to its child windows and descendant window. In this way, all descendant windows of the window being destroyed are also destroyed.

A window with a System menu receives a WM_CLOSE message when the user chooses Close from the System menu. By processing this message, an application can prompt the user for confirmation before destroying the window. If the user confirms that the window should be destroyed, the application can call the **DestroyWindow** function to destroy the window.

If the window being destroyed is the active window, both the active and focus states are transferred to another window. The window that becomes the active window is the next window, as determined by the ALT+ESC key combination. The new active window then determines which window receives the keyboard focus.

1.2 Using Windows

The following sections explain how to create and use windows in an application, how to manage parent-child window relationships, and how to move and size windows.

1.2.1 Creating a Main Window

The first window an application creates is typically the main window. You create the main window by using the **CreateWindowEx** function, specifying the window class, window name, window styles, size, position, menu handle, instance handle, and creation data. A main window belongs to an application-defined window class, so you must register the window class and provide a window procedure for the class before creating the main window.

Most applications typically use the WS_OVERLAPPEDWINDOW style to create the main window. This style gives the window a title bar, a System menu, a sizing border, and minimize and maximize boxes. The **CreateWindowEx** function returns a handle that uniquely identifies the window.

The following example creates a main window belonging to an application-defined window class. The window name, "Main Window", will appear in the window's title bar. By combining the WS_VSCROLL and WS_HSCROLL styles with the WS_OVERLAPPEDWINDOW style, the application creates a main window with horizontal and vertical scroll bars in addition to the components provided by the WS_OVERLAPPED WINDOW style. The four occurrences of the CW_USEDEFAULT constant set the initial size and position of the window to the system-defined default values. Specifying NULL instead of a menu handle means the window will have the menu defined for the window class.

```
HINSTANCE hinst;
HWND hwndMain;

.
. /* Register the window class for the main window. */
.


/* Create the main window. */

hwndMain = CreateWindowEx(
    0,                         /* no extended styles         */
    "MainWClass",              /* class name                 */
    "Main Window",             /* window name                */
    WS_OVERLAPPEDWINDOW |      /* overlapped window          */
        WS_HSCROLL |           /* horizontal scroll bar      */
        WS_VSCROLL,            /* vertical scroll bar        */
    CW_USEDEFAULT,             /* default horizontal position */
    CW_USEDEFAULT,             /* default vertical position  */
    CW_USEDEFAULT,             /* default width              */
    CW_USEDEFAULT,             /* default height             */
    (HWND) NULL,               /* no parent or owner window  */
    (HMENU) NULL,              /* class menu used            */
    hinstance,                 /* instance handle            */
    NULL);                     /* no window creation data    */

if (!hwndMain)
    return FALSE;

/*
 * Show the window using the flag specified by the program
 * that launched the application, and send the application
 * a WM_PAINT message.
 */

ShowWindow(hwndMain, SW_SHOWDEFAULT);
```

```
UpdateWindow(hwndMain);

.
. /* Start the message loop for the application. */
.
```

Notice that the preceding example calls the **ShowWindow** function after creating the main window. This is done because Windows does not automatically display the main window after creating it. By passing the SW_SHOWDEFAULT flag to **ShowWindow**, the application allows the program that launched the application to set the initial show state of the main window. The **UpdateWindow** function sends the window its first WM_PAINT message.

1.2.2 Creating, Enumerating, and Sizing Child Windows

You can divide a window's client area into different functional areas by using child windows. Creating a child window is like creating a main window—you use the **CreateWindowEx** function. To create a window of an application-defined window class, you must register the window class and provide a window procedure before creating the child window. You must give the child window the WS_CHILD style and specify a parent window for the child window when you create it.

The following example divides the client area of an application's main window into three functional areas by creating three child windows of equal size. Each child window is the same height as the main window's client area, but is each one-third its width. The main window creates the child windows in response to the WM_CREATE message, which the main window receives during its own window-creation process. Because each child window has the WS_BORDER style, each has a thin line border. Also, because the WS_VISIBLE style is not specified, each child window is initially hidden. Notice also that each child window is assigned a child-window identifier.

The main window sizes and positions the child windows in response to the WM_SIZE message, which the main window receives when its size changes. In response to WM_SIZE, the main window retrieves the dimensions of its client area by using the **GetWindowRect** function and then passes the dimensions to the **EnumChildWindows** function. **EnumChildWindows** passes the handle of each child window, in turn, to the application-defined **EnumChildProc** callback function. This function sizes and positions each child window by calling the **MoveWindow** function; the size and position are based on the dimensions of the main window's client area and the identifier of the child window. Afterward, **EnumChildProc** calls the **ShowWindow** function to make the window visible.

```
#define ID_FIRSTCHILD  100
#define ID_SECONDCHILD 101
#define ID_THIRDCHILD  102
```

```
LONG APIENTRY MainWndProc(hwnd, uMsg, wParam, lParam)
HWND hwnd;
UINT uMsg;
UINT wParam;
LONG lParam;
{
    RECT rcClient;
    int i;

    switch(uMsg) {
        case WM_CREATE: /* creating main window */

            /* Create three invisible child windows. */

            for (i = 0; i < 3; i++)
                CreateWindowEx(
                    0,
                    "ChildWClass",
                    (LPCTSTR) NULL,
                    WS_CHILD | WS_BORDER,
                    0,0,0,0,
                    hwnd,
                    (HMENU) (int) (ID_FIRSTCHILD + i),
                    hinst,
                    NULL);

            return 0;

        case WM_SIZE: /* main window changed size */

            /*
             * Get the dimensions of the main window's client
             * area, and enumerate the child windows. Pass the
             * dimensions to the child windows during enumeration.
             */

            GetClientRect(hwnd, &rcClient);
            EnumChildWindows(hwnd, EnumChildProc,
                (LPARAM) &rcClient);
            return 0;

        .
        . /* Process other messages. */
        .

    }
    return DefWindowProc(hwnd, uMsg, wParam, lParam);
}
```

```
BOOL CALLBACK EnumChildProc(hwndChild, lParam)
HWND hwndChild;
LPARAM lParam;
{
    LPRECT rcParent;
    int i, idChild;

    /*
     * Retrieve the child-window identifier. Use it to set the
     * position of the child window.
     */

    idChild = GetWindowLong(hwndChild, GWL_ID);

    if (idChild == ID_FIRSTCHILD)
        i = 0;
    else if (idChild == ID_SECONDCHILD)
        i = 1;
    else
        i = 2;

    /* Size and position the child window. */

    rcParent = (LPRECT) lParam;
    MoveWindow(hwndChild,
        (rcParent->right / 3) * i,
        0,
        rcParent->right / 3,
        rcParent->bottom,
        TRUE);

    /* Make sure the child window is visible. */

    ShowWindow(hwndChild, SW_SHOW);

    return TRUE;
}
```

1.2.3 Destroying a Window

You can use the **DestroyWindow** function to destroy a window. Typically, an application sends the WM_CLOSE message before destroying a window, giving the window the opportunity to prompt the user for confirmation before the window is destroyed. A window that includes a System menu automatically receives the WM_CLOSE message when the user chooses the Close command from the menu. If the user confirms that the window should be destroyed, the application calls **DestroyWindow**. Windows sends the WM_DESTROY message to the window after removing it from the screen. In response to WM_DESTROY, the window saves its data and frees any resources it allocated. A main window concludes its processing of WM_DESTROY by calling the **PostQuitMessage** function to quit the application.

The following example shows how to prompt for user confirmation before destroying a window. In response to WM_CLOSE, the example displays a dialog box that contains Yes, OK, and Cancel buttons. If the user clicks the Yes button, **DestroyWindow** is called; otherwise, the window is not destroyed. Because the window being destroyed is a main window, the example calls **PostQuitMessage** in response to WM_DESTROY.

```
case WM_CLOSE:

    /*
     * Create the message box. If the user clicks
     * the Yes button, destroy the main window.
     */

    if (MessageBox(hwnd, szConfirm, szAppName,
            MB_YESNOCANCEL) == IDYES)
        DestroyWindow(hwndMain);
    else
        return 0;

case WM_DESTROY:

    /*
     * Post the WM_QUIT message to
     * quit the application terminate.
     */

    PostQuitMessage(0);
    return 0;
```

1.3 Functions and Messages

Following are the functions and messages to create and manage windows.

Functions
AdjustWindowRect
AdjustWindowRectEx
AnyPopup
ArrangeIconicWindows
BeginDeferWindowPos
BringWindowToTop

ChildWindowFromPoint
CloseWindow
CreateWindow
CreateWindowEx
DeferWindowPos
DestroyWindow
EndDeferWindowPos
EnumChildProc
EnumChildWindows
EnumTaskWindows (Obsolete)
EnumThreadWindows
EnumThreadWndProc
EnumWindows
EnumWindowsProc
FindWindow
GetClientRect
GetDesktopWindow
GetForegroundWindow
GetLastActivePopup
GetNextWindow
GetParent
GetTopWindow
GetWindow
GetWindowPlacement
GetWindowRect
GetWindowTask (Obsolete)
GetWindowText
GetWindowTextLength
GetWindowThreadProcessId
IsChild
IsIconic
IsWindow
IsWindowUnicode
IsWindowVisible
IsZoomed
MoveWindow
OpenIcon
SetDeskWallpaper
SetForegroundWindow
SetParent
SetWindowPlacement
SetWindowPos
SetWindowText
ShowOwnedPopups
ShowWindow

WindowFromPoint
WinMain

Messages

WM_ACTIVATE
WM_ACTIVATEAPP
WM_CANCELMODE
WM_CHILDACTIVATE
WM_CLOSE
WM_COPYDATA
WM_CREATE
WM_DESTROY
WM_ENABLE
WM_ENDSESSION
WM_GETMINMAXINFO
WM_GETTEXT
WM_MOVE
WM_NCACTIVATE
WM_NCCALCSIZE
WM_NCCREATE
WM_NCDESTROY
WM_OPENICON
WM_PARENTNOTIFY
WM_POWER
WM_QUERYENDSESSION
WM_QUERYOPEN
WM_QUIT
WM_SETTEXT
WM_SHOWWINDOW
WM_SIZE
WM_WINDOWPOSCHANGED
WM_WINDOWPOSCHANGING

CHAPTER 2

Messages and Message Queues

2.1 About Messages and Message Queues

Unlike traditional applications, applications written for Microsoft ® Windows ™ do not make explicit function calls (such as to **getchar**) to obtain input. Instead, they wait for Windows to pass input to them.

Windows passes all input for an application to the various windows in the application. Each window has a function, called a *window procedure*, that Windows calls whenever it has input for the window. The window procedure processes the input and returns control to Windows. For more information about window procedures, see Chapter 4, "Window Procedures."

This chapter describes messages and message queues and explains how to use them in your application.

2.1.1 Messages

Windows passes input to a window procedure in the form of *messages*. Messages are generated by Windows and by applications. Windows generates a message at each input event—for example, when the user types, moves the mouse, or clicks a control such as a scroll bar. Windows also generates messages in response to changes in the system brought about by an application, such as when an application changes the pool of system font resources or resizes one of its windows. An application can generate messages to direct its own windows to carry out tasks or to communicate with windows in other applications.

Windows sends a message to a window procedure with a set of four parameters: a window handle, a message identifier, and two 32-bit values called *message parameters*. The window handle identifies the window for which the message is intended. Windows uses it to determine which window procedure to send the message to.

A message identifier is a named constant that identifies the purpose of a message. When a window procedure receives a message, it uses a message identifier to determine how to process the message. For example, the message identifier WM_PAINT tells the window procedure that the window's client area has changed and must be repainted.

Message parameters specify data or the location of data used by a window procedure when processing a message. The meaning and value of the message parameters depend on the message. A message parameter can contain an integer, packed bit flags, a pointer to a structure containing additional data, and so on. When a message does not use message parameters, it typically sets them to NULL. A window procedure must check the message identifier to determine how to interpret the message parameters.

2.1.2 Message Routing

Windows uses two methods to route messages to a window procedure: posting messages to a first-in, first-out queue called a *message queue*, a system-defined memory object that temporarily stores messages, and sending messages directly to a window procedure.

Messages posted to a message queue are called *queued messages*. They are primarily the result of user input entered through the mouse or keyboard, such as WM_MOUSEMOVE, WM_LBUTTONDOWN, WM_KEYDOWN, and WM_CHAR messages. Other queued messages include the timer, paint, and quit messages: WM_TIMER, WM_PAINT, and WM_QUIT. Most other messages, which are sent directly to a window procedure, are called *nonqueued messages*.

2.1.2.1 Queued Messages

Windows can display any number of windows at a time. To route mouse and keyboard input to the appropriate window, Windows uses message queues. It maintains a single system message queue and any number of thread message queues, one for each thread.

Whenever the user moves the mouse, clicks the mouse buttons, or types at the keyboard, the device driver for the mouse or keyboard converts the input into messages and places them in the system message queue. Windows removes the messages, one at a time, from the system message queue, examines them to determine the destination window, and then posts them to the message queue of the thread that created the destination window. A thread's message queue receives all mouse and keyboard messages for the windows created by the thread. The thread removes messages from its queue and directs Windows to send them to the appropriate window procedure for processing. For more information about threads, see Chapter 43, "Processes and Threads."

With the exception of the WM_PAINT message, Windows always posts messages at the end of a message queue. This ensures that a window receives its input messages in the proper first-in, first-out sequence. The WM_PAINT message, however, is kept in the queue and is forwarded to the window procedure only when the queue contains no other messages. Multiple WM_PAINT messages for the same window are combined into a single WM_PAINT message, consolidating all invalid parts of the client area into a single area. Combining WM_PAINT messages reduces the number of times a window must redraw the contents of its client area.

The system posts a message to a thread's message queue by filling an **MSG** structure and then copying it to the message queue. Information in the **MSG** structure includes the handle of the window for which the message is intended, the message identifier, the two message parameters, the message time, and the mouse cursor position. A thread can post a message to its own message queue or to the queue of another thread by using the **PostMessage** or **PostThreadMessage** function.

An application can remove a message from its queue by using the **GetMessage** function. To examine a message without removing it from its queue, an application can use the **PeekMessage** function. This function fills an **MSG** structure with information about the message.

After removing a message from its queue, an application can use the **DispatchMessage** function to direct Windows to send the message to a window procedure for processing. **DispatchMessage** takes a pointer to the **MSG** structure that was filled by a previous call to the **GetMessage** or **PeekMessage** function. **DispatchMessage** passes the window handle, the message identifier, and the two message parameters to the window procedure, but it does not pass the time or mouse cursor position. An application can retrieve this information by calling the **GetMessageTime** and **GetMessagePos** functions while processing a message.

2.1.2.2 Nonqueued Messages

Nonqueued messages are sent immediately to the destination window procedure, bypassing the system message queue and thread message queue. Windows typically sends nonqueued messages to notify a window of events that affect it. For example, when the user activates a new application window, Windows sends the window a series of messages, including WM_ACTIVATE, WM_SETFOCUS, and WM_SETCURSOR. These messages notify the window that it has been activated, that keyboard input is being directed to the window, and that the mouse cursor has been moved within the borders of the window. Nonqueued messages can also result when an application calls certain Windows functions. For example, Windows sends the WM_WINDOWPOSCHANGED message after an application uses the **SetWindowPos** function to move a window.

An application can send a message by calling the **SendMessage**, **SendNotifyMessage**, or **SendDlgItemMessage** function. For more information about sending messages, see Section 2.2.4, "Sending a Message."

2.1.3 Message Handling

An application must remove and process messages posted to the message queues of its threads. A single-threaded application usually uses a *message loop* in its **WinMain** function to remove and send messages to the appropriate window procedures for processing. Applications with multiple threads can include a message loop in each thread that creates a window. The following sections describe how a message loop works and explain the role of a window procedure.

2.1.3.1 Message Loop

A simple message loop consists of one function call to each of these functions: **GetMessage**, **TranslateMessage**, and **DispatchMessage**. The **GetMessage** function retrieves a message from the queue and copies it to an **MSG** structure. **GetMessage** returns TRUE unless it encounters the WM_QUIT message, in which case it returns FALSE and ends the loop. In a single-threaded application, ending the message loop is often the first step in closing the application. An application can end its own loop by using the **PostQuitMessage** function, typically in response to the WM_DESTROY message in the window procedure of the application's main window.

If you specify a window handle in **GetMessage**, only messages for the specified window are retrieved from the queue. **GetMessage** can also filter messages in the queue, retrieving only those messages that fall within a specified range. For more information about filtering messages, see Section 2.1.6, "Message Filtering."

A thread's message loop must include **TranslateMessage** if the thread is to receive character input from the keyboard. Windows generates virtual-key messages (WM_KEYDOWN and WM_KEYUP) each time the user presses a key. A virtual-key message contains a virtual-key code that identifies which key was pressed, but not its character value. To retrieve this value, the message loop must contain **TranslateMessage**, which translates the virtual-key message into a character message (WM_CHAR) and places it back into the application message queue. The character message can then be removed on a subsequent iteration of the message loop and dispatched to a window procedure.

The **DispatchMessage** function sends a message to the window procedure associated with the window handle specified in the **MSG** structure. If the window handle is HWND_TOPMOST, **DispatchMessage** sends the message to the window procedures of all top-level windows in the system. If the window handle is NULL, **DispatchMessage** does nothing with the message.

An application's main thread starts its message loop after initializing the application and creating at least one window. Once started, the message loop continues to retrieve messages from the thread's message queue and to dispatch them to the appropriate windows. The message loop ends when the **GetMessage** function removes the WM_QUIT message from the message queue.

Only one message loop is needed for a message queue, even if an application contains many windows. Because each message in the queue is an **MSG** structure that contains the handle of the window to which the message belongs, **DispatchMessage** always dispatches the message to the proper window.

An application can modify its message loop in a variety of ways. For example, it can retrieve messages from the queue without dispatching them to a window. This is useful for applications that post messages not specifying a window. (These messages apply to the application rather than to a specific window, because they have NULL window handles.) An application can also direct **GetMessage** to search for specific messages, leaving other messages in the queue. This is useful for applications that must temporarily bypass the usual first-in, first-out order of the message queue.

An application that uses accelerator keys must be able to translate keyboard messages into command messages. To do this, the application's message loop must include a call to the **TranslateAccelerator** function. For more information about accelerator keys, see Chapter 17, "Keyboard Accelerators."

2.1.3.2 Window Procedure

A window procedure is a function that receives and processes all messages sent to the window. Every window class has a window procedure, and every window created with that class uses that same window procedure to respond to messages.

The system sends a message to a window procedure by passing the message data as arguments to the procedure. The window procedure then carries out an appropriate action for the message; it checks the message identifier and, while processing the message, uses the information specified by the message parameters.

A window procedure does not usually ignore a message. If it does not process a message, it must send the message back to the system for default processing. The window procedure does this by calling the **DefWindowProc** function, which carries out a default action and returns a message result. The window procedure must then return this value as its own message result. Most window procedures process just a few types of messages and pass the others on to the system by calling **DefWindowProc**.

Because a window procedure is shared by all windows belonging to the same class, it can process messages for several different windows. To identify the specific window affected by the message, a window procedure can examine the window handle passed with a message. For more information about window procedures, see Chapter 4, "Window Procedures."

2.1.4 Posting and Sending Messages

Any application can post and send messages. Like the system, an application posts a message by copying it to a message queue and sends a message by passing the message data as arguments to a window procedure. To post and send messages, an application uses the **PostMessage** and **SendMessage** functions.

An application typically posts a message to notify a specific window to carry out a task. **PostMessage** creates an **MSG** structure for the message and copies the message to the message queue. The application's message loop eventually retrieves the message and dispatches it to the appropriate window procedure.

An application typically sends a message to notify a window procedure to carry out a task immediately. The **SendMessage** function sends the message to the window procedure corresponding to the given window. The function waits until the window procedure completes processing and then returns the message result. Parent and child windows often communicate by sending messages to each other. For example, a parent window that has an edit control as its child window can set the text of the control by sending a message to it. The control can notify the parent window of changes to the text that are carried out by the user by sending messages back to the parent.

Occasionally, an application may be required to send or post a message to all top-level windows in the system. For example, if the application changes the system time, it must notify all top-level windows about the change by sending a WM_TIMECHANGE message. An application can send or post a message to all top-level windows by calling the **SendMessage** or **PostMessage** function and specifying HWND_TOPMOST in the *hwnd* parameter.

An application can post a message without specifying a window. If the application supplies a NULL window handle when calling **PostMessage**, the message is posted to the queue associated with the current thread. Because no window handle is specified, the application must process the message in the message loop. This is one way to create a message that applies to the entire application instead of to a specific window.

By using the **InSendMessage** function, a window procedure can determine whether it is processing a message sent by another thread. This capability is useful when message processing depends on the origin of the message.

A common programming error is to assume that the **PostMessage** function always posts a message. This is not true when the message queue is full. An application should check the return value of the **PostMessage** function to determine whether the message has been posted and, if it has not been, repost it.

2.1.5 Message Types

This section describes the two types of Windows messages: system defined and application defined.

2.1.5.1 System-Defined Messages

The system uses system-defined messages to control the operations of applications and to provide input and other information for applications to process. The system sends or posts a system-defined message when it communicates with an application. An application can also send or post system-defined messages. Applications usually use these messages to control the operation of control windows created by using preregistered window classes.

Each system message has a unique message identifier and a corresponding symbolic constant (defined in the Windows header files) that states the purpose of the message. For example, the WM_PAINT constant requests that a window paint its contents.

Symbolic constants specify the category to which system-defined messages belong. The prefix of the constant identifies the type of window that can interpret and process the message. Following are the prefixes and their related message categories.

Prefix	Message category
BM	Button control
CB	Combo box control
DM	Default push button control
EM	Edit control
LB	List box control
SBM	Scroll bar control
WM	General window

General window messages cover a wide range of information and requests, including messages for mouse and keyboard input, menu and dialog box input, window creation and management, and dynamic data exchange (DDE).

2.1.5.2 Application-Defined Messages

An application can create messages to use in its own windows or to communicate with windows in other processes. If an application creates its own messages, the window procedure that receives them must interpret the messages and provide appropriate processing.

Windows reserves message-identifier values in the range 0x0000 through 0x03FF (the value of WM_USER – 1) and 0x8000 through 0xBFFF for system-defined messages. Applications cannot use these values for private messages.

Values in the range 0x0400 (the value of WM_USER) through 0x7FFF are available for message identifiers defined by an application for its own use. Values in the range 0xC000 through 0xFFFF are available for message identifiers defined by an application for use in communicating with windows in other applications.

Windows returns a message identifier in the range 0xC000 through 0xFFFF when an application calls the **RegisterWindowMessage** function to register a message. The message identifier returned by this function is guaranteed to be unique throughout the system. If your application creates messages to communicate with windows in other applications, it should use **RegisterWindowMessage** to register the message. Use of this function prevents conflicts that can arise if other applications use the same message identifier for different purposes.

2.1.6 Message Filtering

An application can choose specific messages to retrieve from the message queue (while ignoring other messages) by using the **GetMessage** or **PeekMessage** function to specify a message filter. This is a range of message identifiers (specified by a first and last identifier), a window handle, or both. **GetMessage** and **PeekMessage** use a message filter to select which messages to retrieve from the queue. Message filtering is useful if an application must search the message queue for messages that have arrived later in the queue.

Any application that filters messages must ensure that a message satisfying the message filter can be posted. For example, if an application filters for a WM_CHAR message in a window that does not receive keyboard input, the **GetMessage** function does not return. This effectively "hangs" the application.

To filter for keyboard, mouse, and DDE messages, an application can use the WM_KEYFIRST and WM_KEYLAST, WM_MOUSEFIRST and WM_MOUSELAST, and WM_DDE_FIRST and WM_DDE_LAST constants.

2.1.7 Message Deadlocks

A thread that calls the **SendMessage** function to send a message to another thread cannot continue executing until the window procedure that receives the message returns. If the receiving thread yields control while processing the message, the sending thread cannot continue executing, because it is waiting for **SendMessage** to return. This situation is called a *deadlock*. The receiving thread need not yield explicitly; calling any of the following functions can cause a thread to yield control.

DialogBox
DialogBoxIndirect
DialogBoxIndirectParam
DialogBoxParam
GetMessage
MessageBox
PeekMessage

A window procedure can determine whether a message it has received was sent by another thread by calling the **InSendMessage** function. Before calling any of the functions in the preceding list while processing a message, the window procedure should first call **InSendMessage**. If this function returns TRUE, the window procedure must call the **ReplyMessage** function before any function that causes the thread to yield control.

2.2 Using Messages and Message Queues

This section explains how to perform the following tasks:

- Create a message loop
- Examine a message queue
- Post a message
- Send a message

2.2.1 Creating a Message Loop

Windows automatically creates a message queue for each thread. If the thread creates one or more windows, a message loop that retrieves messages from the thread's message queue and dispatches them to the appropriate window procedures must be provided.

Because Windows directs messages to individual windows in an application, a thread must create at least one window before starting its message loop. Most Windows-based applications contain a single thread that creates windows. A typical application registers the window class for its main window, creates and shows the main window, and then starts its message loop—all in the **WinMain** function.

You create a message loop by using the **GetMessage** and **DispatchMessage** functions. If your application must obtain character input from the user, include the **TranslateMessage** function in the loop. **TranslateMessage** translates virtual-key messages into character messages. The following example shows the message loop in the **WinMain** function of a simple Windows-based application.

```
HINSTANCE hinst;
HWND hwndMain;

int APIENTRY WinMain(hInstance, hPrevInstance, lpszCmdLine,
    nCmdShow)
HINSTANCE hInstance;
HINSTANCE hPrevInstance;
LPSTR lpszCmdLine;
int nCmdShow;
{
    MSG msg;
    WNDCLASS wc;
    UNREFERENCED_PARAMETER(lpszCmdLine);

    /* Register the window class for the main window. */

    if (!hPrevInstance) {
        wc.style = 0;
```

```
        wc.lpfnWndProc = (WNDPROC) WndProc;
        wc.cbClsExtra = 0;
        wc.cbWndExtra = 0;
        wc.hInstance = hInstance;
        wc.hIcon = LoadIcon((HINSTANCE) NULL, IDI_APPLICATION);
        wc.hCursor = LoadCursor((HINSTANCE) NULL, IDC_ARROW);
        wc.hbrBackground = GetStockObject(WHITE_BRUSH);
        wc.lpszMenuName =  "MainMenu";
        wc.lpszClassName = "MainWndClass";

        if (!RegisterClass(&wc))
            return FALSE;
    }

    hinst = hInstance;  /* saves handle of application instance */

    /* Create the main window. */

    hwndMain = CreateWindow("MainWndClass", "Sample",
        WS_OVERLAPPEDWINDOW, CW_USEDEFAULT, CW_USEDEFAULT,
        CW_USEDEFAULT, CW_USEDEFAULT, (HWND) NULL,
        (HMENU) NULL, hinst, (LPVOID) NULL);

    /*
     * If the main window cannot be created, terminate
     * the application.
     */

    if (!hwndMain)
        return FALSE;

    /* Show the window and paint its contents. */

    ShowWindow(hwndMain, nCmdShow);
    UpdateWindow(hwndMain);

    /* Start the message loop. */

    while (GetMessage(&msg, (HWND) NULL, 0, 0)) {
        TranslateMessage(&msg);
        DispatchMessage(&msg);
    }

    /* Return the exit code to Windows. */

    return msg.wParam;
}
```

The **GetMessage**, **TranslateMessage**, and **DispatchMessage** functions take a pointer to an **MSG** structure as a parameter. If a message is available, **GetMessage** copies it to the **MSG** structure. If the message is a virtual-key message (such as WM_KEYDOWN or WM_SYSKEYDOWN), **TranslateMessage** generates a character message (WM_CHAR or WM_SYSCHAR) and places it in the message queue. **DispatchMessage** uses the members of the **MSG** structure as arguments for the window procedure but does not return until the window procedure finishes processing the message.

If a thread supports accelerators, its message loop must include the **TranslateAccelerator** function. This function checks for key combinations that match an entry in the thread's accelerator table. When it finds a match, **TranslateAccelerator** translates the key combination into a WM_COMMAND message and dispatches it to the window procedure. For more information about accelerators, see Chapter 17, "Keyboard Accelerators."

If a thread uses a modeless dialog box, the message loop must include the **IsDialogMessage** function so that the dialog box can receive keyboard input. For more information about dialog boxes, see Chapter 18, "Dialog Boxes."

The following example shows a message loop for a thread that uses accelerators and displays a modeless dialog box. When **TranslateAccelerator** or **IsDialogMessage** returns TRUE (indicating that the message has been processed), **TranslateMessage** and **DispatchMessage** are not called. The reason for this is that **TranslateAccelerator** and **IsDialogMessage** perform all necessary translating and dispatching of messages.

```
HWND hwndMain;
HWND hwndDlgModeless = NULL;
MSG msg;
HACCEL haccel;
.
. /* Perform initialization and create a main window. */
.

while (GetMessage(&msg, (HWND) NULL, 0, 0)) {
    if (hwndDlgModeless == (HWND) NULL ||
            !IsDialogMessage(hwndDlgModeless, &msg) &&
            !TranslateAccelerator(hwndMain, haccel, &msg)) {
        TranslateMessage(&msg);
        DispatchMessage(&msg);
    }
}
```

2.2.2 Examining a Message Queue

Occasionally, an application needs to examine the contents of a thread's message queue from outside the thread's message loop. For example, if an application's window procedure performs a lengthy drawing operation, you may want the user to be able to interrupt the operation. Unless your application periodically examines the message queue during the operation for mouse and keyboard messages, it will not respond to user input until after the operation has completed. The reason for this is that the **DispatchMessage** function in the thread's message loop does not return until the window procedure finishes processing a message.

You can use the **PeekMessage** function to examine a message queue during a lengthy operation. **PeekMessage** is similar to the **GetMessage** function; both check a message queue for a message that matches the filter criteria and then copy the message to an **MSG** structure. The main difference between them is that **GetMessage** does not return until a message matching the filter criteria is placed in the queue, whereas **PeekMessage** returns immediately regardless of whether a message is in the queue.

The following example shows how to use **PeekMessage** to examine a message queue for mouse clicks and keyboard input during a lengthy operation.

```
HWND hwnd;
BOOL fDone;
MSG msg;

/*
 * Begin the operation and continue until it is complete
 * or until the user clicks the mouse or presses a key.
 */

fDone = FALSE;
while (!fDone) {
    fDone = DoLengthyOperation(); /* application-defined */

    /*
     * Remove any messages that may be in the queue. If the
     * queue contains any mouse or keyboard
     * messages, end the operation.
     */

    while (PeekMessage(&msg, hwnd,  0, 0, PM_REMOVE)) {
        switch(msg.message) {
            case WM_LBUTTONDOWN:
            case WM_RBUTTONDOWN:
            case WM_KEYDOWN:
                .
                . /* Perform any required cleanup. */
                .
                fDone = TRUE;
        }
    }
}
```

Other functions, including **GetQueueStatus** and **GetInputState**, also allow you to examine the contents of a thread's message queue. **GetQueueStatus** returns an array of flags that indicates the types of messages in the queue; using it is the fastest way to discover whether the queue contains any messages. **GetInputState** returns TRUE if the queue contains mouse or keyboard messages. Both of these functions can be used to determine whether the queue contains messages that need to be processed.

2.2.3 Posting a Message

You can post a message to a message queue by using the **PostMessage** function. **PostMessage** places a message at the end of a thread's message queue and returns immediately, without waiting for the thread to process the message. The function's parameters include a window handle, a message identifier, and two message parameters. Windows copies these parameters to an **MSG** structure, fills the **time** and **pt** members of the structure, and places the structure in the message queue.

Windows uses the window handle passed with the **PostMessage** function to determine which thread message queue should receive the message. If the handle is HWND_TOPMOST, Windows posts the message to the thread message queues of all top-level windows.

You can use the **PostThreadMessage** function to post a message to a specific thread message queue. **PostThreadMessage** is similar to **PostMessage**, except the first parameter is a thread identifier rather than a window handle. You can retrieve the thread identifier by calling the **GetCurrentThreadId** function.

Use the **PostQuitMessage** function to exit a message loop. **PostQuitMessage** posts the WM_QUIT message to the currently executing thread. The thread's message loop terminates and returns control to Windows when it encounters the WM_QUIT message. An application usually calls **PostQuitMessage** in response to the WM_DESTROY message, as shown in the following example.

```
case WM_DESTROY:
    .
    . /* Perform cleanup tasks. */
    .
    PostQuitMessage(0);
    break;
```

2.2.4 Sending a Message

The **SendMessage** function is used to send a message directly to a window procedure. **SendMessage** calls a window procedure and waits for that procedure to process the message and return a result.

A message can be sent to any window in the system; all that is required is a window handle. Windows uses the handle to determine which window procedure should receive the message.

If a window procedure yields control when processing a message sent by another thread, a message deadlock may result (For more information about message deadlocks, see Section 2.1.7, "Message Deadlocks.") Before processing a message that may have been sent from another thread, a window procedure should first call the **InSendMessage** function. If this function returns TRUE, the window procedure should call **ReplyMessage** before any function that causes the thread to yield control, as shown in the following example.

```
case WM_USER + 5:
    if (InSendMessage())
        ReplyMessage(TRUE);

    DialogBox(hInst, "MyDialogBox", hwndMain, (DLGPROC) MyDlgProc);
    break;
```

A number of messages can be sent to controls in a dialog box. These control messages set the appearance, behavior, and content of controls or retrieve information about controls. For example, the CB_ADDSTRING message can add a string to a combo box, and the BM_SETCHECK message can set the check state of a check box or radio button.

Use the **SendDlgItemMessage** function to send a message to a control, specifying the identifier of the control and the handle of the dialog box window that contains the control. The following example, taken from a dialog box procedure, copies a string from a combo box's edit control into its list box. The example uses **SendDlgItemMessage** to send a CB_ADDSTRING message to the combo box.

```
HWND hwndCombo;
int cTxtLen;
PSTR pszMem;

switch (uMsg) {

    case WM_COMMAND:
        switch (LOWORD(wParam)) {

            case IDD_ADDCBITEM:

                /*
                 * Get the handle of the combo box and the
                 * length of the string in the edit control of
                 * the combo box.
                 */

                hwndCombo = GetDlgItem(hwndDlg, IDD_COMBO);
```

```
                              cTxtLen = GetWindowTextLength(hwndCombo);

                              /*
                               * Allocate memory for the string and copy
                               * the string into the memory.
                               */

                              pszMem = (PSTR) VirtualAlloc((LPVOID) NULL,
                                  (DWORD) (cTxtLen + 1), MEM_COMMIT,
                                  PAGE_READWRITE);
                              GetWindowText(hwndCombo, pszMem, cTxtLen + 1);

                              /*
                               * Add the string to the list box of the
                               * combo box and remove the string from the
                               * edit control of the combo box.
                               */

                              if (*pszMem != NULL) {
                                  SendDlgItemMessage(hwndDlg, IDD_COMBO,
                                      CB_ADDSTRING, 0,
                                      (DWORD) ((LPSTR) pszMem));
                                  SetWindowText(hwndCombo, (LPSTR) NULL);
                              }

                              /* Free the memory and return. */

                              VirtualFree(pszMem, 0, MEM_RELEASE);
                              return TRUE;
                          .
                          . /* Process other dialog box commands. */
                          .


                      }

                  .
                  . /* Process other dialog box messages. */
                  .

              }
```

2.3 Functions

Following are the functions used with messages and message queues.

CallWndProc
DefWindowProc
DispatchMessage
GetInputState
GetMessage
GetMessageExtraInfo
GetMessagePos
GetMessageTime
GetMsgProc
GetQueueStatus
InSendMessage
IsDialogMessage
IsWindowUnicode
PeekMessage
PostMessage
PostQuitMessage
PostThreadMessage
RegisterWindowMessage
ReplyMessage
SendDlgItemMessage
SendMessage
SendNotifyMessage
TranslateAccelerator
TranslateMessage
WaitMessage

CHAPTER 3

Window Classes

3.1 About Window Classes

Every window is a member of a window class. A *window class* is a set of attributes that Microsoft ® Windows ™ uses as a template to create a window in an application. Each window class has an associated window procedure shared by all windows of the same class. The window procedure processes messages for all windows of that class and therefore controls their behavior and appearance. For more information about window procedures, see Chapter 4, "Window Procedures."

An application must register a window class before it can create a window of that class. Registering a window class associates a window procedure, class styles, and other class attributes with a class name. When an application specifies a class name in the **CreateWindow** or **CreateWindowEx** function, the operating system creates a window with the window procedure, styles, and other attributes associated with that class name.

3.1.1 Types of Window Classes

There are three types of window classes: system global, application global, and application local. These types differ in scope and in when and how they are registered and destroyed.

3.1.1.1 System Global Classes

When Windows starts, it registers a set of *system global classes* for controls, including buttons, combo boxes, list boxes, scroll bars, edit controls, and static controls. For more information about controls, see Chapter 9, "Controls," through Chapter 15, "Static Controls." Any application can use a system global class at any time. Because Windows registers system global classes on behalf of all applications, an application cannot destroy any of these classes.

3.1.1.2 Application Global Classes

An *application global class* is a window class registered by a dynamic-link library (DLL) and available to all applications in the system. For example, you can register a window class that defines a custom control as an application global class so that all applications can create instances of the custom control.

In Windows, all window classes are process specific. An application can create a global class by creating the window class in a DLL and listing the name of the DLL in the registration database under the following keys:

**HKEY_LOCAL_MACHINE\Software\Microsoft\Windows NT\
    CurrentVersion\Windows\APPINIT_DLLS**

Whenever a process starts, the system loads the specified DLL in the context of the newly started process before calling the **main** function in that process. The DLL must register the class during its initialization procedure and must specify the CS_GLOBALCLASS style. For more information about class styles, see Section 3.1.4.8, "Class Styles." After a class has been registered, any application can use it to create any number of windows belonging to that class.

Windows destroys an application global class when the DLL that registered it is unloaded. For this reason, all applications must destroy all windows that belong to an application global class before unloading that DLL. Use the **UnregisterClass** function to remove an application global class and free the storage associated with it.

3.1.1.3 Application Local Classes

An *application local class* is any window class that an application registers for its exclusive use. Although an application can register any number of local classes, most applications register only one. This window class supports the window procedure of the application's main window.

Registering a local class is similar to registering an application global class, except that the CS_GLOBALCLASS style is not specified in the **style** member of the **WNDCLASS** structure.

Windows destroys a local class when the application that registered it closes. An application can also use the **UnregisterClass** function to remove a local class and free the storage associated with it.

3.1.2 How Windows Locates a Class

Windows maintains a list of **WNDCLASS** structures for each of the three types of window classes. When an application calls the **CreateWindow** or **CreateWindowEx** function to create a window with a specified class, Windows uses the following procedure to locate the class:

1. Windows searches the list of application local classes for a class with the specified name.
2. If the name is not in the application local class list, Windows searches the list of application global classes.
3. If the name is not in the application global class list, Windows searches the list of system global classes.

All windows created by the application use this procedure, including windows created by Windows on the application's behalf, such as dialog boxes. It is possible to override system global classes without affecting other applications. That is, an application can register an application local class having the same name as a system global class. This replaces the system global class in the context of the application but does not prevent other applications from using the system global class.

3.1.3 Class Ownership

The owner of a class is the application or DLL that registered the class. Windows determines class ownership from the **hInstance** member of the **WNDCLASS** structure passed to the **RegisterClass** function when the class is registered. For Windows DLLs, the **hInstance** member *must* be the instance handle of the DLL. The class is destroyed when the owner closes or is unloaded. For this reason, the application must destroy all windows using the class before it closes or the DLL is unloaded.

3.1.4 Elements of a Window Class

The elements of a window class define the default behavior of windows belonging to the class. The application that registers a window class assigns elements to the class by setting appropriate members in a **WNDCLASS** structure and passing the structure to the **RegisterClass** function. The **GetClassInfo** and **GetClassLong** functions retrieve information about a given window class. The **SetClassLong** function changes elements of a local or global class that the application has already registered.

Although a complete window class consists of many elements, Windows requires only that an application supply a class name, the window-procedure address, and an instance handle. Use the other elements to define default attributes for windows of the class, such as the shape of the cursor and the content of the menu for the window. The window class elements are as follows.

Element	Purpose
Class name	Distinguishes the class from other registered classes.
Window-procedure address	Points to the function that processes all messages sent to windows in the class and defines the behavior of the window.
Instance handle	Identifies the application or DLL that registered the class.
Class cursor	Defines the shape of the cursor in a window of the class.
Class icon	Defines the shape of the icon when a window belonging to the class is minimized.
Class background brush	Defines the color and pattern that fill the client area when the window is opened or painted.

Class menu	Specifies the default menu for windows that do not explicitly define a menu.
Class styles	Defines how to update the window after moving or resizing it, how to process double-clicks of the mouse, how to allocate space for the device context, and other aspects of the window.
Extra class memory	Specifies the amount of extra memory, in bytes, that Windows should reserve for the class. All windows in the class share the extra memory and can use it for any application-defined purpose. Windows initializes this memory to zero.
Extra window memory	Specifies the amount of extra memory, in bytes, that Windows should reserve for each window belonging to the class. The extra memory can be used for any application-defined purpose. Windows initializes this memory to zero.

3.1.4.1 Class Name

Every window class needs a *class name* to distinguish one class from another. Assign a class name by setting the **lpszClassName** member of the **WNDCLASS** structure to the address of a null-terminated string that specifies the name. Because window classes are process specific in Windows, window class names need to be unique only within the same process.

The **GetClassName** function retrieves the name of the class to which a given window belongs.

3.1.4.2 Window-Procedure Address

Every class needs a window-procedure address to define the entry point of the window procedure used to process all messages for windows in the class. Windows passes messages to the procedure when it requires the window to carry out tasks, such as painting its client area or responding to input from the user. An application assigns a window procedure to a class by copying its address to the **lpfnWndProc** member of the **WNDCLASS** structure. The window procedure must be exported in the module-definition (.DEF) file. For more information about window procedures, see Chapter 4, "Window Procedures."

3.1.4.3 Instance Handle

Every window class requires an instance handle to identify the application or DLL that registered the class. As a multitasking system, Windows lets several applications or DLLs run at the same time, so it requires instance handles to keep track of all of them. Windows assigns a handle to each copy of a running application or DLL.

Multiple instances of the same application or DLL all use the same code segment, but each has its own data segment. Windows uses an instance handle to identify the data segment that corresponds to a particular instance of an application or DLL.

Windows passes an instance handle to an application or DLL when the application starts. The application or DLL assigns this instance handle to the class by copying it to the **hInstance** member of the **WNDCLASS** structure.

3.1.4.4 Class Cursor

The *class cursor* defines the shape of the cursor when it is in the client area of a window in the class. Windows automatically sets the cursor to the given shape when the cursor enters the window's client area and ensures it keeps that shape while it remains in the client area. To assign a cursor shape to a window class, load a predefined cursor shape by using the **LoadCursor** function and then assign the returned cursor handle to the **hCursor** member of the **WNDCLASS** structure. Alternatively, provide a custom cursor resource and use the **LoadCursor** function to load it from the application's resources.

Windows does not require a class cursor. If an application sets the **hCursor** member of the **WNDCLASS** structure to NULL, a class cursor is not defined. Windows assumes the window sets the cursor shape each time the cursor moves into the window. A window can set the cursor shape by calling the **SetCursor** function whenever the window receives the WM_MOUSEMOVE message. For more information about cursors, see Chapter 21, "Cursors."

3.1.4.5 Class Icon

The *class icon* defines the shape of the icon used when the window of the given class is minimized. To assign an icon to a window class, load the icon from the application's resources by using the **LoadIcon** function and then assign the returned icon handle to the **hIcon** member of the **WNDCLASS** structure. For more information about icons, see Chapter 23, "Icons."

Windows does not require that a window class have a class icon. If an application sets the **hIcon** member of the **WNDCLASS** structure to NULL, a class icon is not defined. In this case, Windows sends the WM_ICONERASEBKGND message to a window of the class whenever it must paint the background of the icon. If the window does not process the WM_ICONERASEBKGND message, Windows draws an image of the contents of the window's client area onto the icon when it is minimized.

3.1.4.6 Class Background Brush

A *class background brush* prepares the client area of a window for subsequent drawing by the application. Windows uses the brush to fill the client area with a solid color or pattern, thereby removing all previous images from that location whether they belonged to the window or not. Windows notifies a window that its background should be painted by sending the WM_ERASEBKGND message to the window. For more information about brushes, see Chapter 30, "Brushes."

To assign a background brush to a class, create a brush by using the appropriate functions from the graphics device interface (GDI) and assign the returned brush handle to the **hbrBackground** member of the **WNDCLASS** structure.

Instead of creating a brush, an application can set the **hbrBackground** member to one of the standard system color values. For a list of the standard system color values, see the description of the **SetSysColors** function in the *Microsoft Win32 Programmer's Reference, Volume 4.*

To use a standard system color, the application must increase the background-color value by one. For example, COLOR_BACKGROUND + 1 is the system background color.

Windows does not require that a window class have a class background brush. If this parameter is set to NULL, the window must paint its own background whenever it receives the WM_ERASEBKGND message.

3.1.4.7 Class Menu

A *class menu* defines the default menu to be used by the windows in the class if no explicit menu is given when the windows are created. A menu is a list of commands from which a user can choose actions for the application to carry out.

To assign a menu to a class, set the **lpszMenuName** member of the **WNDCLASS** structure to the address of a null-terminated string that specifies the resource name of the menu. The menu is assumed to be a resource in the given application. Windows automatically loads the menu when it is needed. Note that if the menu resource is identified by an integer and not by a name, the application can set the **lpszMenuName** member to that integer by applying the **MAKEINTRESOURCE** macro before assigning the value.

Windows does not require a class menu. If an application sets the **lpszMenuName** member of the **WNDCLASS** structure to NULL, Windows assumes the windows in the class have no menu bars. Even if no class menu is given, an application can still define a menu bar for a window when it creates the window.

Windows does not allow menu bars with child windows. If a menu is given for a class and a child window of that class is created, the menu is ignored. For more information about menus, see Chapter 16, "Menus."

3.1.4.8 Class Styles

The class styles define additional elements of the window class. Two or more styles can be combined by using the bitwise OR (|) operator. To assign a style to a window class, assign the style to the **style** member of the **WNDCLASS** structure. The class styles are as follows.

Style	Action
CS_BYTEALIGNCLIENT	Aligns the window's client area on a byte boundary (in the x direction) to enhance performance during drawing operations. This style affects the width of the window and its horizontal placement on the display.
CS_BYTEALIGNWINDOW	Aligns the window on a byte boundary (in the x direction) to enhance performance during operations that involve moving or sizing the window. This style affects the width of the window and its horizontal placement on the display.
CS_CLASSDC	Allocates one device context to be shared by all windows in the class. For more information about device contexts, see Section 3.1.5, "Class and Private Device Contexts," and Chapter 28, "Device Contexts."
CS_DBLCLKS	Instructs Windows to send a double-click message to the window procedure when the user double-clicks the mouse while the cursor is within a window belonging to the class. For more information about double-clicks, see Chapter 6, "Mouse Input."
CS_GLOBALCLASS	Specifies that the window class is an application global class. For more information, see Section 3.1.1.2, "Application Global Classes."
CS_HREDRAW	Specifies that the entire window is to be redrawn if a movement or size adjustment changes the width of the client area.
CS_NOCLOSE	Disables the Close command on the System menu.
CS_OWNDC	Allocates a unique device context for each window in the class. For more information about device contexts, see Section 3.1.5, "Class and Private Device Contexts," and Chapter 28, "Device Contexts."
CS_PARENTDC	Gives the parent window's device context to the child windows. For more information about device contexts, see Section 3.1.5, "Class and Private Device Contexts," and Chapter 28, "Device Contexts."

CS_SAVEBITS | Saves, as a bitmap, the portion of the screen image obscured by a window. Windows uses the saved bitmap to re-create the screen image when the window is removed. Windows displays the bitmap at its original location and does not send WM_PAINT messages to windows obscured by the window if other screen actions have not invalidated the stored image. Use this style for small windows that are displayed briefly and then removed before other screen activity takes place (for example, menus or dialog boxes). This style increases the time required to display the window, because the operating system must first allocate memory to store the bitmap.

CS_VREDRAW | Specifies that the entire window is to be redrawn if a movement or size adjustment changes the height of the client area.

3.1.4.9 Extra Class Memory

Windows maintains a **WNDCLASS** structure internally for each window class in the system. When an application registers a window class, it can direct Windows to allocate and append a number of additional bytes of memory to the end of the **WNDCLASS** structure. This memory is called *extra class memory* and is shared by all windows belonging to the class. Use the extra class memory to store any information pertaining to the class.

The **SetClassWord** and **SetClassLong** functions copy a value to the extra class memory. To retrieve a value from the extra class memory, use the **GetClassWord** and **GetClassLong** functions. The **cbClsExtra** member of the **WNDCLASS** structure specifies the amount of extra class memory to allocate. An application that doesn't use extra class memory must initialize the **cbClsExtra** member to zero.

3.1.4.10 Extra Window Memory

Windows maintains an internal data structure for each window. When registering a window class, an application can specify a number of additional bytes of memory, called *extra window memory*. When creating a window of the class, Windows allocates and appends the specified amount of extra window memory to the end of the window's structure. An application can use this memory to store window-specific data.

The **SetWindowWord** and **SetWindowLong** functions copy a value to the extra memory. The **GetWindowWord** and **GetWindowLong** functions retrieve a value from the extra window memory. The **cbWndExtra** member of the **WNDCLASS** structure specifies the amount of extra window memory to allocate. An application that doesn't use extra window memory must initialize the **cbWndExtra** member to zero.

3.1.5 Class and Private Device Contexts

A device context is a special set of values that applications use for drawing in the client area of their windows. Windows requires a device context for each window on the display but allows some flexibility in how the operating system stores and treats that device context.

If no device-context style is explicitly given, Windows assumes each window uses a device context retrieved from a pool of contexts maintained by Windows. In such cases, each window must retrieve and initialize the device context before painting and free it after painting.

To avoid retrieving a device context each time it needs to paint inside a window, an application can specify the CS_OWNDC style for the window class. This class style directs Windows to create a private device context—that is, to allocate a unique device context for each window in the class. The application need retrieve the context only once and then use it for all subsequent painting. Although the CS_OWNDC style is convenient, use it carefully, because each device context uses a significant portion of system resources.

By specifying the CS_CLASSDC style, an application can create a class device context. A class device context is a rarely used feature that allows multiple windows created from the same window class within a process to use exactly the same device context for drawing.

An application can specify the CS_PARENTDC style to create child windows that inherit the device context of their parent window. This style allows a child window to draw in the client area of its parent.

For more information about device contexts, see Chapter 28, "Device Contexts." For more information about painting, see Chapter 20, "Painting and Drawing."

3.2 Using Window Classes

In Windows, each application must register its own window classes. Your application can register an application local class at any time by using the **RegisterClass** function. You must define the window procedure in the application, fill the members of the **WNDCLASS** structure, and then pass a pointer to the structure to the **RegisterClass** function.

The following example shows how to register a local window class and use it to create your application's main window.

```
#include <windows.h>

/* Global variable */

HINSTANCE hinst;
```

```c
/* Function prototypes */

int WINAPI WinMain(HINSTANCE, HINSTANCE, LPSTR, int);
InitApplication(HINSTANCE);
InitInstance(HINSTANCE, int);
LRESULT CALLBACK MainWndProc(HWND, UINT, WPARAM, LPARAM);

/* Application entry point */

int WINAPI WinMain(hinstance, hPrevInstance, lpCmdLine, nCmdShow)
HINSTANCE hinstance;
HINSTANCE hPrevInstance;
LPSTR lpCmdLine;
int nCmdShow;
{
    MSG msg;

    if (!InitApplication(hinstance))
        return FALSE;

    if (!InitInstance(hinstance, nCmdShow))
        return FALSE;

    while (GetMessage(&msg, (HWND) NULL, 0, 0)) {
        TranslateMessage(&msg);
        DispatchMessage(&msg);
    }
    return msg.wParam;
        UNREFERENCED_PARAMETER(lpCmdLine);
}

BOOL InitApplication(hinstance)
HINSTANCE hinstance;
{
    WNDCLASS wc;

    /*
     * Fill in the window class structure with parameters
     * that describe the main window.
     */

    wc.style = CS_HREDRAW |
        CS_VREDRAW;                      /* redraw if size changes */
    wc.lpfnWndProc = MainWndProc;        /* points to window proc. */
    wc.cbClsExtra = 0;                   /* no extra class memory   */
    wc.cbWndExtra = 0;                   /* no extra window memory  */
    wc.hInstance = hinstance;            /* handle of instance      */
    wc.hIcon = LoadIcon(NULL,
        IDI_APPLICATION);                /* predefined app. icon    */
```

```
        wc.hCursor = LoadCursor(NULL,
            IDC_ARROW);                     /* predefined arrow        */
        wc.hbrBackground = GetStockObject(
            WHITE_BRUSH);                   /* white background brush */
        wc.lpszMenuName = "MainMenu";      /* name of menu resource   */
        wc.lpszClassName = "MainWClass";   /* name of window class    */

        /* Register the window class. */

        return RegisterClass(&wc);
    }

BOOL InitInstance(hinstance, nCmdShow)
HINSTANCE hinstance;
int nCmdShow;
{
    HWND hwnd;

    /* Save the application-instance handle. */

    hinst = hinstance;

    /* Create the main window. */

    hwnd = CreateWindow(
        "MainWClass",         /* name of window class      */
        "Sample",             /* title-bar string          */
        WS_OVERLAPPEDWINDOW,  /* top-level window          */
        CW_USEDEFAULT,        /* default horizontal position */
        CW_USEDEFAULT,        /* default vertical position */
        CW_USEDEFAULT,        /* default width             */
        CW_USEDEFAULT,        /* default height            */
        (HWND) NULL,          /* no owner window           */
        (HMENU) NULL,         /* use class menu            */
        hinstance,            /* handle of app. instance   */
        (LPVOID) NULL);       /* no window-creation data   */

    if (!hwnd)
        return FALSE;

    /*
     * Show the window and send a WM_PAINT message to the window
     * procedure.
     */

    ShowWindow(hwnd, nCmdShow);
    UpdateWindow(hwnd);
    return TRUE;

}
```

Registering an application global class is similar to registering an application local class, with the following exceptions:

- The **style** parameter of the **WNDCLASS** structure must specify the CS_GLOBALCLASS style.

- The class can be registered in the context of either an application or a DLL.

- The application or DLL need not check for a previous instance of the application or DLL before registering the class.

3.3 Functions

Following are the functions used with window classes.

GetClassInfo
GetClassLong
GetClassName
GetClassWord
GetWindowLong
GetWindowWord
RegisterClass
SetClassLong
SetClassWord
SetWindowLong
SetWindowWord
UnregisterClass

CHAPTER 4

Window Procedures

4.1 About Window Procedures

In Microsoft ® Windows ™, every window has an associated *window procedure*—
a function that processes all messages sent or posted to all windows of the class.
All aspects of a window's appearance and behavior depend on the window
procedure's response to these messages.

Each window is a member of a particular window class. The window class
determines the window procedure that an individual window uses to process its
messages. All windows belonging to the same class use the same window
procedure. For example, the system defines a window procedure for the combo
box class (COMBOBOX), and all combo boxes use that window procedure.

An application typically registers at least one new window class and an associated
window procedure. After registering a class, the application can create many
windows of that class, all of which use the same window procedure. Because this
means several sources could simultaneously call the same piece of code, the
developer must be careful when modifying shared resources from a window
procedure. For more information about window classes, see Chapter 3, "Window
Classes."

Dialog box procedures have the same structure and function as window
procedures. All points referring to window procedures in this section also apply to
dialog box procedures. For more information about dialog boxes, see Chapter 18,
"Dialog Boxes."

4.1.1 Structure of a Window Procedure

A window procedure is a function that has four parameters and returns a 32-bit
signed value. The parameters consist of a window handle, a **UINT** message
identifier, and two message parameters declared with the **WPARAM** and
LPARAM data types. The operating system defines a **WPARAM** value as a 32-
bit unsigned integer and an **LPARAM** value as a 32-bit signed integer.

The window procedure parameters are described in the following table.

Parameter	Description
hwnd	Handle of the window receiving the message.
uMsg	Message identifier. The identifier corresponds to one of the predefined constants (for example, WM_CREATE) defined in the system header files or to an application-defined message identifier.
wParam, lParam	Message parameters. Their interpretation depends on the value of the *uMsg* parameter.

Message parameters often contain information in both their low-order and high-order words. The Win32 application programming interface (API) includes several macros an application can use to extract information from the message parameters. The **LOWORD** macro, for example, extracts the low-order word (bits 0 through 15) from a message parameter. Other macros include **HIWORD**, **LOBYTE**, and **HIBYTE**.

The return value of a window procedure is declared as an **LRESULT** data type, which is defined as a 32-bit signed value. The interpretation of the return value depends on the particular message. Consult the description of each message to determine the appropriate return value.

Because it is possible to call a window procedure recursively, it is important to minimize the number of local variables that it uses. When processing individual messages, an application should call functions outside the window procedure to avoid excessive use of local variables, possibly causing the stack to overflow during deep recursion.

4.1.2 Default Window Procedure

The default window procedure function **DefWindowProc** defines certain fundamental behavior shared by all windows. The *default window procedure* provides the minimal functionality for a window. An application-defined window procedure should pass any messages that it does not process to the **DefWindowProc** function for default processing.

4.1.3 Window Procedure Subclassing

When an application creates a window, the operating system allocates a block of memory for storing information specific to the window, including the address of the window procedure that processes messages for the window. When Windows needs to pass a message to the window, it searches the window-specific information for the address of the window procedure and passes the message to that procedure.

Subclassing is a technique that allows an application to intercept and process messages sent or posted to a particular window before the window has a chance to process them. By subclassing a window, an application can augment, modify, or monitor the behavior of the window. An application can subclass any window, including those belonging to a system global class, such as an edit control or a list box. For example, an application could subclass an edit control to prevent the control from accepting certain characters.

An application subclasses a window by replacing the address of the window's original window procedure with the address of a new window procedure, called the *subclass procedure*. Thereafter, the subclass procedure receives any messages sent or posted to the window.

The subclass procedure can take three actions when it receives a message: it can pass the message to the original window procedure, modify the message and pass it to the original window procedure, or process the message and not pass it to the original window procedure. If the subclass procedure processes a message, it can do so before, after, or both before and after it passes the message to the original window procedure.

Windows provides two types of subclassing: instance and global. In *instance subclassing*, an application replaces the window procedure address of a single instance of a window. An application must use instance subclassing to subclass an existing window. In *global subclassing*, an application replaces the address of the window procedure in the **WNDCLASS** structure of a window class. All subsequent windows created with the class have the address of the subclass procedure, but existing windows of the class are not affected.

4.1.3.1 Instance Subclassing

An application subclasses an instance of a window by using the **SetWindowLong** function. The application passes the GWL_WNDPROC flag, the handle of the window to subclass, and the address of the subclass procedure to **SetWindowLong**. The subclass procedure can reside in either the application's module or a dynamic-link library (DLL). An application must list the name of the subclass procedure in the **EXPORTS** statement of the application's or DLL's module-definition (.DEF) file.

SetWindowLong returns the address of the window's original window procedure. The application must save the address, using it in subsequent calls to the **CallWindowProc** function, to pass intercepted messages to the original window procedure. The application also needs the original window procedure address to remove the subclass from the window. To do so, the application calls **SetWindowLong** again, passing the address of the original window procedure with the GWL_WNDPROC flag and the handle of the window.

An application can subclass any window in the system; however, when subclassing a window it does not own, the application must ensure the subclass procedure does not destroy the original behavior of the window. Because the application does not control the window, it must not depend on information about the window that the owner might change in the future.

An application should not use the extra window bytes or the class bytes for a window without knowing exactly what the bytes mean and how the original window procedure uses them. Even so, the application should not use them unless it owns the window. If the application uses the extra window bytes of a window that another application owns and the owner changes some aspect of the extra bytes, the subclass procedure may fail. For this reason, an application should not subclass a window that belongs to a system global control class. Windows owns the system global classes, and aspects of the controls might change from one version of Windows to the next. If the application must subclass a window that belongs to a system global class, the developer may need to update the application when a new version of Windows is released.

Because instance subclassing occurs after a window is created, the application subclassing the window cannot add any extra bytes to the window. Applications that subclass a window should use the window's property list to store any data needed for an instance of the subclassed window. For more information about window properties, see Chapter 24, "Window Properties."

When an application subclasses a subclassed window, it must remove the subclasses in the reverse order they were performed. If the removal order is not reversed, an unrecoverable system error may occur.

4.1.3.2 Global Subclassing

To globally subclass a window class, the application must have a handle of a window of the class. The application also needs the handle to remove the subclass. To get the handle, an application typically creates a hidden window of the class to be subclassed. After obtaining the handle, the application calls the **SetClassLong** function, specifying the handle, the GCL_WNDPROC flag, and the address of the subclass procedure. **SetClassLong** returns the address of the original window procedure for the class.

The original window procedure address is used in global subclassing in the same way it is used in instance subclassing. The subclass procedure passes messages to the original window procedure by calling the **CallWindowProc** function. The application removes the subclass from the window class by calling **SetClassLong** again, specifying the address of the original window procedure, the GCL_WNDPROC flag, and the handle of a window of the class being subclassed. An application that globally subclasses a control class must remove the subclass when the application terminates; otherwise, an unrecoverable system error may occur.

Global subclassing has the same limitations as instance subclassing, plus some additional restrictions. An application should not use the extra bytes for either the class or the window instance without knowing exactly how the original window procedure uses them. If the application must associate data with a window, it should use window properties.

An application must not globally subclass a system global class. An unrecoverable system error may occur if more than one application globally subclasses a control class. If the application could benefit from globally subclassing a control class, use the technique called superclassing, described in the following section.

4.1.4 Window Procedure Superclassing

Superclassing is a technique that allows an application to create a new window class with the basic functionality of the existing class, plus enhancements provided by the application. A superclass is based on an existing window class called the *base class*. Frequently, the base class is a system global window class such as an edit control, but it can be any window class.

Note   An application must not superclass the system global SCROLLBAR class.

A superclass has its own window procedure, called the superclass procedure. The *superclass procedure* can take three actions with a message: it can pass the message to the original window procedure, modify the message and pass it to the original window procedure, or process the message and not pass it to the original window procedure. If the superclass procedure processes a message, it can do so before, after, or both before and after it passes the message to the original window procedure.

Unlike a subclass procedure, a superclass procedure can process window creation messages (WM_NCCREATE, WM_CREATE, and so on), but it must also pass them to the original base-class window procedure so that the base-class window procedure can perform its initialization procedure.

To superclass a window class, an application first calls the **GetClassInfo** function to retrieve information about the base class. **GetClassInfo** fills a **WNDCLASS** structure with the values from the **WNDCLASS** structure of the base class. Next, the application copies its own instance handle into the **hInstance** member of the **WNDCLASS** structure and copies the name of the superclass into the **lpszClassName** member. If the base class has a menu, the application must provide a new menu with the same menu identifiers and copy the menu name into the **lpszMenuName** member. If the superclass procedure processes the WM_COMMAND message and does not pass it to the window procedure of the base class, the menu does not need to have corresponding identifiers. The **GetClassInfo** function does not return the **lpszMenuName**, **lpszClassName**, or **hInstance** member of the **WNDCLASS** structure.

An application must also set the **lpfnWndProc** member of the **WNDCLASS** structure. The **GetClassInfo** function fills this member with the address of the original window procedure for the class. The application must save this address, to pass messages to the original window procedure, and then copy the address of the superclass procedure into the **lpfnWndProc** member. The application can, if necessary, modify any other members of the **WNDCLASS** structure. After it fills the **WNDCLASS** structure, the application registers the superclass by passing the address of the structure to the **RegisterClass** function. The superclass can then be used to create windows.

Because superclassing registers a new window class, an application can add to both the extra class bytes and the extra window bytes. The superclass must not use the original extra bytes for the base class or the window for the same reasons that an instance subclass or a global subclass should not use them. Also, if the application adds extra bytes for its use to either the class or the window instance, it must reference the extra bytes relative to the number of extra bytes used by the original base class. Because the number of bytes used by the base class may vary from one version of the base class to the next, the starting offset for the superclass's own extra bytes may also vary from one version of the base class to the next.

4.2 Using Window Procedures

This section explains how to perform the following tasks:

- Design a window procedure
- Associate a window procedure with a window class
- Subclass a window

4.2.1 Designing a Window Procedure

The following example shows the structure of a typical window procedure. The window procedure uses the message argument in a **switch** statement with individual messages handled by separate **case** statements. Notice that each case returns a specific value for each message. For messages that it does not process, the window procedure calls the **DefWindowProc** function.

```
LRESULT APIENTRY MainWndProc(hwnd, uMsg, wParam, lParam)
HWND hwnd;        /* handle of the window      */
UINT uMsg;        /* message identifier        */
WPARAM wParam;    /* first message parameter   */
LPARAM lParam;    /* second message parameter  */
{

    switch (uMsg) {
        case WM_CREATE:

            /* Initialize the window. */

            return 0;

        case WM_PAINT:

            /* Paint the window's client area. */

            return 0;
```

```
      case WM_SIZE:

          /* Set the size and position of the window. */

          return 0;

      case WM_DESTROY:

          /* Clean up window-specific data objects. */

          return 0;

      .
      . /* Process other messages. */
      .

      default:
          return DefWindowProc(hwnd, uMsg, wParam, lParam);
  }
  return 0;
}
```

At the very least, a window procedure should process the WM_PAINT message to draw itself. Typically, it should handle mouse and keyboard messages as well. Consult the descriptions of individual messages to determine whether your window procedure should handle them.

Your application can call the **DefWindowProc** function as part of the processing of a message. In such a case, the application can modify the message parameters before passing the message to **DefWindowProc**, or it can continue with the default processing after performing its own operations.

A dialog box procedure receives a WM_INITDIALOG message instead of a WM_CREATE message and does not pass unprocessed messages to the **DefDlgProc** function. Otherwise, a dialog box procedure is exactly the same as a window procedure. For more information about dialog box procedures, see Chapter 18, "Dialog Boxes."

4.2.2 Associating a Window Procedure with a Window Class

You associate a window procedure with a window class when registering the class. You must fill a **WNDCLASS** structure with information about the class, and the **lpfnWndProc** member must specify the address of the window procedure. To register the class, pass the address of **WNDCLASS** structure to the **RegisterClass** function. Once the window class is registered, the window procedure is automatically associated with each new window created with that class.

The following example shows how to associate the window procedure in the previous example with a window class.

```
int APIENTRY WinMain(hinstance, hinstPrev, lpCmdLine, nCmdShow)
HINSTANCE hinstance;   /* handle of current instance   */
HINSTANCE hinstPrev;   /* handle of previous instance  */
LPSTR lpCmdLine;       /* address of command-line string */
int nCmdShow;          /* show-window type             */
{
    WNDCLASS wc;

    /* Register the main window class. */

    wc.style = CS_HREDRAW | CS_VREDRAW;
    wc.lpfnWndProc = (WNDPROC) MainWndProc;
    wc.cbClsExtra = 0;
    wc.cbWndExtra = 0;
    wc.hInstance = hinstance;
    wc.hIcon = LoadIcon(NULL, IDI_APPLICATION);
    wc.hCursor = LoadCursor(NULL, IDC_ARROW);
    wc.hbrBackground = GetStockObject(WHITE_BRUSH);
    wc.lpszMenuName =  "MainMenu";
    wc.lpszClassName = "MainWindowClass";

    if (!RegisterClass(&wc))
       return FALSE;


    .
    . /* Process other messages. */
    .

}
```

4.2.3 Subclassing a Window

To subclass an instance of a window, call the **SetWindowLong** function and specify the GWL_WNDPROC flag, the handle of the window to subclass, and a pointer to the subclass procedure. The **SetWindowLong** function returns a pointer to the original window procedure; use this pointer to pass messages to the original procedure.

The following example shows how to subclass an instance of an edit control in a dialog box. The subclass window procedure allows the edit control to receive all keyboard input, including the ENTER and TAB keys, whenever the control has the input focus.

```
WNDPROC wpOrigEditProc;

LRESULT APIENTRY EditBoxProc(hwndDlg, uMsg, wParam, lParam)
```

```
HWND hwndDlg;
UINT uMsg;
WPARAM wParam;
LPARAM lParam;
{
    HWND hwndEdit;

    switch(uMsg) {
        case WM_INITDIALOG:

            /* Retrieve the handle of the edit control. */

            hwndEdit = GetDlgItem(hwndDlg, ID_EDIT);

            /* Subclass the edit control. */

            wpOrigEditProc = (WNDPROC) SetWindowLong(hwndEdit,
                GWL_WNDPROC, (LONG) EditSubclassProc);
            .
            . /* Continue the initialization procedure. */
            .
            return TRUE;

        case WM_DESTROY:

            /* Remove the subclass from the edit control. */

            SetWindowLong(hwndEdit, GWL_WNDPROC,
                (LONG) wpOrigEditProc);
            .
            . /* Continue the cleanup procedure. */
            .
            break;
    }
    return FALSE;
        UNREFERENCED_PARAMETER(lParam);
}

/*
 * Subclass procedure
 */

LRESULT APIENTRY EditSubclassProc(hwnd, uMsg, wParam, lParam)
HWND hwnd;
UINT uMsg;
WPARAM wParam;
LPARAM lParam;
{
    if (uMsg == WM_GETDLGCODE)
        return DLGC_WANTALLKEYS;
```

```
        return CallWindowProc(wpOrigEditProc, hwnd, uMsg,
            wParam, lParam);
}
```

4.3 Functions

Following are the functions used with window classes.

CallWindowProc
DefWindowProc
WindowProc

CHAPTER 5

Keyboard Input

5.1 About Keyboard Input

All applications written for Microsoft ® Windows ™ should accept user input from the keyboard as well as from the mouse. A Windows-based application receives keyboard input in the form of messages posted to its windows. This chapter describes how Windows generates keyboard input and how an application receives and processes that input.

5.1.1 Keyboard Input Model

Windows provides device-independent keyboard support for applications by installing a keyboard device driver appropriate for the current keyboard. Windows provides language-independent keyboard support by using the language-specific keyboard layout currently selected by the user or the application. The keyboard device driver receives scan codes from the keyboard, which are sent to the keyboard layout where they are translated into messages and posted to the appropriate windows in your application.

Assigned to each key on a keyboard is a unique value called a *scan code*, a device-dependent identifier for the key on the keyboard. A keyboard generates two scan codes when the user types a key—one when the user presses the key and another when the user releases the key.

The keyboard device driver interprets a scan code and translates (maps) it to a *virtual-key code*, a device-independent value defined by Windows that identifies the purpose of a key. After translating a scan code, the keyboard layout creates a message that includes the scan code, the virtual-key code, and other information about the keystroke, and then places the message in the system message queue. Windows removes the message from the system message queue and posts it to the message queue of the appropriate thread. Eventually, the thread's message loop removes the message and passes it to the appropriate window procedure for processing. The following figure illustrates the keyboard input model for Windows.

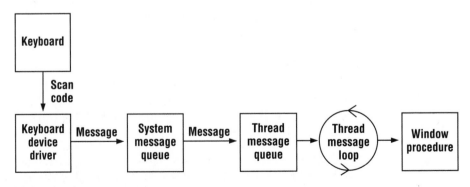

5.1.2 Keyboard Focus and Activation

Windows posts keyboard messages to the message queue of the thread that created the window with the keyboard focus. The *keyboard focus* is a temporary property of a window. Windows shares the keyboard among all windows on the display by shifting the keyboard focus, at the user's direction, from one window to another. The window that has the keyboard focus receives (from the message queue of the thread that created it) all keyboard messages until the focus changes to a different window.

A thread can call the **GetFocus** function to determine which of its windows (if any) currently has the keyboard focus. A thread can give the keyboard focus to one of its windows by calling the **SetFocus** function. When the keyboard focus changes from one window to another, the system sends a WM_KILLFOCUS message to the window that has lost the focus, and then sends a WM_SETFOCUS message to the window that has gained the focus.

The concept of keyboard focus is related to that of the active window. The *active window* is the top-level window the user is currently working with. The window with the keyboard focus is either the active window itself, or a child window of the active window. So the user can easily identify the active window, the system places it at the top of the Z order and highlights its title bar (if it has one) and border.

The user can activate a top-level window by clicking it, by selecting it using the ALT+TAB or ALT+ESC key combination, or by selecting if from Task List. A thread can activate a top-level window by using the **SetActiveWindow** function. It can determine whether a top-level window it created is active by using the **GetActiveWindow** function.

When one window is deactivated and another activated, Windows sends the WM_ACTIVATE message first to the window being deactivated, then to the window being activated. The low-order word of the *wParam* parameter is zero if the window is being deactivated and nonzero if it is being activated. When the default window procedure receives the WM_ACTIVATE message, it sets the keyboard focus to the active window.

5.1.3 Keystroke Messages

Pressing a key results in a WM_KEYDOWN or WM_SYSKEYDOWN message being placed in the thread message queue associated with the window that has the keyboard focus. Releasing a key results in a WM_KEYUP or WM_SYSKEYUP message being placed in the queue.

Key-up and key-down messages typically occur in pairs, but if the user holds down a key long enough to start the keyboard's automatic repeat feature, the system generates a number of WM_KEYDOWN or WM_SYSKEYDOWN messages in a row, then a single WM_KEYUP or WM_SYSKEYUP message when the user releases the key.

5.1.3.1 System and Nonsystem Keystrokes

Windows makes a distinction between system keystrokes and nonsystem keystrokes. System keystrokes produce system keystroke messages: WM_SYSKEYDOWN and WM_SYSKEYUP. Nonsystem keystrokes produce nonsystem keystroke messages: WM_KEYDOWN and WM_KEYUP.

If your window procedure must process a system keystroke message, make sure that after processing the message the procedure passes it to the **DefWindowProc** function. Otherwise, all system operations involving the ALT key will be disabled whenever the window has the keyboard focus. That is, the user won't be able to access the window's menus or System menu, or use the ALT+ESC or ALT+TAB key combination to activate a different window.

System keystroke messages are primarily for use by Windows rather than by an application. Windows uses them to provide its built-in keyboard interface to menus and to allow the user to control which window is active. System keystroke messages are generated when the user types a key in combination with the ALT key, or when the user types and no window has the keyboard focus (for example, when the active application is minimized). In this case, the messages are posted to the message queue associated with the active window.

Nonsystem keystroke messages are for use by application windows; the **DefWindowProc** function does nothing with them. A window procedure can discard any nonsystem keystroke messages that it does not need.

5.1.3.2 Virtual-Key Codes

The *wParam* parameter of a keystroke message contains the virtual-key code of the key that was pressed or released. A window procedure processes or ignores a keystroke message, depending on the value of the virtual-key code. For a list of virtual-key codes, see Appendix B, "Virtual-Key Codes."

A typical window procedure processes only a small subset of the keystroke messages that it receives and ignores the rest. For example, a window procedure might process only WM_KEYDOWN keystroke messages, and only those that contain virtual-key codes for the cursor movement keys, shift keys (also called control keys), and function keys. A typical window procedure does not process keystroke messages from character keys. Instead, it uses the **TranslateMessage** function to convert the message into character messages. For more information about **TranslateMessage** and character messages, see Section 5.1.4, "Character Messages."

5.1.3.3 Keystroke Message Flags

The *lParam* parameter of a keystroke message contains additional information about the keystroke that generated the message. This information includes the repeat count, the scan code, the extended-key flag, the context code, the previous key-state flag, and the transition-state flag. The following illustration shows the locations of these flags and values in the *lParam* parameter:

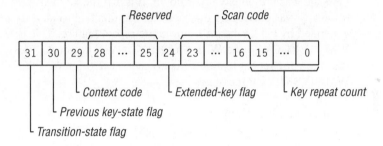

Repeat Count

You can check the repeat count to determine whether a keystroke message represents more than one keystroke. The system increments the count when the keyboard generates WM_KEYDOWN or WM_SYSKEYDOWN messages faster than an application can process them. This often occurs when the user holds down a key long enough to start the keyboard's automatic repeat feature. Instead of filling the system message queue with the resulting key-down messages, the system combines the messages into a single key down message and increments the repeat count. Releasing a key cannot start the automatic repeat feature, so the repeat count for WM_KEYUP and WM_SYSKEYUP messages is always set to 1.

Scan Code

The scan code is the value that the keyboard hardware generates when the user presses a key. It is a device-dependent value that identifies the key pressed, as opposed to the character represented by the key. An application typically ignores scan codes. Instead, it uses the device-independent virtual-key codes to interpret keystroke messages.

Extended-Key Flag

The extended-key flag indicates whether the keystroke message originated from one of the additional keys on the enhanced keyboard. The extended keys consist of the ALT and CTRL keys on the right-hand side of the keyboard; the INS, DEL, HOME, END, PAGE UP, PAGE DOWN and arrow keys in the clusters to the left of the numeric keypad; the NUM LOCK key; the BREAK (CTRL+PAUSE) key; the PRINT SCRN key; and the divide (/) and ENTER keys in the numeric keypad. The extended-key flag is set if the key is an extended key.

Context Code

The context code indicates whether the ALT key was down when the keystroke message was generated. The code is 1 if the ALT key was down and 0 if it was up.

Previous Key-State Flag

The previous key-state flag indicates whether the key that generated the keystroke message was previously up or down. It is 1 if the key was previously down and 0 if the key was previously up. You can use this flag to identify keystroke messages generated by the keyboard's automatic repeat feature. This flag is set to 1 for WM_KEYDOWN and WM_SYSKEYDOWN keystroke messages generated by the automatic repeat feature. It is always set to 0 for WM_KEYUP and WM_SYSKEYUP messages.

Transition-State Flag

The transition-state flag indicates whether pressing a key or releasing a key generated the keystroke message. This flag is always set to 0 for WM_KEYDOWN and WM_SYSKEYDOWN messages; it is always set to 1 for WM_KEYUP and WM_SYSKEYUP messages.

5.1.4 Character Messages

Keystroke messages provide a lot of information about keystrokes, but they don't provide character codes for character keystrokes. To retrieve character codes, an application must include the **TranslateMessage** function in its thread message loop. **TranslateMessage** passes a WM_KEYDOWN or WM_SYSKEYDOWN message to the keyboard layout. The layout examines the message's virtual-key code and, if it corresponds to a character key, provides the character code equivalent (taking into account the state of the SHIFT and CAPS LOCK keys). It then generates a character message that includes the character code and places the message at the top of the message queue. The next iteration of the message loop removes the character message from the queue and dispatches the message to the appropriate window procedure.

5.1.4.1 System and Nonsystem Character Messages

A window procedure can receive four different character messages, including WM_CHAR, WM_DEADCHAR, WM_SYSCHAR, and WM_SYSDEADCHAR. The **TranslateMessage** function generates a WM_CHAR or WM_DEADCHAR message when it processes a WM_KEYDOWN message. Similarly, it generates a WM_SYSCHAR or WM_SYSDEADCHAR message when it processes a WM_SYSKEYDOWN message.

An application that processes keyboard input typically ignores all but the WM_CHAR message, passing any other messages to the **DefWindowProc** function. Windows uses the WM_SYSCHAR and WM_SYSDEADCHAR messages to implement menu mnemonics.

The *wParam* parameter of all character messages contains the character code of the character key that was pressed. The value of the character code depends on the window class of the window receiving the message. If the Unicode™ version of the **RegisterWindowClass** function was used to register the window class, the system provides Unicode characters to all windows of that class. Otherwise, the system provides ASCII character codes from the Windows character set. For more information about Unicode, see Chapter 53, "String Manipulation and Unicode."

The contents of the *lParam* parameter of a character message are identical to the contents of the *lParam* parameter of the key-down message that was translated to produce the character message. For information about the contents of the *lParam* parameter, see Section 5.1.3.3, "Keystroke Message Flags."

5.1.4.2 Dead-Character Messages

Some non-English keyboards contain character keys that are not expected to produce characters by themselves. Instead, they are used to add a diacritic to the character produced by the subsequent keystroke. These keys are called *dead keys*. The circumflex key on a German keyboard is an example of a dead key. To enter the character consisting of an o with an circumflex, a German user would type the circumflex key followed by the o key. The window with the keyboard focus would receive the following sequence of messages:

WM_KEYDOWN
WM_DEADCHAR
WM_KEYUP
WM_KEYDOWN
WM_CHAR
WM_KEYUP

TranslateMessage generates the WM_DEADCHAR message when it processes the WM_KEYDOWN message from a dead key. Although the *wParam* parameter of the WM_DEADCHAR message contains the character code of the diacritic for the dead key, an application typically ignores the message. Instead, it processes the WM_CHAR message generated by the subsequent keystroke. The *wParam* parameter of the WM_CHAR message contains the character code of the letter with the diacritic. If the subsequent keystroke generates a character that cannot be combined with a diacritic, Windows generates two WM_CHAR messages. The *wParam* parameter of the first contains the character code of the diacritic; the *wParam* parameter of the second contains the character code of the subsequent character key.

The **TranslateMessage** function generates the WM_SYSDEADCHAR message when it processes the WM_SYSKEYDOWN message from a system dead key (a dead key that is pressed in combination with the ALT key). An application typically ignores the WM_SYSDEADCHAR message.

5.1.5 Key Status

While processing a keyboard message, an application may need to determine the status of another key besides the one that generated the current message. For example, a word processing application that allows the user to press SHIFT+END to highlight a block of text must check the status of the SHIFT key whenever it receives a keystroke message from the END key. The application can use the **GetKeyState** function to determine the status of a virtual key at the time the current message was generated, and it can use the **GetAsyncKeyState** function to retrieve the current status of a virtual key.

The keyboard layout maintains a list of names. The name of a key that produces a single character is the same as the character produced by the key. The name of a noncharacter key such as TAB and ENTER is stored as a character string. An application can retrieve the name of any key from the device driver by calling **GetKeyNameText**.

5.1.6 Keystroke and Character Translations

Windows includes several special purpose functions that translate scan codes, character codes, and virtual-key codes provided by various keystroke messages. These functions include **MapVirtualKey**, **ToAscii**, **ToUnicode**, and **VkKeyScan**.

5.1.7 Hot Key Support

Windows provides a set of functions that applications can use to define hot keys. A *hotkey* for your application. A *hot key* is a key combination that generates a WM_HOTKEY message, a message the system places at the top of a thread's message queue, bypassing any existing messages in the queue. Applications use hot keys to obtain high-priority keyboard input from the user. For example, by defining a hot key consisting of the CTRL+C key combination, an application can allow the user to cancel a lengthy operation.

To define a hot key, an application calls the **RegisterHotKey** function, specifying the combination of keys that generates the WM_HOTKEY message, the handle of the window to receive the message, and the identifier of the hot key. When the user presses the hot key, a WM_HOTKEY message is placed in the message queue of the thread that created the given window. The *wParam* parameter of the message contains the identifier of the hot key. The application can define multiple hot keys for a thread, but each hot key in the thread must have a unique identifier.

Before the application terminates, it should use the **Unregister Hot Key** function to destroy the hot key.

5.2 Using Keyboard Input

A window receives keyboard input in the form of keystroke messages and character messages. The message loop associated with the window must include code to translate keystroke messages into the corresponding character messages. If the window displays keyboard input in its client area, it should create and display a caret to indicate the position where the next character will be entered. The following sections describe the code involved in receiving, processing, and displaying keyboard input.

5.2.1 Processing Keystroke Messages

The window procedure of the window that has the keyboard focus receives keystroke messages when the user types at the keyboard. The keystroke messages are WM_KEYDOWN, WM_KEYUP, WM_SYSKEYDOWN, and WM_SYSKEYUP. A typical window procedure ignores all keystroke messages except WM_KEYDOWN. Windows posts the WM_KEYDOWN message when the user presses a key.

When the window procedure receives the WM_KEYDOWN message, it should examine the virtual-key code that accompanies the message to determine how to process the keystroke. The virtual-key code is in the message's *wParam* parameter. Typically, an application processes only keystrokes generated by noncharacter keys, including the function keys, the cursor movement keys, and the special-purpose keys such as INS, DEL, HOME and END.

The following example shows the window procedure framework that a typical application uses to receive and process keystroke messages

```
case WM_KEYDOWN:
    switch (wParam) {
        case VK_LEFT:
            .
            . /* Process the LEFT ARROW key. */
            .

            break;

        case VK_RIGHT:
            .
            . /* Process the RIGHT ARROW key. */
            .

            break;
```

```
        case VK_UP:
            .
            . /* Process the UP ARROW key. */
            .

            break;

        case VK_DOWN:
            .
            . /* Process the DOWN ARROW key. */
            .

            break;

        case VK_HOME:
            .
            . /* Process the HOME key. */
            .

            break;

        case VK_END:
            .
            . /* Process the END key. */
            .

            break;

        case VK_INSERT:
            .
            . /* Process the INS key. */
            .

            break;

        case VK_DELETE:
            .
            . /* Process the DEL key. */
            .

            break;

        case VK_F2:
            .
            . /* Process the F2 key. */
            .

            break;
```

```
.
. /* Process other noncharacter keystrokes. */
.

        default:
            break;
    }
```

5.2.2 Translating Character Messages

Any thread that receives character input from the user must include the **TranslateMessage** function in its message loop. This function examines the virtual-key code of a keystroke message and, if the code corresponds to a character, places a character message into the message queue. The character message is removed and dispatched on the next iteration of the message loop; the *wParam* parameter of the message contains the character code.

In general, a thread's message loop should use the **TranslateMessage** function to translate every message, not just virtual-key messages. Although **TranslateMessage** has no effect on other types of messages, it guarantees that keyboard input is translated correctly. The following example shows how to include the **TranslateMessage** function in a typical thread message loop.

```
while (GetMessage(&msg, (HWND) NULL, 0, 0)) {
    if (TranslateAccelerator(hwndMain, haccl, &msg) == 0) {
        TranslateMessage(&msg);
        DispatchMessage(&msg);
    }
}
```

5.2.3 Processing Character Messages

A window procedure receives a character message when the **TranslateMessage** function translates a virtual-key code corresponding to a character key. The character messages are WM_CHAR, WM_DEADKEY, WM_SYSCHAR, and WM_SYSDEADKEY. A typical window procedure ignores all character messages except WM_CHAR. The **TranslateMessage** function generates a WM_CHAR message when the user presses any of the following keys:

Any character key
BACKSPACE
ENTER (carriage return)
ESC
SHIFT+ENTER (linefeed)
TAB

When a window procedure receives the WM_CHAR message, it should examine the character code that accompanies the message to determine how to process the character. The character code is in the message's *wParam* parameter.

The following example shows the window procedure framework that a typical application uses to receive and process character messages.

```
case WM_CHAR:
    switch (wParam) {
        case 0x08:

            .
            . /* Process a backspace. */
            .

            break;

        case 0x0A:

            .
            . /* Process a linefeed. */
            .

            break;

        case 0x1B:

            .
            . /* Process an escape. */
            .

            break;

        case 0x09:

            .
            . /* Process a tab. */
            .

            break;

        case 0x0D:

            .
            . /* Process a carriage return. */
            .

            break;

        default:

            .
            . /* Process displayable characters. */
            .

            break;
```

}

5.2.4 Using the Caret

A window that receives keyboard input typically displays the characters the user types in the window's client area. A window should use a caret to indicate the position in the client area where the next character will appear. The window should also create and display the caret when it receives the keyboard focus, and hide and destroy the caret when it loses the focus. A window can perform these operations in the processing of the WM_SETFOCUS and WM_KILLFOCUS messages. For more information about carets, see Chapter 22, "Carets."

5.2.5 Displaying Keyboard Input

The example in this section shows how an application can receive characters from the keyboard, display them in the client area of a window, and update the position of the caret with each character typed. It also demonstrates how to move the caret in response to the LEFT ARROW, RIGHT ARROW, HOME and END keystrokes, and shows how to highlight selected text in response to the SHIFT+RIGHT ARROW key combination.

During processing of the WM_CREATE message, the window procedure shown in the example allocates a 64K buffer for storing keyboard input. It also retrieves the metrics of the currently loaded font, saving the height and average width of characters in the font. The height and width are used in processing the WM_SIZE message to calculate the line length and maximum number of lines, based on the size of the client area.

The window procedure creates and displays the caret when processing the WM_SETFOCUS message. It hides and deletes the caret when processing the WM_KILLFOCUS message.

When processing the WM_CHAR message, the window procedure displays characters, stores them in the input buffer, and updates the caret position. The window procedure also converts tab characters to four consecutive space characters. Backspace, linefeed, and escape characters generate a beep but are not otherwise processed.

The window procedure performs the left, right, end, and home caret movements when processing the WM_KEYDOWN message. While processing the action of the RIGHT ARROW key, the window procedure checks the state of the SHIFT key and, if it is down, highlights the character to the right of the caret as the caret is moved.

Note that the following code is written so that it can be compiled either as Unicode or as ANSI. If the source code defines Unicode, strings are handled as Unicode characters; otherwise, they are handled as ANSI characters.

```
#define BUFSIZE 65535
#define SHIFTED 0x8000

LONG APIENTRY MainWndProc(hwndMain, uMsg, wParam, lParam)
HWND hwndMain;
UINT uMsg;
UINT wParam;
LONG lParam;
{
    HDC hdc;                        /* handle of device context       */
    TEXTMETRIC tm;                  /* structure for text metrics     */
    static DWORD dwCharX;           /* average width of characters    */
    static DWORD dwCharY;           /* height of characters           */
    static DWORD dwClientX;         /* width of client area           */
    static DWORD dwClientY;         /* height of client area          */
    static DWORD dwLineLen;         /* line length                    */
    static DWORD dwLines;           /* text lines in client area      */
    static int nCaretPosX = 0;      /* horizontal position of caret   */
    static int nCaretPosY = 0;      /* vertical position of caret     */
    static int nCharWidth = 0;      /* width of a character           */
    static int cch = 0;             /* characters in buffer           */
    static int nCurChar = 0;        /* index of current character     */
    static PTCHAR pchInputBuf;      /* address of input buffer        */
    int i, j;                       /* loop counters                  */
    int cCR = 0;                    /* count of carriage returns      */
    int nCRIndex = 0;               /* index of last carriage return  */
    int nVirtKey;                   /* virtual-key code               */
    TCHAR szBuf[128];               /* temporary buffer               */
    TCHAR ch;                       /* current character              */
    PAINTSTRUCT ps;                 /* required by BeginPaint          */
    RECT rc;                        /* output rectangle for DrawText  */
    SIZE sz;                        /* string dimensions              */
    COLORREF crPrevText;            /* previous text color            */
    COLORREF crPrevBk;              /* previous background color      */

    switch (uMsg) {
        case WM_CREATE:

            /* Get the metrics of the current font. */

            hdc = GetDC(hwndMain);
            GetTextMetrics(hdc, &tm);
            ReleaseDC(hwndMain, hdc);

            /* Save the average character width and height. */

            dwCharX = tm.tmAveCharWidth;
            dwCharY = tm.tmHeight;

            /* Allocate a buffer to store keyboard input. */
```

```
            pchInputBuf = (LPTSTR) GlobalAlloc(GPTR,
                BUFSIZE * sizeof(TCHAR));
        return 0;

    case WM_SIZE:

        /* Save the new width and height of the client area. */

        dwClientX = LOWORD(lParam);
        dwClientY = HIWORD(lParam);

        /*
         * Calculate the maximum width of a line and the
         * maximum number of lines in the client area.
         */

        dwLineLen = dwClientX - dwCharX;
        dwLines = dwClientY / dwCharY;
        break;


    case WM_SETFOCUS:

        /*
         * Create, position, and display the caret when the
         * window receives the keyboard focus.
         */

        CreateCaret(hwndMain, (HBITMAP) 1, 0, dwCharY);
        SetCaretPos(nCaretPosX, nCaretPosY * dwCharY);
        ShowCaret(hwndMain);
        break;

    case WM_KILLFOCUS:

        /*
         * Hide and destroy the caret when the window loses the
         * keyboard focus.
         */

        HideCaret(hwndMain);
        DestroyCaret();
        break;

    case WM_CHAR:
        switch (wParam) {
            case 0x08: /* backspace */
            case 0x0A: /* linefeed */
            case 0x1B: /* escape */
```

```
                MessageBeep(0xFFFFFFFF);
                return 0;

        case 0x09: /* tab */

                /* Convert tabs to four consecutive spaces. */

                for (i = 0; i < 4; i++)
                    SendMessage(hwndMain, WM_CHAR, 0x20, 0);
                return 0;

        case 0x0D: /* carriage return */

                /*
                 * Record the carriage return and position the
                 * caret at the beginning of the new line.
                 */

                pchInputBuf[cch++] = 0x0D;
                nCaretPosX = 0;
                nCaretPosY += 1;
                break;

        default: /* displayable character */

                ch = (TCHAR) wParam;
                HideCaret(hwndMain);

                /*
                 * Retrieve the character's width and output
                 * the character.
                 */

                hdc = GetDC(hwndMain);
                GetCharWidth(hdc, (UINT) wParam, (UINT) wParam,
                    &nCharWidth);
                TextOut(hdc, nCaretPosX, nCaretPosY * dwCharY,
                    &ch, 1);
                ReleaseDC(hwndMain, hdc);

                /* Store the character in the buffer. */

                pchInputBuf[cch++] = ch;

                /*
                 * Calculate the new horizontal position of the
                 * caret. If the position exceeds the maximum,
                 * insert a carriage return and move the caret
                 * to the beginning of the next line.
                 */
```

```
                        nCaretPosX += nCharWidth;
                        if ((DWORD) nCaretPosX > dwLineLen) {
                            nCaretPosX = 0;
                            pchInputBuf[cch++] = 0x0D;
                            ++nCaretPosY;
                        }
                        nCurChar = cch;
                        ShowCaret(hwndMain);
                        break;
                }
                SetCaretPos(nCaretPosX, nCaretPosY * dwCharY);
                break;

        case WM_KEYDOWN:
            switch (wParam) {
                case VK_LEFT: /* LEFT ARROW */

                    /*
                     * The caret can move only to the beginning of
                     * the current line.
                     */

                    if (nCaretPosX > 0) {
                        HideCaret(hwndMain);

                        /*
                         * Retrieve the character to the left of
                         * the caret, calculate the character's
                         * width, then subtract the width from the
                         * current horizontal position of the caret
                         * to obtain the new position.
                         */

                        ch = pchInputBuf[--nCurChar];
                        hdc = GetDC(hwndMain);
                        GetCharWidth(hdc, ch, ch, &nCharWidth);
                        ReleaseDC(hwndMain, hdc);
                        nCaretPosX = max(nCaretPosX - nCharWidth,
                            0);
                        ShowCaret(hwndMain);
                    }
                    break;

                case VK_RIGHT: /* RIGHT ARROW */

                    /*
                     * Caret moves to the right or, when a carriage
                     * return is encountered, to the beginning of
                     * the next line.
```

```
                             */

            if (nCurChar < cch) {
                HideCaret(hwndMain);

                /*
                 * Retrieve the character to the right of
                 * the caret. If it's a carriage return,
                 * position the caret at the beginning of
                 * the next line.
                 */

                ch = pchInputBuf[nCurChar];
                if (ch == 0x0D) {
                    nCaretPosX = 0;
                    nCaretPosY++;
                }

                /*
                 * If the character isn't a carriage
                 * return, check to see whether the SHIFT
                 * key is down. If it is, invert the text
                 * colors and output the character.
                 */

                else {
                    hdc = GetDC(hwndMain);
                    nVirtKey = GetKeyState(VK_SHIFT);
                    if (nVirtKey & SHIFTED) {
                        crPrevText = SetTextColor(hdc,
                            RGB(255, 255, 255));
                        crPrevBk = SetBkColor(hdc,
                            RGB(0,0,0));
                        TextOut(hdc, nCaretPosX,
                            nCaretPosY * dwCharY,
                            &ch, 1);
                        SetTextColor(hdc, crPrevText);
                        SetBkColor(hdc, crPrevBk);
                    }

                    /*
                     * Get the width of the character and
                     * calculate the new horizontal
                     * position of the caret.
                     */

                    GetCharWidth(hdc, ch, ch, &nCharWidth);
                    ReleaseDC(hwndMain, hdc);
                    nCaretPosX = nCaretPosX + nCharWidth;
                }
```

```
            nCurChar++;
            ShowCaret(hwndMain);
            break;
    }
    break;

case VK_UP: /* UP ARROW    */
case VK_DOWN: /* DOWN ARROW */
    MessageBeep(0xFFFFFFFF);
    return 0;

case VK_HOME: /* HOME */

    /*
     * Set the caret's position to the upper left
     * corner of the client area.
     */

    nCaretPosX = nCaretPosY = 0;
    nCurChar = 0;
    break;

case VK_END: /* END */

    /* Move the caret to the end of the text. */

    for (i=0; i < cch; i++) {

        /*
         * Count the carriage returns and save the
         * index of the last one.
         */

        if (pchInputBuf[i] == 0x0D) {
            cCR++;
            nCRIndex = i + 1;
        }
    }
    nCaretPosY = cCR;

    /*
     * Copy all text between the last carriage
     * return and the end of the keyboard input
     * buffer to a temporary buffer.
     */

    for (i = nCRIndex, j = 0; i < cch; i++, j++)
        szBuf[j] = pchInputBuf[i];
    szBuf[j] = TEXT('\0');
```

```
                        /*
                         * Retrieve the text extent and use it
                         * to set the horizontal position of the
                         * caret.
                         */

                        hdc = GetDC(hwndMain);
                        GetTextExtentPoint(hdc, szBuf, lstrlen(szBuf),
                            &sz);
                        nCaretPosX = sz.cx;
                        ReleaseDC(hwndMain, hdc);
                        nCurChar = cch;
                        break;

                    default:
                        break;
                }
                SetCaretPos(nCaretPosX, nCaretPosY * dwCharY);
                break;

            case WM_PAINT:
                if (cch == 0)          /* nothing in input buffer */
                    break;

                hdc = BeginPaint(hwndMain, &ps);
                HideCaret(hwndMain);

                /*
                 * Set the clipping rectangle, and then draw the text
                 * into it.
                 */

                SetRect(&rc, 0, 0, dwLineLen, dwClientY);
                DrawText(hdc, pchInputBuf, -1, &rc, DT_LEFT);

                ShowCaret(hwndMain);
                EndPaint(hwndMain, &ps);
                break;
            .
            . /* Process other messages. */
            .
            case WM_DESTROY:
                PostQuitMessage(0);

                /* Free the input buffer. */

                GlobalFree((HGLOBAL) pchInputBuf);
                break;

            default:
```

```
                    return DefWindowProc(hwndMain, uMsg, wParam, lParam);
    }
    return NULL;
}
```

5.3 Functions and Messages

Following are the functions and messages used to receive and process keyboard input:

Functions

EnableWindow
GetActiveWindow
GetAsyncKeyState
GetFocus
GetKeyboardState
GetKeyNameText
GetKeyState
IsWindowEnabled
keybd_event
MapVirtualKey
RegisterHotKey
SetActiveWindow
SetFocus
SetKeyboardState
ToAscii
ToUnicode
UnregisterHotKey
VkKeyScan

Messages

WM_ACTIVATE
WM_CHAR
WM_DEADCHAR
WM_HOTKEY
WM_KEYDOWN
WM_KEYUP
WM_KILLFOCUS
WM_SETFOCUS
WM_SYSCHAR
WM_SYSDEADCHAR
WM_SYSKEYDOWN
WM_SYSKEYUP

C H A P T E R   6

Mouse Input

6.1 About Mouse Input

The mouse is an important, but optional, user-input device for applications written for Microsoft ® Windows ™. A well-written Windows-based application should include a mouse interface, but it should not depend on the mouse as the sole means of acquiring user input. The application should provide full keyboard support as well.

A Windows-based application receives mouse input in the form of messages that are sent or posted to its windows. This chapter describes how Windows generates mouse input and explains how an application receives and processes that input.

6.1.1 Mouse Cursor

When the user moves the mouse, the system moves a bitmap on the screen called the *mouse cursor*. The mouse cursor contains a single-pixel point called the *hot spot*, a point that the system tracks and recognizes as the position of the cursor. When a mouse event occurs, the window that contains the hot spot typically receives the mouse message resulting from the event. The window need not be active or have the keyboard focus to receive a mouse message.

The system maintains a variable that controls the mouse speed—that is, the distance the cursor moves when the user moves the mouse. You can use the **SystemParametersInfo** function with the SPI_GETMOUSE or SPI_SETMOUSE flag to retrieve or set the mouse speed. For more information about mouse cursors, see Chapter 21, "Cursors."

6.1.2 Mouse Capture

The system typically posts a mouse message to the window that contains the cursor hot spot at the time a mouse event occurs. An application can change this behavior by using the **SetCapture** function to route mouse messages to a specific window. The window receives all mouse messages until the application calls the **ReleaseCapture** function or specifies another capture window, or until the user clicks a window created by another thread.

Only the foreground window can capture mouse input. When a background window attempts to capture mouse input, it receives messages only for mouse events that occur when the cursor hot spot is within the visible portion of the window.

Capturing mouse input is useful if a window must receive all mouse input, even when the cursor moves outside the window. For example, an application typically tracks the cursor position after a mouse "button down" event, following the cursor until a "button up" event occurs. If an application has not captured mouse input and the user releases the mouse button outside the window, the window does not receive the button up message.

A thread can use the **GetCapture** function to determine whether one of its windows has captured the mouse. If one of the thread's windows has captured the mouse, **GetCapture** retrieves the handle of the window.

6.1.3 Mouse Configuration

Although the mouse is an important input device for Windows-based applications, not every user necessarily has a mouse. An application can determine whether the system includes a mouse by passing the SM_MOUSEPRESENT value to the **GetSystemMetrics** function.

Windows supports a mouse having up to three buttons. On a three-button mouse, the buttons are designated as the left, middle, and right buttons. Windows messages and named constants related to the mouse buttons use the letters L, M, and R to identify the buttons. The button on a single-button mouse is considered to be the left button. Although Windows supports a mouse with multiple buttons, most applications use the left button primarily and use the others little, if at all.

An application can determine the number of buttons on the mouse by passing the SM_CMOUSEBUTTONS value to the **GetSystemMetrics** function. To configure the mouse for a left-handed user, the application can use the **SwapMouseButton** function to reverse the meaning of the left and right mouse buttons. Passing the SPI_SETMOUSEBUTTONSWAP value to the **SystemParametersInfo** function is another way to reverse the meaning of the buttons. Note, however, that the mouse is a shared resource, so reversing the meaning of the buttons affects all applications.

6.1.4 Mouse Messages

The mouse generates an input event whenever the user moves the mouse, or presses or releases a mouse button. Windows converts mouse input events into messages and posts them to the appropriate thread's message queue. When mouse messages are posted faster than a thread can process them, Windows discards all but the most recent mouse message.

A window receives a mouse message when a mouse event occurs while the cursor is within the borders of the window, or when the window has captured the mouse. Mouse messages are divided into two groups: client area messages and nonclient area messages. Typically, an application processes client area messages and ignores nonclient area messages.

6.1.4.1 Client Area Mouse Messages

A window receives a client area mouse message when a mouse event occurs within the window's client area. The system posts the WM_MOUSEMOVE message to the window when the user moves the cursor within the client area. It posts one of the following messages when the user presses or releases a mouse button while the cursor is within the client area.

Message	Meaning
WM_LBUTTONDBLCLK	The left mouse button was double-clicked.
WM_LBUTTONDOWN	The left mouse button was pressed.
WM_LBUTTONUP	The left mouse button was released.
WM_MBUTTONDBLCLK	The middle mouse button was double-clicked.
WM_MBUTTONDOWN	The middle mouse button was pressed.
WM_MBUTTONUP	The middle mouse button was released.
WM_RBUTTONDBLCLK	The right mouse button was double-clicked.
WM_RBUTTONDOWN	The right mouse button was pressed.
WM_RBUTTONUP	The right mouse button was released.

Message Parameters

The *lParam* parameter of a client area mouse message indicates the position of the cursor hot spot. The low-order word indicates the x-coordinate of the hot spot, and the high-order word indicates the y-coordinate. The coordinates are given in *client coordinates*. In the client coordinate system, all points on the screen are given relative to the coordinates (0,0) of the upper-left corner of the client area.

The *wParam* parameter contains flags that indicate the status of the other mouse buttons and the CTRL and SHIFT keys at the time of the mouse event. You can check for these flags when mouse-message processing depends on the state of another mouse button or of the CTRL or SHIFT key. The *lParam* parameter can be a combination of the following values.

Value	Meaning
MK_CONTROL	The CTRL key is down.
MK_LBUTTON	The left mouse button is down.
MK_MBUTTON	The middle mouse button is down.
MK_RBUTTON	The right mouse button is down.
MK_SHIFT	The SHIFT key is down.

Double-Click Messages

The system generates a double-click message when the user clicks a mouse button twice in quick succession. When the user clicks a button, the system establishes a rectangle centered around the cursor hot spot. It also marks the time at which the click occurred. When the user clicks the same button a second time, the system determines whether the hot spot is still within the rectangle and calculates the time elapsed since the first click. If the hot spot is still within the rectangle and the elapsed time does not exceeded the double-click time-out value, the system generates a double-click message.

An application can get and set double-click time-out values by using the **GetDoubleClickTime** and **SetDoubleClickTime** functions, respectively. Alternatively, the application can set the double-click time-out value by using the SPI_SETDOUBLECLICKTIME flag with the **SystemParametersInfo** function. It can also set the size of the rectangle that Windows uses to detect double-clicks by passing the SPI_SETDOUBLECLKWIDTH and SPI_SETDOUBLECLKHEIGHT flags to **SystemParametersInfo**. Note, however, that setting the double-click time-out value and rectangle affects all applications.

An application-defined window does not, by default, receive double-click messages. Because of the system overhead involved in generating double-click messages, these messages are generated only for windows belonging to classes that have the CS_DBLCLKS class style. Your application must set this style when registering the window class. For more information about window classes, see Chapter 3, "Window Classes."

A double-click message is always the third message in a four-message series. The first two messages are the button down and button up messages generated by the first click. The second click generates the double-click message followed by another button up message. For example, double-clicking the left mouse button generates the following message sequence:

WM_LBUTTONDOWN
WM_LBUTTONUP
WM_LBUTTONDBLCLK
WM_LBUTTONUP

Because a window always receives a button down message before receiving a double-click message, an application typically uses a double-click message to extend a task it began during a button down message. For example, when the user clicks a color in the color palette of Windows PaintBrush, PaintBrush displays the selected color next to the palette. When the user double-clicks a color, PaintBrush displays the color and opens the Edit Colors dialog box.

6.1.4.2 Nonclient Area Mouse Messages

A window receives a nonclient area mouse message when a mouse event occurs in any part of a window except the client area. A window's *nonclient area* consists of its border, menu bar, title bar, scroll bar, System menu, Minimize button, and Maximize button.

Windows generates nonclient area messages primarily for its own use. For example, Windows uses nonclient area messages to change the cursor to a two-headed arrow when the cursor hot spot moves into a window's border. A window must pass nonclient area mouse messages to the **DefWindowProc** function to take advantage of the built-in mouse interface found in Windows.

There is a corresponding nonclient area mouse message for each client area mouse message. The names of these messages are similar except that the named constants for the nonclient area messages include the letters "NC". For example, moving the cursor in the nonclient area generates a WM_NCMOUSEMOVE message, and pressing the left mouse button while the cursor is in the nonclient area generates a WM_NCLBUTTONDOWN message.

The *lParam* parameter of a nonclient area mouse message is a **POINTS** structure that contains the x- and y-coordinates of the cursor hot spot. Unlike coordinates of client area mouse messages, the coordinates are given in *screen coordinates* rather than client coordinates. In the screen coordinate system, all points on the screen are relative to the coordinates (0,0) of the upper-left corner of the screen.

The *wParam* parameter contains a *hit-test code*, a value that indicates where in the nonclient area the mouse event occurred. The following section explains the purpose of hit-test codes.

6.1.5 The WM_NCHITTEST Message

Whenever a mouse event occurs, the system sends a WM_NCHITTEST message to either the window that contains the cursor hot spot or the window that has captured the mouse. Windows uses this message to determine whether to send a client area or nonclient area mouse message. An application that must receive mouse movement and mouse button messages must pass the WM_NCHITTEST message to the **DefWindowProc** function.

The *lParam* parameter of the WM_NCHITTEST message contains the screen coordinates of the cursor hot spot. The **DefWindowProc** function examines the coordinates and returns a hit-test code that identifies the location of the hot spot. The hit-test code can be one of the following values.

Value	Location of hot spot
HTBORDER	In the border of a window that does not have a sizing border
HTBOTTOM	In the lower horizontal border of a window
HTBOTTOMLEFT	In the lower left corner of a window border
HTBOTTOMRIGHT	In the lower right corner of a window border
HTCAPTION	In a title bar
HTCLIENT	In a client area

HTERROR	On the screen background or on a dividing line between windows (same as HTNOWHERE, except that the **DefWindowProc** function produces a system beep to indicate an error)
HTGROWBOX	In a size box (same as HTSIZE)
HTHSCROLL	In a horizontal scroll bar
HTLEFT	In the left border of a window
HTMENU	In a menu
HTNOWHERE	On the screen background or on a dividing line between windows
HTREDUCE	In a Minimize button
HTRIGHT	In the right border of a window
HTSIZE	In a size box (same as HTGROWBOX)
HTSYSMENU	In a System menu or in a Close button in a child window
HTTOP	In the upper horizontal border of a window
HTTOPLEFT	In the upper left corner of a window border
HTTOPRIGHT	In the upper right corner of a window border
HTTRANSPARENT	In a window currently covered by another window
HTVSCROLL	In the vertical scroll bar
HTZOOM	In a Maximize button

If the cursor is in the client area of a window, **DefWindowProc** returns the HTCLIENT hit-test code to the window procedure. When the window procedure returns this code to the system, Windows converts the screen coordinates of the cursor hot spot to client coordinates, and then posts the appropriate client area mouse message.

The **DefWindowProc** function returns one of the other hit-test codes when the cursor hot spot is in a window's nonclient area. When the window procedure returns one of these hit-test codes, Windows posts a nonclient area mouse message, placing the hit-test code in the message's *wParam* parameter and the cursor coordinates in the *lParam* parameter.

6.1.6 Window Activation

When the user clicks an inactive top-level window or the child window of a inactive top-level window, Windows sends the WM_MOUSEACTIVATE message (among others) to the top-level or child window. Windows sends this message after posting the WM_NCHITTEST message to the window, but before posting the button down message. When WM_MOUSEACTIVATE is passed to the **DefWindowProc** function, Windows activates the top-level window and then posts the button down message to the top-level or child window.

By processing WM_MOUSEACTIVATE, a window can control whether the top-level window becomes the active window as a result of a mouse click, and whether the window that was clicked receives the subsequent button down message. It does so by returning one of the following values after processing WM_MOUSEACTIVATE.

Value	Meaning
MA_ACTIVATE	Activate the window, and do not discard the mouse message.
MA_NOACTIVATE	Do not activate the window, and do not discard the mouse message.
MA_ACTIVATEANDEAT	Activate the window, and discard the mouse message.
MA_NOACTIVATEANDEAT	Do not activate the window, but discard the mouse message.

6.2 Using Mouse Input

This section explains how to perform the following tasks:

- Track the mouse cursor.
- Process double-click messages.

6.2.1 Tracking the Mouse Cursor

Windows-based applications often perform tasks that involve tracking the position of the mouse cursor. Most drawing applications, for example, track it during drawing operations, allowing the user to draw in a window's client area by dragging the mouse. Word-processing applications also track the cursor, enabling the user to select a word or block of text by clicking and dragging the mouse.

Tracking the cursor typically involves processing the WM_LBUTTONDOWN, WM_MOUSEMOVE, and WM_LBUTTONUP messages. A window determines when to begin tracking the cursor by checking the cursor position provided in the *lParam* parameter of the WM_LBUTTONDOWN message. For example, a word-processing application would begin tracking the cursor only if the WM_LBUTTONDOWN message occurred while the cursor was on a line of text, but not if it was past the end of the document.

A window tracks the position of the cursor by processing the stream of WM_MOUSEMOVE messages posted to the window as the mouse moves. Processing the WM_MOUSEMOVE message typically involves a repetitive painting or drawing operation in the client area. For example, a drawing application might redraw a line repeatedly as the mouse moves. A window uses the WM_LBUTTONUP message as a signal to stop tracking the cursor.

6.2.2 Drawing Lines with the Mouse

The example in this section demonstrates how to track the mouse cursor. It contains portions of a window procedure that enables the user to draw lines in a window's client area by dragging the mouse.

When the window procedure receives a WM_LBUTTONDOWN message, it captures the mouse and saves the coordinates of the cursor, using the coordinates as the starting point of the line. It also uses the **ClipCursor** function to confine the cursor to the client area during the line drawing operation.

During the first WM_MOUSEMOVE message, the window procedure draws a line from the starting point to the current position of the cursor. During subsequent WM_MOUSEMOVE messages, the window procedure erases the previous line by drawing over it with an inverted pen color. Then it draws a new line from the starting point to the new position of the cursor.

The WM_LBUTTONUP message signals the end of the drawing operation. The window procedure releases the mouse capture and frees the mouse from the client area.

```
LRESULT APIENTRY MainWndProc(hwndMain, uMsg, wParam, lParam)
HWND hwndMain;
UINT uMsg;
WPARAM wParam;
LPARAM lParam;
{
    HDC hdc;                        /* handle of device context  */
    RECT rcClient;                  /* client area rectangle     */
    POINT ptClientUL;               /* client upper-left corner  */
    POINT ptClientLR;               /* client lower-right corner */
    static POINTS ptsBegin;         /* beginning point           */
    static POINTS ptsEnd;           /* new endpoint              */
    static POINTS ptsPrevEnd;       /* previous endpoint         */
    static BOOL fPrevLine = FALSE;  /* previous line flag        */

    switch (uMsg) {
        case WM_LBUTTONDOWN:

            /* Capture mouse input. */

            SetCapture(hwndMain);

            /*
             * Retrieve the screen coordinates of the client area,
             * and convert them into client coordinates.
```

```
                        /*

            GetClientRect(hwndMain, &rcClient);
            ptClientUL.x = rcClient.left;
            ptClientUL.y = rcClient.top;

            /*
             * Add one to the right and bottom sides, because the
             * coordinates retrieved by GetClientRect do not
             * include the far left and lowermost pixels.
             */

            ptClientLR.x = rcClient.right + 1;
            ptClientLR.y = rcClient.bottom + 1;
            ClientToScreen(hwndMain, &ptClientUL);
            ClientToScreen(hwndMain, &ptClientLR);

            /*
             * Copy the client coordinates of the client area
             * to the rcClient structure. Confine the mouse cursor
             * to the client area by passing the rcClient structure
             * to the ClipCursor function.
             */

            SetRect(&rcClient, ptClientUL.x, ptClientUL.y,
                ptClientLR.x, ptClientLR.y);
            ClipCursor(&rcClient);

            /*
             * Convert the cursor coordinates into a POINTS
             * structure, which defines the beginning point of the
             * line drawn during a WM_MOUSEMOVE message.
             */

            ptsBegin = MAKEPOINTS(lParam);
            return 0;

        case WM_MOUSEMOVE:

            /*
             * When moving the mouse, the user must hold down
             * the left mouse button to draw lines.
             */

            if (wParam & MK_LBUTTON) {

                /*
                 * Retrieve a device context (DC) for the client
                 * area.
                 */
```

```
hdc = GetDC(hwndMain);

/*
 * The following function ensures that pixels of
 * the previously drawn line are set to white and
 * those of the new line are set to black.
 */

SetROP2(hdc, R2_NOTXORPEN);

/*
 * If a line was drawn during an earlier
 * WM_MOUSEMOVE message, draw over it. This erases
 * the line by setting the color of its pixels to
 * white.
 */

if (fPrevLine) {
    MoveToEx(hdc, ptsBegin.x, ptsBegin.y,
        (LPPOINT) NULL);
    LineTo(hdc, ptsPrevEnd.x, ptsPrevEnd.y);
}

/*
 * Convert the current cursor coordinates to a
 * POINTS structure, and then draw a new line.
 */

ptsEnd = MAKEPOINTS(lParam);
MoveToEx(hdc, ptsBegin.x, ptsBegin.y,
    (LPPOINT) NULL);
LineTo(hdc, ptsEnd.x, ptsEnd.y);

/*
 * Set the previous line flag, save the ending
 * point of the new line, and then release the DC.
 */

fPrevLine = TRUE;
ptsPrevEnd = ptsEnd;
ReleaseDC(hwndMain, hdc);
}
break;

case WM_LBUTTONUP:

/*
 * The user has finished drawing the line. Reset the
 * previous line flag, release the mouse cursor, and
```

```
                              * release the mouse capture.
                              */

                              fPrevLine = FALSE;
                              ClipCursor(NULL);
                              ReleaseCapture();
                              return 0;

                       case WM_DESTROY:
                              PostQuitMessage(0);
                              break;

                       .
                       . /* Process other messages. */
                       .
```

6.2.3 Processing a Double-Click Message

To receive double-click messages, a window must belong to a window class that
has the CS_DBLCLKS class style. You set this style when registering the window
class, as shown in the following example.

```
BOOL InitApplication(hInstance)
HINSTANCE hInstance;
{
    WNDCLASS wc;

    wc.style = CS_DBLCLKS | CS_HREDRAW | CS_VREDRAW;
    wc.lpfnWndProc = (WNDPROC) MainWndProc;
    wc.cbClsExtra = 0;
    wc.cbWndExtra = 0;
    wc.hInstance = hInstance;
    wc.hIcon = LoadIcon(NULL, IDI_APPLICATION);
    wc.hCursor = LoadCursor(NULL, IDC_IBEAM);
    wc.hbrBackground = GetStockObject(WHITE_BRUSH);
    wc.lpszMenuName = "MainMenu";
    wc.lpszClassName = "MainWClass";

    return RegisterClass(&wc);
}
```

A double-click message is always preceded by a button down message. For this
reason, applications typically use a double-click message to extend a task that it
began during a button down message.

6.2.4 Selecting a Line of Text

The example in this section is taken from a simple word-processing application. It
includes code that enables the user to set the position of the caret by clicking
anywhere on a line of text, and to select (highlight) a line of text by double-
clicking anywhere on the line.

```
LRESULT APIENTRY MainWndProc(hwndMain, uMsg, wParam, lParam)
HWND hwndMain;
UINT uMsg;
WPARAM wParam;
LPARAM lParam;
{
    HDC hdc;                         /* handle of device context   */
    TEXTMETRIC tm;                   /* font size data             */
    int i, j;                        /* loop counters              */
    int cCR = 0;                     /* count of carriage returns  */
    char ch;                         /* character from input buffer */
    static int nBegLine;             /* beginning of selected line */
    static int nCurrentLine = 0;     /* currently selected line    */
    static int nLastLine = 0;        /* last text line             */
    static int nCaretPosX = 0;       /* x-coordinate of caret      */
    static int cch = 0;              /* number of characters entered */
    static int nCharWidth = 0;       /* exact width of a character  */
    static char szHilite[128];       /* text string to highlight   */
    static DWORD dwCharX;            /* average width of characters */
    static DWORD dwLineHeight;       /* line height                */
    static POINTS ptsCursor;         /* coordinates of mouse cursor */
    static COLORREF crPrevText;      /* previous text color        */
    static COLORREF crPrevBk;        /* previous background color  */
    static PTCHAR pchInputBuf;       /* address of input buffer    */
    static BOOL fTextSelected = FALSE; /* text-selection flag      */


    switch (uMsg) {
        case WM_CREATE:

            /* Get the metrics of the current font. */

            hdc = GetDC(hwndMain);
            GetTextMetrics(hdc, &tm);
            ReleaseDC(hwndMain, hdc);

            /* Save the average character width and height. */

            dwCharX = tm.tmAveCharWidth;
            dwLineHeight = tm.tmHeight;

            /* Allocate a buffer to store keyboard input. */
```

```
                    pchInputBuf = (LPSTR) GlobalAlloc(GPTR,
                        BUFSIZE * sizeof(TCHAR));

                return 0;

            case WM_CHAR:
                switch (wParam) {
                    case 0x08: /* backspace */
                    case 0x0A: /* linefeed  */
                    case 0x1B: /* escape    */
                        MessageBeep(0xFFFFFFFF);
                        return 0;

                    case 0x09: /* tab */

                        /* Convert tabs to four consecutive spaces. */

                        for (i = 0; i < 4; i++)
                            SendMessage(hwndMain, WM_CHAR, 0x20, 0);
                        return 0;

                    case 0x0D: /* carriage return */

                        /*
                         * Record the carriage return, and position
                         * the caret at the beginning of the new line.
                         */

                        pchInputBuf[cch++] = 0x0D;
                        nCaretPosX = 0;
                        nCurrentLine += 1;
                        break;

                    default: /* displayable character */

                        ch = (char) wParam;
                        HideCaret(hwndMain);

                        /*
                         * Retrieve the character's width, and display
                         * the character.
                         */

                        hdc = GetDC(hwndMain);
                        GetCharWidth(hdc, (UINT) wParam, (UINT) wParam,
                            &nCharWidth);
                        TextOut(hdc, nCaretPosX,
                            nCurrentLine * dwLineHeight, &ch, 1);
                        ReleaseDC(hwndMain, hdc);
```

```
                          /* Store the character in the buffer. */

                          pchInputBuf[cch++] = ch;

                          /*
                           * Calculate the new horizontal position of
                           * the caret. If the new position exceeds the
                           * maximum, insert a carriage return and
                           * reposition the caret at the beginning of
                           * the next line.
                           */

                          nCaretPosX += nCharWidth;
                          if ((DWORD) nCaretPosX > dwMaxCharX) {
                              nCaretPosX = 0;
                              pchInputBuf[cch++] = 0x0D;
                              ++nCurrentLine;
                          }

                          ShowCaret(hwndMain);

                          break;
                  }
                  SetCaretPos(nCaretPosX, nCurrentLine * dwLineHeight);
                  nLastLine = max(nLastLine, nCurrentLine);
                  break;

          .
          . /* Process other messages. */
          .

          case WM_LBUTTONDOWN:

              /*
               * If a line of text is currently highlighted, redraw
               * the text to remove the highlighting.
               */

              if (fTextSelected) {
                  hdc = GetDC(hwndMain);
                  SetTextColor(hdc, crPrevText);
                  SetBkColor(hdc, crPrevBk);
                  TextOut(hdc, 0, nCurrentLine * dwLineHeight,
                      szHilite, lstrlen(szHilite));
                  ReleaseDC(hwndMain, hdc);
                  ShowCaret(hwndMain);
                  fTextSelected = FALSE;
              }
```

```
/* Save the current mouse-cursor coordinates. */

ptsCursor = MAKEPOINTS(lParam);

/*
 * Determine which line the cursor is on, and save
 * the line number. Do not allow line numbers greater
 * than the number of the last line of text. The
 * line number is later multiplied by the average
 * height of the current font. The result is used to
 * set the y-coordinate of the caret.
 */

nCurrentLine = min((int)(ptsCursor.y / dwLineHeight),
    nLastLine);

/*
 * Parse the text input buffer to find the first
 * character in the selected line of text. Each
 * line ends with a carriage return, so it is possible
 * to count the carriage returns to find the selected
 * line.
 */

cCR = 0;
nBegLine = 0;
if (nCurrentLine != 0) {
    for (i = 0; (i < cch) &&
            (cCR < nCurrentLine); i++) {
        if (pchInputBuf[i] == 0x0D)
            ++cCR;
    }
    nBegLine = i;
}

/*
 * Starting at the beginning of the selected line,
 * measure the width of each character, summing the
 * width with each character measured. Stop when the
 * sum is greater than the x-coordinate of the cursor.
 * The sum is used to set the x-coordinate of the
 * caret.
 */

hdc = GetDC(hwndMain);
nCaretPosX = 0;
for (i = nBegLine;
        (pchInputBuf[i] != 0x0D) && (i < cch); i++) {
    ch = pchInputBuf[i];
    GetCharWidth(hdc, (int) ch, (int) ch, &nCharWidth);
```

```
                    if ((nCaretPosX + nCharWidth) > ptsCursor.x)
                        break;
                    else
                        nCaretPosX += nCharWidth;
                }
                ReleaseDC(hwndMain, hdc);

                /* Set the caret to the user-selected position. */

                SetCaretPos(nCaretPosX, nCurrentLine * dwLineHeight);
                break;

            case WM_LBUTTONDBLCLK:

                /* Copy the selected line of text to a buffer. */

                for (i = nBegLine, j = 0; (pchInputBuf[i] != 0x0D) &&
                        (i < cch); i++)
                    szHilite[j++] = pchInputBuf[i];
                szHilite[j] = '\0';

                /*
                 * Hide the caret, invert the background and
                 * foreground colors, and then redraw the selected
                 * line.
                 */

                HideCaret(hwndMain);
                hdc = GetDC(hwndMain);
                crPrevText = SetTextColor(hdc, RGB(255, 255, 255));
                crPrevBk = SetBkColor(hdc, RGB(0, 0, 0));
                TextOut(hdc, 0, nCurrentLine * dwLineHeight, szHilite,
                    lstrlen(szHilite));
                SetTextColor(hdc, crPrevText);
                SetBkColor(hdc, crPrevBk);
                ReleaseDC(hwndMain, hdc);

                fTextSelected = TRUE;
                break;
                .
                . /* Process other messages. */
                .
            default:
                return DefWindowProc(hwndMain, uMsg, wParam, lParam);
        }
        return NULL;
    }
```

6.3 Functions and Messages

Following are the functions and messages used to receive and process mouse input.

Functions

GetCapture
GetDoubleClickTime
mouse_event
ReleaseCapture
SetCapture
SetDoubleClickTime
SwapMouseButton

Messages

WM_LBUTTONDBLCLK
WM_LBUTTONDOWN
WM_LBUTTONUP
WM_MBUTTONDBLCLK
WM_MBUTTONDOWN
WM_MBUTTONUP
WM_MOUSEACTIVATE
WM_MOUSEMOVE
WM_NCHITTEST
WM_NCLBUTTONDBLCLK
WM_NCLBUTTONDOWN
WM_NCLBUTTONUP
WM_NCMBUTTONDBLCLK
WM_NCMBUTTONDOWN
WM_NCMBUTTONUP
WM_NCMOUSEMOVE
WM_NCRBUTTONDBLCLK
WM_NCRBUTTONDOWN
WM_NCRBUTTONUP
WM_RBUTTONDBLCLK
WM_RBUTTONDOWN
WM_RBUTTONUP

CHAPTER 7

Timers

7.1 About Timers

A *timer* is an internal routine that repeatedly measures a specified interval, in milliseconds. Each time the interval called a *time-out value* elapses, the system notifies the window associated with the timer. Because the accuracy of a timer depends on the system clock rate and how often the application retrieves messages from the message queue, the time-out value is only approximate.

An application written for Microsoft ® Windows ™ creates a timer by using the **SetTimer** function. If a window handle is given in this function, the application creates the timer for that window. Then, whenever the time-out value elapses, the system posts a WM_TIMER message to the window. If no window handle is given in the **SetTimer** function, the application that created the timer must monitor its message queue for WM_TIMER messages and dispatch them to the appropriate window.

A new timer starts timing as soon as it is created. An application can change a timer's time-out value by using **SetTimer** and can destroy a timer by using the **KillTimer** function. To use system resources efficiently, applications should destroy timers that are no longer necessary.

Each timer has a unique identifier. When creating a timer, an application can either specify an identifier or have the system create a unique value. The first parameter of a WM_TIMER message contains the identifier of the timer that posted the message.

7.2 Using Timers

This section shows how to perform the following tasks:

- Create a timer.
- Destroy a timer.
- Process the WM_TIMER message.
- Use a **TimerProc** callback function.

7.2.1 Creating a Timer

The following code sample uses the **SetTimer** function to create two timers. The first timer is set for every 10 seconds, the second for every 5 minutes.

```
/* Set two timers. */

SetTimer(hwnd,              /* handle of main window */
    IDT_TIMER1,            /* timer identifier      */
    10000,                 /* 10-second interval    */
```

```
    (TIMERPROC) NULL);        /* no timer callback      */

SetTimer(hwnd,              ·  /* handle of main window */
    IDT_TIMER2,               /* timer identifier      */
    300000,                   /* 5-minute interval     */
    (TIMERPROC) NULL);        /* no timer callback     */
```

To process the WM_TIMER messages generated by these timers, add a
WM_TIMER case statement to the window procedure for *hwnd*.

```
case WM_TIMER:

    switch (wParam) {

        case IDT_TIMER1:

            .
            . /* Process the 10-second timer. */
            .

            return 0;

        case IDT_TIMER2:

            .
            . /* Process the 5-minute timer. */
            .

            return 0;
    }
```

An application can also create a timer whose WM_TIMER messages are
processed not by the main window procedure but by an application-defined
callback function, as in the following code sample, which creates a timer and uses
the callback function MyTimerProc to process the timer's WM_TIMER
messages.

```
/* Set the timer. */

SetTimer(hwnd,                    /* handle of main window */
    IDT_TIMER3,                   /* timer identifier      */
    5000,                         /* 5-second interval     */
    (TIMERPROC) MyTimerProc);     /* timer callback        */
```

The calling convention for MyTimerProc must be based on the Microsoft ®
Win32 ™ callback function **TimerProc**.

If your application creates a timer without specifying a window handle, your application must monitor the message queue for WM_TIMER messages and dispatch them to the appropriate window.

```
HWND hwndTimer;    /* handle of window for timer messages */
MSG msg;           /* message structure */

    while (GetMessage(&msg, /* message structure              */
            NULL,           /* handle of window receiving msg. */
            NULL,           /* lowest message to examine       */
            NULL))          /* highest message to examine      */
    {

        /* Post WM_TIMER messages to the hwndTimer procedure. */

        if (msg.message == WM_TIMER) {
            msg.hwnd = hwndTimer;
        }

        TranslateMessage(&msg); /* translates virtual-key codes */
        DispatchMessage(&msg);  /* dispatches message to window */
    }
```

7.2.2 Destroying a Timer

Applications should use the **KillTimer** function to destroy timers that are no longer necessary. The following example destroys the timers identified by the constants IDT_TIMER1, IDT_TIMER2, and IDT_TIMER3.

```
/* Destroy the timers. */

KillTimer(hwnd, IDT_TIMER1);
KillTimer(hwnd, IDT_TIMER2);
KillTimer(hwnd, IDT_TIMER3);
```

7.2.3 Creating a Mousetrap

Sometimes it is necessary to prevent more input while you have a cursor on the screen. One way to accomplish this is to create a special routine that traps mouse input until a specific event occurs. Many developers refer to this routine as "building a mousetrap."

The following code sample uses the **SetTimer** and **KillTimer** functions to create a simple mousetrap. **SetTimer** creates a timer that sends a WM_TIMER message every 10 seconds. Each time the application receives a WM_TIMER message, it records the cursor location. If the current location is the same as the previous location and the application's main window is minimized, the application moves the cursor to the icon. When the application closes, **KillTimer** stops the timer.

```
HICON hIcon1;                  /* icon handle                    */
POINT ptOld;                   /* previous cursor location       */
UINT uResult;                  /* SetTimer's return value        */
HINSTANCE hinstance;           /* handle of current instance     */

.
. /* Perform application initialization here. */
.

wc.hIcon = LoadIcon(hinstance, MAKEINTRESOURCE(400));
wc.hCursor = LoadCursor(hinstance, MAKEINTRESOURCE(200));

/* Record the initial cursor position. */

GetCursorPos(&ptOld);

/* Set the timer for the mousetrap. */

uResult = SetTimer(hwnd,            /* handle of main window */
    IDT_MOUSETRAP,                  /* timer identifier      */
    10000,                          /* 10-second interval    */
    (TIMERPROC) NULL);              /* no timer callback     */

if (uResult == 0) {
    ErrorHandler("No timer is available.");
}

LONG APIENTRY MainWndProc(
HWND hwnd,             /* handle of main window  */
UINT message,         /* type of message        */
UINT wParam,          /* additional information */
LONG lParam)          /* additional information */
{

    HDC hdc;          /* handle of device context      */
    POINT pt;         /* current cursor location       */
    RECT rc;          /* location of minimized window  */

    switch (message) {

        .
        . /* Process other messages. */
        .

        case WM_TIMER:

            /*
             * If the window is minimized, compare the current
             * cursor position with the one from 10 seconds
             * earlier. If the cursor position has not changed,
```

```
                              * move the cursor to the icon.
                              */

                     if (IsIconic(hwnd)) {
                         GetCursorPos(&pt);

                         if ((pt.x == ptOld.x) && (pt.y == ptOld.y)) {
                             GetWindowRect(hwnd, &rc);
                             SetCursorPos(rc.left, rc.top);
                         }
                         else {
                             ptOld.x = pt.x;
                             ptOld.y = pt.y;
                         }
                     }

                     return 0;

                 case WM_DESTROY:

                     /* Destroy the timer. */

                     KillTimer(hwnd, IDT_MOUSETRAP);
                     PostQuitMessage(0);
                     break;

                 .
                 . /* Process other messages. */
                 .

             }
```

Although the following code sample also creates a mousetrap, it processes the
WM_TIMER message through the application-defined callback function
MyTimerProc, rather than through the application's message queue.

```
UINT uResult;                 /* SetTimer's return value     */
HICON hIcon1;                 /* icon handle                 */
POINT ptOld;                  /* previous cursor location    */
HINSTANCE hinstance;          /* handle of current instance  */

.
. /* Perform application initialization here. */
.

wc.hIcon = LoadIcon(hinstance, MAKEINTRESOURCE(400));
wc.hCursor = LoadCursor(hinstance, MAKEINTRESOURCE(200));

/* Record the current cursor position. */
```

```
GetCursorPos(&ptOld);

/* Set the timer for the mousetrap. */

uResult = SetTimer(hwnd,          /* handle of main window */
    IDT_MOUSETRAP,                /* timer identifier      */
    10000,                        /* 10-second interval    */
    (TIMERPROC) MyTimerProc);     /* timer callback        */

if (uResult == 0) {
    ErrorHandler("No timer is available.");
}

LONG APIENTRY MainWndProc(
HWND hwnd,              /* handle of main window  */
UINT message,          /* type of message        */
UINT wParam,           /* additional information */
LONG lParam)           /* additional information */
{

    HDC hdc;           /* handle of device context */

    switch (message) {


        . /* Process other messages. */
        .

        case WM_DESTROY:

            /* Destroy the timer. */

            KillTimer(hwnd, IDT_MOUSETRAP);
            PostQuitMessage(0);
            break;


        . /* Process other messages. */
        .

}

/*
 * MyTimerProc is an application-defined callback function that
 * processes WM_TIMER messages.
 */

VOID CALLBACK MyTimerProc(
    HWND hwnd,         /* handle of window for timer messages */
    UINT message,      /* WM_TIMER message                   */
```

```
                    UINT idTimer,    /* timer identifier              */
                    DWORD dwTime)    /* current system time           */
               {

                    RECT rc;
                    POINT pt;

                    /*
                     * If the window is minimized, compare the current
                     * cursor position with the one from 10 seconds earlier.
                     * If the cursor position has not changed, move the
                     * cursor to the icon.
                     */

                    if (IsIconic(hwnd)) {
                        GetCursorPos(&pt);

                        if ((pt.x == ptOld.x) && (pt.y == ptOld.y)) {
                            GetWindowRect(hwnd, &rc);
                            SetCursorPos(rc.left, rc.top);
                        }
                        else {
                            ptOld.x = pt.x;
                            ptOld.y = pt.y;
                        }
                    }
               }
```

7.3 Functions

The following functions are used with timers.

KillTimer
SetTimer
TimerProc

C H A P T E R 8

Hooks

8.1 About Hooks

A *hook* is a point in the Microsoft ® Windows ™ message-handling mechanism where an application can install a subroutine to monitor the message traffic in the system and process certain types of messages before they reach the target window procedure. This chapter describes Windows hooks and explains how to use them in a Windows-based application.

8.1.1 Hook Chains

Windows contains many different types of hooks; each type provides access to a different aspect of the Windows message-handling mechanism. For example, an application can use the WH_MOUSE hook to monitor the message traffic for mouse messages.

Windows maintains a separate hook chain for each type of hook. A *hook chain* is a list of pointers to special, application-defined callback functions called *hook procedures*. When a message occurs that is associated with a particular type of hook, Windows passes the message to each hook procedure referenced in the hook chain, one after the other. The action a hook procedure can take depends on the type of hook involved. The hook procedures for some types of hooks can only monitor messages; others can modify messages or stop their progress though the chain, preventing them from reaching the next hook procedure or the destination window.

Hooks tend to slow down the system because they increase the amount of processing the system must perform for each message. A developer should install a hook only when necessary, and remove it as soon as possible.

8.1.2 Hook Procedures

To take advantage of a particular type of hook, the developer provides a hook procedure and uses the **SetWindowsHookEx** function to install it into the chain associated with the hook. A hook procedure must have the following syntax:

LRESULT CALLBACK *HookProc(nCode, wParam, lParam)*
int *nCode*;
WPARAM *wParam*;
LPARAM *lParam*;

HookProc is a placeholder for an application-defined name. Because Windows must call the hook procedure, the actual name must be exported by listing it and, optionally, its ordinal value, in the **EXPORTS** statement of the application's module-definition file.

The *nCode* parameter is a hook code that the hook procedure uses to determine the action to perform. The value of the hook code depends on the type of the hook; each type has its own characteristic set of hook codes. The values of the *wParam* and *lParam* parameters depend on the hook code, but they typically contain information about a message that was sent or posted.

SetWindowsHookEx always installs a hook procedure at the beginning of a hook chain. When an event occurs that is monitored by a particular type of hook, Windows calls the procedure at the beginning of the hook chain associated with the hook. Each hook procedure in the chain determines whether to pass the event to the next procedure. A hook procedure passes an event to the next procedure by calling the **CallNextHookEx** function.

Note that the hook procedures for some types of hooks can only monitor messages. Windows passes messages to each hook procedure, regardless of whether a particular procedure calls **CallNextHookEx**.

A hook procedure can be global, monitoring messages for all threads in the system, or it can be thread specific, monitoring messages for only an individual thread. A global hook procedure can be called in the context of any application, so the procedure must be in a separate dynamic-link library (DLL) module. A thread specific hook procedure is called only in the context of the associated thread. If an application installs a hook procedure for one of its own threads, the hook procedure can be in either the same module as the rest of the application's code or in a DLL. If the application installs a hook procedure for a thread of a different application, the procedure must be in a DLL. For information about DLLs, see Chapter 50, "Dynamic-Link Libraries."

8.1.3 Hook Types

Each type of hook enables an application to monitor a different aspect of the Windows message-handling mechanism. The following sections describe the types of hooks available in Windows. For more information about each type of hook, see the description of the appropriate hook procedure in the *Microsoft Win32 Programmer's Reference, Volumes 3* and *4*.

8.1.3.1 WH_CALLWNDPROC Hook

The WH_CALLWNDPROC hook enables an application to monitor messages sent to window procedures by the **SendMessage** function. Windows calls a WH_CALLWNDPROC hook procedure before passing the message to the receiving window procedure.

8.1.3.2 WH_CBT Hook

Windows calls a WH_CBT hook procedure before activating, creating, destroying, minimizing, maximizing, moving, or sizing a window; before completing a system command; before removing a mouse or keyboard event from the system message queue; before setting the input focus; or before synchronizing with the system message queue. The value the hook procedure returns determines whether Windows allows or prevents one of these operations. The WH_CBT hook is intended primarily for Windows computer-based training (CBT) applications.

8.1.3.3 WH_DEBUG Hook

Windows calls a WH_DEBUG hook procedure before calling hook procedures associated with any other hook in the system. An application can use this hook to determine whether to allow the system to call hook procedures associated with other types of hooks.

8.1.3.4 WH_GETMESSAGE Hook

The WH_GETMESSAGE hook enables an application to monitor messages about to be returned by the **GetMessage** or **PeekMessage** function. An application uses the WH_GETMESSAGE hook to monitor mouse and keyboard input and other messages posted to a queue.

8.1.3.5 WH_JOURNALRECORD Hook

The WH_JOURNALRECORD hook enables an application to monitor and record input events. Typically, an application uses this hook to record a sequence of mouse and keyboard events it can play back later by using the WH_JOURNALPLAYBACK hook. The WH_JOURNALRECORD hook is a global hook—it cannot be used as a thread-specific hook.

8.1.3.6 WH_JOURNALPLAYBACK Hook

The WH_JOURNALPLAYBACK hook enables an application to insert messages into the system message queue. An application might use this hook to play back a series of mouse and keyboard events recorded earlier by using the WH_JOURNALRECORD hook. Regular mouse and keyboard input is disabled as long as a WH_JOURNALPLAYBACK hook is installed. A WH_JOURNALPLAYBACK hook is a global hook—it cannot be used as a thread-specific hook.

The WH_JOURNALPLAYBACK hook returns a time-out value. This value tells the system how many milliseconds to wait before processing the current message from the playback hook. This enables the hook to control the timing of the events it plays back.

8.1.3.7 WH_KEYBOARD Hook

The WH_KEYBOARD hook enables an application to monitor message traffic for WM_KEYDOWN and WM_KEYUP messages about to be returned by the **GetMessage** or **PeekMessage** function. An application uses the WH_KEYBOARD hook to monitor keyboard input posted to a message queue.

8.1.3.8 WH_MOUSE Hook

The WH_MOUSE hook enables an application to monitor mouse messages about to be returned by the **GetMessage** or **PeekMessage** function. An application uses the WH_MOUSE hook to monitor mouse input posted to a message queue.

8.1.3.9 WH_MSGFILTER and WH_SYSMSGFILTER Hooks

The WH_MSGFILTER and WH_SYSMSGFILTER hooks enable an application to monitor messages about to be processed by a menu, scroll bar, message box, or dialog box, and to detect when a different window is about to be activated as a result of the user's pressing the ALT+TAB or ALT+ESC key combination. The WH_MSGFILTER hook can monitor only messages passed to a menu, scroll bar, message box, or dialog box created by the application that installed the hook procedure. The WH_SYSMSGFILTER hook monitors such messages for all applications.

The WH_MSGFILTER and WH_SYSMSGFILTER hooks enable an application to perform message filtering during modal loops that is equivalent to the filtering done in the main message loop. For example, an application often examines a new message in the main loop between the time it retrieves the message from the queue and the time it dispatches the message, performing special processing as appropriate. However, during a modal loop, the system retrieves and dispatches messages without allowing an application the chance to filter the messages in its main message loop. If an application installs a WH_MSGFILTER or WH_SYSMSGFILTER hook procedure, the system calls the procedure during the modal loop. For more information about modal loops, see Chapter 1, "Windows."

An application can call the WH_MSGFILTER hook directly by calling the **CallMsgFilter** function. By using this function, the application can use the same code to filter messages during modal loops as it uses in the main message loop. To do so, the application encapsulates the filtering operations in a WH_MSGFILTER hook procedure and calls **CallMsgFilter** between the calls to the **GetMessage** and **DispatchMessage** functions.

```
while (GetMessage(&msg, (HWND) NULL, 0, 0)) {
    if (!CallMsgFilter(&qmsg, 0))
        DispatchMessage(&qmsg);
}
```

The last argument of **CallMsgFilter** is simply passed to the hook procedure; the application can enter any value. The hook procedure, by defining a constant such as MSGF_MAINLOOP, can use this value to determine where the procedure was called from.

8.1.3.10 WH_SHELL Hook

A Windows shell application can use the WH_SHELL hook to receive important notifications. Windows calls a WH_SHELL hook procedure when the shell application is about to be activated and when a top-level window is created or destroyed.

8.2 Using Hooks

This section explains how to install and release hook procedures. It also contains an example demonstrating how to use hooks to monitor the system for a variety of events.

8.2.1 Installing and Releasing Hook Procedures

You can install a hook procedure by calling the **SetWindowsHookEx** function and specifying the type of hook calling the procedure, whether the procedure should be associated with all threads or with a particular thread, and a pointer to a procedure entry point.

You must place a global hook procedure in a DLL separate from the application installing the hook procedure. The installing application must have the handle of the DLL module before it can install the hook procedure. The **LoadLibrary** function, when given the name of the DLL, returns the handle of the DLL module. After you have the handle, you can call the **GetProcAddress** function to retrieve the address of the hook procedure. Finally, you use **SetWindowsHookEx** to install the hook procedure address in the appropriate hook chain. **SetWindowsHookEx** passes the module handle, a pointer to the hook-procedure entry point, and 0 for the thread identifier, indicating that the hook procedure should be associated with all threads in the system. This sequence is shown in the following example.

```
HOOKPROC hkprcSysMsg;
static HINSTANCE hinstDLL;
static HHOOK hhookSysMsg;

    .
    .
    .

hinstDLL = LoadLibrary((LPCTSTR) "c:\\windows\\sysmsg.dll");
hkprcSysMsg = (HOOKPROC)GetProcAddress(hinstDLL, "SysMessageProc");
hhookSysMsg = SetWindowsHookEx(WH_SYSMSGFILTER,
    hkprcSysMsg, hinstDLL, 0);

    .
    .
    .
```

You can release a thread-specific hook procedure (remove its address from the hook chain) by calling the **UnhookWindowsHookEx** function, specifying the handle of the hook procedure to release. Release a hook procedure as soon as your application no longer needs it.

You can release a global hook procedure by using **UnhookWindowsHookEx**, but this function does not free the DLL containing the hook procedure. This is because global hook procedures are called in the process context of every Windows-based application in the system, causing an implicit call to the **LoadLibrary** function for all of those processes. Because a call to the **FreeLibrary** function cannot be made for another process, there is then no way to free the DLL. Windows eventually frees the DLL after all processes explicitly linked to the DLL have either terminated or called **FreeLibrary** and all processes that called the hook procedure have resumed processing outside the DLL.

An alternative method for installing a global hook procedure is to provide an installation function in the DLL, along with the hook procedure. With this method, the installing application does not need the handle of the DLL module. By linking with the DLL, the application gains access to the installation function. The installation function can supply the DLL module handle and other details in the call to **SetWindowsHookEx**. The DLL can also contain a function that releases the global hook procedure; the application can call this hook-releasing function when terminating.

8.2.2 Monitoring System Events

The example in this section uses a variety of thread-specific hook procedures to monitor the system for events affecting a thread. It demonstrates how to process events for the following types of hook procedures:

WH_CALLWNDPROC
WH_CBT
WH_DEBUG
WH_GETMESSAGE
WH_KEYBOARD
WH_MOUSE
WH_MSGFILTER

In this example, the user can install and remove a hook procedure by using the menu. When a hook procedure is installed and an event that is monitored by the procedure occurs, the procedure writes information about the event to the client area of the application's main window.

```
#define NUMHOOKS 7

/* Global variables */

typedef struct _MYHOOKDATA {
    int nType;
    HOOKPROC hkprc;
    HHOOK hhook;
} MYHOOKDATA;

MYHOOKDATA myhookdata[NUMHOOKS];

LONG APIENTRY MainWndProc(hwndMain, uMsg, wParam, lParam)
HWND hwndMain;
UINT uMsg;
UINT wParam;
LONG lParam;
{
    static BOOL afHooks[NUMHOOKS];
    int index;
    static HMENU hmenu;

    switch (uMsg) {
        case WM_CREATE:

            /* Save the menu handle. */

            hmenu = GetMenu(hwndMain);

            /*
             * Initialize structures with hook data. The menu-item
             * identifiers are defined as 0 through 6 in the
             * header file. They can be used to identify array
             * elements both here and during the WM_COMMAND
             * message.
             */

            myhookdata[IDM_CALLWNDPROC].nType = WH_CALLWNDPROC;
            myhookdata[IDM_CALLWNDPROC].hkprc = CallWndProc;
            myhookdata[IDM_CBT].nType = WH_CBT;
            myhookdata[IDM_CBT].hkprc = CBTProc;
            myhookdata[IDM_DEBUG].nType = WH_DEBUG;
            myhookdata[IDM_DEBUG].hkprc = DebugProc;
            myhookdata[IDM_GETMESSAGE].nType = WH_GETMESSAGE;
            myhookdata[IDM_GETMESSAGE].hkprc = GetMsgProc;
            myhookdata[IDM_KEYBOARD].nType = WH_KEYBOARD;
            myhookdata[IDM_KEYBOARD].hkprc = KeyboardProc;
            myhookdata[IDM_MOUSE].nType = WH_MOUSE;
            myhookdata[IDM_MOUSE].hkprc = MouseProc;
            myhookdata[IDM_MSGFILTER].nType = WH_MSGFILTER;
```

```
                    myhookdata[IDM_MSGFILTER].hkprc = MessageProc;

                    /* Initialize all flags in the array to FALSE. */

                    memset(afHooks, FALSE, sizeof(afHooks));

                    return 0;

                case WM_COMMAND:
                    switch (LOWORD(wParam)) {

                        /*
                         * The user selected a hook command from the menu.
                         */

                        case IDM_CALLWNDPROC:
                        case IDM_CBT:
                        case IDM_DEBUG:
                        case IDM_GETMESSAGE:
                        case IDM_KEYBOARD:
                        case IDM_MOUSE:
                        case IDM_MSGFILTER:

                            /*
                             * Use the menu-item identifier as an index
                             * into the array of structures with hook data.
                             */

                            index = LOWORD(wParam);

                            /*
                             * If the selected type of hook procedure isn't
                             * installed yet, install it and check the
                             * associated menu item.
                             */

                            if (!afHooks[index]) {
                                myhookdata[index].hhook = SetWindowsHookEx(
                                    myhookdata[index].nType,
                                    myhookdata[index].hkprc,
                                    (HINSTANCE) NULL, GetCurrentThreadId());
                                CheckMenuItem(hmenu, index,
                                    MF_BYCOMMAND | MF_CHECKED);
                                afHooks[index] = TRUE;
                            }

                            /*
                             * If the selected type of hook procedure is
                             * already installed, remove it and remove the
                             * check mark from the associated menu item.
```

```
                              */
                        else {
                            UnhookWindowsHookEx(myhookdata[index].hhook);
                            CheckMenuItem(hmenu, index,
                                MF_BYCOMMAND | MF_UNCHECKED);
                            afHooks[index] = FALSE;
                        }

                    default:
                        return (DefWindowProc(hwndMain, uMsg, wParam,
                            lParam));
                }
                break;

                .
                . /* Process other messages. */
                .

        default:
            return DefWindowProc(hwndMain, uMsg, wParam, lParam);
    }
    return NULL;
}

/******************************************************************
  WH_CALLWNDPROC hook procedure
 ******************************************************************/

LRESULT CALLBACK CallWndProc(nCode, wParam, lParam)
int nCode;
WPARAM wParam;
LPARAM lParam;
{
    CHAR szCWPBuf[256];
    CHAR szMsg[16];
    HDC hdc;
    static int c = 0;
    int cch;

    if (nCode < 0)  /* do not process message */
        return CallNextHookEx(myhookdata[CALLWNDPROC].hhook, nCode,
                wParam, lParam);

    /*
     * Call an application-defined function that converts a message
     * constant to a string and copies it to a buffer.
     */

    LookUpTheMessage((PMSG) lParam, szMsg);
```

```
                hdc = GetDC(hwndMain);

                switch (nCode) {
                    case HC_ACTION:
                        cch = wsprintf(szCWPBuf,
                            "CALLWNDPROC - tsk: %ld, msg: %s, %d times    ",
                            wParam, szMsg, c++);
                        TextOut(hdc, 2, 15, szCWPBuf, cch);
                        break;

                    default:
                        break;
                }

            ReleaseDC(hwndMain, hdc);
            return CallNextHookEx(myhookdata[CALLWNDPROC].hhook, nCode,
                wParam, lParam);
        }


/****************************************************************
    WH_GETMESSAGE hook procedure
 ****************************************************************/

LRESULT CALLBACK GetMsgProc(nCode, wParam, lParam)
int nCode;
WPARAM wParam;
LPARAM lParam;
{
    CHAR szMSGBuf[256];
    CHAR szRem[16];
    CHAR szMsg[16];
    HDC hdc;
    static int c = 0;
    int cch;

    if (nCode < 0) /* do not process message */
        return CallNextHookEx(myhookdata[GETMESSAGE].hhook, nCode,
            wParam, lParam);

    switch (nCode) {
        case HC_ACTION:
            switch (wParam) {
                case PM_REMOVE:
                    lstrcpy(szRem, "PM_REMOVE");
                    break;

                case PM_NOREMOVE:
                    lstrcpy(szRem, "PM_NOREMOVE");
                    break;
```

```
                    default:
                        lstrcpy(szRem, "Unknown");
                        break;
                }

                /*
                 * Call an application-defined function that converts a
                 * message constant to a string and copies it to a
                 * buffer.
                 */

                LookUpTheMessage((PMSG) lParam, szMsg);

                hdc = GetDC(hwndMain);
                cch = wsprintf(szMSGBuf,
                    "GETMESSAGE - wParam: %s, msg: %s, %d times    ",
                    szRem, szMsg, c++);
                TextOut(hdc, 2, 35, szMSGBuf, cch);
                break;

            default:
                break;
        }

        ReleaseDC(hwndMain, hdc);
        return CallNextHookEx(myhookdata[GETMESSAGE].hhook, nCode,
            wParam, lParam);
}

/****************************************************************
  WH_DEBUG hook procedure
 ****************************************************************/

LRESULT CALLBACK DebugProc(nCode, wParam, lParam)
int nCode;
WPARAM wParam;
LPARAM lParam;
{
    CHAR szBuf[128];
    HDC hdc;
    static int c = 0;
    int cch;

    if (nCode < 0)  /* do not process message */
        return CallNextHookEx(myhookdata[DEBUG].hhook, nCode,
            wParam, lParam);

    hdc = GetDC(hwndMain);
```

```
            switch (nCode) {
                case HC_ACTION:
                    cch = wsprintf(szBuf,
                        "DEBUG - nCode: %d, tsk: %ld, %d times    ",
                        nCode,wParam, c++);
                    TextOut(hdc, 2, 55, szBuf, cch);
                    break;

                default:
                    break;
            }

        ReleaseDC(hwndMain, hdc);
        return CallNextHookEx(myhookdata[DEBUG].hhook, nCode, wParam,
            lParam);
    }

    /****************************************************************
      WH_CBT hook procedure
    ****************************************************************/

    LRESULT CALLBACK CBTProc(nCode, wParam, lParam)
    int nCode;
    WPARAM wParam;
    LPARAM lParam;
    {
        CHAR szBuf[128];
        CHAR szCode[128];
        HDC hdc;
        static int c = 0;
        int cch;

        if (nCode < 0)  /* do not process message */
            return CallNextHookEx(myhookdata[CBT].hhook, nCode, wParam,
                lParam);

        hdc = GetDC(hwndMain);

        switch (nCode) {
            case HCBT_ACTIVATE:
                lstrcpy(szCode, "HCBT_ACTIVATE");
                break;

            case HCBT_CLICKSKIPPED:
                lstrcpy(szCode, "HCBT_CLICKSKIPPED");
                break;

            case HCBT_CREATEWND:
                lstrcpy(szCode, "HCBT_CREATEWND");
                break;
```

```
        case HCBT_DESTROYWND:
            lstrcpy(szCode, "HCBT_DESTROYWND");
            break;

        case HCBT_KEYSKIPPED:
            lstrcpy(szCode, "HCBT_KEYSKIPPED");
            break;

        case HCBT_MINMAX:
            lstrcpy(szCode, "HCBT_MINMAX");
            break;

        case HCBT_MOVESIZE:
            lstrcpy(szCode, "HCBT_MOVESIZE");
            break;

        case HCBT_QS:
            lstrcpy(szCode, "HCBT_QS");
            break;

        case HCBT_SETFOCUS:
            lstrcpy(szCode, "HCBT_SETFOCUS");
            break;

        case HCBT_SYSCOMMAND:
            lstrcpy(szCode, "HCBT_SYSCOMMAND");
            break;

        default:
            lstrcpy(szCode, "Unknown");
            break;
    }

    cch = wsprintf(szBuf, "CBT - nCode: %s, tsk: %ld, %d times     ",
        szCode, wParam, c++);
    TextOut(hdc, 2, 75, szBuf, cch);
    ReleaseDC(hwndMain, hdc);
    return CallNextHookEx(myhookdata[CBT].hhook, nCode, wParam,
        lParam);
}


/****************************************************************
  WH_MOUSE hook procedure
 ****************************************************************/

LRESULT CALLBACK MouseProc(nCode, wParam, lParam)
int nCode;
WPARAM wParam;
LPARAM lParam;
```

```
{
    CHAR szBuf[128];
    CHAR szMsg[16];
    HDC hdc;
    static int c = 0;
    int cch;

    if (nCode < 0)   /* do not process the message */
        return CallNextHookEx(myhookdata[MOUSE].hhook, nCode,
            wParam, lParam);

    /*
     * Call an application-defined function that converts a message
     * constant to a string and copies it to a buffer.
     */

    LookUpTheMessage((PMSG) lParam, szMsg);

    hdc = GetDC(hwndMain);
    cch = wsprintf(szBuf,
        "MOUSE - nCode: %d, msg: %s, x: %d, y: %d, %d times     ",
        nCode, szMsg, LOWORD(lParam), HIWORD(lParam), c++);
    TextOut(hdc, 2, 95, szBuf, cch);
    ReleaseDC(hwndMain, hdc);
    return CallNextHookEx(myhookdata[MOUSE].hhook, nCode, wParam,
        lParam);
}

/******************************************************************
  WH_KEYBOARD hook procedure
 ******************************************************************/

LRESULT CALLBACK KeyboardProc(nCode, wParam, lParam)
int nCode;
WPARAM wParam;
LPARAM lParam;
{
    CHAR szBuf[128];
    HDC hdc;
    static int c = 0;
    int cch;

    if (nCode < 0)   /* do not process message */
        return CallNextHookEx(myhookdata[KEYBOARD].hhook, nCode,
            wParam, lParam);

    hdc = GetDC(hwndMain);
    cch = wsprintf(szBuf, "KEYBOARD - nCode: %d, vk: %d, %d times ",
        nCode, wParam, c++);
    TextOut(hdc, 2, 115, szBuf, cch);
```

```
            ReleaseDC(hwndMain, hdc);
            return CallNextHookEx(myhookdata[KEYBOARD].hhook, nCode, wParam,
                lParam);
        }


        /****************************************************************
          WH_MSGFILTER hook procedure
        ****************************************************************/

        LRESULT CALLBACK MessageProc(nCode, wParam, lParam)
        int nCode;
        WPARAM wParam;
        LPARAM lParam;
        {
            CHAR szBuf[128];
            CHAR szMsg[16];
            CHAR szCode[32];
            HDC hdc;
            static int c = 0;
            int cch;

            if (nCode < 0)  /* do not process message */
                return CallNextHookEx(myhookdata[MSGFILTER].hhook, nCode,
                    wParam, lParam);

            switch (nCode) {
                case MSGF_DIALOGBOX:
                    lstrcpy(szCode, "MSGF_DIALOGBOX");
                    break;

                case MSGF_MENU:
                    lstrcpy(szCode, "MSGF_MENU");
                    break;

                case MSGF_SCROLLBAR:
                    lstrcpy(szCode, "MSGF_SCROLLBAR");
                    break;

                case MSGF_NEXTWINDOW:
                    lstrcpy(szCode, "MSGF_NEXTWINDOW");
                    break;

                default:
                    wsprintf(szCode, "Unknown: %d", nCode);
                    break;
            }

            /*
             * Call an application-defined function that converts a message
             * constant to a string and copies it to a buffer.
```

```
    */

    LookUpTheMessage((PMSG) lParam, szMsg);

    hdc = GetDC(hwndMain);
    cch = wsprintf(szBuf,
        "MSGFILTER  nCode: %s, msg: %s, %d times     ",
        szCode, szMsg, c++);
    TextOut(hdc, 2, 135, szBuf, cch);
    ReleaseDC(hwndMain, hdc);
    return CallNextHookEx(myhookdata[MSGFILTER].hhook, nCode,
        wParam, lParam);
}
```

8.3 Functions

Following are the Windows functions and the message used with hooks.

Functions
CallMsgFilter
CallNextHookEx
CallWndProc
CBTProc
DebugProc
DefHookProc
GetMsgProc
HardwareProc
JournalPlaybackProc
JournalRecordProc
KeyboardProc
MessageProc
MouseProc
SetWindowsHook
SetWindowsHookEx
ShellProc
SysMsgProc
UnhookWindowsHook
UnhookWindowsHookEx

Message
WM_QUEUESYNC

CHAPTER 9

Controls

9.1 About Controls

In Microsoft ® Windows ™, a *control* is a child window an application uses in conjunction with another window to carry out simple input and output (I/O) tasks. Controls are most often used within dialog boxes, but they can also be used in other windows. Controls within dialog boxes provide the user with the means to type text, choose options, and direct a dialog box to complete its action. Controls in other windows provide a variety of services, such as letting the user choose commands, view status, and view and edit text.

Like other windows, each control belongs to a window class, either predefined or application defined. The window class and the corresponding window procedure define the properties of the control, its appearance, behavior, and purpose. An application can create controls individually by specifying the name of the window class when calling the **CreateWindow** or **CreateWindowEx** function. An application can also direct Windows to create controls for a dialog box by specifying the controls in the dialog box template.

Controls are child windows. When Windows creates controls for a dialog box, each control is the child of the dialog box. When an application creates a control, the control is the child of a window identified by the application. This relationship is important because a control sends messages, called *notification messages*, to its parent window when events, such as input from the user, occur in the control. The application relies on these notification messages to determine what action the user wants the application to take.

Because controls are windows, an application can manipulate them by using the window-management functions, such as the **ShowWindow** and **EnableWindow** functions. If the window class for a control supports *control messages*, an application can also manipulate a control of that class by using the **SendMessage** function to send these messages to the control. The purpose and function of each control message is specific to the window class and is defined by the control's window procedure.

9.1.1 Predefined Controls

Windows provides several predefined window classes for controls. Controls belonging to these window classes are called *predefined controls*. An application creates a predefined control of a particular type by specifying the appropriate window class name in either the **CreateWindow** function or the dialog box template. Following are the predefined window classes.

Name	Description
BUTTON	Creates button controls. These controls typically notify the parent window when the user chooses the control.
LISTBOX	Creates list boxes. These controls display a list from which the user can select one or more items.
EDIT	Creates edit controls. These controls let the user view and edit text.
COMBOBOX	Creates combo boxes. These controls are a combination of list boxes and edit controls, letting the user choose and edit items.
SCROLLBAR	Creates scroll bar controls. These controls let the user choose the direction and distance to scroll information in a related window.
STATIC	Creates static controls. These controls often act as labels for other controls.

Each predefined window class has a corresponding set of *control styles* that enable an application to vary the appearance and behavior of the controls it creates. For example, the BUTTON class supports styles to create push buttons, radio buttons, check boxes, and group boxes. An application specifies the style when creating the control.

Each predefined window class has a corresponding set of notification and control messages. Applications rely on the notification messages to determine when the user has provided input to the controls. For example, a push button sends a BN_CLICKED message to the parent window when the user chooses the button. Applications use the control messages to retrieve information from the controls and to manipulate the appearance and behavior of the controls. For example, an application can send a BM_GETCHECK message to a check box to determine whether it currently contains a check mark.

Most applications make extensive use of predefined controls in dialog boxes and other windows. Because predefined controls offer many capabilities, a full discussion of each is beyond the scope of this chapter. For more information about the predefined controls, see the individual chapters for each window class following this chapter.

9.1.2 Custom Controls

Applications can create custom controls to carry out tasks not supported by predefined controls. Windows provides the following ways to create custom controls:

- Use owner-drawn buttons, list boxes, and combo boxes.
- Subclass an existing control-window class.
- Register and implement from scratch an application-defined window class.

Buttons, list boxes, and combo boxes have owner-drawn styles available that direct the control to send a message to the parent window whenever the control must be drawn. This feature permits an application to alter the appearance of a control. For buttons, the owner-drawn style affects how the system draws the entire control. For list boxes and combo boxes, the parent window draws the items within the control, and the control draws its own outline. For example, an application can customize a list box so that it displays a small bitmap beside each item in the list.

An application can designate list boxes, combo boxes, and buttons as owner-drawn controls by creating them with the appropriate style. When a control has the owner-drawn style, Windows handles the user's interaction with the control as usual, performing such tasks as detecting when a user has chosen a button and notifying the button's owner of the event. However, because the control is owner drawn, the parent window of the control is responsible for the visual appearance of the control. For more information about owner-drawn controls, see the individual chapters for buttons, list boxes, and combo boxes.

Subclassing an existing control is another way to create a custom control. The subclass procedure can alter selected behaviors of the control by processing those messages that affect the selected behaviors. All other messages pass to the original window procedure for the control. For example, an application can display a small bitmap next to the text in a read-only, single-line edit control by subclassing the control and processing the WM_PAINT message. For more information about subclassing, see Chapter 3, "Window Classes."

Although an application may subclass a predefined control, it relies on the window procedure of the control to provide all other aspects of the control's behavior. For more information about a control's behavior, see the individual chapters for the predefined controls.

An application can create custom controls by registering an application-defined window class and specifying the name of the window class in the **CreateWindow** or **CreateWindowEx** function or in the dialog box template. The process for registering an application-defined window class for a custom control is the same as for registering a class for an ordinary window. Each class must have a unique name, a corresponding window procedure, and other information.

At a minimum, the window procedure draws the control. If an application uses the control to let the user type information, the window procedure also processes input messages from the keyboard and mouse and sends notification messages to the parent window. In addition, if the control supports control messages, the window procedure processes messages sent to it by the parent window or other windows. For example, controls often process the WM_GETDLGCODE message sent by dialog boxes to direct a dialog box to process keyboard input in a given way.

9.1.3 Notification Messages

A control should send a notification message to its parent window to notify the parent about user input or changes to the control. The notification message is a WM_COMMAND message that includes a control identifier and a notification code identifying the nature of the event. A *control identifier* is a unique number the application uses to identify the control sending the message. The application sets the identifier for a control when it creates the control. The application specifies the identifier either in the *hMenu* parameter of the **CreateWindow** or **CreateWindowEx** function or in the **id** member of the dialog box template.

Because the control does not set the control identifier, the control must retrieve the identifier before it can send notification messages. A control must use the **GetDlgCtrlID** function to retrieve its own control identifier. Although the control identifier is specified as the menu handle when the control is created, the **GetMenu** function cannot be used to retrieve the identifier. Alternatively, a control can retrieve the identifier from the **hMenu** member in the **CREATESTRUCT** structure while processing the WM_CREATE message.

9.1.4 Control Messages

A parent window or other windows send control messages to direct a control to carry out specific tasks. The window procedure processes these messages and carries out the requested action.

Control messages can be predefined or application defined. Windows has several predefined messages, such as WM_GETTEXT and WM_GETDLGCODE, that it sends to controls. These messages typically correspond to window-management functions that carry out actions on windows. In general, the window procedure for an application-defined control should process any predefined control message in the following table if the message affects the operation of the control.

Message	Recommendation
WM_GETDLGCODE	Process if the control uses the ENTER, ESC, TAB, or direction keys. The **IsDialogMessage** function sends this message to controls in a dialog box to determine whether to process the keys or pass them to the control.
WM_GETFONT	Process if the WM_SETFONT message is also processed.
WM_GETTEXT	Process if the control text is not the same as the title specified by the **CreateWindow** or **CreateWindowEx** function.
WM_GETTEXTLENGTH	Process if the control text is not the same as the title specified by the **CreateWindow** or **CreateWindowEx** function.

WM_KILLFOCUS	Process if the control displays a caret, a focus rectangle, or another item to indicate that it has the input focus.
WM_SETFOCUS	Process if the control displays a caret, a focus rectangle, or another item to indicate that it has the input focus.
WM_SETTEXT	Process if the control text is not the same as the title specified by the **CreateWindow** or **CreateWindowEx** function.
WM_SETFONT	Process if the control displays text. Windows sends this message when creating a dialog box that has the DS_SETFONT style.

Application-defined control messages are specific to the given control and must be explicitly sent to the control by using a **SendMessage** or **SendDlgItemMessage** function. The numeric value for each message must be unique and must not conflict with the values of other window messages. To ensure that application-defined message values do not conflict, an application should create each value by adding a unique number to the WM_USER value.

9.2 Messages

Following are the messages used with controls.

WM_GETFONT
WM_SETFONT
WM_SETTEXT

C H A P T E R   1 0

Buttons

10.1 About Buttons

Microsoft ® Windows ™ provides dialog boxes and controls to support communication between an application and the user. A *button* is a control the user can turn on or off to provide input to an application. There are several types of buttons and, within each type, one or more styles to distinguish among buttons of the same type. The user turns a button on or off by selecting it using the mouse or keyboard. Selecting a button typically changes its visual appearance and state (from checked to unchecked, for example). Windows, the button, and the application cooperate in changing the button's appearance and state. A button can send messages to its parent window, and a parent window can send messages to a button. Some buttons are painted by Windows, some by the application. Buttons can be used alone or in groups and can appear with or without a label. They belong to the BUTTON window class.

Although an application can use buttons in overlapped, pop-up, and child windows, they are designed for use in dialog boxes, where Windows standardizes their behavior. If an application uses buttons outside dialog boxes, it increases the risk that the application may behave in a nonstandard fashion. Applications typically either use buttons in dialog boxes or use window subclassing to create customized buttons.

For general information about controls, see Chapter 9, "Controls." For more information about dialog boxes, see Chapter 18, "Dialog Boxes." For more information about window subclassing, see Chapter 4, "Window Procedures."

10.1.1 Button Types and Styles

Windows provides five kinds of buttons: push buttons, check boxes, radio buttons, group boxes, and owner-drawn buttons. Each type has one or more styles.

10.1.1.1 Push Buttons

A *push button* is a round-cornered rectangle containing application-defined text (label) that specifies what the button does when the user selects it. The push button includes the following styles: push button and default push button, defined by the constants BS_PUSHBUTTON and BS_DEFPUSHBUTTON, respectively. A standard push button is typically used to start an operation. It receives the keyboard focus when the user selects it. A default push button, on the other hand, is typically used to cancel an operation. It receives the keyboard focus when it is created (thus, becoming the default).

When the user selects a push button (of either style), it receives the keyboard focus from Windows, which sends the button's parent window a WM_COMMAND message containing the BN_CLICKED notification code. In response, the parent window typically sets the button's highlight state to highlighted, closes the dialog box, and starts (or cancels) the operation.

The following figure shows both a standard and a default push button.

The labels on push buttons are always centered on the button.

10.1.1.2 Check Boxes

A *check box* consists of a square box and application-defined text (label) that specifies a choice the user can make by selecting the button. Applications typically display check boxes in a group box to permit the user to choose from a set of related but independent options. For example, an application might present a group of check boxes from which the user can select error conditions that produce warning beeps.

A check box can be one of four styles: check box, automatic check box, three-state check box, and automatic three-state check box, which are defined by the constants BS_CHECKBOX, BS_AUTOCHECKBOX, BS_3STATE, and BS_AUTO3STATE, respectively. All four styles can assume two check states: checked (an X inside the box) or unchecked (no X). In addition, a three-state check box can assume a disabled state (the box is grayed). Repeatedly selecting a standard or automatic check box toggles it from checked to unchecked and back again. Repeatedly selecting a three-state check box toggles it from checked to unchecked to grayed and back again.

The following figure shows all three states of a three-state check box.

☐ Unchecked
☒ Checked
▨ Disabled (Gray)

When the user selects a check box (of any style), the check box receives the keyboard focus from Windows, which sends the check box's parent window a WM_COMMAND message containing the BN_CLICKED notification code. The parent window doesn't acknowledge this message if it comes from an automatic check box or automatic three-state check box, because Windows automatically sets the check state and the highlight state for those styles. But the parent window must acknowledge the message if it comes from a check box or three-state check box because the parent window, not Windows, is responsible for setting the check state and highlight state for those styles. Regardless of the check box style, Windows automatically repaints the check box once its state is changed.

By default, a label is placed on the right of a check box. An application can place labels on the left instead by using the left-text style (BS_LEFTTEXT). The left-text style is only a style, not a distinct button type.

10.1.1.3 Radio Buttons

A *radio button* consists of a round button and application-defined text (a label) that specifies a choice the user can make by selecting the button. An application typically uses radio buttons in a group box to permit the user to choose from a set of related but mutually exclusive options. For example, the application might present a group of radio buttons from which the user can select a format preference for text selected in the client area. The user could select a left-aligned, right-aligned, or centered format by selecting the corresponding radio button. Typically, the user can select only one option at a time from a set of radio buttons.

The radio button includes the following styles: radio button and automatic radio button, defined by the constants BS_RADIOBUTTON and BS_AUTORADIOBUTTON, respectively. Both styles can assume two check states: checked (a black dot on the button) or unchecked (no dot on the button). Repeatedly selecting a check box (standard or automatic) toggles it from checked to unchecked and back again. Repeatedly selecting a three-state check box (standard or automatic) toggles it from checked to unchecked to grayed and back again.

The following figure shows both states of a radio button.

○ Unchecked
◉ Checked

When the user selects either state, the radio button receives the keyboard focus from Windows, which sends the button's parent window a WM_COMMAND message containing the BN_CLICKED notification code. The parent window doesn't acknowledge this message if it comes from an automatic radio button because Windows automatically sets the check state and the highlight state for that style. But the parent window should acknowledge the message if it comes from a radio button because the parent window, not Windows, is responsible for setting the check state and highlight state for that style. Regardless of the radio button style, Windows automatically repaints the button as its state changes.

When the user selects an automatic radio button, Windows automatically removes the highlighting from any previously selected automatic radio button within the same group. The same behavior is available for standard radio buttons by using the WS_GROUP style, as discussed in Chapter 18, "Dialog Boxes."

By default, a label is placed on the right of a radio button. An application can place labels on the left instead by using the left-text style (BS_LEFTTEXT). The left-text style is only a style, not a distinct button type.

10.1.1.4 Owner-Drawn Buttons

Unlike radio buttons, an *owner-drawn button* is painted by the application, not Windows, and has no predefined appearance or usage. Its purpose is to provide a button whose appearance and behavior are defined by the application alone. There is only one owner-drawn button style: BS_OWNERDRAW.

When the user selects an owner-drawn button, Windows sends the button's parent window a WM_COMMAND message containing the BN_CLICKED notification code, just as it does for a button that is not owner-drawn. The application must respond appropriately.

10.1.1.5 Group Boxes

A *group box* is a rectangle that surrounds a set of controls, such as check boxes or radio buttons, with application-defined text (label) in its upper-left corner. The sole purpose of a group box is to organize controls related by a common purpose (usually indicated by the label). The group box has only one style, defined by the constant BS_GROUPBOX.

The following figure shows a group box containing two radio buttons.

Because a group box cannot be selected, it has no check state, focus state, highlight state, or enabled state. An application cannot send messages to a group box.

10.1.1.6 Button Styles

Many developers create dialog boxes by using stand-alone tools not requiring them to specify button styles. However, if an application creates a button by using the **CreateWindow** or **CreateWindowEx** function, the following table of constants can be used to define the button style.

Style	Meaning
BS_3STATE	Creates a button that is the same as a check box, except that the box can be grayed as well as checked. Use the grayed state to show that the state of the check box is not determined.
BS_AUTO3STATE	Creates a button that is the same as a three-state check box, except that the box changes its state when the user selects it. The state cycles through checked, grayed, and normal.
BS_AUTOCHECKBOX	Creates a button that is the same as a check box, except that an X appears in the check box when the user selects the box; the X disappears the next time the user selects the box.

BS_AUTORADIOBUTTON	Creates a button that is the same as a radio button, except that when the user selects it, the button automatically highlights itself and removes the selection from any other buttons in the same group.
BS_CHECKBOX	Creates a small empty square, with text displayed to its right, unless this style is combined with the BS_LEFTTEXT style.
BS_DEFPUSHBUTTON	Creates a button that has a heavy black border. The user can select this button by pressing the ENTER key. This style is useful for enabling the user to quickly select the most likely (default) option.
BS_GROUPBOX	Creates a rectangle in which other controls can be grouped. Any text associated with this style is displayed in the rectangle's upper left corner.
BS_LEFTTEXT	Places text on the left side of the radio button or check box when combined with a radio button or check box style.
BS_OWNERDRAW	Creates an owner-drawn button. The owner window receives a WM_MEASUREITEM message when the button is created and a WM_DRAWITEM message when a visual aspect of the button has changed. Do not combine the BS_OWNERDRAW style with any other button styles.
BS_PUSHBOX	Unsupported. Applications should use BS_PUSHBUTTON instead.
BS_PUSHBUTTON	Creates a push button that posts a WM_COMMAND message to the owner window when the user selects the button.
BS_RADIOBUTTON	Creates a small circle that has text displayed to its right, unless this style is combined with the BS_LEFTTEXT style. Use radio buttons for groups of related but mutually exclusive choices.
BS_USERBUTTON	Obsolete. Applications should use BS_OWNERDRAW instead.

10.1.2 Button States

This section discusses how selecting a button changes its state and how the application should respond.

10.1.2.1 Button Selection

The user can select a button in three ways: by clicking it with the mouse, by tabbing to it and then pressing the ENTER key, or (if the button is part of a group defined by the WS_GROUP style) by tabbing to the selected button in the group and using the arrow keys to move within that group. The two tabbing methods are part of the predefined keyboard interface provided by Windows. For a complete description of this interface, see Chapter 18, "Dialog Boxes."

Selecting a button typically causes the following events:

- Windows gives the button the keyboard focus.
- The button sends its parent window a message to notify it of the selection.
- The parent window (or Windows) sends the button a message to change its state.
- The parent window (or Windows) repaints the button to reflect its new state.

The following paragraphs discuss these events and button states in greater detail.

10.1.2.2 Elements of a Button State

A button's state can be characterized by its focus state, highlight state, check state, and enabled state. The focus state applies to a check box, radio button, push button, or owner-drawn button. A button receives the keyboard focus when the user selects it and loses the focus when the user selects another button. Only one button can have the keyboard focus at a time. For example, when one radio button in a group receives the focus, the previously selected radio button in the group loses it, to preserve the mutually exclusive nature of radio buttons.

The highlight state applies to a check box, radio button, push button, or owner-drawn button. A button is highlighted when it receives the keyboard focus and loses its highlighting when it loses the focus. Typically, a highlighted button surrounds its text with a dotted line and has a heavy dark border. Windows automatically changes the highlight state for an automatic button, but the application must change the highlight state for a non-automatic button.

The check state applies to a check box, radio button, or three-state check box, but does not apply to other buttons. The state can be checked, unchecked, or (for three-state check boxes) disabled. A check box is checked when it contains an X, and is unchecked when it does not. A radio button is checked when it contains a black dot, and is unchecked when it does not. A three-state check box is checked when it contains an X, unchecked when it does not, and is disabled when it is grayed. Windows changes the check state of an automatic button automatically, but the application must change the check state of a non-automatic button.

The enabled state applies to a standard or automatic three-state check box, but does not apply to other buttons. The state can be enabled or disabled.

10.1.2.3 Changes to a Button State

When the user selects a button, it is generally necessary to change one or more of the button's state elements. Windows automatically changes the focus state for all button types and the highlight, check, and enabled states for all automatic buttons, but the application must make all other state changes, taking into account the button's type, style, and current state. The following list shows the state elements that must be changed for each button type:

- A push button must change the highlight state but not the check state or the enabled state, because push buttons cannot be checked or disabled.

- A check box must change the check state, the highlight state, and the enabled state for three-state check boxes.

- A radio button must change the check state and the highlight state, but not the enabled state (because radio buttons cannot be disabled). It may also be necessary to change other radio buttons in the same group to ensure the mutually exclusive nature of radio buttons.

- Because the state of an owner-drawn button is application dependent, what the application must change in the button can vary. No elements of a group box must be changed, because users cannot select group boxes.

An application can determine a button's state by sending it a BM_GETCHECK or BM_GETSTATE message; the application can set a button's state by sending it a BM_SETCHECK or BM_SETSTATE message.

10.1.3 Notification Messages from Buttons

When the user selects a button, its state changes, and the button sends notification messages to its parent window. For example, a push button control sends the BN_CLICKED notification message whenever the user chooses the button. In all cases, the low word of the *wParam* parameter contains the control identifier, the high word of *wParam* contains the notification code, and the *lParam* parameter contains the control window handle.

Portability Issue In Windows ® NT ™, the placement of the notification code in a notification message has moved from the *lParam* parameter to the *wParam* parameter. To accommodate this change in placement, when porting your Windows 3.*x*–based application to Windows NT, you must modify the code that processes notification messages.

Both the message and the parent window's response depend on the type, style, and current state of the button. Following are the button notification messages an application should monitor and process.

Message	Description
BN_CLICKED	The user clicked a button.
BN_DISABLE	A button is disabled.
BN_DOUBLECLICKED	The user double-clicked a button.

BN_HILITE	The user highlighted a button.
BN_PAINT	The button should be painted.
BN_UNHILITE	The highlight should be removed.

For automatic buttons, the operating system performs disabling, highlighting, unhighlighting, and painting. In this case, the application typically processes only the BN_CLICKED and BN_DOUBLECLICKED notification messages. For buttons that are not automatic, the application typically responds to the notification message by sending a message to change the state of the button. For information about sending messages to buttons, see Section 10.1.4, "Messages to Buttons."

When the user selects an owner-drawn button, the button sends its parent window a WM_DRAWITEM message containing the identifier of the control to be drawn and information about its dimensions and state. For more information about this message, see Section 10.2.3, "Using Owner-Drawn Buttons."

10.1.4 Messages to Buttons

A parent window can send messages to a button in an overlapped or child window by using the **SendMessage** function, or it can send messages to a button in a dialog box by using the **SendDlgItemMessage**, **CheckDlgButton**, **CheckRadioButton**, and **IsDlgButtonChecked** functions.

An application can use the BM_GETCHECK message to retrieve the check state of two-state buttons (check boxes, automatic check boxes, radio buttons, and automatic radio buttons). An application can also use the BM_GETSTATE message to retrieve the button's current states (the check state, highlight state, and focus state). It retrieves the check state of a three-state check box or the focus or highlight state of a button. To get information about a specific state, use a bitmask on the returned state value.

The BM_SETCHECK message sets the check state of a check box or radio button; the message returns zero. The BM_SETSTATE message sets the highlight state of a button; this message also returns zero. The BM_SETSTYLE message changes the style of a button. It is designed for changing button styles within a type (for example, changing a check box to an automatic check box). It is not designed for changing between types (for example, changing a check box to a push button). An application should not change a button from one type to another.

An application can also use the DM_GETDEFID message to retrieve the identifier of the default push button control. An application can use the DM_SETDEFID message to set the default push button for a dialog box.

Calling the **CheckDlgButton** or **CheckRadioButton** function is equivalent to sending a BM_SETCHECK message. Calling the **IsDlgButtonChecked** function is equivalent to sending a BM_GETCHECK message.

10.1.5 Button Color Messages

Windows provides default color values for buttons. The system sends a WM_CTLCOLORBTN message to a button's parent window before the button is drawn. This message contains a handle of the button's device context and a handle of the child window. The parent window can use these handles to change the button's text and background colors. The following table shows the default button-color values.

Value	Element colored
COLOR_BTNFACE	Button faces.
COLOR_BTNHIGHLIGHT	Highlight area (the top and left edges) of a button.
COLOR_BTNSHADOW	Shadow area (the bottom and right edges) of a button.
COLOR_BTNTEXT	Regular (non-gray) text in buttons.
COLOR_GRAYTEXT	Disabled (gray) text in buttons. This color is set to 0 if the current display driver does not support a solid gray color.
COLOR_WINDOW	Window backgrounds.
COLOR_WINDOWFRAME	Window frames.
COLOR_WINDOWTEXT	Text in windows.

An application can retrieve the default values for these colors by calling the **GetSysColor** function, or set the values by calling the **SetSysColor** function. For more information about system colors, see Chapter 67, "System Information." For more information about how colors are used with controls, see Chapter 9, "Controls."

Portability Issue In Windows NT, the WM_CTLCOLOR message has been replaced by the set of control-color messages. When porting your Windows 3.x–based application to Windows NT, you must modify any code that processes the WM_CTLCOLOR message.

10.1.6 Default Message Processing

The window procedure for the predefined button control window class carries out default processing for all messages that the button control procedure does not process. When the button control procedure returns FALSE for any message, the predefined window procedure checks the messages and carries out the default actions listed in the following table.

Message	Default action
BM_GETCHECK	Returns the check state of the button.

BM_GETSTATE	Returns the current state of the button.
BM_SETCHECK	Sets the check mark for all styles of radio buttons and check boxes. If the *wParam* parameter is greater than zero for radio buttons, the button is given the WS_TABSTOP style.
BM_SETSTATE	Highlights or unhighlights the button. For owner-drawn buttons, a WM_DRAWITEM message is sent to the parent window if the state of the button has changed.
BM_SETSTYLE	Sets the button style. If the low word of the *lParam* parameter is TRUE, the button is redrawn.
WM_CHAR	Checks a check box or automatic check box when the user presses the + or = keys. Removes the check mark from a check box or automatic check box when the user presses the − key.
WM_ENABLE	Paints the button.
WM_ERASEBKGND	Erases the background for owner-drawn buttons. The backgrounds of other buttons are erased as part of the WM_PAINT and WM_ENABLE processing.
WM_GETDLGCODE	Returns values indicating the type of input processed by the default button procedure, as shown in the following.

Button style	Returns
BS_AUTOCHECKBOX	
	DLGC_WANTCHARS | DLGC_BUTTON
BS_AUTORADIOBUTTON	
	DLGC_RADIOBUTTON
BS_CHECKBOX	
	DLGC_WANTCHARS | DLGC_BUTTON
BS_DEFPUSHBUTTON	
	DLGC_DEFPUSHBUTTON
BS_GROUPBOX	
	DLGC_STATIC
BS_PUSHBUTTON	
	DLGC_UNDEFPUSHBUTTON
BS_RADIOBUTTON	
	DLGC_RADIOBUTTON

WM_GETFONT	Returns a handle of the current font.
WM_KEYDOWN	Highlights the button if the user presses the SPACEBAR.
WM_KEYUP	Releases the mouse capture for all cases except the TAB key.
WM_KILLFOCUS	Removes the focus rectangle from a button. For push buttons and default push buttons, the focus rectangle is invalidated. If the button has the mouse capture, the capture is released, the button is not clicked, and any highlighting is removed.
WM_LBUTTONDBLCLK	Sends a BN_DOUBLECLICKED notification message to the parent window for radio buttons and owner-drawn buttons. For other buttons, a double-click is processed as a WM_LBUTTONDOWN message.
WM_LBUTTONDOWN	Highlights the button if the position of the mouse cursor is within the button's client rectangle.
WM_LBUTTONUP	Releases the mouse capture if the button had the mouse capture.
WM_MOUSEMOVE	Performs the same action as WM_LBUTTONDOWN if the button has the mouse capture. Otherwise, no action is performed.
WM_NCCREATE	Turns any BS_USERBUTTON button into a BS_PUSHBUTTON button.
WM_NCHITTEST	Returns HTTRANSPARENT if the button control is a group box.
WM_PAINT	Draws the button according to its style and current state.
WM_SETFOCUS	Draws a focus rectangle on the button getting the focus. For radio buttons and automatic radio buttons, the parent window is sent a BN_CLICKED notification message.
WM_SETFONT	Sets a new font and optionally updates the window.
WM_SETTEXT	Sets the text of the button. In the case of a group box, paints over the preexisting text before repainting the group box with the new text.
WM_SYSKEYUP	Releases the mouse capture for all cases except the TAB key.

The predefined window procedure passes all other messages to the
DefWindowProc function for default processing.

10.2 Using Buttons

This section explains how to perform the following tasks:

- Create a button outside a dialog box.
- Use system-drawn buttons.
- Use owner-drawn buttons.

10.2.1 Creating a Button Outside a Dialog Box

The following code sample shows how to use the **CreateWindow** function to create a default push button.

```
hwndButton = CreateWindow(
    "BUTTON",   /* predefined class                              */
    "OK",       /* button text                                   */
    WS_VISIBLE | WS_CHILD | BS_DEFPUSHBUTTON, /* styles          */

    /*
     * Size and position values are given explicitly, because
     * the CW_USEDEFAULT constant gives zero values for buttons.
     */

    10,         /* starting x position                           */
    10,         /* starting y position                           */
    100,        /* button width                                  */
    100,        /* button height                                 */
    hwnd,       /* parent window                                 */
    NULL,       /* No menu                                        */
    (HINSTANCE) GetWindowLong(hwnd, GWL_HINSTANCE),
    NULL);      /* pointer not needed                            */
```

10.2.2 Using Buttons That Are Not Owner-Drawn

The code example in this section is the window procedure for a dialog box, as shown in the following illustration.

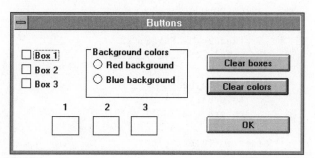

The check boxes and radio buttons in the Buttons dialog box are automatic. The check boxes are three-state. The Clear colors push button is a default push button. The check boxes, radio buttons, and push buttons are defined as follows in the application's header file.

```
#define IDB_BOX1       101         /* first check box       */
#define IDB_BOX2       102         /* second check box      */
#define IDB_BOX3       103         /* third check box       */
#define IDB_REDBACK    104         /* top radio button      */
#define IDB_BLUEBACK   105         /* bottom radio button   */
#define IDB_CLEARBOXES 107         /* top push button       */
#define IDB_CLEARBACK  108         /* bottom push button    */


HBRUSH hbrRed, hbrBlue, hbrWhite;
BOOL fRedBack, fBlueBack, fClearColor; /* background-state flags */
```

Note that it is not necessary to define IDOK, the identifier for the OK push button.

In the following window procedure, the WM_CTLCOLORDLG message notifies the application that the dialog box is about to be drawn. If the user presses the Clear colors button (signified by the fClearColor flag), the procedure uses the **SendDlgItemMessage** function to uncheck the check boxes and radio buttons. The BN_CLICKED notification message contains the identifiers of the buttons.

```
LRESULT APIENTRY ButtonProc(hDlg, message, wParam, lParam)
HWND hDlg;                  /* window handle of dialog box  */
UINT message;               /* type of message              */
UINT wParam;                /* message-specific information  */
LONG lParam;
{
    LRESULT lState;

    switch (message) {
        case WM_INITDIALOG:
            hbrRed = CreateSolidBrush(RGB(255, 0, 0));
            hbrBlue = CreateSolidBrush(RGB(0, 0, 255));
            hbrWhite = GetStockObject(WHITE_BRUSH);
            return TRUE;

        case WM_CTLCOLORDLG:
            if (fRedBack) {
                fRedBack = FALSE;
                return (LRESULT) hbrRed;
            }
            else if (fBlueBack) {
                fBlueBack = FALSE;
                return (LRESULT) hbrBlue;
            }
            else if (fClearColor) {
```

```
                    fClearColor = FALSE;

                    /*
                     * Uncheck all check boxes and radio buttons.
                     */

                    SendDlgItemMessage(hDlg, /* window handle         */
                        IDB_BOX1,            /* button identifier     */
                        BM_SETCHECK,         /* message               */
                        0,                   /* check state (unchecked) */
                        0);                  /* must be zero          */
                    SendDlgItemMessage(hDlg, IDB_BOX2,
                        BM_SETCHECK, 0, 0);
                    SendDlgItemMessage(hDlg, IDB_BOX3,
                        BM_SETCHECK, 0, 0);
                    SendDlgItemMessage(hDlg, IDB_REDBACK,
                        BM_SETCHECK, 0, 0);
                    SendDlgItemMessage(hDlg, IDB_BLUEBACK,
                        BM_SETCHECK, 0, 0);
                }
            return (LRESULT) hbrWhite;

        case WM_COMMAND:
            if (wParam == IDOK) {
                EndDialog(hDlg, TRUE);
                return TRUE;
            }

            if (HIWORD(wParam) == BN_CLICKED) {
                switch (LOWORD(wParam)) {
                    case IDB_BOX1:

                        /* Retrieve the state of the check box. */

                        lState = SendDlgItemMessage(hDlg,
                            IDB_BOX1, BM_GETSTATE, 0, 0);

                        /*
                         * The box-painting function is
                         * application defined.
                         */

                        BoxPainter(hDlg, /* window handle    */
                            1,           /* box to paint     */
                            lState);     /* check box state  */
                        break;

                    case IDB_BOX2:
                        lState = SendDlgItemMessage(hDlg,
                            IDB_BOX2, BM_GETSTATE, 0, 0);
```

```
                                BoxPainter(hDlg, 2, lState);
                                break;

                        case IDB_BOX3:
                            lState = SendDlgItemMessage(hDlg,
                                IDB_BOX3, BM_GETSTATE, 0, 0);
                            BoxPainter(hDlg, 3, lState);
                            break;

                        case IDB_REDBACK:
                            fRedBack = TRUE;
                            InvalidateRect(hDlg, NULL, TRUE);
                            break;

                        case IDB_BLUEBACK:
                            fBlueBack = TRUE;
                            InvalidateRect(hDlg, NULL, TRUE);
                            break;

                        case IDB_CLEARBACK:
                            fClearColor = TRUE;
                            InvalidateRect(hDlg, NULL, TRUE);
                            break;

                        case IDB_CLEARBOXES:
                            BoxPainter(hDlg, 4, (LRESULT) 0);
                            break;
                    }
                }

        case WM_DESTROY:
            DeleteObject(hbrRed);
            DeleteObject(hbrBlue);

            /*
             * Do not delete hbrWhite, because it is a stock
             * object.
             */

            break;

    }
    return FALSE;        /* did not process a message */
        UNREFERENCED_PARAMETER(lParam);
}
```

10.2.3 Using Owner-Drawn Buttons

The parent window of an owner-drawn button typically responds to at least three messages for the button: WM_INITDIALOG, WM_COMMAND, and WM_DRAWITEM. It is not necessary to process the WM_MEASUREITEM message for owner-drawn buttons.

When you must paint an owner-drawn button, Windows sends the parent window a WM_DRAWITEM message whose *lParam* parameter points to a **DRAWITEMSTRUCT** structure. Use this structure with all owner-drawn controls to provide the application with the information it requires to paint the control. The **itemAction** and **itemState** structure members define how to paint an owner-drawn button.

The following code sample shows how to process WM_INITDIALOG, WM_DRAWITEM, and WM_COMMAND messages for owner-drawn buttons. This code demonstrates how to draw one of two bitmaps for a control, depending on whether the control is selected. You would typically use the *wParam* parameter of the WM_DRAWITEM message to identify the control; in this example, only one control is assumed.

```
LRESULT APIENTRY OwnDrawProc(hDlg, message, wParam, lParam)
HWND hDlg;       /* window handle of dialog box        */
UINT message;    /* type of message                    */
UINT wParam;     /* message-specific information        */
LONG lParam;
{
    HDC hdcMem;
    LPDRAWITEMSTRUCT lpdis;

    switch (message) {
        case WM_INITDIALOG:

            /* hinst, hbm1 and hbm2 are defined globally. */

            hbm1 = LoadBitmap((HANDLE) hinst, "OwnBit1");
            hbm2 = LoadBitmap((HANDLE) hinst, "OwnBit2");
            return TRUE;

        case WM_DRAWITEM:
            lpdis = (LPDRAWITEMSTRUCT) lParam;
            hdcMem = CreateCompatibleDC(lpdis->hDC);

            if (lpdis->itemState & ODS_SELECTED) /* if selected     */
                SelectObject(hdcMem, hbm2);
            else
                SelectObject(hdcMem, hbm1);

            StretchBlt(
```

```
                    lpdis->hDC,           /* destination device context   */
                    lpdis->rcItem.left,  /* x upper-left destination      */
                    lpdis->rcItem.top,   /* y upper-left destination      */

                    /* The next two lines specify the width and height. */

                    lpdis->rcItem.right - lpdis->rcItem.left,
                    lpdis->rcItem.bottom - lpdis->rcItem.top,
                    hdcMem,     /* handle of source device context        */
                    0,          /* x-coordinate upper-left source         */
                    0,          /* y-coordinate upper-left source         */
                    32,         /* source bitmap width                    */
                    32,         /* source bitmap height                   */
                    SRCCOPY);   /* raster operation                       */

                DeleteDC(hdcMem);
                return TRUE;

            case WM_COMMAND:
                if (wParam == IDOK
                    || wParam == IDCANCEL) {
                    EndDialog(hDlg, TRUE);
                    return TRUE;
                }
                if (HIWORD(wParam) == BN_CLICKED) {
                    switch (LOWORD(wParam)) {
                        case IDB_OWNERDRAW:


                            .
                            . /* application-defined processing */
                            .


                            break;
                    }
                }
                break;

            case WM_DESTROY:
                DeleteObject(hbm1); /* delete bitmaps                 */
                DeleteObject(hbm2);

                break;

    }
    return FALSE;
        UNREFERENCED_PARAMETER(lParam);
}
```

10.3 Functions and Messages

The following functions and messages can be used with buttons.

Functions

CheckDlgButton
CheckRadioButton
IsDlgButtonChecked

Messages

BM_GETCHECK
BM_GETSTATE
BM_SETCHECK
BM_SETSTATE
BM_SETSTYLE
BN_CLICKED
BN_DISABLE
BN_DOUBLECLICKED
BN_HILITE
BN_PAINT
BN_UNHILITE
DM_GETDEFID
DM_SETDEFID
WM_CTLCOLORBTN

CHAPTER 11

List Boxes

11.1 About List Boxes

Microsoft ® Windows ™ provides dialog boxes and controls to support communication between an application and the user. A *list box* is a control window that contains a list of items from which the user can choose. List box items can be represented by text strings, bitmaps, or both. If the list box is not large enough to display all the list box items at once, the list box can provide a scroll bar.

The user selects a list box item or cancels a selection by using the mouse or keyboard. Selecting a list box item changes its visual appearance, usually by changing the text and background colors to the colors specified by the operating system metrics for selected items. When the user selects or cancels an item, Windows sends a notification message to the parent window of the list box.

Although an application can use a list box in an overlapped, child, or pop-up window, list boxes are mainly designed for use in dialog boxes, where most of their functionality is predefined by Windows. When using a list box in windows other than dialog boxes, it is difficult to maintain a consistent user interface. Therefore, you should use window subclassing to implement a list box outside a dialog box. This chapter primarily discusses the use of list boxes within dialog boxes, but this discussion also applies to the use of list boxes in any parent window. For more information about window subclassing, see Chapter 4, "Window Procedures."

A dialog box procedure is responsible for initializing and monitoring its child windows, including any list boxes. The dialog box procedure communicates with the list box by sending messages to it and by processing the notification messages sent by the list box. For more information about dialog boxes, see Chapter 18, "Dialog Boxes."

For general information about controls, see Chapter 9, "Controls."

11.1.1 List Box Styles

Windows provides two general styles of list box: single-selection and multiple-selection. In a *single-selection list box* (the default), the user can select only one item at a time. In a *multiple-selection list box*, the user can select more than one item at a time. Either the LBS_MULTIPLESEL or the LBS_EXTENDEDSEL style must be specified for a multiple-selection list box.

Windows provides many other list box and window styles that control the appearance and operation of a list box. These styles indicate whether list box items are sorted, arranged in multiple columns, drawn by the application, and so on. The dimensions and styles of a list box are typically defined in a dialog box template included in an application's resources. For information about how to create a dialog box template and include it in an application, refer to the documentation provided with your application-development tools.

To create a list box by using the **CreateWindow** or **CreateWindowEx** function, use the LISTBOX class, appropriate window-style constants, and the following list box–style constants to define the list box.

Style	Meaning

LBS_DISABLENOSCROLL

Shows a disabled vertical scroll bar for the list box when the box does not contain enough items to scroll. If an application does not specify this style, the scroll bar is hidden when the list box does not contain enough items.

LBS_EXTENDEDSEL

Allows multiple items to be selected by using the SHIFT key and the mouse or special key combinations.

LBS_HASSTRINGS

Specifies that a list box contains items consisting of strings. The list box maintains the memory and addresses for the strings so the application can use the LB_GETTEXT message to retrieve the text for a particular item. By default, all list boxes except owner-drawn list boxes have this style. An application can create an owner-drawn list box either with or without this style.

LBS_MULTICOLUMN

Specifies a multicolumn list box with horizontal scrolling. The LB_SETCOLUMNWIDTH message sets the width of the columns.

LBS_MULTIPLESEL

Turns string selection on or off each time the user clicks or double-clicks the string. The user can select any number of strings.

LBS_NODATA

Specifies a no-data list box. To use memory efficiently, an application should specify this style when the count of items in the list box exceed one thousand. A no-data list box must also have the LBS_OWNERDRAWFIXED style, but must not have the LBS_SORT or LBS_HASSTRINGS style.

LBS_NOINTEGRALHEIGHT

Specifies that the size of the list box is exactly the size specified by the application when it created the list box. By default, Windows sizes a list box so that the list box does not display partial items.

LBS_NOREDRAW

Specifies that the appearance of the list box is not updated when changes are made. An application can change this style at any time by sending a WM_SETREDRAW message.

LBS_NOTIFY

Sends an input message to the parent window whenever the user clicks or double-clicks a string.

LBS_OWNERDRAWFIXED

Specifies that the owner of the list box is responsible for drawing its contents and that the items in the list box are the same height. The owner window receives a WM_MEASUREITEM message when the list box is created and a WM_DRAWITEM message whenever a visual aspect of the list box changes.

LBS_OWNERDRAWVARIABLE

Specifies that the owner of the list box is responsible for drawing its contents and that the items in the list box are variable in height. The owner window receives a WM_MEASUREITEM message for each item in the list box when the list box is created and a WM_DRAWITEM message whenever the visual aspect of the list box changes.

LBS_SORT

Sorts strings in the list box alphabetically.

LBS_STANDARD

Specifies a standard list box. Specifying this style is equivalent to specifying LBS_SORT, LBS_NOTIFY, and LBS_BORDER.

LBS_USETABSTOPS

Allows a list box to recognize and expand tab characters when drawing its strings. The default tab positions are 32 dialog box units. Windows computes the dialog box base units based on the height and width of the current operating system font. One horizontal dialog box unit is equal to one-fourth of the current dialog box base width unit. The **GetDialogBaseUnits** function returns the current dialog box base units in pixels.

LBS_WANTKEYBOARDINPUT

Specifies that the owner of the list box receives WM_VKEYTOITEM messages whenever the user presses a key and the list box has the input focus. This allows an application to perform special processing on the keyboard input.

11.1.2 List Box Functions

Windows supports two functions specific to list boxes. The **DlgDirList** function fills a list box with the files and directories in a specified path. The **DlgDirSelectEx** function retrieves the current selection in a list box initialized by **DlgDirList**. These functions make it possible for the user to select a file from a list box without typing the location and name of the file.

11.1.3 Notification Messages from List Boxes

When an event occurs in a list box, the list box sends a notification message to the dialog box procedure of the owner window. List box notification messages are sent when a user selects, double-clicks, or cancels a list box item; when the list box receives or loses the keyboard focus; and when the operating system cannot allocate enough memory for a list box request. A notification message is sent as a WM_COMMAND message in which the low-order word of the *wParam* parameter contains the list box identifier, the high-order word of *wParam* contains the notification code, and the *lParam* parameter contains the control window handle.

Portability Issue   In Microsoft ® Windows NT ™, the placement of the notification code has moved from the *lParam* parameter to the *wParam* parameter. Windows 3.*x* applications that process notification messages must be modified in this respect when they are ported to Windows NT.

A dialog box procedure is not required to process these messages; the default window procedure processes them.

An application should monitor and process the following list box notification messages.

Notification code	Meaning
LBN_DBLCLK	The user double-clicks an item in the list box.
LBN_ERRSPACE	The list box cannot allocate enough memory to fulfill a request.
LBN_KILLFOCUS	The list box loses the keyboard focus.
LBN_SELCANCEL	The user cancels the selection of an item in the list box.
LBN_SELCHANGE	The selection in a list box is about to change.
LBN_SETFOCUS	The list box receives the keyboard focus.

11.1.4 Messages to List Boxes

A dialog box procedure can send messages to a list box to add, delete, examine, and change list box items. For example, a dialog box procedure could send an LB_ADDSTRING message to a list box to add an item, and the LB_GETSEL message to determine whether the item is selected. Other messages set and retrieve information about the size, appearance, and behavior of the list box. For example, the LB_SETHORIZONTALEXTENT message sets the scrollable width of a list box. A dialog box procedure can send any message to a list box by using the **SendMessage** or **SendDlgItemMessage** function.

A list box item is often referenced by its index, an integer that represents the item's position in the list box. The index of the first item in a list box is 0, the index of the second item is 1, and so on.

The following table describes how the predefined list box procedure responds to list box messages.

Message	Response
LB_ADDFILE	Inserts a file into a directory list box filled by the **DlgDirList** function and retrieves the list box index of the inserted item.
LB_ADDSTRING	Adds a string to a list box and returns its index.
LB_DELETESTRING	Removes a string from a list box and returns the number of strings remaining in the list.
LB_DIR	Adds a list of filenames to a list box and returns the index of the last filename added.
LB_FINDSTRING	Returns the index of the first string in the list box that matches a given prefix.
LB_FINDSTRINGEXACT	Returns the index of the string that is equivalent to or prefixed by a given prefix.
LB_GETANCHORINDEX	Returns the index of the item that the mouse last selected.
LB_GETCARETINDEX	Returns the index of the item that has the focus rectangle.
LB_GETCOUNT	Returns the number of items in the list box.
LB_GETCURSEL	Returns the index of the currently selected item in a single-selection list box.
LB_GETHORIZONTALEXTENT	Returns the scrollable width, in pixels, of a list box.
LB_GETITEMDATA	Returns the 32-bit value associated with the given item.
LB_GETITEMHEIGHT	Returns the height, in pixels, of an item in a list box.
LB_GETITEMRECT	Retrieves the client coordinates of the given list box item.
LB_GETLOCALE	Retrieves the locale of the list box. The high-order word contains the country code and the low-order word contains the language identifier.
LB_GETSEL	Returns the selection state of a list box item.
LB_GETSELCOUNT	Returns the number of selected items in a multiple-selection list box.

LB_GETSELITEMS	Creates an array of the indexes of all selected items in a multiple-selection list box and returns the total number of selected items.
LB_GETTEXT	Retrieves the string associated with a given item and the length of the string.
LB_GETTEXTLEN	Returns the length, in characters, of the string associated with a given item.
LB_GETTOPINDEX	Returns the index of the first visible item in a list box.
LB_INSERTSTRING	Inserts a string at a given index in a list box.
LB_RESETCONTENT	Removes all items from a list box.
LB_SELECTSTRING	Selects the first string it finds that matches a given prefix.
LB_SELITEMRANGE	Selects a given range of items in a list box.
LB_SELITEMRANGEEX	Selects a given range of items if the index of the first item in the range is less than the index of the last item in the range. Cancels the selection in the range if the index of the first item is greater than the last.
LB_SETANCHORINDEX	Sets the item that the mouse last selected to a given item.
LB_SETCARETINDEX	Sets the focus rectangle to a given list box item.
LB_SETCOLUMNWIDTH	Sets the width, in pixels, of all columns in a list box.
LB_SETCOUNT	Sets the number of items in a list box.
LB_SETCURSEL	Selects a given list box item.
LB_SETHORIZONTALEXTENT	Sets the scrollable width, in pixels, of a list box.
LB_SETITEMDATA	Associates a 32-bit value with a list box item.
LB_SETITEMHEIGHT	Sets the height, in pixels, of an item or items in a list box.
LB_SETLOCALE	Sets the locale of a list box and returns the previous locale identifier.
LB_SETSEL	Selects an item in a multiple-selection list box.
LB_SETTABSTOPS	Sets the tab stops to those specified in a given array.
LB_SETTOPINDEX	Scrolls the list box so the specified item is at the top of the visible range.

11.1.5 Default Window-Message Processing

The window procedure for the predefined list box window class carries out default processing for all messages that the list box does not process. When the list box procedure returns FALSE for a message, the predefined window procedure checks the message and carries out default actions, as shown in the following table.

Message	Default
WM_CHAR	Moves the selection to the first item that begins with the character the user typed. If the list box has the LBS_OWNERDRAW style, nothing happens.
WM_COPYGLOBALDATA	Passes the message to the dialog box procedure or parent window process.
WM_CREATE	Creates an empty list box.
WM_DESTROY	Destroys the list box and frees any resources it uses.
WM_DRAGLOOP	Passes the message to the dialog box procedure or parent window process.
WM_DRAGMOVE	Passes the message to the dialog box procedure or parent window process.
WM_DRAGSELECT	Passes the message to the dialog box procedure or parent window process.
WM_DROPFILES	Passes the message to the dialog box procedure or parent window process.
WM_DROPOBJECT	Sets control data and sends the message to the dialog box procedure or parent window process.
WM_ENABLE	If the control is visible, invalidates the rectangle so the strings can be painted gray.
WM_ERASEBACKGROUND	Erases the background of a list box. If the list box has the LBS_OWNERDRAW style, the background is not erased.
WM_GETDLGCODE	Returns DLGC_WANTARROWS	DLGC_WANTCHARS, indicating the default list box procedure processes the arrow keys and WM_CHAR messages.
WM_GETFONT	Returns a handle of the current font for the list box.
WM_HSCROLL	Scrolls the list box horizontally.
WM_KEYDOWN	Processes virtual keys for scrolling. The virtual key is the index of the item to move the caret to. The selection is not changed.

WM_KILLFOCUS	Turns the caret off and destroys it. Sends an LBN_KILLFOCUS message to the owner of the list box.
WM_LBUTTONDBLCLK	Tracks the mouse in the list box client area. This enables the user to cancel a selection if the mouse button is released outside the list box client area.
WM_LBUTTONDOWN	Tracks the mouse in the list box client area. This enables the user to cancel a selection if the mouse button is released outside the list box client area.
WM_LBUTTONUP	Tracks the mouse in the list box client area. This enables the user to cancel a selection if the mouse button is released outside the list box client area.
WM_MOUSEMOVE	Tracks the mouse in the list box client area. This enables the user to cancel a selection if the mouse button is released outside the list box client area.
WM_PAINT	Performs a subclassed paint operation by using the list box handle of the device context.
WM_QUERYDROPOBJECT	Sets control data and sends the message to the dialog box procedure or parent window process.
WM_SETFOCUS	Turns the caret on and sends an LBN_SETFOCUS message to the owner of the list box.
WM_SETFONT	Sets a new font for the list box.
WM_SETREDRAW	Sets or clears the redraw flag based on the value of *wParam*.
WM_SIZE	Resizes the list box to an integral number of items.
WM_SYSTIMER	Notifies the list box window procedure that the timer set for tracking the mouse in the list box has elapsed.
WM_VSCROLL	Scrolls the list box vertically.

The predefined list box procedure passes all other messages to the **DefWindowProc** function for default processing.

11.2 Using List Boxes

This section shows how to perform the following tasks:

- Create a simple list box.
- Create a directory listing in a single-selection list box.
- Create a directory listing in a multiple-selection list box.
- Create an owner-drawn list box.

11.2.1 Creating a Simple List Box

The following code sample demonstates how a dialog box procedure creates a
simple list box and fills it with the names of people on a softball team. When a
name in the list is selected, additional information about the player is displayed in
the dialog box. The following illustration shows the dialog box.

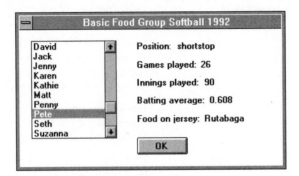

The list box has the LBS_STANDARD style, a combination of LBS_SORT,
LBS_NOTIFY, WS_VSCROLL, and WS_BORDER. The code initializes the
dialog box while processing the WM_INITDIALOG message. For each name that
appears in the list box, the code sends an LB_ADDSTRING message to the list
box. By processing the LBN_SELCHANGE notification, the code also keeps
track of when the selection changes.

```
#define BUFFER MAX_PATH

#define NAMELENGTH 15
#define POSITIONLENGTH 20
#define TEAMSIZE 15

typedef struct {
    TCHAR tchName[NAMELENGTH];
    TCHAR tchPosition[POSITIONLENGTH];
    int nGamesPlayed;
    int nInningsPlayed;
    double xBattingAverage;
    TCHAR tchFoodName[NAMELENGTH];
} Player;

Player Roster[] = {
        {"Pete", "shortstop", 26, 90, .608, "Rutabaga"},
        {"Suzanna", "catcher", 16, 53, .286, "Toast"},
        {"Jack", "pitcher", 27, 110, .542, "Animal Crackers"},
        {"Karen", "second base", 26, 140, .238, "Pez"},
        {"Dave", "first base", 28, 138, .508, "Suds"},
        {"Wendy", "third base", 25, 154, .493, "Ham"},
        {"Matt", "shortstop", 24, 112, .579, "Oats"},
```

```
             {"Jenny", "right field", 22, 101, .509, "Mashed Potatoes"},
             {"Seth", "left-center field", 20, 76, .407, "Otter Pop"},
             {"Kathie", "left field", 26, 127, .353, "Baba Ganouj"},
             {"Colin", "pitcher", 26, 96, .456, "Lefse"},
             {"Penny", "right field", 24, 112, .393, "Zotz"},
             {"Art", "left-center field", 17, 56, .375, "Cannelloni"},
             {"Cindy", "second base", 13, 58, .207, "Tequila"},
             {"David", "center field", 18, 101, .612, "Bok Choy"}
          };

    /*
     * FUNCTION: DlgTeamProc(HWND, unsigned, WORD, LONG)
     *
     * PURPOSE: Dialog box for "BFG Softball Statistics"
     */

BOOL APIENTRY DlgTeamProc(
       HWND hDlg,              /* window handle of dialog box    */
       UINT message,          /* type of message               */
       UINT wParam,           /* message-specific information   */
       LONG lParam)           /* message-specific information   */
{

   TCHAR tchName[NAMELENGTH];
   TCHAR tchBuffer[BUFFER];
   int nItem;
   int i;


   switch (message) {

     case WM_INITDIALOG:

        /* Initialize the list box (fill it with player names). */

        for (i = 0; i < TEAMSIZE; i++) {
            SendMessage(GetDlgItem(hDlg, IDL_SOFTBALL),
                LB_ADDSTRING, 0, (LPARAM) Roster[i].tchName);
        }

        SetFocus(GetDlgItem(hDlg, IDL_SOFTBALL));

        return FALSE;

     case WM_COMMAND:

        switch (LOWORD(wParam)) {

          case IDL_SOFTBALL:
```

```
                    switch (HIWORD(wParam)) {

                  case LBN_SELCHANGE:

                    /* Display the selected player's statistics. */

                    nItem = SendMessage(GetDlgItem(hDlg, IDL_SOFTBALL),
                        LB_GETCURSEL, 0, 0);

                    SendMessage(GetDlgItem(hDlg, IDL_SOFTBALL),
                        LB_GETTEXT, nItem, (LPARAM) tchName);

                    for (i = 0; strcmp(tchName, Roster[i].tchName); i++);

                    SetDlgItemText(hDlg, IDS_POS, Roster[i].tchPosition);
                    SetDlgItemText(hDlg, IDS_GAME,
                        _itoa(Roster[i].nGamesPlayed, tchBuffer, 10));
                    SetDlgItemText(hDlg, IDS_INN,
                        _itoa(Roster[i].nInningsPlayed, tchBuffer, 10));
                    SetDlgItemText(hDlg, IDS_BA,
                        _gcvt(Roster[i].xBattingAverage, 3, tchBuffer));
                    SetDlgItemText(hDlg, IDS_FOOD,
                        Roster[i].tchFoodName);

                    return TRUE;
                  }
                  break;

                case IDOK:
                case IDCANCEL:

                  /* Destroy the dialog box. */

                  EndDialog(hDlg, TRUE);
                  return TRUE;

                default:
                  return FALSE;

              }

            default:
              return FALSE;

          }
        }
```

11.2.2 Creating a Directory Listing in a Single-Selection List Box

The following code sample demonstrates how to display the contents of the current directory in a list box and enable the user to delete one file at a time. The following illustration shows the dialog box.

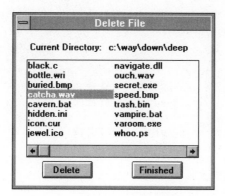

In addition to the standard list box styles, this list box has the LBS_MULTICOLUMN and LBS_HSCROLL styles. The code initializes the list box by using the **DlgDirList** function to fill the list box with the names of all the files in the current directory. When the user selects the Delete button, the **DlgDirSelectEx** function retrieves the name of the selected file. The code deletes the file by using the **DeleteFile** function and updates the directory list box by sending the LB_DELETESTRING message.

```
#define BUFFER MAX_PATH

    /*
     * FUNCTION: DlgDelFileProc(HWND, unsigned, WORD, LONG)
     *
     * PURPOSE: "Delete File" dialog box
     */

BOOL APIENTRY DlgDelFileProc(
    HWND hDlg,            /* window handle of dialog box       */
    UINT message,        /* type of message                   */
    UINT wParam,         /* message-specific information      */
    LONG lParam)
{

    DWORD cchCurDir;
    LPSTR lpszCurDir;
    LPSTR lpszFileToDelete;
    int nItem;
    int nTotal;
    TCHAR tchBuffer[BUFFER];
    BOOL fResult;
```

```
switch (message) {

  case WM_INITDIALOG:

    /*
     * Initialize the list box by filling it with files from
     * the current directory.
     */

    lpszCurDir = tchBuffer;
    GetCurrentDirectory(cchCurDir, lpszCurDir);
    DlgDirList(hDlg, lpszCurDir, IDL_FILES, IDS_PATHTOFILL, 0);

    SetFocus(GetDlgItem(hDlg, IDL_FILES));

    return FALSE;

  case WM_COMMAND:

    switch (LOWORD(wParam)) {

      case IDOK:

        /*
         * When the user presses the DEL (IDOK) button,
         * delete the selected file.
         */

        lpszFileToDelete = tchBuffer;

        DlgDirSelectEx(hDlg, lpszFileToDelete, MAX_PATH,
            IDL_FILES);
        fResult = DeleteFile(lpszFileToDelete);
        if (!fResult) {
            MessageBox(hDlg, "Could not delete file.",
                NULL, MB_OK);
        } else {

            nItem = SendMessage(GetDlgItem(hDlg, IDL_FILES),
                LB_GETCURSEL, 0, 0);

            nTotal = SendMessage(GetDlgItem(hDlg, IDL_FILES),
                LB_DELETESTRING, nItem, 0);

            /* Update the list box. */

            if (nTotal > nItem) {
                SendMessage(GetDlgItem(hDlg, IDL_FILES),
                    LB_SETCURSEL, nItem, 0);
```

```
            } else {
                SendMessage(GetDlgItem(hDlg, IDL_FILES),
                    LB_SETCURSEL, nTotal, 0);
            }

        }
        return TRUE;

    case IDCANCEL:

        /* Destroy the dialog box. */

        EndDialog(hDlg, TRUE);
        return TRUE;

    default:
        return FALSE;

    }

    default:
        return FALSE;

  }
}
```

11.2.3 Creating a Multiple-Selection List Box

The following code sample displays and initializes the same dialog box used in the preceding example. However, this code uses the LBS_MULTIPLESEL style to enable the user to select more than one file at a time. When the user selects the Delete button, the example sends the LB_GETSELCOUNT message (to retrieve the number of files selected) and the LB_GETSELITEMS message (to retrieve an array of selected list box items). After deleting a file, the code removes the corresponding item from the list box by sending the LB_DELETESTRING message.

```
#define BUFFER MAX_PATH

#define BIGBUFF 8192

    /*
     * FUNCTION: DlgDelFilesProc(HWND, unsigned, WORD, LONG)
     *
     * PURPOSE: "Delete files" dialog box
     */

BOOL APIENTRY DlgDelFilesProc(
```

```
            HWND hDlg,              /* window handle of dialog box  */
            UINT message,           /* type of message             */
            UINT wParam,            /* message-specific information */
            LONG lParam)
    {

        DWORD cchCurDir;
        LPTSTR lpszCurDir;
        LPTSTR lpszFileToDelete;
        int nSelItems;
        int nSelItemsInBuffer;
        TCHAR tchBuffer[BUFFER];
        TCHAR tchMsgBuff[BUFFER];
        int nBuffer[BIGBUFF];
        int i;
        BOOL fResult;
        HWND hListBox;

        switch (message) {

            case WM_INITDIALOG:

                /*
                 * Initialize the list box by filling it with files from
                 * the current directory.
                 */

                lpszCurDir = tchBuffer;
                GetCurrentDirectory(cchCurDir, lpszCurDir);
                DlgDirList(hDlg, lpszCurDir, IDL_FILES, IDS_PATHTOFILL, 0);

                SetFocus(GetDlgItem(hDlg, IDL_FILES));

                return FALSE;

            case WM_COMMAND:

                switch (LOWORD(wParam)) {

                    case IDOK:

                        /*
                         * When the user presses the Delete (IDOK) button,
                         * delete all the selected files.
                         */

                        lpszFileToDelete = tchBuffer;

                        hListBox = GetDlgItem(hDlg, IDL_FILES);
```

```
                    nSelItems = SendMessage(hListBox, LB_GETSELCOUNT, 0, 0);

                    nSelItemsInBuffer = SendMessage(hListBox, LB_GETSELITEMS,
                        512, (LPARAM) nBuffer);

                    if (nSelItems > nSelItemsInBuffer) {
                        MessageBox(hDlg, "Too many items selected.",
                            NULL, MB_OK);
                    } else {

                        for (i = nSelItemsInBuffer - 1; i > -1; i--) {

                            SendMessage(hListBox, LB_GETTEXT, nBuffer[i],
                                (LPARAM) lpszFileToDelete);

                            fResult = DeleteFile(lpszFileToDelete);
                            if (!fResult) {
                                sprintf(tchMsgBuff,
                                    "Could not delete file: %s GetLastError = %u",
                                    (LPARAM) lpszFileToDelete);
                                ErrorHandler(tchMsgBuff);    /* app-defined */
                            } else {
                                SendMessage(hListBox, LB_DELETESTRING,
                                    nBuffer[i], 0);
                            }
                        }

                        SendMessage(hListBox, LB_SETCARETINDEX, 0, 0);

                    }
                    return TRUE;

                case IDCANCEL:

                    /* Destroy the dialog box. */

                    EndDialog(hDlg, TRUE);
                    return TRUE;

                default:
                    return FALSE;

            }

        default:
            return FALSE;

    }
}
```

11.2.4 Creating an Owner-Drawn List Box

The following code sample shows how to draw a list box that contains five owner-drawn items and prompts the user to select the item not like the others. The following illustration shows the dialog box.

The list box has the **LBS_OWNERDRAW** and **LBS_HASSTRINGS** styles, in addition to the standard list box styles. The code initializes the list box by sending the **LB_ADDSTRING** message to set the text, and then sends the **LB_SETITEMDATA** message to associate a bitmap with each list box item. The code also sets the height of each list box item by processing the **WM_MEASUREITEM** message and draws the text and bitmap for each item by processing the **WM_DRAWITEM** message.

```
#define XBITMAP 80
#define YBITMAP 20

#define BUFFER MAX_PATH

HBITMAP hbmpPencil, hbmpCrayon, hbmpMarker, hbmpPen, hbmpFork;
HBITMAP hbmpPicture, hbmpOld;

    /*
     * FUNCTION: DlgDrawProc(HWND, unsigned, WORD, LONG)
     *
     * PURPOSE: "One of these things..." dialog box
     */

DWORD APIENTRY DlgDrawProc(
        HWND hDlg,              /* window handle of dialog box    */
        UINT message,          /* type of message                */
        UINT wParam,           /* message-specific information   */
        LONG lParam)
{

  int nItem;
  TCHAR tchBuffer[BUFFER];
```

```
HWND hListBox;
TEXTMETRIC tm;
int y;
HDC hdcMem;
LPMEASUREITEMSTRUCT lpmis;
LPDRAWITEMSTRUCT lpdis;
RECT rcBitmap;

switch (message) {

  case WM_INITDIALOG:

    /* Load bitmaps. */

    hbmpPencil = LoadBitmap(hinst, MAKEINTRESOURCE(700));
    hbmpCrayon = LoadBitmap(hinst, MAKEINTRESOURCE(701));
    hbmpMarker = LoadBitmap(hinst, MAKEINTRESOURCE(702));
    hbmpPen = LoadBitmap(hinst, MAKEINTRESOURCE(703));
    hbmpFork = LoadBitmap(hinst, MAKEINTRESOURCE(704));

    /* Retrieve list box handle. */

    hListBox = GetDlgItem(hDlg, IDL_STUFF);

    /*
     * Initialize the list box text and associate a bitmap
     * with each list box item.
     */

    nItem = SendMessage(hListBox, LB_ADDSTRING, 0,
        (LPARAM) "pencil");
    SendMessage(hListBox, LB_SETITEMDATA, nItem,
        (LPARAM) hbmpPencil);

    nItem = SendMessage(hListBox, LB_ADDSTRING, 0,
        (LPARAM) "crayon");
    SendMessage(hListBox, LB_SETITEMDATA, nItem,
        (LPARAM) hbmpCrayon);

    nItem = SendMessage(hListBox, LB_ADDSTRING, 0,
        (LPARAM) "marker");
    SendMessage(hListBox, LB_SETITEMDATA, nItem,
        (LPARAM) hbmpMarker);

    nItem = SendMessage(hListBox, LB_ADDSTRING, 0,
        (LPARAM) "pen");
    SendMessage(hListBox, LB_SETITEMDATA, nItem,
        (LPARAM) hbmpPen);

    nItem = SendMessage(hListBox, LB_ADDSTRING, 0,
```

```
            (LPARAM) "fork");
        SendMessage(hListBox, LB_SETITEMDATA, nItem,
            (LPARAM) hbmpFork);

        SetFocus(hListBox);

        SendMessage(hListBox, LB_SETCURSEL, 0, 0);

        return TRUE;

case WM_MEASUREITEM:

    lpmis = (LPMEASUREITEMSTRUCT) lParam;

    /* Set the height of the list box items. */

    lpmis->itemHeight = 20;

    return TRUE;

case WM_DRAWITEM:

    lpdis = (LPDRAWITEMSTRUCT) lParam;

    /* If there are no list box items, skip this message. */

    if (lpdis->itemID == -1) {
      break;
    }

    /*
     * Draw the bitmap and text for the list box item. Draw a
     * rectangle around the bitmap if it is selected.
     */

    switch (lpdis->itemAction) {

      case ODA_SELECT:
      case ODA_DRAWENTIRE:

        /* Display the bitmap associated with the item. */

        hbmpPicture = (HBITMAP) SendMessage(lpdis->hwndItem,
            LB_GETITEMDATA, lpdis->itemID, (LPARAM) 0);

        hdcMem = CreateCompatibleDC(lpdis->hDC);
        hbmpOld = SelectObject(hdcMem, hbmpPicture);

        BitBlt(lpdis->hDC,
            lpdis->rcItem.left, lpdis->rcItem.top,
```

```
        lpdis->rcItem.right - lpdis->rcItem.left,
        lpdis->rcItem.bottom - lpdis->rcItem.top,
        hdcMem, 0, 0, SRCCOPY);

    /* Display the text associated with the item. */

    SendMessage(lpdis->hwndItem, LB_GETTEXT, lpdis->itemID,
        (LPARAM) tchBuffer);

    GetTextMetrics(lpdis->hDC, &tm);

    y = (lpdis->rcItem.bottom + lpdis->rcItem.top -
        tm.tmHeight) / 2;

    TextOut(lpdis->hDC,
        XBITMAP + 6,
        y,
        tchBuffer,
        strlen(tchBuffer));

    SelectObject(hdcMem, hbmpOld);

    DeleteDC(hdcMem);

    /* Is the item selected? */

    if (lpdis->itemState & ODS_SELECTED) {

        /* Set RECT coordinates to surround only the bitmap. */

        rcBitmap.left = lpdis->rcItem.left;
        rcBitmap.top = lpdis->rcItem.top;
        rcBitmap.right = lpdis->rcItem.left + XBITMAP;
        rcBitmap.bottom = lpdis->rcItem.top + YBITMAP;

        /* Draw a rectangle around bitmap to indicate the selection. */

        DrawFocusRect(lpdis->hDC, &rcBitmap);

    }

    break;

case ODA_FOCUS:

    /*
     * Do not process focus changes. The focus caret (outline
     * rectangle) indicates the selection. The Which one? (IDOK)
     * button indicates the final selection.
     */
```

```
            break;
        }

        return TRUE;

    case WM_COMMAND:

        switch (LOWORD(wParam)) {

            case IDOK:

                /* Get the selected item's text. */

                nItem = SendMessage(GetDlgItem(hDlg, IDL_STUFF),
                    LB_GETCURSEL, 0, (LPARAM) 0);
                SendMessage(GetDlgItem(hDlg, IDL_STUFF), LB_GETTEXT,
                    nItem, (LPARAM) tchBuffer);

                /*
                 * If the item is not the correct answer, tell the
                 * user to try again.
                 *
                 * If the item is the correct answer, congratulate
                 * the user and destroy the dialog box.
                 */

                if (strcmp(tchBuffer, "fork")) {
                    MessageBox(hDlg, "Try again!", "Oops.", MB_OK);
                    return FALSE;
                } else {
                    MessageBox(hDlg, "You're right!", "Congratulations.",
                        MB_OK);

                    /* Fall through. */

                }

            case IDCANCEL:

                /* Destroy the dialog box. */

                EndDialog(hDlg, TRUE);
                return TRUE;

            default:

                return FALSE;

        }
```

```
    case WM_DESTROY:

        /* Free any resources used by the bitmaps. */

        DeleteObject(hbmpPencil);
        DeleteObject(hbmpCrayon);
        DeleteObject(hbmpMarker);
        DeleteObject(hbmpPen);
        DeleteObject(hbmpFork);

        return TRUE;

    default:
        return FALSE;

    }
    return FALSE;
}
```

11.3 Functions and Messages

Following are the functions and messages used with list boxes.

Functions
DigDirList
DigDirSelectEx

Messages
LB_ADDFILE
LB_ADDSTRING
LB_DELETESTRING
LB_DIR
LB_FINDSTRING
LB_FINDSTRINGEXACT
LB_GETANCHORINDEX
LB_GETCARETINDEX
LB_GETCOUNT
LB_GETCURSEL
LB_GETHORIZONTALEXTENT
LB_GETITEMDATA
LB_GETITEMHEIGHT
LB_GETITEMRECT
LB_GETLOCALE

LB_GETSEL
LB_GETSELCOUNT
LB_GETSELITEMS
LB_GETTEXT
LB_GETTEXTLEN
LB_GETTOPINDEX
LB_INSERTSTRING
LB_RESETCONTENT
LB_SELECTSTRING
LB_SELITEMRANGE
LB_SELITEMRANGEEX
LB_SETANCHORINDEX
LB_SETCARETINDEX
LB_SETCOLUMNWIDTH
LB_SETCOUNT
LB_SETCURSEL
LB_SETHORIZONTALEXTENT
LB_SETITEMDATA
LB_SETITEMHEIGHT
LB_SETLOCALE
LB_SETSEL
LB_SETTABSTOPS
LB_SETTOPINDEX
LBN_DBLCLK
LBN_ERRSPACE
LBN_KILLFOCUS
LBN_SELCANCEL
LBN_SELCHANGE
LBN_SETFOCUS
WM_CHARTOITEM
WN_DELETEITEM
WN_VKEYTOITEM

CHAPTER 12

Edit Controls

12.1 About Edit Controls

Microsoft ® Windows ™ provides dialog boxes and controls to support communication between the application and the user. An *edit control* is a rectangular control window typically used in a dialog box to permit the user to enter and edit text from the keyboard. The user selects an edit control giving it the input focus by clicking the mouse inside it or by pressing the TAB key. After it is selected, the edit control displays its text (if any) and a flashing caret that indicates the insertion point. The user can then enter text, move the insertion point, or select text to be moved or deleted by using the keyboard or the mouse. An edit control can send notification messages to its parent window in the form of WM_COMMAND messages. For more information about messages from an edit control, see Section 12.1.5, "Edit Control Notifications." A parent window can send messages to an edit control in a dialog box by calling the **SendDlgItemMessage** function. Each of the messages sent to edit controls are discussed in this chapter.

Edit controls can be single-line (the default) or multiline. Multiline edit controls (sometimes called MLEs) can have scroll bars. Edit controls belong to the EDIT window class.

Although edit controls can be used in overlapped, pop-up, and child windows, they are designed for use in dialog boxes, where Windows standardizes their behavior. If the application uses edit controls outside dialog boxes, this creates extra work and increases the risk that the application may behave in a nonstandard fashion. For these reasons, the application should either use edit controls in dialog boxes or use window subclassing to create customized edit controls. For more information about dialog boxes, see Chapter 18, "Dialog Boxes"; for more information about window subclassing, see Chapter 4, "Window Procedures."

A combo box is a control that combines much of the functionality of an edit control and a list box. In a combo box, the edit control displays the current selection and the list box presents options a user can select. For more information about combo boxes, see Chapter 13, "Combo Boxes."

Many developers use the dialog boxes provided in the common dialog box library (COMDLG32.DLL) to perform tasks that otherwise might require customized edit controls. For information about common dialog boxes, see Chapter 76, "Common Dialog Box Library."

12.1.1 Edit Control Styles

Windows provides 13 edit control styles. An individual edit control can have several styles at the same time. Most developers use stand-alone tools to develop dialog boxes and so may not need to specify edit control styles explicitly. If an application creates an edit control using the **CreateWindow** or **CreateWindowEx** function, however, it must specify these edit control styles.

Every edit control specifies a combination of style values that define the appearance and features of the edit control. The style values can establish the appearance of a single-line or multiline edit control, align the text in the control, and determine how, and even if, text appears in the edit control. The number and type of styles the application uses depend on the type and purpose of the edit control.

There are two line styles for edit controls. The default is a single-line edit control that doesn't require an associated style. An application can create a multiline edit control by using the ES_MULTILINE style.

There are three styles that cause Windows to align the text in an edit control. The ES_LEFT, ES_CENTER, and ES_RIGHT styles determine whether text is aligned on the left, center, or right, respectively. These styles apply only to multiline edit controls.

An application can use a style to determine how Windows displays text that a user enters in an edit control. The ES_LOWERCASE style converts the text into lowercase characters; the ES_UPPERCASE style converts the text into uppercase characters. Some applications may need to convert the text in a Windows string (such as a filename) into a specific character set. The ES_OEMCONVERT style ensures the proper conversion of characters in these instances. For more information about character sets, see Chapter 57, "Consoles and Character-Mode Support."

When the amount of text to be displayed exceeds the size of the edit control, an application can use two styles to scroll the text through the edit control. The ES_AUTOHSCROLL style automatically scrolls text horizontally in single-line and multiline edit controls. When the application has a multiline edit control, it can also use the ES_AUTOVSCROLL style to automatically scroll text vertically, if necessary.

Other available styles define different aspects of an edit control. The ES_NOHIDESEL style specifies that the selected text is not hidden when the edit control loses the keyboard focus. The ES_READONLY style makes the edit control read-only. The ES_PASSWORD style displays all characters in the edit control as asterisks. (An application can define a different character to display by using the EM_SETPASSWORDCHAR message, as described later in this chapter.) In multiline edit controls, an application can specify the ES_WANTRETURN style to request that Windows insert a carriage return when the user presses the ENTER key in the edit control.

By default, an edit control has no border. To give it one, an application can use the WS_BORDER window style.

12.1.2 The Text Buffer

Windows stores edit control text in a buffer and copies it to the control as necessary. This section discusses the tools Windows provides to allocate and initialize the buffer and to change its characteristics.

12.1.2.1 Allocating a Text Buffer

When Windows creates an edit control, it automatically creates a text buffer, sets its initial size, and increases the size as necessary, up to a predefined limit of approximately 32 kilobytes for single-line edit controls. Because this limit can change, it is called a soft limit. An application can set a hard limit to the buffer size by sending an EM_LIMITTEXT message to the edit control. If the buffer exceeds either limit, Windows sends the application an EN_ERRSPACE message.

Windows typically creates an edit control buffer in a dialog box, using memory outside the application's data segment. An application can suppress this default allocation behavior and create the buffer from its local heap by using the DS_LOCALEDIT style when creating the edit control. An application that uses the DS_LOCALEDIT style is responsible for all buffer allocations. To make the initial allocation, an application can call the **LocalAlloc** function and pass the returned buffer handle to the edit control by sending it an EM_SETHANDLE message. To make subsequent allocations (in response to an EN_ERRSPACE message, for example), an application should save the current buffer contents (if necessary) and obtain a new buffer as follows:

1. Retrieve the handle of the memory currently allocated for the text in a multiline edit control by sending the control an EM_GETHANDLE message.
2. Free the buffer by calling the **LocalFree** function.
3. Obtain a new buffer (and buffer handle) by calling **LocalAlloc**.
4. Give the buffer handle to Windows by sending the control an EM_SETHANDLE message.

The EM_SETHANDLE and EM_GETHANDLE messages apply only to multiline edit controls.

An application that uses the default allocation behavior (that is, does not use the DS_LOCALEDIT style) must not send EM_SETHANDLE and EM_GETHANDLE messages to the edit control.

Sending an EM_SETHANDLE message has several side effects: it clears the undo flag (making the EM_CANUNDO message return zero), it clears the modify flag (making the EM_GETMODIFY message return zero), and it redraws the edit control window.

12.1.2.2 Initializing a Text Buffer

An application can initialize or reinitialize an edit control's text buffer by calling the **SetDlgItemText** function. An application can retrieve the contents of a text buffer by calling the **GetDlgItemText** function.

12.1.2.3 Making a Text Buffer Read-Only

For each edit control, Windows maintains a read-only flag that indicates whether the control's text is read-write (the default) or read-only. An application can set the read-write or read-only flag for the text by sending the control an EM_SETREADONLY message. To determine whether an edit control is read-only, an application can call the **GetWindowLong** function using the GWL_STYLE constant. The EM_SETREADONLY message applies to both single-line and multiline edit controls.

12.1.3 Changing the Formatting Rectangle

The visibility of an edit control's text is governed by the dimensions of its window rectangle and its formatting rectangle. The window rectangle is the client area of the window containing the edit control. The formatting rectangle is a construct maintained by Windows for formatting the text displayed in the window rectangle. When an edit control is first displayed, the two rectangles are identical on the screen. An application can make the formatting rectangle larger than the window rectangle (thereby limiting the visibility of the edit control's text) or smaller than the window rectangle (thereby creating extra white space around the text).

An application can set the coordinates of an edit control's formatting rectangle by sending it an EM_SETRECT message. The EM_SETRECT message also automatically redraws the edit control's text. To establish the coordinates of the formatting rectangle without redrawing the control's text, an application can send the control an EM_SETRECTNP message. To retrieve the coordinates of the formatting rectangle, an application can send the control an EM_GETRECT message. These messages apply to multiline edit controls only.

12.1.4 Text Operations

Windows automatically processes all user-initiated text operations and notifies the application when the operations are completed. This section discusses user-initiated text operations and the application's response.

12.1.4.1 Character Sets

Windows supports two character sets: Unicode, a two-byte character set, and ANSI, a one-byte character set that is a strict subset of Unicode. In ANSI, n characters equals n bytes, but in Unicode, n characters equals $2n$ bytes. For more information about Unicode and character sets, see Chapter 53, "String Manipulation and Unicode."

12.1.4.2 Fonts

An application can change the font that an edit control uses by sending the WM_SETFONT message. Most applications do this while processing the WM_INITDIALOG message. Changing the font does not change the size of the edit control; applications that send the WM_SETFONT message may have to retrieve the font metrics for the text and recalculate the size of the edit control. For more information about fonts and font metrics, see Chapter 35, "Fonts and Text."

12.1.4.3 Selecting an Edit Control

The user can select an edit control in three ways: by clicking it with the mouse, by tabbing to it and pressing the SPACEBAR, or (when the edit control is part of a group defined using the WS_GROUP style) by tabbing to the selected edit control in the group and using the arrow keys to move within the group. (The latter two "tabbing" methods are part of a predefined keyboard interface that Windows provides. For a complete description of this interface, see Chapter 18, "Dialog Boxes.") When the user selects an edit control, Windows gives the control the keyboard focus and highlights its text by using reverse video.

12.1.4.4 Selecting Text

After selecting an edit control, the user can select text in the control by using the mouse or the keyboard. An application can retrieve the starting and ending character positions of the current selection in an edit control by sending the control an EM_GETSEL message. The return value for the ending position is one greater than the last character in the selection (that is, the position of the first character following the last selected character).

An application can also select text in an edit control by sending the control an EM_SETSEL message with the starting and ending character indices for the selection. For example, the application can use EM_SETSEL with EM_REPLACESEL to delete text from an edit control.

These three messages apply to both single-line and multiline edit controls.

12.1.4.5 Replacing Text

An application can replace selected text in an edit control by sending the control an EM_REPLACESEL message with a pointer to the replacement text. If there is no current selection, EM_REPLACESEL inserts the replacement text at the insertion point. The application may receive an EN_ERRSPACE message if the replacement text exceeds the available memory. This message applies to both single-line and multiline edit controls.

An application can use EM_REPLACESEL to replace part of an edit control's text or the **SetDlgItemText** function to replace all of it.

12.1.4.6 Cut, Copy, Paste, and Clear Operations

Windows provides four messages for moving text between an edit control and the Clipboard. The WM_COPY message copies the current selection (if any) from an edit control to the Clipboard without deleting it from the edit control. The WM_CUT message deletes the current selection, if any, in the edit control and copies the deleted text to the Clipboard. The WM_CLEAR message deletes the current selection (if any) from an edit control, but does not copy it to the Clipboard (unless the user pressed the SHIFT key). The WM_PASTE message copies text from the Clipboard into an edit control at the insertion point. These four messages apply to both single-line and multiline edit controls.

12.1.4.7 Modifying Text

The user can select, delete, or move text in an edit control. Windows maintains an internal flag for each edit control indicating whether the contents of the control have been modified. Windows clears this flag when it creates the control and sets the flag whenever the text in the control is modified. An application can retrieve the modification flag by sending the control an EM_GETMODIFY message and set or clear the modification flag by sending the control an EM_SETMODIFY message. These messages apply to both single-line and multiline edit controls.

12.1.4.8 Limiting User-Entered Text

The default limit to the amount of text a user can enter in an edit control is 32 kilobytes. An application can change the amount of text the user can enter by sending the control an EM_LIMITTEXT message. This message sets a hard limit to the number of bytes the user can enter into an edit control, but affects neither text in the control when the message was sent nor text copied to the control by the **SetDlgItemText** function. For example, suppose that the application uses the **SetDlgItemText** function to place 500 bytes in an edit control, and the user also enters 500 bytes (1000 bytes total). If the application then sends an EM_LIMITTEXT message limiting user-entered text to 300 bytes, the 1000 bytes already in the edit control remain there, and the user cannot add any more text (having entered 500 bytes already). On the other hand, if the application sends an EM_LIMITTEXT message limiting user-entered text to 1300 bytes, the 1000 bytes remain, but the user can add 800 more bytes (having entered only 500 bytes).

When the user reaches the character limit of an edit control, Windows sends the application a WM_COMMAND message containing an EN_MAXTEXT notification message. This notification message does not mean that memory has been exhausted, but that the limit for user-entered text has been reached and the user cannot enter any more text. To change this limit, an application must send the control a new EM_LIMITTEXT message with a higher limit.

As an example of the use of EM_LIMITTEXT and EN_MAXTEXT, suppose that the application must limit the user to no more than four characters in an edit control. The application would use EM_LIMITTEXT to specify a four-character limit. If the user tried to enter a fifth character, Windows would send an EN_MAXTEXT notification message to the application.

12.1.4.9 Character and Line Operations

The Win32 application programming interface (API) provides several messages that return information about the characters and lines in an edit control. Most of the messages return an index, usually a zero-based number, to refer to a character or line. Given this, a single-line edit control containing n characters, the line index is zero and the characters are indexed from zero to $n - 1$. In a multiline edit control containing m lines and n characters, the lines are indexed from zero to $m - 1$, and the characters are indexed from zero to $n - 1$. Note that character indexing ignores line breaks.

An application can determine the number of characters in an edit control by sending the WM_GETTEXTLENGTH message to the edit control. This message returns the length, in characters (not including the terminating null character), of the text in a single-line or multiline edit control. The EM_LINELENGTH message returns the length, in characters, of a line specified by the character index of a character in the line. The returned length does not include any selected characters. An application can use these messages in a single-line or multiline edit control.

The EM_GETFIRSTVISIBLELINE message returns the zero-based index of the uppermost visible line in a multiline edit control, or the zero-based index of the first visible character in a single-line edit control. An application can copy a line from an edit control to a buffer by sending the EM_GETLINE message to the edit control. The line is specified by its line index and the first word of the receiving buffer contains the maximum number of bytes to be copied to the buffer. The return value is the number of bytes copied. This message can also be used in a single-line or multiline edit control.

There are unique messages available to return the information about a line in a multiline edit control. The EM_GETLINECOUNT message returns the number of lines in an edit control. An application can determine the index of a character in a specific line by using the EM_LINEFROMCHAR and EM_LINEINDEX messages. The EM_LINEFROMCHAR message returns the index of the line containing a specified character index. This message is the reverse of the EM_LINEINDEX message, which returns the index of the first character in a specified line.

12.1.4.10 Scrolling Text

An application can implement scrolling in an edit control by using the automatic scrolling styles discussed in Section 12.1.1, "Edit Control Styles," or by explicitly adding scroll bars to the control. To add a horizontal scroll bar, use the style WS_HSCROLL; to add a vertical scroll bar, use the style WS_VSCROLL. An edit control with scroll bars processes its own scroll bar messages. For detailed information about adding scroll bars to edit controls, see Chapter 14, "Scroll Bars."

Windows provides two messages that an application can send to an edit control with scroll bars. The EM_LINESCROLL message scrolls a multiline edit control vertically, or horizontally if the control has the ES_LEFT style. The *lParam* parameter specifies the number of lines to scroll vertically starting from the current line and the *wParam* parameter specifies the number of characters to scroll horizontally, starting from the current character. The edit control doesn't acknowledge horizontal scrolling messages if it has the ES_CENTER or ES_RIGHT style. This message applies to multiline edit controls only.

The EM_SCROLL message scrolls a multiline edit control vertically, which is the same effect as sending a WM_VSCROLL message. The *wParam* parameter specifies the scrolling action. The EM_SCROLL message applies to multiline edit controls only.

The EM_SCROLLCARET message scrolls the caret into view in an edit control. This was done in previous versions of Windows by specifying fScroll = FALSE in an EM_SETSEL message. A Win32 application should use the EM_SCROLLCARET message for the task.

12.1.4.11 Tab Stops

An application can set tab stops in a multiline edit control by using the EM_SETTABSTOPS message. (The default for a tab stop is eight characters.) When an application adds text to the edit control, tab characters in the text automatically generate space up to the next tab stop. The EM_SETTABSTOPS message does not automatically cause Windows to redraw the text. To do that, an application can call the **InvalidateRect** function. The EM_SETTABSTOPS message applies to multiline edit controls only.

12.1.4.12 Password Characters

An application can use a password character in an edit control to conceal user input. When a password character is set, it is displayed in place of each character the user types. When a password character is removed, the control displays the characters the user types. If the application creates an edit control using the style ES_PASSWORD, the default password character is an asterisk (*). An application can use the EM_SETPASSWORDCHAR message to remove or define a different password character and the EM_GETPASSWORDCHAR message to retrieve the current password character. These messages apply to single-line edit controls only.

12.1.4.13 Using Integers

Windows provides two integer-conversion functions for edit controls designed to contain numbers only. The **SetDlgItemInt** function creates the string representation of a specified integer (signed or unsigned) and sends the string to an edit control. **SetDlgItemInt** returns no value. The **GetDlgItemInt** function creates an integer (signed or unsigned) from its string representation in an edit control. **GetDlgItemInt** returns the integer (or an error code).

12.1.4.14 Undoing Text Operations

Every edit control maintains an undo flag that indicates whether an application can reverse (undo) the most recent operation on the edit control (to undo a text deletion, for example). The edit control sets the undo flag to indicate that the operation can be undone and resets it to indicate that the operation cannot be undone. An application can determine the setting of the undo flag by sending the control an EM_CANUNDO message.

An application can undo the most recent operation by sending the control an EM_UNDO message. An operation can be undone provided no other edit control operation occurs first. For example, the user can delete text, replace the text (undo the deletion), and then delete the text again (undo the replacement). The EM_UNDO message applies to both single-line and multiline edit controls and always works for single-line edit controls.

An application can reset an edit control's undo flag by sending the control an EM_EMPTYUNDOBUFFER message. Windows automatically resets the undo flag whenever an edit control receives an EM_SETHANDLE or WM_SETTEXT message. The **SetDlgItemText** function sends a WM_SETTEXT message.

12.1.4.15 Wordwrap Functions

An application can use wordwrap functions with multiline edit controls to locate the word or word fragment that should be wrapped to the next line. Using the default wordwrap function provided by Windows, lines always end at the spaces between words. An application can specify its own wordwrap function by supplying a **WordBreakProc** wordwrap function and sending an edit control an EM_SETWORDBREAKPROC message. An application can retrieve the address of the current wordwrap function by sending the control an EM_GETWORDBREAKPROC message.

An application may direct a multiline edit control to add or remove a soft line-break character (two carriage returns and a linefeed) automatically at the end of wrapped text lines. An application can turn this feature on or off by sending the edit control an EM_FMTLINES message. This message applies only to multiline edit controls and does not affect a line that ends with a hard line break (one carriage return and a linefeed entered by the user).

12.1.5 Edit Control Notifications

The user makes editing requests by using the keyboard and mouse. Windows sends each request to the edit control's parent window in the form of a WM_COMMAND message. The message includes the edit control identifier in the low-order word of the *wParam* parameter, the handle of the edit control in the *lParam* parameter, and an edit control notification message corresponding to the user's action in the high-order word of the *wParam* parameter.

Portability issue In Microsoft ® Windows NT ™, the placement of the notification code in a notification message has moved from the *lParam* parameter to the *wParam* parameter. Windows 3.*x* applications that process notification messages must modify this code when porting to Windows NT.

An application should examine each notification message and respond appropriately. The following table lists each edit control notification message and the action that generates it.

Notification message	User action
EN_CHANGE	The user has modified text in an edit control. Windows updates the display before sending this message (unlike EN_UPDATE).
EN_ERRSPACE	The edit control cannot allocate enough memory to meet a specific request.
EN_HSCROLL	The user has clicked the edit control's horizontal scroll bar. Windows sends this message before updating the screen.
EN_KILLFOCUS	The user has selected another control.
EN_MAXTEXT	While inserting text, the user has exceeded the specified number of characters for the edit control. Insertion has been truncated. This message is also sent either when an edit control does not have the ES_AUTOHSCROLL style and the number of characters to be inserted exceeds the width of the edit control or when an edit control does not have the ES_AUTOVSCROLL style and the total number of lines to be inserted exceeds the height of the edit control.
EN_SETFOCUS	The user has selected this edit control.
EN_UPDATE	The user has altered the text in the edit control and Windows is about to display the new text. Windows sends this message after formatting the text, but before displaying it, so that the application can resize the edit control window.

EN_VSCROLL   The user has clicked the edit control's vertical scroll bar. Windows sends this message before updating the screen.

In addition, the system sends a WM_CTLCOLOREDIT message to an edit control's parent window before the edit control is drawn. This message contains a handle of the edit control's display context and a handle of the child window. The parent window can use these handles to change the edit control's text and background colors.

12.1.6 Default Message Processing

The window procedure for the predefined edit control window class carries out default processing for all messages that the edit control procedure does not process. When the edit control procedure returns FALSE for any message, the predefined window procedure checks the messages and carries out the following default actions.

Message	Default action
EM_CANUNDO	Returns TRUE if the edit control operation can be undone.
EM_EMPTYUNDOBUFFER	Empties the undo buffer and sets the undo flag retrieved by the EM_CANUNDO message to FALSE. Windows automatically clears the undo flag whenever the edit control receives a WM_SETTEXT or EM_SETHANDLE message.
EM_FMTLINES	Adds or removes soft line-break characters (two carriage returns and a linefeed) to the ends of wrapped lines in a multiline edit control. It is not processed by single-line edit controls.
EM_GETFIRSTVISIBLELINE	Returns the zero-based index of the first visible character in a single-line edit control or the zero-based index of the uppermost visible line in a multiline edit control.
EM_GETHANDLE	Returns a handle identifying the buffer containing the multiline edit control's text. It is not processed by single-line edit controls.
EM_GETLINE	Copies characters in a single-line edit control to a buffer and returns the number of characters copied. In a multiline edit control, retrieves a line of text from the control and returns the number of characters copied.
EM_GETLINECOUNT	Returns the number of lines in the edit control.
EM_GETMODIFY	Returns a flag indicating whether the contents of an edit control have been modified.

EM_GETPASSWORDCHAR	Returns the character that edit controls use in conjunction with the ES_PASSWORD style.
EM_GETRECT	Returns the coordinates of the formatting rectangle in an edit control.
EM_GETSEL	Returns the starting and ending character positions of the current selection in the edit control.
EM_GETTHUMB	Unsupported.
EM_GETWORDBREAKPROC	Returns the address of the current wordwrap function in an edit control.
EM_LIMITTEXT	Sets the maximum number of characters the user may enter in the edit control. For single-line edit controls, this value is either 0x7FFFFFFE or the value of the *wParam* parameter, whichever is smaller. For multiline edit controls, this value is either 0xFFFFFFFF or the value of the *wParam* parameter, whichever is smaller.
EM_LINEFROMCHAR	Returns the zero-based number of the line in a multiline edit control that contains a specified character index This message is the reverse of the EM_LINEINDEX message. It is not processed by single-line edit controls.
EM_LINEINDEX	Returns the character of a line in a multiline edit control. This message is the reverse of the EM_LINEFROMCHAR message. It is not processed by single-line edit controls.
EM_LINELENGTH	Returns the length, in characters, of a single-line edit control. In a multiline edit control, returns the length, in characters, of a specified line.
EM_LINESCROLL	Scrolls the text vertically in a single-line edit control or horizontally in a multiline edit control (when the control has the ES_LEFT style). The *lParam* parameter specifies the number of lines to scroll vertically, starting from the current line. The *wParam* parameter specifies the number of characters to scroll horizontally, starting from the current character.
EM_MSGMAX	Unsupported.
EM_REPLACESEL	Replaces the current selection with the text in an application-supplied buffer, sends the parent window EN_UPDATE and EN_CHANGE messages, and updates the undo buffer.
EM_SCROLL	Scrolls the text vertically in a multiline edit control. This message is equivalent to sending a WM_VSCROLL message to the edit control. It is not processed by single-line edit controls.

EM_SCROLLCARET	Scrolls the caret into view in an edit control. In previous versions of Windows this was done via EM_SETSEL using particular parameters. A Win32 application should use EM_SCROLLCARET.
EM_SETFONT	Unsupported.
EM_SETHANDLE	Sets a handle to the memory used as a text buffer, empties the undo buffer, resets the scroll positions to zero, and redraws the window.
EM_SETMODIFY	Sets or clears the modification flag to indicate whether the edit control has been modified.
EM_SETPASSWORDCHAR	Defines the character that edit controls use in conjunction with the ES_PASSWORD style.
EM_SETREADONLY	Sets or removes the read-only style (ES_READONLY) in an edit control.
EM_SETRECT	Sets the formatting rectangle for the multiline edit control and redraws the window. It is not processed by single-line edit controls.
EM_SETRECTNP	Sets the formatting rectangle for the multiline edit control but does not redraw the window. It is not processed by single-line edit controls.
EM_SETSEL	Selects a range of characters in the edit control by setting the starting and ending positions to be selected.
EM_SETTABSTOPS	Sets tab-stop positions in the multiline edit control. It is not processed by single-line edit controls.
EM_SETWORDBREAKPROC	Replaces the default wordwrap function with an application-defined wordwrap function.
EM_UNDO	Removes any text that was just inserted or inserts any deleted characters and sets the selection to the inserted text. If necessary, sends the EN_UPDATE and EN_CHANGE notification messages to the parent window.
WM_CHAR	Writes a character to the single-line edit control and sends the EN_UPDATE and EN_CHANGE notification messages to the parent window. Writes a character to the multiline edit control. Handles the accelerator keys for standard functions, such as CTRL+C for copying and CTRL+V for pasting. In multiline edit controls, also processes TAB, and CTRL+TAB keystrokes to move among the controls in a dialog box and to insert tabs into multiline edit controls. Uses the **MessageBeep** function for illegal characters.

WM_CLEAR	Clears the current selection, if any, in an edit control. If there is no current selection, deletes the character to the right of the caret. If the user presses the SHIFT key, this cuts the selection to the Clipboard, or deletes the character to the left of the caret when there is no selection. If the user presses the CTRL key, this deletes the selection, or deletes to the end of the line when there is no selection.
WM_COPY	Copies text to the Clipboard unless the style is ES_PASSWORD, in which case the message returns zero.
WM_CREATE	Creates the edit control and notifies the parent window with TRUE for success or –1 for failure.
WM_CUT	Cuts the selection to the Clipboard, or deletes the character to the left of the cursor if there is no selection.
WM_ENABLE	Causes the rectangle to be redrawn in gray for single-line edit controls. Returns the enabled state for single-line and multiline edit controls.
WM_ERASEBKGND	Fills the multiline edit control window with the current color of the edit control.
WM_GETDLGCODE	Returns the following values: DLGC_WANTCHARS, DLGC_HASSETSEL, and DLGC_WANTARROWS. In multiline edit controls, it also returns DLGC_WANTALLKEYS. If the user presses ALT+BACKSPACE, it also returns DLGC_WANTMESSAGE.
WM_GETFONT	Returns the handle of the font being used by the control, or NULL if the control uses the system font.
WM_GETTEXT	Copies the specified number of characters to a buffer and returns the number of characters copied.
WM_GETTEXTLENGTH	Returns the length, in characters, of the text in an edit control. The length does not include the null-terminating character.
WM_HSCROLL	Scrolls the text in a multiline edit control horizontally and handles scroll box movement.
WM_KEYDOWN	Performs standard processing of the virtual-key codes.

WM_KILLFOCUS	Removes the keyboard focus of an edit control window, destroys the caret, hides the current selection, and notifies the parent window that the edit control has lost the focus.
WM_LBUTTONDBLCLK	Clears the current selection and selects the word under the cursor. If the SHIFT key is down, extends the selection to the word under the cursor.
WM_LBUTTONDOWN	Changes the current insertion point. If the SHIFT key is down, it extends the selection to the position of the cursor. In multiline edit controls, also sets the timer to automatically scroll when the user holds down the mouse button outside the multiline edit control window.
WM_LBUTTONUP	Releases the mouse capture and sets the text insertion point in the single-line edit control. In a multiline edit control, it also kills the timer set in the WM_LBUTTONDOWN message.
WM_MOUSEMOVE	Changes the current selection in the single-line edit control, if mouse button is down. In a multiline edit controls, also sets the timer to automatically scroll if the user holds down the mouse button outside the multiline edit control window.
WM_NCCREATE	Points to the **CREATESTRUCT** structure for the window. This message is sent to the WM_CREATE message when a window is first created.
WM_NCDESTROY	Frees all memory associated with the edit control window, including the text buffer, undo buffer, tab-stop buffer, and highlight brush.
WM_PAINT	Erases the background, fills the window with the current color of the edit control window, draws the border (if any), sets the font and draws any text, and shows the text-insertion caret.
WM_PASTE	Pastes text from the Clipboard into the edit control window at the caret position.
WM_SETFOCUS	Sets the keyboard focus of an edit control window (shows the current selection, if it was hidden, and creates the caret).
WM_SETFONT	Sets the font and optionally redraws the edit control.

WM_SETTEXT	Copies text to the single-line edit control, notifies the parent window when there is insufficient memory, empties the undo buffer, and sends the EN_UPDATE and EN_CHANGE notification messages to the parent window. In multiline edit controls, also rewraps the lines (if necessary) and sets the scroll positions.
WM_SIZE	Changes the size of the edit control window and ensures that the minimum size accommodates the height and width of a character.
WM_SYSCHAR	Returns TRUE if the user presses ALT+BACKSPACE; otherwise, it takes no action.
WM_SYSKEYDOWN	Undoes the last action if the user presses ALT+BACKSPACE; otherwise, it takes no action.
WM_TIMER	Scrolls the text in the edit control window if the user holds down the mouse button outside the multiline edit control window.
WM_UNDO	Removes any text that was just inserted or inserts any deleted characters and sets the selection to the inserted text. If necessary, sends the EN_UPDATE and EN_CHANGE notification messages to the parent window.
WM_VSCROLL	Scrolls a multiline edit control vertically and handles scroll box movement. It is not processed by single-line edit controls.

The predefined edit control window procedure passes all other messages to the **DefWindowProc** function for default processing.

12.2 Using Edit Controls

Edit controls are typically used in dialog boxes, but you can use them in the client area of a standard window as well. Single-line edit controls are useful for retrieving a single string from the user. Multiline edit controls make it easy for your application to implement most of the features of a simple word processor.

12.2.1 Simple Word Processing with an Edit Control

The following code sample implements much of the functionality of a simple word processor by filling the client area of a window with a multiline edit control. The system automatically performs wordwrap operations for this edit control and also handles the processing for the vertical scroll bar (created by specifying ES_AUTOVSCROLL in the call to the **CreateWindow** function). The WM_COMMAND message processes menu items; they allow the user to undo

the previous action, cut or copy selections to the Clipboard, paste text from the
Clipboard, and delete the current selection.

```
LONG APIENTRY MainWndProc(
HWND hwnd,                      /* window handle             */
UINT message,                  /* type of message           */
UINT wParam,                   /* additional information    */
LONG lParam)                   /* additional information    */
{
    static HWND hwndEdit;

    CHAR lpszTrouble[] = "When in the Course of human Events "
                         "it becomes necessary for one People "
                         "to dissolve the Political Bands which "
                         "have connected them with another, and "
                         "to assume among the Powers of the "
                         "Earth, the separate and equal Station "
                         "to which the Laws of Nature and of "
                         "Nature's God entitle them, a decent "
                         "Respect to the Opinions of Mankind "
                         "requires that they should declare the "
                         "causes which impel them to the "
                         "Separation. ";

    switch (message) {
        case WM_CREATE:
            hwndEdit = CreateWindow(
                "EDIT",      /* predefined class            */
                NULL,        /* no window title             */
                WS_CHILD | WS_VISIBLE | WS_VSCROLL |
                    ES_LEFT | ES_MULTILINE | ES_AUTOVSCROLL,
                0, 0, 0, 0, /* set size in WM_SIZE message   */
                hwnd,        /* parent window               */
                (HMENU) ID_EDITCHILD, /* edit control ID    */
                (HINSTANCE) GetWindowLong(hwnd, GWL_HINSTANCE),
                NULL);                 /* pointer not needed */

            /* Add text to the window. */

            SendMessage(hwndEdit, WM_SETTEXT, 0,
                (LPARAM) lpszTrouble);

            return 0;

        case WM_COMMAND:
            switch (wParam) {
                case IDM_EDUNDO:

                    SingleLine
                    /*
```

```
                                 * Send WM_UNDO only if there is something
                                 * to be undone.
                                 */

                                if (SendMessage(hwndEdit, EM_CANUNDO, 0, 0))
                                    SendMessage(hwndEdit, WM_UNDO, 0, 0);
                                else
                                    MessageBox(hwndEdit,
                                        "Nothing to undo.",
                                        "Undo notification", MB_OK);
                                break;

                        case IDM_EDCUT:
                            SendMessage(hwndEdit, WM_CUT, 0, 0);
                            break;

                        case IDM_EDCOPY:
                            SendMessage(hwndEdit, WM_COPY, 0, 0);
                            break;

                        case IDM_EDPASTE:
                            SendMessage(hwndEdit, WM_PASTE, 0, 0);
                            break;

                        case IDM_EDDEL:
                            SendMessage(hwndEdit, WM_CLEAR, 0, 0);
                            break;

                        default:
                            return DefWindowProc(hwnd, message, wParam, lParam);
                    }
                    break;

                case WM_SETFOCUS:
                    SetFocus(hwndEdit);
                    return 0;

                case WM_SIZE:

                    /*
                     * Make the edit control the size of the window's
                     * client area.
                     */

                    MoveWindow(hwndEdit,
                        0, 0,            /* starting x- and y-coordinates */
                        LOWORD(lParam), /* width of client area          */
                        HIWORD(lParam), /* height of client area         */
                        TRUE);          /* repaint window                */
                    return 0;
```

```
                        case WM_DESTROY:
                            PostQuitMessage(0);
                            return 0;

                    default:
                            return DefWindowProc(hwnd, message, wParam, lParam);
                }
                return NULL;
            }
```

12.2.2 Using Single-Line Edit Controls

The code sample in this section demonstrates how to use a window procedure to produce a dialog box, as shown in the following illustration.

The single-line edit control in the Password dialog box has the ES_PASSWORD style. By default, edit controls with this style display an asterisk for each character the user types. This example, however, uses the EM_SETPASSWORDCHAR message to change the default character from an asterisk to a plus sign (+).

This window procedure changes the default push button from Cancel to OK as soon as the user enters text in the edit control. If the user presses the OK button, the window procedure uses the EM_LINELENGTH and EM_GETLINE messages to retrieve the text.

```
LRESULT CALLBACK PassProc(hDlg, message, wParam, lParam)
HWND hDlg;                      /* window handle of the dialog box */
UINT message;                   /* type of message                */
UINT wParam;                    /* message-specific information    */
LONG lParam;
{
    CHAR lpszPassword[16];
    WORD cchPassword;

    switch (message) {
        case WM_INITDIALOG:

            /* Set password character to a plus sign (+) */
```

```
                    SendDlgItemMessage(hDlg,
                        IDE_PASSWORDEDIT,
                        EM_SETPASSWORDCHAR,
                        (WPARAM) '+',
                        (LPARAM) 0);

                    /* Set the default push button to "Cancel." */

                    SendMessage(hDlg,
                        DM_SETDEFID,
                        (WPARAM) IDCANCEL,
                        (LPARAM) 0);

                    return TRUE;

                case WM_COMMAND:

                    /*
                     * Set the default push button to "OK" when the user
                     * enters text.
                     */

                    if(HIWORD (wParam) == EN_CHANGE &&
                            LOWORD(wParam) == IDE_PASSWORDEDIT)
                        SendMessage(hDlg,
                            DM_SETDEFID,
                            (WPARAM) IDOK,
                            (LPARAM) 0);

                    switch(wParam) {
                        case IDOK:

                            /* Get number of characters. */

                            cchPassword = (WORD) SendDlgItemMessage(hDlg,
                                IDE_PASSWORDEDIT,
                                EM_LINELENGTH,
                                (WPARAM) 0,
                                (LPARAM) 0);

                            if (cchPassword >= 16) {
                                MessageBox(hDlg,
                                    "Too many characters.",
                                    "Error",
                                    MB_OK);
                                EndDialog(hDlg, TRUE);
                                return FALSE;
                            }
                            else if (cchPassword == 0) {
```

```
                                MessageBox(hDlg,
                                    "No characters entered.",
                                    "Error",
                                    MB_OK);
                                EndDialog(hDlg, TRUE);
                                return FALSE;
                            }

                            /*
                             * Put the number of characters into first word
                             * of buffer.
                             */

                            *((LPWORD)lpszPassword) = cchPassword;

                            /* Get the characters. */

                            SendDlgItemMessage(hDlg,
                                IDE_PASSWORDEDIT,
                                EM_GETLINE,
                                (WPARAM) 0,         /* line 0 */
                                (LPARAM) lpszPassword);

                            /* Null-terminate the string. */

                            lpszPassword[cchPassword] = 0;

                            /* Call a local password-parsing function. */

                            ParsePassword(lpszPassword);

                            EndDialog(hDlg, TRUE);
                            return TRUE;

                    case IDCANCEL:
                            EndDialog(hDlg, TRUE);
                            return TRUE;
                }
                return 0;
        }
    return FALSE;
        UNREFERENCED_PARAMETER(lParam);
}
```

12.3 Functions and Messages

Following are the function and messages used with edit controls.

Function

WordBreakProc

Messages

EM_CANUNDO
EM_EMPTYUNDOBUFFER
EM_FMTLINES
EM_GETFIRSTVISIBLELINE
EM_GETHANDLE
EM_GETLINE
EM_GETLINECOUNT
EM_GETMODIFY
EM_GETPASSWORDCHAR
EM_GETRECT
EM_GETSEL
EM_GETWORDBREAKPROC
EM_LIMITTEXT
EM_LINEFROMCHAR
EM_LINEINDEX
EM_LINELENGTH
EM_LINESCROLL
EM_REPLACESEL
EM_SCROLL
EM_SCROLLCARET
EM_SETHANDLE
EM_SETMODIFY
EM_SETPASSWORDCHAR
EM_SETREADONLY
EM_SETRECT
EM_SETRECTNP
EM_SETSEL
EM_SETTABSTOPS
EM_SETWORDBREAKPROC
EM_UNDO
EN_CHANGE
EN_ERRSPACE
EN_HSCROLL
EN_KILLFOCUS
EN_MAXTEXT
EN_SETFOCUS

EN_UPDATE
EN_VSCROLL
WM_COMMAND
WM_COPY
WM_CTLCOLOREDIT
WM_CUT
WM_PASTE
WM_UNDO

Terms

Term	Definition
edit control	An element of the Windows user interface that allows the user to enter and edit text. Edit controls are typically used in dialog boxes.

CHAPTER 13

Combo Boxes

13.1 About Combo Boxes

As discussed in Chapter 9, "Controls," dialog boxes and controls provide users of the Microsoft ® Windows ™ operating system with the means to enter text, choose options, and complete actions. A combo box, however, is a unique type of control. It is defined by the COMBOBOX class and combines much of the functionality of a list box and an edit control.

Windows provides three types of combo box: simple combo boxes (CBS_SIMPLE), drop-down combo boxes (CBS_DROPDOWN), and drop-down list boxes (CBS_DROPDOWNLIST).

There are also a number of combo box styles that define specific properties. For example, two styles enable an application to create an *owner-drawn* combo box, making the application responsible for displaying information in the control.

A combo box consists of a list and a selection field. The list presents the options a user can select and the selection field displays the current selection. Except in drop-down list boxes, the selection field is an edit control and can be used to enter text not in the list.

Combo boxes are used primarily in dialog boxes. Dialog boxes can process keyboard input messages that combo boxes cannot, such as the TAB, ENTER, and ESCAPE keys. However, an application can provide this functionality outside a dialog box by using window subclassing. For more information about dialog boxes, see Chapter 18, "Dialog Boxes."

This chapter describes the types and styles of combo box, the parts of a combo box, the use of an owner-drawn combo box, and how to subclass a combo box. Additional features of combo boxes are also discussed.

13.1.1 Combo Box Types and Styles

Combo boxes can be characterized by type and style. Combo box types determine whether the combo box list is a drop-down list and whether the selection field is an edit control. A drop-down list appears only when the user opens it, so it uses less screen space than a list that is always visible. If the selection field is an edit control, the user can enter information not in the list; otherwise, the user can only select items in the list.

The following table shows the three combo box types and indicates whether each includes a drop-down list and an edit control.

Combo box type	Drop-down list	Edit control
Simple combo box	No	Yes
Drop-down combo box	Yes	Yes
Drop-down list box	Yes	No

Combo box styles define specific properties of a combo box. An application can combine styles; however some styles only apply to certain combo box types. The following table describes the combo box styles.

Style	Desription
CBS_AUTOHSCROLL	Automatically scrolls text to the left when the user types beyond the right end of the selection field. If an application does not specify this style, only text that fits within the edit control is allowed. This style does not apply to drop-down list boxes.
CBS_DISABLENOSCROLL	Displays a scroll bar in the list even if the entire contents are visible at once. Ordinarily, the scroll bar only appears if the list contains enough items to scroll through.
CBS_HASSTRINGS	Keeps track of strings for list items in an owner-drawn combo box. For more information, see Section 13.1.4, "Owner-Drawn Combo Boxes."
CBS_NOINTEGRALHEIGHT	Specifies that the combo box is exactly the size set forth by the application when it created the combo box. Ordinarily, Windows adjusts the size of a combo box so it does not display partial items.
CBS_OEMCONVERT	Specifies that text in the selection field is in the OEM character set. Windows automatically converts text to and from the OEM character set as it is entered in and retrieved from the selection field. This style does not apply to drop-down list boxes.
CBS_OWNERDRAWFIXED	Assigns responsibility for displaying information to the parent window or dialog box procedure It specifies that list items are all the same size. For more information, see Section 13.1.4, "Owner-Drawn Combo Boxes."

| CBS_OWNERDRAWVARIABLE | Assigns responsibility for displaying information to the parent window or dialog box procedure It specifies that list items vary in size. For more information, see Section 13.1.4, "Owner-Drawn Combo Boxes." |
| CBS_SORT | Automatically sorts the contents of the list. An application can ensure that sorted combo box items are correct for a given language and sublanguage by using CB_SETLOCALE message. To retrieve the current locale for a combo box, use the CB_GETLOCALE message. |

13.1.2 Combo Box List

The list is the portion of a combo box that displays the items a user can select. Typically, an application initializes the contents of the list when it creates a combo box. Any list item selected by the user is the *current selection*. In simple and drop-down combo boxes, the user can type in the selection field instead of selecting a list item. In these cases, there is no current selection. For more information, see Section 13.1.3, "Edit Control Selection Fields."

13.1.2.1 List Contents

When an application creates a combo box, it typically initializes the combo box by adding one or more strings to the list. Later, an application may add or delete list items reinitialize the list, or retrieve strings from it.

An application adds list items to a combo box by sending the CB_ADDSTRING message to it. The specified string is added to the end of the list or, in a sorted combo box, in its correct sorted position. In an unsorted combo box, an application can use the CB_INSERTSTRING message to insert a string at a specific position. Once added, a list item is identified by its position.

An application can determine the position of a list item by using the CB_FINDSTRING or CB_FINDSTRINGEXACT message. The CB_FINDSTRING message finds an item beginning with the specified string. The CB_FINDSTRINGEXACT message finds an item that matches the string exactly. Neither message is case sensitive.

An application can remove a list item by using the CB_DELETESTRING message. If an application needs to reinitialize the combo box list, it can first clear its entire contents by using the CB_RESETCONTENT message. When adding multiple strings to the list after a combo box has already been shown, an application can clear the redraw flag to prevent the combo box from being repainted after each string is added. For more information, see the WM_SETREDRAW message.

To retrieve the text for a list entry, an application can use the CB_GETLBTEXT message. The string is copied to the buffer specified by the application. To ensure that the buffer is large enough to receive the string, the application can first use the CB_GETLBTEXTLEN message to determine the length of the string. To get the number of list items in a combo box, an application can use the CB_GETCOUNT message.

13.1.2.2 Current Selection

The current selection is a list item the user has selected; the selected text appears in the selection field edit control in the combo box. However, the current selection is only one form of possible user input in a combo box. The user can also type text in the selection field. In a drop-down list box, the current selection is the only form of user input.

The current selection is identified by the zero-based index of the selected list item. An application can set and retrieve it at any time. The parent window or dialog box procedure receives notifications when the current selection for a combo box changes.

When a combo box is created, there is no current selection. This is also true for a simple or drop-down combo box if the user has edited the contents of the selection field. To set the current selection, an application sends the CB_SETCURSEL message to the combo box. An application can also use the CB_SELECTSTRING message to set the current selection to a list item beginning with a specified string. To determine the current selection, an application sends the CB_GETCURSEL message to the combo box. If there is no current selection, this message returns CB_ERR.

When the current selection in a combo box changes, the parent window or dialog-box procedure receives a WM_COMMAND message with the CBN_SELCHANGE notification code in the high-order word of *wParam*. As a result, the application can respond to this notification message and execute a specific process each time the user selects a list item. This notification is not sent when the current selection is set using the CB_SETCURSEL message nor when the user modifies the current selection in a simple or drop-down combo box.

In a drop-down combo box or drop-down list box, an application can close the list and wait to process a change in the current selection until the user selects a new item. This can be useful when significant processing is required. For example, to update a directory list based on the selected drive, an application can process the CBN_CLOSEUP message instead of CBN_SELCHANGE to update a directory list after the user selects a drive.

Alternatively, an application can process the CBN_SELENDOK and CBN_SELENDCANCEL messages. The system sends the CBN_SELENDOK notification when the user clicks a list item or selects an item and then closes the list. This indicates the user has finished and the selection should be processed. The CBN_SELENDCANCEL notification is sent when the user selects an item but then selects another control or closes the dialog box. This indicates the user's selection should be ignored. In a simple combo box, a CBN_SELENDOK notification is sent before every CBN_SELCHANGE message. The system does not send the CBN_SELENDOK and CBN_SELENDCANCEL messages if the WS_EX_NOPARENTNOTIFY extended window style is specified for the combo box.

In a simple combo box, the system sends the CBN_DBLCLK notification when the user double-clicks a list item. In a drop-down combo box or drop-down list, however, a single click hides the list so it is not possible to double-click an item.

13.1.2.3 Drop-Down Lists

Certain notifications and messages apply only to combo boxes containing drop-down lists. When a drop-down list is open or closed, the parent window of a combo box receives a notification in the form of a WM_COMMAND message. If the list is being opened, the high-order word of *wParam* is CBN_DROPDOWN. If the list is being closed, it is CBN_CLOSEUP.

An application can open the list of a drop-down combo box or drop-down list box by using the CB_SHOWDROPDOWN message. It can determine whether the list is open by using the CB_GETDROPPEDSTATE message and can determine the coordinates of a drop-down list by using the CB_GETDROPPEDCONTROLRECT message.

13.1.3 Edit Control Selection Fields

The selection field is the portion of a combo box that displays the currently selected list item. In simple and drop-down combo boxes, the selection field is an edit control and can be used to enter text that is not in the list.

An application can retrieve or set the contents of the selection field and can determine or set the edit selection. The application can also limit the amount of text a user can type in the selection field. When the contents of the selection field change, Windows sends notification messages to the parent window or dialog box procedure.

To retrieve the contents of the selection field of a simple or drop-down combo box, an application can send the WM_GETTEXT message to the combo box. To set the contents of the selection field, an application can send the WM_SETTEXT message to the combo box.

The *edit selection* is the range of selected text, if any, in the selection field of a simple or drop-down combo box. An application can determine the starting and ending character positions of the current selection by using the

CB_GETEDITSEL message. It can also select characters in the edit selection by using the CB_SETEDITSEL message.

By using the CB_LIMITTEXT message, an application can limit the amount of text a user can type into the selection field.

When the user edits the contents of the selection field, the parent window or dialog box procedure receives notification messages. Windows sends the CBN_EDITUPDATE notification first, indicating that the text in the selection field has been edited. After the altered text is displayed, Windows sends the CBN_EDITCHANGE notification. When the contents of the selection field change as the result of a list item being selected, these notifications are not sent.

13.1.4 Owner-Drawn Combo Boxes

An application can create an *owner-drawn* combo box to take responsibility for painting list items. The parent window or dialog box of an owner-drawn combo box (its *owner*) receives WM_DRAWITEM messages when a portion of the combo box needs to be painted. An owner-drawn combo box can list information other than, or in addition to, text strings. Owner-drawn combo boxes can be of any type. However, the edit control in a simple or drop-down combo box can only display text, while the owner paints the selection field in a drop-down list box.

The owner of an owner-drawn combo box must process the WM_DRAWITEM message. This message is sent whenever a portion of the combo box must be redrawn. The owner may need to process other messages, depending on the styles specified for the combo box.

An application can create an owner-drawn combo box by specifying the CBS_OWNERDRAWFIXED or CBS_OWNERDRAWVARIABLE style. If all list items in the combo box are the same height, such as strings or icons, an application can use the CBS_OWNERDRAWFIXED style. If list items are of varying height, bitmaps of different size, for example, an application can use the CBS_OWNERDRAWVARIABLE style.

The owner of an owner-drawn combo box can process a WM_MEASUREITEM message to specify the dimensions of list items in the combo box. If the application creates the combo box by using the CBS_OWNERDRAWFIXED style, Windows sends the WM_MEASUREITEM message only once. The dimensions specified by the owner are used for all list items. If the CBS_OWNERDRAWVARIABLE style is used, Windows sends a WM_MEASUREITEM message for each list item added to the combo box. The owner can determine or set the height of a list item at any time by using the CB_GETITEMHEIGHT and CB_SETITEMHEIGHT messages, respectively.

If the information displayed in an owner-drawn combo box includes text, an application can keep track of the text for each list item by specifying the

CBS_HASSTRINGS style. Combo boxes with the CBS_SORT style are sorted based on this text. If a combo box is sorted and does not have the CBS_HASSTRINGS style, the owner must process the WM_COMPAREITEM message.

In an owner-drawn combo box, the owner must keep track of list items containing information other than or in addition to text. One convenient way to do this is to save the handle of the information as *item data*. For more information about item data, see Section 13.1.6.2, "Data Associated With List Items." To free data objects associated with items in a combo box, the owner can process the WM_DELETEITEM message.

For an example of an owner-drawn combo box, see Section 13.2.2, "Creating an Owner-Drawn Combo Box."

13.1.5 Subclassing Combo Boxes

Subclassing is a procedure that allows an application to intercept and process messages sent or posted to a window. By using subclassing, an application can substitute its own processing for certain messages, while leaving most message processing to the class-defined window procedure.

When the operating system creates a window, it saves information about it in an internal data structure that includes the address of the window procedure. To subclass a window, an application calls the **SetClassLong** function to replace the address of that procedure with the instance address of an application-defined subclass procedure. Thereafter, all messages to the window are sent to the subclass procedure. This procedure then uses the **CallWindowProc** function to pass unprocessed messages to the original window procedure. For a description of the message processing performed by the COMBOBOX class window procedure, see Section 13.1.8, "Default Combo Box Behavior."

When the combo box is outside a dialog box, an application cannot process the TAB, ENTER, and ESCAPE keys unless it uses a subclass procedure. When a simple or drop-down combo box receives the input focus, it immediately sets the focus to its child edit control. Therefore, an application must subclass the edit control to intercept keyboard input for a simple or drop-down combo box. For an example of this, see Section 13.2.3, "Subclassing a Combo Box."

If a subclass procedure processes the WM_PAINT message, it must use the **BeginPaint** function to prepare for painting. Before calling the **EndPaint** function, it passes the device-context handle as the *wParam* parameter for the window procedure. If **EndPaint** is called first, the class window procedure does no painting because **EndPaint** validates the entire window.

A technique related to subclassing is *superclassing*. A superclass resembles any other class except that its window procedure does not call **DefWindowProc** to handle unprocessed messages. Instead, it passes unprocessed messages to the window procedure for the parent window class. Follow the guidelines in Chapter 4, "Window Procedures," to avoid problems that can occur with subclassing and superclassing.

13.1.6 Special Combo Box Features

The Win32 API provides special-purpose messages and functions that enable an application to display a directory listing in a combo box, associate data with list items in a combo box, and change the keyboard interface for a drop-down combo box or drop-down list box.

13.1.6.1 Directory Lists

An application can add the names of files or subdirectories to a combo box by sending the CB_DIR message to it. The *wParam* parameter for the window procedure specifies the attributes of the files to add, and the *lParam* parameter points to the text string that defines the file specification.

Within a dialog box, an application can also use the **DlgDirListComboBox** function. If the specified filename includes a drive, path, or both, the **DlgDirListComboBox** function changes the current drive or directory and removes the drive and path from the filename string. To show the directory name, the function updates the specified static control, if any. It then resets the contents of the combo box, and sends the CB_DIR message to the combo box to add the specified filenames.

To remove the selected filename, directory name, or drive letter from a combo box that has been filled by using the **DlgDirListComboBox** function, an application can use the **DlgDirSelectComboBoxEx** function.

The CB_DIR message and the **DlgDirListComboBox** and **DlgDirSelectComboBoxEx** functions are similar to the LB_DIR message and the **DlgDirList** and **DlgDirSelectEx** functions used with list boxes.

13.1.6.2 Data Associated With List Items

An application can associate data with the list items in a combo box. The CB_SETITEMDATA message associates a DWORD value with a list item, and the CB_GETITEMDATA retrieves the value associated with a list item.

The example in Section 13.2.2, "Creating an Owner-Drawn Combo Box," uses item data to associate a constant with each item in a drop-down list box. Such a unique value identifies each item independent of its sorted position.

Other applications might use item data to associate a handle or pointer with a list item. If so, an application can process a WM_DELETEITEM message to delete or free the specified object when the list item is deleted.

13.1.6.3 The Extended User Interface

Drop-down combo boxes and drop-down list boxes support an alternative keyboard interface called the *extended user interface*. By default, the F4 key opens or closes the list, and the DOWN ARROW changes the current selection. In a combo box with the extended user interface, however, the F4 key is disabled and pressing the DOWN ARROW key opens the drop-down list.

To select the user interface for a combo box, an application can send the CB_SETEXTENDEDUI message to the combo box. A TRUE value for the *wParam* parameter enables the extended user interface; a FALSE value sets the default user interface. To determine whether a combo box uses the extended user interface, an application can send the CB_GETEXTENDEDUI message to the combo box.

13.1.7 Combo Box Notifications

Messages from combo boxes are sent as notifications in the form of WM_COMMAND messages. The notification code is stored in the high word of the *wParam* parameter and an application can process the following combo box notification messages:

Notification code	Description
CBN_CLOSEUP	Indicates the list in a drop-down combo box or drop-down list box is about to close.
CBN_DBLCLK	Indicates the user has double-clicked a list item in a simple combo box.
CBN_DROPDOWN	Indicates the list in a drop-down combo box or drop-down list box is about to open.
CBN_EDITCHANGE	Indicates the user has changed the text in the edit control of a simple or drop-down combo box. This notification is sent after the altered text is displayed.
CBN_EDITUPDATE	Indicates the user has changed the text in the edit control of a simple or drop-down combo box. This notification is sent before the altered text is displayed.
CBN_ERRSPACE	Indicates the combo box cannot allocate enough memory to carry out a request, such as adding a list item.
CBN_KILLFOCUS	Indicates the combo box is about to lose the input focus.
CBN_SELCHANGE	Indicates the current selection has changed.
CBN_SETFOCUS	Indicates the combo box has received the input focus.

13.1.8 Default Combo Box Behavior

This section describes the messages specifically handled by the predefined COMBOBOX class window procedure.

Message	Description
CB_ADDSTRING	Sends an LB_ADDSTRING message to the list window to add a list item.
CB_DELETESTRING	Sends an LB_DELETESTRING message to the list window to delete a list item.
CB_DIR	Adds the filenames matching the specified attributes and path to the list.
CB_FINDSTRING	Sends an LB_FINDSTRING message to the list window. This message returns the index of the first list item that begins with the specified text.
CB_FINDSTRINGEXACT	Sends an LB_FINDSTRING message to the list window. This message returns the index of the first list item exactly matching the specified text.
CB_GETCOUNT	Sends an LB_GETCOUNT message to the list window. It returns the number of list items.
CB_GETCURSEL	Sends an LB_GETCURSEL message to the list window. It returns the index of the currently selected item, if any.
CB_GETDROPPEDCONTROLRECT	Fills the specified rectangle structure with the screen coordinates of a drop-down list.
CB_GETDROPPEDSTATE	Returns TRUE if a drop-down list is open. Otherwise, it returns FALSE.
CB_GETEDITSEL	Sends an EM_GETSEL message to the edit control, and it returns the starting and ending position of the current selection. In drop-down list boxes, the window procedure returns CB_ERR.
CB_GETEXTENDEDUI	Returns TRUE if the combo box is a drop-down combo box or drop-down list box and the extend user-interface flag is set. Otherwise, it returns FALSE.
CB_GETITEMDATA	Sends an LB_GETITEMDATA message to the list window. It returns the 32-bit value associated with the specified list item.

CB_GETITEMHEIGHT	Sends an LB_GETITEMHEIGHT message to the list window. It returns the height, in pixels, of the specified owner-drawn list item.
CB_GETLBTEXT	Sends an LB_GETTEXT message to the list window. It copies the specified list text to the specified buffer.
CB_GETLBTEXTLEN	Sends an LB_GETTEXTLEN message to the list window. It returns the length, in bytes, of the specified list text.
CB_GETLOCALE	Sends an LB_GETLOCALE message to the list window. It returns the current locale for the list.
CB_INSERTSTRING	Sends an LB_INSERTSTRING message to the list window. It inserts a list item at the specified position.
CB_LIMITTEXT	Sends an EM_LIMITTEXT message to the edit control. It sets the maximum number of characters a user can enter in the edit control. In drop-down list boxes, the window procedure returns CB_ERR.
CB_RESETCONTENT	Sends an LB_RESETCONTENT message to the list window, and it removes the contents of the list.
CB_SELECTSTRING	Sends an LB_SELECTSTRING message to the list window. It selects the first list item, if any, that begins with the characters in the specified text.
CB_SETCURSEL	Sends an LB_SETCURSEL message to the list window, and it sets the current selection.
CB_SETEDITSEL	Sends an EM_SETSEL message to the edit control. It selects the specified range of text. In drop-down list boxes, the window procedure returns CB_ERR.
CB_SETEXTENDEDUI	Sets or clears the extended user interface flag. This flag changes the keys that open and close the list in a drop-down combo box or drop-down list box. if the combo box is a simple combo box, the window procedure returns CB_ERR.
CB_SETITEMDATA	Sends an LB_SETITEMDATA message to the list window. It associates the specified 32-bit value with a list item.

CB_SETITEMHEIGHT	Sends an **LB_SETITEMHEIGHT** message to the list window. It sets the height of the specified owner-drawn list item or the selection field.
CB_SETLOCALE	Sends an **LB_SETLOCALE** message to the list window, and it sets the current locale for the list. The locale affects how the list is sorted if it has the **CBS_SORT** style and strings are added using **CB_ADDSTRING**.
CB_SHOWDROPDOWN	Shows or hides the drop-down list. This message has no effect on simple combo boxes.
WM_CHAR	Processes character input. In drop-down list boxes, this message is passed on to the list window, which moves the selection to the first item beginning with the specified character. In simple and drop-down combo boxes, this message is passed on to the edit control.
WM_CLEAR	Deletes the edit selection. In simple and drop-down combo boxes, the edit control processes this message. In drop-down list boxes, the window procedure returns **CB_ERR**.
WM_COMMAND	Processes notification messages from the edit control and list window and sends corresponding combo box notifications to the parent window.
	For edit control notifications, the window procedure may update the list window's current selection, caret index, and top index. For list notifications, the window procedure may update the contents of the selection field.
WM_COMPAREITEM	Passes the message on to the parent window, enabling the application to specify the relative sort position of two owner-drawn list items. The combo box window receives this message from the list window.
WM_COPY	Copies the edit selection to the clipboard. In simple and drop-down combo boxes, the edit control processes this message. In drop-down list boxes, the window procedure returns **CB_ERR**.
WM_CREATE	Initializes the combo box.

WM_CUT	Deletes the edit selection and places it on the clipboard. In simple and drop-down combo boxes, the edit control processes this message. In drop-down list boxes, the window procedure returns CB_ERR.
WM_DELETEITEM	Passes the message on to the parent window, notifying the application that a list item has been deleted. The combo box window receives this message from the list window.
WM_DRAWITEM	Passes the message on to the parent window enabling the application to paint the specified list item. The combo box window receives this message from the list window. The window procedure can also originate this message to have the application paint the selection field of a drop-down list box.
WM_ENABLE	Sets the state to enable or prohibit mouse and keyboard input.
WM_ERASEBKGND	Returns 1, indicating that the background is erased.
WM_GETDLGCODE	Returns a combination of the DLG_WANTCHARS and DLGC_WANTARROWS values.
WM_GETFONT	Returns the handle of the current font with which the combo box will draw its text.
WM_GETTEXT	Copies the contents of the selection field to the specified buffer. In simple and drop-down combo boxes, the edit control processes this message.
WM_GETTEXTLENGTH	Returns the length, in characters, of the text in the selection field. In simple and drop-down combo boxes, the edit control processes this message.
WM_KEYDOWN	Processes non-character keyboard input. In drop-down list boxes, this message is passed on to the list window, and it can be open or close, or change the current selection or caret index. In simple and drop-down combo boxes, this message is passed on to the edit control. The edit control passes certain keys to the list window, such as the UP and DOWN ARROW keys and the F4 key.

WM_KILLFOCUS	Hides the highlight in the selection field and closes the drop-down list, if necessary. If the window receiving the input focus is part of the combo box (for example, the edit control), this message is ignored.
WM_LBUTTONDBLCLK	Same as WM_LBUTTONDOWN.
WM_LBUTTONDOWN	Sets the focus to the combo box and, for drop-down combo boxes and drop-down lists, can open or close the list. If it opens the list, the window procedure captures the mouse to enable selection by dragging and releasing the mouse button.
WM_LBUTTONUP	Releases the mouse capture if the mouse opened the list.
WM_MEASUREITEM	Posts the message to the parent window, enabling the application to modify the contents of the specified **MEASUREITEMSTRUCT** structure. The combo box window receives this message from the list window.
WM_MOUSEMOVE	Posts the message to the list window if the mouse has opened the list and the mouse button is still down. This enables a user to select an item by dragging the mouse pointer to a list item and then releasing the button.
WM_NCCREATE	Allocates an internal data structure used by the combo box window procedure.
WM_NCDESTROY	Frees resources allocated in response to the WM_NCCREATE message.
WM_PAINT	Paints the invalid region of the combo box. If *wParam* is not NULL, it is assumed to be a device context handle passed from a subclass function. The window procedure uses the specified device context instead of calling **BeginPaint** and **EndPaint**.
WM_PASTE	Replaces the edit selection with the contents of the clipboard. In simple and drop-down combo boxes, the edit control processes this message. In drop-down list boxes, the window procedure returns CB_ERR.
WM_SETFOCUS	Sets the focus to the edit control or, in drop-down list boxes, inverts the selection field and turns on the caret in the list window.

WM_SETFONT	Saves the specified font handle in an internal structure, adjusts the dimensions of the selection field and list, and invalidates the combo box window. Text in the selection field and the list is displayed in the saved font.
WM_SETREDRAW	Sets or clears the redraw flag. If the redraw flag is cleared, the combo box is not repainted until the flag is set again.
WM_SETTEXT	Sets the contents of the edit control. In simple and drop-down combo boxes, the edit control processes this message. In drop-down list boxes, the window procedure returns CB_ERR.
WM_SIZE	Resizes the child windows, if necessary.
WM_SYSKEYDOWN	Opens or closes the drop-down list depending on which arrow key the user pressed.

All other messages are passed to the **DefWindowProc** function for default processing.

13.2 Using Combo Boxes

This section explains how to perform the following tasks:

- Use a simple combo box in a dialog box.
- Use an owner-drawn combo box in a dialog box.
- Subclass a combo box for use outside dialog box.

13.2.1 Creating a Simple Combo Box

This section describes how to use a simple combo box in a dialog box. The code example in Section 13.2.1.4, "Creating a Spell Dialog Box," uses a simple combo box in a dialog box for a spelling checker. When it finds a misspelled word, the spelling checker suggests alternative spellings. The user can ignore the misspelling, change to one of the suggested spellings, or type a spelling not suggested. A simple combo box is well suited for receiving this kind of user input.

13.2.1.1 Creating the Dialog Box

The dialog box template defines the window styles, buttons, and control identifiers for the combo box. In this example, the combo box uses the CBS_SIMPLE, CBS_SORT, WS_VSCROLL, and WS_TABSTOP styles.

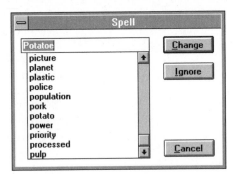

The dialog box also contains three buttons: Change (IDOK), Ignore (IDSKIP), and Cancel (IDCANCEL). The constants IDOK and IDCANCEL are defined by the Win32 API. The constant IDSKIP is defined in the application's header file, as is the control identifier, IDCOMBO.

For more information about dialog boxes, see Chapter 18, "Dialog Boxes."

13.2.1.2 Processing the WM_INITDIALOG and WM_DESTROY Messages

When you use a combo box in a dialog box, you usually respond to the WM_INITDIALOG message by initializing the combo box. The code example in Section 13.2.1.4, "Creating a Spell Dialog Box," calls the application-defined OpenDictionary function to load the dictionary. It then calls the application-defined SelectNextWord and InitSpellList functions to select the first misspelled word.

SelectNextWord selects the next word in the edit control and copies it to the specified buffer. InitSpellList determines whether the selected word is in the dictionary. If not, it places the word in the selection field of the combo box and adds suggested spellings to the list.

The dialog box procedure processes the WM_DESTROY message to free the resources allocated to the spelling dictionary.

13.2.1.3 Processing the WM_COMMAND Message

When an event occurs in a dialog box control, the control sends a WM_COMMAND message to the dialog box procedure.

For edit controls, the window procedure may update the current selection in the list window. Once the user types something in the edit control, triggering an edit control notification, there is no current selection. The window procedure also sets the top index, specifying the zero-based index of the list item at the top of the window. It may also set the caret index, indicating the index of the highlighted list item when the list window has the input focus.

The code example in Section 13.2.1.4, "Creating a Spell Dialog Box," processes notification messages from the combo box, the Change button, the Ignore button, and the Cancel button. The control identifier is in the low-order word of *wParam*, and the notification code is in the high-order word of *wParam*.

The control identifier IDCOMBO signifies that an event occurred in the combo box, although the dialog box procedure ignores all events in it except one. CBN_DBLCLK indicates the user has double-clicked a list item; this event is processed in the same way as a Change button click.

The control identifier IDOK signifies the user clicked the Change button. The dialog box procedure replaces the current selection in the application's edit control with the contents of the selection field in the combo box. The selection field may contain either the selected list item or text the user has typed. The dialog box procedure then selects the next misspelled word in the same way it processes an Ignore button click.

The control identifier IDSKIP signifies the user has clicked the Ignore button. The dialog box procedure calls SelectNextWord and InitSpellList to select the next misspelled word in the application's edit control. InitSpellList places the misspelled word in the selection field of the combo box and adds suggested spellings to the combo box list.

The control identifier IDCANCEL indicates the user clicked the Cancel button. The dialog box procedure calls the **EndDialog** function to close the dialog box.

13.2.1.4 Creating a Spell Dialog Box

Following are the dialog box procedure and supporting functions for the spelling checker dialog box.

```
HWND hwndMain;
HWND hwndEdit;
char achTemp[256];          /* temporary buffer          */

LPSTR lpstrDict;            /* buffer for dictionary file */
LPSTR *paLpDict;            /* array of pointers to words */
```

```
    UINT  cWords;                /* number of words            */

    /**********************************************************

        FUNCTION: SpellDlgProc

        PURPOSE: Dialog procedure for Spell dialog box.

    **********************************************************/

    BOOL CALLBACK SpellDlgProc(hwndDlg, msg, wParam, lParam)
    HWND hwndDlg;
    UINT msg;
    WPARAM wParam;
    LPARAM lParam;
    {
        switch (msg) {
            case WM_INITDIALOG:
                if (!OpenDictionary()) {
                    EndDialog(hwndDlg, 0);
                    break;
                }
                SendMessage(hwndEdit, EM_SETSEL, 0, 0);
                do
                    if (!SelectNextWord(hwndEdit, achTemp)) {
                        GlobalFree((HGLOBAL) lpstrDict);
                        LocalFree((HLOCAL) paLpDict);
                        EndDialog(hwndDlg, 0);
                        break;
                    }
                while (!InitSpellList(
                    GetDlgItem(hwndDlg, IDCOMBO), achTemp));
                break;

            case WM_COMMAND:
                switch (LOWORD(wParam)) {
                    case IDCOMBO:
                        if (HIWORD(wParam) != CBN_DBLCLK)
                            break;

                        /* For a double-click, process the OK case. */

                    case IDOK:
                        SendDlgItemMessage(hwndDlg, IDCOMBO,
                            WM_GETTEXT, sizeof(achTemp),
                            (LPARAM) achTemp);
                        SendMessage(hwndEdit, EM_REPLACESEL, 0,
                            (LPARAM) achTemp);

                        /* Fall through to get the next word. */
```

```
                    case IDSKIP:
                        do
                            if (!SelectNextWord(hwndEdit, achTemp)) {
                                EndDialog(hwndDlg, 0);
                                break;
                            }
                        while (!InitSpellList(GetDlgItem(hwndDlg,
                            IDCOMBO), achTemp));
                        break;

                    case IDCANCEL:
                        EndDialog(hwndDlg, 0);
                }
                break;

        case WM_DESTROY:
            GlobalFree((HGLOBAL) lpstrDict);
            LocalFree((HLOCAL) paLpDict);
            break;

        default:
            return FALSE;
    }
    return TRUE;
}


/***********************************************************

    FUNCTION: InitSpellList

    PURPOSE: Initializes the selection field and list
             of suggestions for the specified word, if
             it is not in the dictionary.

    RETURNS: If the list is initialized, the return
             value is TRUE. If an error occurs or the
             word is in the dictionary, the return
             value is FALSE.

***********************************************************/

BOOL PASCAL InitSpellList(HWND hwndCombo, LPSTR lpszWord)
{
    int min = 0;        /* beginning of search range */
    int max = cWords;   /* end of search range       */
    int n;              /* index of word             */
    int cmp;            /* result of comparison      */
    char ch;            /* first character in word   */
```

```
ch = *lpszWord;
AnsiLowerBuff(&ch, 1);

/*
 * Perform a binary search for the word.
 *
 * The global array paLpDict contains pointers to words
 * in the global array lpstrDict. These two variables are
 * initialized by the OpenDictionary function.
 */

n = max / 2;
while (min < max) {
    cmp = lstrcmpi(lpszWord, paLpDict[n]);
    if (cmp == 0)
        return FALSE;          /* not misspelled */

    if (cmp < 0)
        max = n;
    else
        min = n + 1;
    n = (min + max) / 2;
}

/* List the words beginning with the same letter as lpszWord. */

SendMessage(hwndCombo, CB_RESETCONTENT, 0, 0);
while (n > 0 && *paLpDict[n - 1] == ch)
    n--;
while (*paLpDict[n] == ch)
    SendMessage(hwndCombo, CB_ADDSTRING,
        0, (LPARAM) paLpDict[n++]);

/* Place the word in the selection field. */

SendMessage(hwndCombo, WM_SETTEXT, 0, (LPARAM) lpszWord);

return TRUE;
}
```

13.2.2 Creating an Owner-Drawn Combo Box

This section describes how to use an owner-drawn combo box. The code example in Section 13.2.2.6, "Creating a Square Meal Dialog Box," uses an owner-drawn drop-down list box to display the four food groups, each represented by a bitmap and a name. Selecting a food group causes the foods in that group to appear in a list.

13.2.2.1 Creating the Dialog Box

The dialog box template defines the window styles, buttons, and control identifiers for the combo box. The combo box in this example uses the CBS_DROPDOWNLIST, CBS_OWNERDRAWFIXED, CBS_SORT, CBS_HASSTRINGS, WS_VSCROLL, and WS_TABSTOP styles.

The dialog box also contains a list box (IDLIST) and two buttons: OK (IDOK) and Cancel (IDCANCEL). The constants IDOK and IDCANCEL are defined by the Win32 API. The constant IDLIST is defined in the application's header file, as is the control identifier, IDCOMBO.

For more information about dialog boxes, see Chapter 18, "Dialog Boxes."

13.2.2.2 Processing the WM_INITDIALOG and WM_DESTROY Messages

When you use a combo box in a dialog box, you usually respond to a WM_INITDIALOG message by initializing the combo box. The code example in Section 13.2.2.6, "Creating a Square Meal Dialog Box," loads the bitmaps used for the owner-drawn combo box, then calls the application-defined InitGroupList function to initialize the combo box. It also selects the first list item in the combo box, then calls the application-defined InitFoodList function to initialize the list box.

In the example, the owner-drawn combo box is a drop-down list box containing the names of each of the four food groups. InitGroupList adds the name of each food group, and calls SetItemData to associate a constant with each list item that identifies a corresponding food group.

The list box in the example contains the names of foods in the selected food group. InitFoodList resets the contents of the list box, then adds the names of the current food selection in the current food group drop-down list box.

The dialog box procedure processes the WM_DESTROY message to delete the bitmaps in the owner-drawn combo box.

13.2.2.3 Processing the WM_MEASUREITEM Message

An owner-drawn combo box sends the WM_MEASUREITEM message to its parent window or dialog box procedure so the application can set the dimensions of each list item. Because the example combo box has the CBS_OWNERDRAWFIXED style, the system sends the WM_MEASUREITEM message only once. Combo boxes with the CBS_OWNERDRAWVARIABLE style send a WM_MEASUREITEM message for each list item.

The *lParam* parameter points to a **MEASUREITEMSTRUCT** structure that identifies the control and list item. It also contains the default dimensions of the list item. The code example in Section 13.2.2.6, "Creating a Square Meal Dialog Box," modifies the **itemHeight** structure member to ensure that the list items are high enough to accommodate the food-group bitmaps.

13.2.2.4 Processing the WM_DRAWITEM Message

An owner-drawn combo box sends the WM_DRAWITEM message to its parent window or dialog box procedure each time the application must repaint a list item. The *lParam* parameter points to a **DRAWITEMSTRUCT** structure that identifies the control and list item. It also contains information needed to paint the item.

The code example in Section 13.2.2.6, "Creating a Square Meal Dialog Box," displays the list-item text and the bitmap associated with the food group. If the item has the focus, it also draws a focus rectangle. Before displaying the text, the example sets the foreground and background colors, based on the item selected. Because the combo box has the CBS_HASSTRINGS style, the combo box maintains the text for each list item, that can be retrieved using the CB_GETLBTEXT message.

The bitmaps used for the list item depend on the food group. InitGroupList uses the CB_SETITEMDATA message to associate a constant with each list item, identifying the corresponding food group. The window procedure uses this value, contained in the **itemData** member of the **DRAWITEMSTRUCT** structure, to determine which bitmaps to display. The system uses two bitmaps for each food group symbol: a monochrome bitmap with the SRCAND raster operation to erase the irregular region behind the image and a color bitmap with the SRCPAINT raster operation to paint the image.

13.2.2.5 Processing the WM_COMMAND Message

When an event occurs in a dialog box control, the control notifies the dialog box procedure, by means of a WM_COMMAND message. The code example in Section 13.2.2.6, "Creating a Square Meal Dialog Box," processes notification messages from the combo box, the list box, and the OK button. The control identifier is in the low-order word of *wParam*, and the notification code is in the high-order word of *wParam*.

If the control identifier is IDCOMBO, an event has occurred in the combo box. In response, the dialog box procedure ignores all other combo box events except CBN_SELCHANGE, used to indicate that the current selection has changed. The dialog box procedure calls InitFoodList to reset the contents of the list box and to add the names of the current selection in the drop-down list box.

If the control identifier is IDLIST, an event has occurred in the list box. This causes the dialog box procedure to ignore all list box events except LBN_DBLCLK, used to indicate that the user has double-clicked a list item. This event is processed in the same way as an OK button click.

If the control identifier is IDOK, the user has clicked the OK button. In response, the dialog box procedure inserts the name of the selected food into the application's multiline edit control, then calls the **EndDialog** function to close the dialog box.

If the control identifier is IDCANCEL, the user has clicked the Cancel button. In response, the dialog box procedure calls **EndDialog** to close the dialog box.

13.2.2.6 Creating a Square Meal Dialog Box

Following are the dialog box procedure and supporting functions for the Square Meal dialog box.

```
HWND hwndMain;
HWND hwndEdit;
char achTemp[256];          /* temporary buffer              */

HBITMAP hbmBread;
HBITMAP hbmDairy;
HBITMAP hbmFruit;
HBITMAP hbmMeat;
HBITMAP hbmBreadMask;
HBITMAP hbmDairyMask;
HBITMAP hbmFruitMask;
HBITMAP hbmMeatMask;


/**********************************************************
```

```
   FUNCTION: FoodDlgProc

   PURPOSE: Dialog procedure for Food dialog box.

**********************************************************/

BOOL CALLBACK FoodDlgProc(hwndDlg, msg, wParam, lParam)
HWND hwndDlg;
UINT msg;
WPARAM wParam;
LPARAM lParam;
{
    LPMEASUREITEMSTRUCT lpmis;
    LPDRAWITEMSTRUCT lpdis;
    HBITMAP hbmIcon;
    HBITMAP hbmMask;
    COLORREF clrBackground;
    COLORREF clrForeground;
    TEXTMETRIC tm;
    HDC hdc;
    HWND hwnd;
    int x;
    int y;

    switch (msg) {
        case WM_INITDIALOG:

            /*
             * Call an application-defined function to load
             * bitmap resources.
             */

            if (!LoadIconBitmaps()) {
                EndDialog(hwndDlg, -1);
                break;
            }

            /* Initialize the drop-down list box. */

            if (!InitGroupList(hwndDlg)) {
                DeleteIconBitmaps();
                EndDialog(hwndDlg, -1);
                break;
            }

            /* Select the first food group. */

            SendDlgItemMessage(hwndDlg, IDCOMBO, CB_SETCURSEL,
                0, 0);
```

```
                          /* List the foods and select the first food. */

                          InitFoodList(hwndDlg);
                          SendDlgItemMessage(hwndDlg, IDLIST, LB_SETCURSEL,
                              0, 0);
                          break;

              case WM_MEASUREITEM:
                          lpmis = (LPMEASUREITEMSTRUCT) lParam;

                          if (lpmis->itemHeight < CY_BITMAP + 2)
                              lpmis->itemHeight = CY_BITMAP + 2;

                          break;

              case WM_DRAWITEM:
                          lpdis = (LPDRAWITEMSTRUCT) lParam;
                          if (lpdis->itemID == -1)                /* empty item */
                              break;

                          /* Determine the bitmaps used to draw the icon. */

                          switch (lpdis->itemData) {
                              case ID_BREAD:
                                  hbmIcon = hbmBread;
                                  hbmMask = hbmBreadMask;
                                  break;

                              case ID_DAIRY:
                                  hbmIcon = hbmDairy;
                                  hbmMask = hbmDairyMask;
                                  break;

                              case ID_FRUIT:
                                  hbmIcon = hbmFruit;
                                  hbmMask = hbmFruitMask;
                                  break;

                              default: /* meat */
                                  hbmIcon = hbmMeat;
                                  hbmMask = hbmMeatMask;
                                  break;
                          }

                          /* The colors depend on whether the item is selected. */

                          clrForeground = SetTextColor(lpdis->hDC,
                              GetSysColor(lpdis->itemState & ODS_SELECTED ?
                              COLOR_HIGHLIGHTTEXT : COLOR_WINDOWTEXT));
```

```
            clrBackground = SetBkColor(lpdis->hDC,
                GetSysColor(lpdis->itemState & ODS_SELECTED ?
                COLOR_HIGHLIGHT : COLOR_WINDOW));

            /* Calculate the vertical and horizontal position. */

            GetTextMetrics(lpdis->hDC, &tm);
            y = (lpdis->rcItem.bottom + lpdis->rcItem.top -
                tm.tmHeight) / 2;
            x = LOWORD(GetDialogBaseUnits()) / 4;

            /* Get and display the text for the list item. */

            SendMessage(lpdis->hwndItem, CB_GETLBTEXT,
                lpdis->itemID, (LPARAM) (LPCSTR) achTemp);

            ExtTextOut(lpdis->hDC, CX_BITMAP + 2 * x, y,
                ETO_CLIPPED | ETO_OPAQUE, &lpdis->rcItem,
                achTemp, lstrlen(achTemp), NULL);

            /* Restore the previous colors. */

            SetTextColor(lpdis->hDC, clrForeground);
            SetBkColor(lpdis->hDC, clrBackground);

            /* Show the icon. */

            hdc = CreateCompatibleDC(lpdis->hDC);
            if (hdc == NULL)
                break;

            SelectObject(hdc, hbmMask);
            BitBlt(lpdis->hDC, x, lpdis->rcItem.top + 1,
                CX_BITMAP, CY_BITMAP, hdc, 0, 0, SRCAND);

            SelectObject(hdc, hbmIcon);
            BitBlt(lpdis->hDC, x, lpdis->rcItem.top + 1,
                CX_BITMAP, CY_BITMAP, hdc, 0, 0, SRCPAINT);

            DeleteDC(hdc);

            /* If the item has the focus, draw focus rectangle. */

            if (lpdis->itemState & ODS_FOCUS)
                DrawFocusRect(lpdis->hDC, &lpdis->rcItem);

            break;

    case WM_COMMAND:
        switch (LOWORD(wParam)) {
```

```
            case IDCOMBO:
                if (HIWORD(wParam) == CBN_SELCHANGE) {
                    InitFoodList(hwndDlg);
                    SendDlgItemMessage(hwndDlg, IDLIST,
                        LB_SETCURSEL, 0, 0);
                }
                break;

            case IDLIST:
                if (HIWORD(wParam) != LBN_DBLCLK)
                    break;

                /* For a double-click, process the OK case. */

            case IDOK:

                /* Get the text for the selected list item. */

                hwnd = GetDlgItem(hwndDlg, IDLIST);
                SendMessage(hwnd, LB_GETTEXT,
                    SendMessage(hwnd, LB_GETCURSEL, 0, 0),
                    (LPARAM) achTemp);

                /* Insert the text into the edit window. */

                SendMessage(hwndEdit, EM_REPLACESEL, 0,
                    (LPARAM) achTemp);

                EndDialog(hwndDlg, 0);
                break;

            case IDCANCEL:
                hwnd = GetDlgItem(hwndDlg, IDCOMBO);
                if (SendMessage(hwnd, CB_GETDROPPEDSTATE,
                        0, 0))
                    SendMessage(hwnd, CB_SHOWDROPDOWN,
                        FALSE, 0);
                else
                    EndDialog(hwndDlg, 0);
        }
        break;

    case WM_DESTROY:

        /*
         * Call the application-defined function to free
         * bitmap resources.
         */

        DeleteIconBitmaps();
```

```
                        break;

                default:
                        return FALSE;
        }
        return TRUE;
}


/***********************************************************

        FUNCTION: InitGroupList

        PURPOSE: Initializes the "food groups" drop-down
                    list box.

        COMMENTS: The ID of the food group associated with
                    each list item is saved as item data.

***********************************************************/

BOOL PASCAL InitGroupList(HWND hwndDlg)
{
        HWND hwndCombo = GetDlgItem(hwndDlg, IDCOMBO);
        DWORD dwIndex;

        /* Add an item for each food group. */

        LoadString(hinst, ID_BREAD, achTemp, sizeof(achTemp));
        dwIndex = SendMessage(hwndCombo, CB_ADDSTRING, 0,
                (LPARAM) (LPCSTR) achTemp);
        SendMessage(hwndCombo, CB_SETITEMDATA, dwIndex, ID_BREAD);

        LoadString(hinst, ID_DAIRY, achTemp, sizeof(achTemp));
        dwIndex = SendMessage(hwndCombo, CB_ADDSTRING, 0,
                (LPARAM) (LPCSTR) achTemp);
        SendMessage(hwndCombo, CB_SETITEMDATA, dwIndex, ID_DAIRY);

        LoadString(hinst, ID_FRUIT, achTemp, sizeof(achTemp));
        dwIndex = SendMessage(hwndCombo, CB_ADDSTRING, 0,
                (LPARAM) (LPCSTR) achTemp);
        SendMessage(hwndCombo, CB_SETITEMDATA, dwIndex, ID_FRUIT);

        LoadString(hinst, ID_MEAT, achTemp, sizeof(achTemp));
        dwIndex = SendMessage(hwndCombo, CB_ADDSTRING, 0,
                (LPARAM) (LPCSTR) achTemp);
        SendMessage(hwndCombo, CB_SETITEMDATA, dwIndex, ID_MEAT);

        return TRUE;
}
```

```
/*********************************************************

    FUNCTION: InitFoodList

    PURPOSE: Clears the contents of the food list, and
             adds the names of foods for the current
             food group.

*********************************************************/

void PASCAL InitFoodList(HWND hwndDlg)
{
    HWND hwndCombo = GetDlgItem(hwndDlg, IDCOMBO);
    HWND hwndList = GetDlgItem(hwndDlg, IDLIST);
    UINT idFoodGroup;
    LPSTR lpsz;
    LPSTR lpszEnd;

    /* Determine the current food group. */

    idFoodGroup = SendMessage(
        hwndCombo,
        CB_GETITEMDATA,
        SendMessage(hwndCombo, CB_GETCURSEL, 0, 0),
        0
    );

    /* Clear the list contents. */

    SendMessage(hwndList, LB_RESETCONTENT, 0, 0);

    .
    . /* Add food names for the current food group. */
    .

}
```

13.2.3 Subclassing a Combo Box

This section demonstrates how to subclass combo boxes so your application can use them outside a dialog box. The code example in Section 13.2.3.4, "Creating a Tool Bar," shows the window procedure for a tool bar window containing two combo boxes. By subclassing the edit controls within the combo boxes, the tool bar window intercepts TAB, ENTER, and ESC keys that would otherwise be ignored.

The following illustration shows the tool bar window:

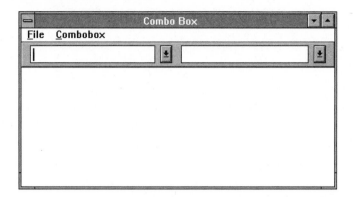

13.2.3.1 Processing the WM_CREATE Message

The code example in Section 13.2.3.4, "Creating a Tool Bar," processes the WM_CREATE message to create two combo box controls as child windows. It then subclasses the edit controls (selection fields) in each combo box because they receive the character input for simple and drop-down combo box. The application gets the handle of each edit control by using the **ChildWindowFromPoint** function.

To subclass the edit controls, the application calls the **SetWindowLong** function, replacing the address of the class window procedure with the address of the application-defined SubClassProc function. The address of the original window procedure is saved in the global variable *lpfnEditWndProc*.

The SubClassProc function intercepts TAB, ESC, and ENTER keys and notifies the tool bar window by sending application-defined messages (WM_TAB, WM_ESC, and WM_ENTER). SubClassProc uses the **CallWindowProc** function to pass most messages to the original window procedure, *lpfnEditWndProc*.

13.2.3.2 Processing the WM_SETFOCUS Message

When the tool bar window receives the input focus, it immediately sets the focus to the first combo box in the tool bar. To do so, the code example in Section 13.2.3.4, "Creating a Tool Bar," calls the **SetFocus** function in response to the WM_SETFOCUS message.

13.2.3.3 Processing the Application-Defined Messages

In the code example in Section 13.2.3.4, "Creating a Tool Bar," SubClassProc sends application-defined messages to the tool bar window when the user presses the TAB, ESC, or ENTER key in a combo box. The WM_TAB message is sent for the TAB key, the WM_ESC message for the ESC key, and the WM_ENTER message for the ENTER key.

The example processes the WM_TAB message by setting the focus to the next combo box in the tool bar. It processes the WM_ESC message by setting the focus to the main application window.

In response to the WM_ENTER message, the example ensures that the current selection for the combo box is valid and then sets the focus to the main application window. If the combo box contains no current selection, the example uses the CB_FINDSTRINGEXACT message to search for a list item that matches the contents of the selection field. If there is a match, the example sets the current selection; otherwise, it adds a new list item.

13.2.3.4 Creating a Tool Bar

Following are the window procedure for the tool bar and the subclass procedure for the two combo boxes.

```
#define WM_TAB (WM_USER)
#define WM_ESC (WM_USER + 1)
#define WM_ENTER (WM_USER + 2)

HWND hwndMain;
HWND hwndEdit;
WNDPROC lpfnEditWndProc; /* original window procedure for */
                         /*    the combo box edit windows  */

int cyToolbar;           /* tool bar window height         */


/***********************************************************

    FUNCTION: ToolbarWindowProc

    PURPOSE: Window procedure for the tool bar window

***********************************************************/

LRESULT CALLBACK ToolbarWindowProc(hwnd, msg, wParam, lParam)
HWND hwnd;
UINT msg;
WPARAM wParam;
LPARAM lParam;
{
    static HWND    hwndEdit1;
    static HWND    hwndEdit2;
    static HWND    hwndCombo1;
    static HWND    hwndCombo2;
    .
    .
    .

    FARPROC    lpfnSubClassProc;
```

```
POINT       pt;
DWORD       dwBaseUnits;
HWND        hwndCombo;
DWORD       dwIndex;

switch (msg) {
    case WM_CREATE:

        /* Create two combo box child windows. */

        dwBaseUnits = GetDialogBaseUnits();

        hwndCombo1 = CreateWindow("COMBOBOX", "",
            CBS_DROPDOWN | WS_CHILD | WS_VISIBLE,
            (6 * LOWORD(dwBaseUnits)) / 4,
            (2 * HIWORD(dwBaseUnits)) / 8,
            (100 * LOWORD(dwBaseUnits)) / 4,
            (50 * HIWORD(dwBaseUnits)) / 8,
            hwnd, NULL, hinst, NULL);

        hwndCombo2 = CreateWindow("COMBOBOX", "",
            CBS_DROPDOWN | WS_CHILD | WS_VISIBLE,
            (112 * LOWORD(dwBaseUnits)) / 4,
            (2 * HIWORD(dwBaseUnits)) / 8,
            (100 * LOWORD(dwBaseUnits)) / 4,
            (50 * HIWORD(dwBaseUnits)) / 8,
            hwnd, NULL, hinst, NULL);

        /* Get the edit window handle for each combo box. */

        pt.x = 1;
        pt.y = 1;
        hwndEdit1 = ChildWindowFromPoint(hwndCombo1, pt);
        hwndEdit2 = ChildWindowFromPoint(hwndCombo2, pt);

        /*
         * Change the window procedure for both edit windows
         * to the subclass procedure.
         */

        lpfnSubClassProc = MakeProcInstance(
            (FARPROC) SubClassProc, hinst);

        lpfnEditWndProc = (WNDPROC) SetWindowLong(hwndEdit1,
            GWL_WNDPROC, (DWORD) lpfnSubClassProc);

        SetWindowLong(hwndEdit2, GWL_WNDPROC,
            (DWORD) lpfnSubClassProc);

        break;
```

```
case WM_SETFOCUS:
    SetFocus(hwndCombo1);
    break;

case WM_TAB:
    if (GetFocus() == hwndEdit1)
        SetFocus(hwndCombo2);
    else
        SetFocus(hwndCombo1);
    break;

case WM_ESC:

    hwndCombo = GetFocus() == hwndEdit1 ?
        hwndCombo1 : hwndCombo2;

    /* Clear the current selection. */

    SendMessage(hwndCombo, CB_SETCURSEL, (WPARAM) (-1), 0);

    /* Set the focus to the main window. */

    SetFocus(hwndMain);
    break;

case WM_ENTER:
    hwndCombo = GetFocus() == hwndEdit1 ?
        hwndCombo1 : hwndCombo2;
    SetFocus(hwndMain);

    /* If there is no current selection, set one. */

    if (SendMessage(hwndCombo, CB_GETCURSEL, 0, 0)
            == CB_ERR) {
        if (SendMessage(hwndCombo, WM_GETTEXT,
                sizeof(achTemp), (LPARAM) achTemp) == 0)
            break;          /* empty selection field */
        dwIndex = SendMessage(hwndCombo,
            CB_FINDSTRINGEXACT, (WPARAM) (-1),
            (LPARAM) achTemp);

        /* Add the string, if necessary, and select it. */

        if (dwIndex == CB_ERR)
            dwIndex = SendMessage(hwndCombo, CB_ADDSTRING,
                0, (LPARAM) achTemp);
        if (dwIndex != CB_ERR)
            SendMessage(hwndCombo, CB_SETCURSEL,
                dwIndex, 0);
```

```
            }
            break;


            .
            . /* Process additional messages. */
            .

        default:
            return DefWindowProc(hwnd, msg, wParam, lParam);
    }
    return 0;
}



/**********************************************************

    FUNCTION: SubClassProc

    PURPOSE: Process TAB and ESCAPE keys, and pass all
             other messages to the class window
             procedure.

**********************************************************/

LRESULT CALLBACK SubClassProc(hwnd, msg, wParam, lParam)
HWND hwnd;
UINT msg;
WPARAM wParam;
LPARAM lParam;
{
    switch (msg) {
        case WM_KEYDOWN:
            switch (wParam) {
                case VK_TAB:
                    SendMessage(hwndToolbar, WM_TAB, 0, 0);
                    return 0;
                case VK_ESCAPE:
                    SendMessage(hwndToolbar, WM_ESC, 0, 0);
                    return 0;
                case VK_RETURN:
                    SendMessage(hwndToolbar, WM_ENTER, 0, 0);
                    return 0;
            }
            break;

        case WM_KEYUP:
        case WM_CHAR:
            switch (wParam) {
                case VK_TAB:
                case VK_ESCAPE:
```

```
                            case VK_RETURN:
                                return 0;
                    }
            }

            /* Call the original window procedure for default processing. */

            return CallWindowProc(lpfnEditWndProc, hwnd,
                msg, wParam, lParam);
    }
```

13.3 Functions and Messages

Following are the functions and messages used with combo boxes.

Functions

DlgDirListComboBox
DlgDirSelect
DlgDirSelectComboBox
DlgDirSelectComboBoxEx

Messages

CB_ADDSTRING
CB_DELETESTRING
CB_DIR
CB_FINDSTRING
CB_FINDSTRINGEXACT
CB_GETCOUNT
CB_GETCURSEL
CB_GETDROPPEDCONTROLRECT
CB_GETDROPPEDSTATE
CB_GETEDITSEL
CB_GETEXTENDEDUI
CB_GETITEMDATA
CB_GETITEMHEIGHT
CB_GETLBTEXT
CB_GETLBTEXTLEN
CB_GETLOCALE
CB_INSERTSTRING
CB_LIMITTEXT
CB_RESETCONTENT
CB_SELECTSTRING
CB_SETCURSEL
CB_SETEDITSEL

CB_SETEXTENDEDUI
CB_SETITEMDATA
CB_SETITEMHEIGHT
CB_SETLOCALE
CB_SHOWDROPDOWN
CBN_CLOSEUP
CBN_DBLCLK
CBN_DROPDOWN
CBN_EDITCHANGE
CBN_EDITUPDATE
CBN_ERRSPACE
CBN_KILLFOCUS
CBN_SELCHANGE
CBN_SETFOCUS
WM_COMPAREITEM
WM_DRAWITEM
WM_MEASUREITEM

C H A P T E R   1 4

Scroll Bars

14.1 About Scroll Bars

A window in an application written for Microsoft ® Windows ™ can display a data object, such as a document or a bitmap, that is larger than the window's client area. When provided with a *scroll bar*, the user can scroll a data object in the client area to bring into view the portions of the object that extend beyond the borders of the window. Scroll bars should be included in any window sized such that the contents of the client area extend beyond the window's borders.

A scroll bar's orientation determines the direction in which scrolling occurs when the user operates the scroll bar. A horizontal scroll bar enables the user to scroll the contents of a window to the left or right. A vertical scroll bar enables the user to scroll the contents up or down. The following illustration shows horizontal and vertical scroll bars in Windows Write.

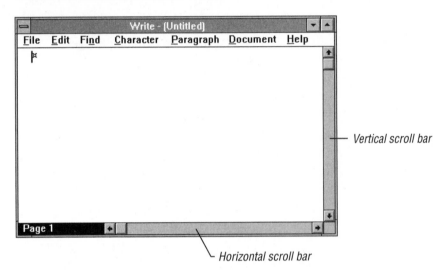

Vertical scroll bar

Horizontal scroll bar

14.1.1 Parts of a Scroll Bar

A scroll bar consists of a shaded shaft with an arrow button at each end and a *scroll box* (sometimes called a thumb) between the arrow buttons. The following illustration shows the parts of a scroll bar.

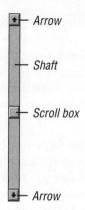

A scroll bar represents the overall length or width of a data object in a window's client area; the scroll box represents the portion of the object that is visible in the client area. The position of the scroll box changes whenever the user scrolls a data object to display a different portion of it.

The user scrolls the contents of a window by clicking one of the arrow buttons, by clicking the area in the shaded shaft, or by dragging the scroll box. When the user clicks an arrow button, the application scrolls the contents by one unit (typically a single line or column). When the user clicks the shaded areas, the application scrolls the contents by one window. The amount of scrolling that occurs when the user drags the scroll box depends on the distance the user drags the scroll box and on the *scrolling range* of the scroll bar. For more information about the scrolling range, see Section 14.1.3, "Scroll Box Position and Scrolling Range."

14.1.2 Standard Scroll Bars and Scroll Bar Controls

A scroll bar is included in a window either as a standard scroll bar or as a scroll bar control. A *standard scroll bar* is located in the nonclient area of a window. It is created with the window and displayed when the window is displayed. The sole purpose of a standard scroll bar is to enable the user to generate scrolling requests for viewing the entire contents of the client area. You can include a standard scroll bar in a window by specifying WS_HSCROLL, WS_VSCROLL, or both styles when you create the window. The WS_HSCROLL style creates a horizontal scroll bar positioned at the bottom of the client area. The WS_VSCROLL style creates a vertical scroll bar positioned at the right of the client area. The SM_CXHSCROLL and SM_CYHSCROLL system metric values define the width and height of a standard horizontal scroll bar. The SM_CXVSCROLL and SM_CYVSCROLL values define the width and height of a standard vertical scroll bar.

A *scroll bar control* is a control window that belongs to the SCROLLBAR window class. A scroll bar control appears and functions like a standard scroll bar, but it is a separate window. As a separate window, a scroll bar control receives direct input focus, indicated by a flashing caret displayed in the scroll box. Unlike a standard scroll bar, a scroll bar control also has a built-in keyboard interface that enables the user to direct scrolling. You can use as many scroll bar controls as needed in a single window. When you create a scroll bar control, you must specify the scroll bar's size and position. However, if a scroll bar control's window can be resized, adjustments to the scroll bar's size must be made whenever the size of the window changes.

The advantage of using a standard scroll bar is that Windows creates the scroll bar and automatically sets its size and position. However, standard scroll bars are sometimes too restrictive. For example, suppose that you want to divide a client area into quadrants and use a separate set of scroll bars to control the contents of each quadrant. You cannot use standard scroll bars, because you can only create one set of scroll bars for a particular window. Use scroll bar controls instead, because you can add as many of them to a window as you want.

Applications can provide scroll bar controls for purposes other than scrolling the contents of a window. For example, the Mouse application in Windows Control Panel provides scroll bar controls making it possible for the user to set the mouse tracking speed and double-click speed. The following figure shows the Double-Click Speed scroll bar control in the Mouse application.

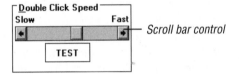
— Scroll bar control

A scroll bar control can have a number of styles that serves to control the orientation and position of the scroll bar. You specify the styles that you want when you call the **CreateWindowEx** function to create a scroll bar control. Some of the styles create a scroll bar control that uses a default width or height. However, you must always specify the x- and y-coordinates and the other dimensions of the scroll bar. Following are the scroll bar control styles.

Style	Description
SBS_BOTTOMALIGN	Positions a horizontal scroll bar at the bottom of the rectangle specified by the *x, y, nWidth* and *nHeight* parameters of the **CreateWindowEx** function. The SBS_HORZ style must also be specified. The scroll bar uses the default height for standard horizontal scroll bars.
SBS_HORZ	Creates a horizontal scroll bar. If neither the SBS_BOTTOMALIGN nor SBS_TOPALIGN style is specified, the scroll bar uses the height, width, and position given in the **CreateWindowEx** function.

SBS_LEFTALIGN	Positions a vertical scroll bar at the left side of the rectangle specified by the *x*, *y*, *nWidth* and *nHeight* parameters of the **CreateWindowEx** function. The SBS_VERT style must also be specified. The scroll bar uses the default width for standard vertical scroll bars.
SBS_RIGHTALIGN	Positions a vertical scroll bar at the right side of the rectangle specified by the *x*, *y*, *nWidth* and *nHeight* parameters of the **CreateWindowEx** function. The SBS_VERT style must also be specified. The scroll bar uses the default width for standard vertical scroll bars.
SBS_TOPALIGN	Positions a horizontal scroll bar at the top of the rectangle specified by the *x*, *y*, *nWidth* and *nHeight* parameters of the **CreateWindowEx** function. The SBS_HORZ style must also be specified. The scroll bar uses the default height for standard horizontal scroll bars.
SBS_VERT	Creates a vertical scroll bar. If neither the SBS_RIGHTALIGN nor SBS_LEFTALIGN style is specified, the scroll bar uses the height, width, and position given by the **CreateWindowEx** function.

14.1.3 Scroll Box Position and Scrolling Range

The position of the scroll box is represented as an integer; it is relative to the left or upper end of the scroll bar, depending on whether the scroll bar is horizontal or vertical. The position must be within the minimum and maximum values of the scrolling range. For example, in a scroll bar with a range of 0 through 100, position 50 is in the middle, with the remaining positions distributed equally along the scroll bar. The initial range depends on the scroll bar. Standard scroll bars have an initial range of 0 through 100; scroll bar controls have an empty range (both minimum and maximum values are zero), unless you supply an explicit range when the control is created. You can change the range at any time by using the **SetScrollRange** function to set new minimum and maximum values. The **GetScrollRange** function retrieves the current minimum and maximum values.

You can adjust the scroll range to convenient integers by using the **SetScrollRange** function. This function makes it easy to translate the scroll box position into a value corresponding to the scrolled data. For example, if an application must display 260 lines of text in a window that can show only 16 lines at a time, the vertical scroll bar range can be set to 1 through 244. If the scroll box is at position 1, the first line will be at the top of the window. If the scroll box is at position 244, the last line (line 260) will be at the bottom of the window. If the **SetScrollPos** function specifies a position value that is less than the minimum or more than the maximum, the minimum or maximum scrolling range value is used instead.

To establish a useful relationship between the scroll bar range and the data, an application must adjust the range whenever the data or the size of the window changes. The application must, therefore, adjust the scroll bar range when processing WM_SIZE messages.

As the user moves the scroll box in a scroll bar, the scroll bar reports the scroll box position as an integer in the scrolling range. If the position is the minimum value, the scroll box is at the top of a vertical scroll bar or at the left end of a horizontal scroll bar. If the position is the maximum value, the scroll box is at the bottom of a vertical scroll bar or at right end of a horizontal scroll bar.

An application must move the scroll box in a scroll bar. Although the user makes a request for scrolling in a scroll bar, the scroll bar does not update the scroll box position. Instead, it passes the request to the parent window, which must scroll the data and update the scroll box position by using the **SetScrollPos** function. Because it controls the scroll box movement, the application can move the scroll box in increments that work best for the data being scrolled.

14.1.4 Scroll Bar Requests

The user makes scrolling requests by clicking various parts of a scroll bar. Windows sends the request to the given window in the form of a WM_HSCROLL or WM_VSCROLL message. A horizontal scroll bar sends the WM_HSCROLL message; a vertical scroll bar sends the WM_VSCROLL message. Each message includes a notification code that corresponds to the user's action, to the handle of the scroll bar (scroll bar controls only), and, in some cases, to the position of the scroll box.

The following figure shows the notification codes that the user generates when clicking various parts of a scroll bar.

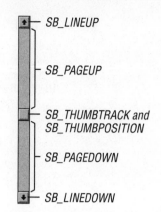

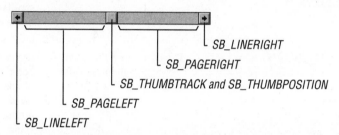

The scroll bar notification codes specify the action the user takes. An application examines the codes that accompany the WM_HSCROLL and WM_VSCROLL messages and then performs the appropriate scrolling operation. In the following table of notification codes, the user's action is specified for each code, followed by the application's response. In each case, a *unit* is defined by the application as appropriate for the given data. For example, the typical unit for scrolling text vertically is a line.

Notification code	Action	Response
SB_LINEUP	The user clicks the top scroll arrow.	Decrement of the scroll box position; scrolls toward the top of the data by one unit.
SB_LINEDOWN	The user clicks the bottom scroll arrow.	Increment of the scroll box position; scrolls toward the bottom of the data by one unit.
SB_LINELEFT	The user clicks the left scroll arrow.	Decrement of the scroll box position; scrolls toward the left end of the data by one unit.

SB_LINERIGHT	The user clicks the right scroll arrow.	Increment of the scroll box position; scrolls toward the right end of the data by one unit.
SB_PAGEUP	The user clicks the scroll bar shaft above the scroll box.	Decrement of the scroll box position by the number of data units in the window; scrolls toward the top of the data by the same number of units.
SB_PAGEDOWN	The user clicks the scroll bar shaft below the scroll box.	Increment of the scroll box position by the number of data units in the window; scrolls toward the bottom of the data by the same number of units.
SB_PAGELEFT	The user clicks the scroll bar shaft to the left of the scroll box.	Decrement of the scroll box position by the number of data units in the window; scrolls toward the left end of the data by the same number of units.
SB_PAGERIGHT	The user clicks the scroll bar shaft to the right of the scroll box.	Increment of the scroll box position by the number of data units in the window; scrolls toward the right end of the data by the same number of units.
SB_THUMBPOSITION	The user releases the scroll box after dragging it.	Setting of the scroll box to the position given in the message; scrolls the data by the same number of units the scroll box has moved.
SB_THUMBTRACK	The user drags the scroll box.	Applications that draw data quickly can set the scroll box to the position given in the message and scroll the data by the same number of units the scroll box has moved. Applications that cannot draw data quickly must wait for the SB_THUMBPOSITION code before moving the scroll box and scrolling the data.

SB_ENDSCROLL	The user releases the mouse after holding it on an arrow or in the scrollbar shaft.	No response is needed.

A scroll bar generates the SB_THUMBPOSITION and SB_THUMBTRACK notification codes when the user clicks and drags the scroll box. An application should be programmed to process either the SB_THUMBTRACK or the SB_THUMBPOSITION notification code.

The SB_THUMBPOSITION notification code occurs when the user releases the mouse button after clicking the scroll box. An application that processes this code performs the scrolling operation after the user has dragged the scroll box to the desired position and released the mouse button.

SB_THUMBTRACK notification codes occur as the user drags the scroll box. If an application processes SB_THUMBTRACK messages, it can scroll the contents of a window as the user drags the scroll box. However, a scroll bar can generate many SB_THUMBTRACK notification codes in a short period, so an application should process these codes only if it can quickly repaint the contents of the window.

14.1.5 Keyboard Interface for a Scroll Bar

A scroll bar control provides a built-in keyboard interface that enables the user to issue scrolling requests by using the keyboard; a standard scroll bar does not. When a scroll bar control has the keyboard focus, it sends WM_HSCROLL and WM_VSCROLL messages to its parent window when the user presses the arrow keys. The notification code is sent with each message corresponding to the arrow key the user has pressed. Following are the arrow keys and their corresponding notification codes.

Arrow key	Notification code
UP	SB_LINEUP or SB_LINELEFT
DOWN	SB_LINEDOWN or SB_LINERIGHT
LEFT	SB_LINEUP or SB_LINELEFT
RIGHT	SB_LINEDOWN or SB_LINERIGHT
PGUP	SB_PAGEUP or SB_PAGELEFT
PGDN	SB_PAGEDOWN or SB_PAGERIGHT
HOME	SB_TOP
END	SB_BOTTOM

Note that the keyboard interface of a scroll bar control sends the SB_TOP and SB_BOTTOM notification codes. The SB_TOP code indicates that the user has reached the top value of the scrolling range. An application scrolls the window contents downward so that the top of the data object is visible. The SB_BOTTOM code indicates that the user has reached the bottom value of the scrolling range. If an application processes the SB_BOTTOM code, it scrolls the window contents upward so that the bottom of the data object is visible.

If you want a keyboard interface for a standard scroll bar, you can create one yourself by processing the WM_KEYDOWN message in your window procedure and then performing the appropriate scrolling action based on the virtual-key code that accompanies the message. For information about how to create a keyboard interface for a scroll bar, see Section 14.2.4, "Creating a Keyboard Interface for a Standard Scroll Bar."

14.1.6 Scrolling the Client Area

The simplest way to scroll the contents of a client area is to erase and then redraw it. This is the method an application is likely to use with SB_PAGEUP, SB_PAGEDOWN, SB_TOP, and SB_END commands, which typically require completely new contents.

For some commands, such as SB_LINEUP and SB_LINEDOWN, not all the contents need be erased, since some remain visible after scrolling occurs. The **ScrollWindow** and **ScrollWindowEx** functions preserve a portion of the client area's contents, move the preserved portion a specified amount, and then prepare the rest of the client area for painting new information. **ScrollWindow** and **ScrollWindowEx** use the **BitBlt** function to move a specific part of the data object to a new location within the client area. Any uncovered part of the client area (anything not preserved) is invalidated, erased, and painted when the next WM_PAINT message occurs.

The **ScrollWindow** and **ScrollWindowEx** functions can be used to exclude a portion of the client area from the scrolling operation. This keeps items with fixed positions, such as child windows, from moving within the client area. It automatically invalidates the portion of the client area that is to receive the new information, so the application does not have to compute its own clipping regions. For more information on clipping, see Chapter 38, "Clipping."

Usually an application scrolls the contents of a window in the direction opposite that indicated by the scroll bar. For example, when the user clicks the shaft in the area below the scroll box, an application scrolls the object in the window upward to reveal a portion of the object that is below the visible portion. The following figure shows the scrolling operation an application performs when processing the SB_PAGEDOWN notification code.

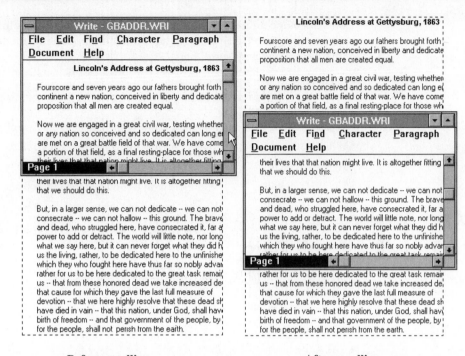

Before scrolling   **After scrolling**

14.1.7 Scroll Bar Visibility

The **SetScrollRange** function hides and disables a standard scroll bar when equal minimum and maximum values are specified. This is the way to temporarily hide a scroll bar when it is not needed for the contents of the client area. There is no need to make scrolling requests through the scroll bar when it is hidden. **SetScrollRange** enables the scroll bar and shows it again when it sets the minimum and maximum values to unequal values. The **ShowScrollBar** function can also be used to hide or show a scroll bar. It does not affect the scroll bar's range or scroll box position.

The **EnableScrollBar** function can be used to disable one or both arrows of a scroll bar. An application displays disabled arrows in gray and does not respond to user input.

14.1.8 Scroll Bar Colors and Metrics

The system-defined color value, COLOR_SCROLLBAR, controls the color within a scroll bar's shaft. Use the **GetSysColor** function to determine the color of the shaft and the **SetSysColor** function to set the color of the shaft. Note, however, that this change of color affects all scroll bars in the system.

You can get the dimensions of the bitmaps that Windows uses in standard scroll bars by calling the **GetSystemMetrics** function. Following are the system metric values associated with scroll bars.

System metric	Description
SM_CXHSCROLL	Width of arrow bitmap on horizontal scroll bar
SM_CYHSCROLL	Height of arrow bitmap on horizontal scroll bar
SM_CXVSCROLL	Width of arrow bitmap on vertical scroll bar
SM_CYVSCROLL	Height of arrow bitmap on vertical scroll bar
SM_CXHTHUMB	Width of scroll box on horizontal scroll bar
SM_CYVTHUMB	Height of scroll box on vertical scroll bar

14.2 Using Scroll Bars

This section explains how to perform the following tasks:

- Create scroll bars
- Scroll text
- Scroll a bitmap
- Create a keyboard interface for a standard scroll bar

14.2.1 Creating Scroll Bars

When creating an overlapped, pop-up, or child window, you can add standard scroll bars by using the **CreateWindowEx** function and specifying WS_HSCROLL, WS_VSCROLL, or both styles. Doing this adds a horizontal or vertical scroll bar, or both, to the window. The code in the following example creates a window with standard horizontal and vertical scroll bars.

```
hwnd = CreateWindowEx(
    0L,                         /* no extended styles        */
    "MyAppClass",               /* window class              */
    "Scroll Bar Application",   /* text for window title bar */
    WS_OVERLAPPEDWINDOW |       /* window styles             */
        WS_HSCROLL |
        WS_VSCROLL,
    CW_USEDEFAULT,              /* default horizontal position */
    CW_USEDEFAULT,              /* default vertical position   */
    CW_USEDEFAULT,              /* default width               */
    CW_USEDEFAULT,              /* default height              */
    (HWND) NULL,                /* no parent for overlapped windows */
    (HMENU) NULL,               /* window class menu           */
    hinst,                      /* instance owning this window */
    (LPVOID) NULL               /* pointer not needed          */
);
```

To process scroll bar messages for these scroll bars, you must include appropriate code in the main window procedure.

When using the **CreateWindowEx** function to create a window, you can add a scroll bar control by specifying the SCROLLBAR window class. This creates a horizontal or vertical scroll bar, depending on whether SBS_HORZ or SBS_VERT is specified as the window style. The scroll bar size and its position relative to its parent window can also be specified. The following code example creates a horizontal scroll bar control and positions it in the upper-right corner of the window.

```
hwndScroll = CreateWindowEx(
    0L,                     /* no extended styles       */
    "SCROLLBAR",            /* scroll bar control class */
    (LPSTR) NULL,           /* text for window title bar */
    WS_CHILD | SBS_HORZ,    /* scroll bar styles        */
    0,                      /* horizontal position      */
    0,                      /* vertical position        */
    200,                    /* width of the scroll bar  */
    CW_USEDEFAULT,          /* default height           */
    hwnd,                 /* handle of main window      */
    (HMENU) NULL,         /* no menu for a scroll bar   */
    hinst,                /* instance owning this window */
    (LPVOID) NULL         /* pointer not needed         */
);
```

14.2.2 Scrolling Text

This section describes the changes you can make to an application's main window procedure to enable a user to scroll text. The example in Section 14.2.2.5, "Example of Scrolling Text," creates and displays an array of text strings and processes WM_HSCROLL and WM_VSCROLL messages generated by the scroll bars so that the user can scroll text both vertically and horizontally.

14.2.2.1 Processing the WM_CREATE Message

Scrolling units are typically set while processing the WM_CREATE message. It is convenient to base the scrolling units on the dimensions of the font associated with the window's display context. To retrieve the font dimensions for a specific display context, use the **GetTextMetrics** function.

In the example in Section 14.2.2.5, "Example of Scrolling Text," one vertical scrolling unit is equivalent to the height of a character cell, plus external leading. One horizontal scrolling unit is equivalent to the average width of a character cell. The horizontal scrolling positions, therefore, do not correspond to actual characters, unless the screen font is fixed-width.

14.2.2.2 Processing the WM_SIZE Message

When processing the WM_SIZE message, it is convenient to adjust the scrolling range and scrolling position to reflect the dimensions of the client area as well as the number of lines of text that will be displayed.

The **SetScrollRange** function sets the minimum and maximum position values for a scroll bar. The **SetScrollPos** function adjusts the scroll box to reflect the scrolling position.

14.2.2.3 Processing the WM_HSCROLL and WM_VSCROLL Messages

The scroll bar sends WM_HSCROLL and WM_VSCROLL messages to the window procedure whenever the user clicks the scroll bar or drags the scroll box. The low-order words of WM_VSCROLL and WM_HSCROLL each contain a notification code that indicates the direction and magnitude of the scrolling action.

When the WM_HSCROLL and WM_VSCROLL messages are processed, the scroll bar notification code is examined and the scrolling increment is calculated. After the increment is applied to the current scrolling position, the window is scrolled to the new position by using the **ScrollWindow** function, and the position of the scroll box is adjusted by using the **SetScrollPos** function.

After a window is scrolled, part of its client area is made invalid. To ensure that the invalid region is updated, the **UpdateWindow** function is used to generate a WM_PAINT message.

14.2.2.4 Processing the WM_PAINT Message

When processing the WM_PAINT message, it is convenient to draw the lines of text that you want to appear in the invalid portion of the window. The example code uses the current scrolling position and the dimensions of the invalid region to determine the range of lines within the invalid region to display them.

14.2.2.5 Example of Scrolling Text

The following example shows how to have your application scroll text in response to input from the horizontal and vertical scroll bars.

```
HDC hdc;
PAINTSTRUCT ps;
TEXTMETRIC tm;

/* These variables are required to display text. */

static int xClient;    /* width of client area            */
static int yClient;    /* height of client area           */
```

```
static int xClientMax;   /* maximum width of client area           */

static int xChar;        /* horizontal scrolling unit              */
static int yChar;        /* vertical scrolling unit                */
static int xUpper;       /* average width of uppercase letters     */

static int xPos;         /* current horizontal scrolling position  */
static int yPos;         /* current vertical scrolling position    */

static int xMax;         /* maximum horiz. scrolling position      */
static int yMax;         /* maximum vert. scrolling position       */

int xInc;                /* horizontal scrolling increment         */
int yInc;                /* vertical scrolling increment           */

int i;                   /* loop counter                           */
int x, y;                /* horiz. and vert. printing coords       */

int FirstLine;           /* first line in the invalidated area     */
int LastLine;            /* last line in the invalidated area      */

/* Create an array of lines to display. */

#define LINES 27
static char *abc[] = { "anteater", "bear", "cougar", "dingo",
   "elephant", "frog", "gazelle", "hyena", "iguana", "jackal",
   "kangaroo", "llama", "moose", "newt", "octopus", "penguin",
   "quail", "rat", "squid", "tortoise", "urus", "vole",
   "walrus", "xylophone", "yak", "zebra",
   "This line contains many words, but no character. Go figure." };

switch (uMsg) {

    case WM_CREATE :

        /* Get the handle of the client area's device context. */

        hdc = GetDC (hwnd);

        /* Extract font dimensions from the text metrics. */

        GetTextMetrics (hdc, &tm);
        xChar = tm.tmAveCharWidth;
        xUpper = (tm.tmPitchAndFamily & 1 ? 3 : 2) * xChar/2;
        yChar = tm.tmHeight + tm.tmExternalLeading;

        /* Free the device context. */

        ReleaseDC (hwnd, hdc);
```

```
        /*
         * Set an arbitrary maximum width for client area.
         * (xClientMax is the sum of the widths of 48 average
         * lowercase letters and 12 uppercase letters.)
         */

        xClientMax = 48 * xChar + 12 * xUpper;

        return 0;

    case WM_SIZE:

        /* Retrieve the dimensions of the client area. */

        yClient = HIWORD (lParam);
        xClient = LOWORD (lParam);

        /*
         * Determine the maximum vertical scrolling position.
         * The two is added for extra space below the lines
         * of text.
         */

        yMax = max (0, LINES + 2 - yClient/yChar);

        /*
         * Make sure the current vertical scrolling position
         * does not exceed the maximum.
         */

        yPos = min (yPos, yMax);

        /*
         * Adjust the vertical scrolling range and scroll box
         * position to reflect the new yMax and yPos values.
         */

        SetScrollRange (hwnd, SB_VERT, 0, yMax, TRUE);
        SetScrollPos (hwnd, SB_VERT, yPos, TRUE);

        /*
         * Determine the maximum horizontal scrolling position.
         * The two is added for extra space to the right of the
         * lines of text.
         */

        xMax = max (0, 2 + (xClientMax - xClient)/xChar);

        /*
         * Make sure the current horizontal scrolling position
```

```
                      * does not exceed the maximum.
                      */

                     xPos = min (xPos, xMax);

                     /*
                      * Adjust the horizontal scrolling range and scroll box
                      * position to reflect the new xMax and xPos values.
                      */

                     SetScrollRange (hwnd, SB_HORZ, 0, xMax, TRUE);
                     SetScrollPos (hwnd, SB_HORZ, xPos, TRUE);

                     return 0;

            case WM_PAINT:

                     /* Prepare the window for painting. */

                     hdc = BeginPaint(hwnd, &ps);

                     /*
                      * Use the current vertical scrolling position and
                      * coordinates of the invalid rectangle to determine
                      * the range of new lines that should be drawn in the
                      * client area.
                      */

                     FirstLine = max (0, yPos + ps.rcPaint.top/yChar - 1);
                     LastLine = min (LINES, yPos + ps.rcPaint.bottom/yChar);

                     /* Display these lines. */

                     for (i = FirstLine;i < LastLine;i++) {
                         x = xChar * (1 - xPos);
                         y = yChar * (1 - yPos + i);

                         TextOut (hdc, x, y, abc[i], lstrlen(abc[i]));
                         }

                     /* Indicate that painting is finished. */

                     EndPaint(hwnd, &ps);
                     break;

            case WM_HSCROLL:
                     switch(LOWORD (wParam)) {

                         /* User clicked shaft left of the scroll box. */
```

```
            case SB_PAGEUP:
                xInc = -8;
                break;

            /* User clicked shaft right of the scroll box. */

            case SB_PAGEDOWN:
                xInc = 8;
                break;

            /* User clicked the left arrow. */

            case SB_LINEUP:
                xInc = -1;
                break;

            /* User clicked the right arrow. */

            case SB_LINEDOWN:
                xInc = 1;
                break;

            /* User dragged the scroll box. */

            case SB_THUMBTRACK:
                xInc = HIWORD(wParam) - xPos;
                break;

            default:
                xInc = 0;

        }

        /*
         * If applying the horizontal scrolling increment does not
         * take the scrolling position out of the scrolling range,
         * increment the scrolling position, adjust the position
         * of the scroll box, and update the window.
         */

        if (xInc = max (-xPos, min (xInc, xMax - xPos))) {
            xPos += xInc;
            ScrollWindow (hwnd, -xChar * xInc, 0,
                (CONST RECT *) NULL, (CONST RECT *) NULL);
            SetScrollPos (hwnd, SB_HORZ, xPos, TRUE);
            UpdateWindow (hwnd);
        }

        return 0;
```

```
case WM_VSCROLL:
        switch(LOWORD (wParam)) {

        /* User clicked the shaft above the scroll box. */

        case SB_PAGEUP:
            yInc = min(-1, -yClient / yChar);
            break;

        /* User clicked the shaft below the scroll box. */

        case SB_PAGEDOWN:
            yInc = max(1, yClient / yChar);
            break;

        /* User clicked the top arrow. */

        case SB_LINEUP:
            yInc = -1;
            break;

        /* User clicked the bottom arrow. */

        case SB_LINEDOWN:
            yInc = 1;
            break;

        /* User dragged the scroll box. */

        case SB_THUMBTRACK:
            yInc = HIWORD(wParam) - yPos;
            break;

        default:
            yInc = 0;

        }

        /*
         * If applying the vertical scrolling increment does not
         * take the scrolling position out of the scrolling range,
         * increment the scrolling position, adjust the position
         * of the scroll box, and update the window. UpdateWindow
         * sends the WM_PAINT message.
         */

        if (yInc = max(-yPos, min(yInc, yMax - yPos))) {
            yPos += yInc;
            ScrollWindow(hwnd, 0, -yChar * yInc,
```

```
                    (CONST RECT *) NULL, (CONST RECT *) NULL);
                SetScrollPos(hwnd, SB_VERT, yPos, TRUE);
                UpdateWindow(hwnd);
            }

        return 0;
```

14.2.3 Scrolling a Bitmap

This section describes changes you can make to an application's main window procedure to enable the user to scroll a bitmap. The example in Section 14.2.3.5, "Example of Scrolling a Bitmap," includes a menu item that copies the screen contents to a bitmap and displays the bitmap in the client area.

The example also processes the WM_HSCROLL and WM_VSCROLL messages generated by the scroll bars so that the user may scroll the bitmap horizontally and vertically. Unlike the example for scrolled text, the bitmap example employs the **BitBlt** function to draw the invalid portion of the client area.

14.2.3.1 Processing the WM_CREATE Message

When the WM_CREATE message is processed, the variables required for scrolling are initialized. Then the **CreateCompatibleDC** function is used to create a compatible device context (DC), the **CreateBitmap** function is used to create a bitmap, and the **SelectObject** function is used to select the bitmap for the device context. Note that a compatible DC is also known as a memory DC.

The device-specific information about the display device is retrieved. If a compatible DC is created for the screen, as in the example, the **GetDeviceCaps** function can be used to get this information. The information includes the number of adjacent color bits per pixel, the number of color planes, and the height and width of the DC.

14.2.3.2 Processing the WM_SIZE Message

Processing of the WM_SIZE message requires adjusting the scrolling range and position, so it reflects the dimensions of the client area and the bitmap that will be displayed.

The **SetScrollRange** function sets the minimum and maximum position values for a scroll bar. The **SetScrollPos** function adjusts the scroll box to reflect the scrolling position.

14.2.3.3 Processing the WM_HSCROLL and WM_VSCROLL Messages

When the WM_HSCROLL and WM_VSCROLL messages are processed, the scroll bar notification code is examined and the scrolling position is set to a new value that reflects the scrolling action of the user. If the scrolling position is within the scrolling range, the window is scrolled to the new position by using the **ScrollWindow** function. The position of the scroll box is then adjusted by using the **SetScrollPos** function.

After a window is scrolled, part of its client area is made invalid. To ensure that the invalid region is updated, the **UpdateWindow** function is used to generate a WM_PAINT message.

The following figure shows the client area before the **ScrollWindow** function is called.

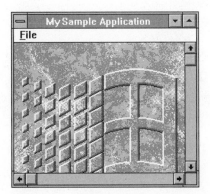

The next figure shows the same client area after the operating system has processed the **ScrollWindow** function.

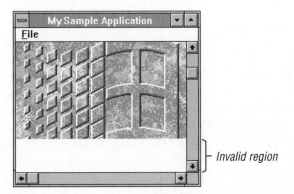

When processing the WM_PAINT message, an application must repaint the invalid region at the bottom of the client area.

14.2.3.4 Processing the WM_PAINT Message

When scrolling or resizing the client area, the example uses the **BitBlt** function to copy the appropriate portion of the bitmap to the invalid portion of the client area.

The following figure shows the client area after the application has processed the WM_PAINT message and called the **BitBlt** function to repaint the invalid region.

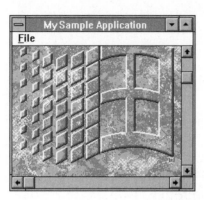

14.2.3.5 Example of Scrolling a Bitmap

The following example enables the user to capture the screen contents into a bitmap and scroll the bitmap in the client area.

```
HDC hdc;
PAINTSTRUCT ps;

/* These variables are required by BitBlt. */

static HDC hdcWin;              /* window DC                      */
static HDC hdcScreen;           /* DC for entire screen           */
static HDC hdcScreenCompat;     /* memory DC for screen           */
static HBITMAP hbmpCompat;      /* bitmap handle for old DC       */
static BITMAP bmp;              /* bitmap data structure          */
static BOOL fBlt;               /* TRUE if BitBlt occurred        */
static BOOL fScroll;            /* TRUE if scrolling occurred     */
static BOOL fSize;              /* TRUE if fBlt & WM_SIZE         */

/* These variables are required for horizontal scrolling. */

static int xMinScroll;          /* minimum horizontal scroll value */
static int xCurrentScroll;      /* current horizontal scroll value */
static int xMaxScroll;          /* maximum horizontal scroll value */

/* These variables are required for vertical scrolling. */

static int yMinScroll;          /* minimum vertical scroll value   */
```

```
static int yCurrentScroll;    /* current vertical scroll value  */
static int yMaxScroll;        /* maximum vertical scroll value  */

switch (uMsg) {
    case WM_CREATE:

        /*
         * Create a normal DC and a memory DC for the entire
         * screen. The normal DC provides a snapshot of the
         * screen contents. The memory DC keeps a copy of this
         * snapshot in the associated bitmap.
         */

        hdcScreen = CreateDC("DISPLAY", (LPCSTR) NULL,
            (LPCSTR) NULL, (CONST DEVMODE *) NULL);
        hdcScreenCompat = CreateCompatibleDC(hdcScreen);

        /*
         * Retrieve the metrics for the bitmap associated with the
         * regular device context.
         */

        bmp.bmBitsPixel =
            (BYTE) GetDeviceCaps(hdcScreen, BITSPIXEL);
        bmp.bmPlanes = (BYTE) GetDeviceCaps(hdcScreen, PLANES);
        bmp.bmWidth = GetDeviceCaps(hdcScreen, HORZRES);
        bmp.bmHeight = GetDeviceCaps(hdcScreen, VERTRES);

        /* The width must be byte-aligned. */

        bmp.bmWidthBytes = ((bmp.bmWidth + 15) &~15)/8;

        /* Create a bitmap for the compatible DC. */

        hbmpCompat = CreateBitmap(bmp.bmWidth, bmp.bmHeight,
            bmp.bmPlanes, bmp.bmBitsPixel, (CONST VOID *) NULL);

        /* Select the bitmap for the compatible DC. */

        SelectObject(hdcScreenCompat, hbmpCompat);

        /* Initialize the flags. */

        fBlt = FALSE;
        fScroll = FALSE;
        fSize = FALSE;

        /* Initialize the horizontal scrolling variables. */

        xMinScroll = 0;
```

```
            xCurrentScroll = 0;
            xMaxScroll = 0;

            /* Initialize the vertical scrolling variables. */

            yMinScroll = 0;
            yCurrentScroll = 0;
            yMaxScroll = 0;

            break;

        case WM_SIZE: {

            int xNewSize;
            int yNewSize;

            xNewSize = LOWORD(lParam);
            yNewSize = HIWORD(lParam);

            if (fBlt)
                fSize = TRUE;

            /*
             * The horizontal scrolling range is defined by
             * (bitmap_width) - (client_width).
             */

            xMaxScroll = max(bmp.bmWidth-xNewSize, 0);
            SetScrollRange(hwnd, SB_HORZ, xMinScroll, xMaxScroll,
                FALSE);

            /*
             * The current horizontal scroll value remains within the
             * horizontal scrolling range.
             */

            xCurrentScroll = min(xCurrentScroll, xMaxScroll);
            SetScrollPos(hwnd, SB_HORZ, xCurrentScroll, TRUE);


            /*
             * The vertical scrolling range is defined by
             * (bitmap_height) - (client_height).
             */

            yMaxScroll = max(bmp.bmHeight - yNewSize, 0);
            SetScrollRange(hwnd, SB_VERT,
                yMinScroll, yMaxScroll, FALSE);

            /*
```

```
              * The current vertical scroll value remains within the
              * vertical scrolling range.
              */

            yCurrentScroll = min(yCurrentScroll, yMaxScroll);
            SetScrollPos(hwnd, SB_VERT, yCurrentScroll, TRUE);

        }

        break;

    case WM_PAINT: {

        PRECT prect;

        hdc = BeginPaint(hwnd, &ps);

        /*
         * If the window has been resized and the user has
         * captured the screen, use the following call to
         * BitBlt to paint the window's client area.
         */

        if (fSize) {
            BitBlt(ps.hdc,
                0, 0,
                bmp.bmWidth, bmp.bmHeight,
                hdcScreenCompat,
                xCurrentScroll, yCurrentScroll,
                SRCCOPY);

            fSize = FALSE;
        }

        /*
         * If scrolling has occurred, use the following call to
         * BitBlt to paint the invalid rectangle.
         *
         * The coordinates of this rectangle are specified in the
         * RECT structure to which prect points.
         *
         * Note that it is necessary to increment the seventh
         * argument (prect->left) by xCurrentScroll and the
         * eighth argument (prect->top) by yCurrentScroll in
         * order to map the correct pixels from the source bitmap.
         */

        if (fScroll) {
            prect = &ps.rcPaint;

            BitBlt(ps.hdc,
```

```
                    prect->left, prect->top,
                    (prect->right - prect->left),
                    (prect->bottom - prect->top),
                    hdcScreenCompat,
                    prect->left + xCurrentScroll,
                    prect->top + yCurrentScroll,
                    SRCCOPY);

            fScroll = FALSE;
        }

        EndPaint(hwnd, &ps);
    }
        break;

    case WM_HSCROLL: {

        int xDelta;     /* xDelta = new_pos - current_pos */
        int xNewPos;    /* new position */
        int yDelta = 0;

        switch (LOWORD(wParam)) {

            /* User clicked the shaft left of the scroll box. */

            case SB_PAGEUP:
                xNewPos = xCurrentScroll - 50;
                break;

            /* User clicked the shaft right of the scroll box. */

            case SB_PAGEDOWN:
                xNewPos = xCurrentScroll + 50;
                break;

            /* User clicked the left arrow. */

            case SB_LINEUP:
                xNewPos = xCurrentScroll - 5;
                break;

            /* User clicked the right arrow. */

            case SB_LINEDOWN:
                xNewPos = xCurrentScroll + 5;
                break;

            /* User dragged the scroll box. */

            case SB_THUMBPOSITION:
```

```
                    xNewPos = HIWORD(wParam);
                    break;

            default:
                    xNewPos = xCurrentScroll;
        }

        /* New position must be between 0 and the screen width. */

        xNewPos = max(0, xNewPos);
        xNewPos = min(xMaxScroll, xNewPos);

        /* If the current position does not change, do not scroll.*/

        if (xNewPos == xCurrentScroll)
            break;

        /* Set the scroll flag to TRUE. */

        fScroll = TRUE;

        /* Determine the amount scrolled (in pixels). */

        xDelta = xNewPos - xCurrentScroll;

        /* Reset the current scroll position. */

        xCurrentScroll = xNewPos;

        /*
         * Scroll the window. (The system repaints most of the
         * client area when ScrollWindow is called; however, it is
         * necessary to call UpdateWindow in order to repaint the
         * rectangle of pixels that were invalidated.)
         */

        ScrollWindow(hwnd, -xDelta, -yDelta, (CONST RECT *) NULL,
            (CONST RECT *) NULL);
        UpdateWindow(hwnd);

        /* Reset the scroll bar. */

        SetScrollPos(hwnd, SB_HORZ, xCurrentScroll, TRUE);
    }
        break;


case WM_VSCROLL: {

    int xDelta = 0;
```

```
int yDelta;      /* yDelta = new_pos - current_pos */
int yNewPos;     /* new position */

switch (LOWORD(wParam)) {

    /* User clicked the shaft above the scroll box. */

    case SB_PAGEUP:
        yNewPos = yCurrentScroll - 50;
        break;

    /* User clicked the shaft below the scroll box. */

    case SB_PAGEDOWN:
        yNewPos = yCurrentScroll + 50;
        break;

    /* User clicked the top arrow. */

    case SB_LINEUP:
        yNewPos = yCurrentScroll - 5;
        break;

    /* User clicked the bottom arrow. */

    case SB_LINEDOWN:
        yNewPos = yCurrentScroll + 5;
        break;

    /* User dragged the scroll box. */

    case SB_THUMBPOSITION:
        yNewPos = HIWORD(wParam);
        break;

    default:
        yNewPos = yCurrentScroll;
}

/* New position must be between 0 and the screen height. */

yNewPos = max(0, yNewPos);
yNewPos = min(yMaxScroll, yNewPos);


/* If the current position does not change, do not scroll.*/

if (yNewPos == yCurrentScroll)
    break;
```

```
          /* Set the scroll flag to TRUE. */

          fScroll = TRUE;

          /* Determine the amount scrolled (in pixels). */

          yDelta = yNewPos - yCurrentScroll;

          /* Reset the current scroll position. */

          yCurrentScroll = yNewPos;

          /*
           * Scroll the window. (The system repaints most of the
           * client area when ScrollWindow is called; however, it is
           * necessary to call UpdateWindow in order to repaint the
           * rectangle of pixels that were invalidated.)
           */

          ScrollWindow(hwnd, -xDelta, -yDelta, (CONST RECT *) NULL,
              (CONST RECT *) NULL);
          UpdateWindow(hwnd);

          /* Reset the scroll bar. */

          SetScrollPos(hwnd, SB_VERT, yCurrentScroll, TRUE);
      }
      break;

  case WM_COMMAND: /* uMsg: command from app. menu */
      switch(wParam) {
          case IDM_STC:

              /*
               * Copy the contents of the current screen
               * into the compatible DC.
               */

              BitBlt(hdcScreenCompat, 0, 0, bmp.bmWidth,
                  bmp.bmHeight, hdcScreen, 0, 0, SRCCOPY);

              /*
               * Copy the compatible DC to the client area.
               */

              hdcWin = GetDC(hwnd);

              BitBlt(hdcWin, 0, 0, bmp.bmWidth, bmp.bmHeight,
                  hdcScreenCompat, 0, 0, SRCCOPY);
```

```
                              ReleaseDC(hwnd, hdcWin);

                              fBlt = TRUE;
                              break;

                     default:
                              return (DefWindowProc(hwnd, uMsg,
                                   wParam, lParam));
                 }
                 break;
```

14.2.4 Creating a Keyboard Interface for a Standard Scroll Bar

Although a scroll bar control provides a built-in keyboard interface, a standard scroll bar does not. To implement a keyboard interface for a standard scroll bar, a window procedure must process the WM_KEYDOWN message and examine the virtual-key code specified by the *wParam* parameter. If the virtual-key code corresponds to an arrow key, the window procedure sends itself a WM_HSCROLL or WM_VSCROLL message with the *wParam* parameter set to the appropriate scroll bar notification code. For example, when the user presses the UP ARROW key, the window procedure receives a WM_KEYDOWN message with *wParam* equal to VK_UP. In response, the window procedure sends itself a WM_VSCROLL message with the low-order word of *wParam* set to the SB_LINEUP notification code.

The following example shows how to include a keyboard interface for a standard scroll bar.

```
WORD wScrollNotify = 0xFFFF;

    .
    .
    .

case WM_KEYDOWN:
    switch (wParam) {
        case VK_UP:
            wScrollNotify = SB_LINEUP;
            break;

        case VK_PRIOR:
            wScrollNotify = SB_PAGEUP;
            break;

        case VK_NEXT:
            wScrollNotify = SB_PAGEDOWN;
            break;
```

```
            case VK_DOWN:
                wScrollNotify = SB_LINEDOWN;
                break;

            case VK_HOME:
                wScrollNotify = SB_TOP;
                break;

            case VK_END:
                wScrollNotify = SB_BOTTOM;
                break;
        }

        if (wScrollNotify != -1)
            SendMessage(hwnd, WM_VSCROLL,
                MAKELONG(wScrollNotify, 0), 0L);


        break;
        .
        .
        .
```

14.3 Functions and Messages

Following are the functions and messages used with scroll bars.

Functions

EnableScrollBar
ScrollWindowEx
GetScrollPos
SetScrollPos
GetScrollRange
SetScrollRange
ScrollDC
ShowScrollBar
ScrollWindow

Messages

SBM_ENABLE_ARROWS
SBM_GETPOS
SBM_GETRANGE
SBM_SETPOS
SBM_SETRANGE
SBM_SETRANGEREDRAW

WM_CTLCOLORSCROLLBAR
WM_HSCROLL
WM_VSCROLL

CHAPTER 15

Static Controls

15.1 About Static Controls

Microsoft ® Windows ™ provides dialog boxes and controls to support communications between an application and the user. A *static control* is a control that enables an application to provide the user with certain types of text and graphics that require no response. Applications often use static controls to label other controls or to separate a group of controls. Although static controls are child windows, they cannot be selected. Therefore, they cannot receive the keyboard focus, cannot have a keyboard interface, and cannot receive user input. A static control does not send messages to its parent window. Static controls belong to the STATIC window class.

Although static controls can be used in overlapped, pop-up, and child windows, they are designed for use in dialog boxes, where Windows standardizes their behavior. If a developer uses static controls outside dialog boxes, it increases the risk that the application might behave in a nonstandard fashion. Typically, developers either use static controls in dialog boxes or use window subclassing to create customized static controls.

For more information about dialog boxes, see Chapter 18, "Dialog Boxes." For more information about window classes, see Chapter 3, "Window Classes." For more information about window subclassing, see Chapter 4, "Window Procedures."

15.1.1 Static Control Types and Styles

Windows provides four types of static controls: rectangle, frame, text, and icon. Each type has one or more styles.

15.1.1.1 Rectangle

A rectangle static control displays a rectangle filled with color in one of three styles: black, gray, or white. These styles are defined by the constants SS_BLACKRECT, SS_GRAYRECT, and SS_WHITERECT. The following figure shows the three rectangle styles. For clarity, the illustration shows the white rectangle on a black background; the actual display does not contain a black rectangle.

SS_BLACKRECT   SS_GRAYRECT   SS_WHITERECT

15.1.1.2 Frame

A frame static control displays a colored frame in one of three styles: black, gray, or white. These styles are defined by the constants SS_BLACKFRAME, SS_GRAYFRAME, and SS_WHITEFRAME. The following figure shows the three frame styles. For clarity, the illustration shows the white frame on a black background; the actual display does not contain a black rectangle.

SS_BLACKFRAME   SS_GRAYFRAME   SS_WHITEFRAME

15.1.1.3 Text

A text static control displays text in a rectangle in one of five styles: centered, left aligned with word wrap, left aligned without word wrap, right aligned, or "simple." These styles are defined by the constants SS_CENTER, SS_LEFT, SS_LEFTNOWORDWRAP, SS_RIGHT, and SS_SIMPLE, respectively. Windows rearranges the text in these controls in predefined ways, except for "simple" text, which is not rearranged. The following figure shows three text styles: centered, left aligned, and right aligned. For clarity, the illustration shows the text inside a box; the actual display does not contain a box.

```
        SS_CENTER
SS_LEFT
            SS_RIGHT
```

An application can change the text in a text static control at any time by using the **SetWindowText** function or the WM_SETTEXT message.

The system displays as much text as it can in the static control and clips whatever does not fit. Retrieve the font metrics for the text to calculate an appropriate size for the control. For more information about fonts and font metrics, see Chapter 35, "Fonts and Text."

15.1.1.4 Icon

An icon static control displays an icon in an icon control. There is one icon style, defined by the constant SS_ICON. An application can use this type of control only in dialog boxes. An icon is also the only type of static control that can receive messages from its parent window. The following figure shows a sample icon.

15.1.1.5 Static Control Styles

Many developers develop dialog boxes by using stand-alone tools and so may not need to specify static control styles. However, if a developer uses the **CreateWindow** or **CreateWindowEx** function to create a static control for an application, the developer must use the following constants to define the style.

Style	Description
SS_BLACKFRAME	Specifies a box with a frame drawn in the same color as the window frames. This color is black in the default Windows color scheme.
SS_BLACKRECT	Specifies a rectangle filled with the current window frame color. This color is black in the default Windows color scheme.
SS_CENTER	Specifies a simple rectangle and centers the given text in the rectangle. The text is formatted before it is displayed. Words that extend past the end of a line are automatically wrapped to the beginning of the next centered line.
SS_GRAYFRAME	Specifies a box with a frame drawn with the same color as the screen background (desktop). This color is gray in the default Windows color scheme.
SS_GRAYRECT	Specifies a rectangle filled with the current screen background color. This color is gray in the default Windows color scheme.
SS_ICON	Specifies an icon displayed in the dialog box. The given text is the name of an icon (not a filename) defined elsewhere in the resource file. The style ignores the *nWidth* and *nHeight* parameters; the icon automatically sizes itself.
SS_LEFT	Specifies a simple rectangle and left-aligns the given text in the rectangle. The text is formatted before it is displayed. Words that extend past the end of a line are automatically wrapped to the beginning of the next left-aligned line.
SS_LEFTNOWORDWRAP	Specifies a simple rectangle and left-aligns the given text in the rectangle. Tabs are expanded but words are not wrapped. Text that extends past the end of a line is clipped.
SS_NOPREFIX	Prevents interpretation of any ampersand (&) characters in the control's text as accelerator prefix characters. These are displayed with the ampersand removed and the next character in the string underlined. This static control style may be included with any of the defined static controls.
	An application can combine SS_NOPREFIX with other styles by using the bitwise OR (|) operator. This can be useful when filenames or other strings that may contain an ampersand (&) must be displayed in a static control in a dialog box.

SS_RIGHT	Specifies a simple rectangle and right-aligns the given text in the rectangle. The text is formatted before it is displayed. Words that extend past the end of a line are automatically wrapped to the beginning of the next right-aligned line.
SS_SIMPLE	Specifies a simple rectangle and displays a single line of left-aligned text in the rectangle. The text line cannot be shortened or altered in any way. The control's parent window or dialog box must not process the WM_CTLCOLOR message.
SS_WHITEFRAME	Specifies a box with a frame drawn with the same color as the window backgrounds. This color is white in the default Windows color scheme.
SS_WHITERECT	Specifies a rectangle filled with the current window background color. This color is white in the default Windows color scheme.

For more information about the colors used by static controls, see Section 15.1.3, "Static Control Color Messages."

15.1.2 Messages for Icons

An application can retrieve the handle of the current icon or change it by sending a message to the icon control using the **SendDlgItemMessage** function. An icon is the only static control that can receive messages from its parent window. The following table describes these messages.

Message	Response
STM_GETICON	Returns the handle of the icon associated with the icon control.
STM_SETICON	Associates an icon with an icon control. This message returns the handle of the icon previously associated with the icon control (or zero, if an error occurs).

15.1.3 Static Control Color Messages

Windows provides default color values for static controls. The system sends a WM_CTLCOLORSTATIC message to a static control's parent window before the control is drawn. This message contains a handle of the static control's device context (DC) and a handle of the child window. The parent window can use these handles to change the static control's text and background colors. The following table shows the default static control color messages.

Value	Use
COLOR_BACKGROUND	For coloring black rectangles and frames
COLOR_WINDOW	For coloring gray rectangles and frames
COLOR_WINDOWFRAME	For coloring white rectangles and frames
COLOR_WINDOWTEXT	For coloring text in text controls

An application can obtain the default values for these colors by calling the **GetSysColor** function or set the color values by calling the **SetSysColor** function. For more information about system colors, see Chapter 67, "System Information." For more information about how colors are used with controls, see Chapter 9, "Controls."

Portability Issue In Windows NT, the WM_CTLCOLOR message has been replaced by the set of control color messages. For applications written for earlier versions of Windows, the developer must modify the code for processing the WM_CTLCOLOR message when porting the application to Windows NT.

15.1.4 Default Message Processing

The window procedure for the predefined static control window class carries out default processing for all messages that the static control procedure does not process. When the static control returns FALSE for any message, the predefined window procedure checks the messages and carries out the default action described in the following table. In the table, a text static control is a static control with the SS_LEFT, SS_CENTER, SS_RIGHT, SS_SIMPLE, or SS_LEFTNOWORDWRAP style.

Message	Default action
STM_GETICON	Returns the handle of the icon if the static control is an icon; otherwise, returns zero.
STM_SETICON	Sets a new icon for the static control; invalidates the rectangle to draw the new icon; returns a handle of the previous icon.
WM_CREATE	Loads the icon and sizes the window to the icon size, for icon controls. Takes no action for other static controls.
WM_DESTROY	Frees and destroys any icon, for icon controls. Takes no action for other static controls.
WM_ENABLE	Repaints visible static controls.
WM_GETDLGCODE	Returns DLGC_STATIC.
WM_GETFONT	Returns the handle of the font for text static controls.

WM_GETTEXT	Returns 2 if the control is an icon that was set by using the STM_SETICON message; otherwise, copies the text of the control into an application-defined buffer.
WM_GETTEXTLENGTH	Returns the length, in characters, of the text for a text static control.
WM_NCCREATE	Sets the window text for text static controls; otherwise, returns TRUE.
WM_NCDESTROY	Takes no action if the control style is SS_LEFT, SS_CENTER, SS_RIGHT, or SS_SIMPLE; otherwise, calls the **DefWindowProc** function.
WM_NCHITTEST	Returns HTTRANSPARENT.
WM_PAINT	Repaints the control.
WM_SETFONT	Sets the font and repaints for text static controls.
WM_SETTEXT	Sets the text and repaints for text static controls.

The predefined window procedure passes all other messages to **DefWindowProc** for default processing.

15.2 Using Static Controls

The following code example uses a timer and the STM_SETICON message to animate an icon in a dialog box. The icon handles and the icon identifier (IDI_ICON) are defined in a global header file.

```
LRESULT APIENTRY StaticProc(hDlg, message, wParam, lParam)
HWND hDlg;       /* window handle of dialog box          */
UINT message;    /* type of message                      */
UINT wParam;     /* message-specific information          */
LONG lParam;
{
    UINT idTimer = 1;
    static UINT i;

    static HICON aIcons[11];

    switch (message) {
        case WM_INITDIALOG: /* initialize dialog box */
            i = 0;

            /* Load icons("hinst" is defined globally). */

            hiconOne    = LoadIcon(hinst, "OneIco");
            aIcons[i]   = hiconOne;
            hiconTwo    = LoadIcon(hinst, "TwoIco");
            aIcons[++i] = hiconTwo;
```

```
            .  /* Continue with the remaining icons. */
            .

        i = 0;

         /*
          * Use STM_SETICON to associate an icon with the
          * IDI_ICON identifier.
          */

        SendDlgItemMessage(hDlg, /* dialog box window handle */
            IDI_ICON,                /* icon identifier          */
            STM_SETICON,             /* message to send          */
            (WPARAM) aIcons[i++],    /* icon handle              */
            0);                      /* not used                 */

        /* Set a timer for 50-millisecond intervals. */

        SetTimer(hDlg, idTimer, 50, (TIMERPROC) NULL);
        return TRUE;


    case WM_TIMER:

         /*
          * Use STM_SETICON to associate a new icon with
          * the IDI_ICON identifier whenever a WM_TIMER
          * message is received.
          */

        SendDlgItemMessage(hDlg, /* dialog box window handle */
            IDI_ICON,                /* icon identifier          */
            STM_SETICON,             /* message to send          */
            (WPARAM) aIcons[i++],    /* new icon handle          */
            0);                      /* not used                 */
        if (i == 10)
            i = 0;

        break;

    case WM_COMMAND:
        if (wParam == IDOK
            || wParam == IDCANCEL) {
            EndDialog(hDlg, TRUE);
            return TRUE;
        }
        return 0;

    case WM_DESTROY: /* clean up  */
```

```
                KillTimer(hDlg, idTimer);
                DeleteObject(hiconOne);
                DeleteObject(hiconTwo);
                    .
                    . /* Continue with the remaining icons. */
                    .

                return 0;
        }
        return FALSE;
            UNREFERENCED_PARAMETER(lParam);
    }
```

15.3 Messages

Following are the messages used with static controls. (STM_GETICON and STM_SETICON are used only with icons.)

STM_GETICON
STM_SETICON
WM_CTLCOLORSTATIC

CHAPTER 16

Menus

16.1 About Menus

A *menu* is one or more lists of application commands. Each command, which is represented by a text string or bitmap, is called a *menu item*. By using the mouse or the keyboard to choose a menu item, the user directs the application to perform the command associated with that menu item. When the user chooses a menu item, Microsoft ® Windows ™ sends the application a command message that indicates which menu item the user chose.

This chapter describes menus and explains how to use them in a Win32 application.

16.1.1 Menu Bars and Pop-up Menus

The menus in an application written for Microsoft Windows are arranged hierarchically. A *menu bar* (sometimes called a top-level menu) resides at the uppermost level of the hierarchy; the lower levels consist of *pop-up menus* (also known as submenus).

The items in a menu bar represent the main categories of commands provided by an application. Selecting an item from the menu bar typically activates a pop-up menu whose items correspond to the commands in a given category. For example, a menu bar might contain a File item that, when the user selects it, activates a pop-up menu with menu items such as New, Open, Save, and so on. The following illustration shows the menu bar and the pop-up menu for the file command in Windows Notepad.

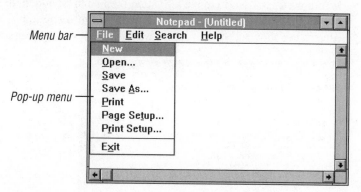

Only an overlapped or pop-up window can contain a menu bar; a child window cannot contain one. A menu bar is always visible. If the window has a title bar, Windows positions the menu bar just below it. By contrast, a pop-up menu is not visible until the user selects a menu item that activates it. When this menu is displayed, it is attached to the title bar.

Every menu must have an owner window. Windows sends messages to a menu's owner window when the user selects the menu or chooses a command from the menu. These messages are described in Section 16.1.9, "Menu Messages."

16.1.1.1 Floating Pop-up Menus

Windows provides a special type of pop-up menu called a *floating pop-up menu*. A floating pop-up menu is not attached to the menu bar; it can appear anywhere on the screen. An application typically associates a floating pop-up menu with a portion of a window such as the client area or with a specific object such as an icon.

A floating pop-up menu remains hidden until the user selects it (for example, by clicking the appropriate screen location with the mouse.) A floating pop-up menu is typically displayed at the position of the caret or mouse cursor.

16.1.1.2 The System Menu

A *System menu* (also known as the Control menu) is a pop-up menu defined and managed almost exclusively by the system. It is represented by a small box containing a horizontal line that is displayed at the left end of the title bar. When the user clicks the box, Windows displays the System menu. Windows also displays the System menu when the user clicks the icon of a minimized application.

A System menu provides a standard set of menu items the user can choose to change a window's size or position, close the application, or activate the Windows Task List. Items in a System menu can be added, deleted, and modified, but most applications just use the standard set of menu items. The following illustration shows a System Menu with the standard menu items.

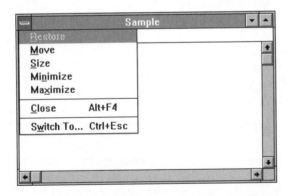

An overlapped, pop-up, or child window can have a System menu. It is uncommon for an overlapped or pop-up window not to include a System menu.

When the user chooses a command from a System menu, Windows sends a WM_SYSCOMMAND message to the menu's owner window. In most applications, the window procedure does not process messages from a System menu. Instead, it simply passes the messages to the **DefWindowProc** function for system-default processing of the message. If a command is added to a System menu, the window procedure must process the command.

16.1.2 Menu Handles

The system generates a unique handle for each menu. A *menu handle* is a value of the **HMENU** type. An application must specify a menu handle in many of the Windows menu functions. The developer receives the handle of a menu bar when he or she creates the menu or loads a menu resource. For information about creating menus and loading menus, see Section 16.1.6, "Menu Creation."

The **GetMenu** or **GetSubMenu** function is used to retrieve the handle of a menu that has been created or loaded. **GetMenu** returns the handle of the menu bar assigned to the specified window. **GetSubMenu** returns the handle of a pop-up menu within the specified menu bar or pop-up menu. The **GetSystemMenu** function is used to retrieve the handle of a window's System menu.

16.1.3 Class Menus

When registering a window class, the developer can specify a default menu for that class. This default menu is known as the *class menu*. To specify a class menu, the developer must assign the name of the menu, as given in your application's resource-definition file, to the **lpszMenuName** member of the **WNDCLASS** structure used to register the window class. After the window class has been registered, each window of that class will have the specified class menu. The developer can override the class menu by specifying the handle of a different menu when creating a window of that class. For more information about window classes, see Chapter 3, "Window Classes."

16.1.4 Menu Items

There are two kinds of menu items in Win32 applications: *command items* and *pop-up items*. When the user chooses a command item, Windows sends a WM_COMMAND or WM_SYSCOMMAND message to the window procedure of the menu's owner window. A command item on a System menu generates a WM_SYSCOMMAND message; command items in other menus generate WM_COMMAND messages. When the user selects a pop-up item, Windows displays a pop-up menu but doesn't send a command message to the window procedure.

As a rule, menu items in a menu bar consist of pop-up items; menu items in a pop-up menu consist of command items. Because a pop-up menu can contain pop-up items, pop-up menus can originate from within pop-up menus, producing a cascading effect as shown in the following illustration.

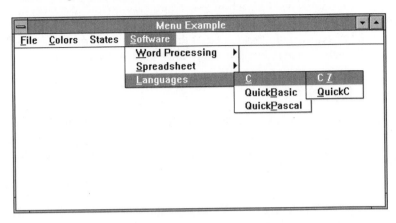

When a pop-up item is included in a pop-up menu, Windows automatically adds a small arrow to the right of the menu item's text string or bitmap (see the Word Processing and Spreadsheet items in the preceding illustration). The arrow is a visual cue to the user that Windows will display another pop-up menu when the item is selected.

16.1.4.1 Menu-Item Identifier

Each command item has an identifier associated with it. An identifier is an application-defined integer value that Windows sends to the window procedure of the menu's owner window when the user chooses a command item. Windows sends the identifier as part of a WM_COMMAND message. The window procedure examines the identifier to determine the source of the message, and then processes the message accordingly.

A menu identifier must be a value from 0 to 65,535, even though it is a 32-bit integer. This is because the WM_COMMAND message passes a menu identifier as the low-order word of its *wParam* parameter.

A pop-up item has no identifier. A pop-up item does not need an identifier, because Windows does not send a WM_COMMAND message when the user selects a pop-up item. Instead, Windows activates the pop-up menu associated with the pop-up item.

16.1.4.2 Checked and Unchecked Menu Items

A menu item can be either checked or unchecked. When a menu item is checked, Windows uses a bitmap to display a check mark to the left of the menu item. When the menu item is unchecked, Windows does not display the check mark. Only menu items in a pop-up menu can be checked; menu items in a menu bar can not be checked.

An application typically uses check marks to indicate menu options that are in effect. For example, when the user selects paragraph formatting options from a menu in a word processing application, the application places check marks next to the selected options. The following illustration shows check marks next to the Left and Single Space options in a word processing application's Paragraph menu.

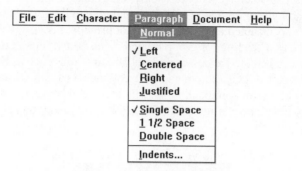

A check mark attribute controls whether a menu item is checked or not. A menu item's check mark attribute can be set by using the **CheckMenuItem** function. The **GetMenuState** function is used to determine whether a menu item is currently checked or unchecked.

Windows provides a default bitmap for displaying check marks. The developer, however, can substitute other bitmaps and direct Windows to use them instead of the default. Windows requires, however, that these check mark bitmaps have the same dimensions as the default check mark bitmap. The **GetMenuCheckMarkDimensions** function can be used to retrieve the default dimensions.

Two bitmaps can be associated with each menu item: one for when the menu item is checked and another for when it is unchecked. The **SetMenuItemBitmaps** function can be used to associate bitmaps with a menu item.

The developer can either provide check mark bitmaps as bitmap resources or create the bitmaps at run time by using graphic device interface (GDI) bitmap functions. A bitmap resource, however, isn't suitable for all video resolutions and aspect ratios, so the bitmap must be sized appropriately. The check mark bitmaps can be either monochrome or color. However, on a color screen the bitmap colors are inverted when the menu item is highlighted, and this result may be undesirable. For more information about bitmaps, see Chapter 29, "Bitmaps."

16.1.4.3 Enabled, Disabled, and Grayed Menu Items

A menu item can be enabled, disabled, or grayed. By default, a menu item is enabled. When the user chooses an enabled menu item, Windows sends a command message to the corresponding window procedure or displays the corresponding pop-up menu, depending on whether the menu item is a command item or a pop-up item.

When menu items are not available to the user, they should be disabled or grayed. Disabled or grayed menu items do not generate a command message or display a pop-up menu when a user chooses them. Typically, applications gray an unavailable menu item to provide a visual clue to the user that a command is not available. A disabled menu item does not provide this visual clue. A disabled item can serve as a heading for group related menu items. (For example, a Save heading can be listed and then a series of commands such as Save File, Save All, and Save As). A grayed item can be used when an action is not appropriate. (For example, the Print command in the File menu can be grayed when the system does not have a printer installed.) The following illustration shows grayed items in an Edit menu.

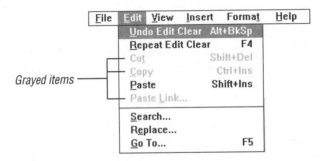

The **EnableMenuItem** function is used to enable, disable, or gray a menu item, and the **GetMenuState** function is used to determine whether a menu item is enabled, disabled, or grayed.

16.1.4.4 Menu-Item Separators and Line Breaks

Windows provides a special type of menu item, called a separator, that consists of a horizontal line. A separator menu item can be used in a pop-up menu to divide a menu into groups of related items. A separator item cannot be used in a menu bar. The user cannot select a separator menu item, and a separator does not send command messages to the window procedure.

When a menu bar contains more items than will fit on one line, Windows automatically breaks it into two or more lines. You can force a line break at a specific item on a menu bar by assigning the MF_MENUBREAK flag to the item. Windows places that item and all remaining items on a new line.

The MF_MENUBREAK and MF_MENUBARBREAK flags are used to divide items in a pop-up menu into multiple columns. When MF_MENUBREAK flag is assigned to an item, Windows places it and all remaining items in a new column. The MF_MENUBARBREAK flag creates a similar effect, except Windows includes a vertical line in the menu to separate the new column from the old one.

16.1.4.5 Menu-Item Position

Windows assigns an integer position value to each item on a menu and uses the value to keep track of each item's position in the menu. Position values are zero-based; that is, the first item on a menu occupies position zero, the next position one, and so on. In a menu bar, the leftmost menu item is considered the first item, so it occupies position zero; in a pop-up menu, the uppermost menu item occupies position zero. Windows assigns position values to menu-item separators. The following illustration shows the position values of both items and separators in a menu bar and a pop-up menu.

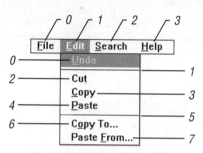

A number of functions are used to add an item to a menu, delete an item from a menu, or modify an existing item on a menu. When one of these functions is called, the item to be modified is identified either by its position value or, if it is a command item, by its identifier. Either the MF_BYPOSITION or MF_BYCOMMAND flag is also specified. For more information about modifying the contents of a menu, see Section 16.1.10, "Menu Modifications."

16.1.4.6 Highlighted Menu Items

Windows automatically highlights menu items as the user selects them. Highlighting can, however, be explicitly added or removed from a menu item on the menu bar by calling the **HiliteMenuItem** function. This function has no effect on menu items in pop-up menus. When you use **HiliteMenuItem** to highlight a menu item, however, the menu item only appears to be selected; if the user presses the ENTER key, the highlighted item is not chosen.

16.1.4.7 Owner-drawn Menu Items

An application can completely control the appearance of a menu item by using an *owner-drawn item*. Owner-drawn items require an application to take total responsibility for drawing selected (highlighted), checked, and unchecked states. For example, if an application provided a font menu it could draw each menu item by using the corresponding font; the item for roman would be drawn with a roman font, the item for italic would be drawn in italic, and so on.

For information on how to create owner-drawn menu items, see Section 16.2.4, "Creating Owner-drawn Menu Items."

16.1.4.8 Help Item

The developer should provide a standard interface for the user, including a Help item on an application's menu bars. The item should read "Help," and it should be the rightmost item on the menu bar.

16.1.5 Keyboard Access to Menus

Windows provides a standard keyboard interface for menus. You can enhance this interface by including mnemonics and accelerator keys for your menu items. The following three sections describe the standard keyboard interface, mnemonics, and accelerator keys.

16.1.5.1 Standard Keyboard Interface

Windows is designed to work with or without a mouse or other pointing device. Because Windows provides a standard keyboard interface the user can use the keyboard to select menu items. Special code is not needed to support this keyboard interface. An application receives a command message whether a menu item is selected through the keyboard or by using a mouse. The standard keyboard interface processes the following keystrokes.

Keystroke	Action
ALT	Toggles in and out of menu bar mode.
ALT+SPACEBAR	Displays the System menu.
ESC	Exits menu mode.
RIGHT ARROW	Cycles to the next top-level menu item. This keystroke cycles between the application and System menus. If the selected item is in a pop-up menu, the next column in the pop-up menu is selected or the next top-level menu item is selected.
LEFT ARROW	Works like the RIGHT ARROW key, except in the opposite direction. In pop-up menus, this keystroke backs up one column; when the currently selected item is in the far-left column, the previous pop-up menu is selected.
UP or DOWN ARROWS	Activate a pop-up menu when pressed in a top-level menu. When pressed in a pop-up menu, either keystroke selects the next or previous item.

ENTER

Activates a pop-up menu and highlights the first item if an item has a pop-up menu associated with it; otherwise, this keystroke chooses the item as if the user released the mouse button while the item was selected.

Alphabetic character

Selects the first menu item with the specified character as its mnemonic. If the selected item onvokes a pop-up menu, the menu is displayed and the first item is highlighted; otherwise, the item is chosen.

16.1.5.2 Mnemonics

The standard keyboard interface for menus can be enhanced by adding mnemonics to menu items. A mnemonic is a underlined letter in the text of a menu item. When a menu is active, the user can select a menu item by pressing the key that corresponds to the item's underlined letter. The menu bar is active when the user presses and releases the ALT key and the first item on the menu bar is highlighted. A pop-up menu is active when it is displayed.

A mnemonic keystroke for a menu item is created by preceding a character in the item's text string with an ampersand. For example, "&Move" causes Windows to underline the "*M*" character. The following illustration shows the mnemonics in the System menu.

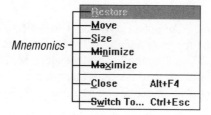

Mnemonics

16.1.5.3 Keyboard Accelerators

In addition to having a mnemonic, a menu item can have a keyboard accelerator associated with it. A keyboard accelerator is different from a mnemonic in that the menu need not be active for the accelerator key to work. Also, a mnemonic is always associated with a menu item, while a keyboard accelerator is usually associated with a menu item, but it does not have to be.

Text to identify the keyboard accelerator is added to the menu-item text string. The accelerator text appear to the right of the menu-item name after a backslash and tab character. For example, "$ClosetF4" represents a Close item with the F4 key as its keyboard accelerator and with C as its mnemonic. For more information on accelerators, see Chapter 17, "Keyboard Accelerators." The following illustration shows accelerators in the System menu.

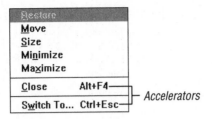

Accelerators

16.1.6 Menu Creation

The developer can use the following methods to create a menu for use in an application:

- Load a menu from a menu-template resource.
- Build a menu from a menu template created at run time.
- Use the menu creation functions to build a menu at run time.

The following sections describe how to use these three methods to create menus.

16.1.6.1 Menu-Template Resources

Most developers implement menus by creating a menu-template resource that is loaded at run time. A menu template defines a menu, including the items in the menu bar and all pop-up menus.

The first step in using a menu-template resource is to define a menu template in the resource-definition file for an application. Then a resource compiler is used to create the resource and add it to the application's executable file. At run time, the **LoadMenu** function is called to load the menu-template resource into memory and to retrieve the handle of the menu. Then a call the **SetMenu** function assigns the menu to a window.

Implementing menus as resources makes an application easier to localize for use in other countries. The resource-definition file is edited and recompiled, and the new resources are added to the application's executable file. For more information on creating a menu resource, see Section 16.2.1, "Using a Menu-Template Resource."

16.1.6.2 Menu Template in Memory

A menu can be created from a menu template that is built in memory at run time. A menu is created from the menu template by passing the address of the **MENUITEMTEMPLATEHEADER** structure to the **LoadMenuIndirect** function. The last member of the **MENUITEMTEMPLATEHEADER** structure specifies the offset of the array of **MENUITEMTEMPLATE** structures. Each member of the array describes a menu item. **LoadMenuIndirect** returns the handle of the menu.

16.1.6.3 Menu-Creation Functions

Another way to create a menu at run time is to use the **CreateMenu** and **CreatePopupMenu** functions to create empty menus. **CreateMenu** creates an empty menu bar; **CreatePopupMenu** creates an empty pop-up menu. Then menu items are added to the menus by using the **AppendMenu** or **InsertMenu** functions.

16.1.7 Menu Display

After a menu has been loaded or created, it must be assigned to a window before Windows can display it. This can be done by creating a class menu (see Section 16.1.3, "Class Menus"), by specifying the handle of the menu as the *hmenu* parameter of the **CreateWindowEx** function, or by calling the **SetMenu** function.

The **TrackPopupMenu** function can be used to display a pop-up menu. To do so, the handle of a pop-up menu is passed to the function. The menu's owner window, the screen position where Windows should display the menu, and the mouse button the user must use to choose an item must also be specified.

16.1.8 Menu Destruction

If a menu is assigned to a window and that window is destroyed, Windows automatically destroys the menu, freeing the menu's handle and the memory occupied by the menu. Windows does not automatically destroy a menu that is not assigned to a window. An application must destroy the unassigned menu by calling the **DestroyMenu** function; otherwise, the menu continues to exist in memory even after the application closes.

16.1.9 Menu Messages

Windows reports menu-related activity by sending messages to the window procedure of the window that owns the menu. The first menu-related message the window procedure receives is WM_SYSCOMMAND. Windows sends this message when the user activates the menu by clicking the menu bar or by pressing a key that activates the menu (for more information, see Section 16.1.5.1, "Standard Keyboard Interface"). The WM_SYSCOMMAND message includes a flag, either SC_KEYMENU or SC_MOUSEMENU, that indicates the hardware device used to activate the menu.

Next, Windows sends the WM_INITMENU message to the window procedure before Windows displays any pop-up menus, so an application can modify the menus before the user sees them. Windows sends the WM_INITMENU message only once per menu activation.

When the user selects a pop-up item, Windows sends the owner window the WM_INITMENUPOPUP message before displaying the pop-up menu. This message gives the application a second opportunity to modify the pop-up menu before it is displayed.

Each time the user moves the highlighting from one item to another, Windows sends a WM_MENUSELECT message to the window procedure of the menu's owner window. This message identifies the currently selected menu item. Many applications provide an information area at the bottom of their main windows and use this message to display additional information about the selected menu item.

Windows sends a WM_COMMAND message to the window procedure when the user chooses a command item from a menu. The low-order word of the WM_COMMAND message's *wParam* parameter contains the identifier of the chosen item. The window procedure should examine the identifier and process the message accordingly.

16.1.10 Menu Modifications

A number of functions can be used to modify a menu after it has been loaded or created. The **AppendMenu** and **InsertMenu** functions are used to add items to a menu. **AppendMenu** appends a menu item to the end of a menu; **InsertMenu** inserts a menu item at a specified position in a menu. Both functions permit the attributes of the menu item to be specified, including whether the menu item is enabled, checked, grayed, and so on.

The **ModifyMenu** function is used to change the appearance or attributes of an existing menu item. For example, the text string or bitmap of a menu item can be enabled, disabled, grayed, checked, or unchecked. **ModifyMenu** replaces the specified menu item with a new item.

The **DeleteMenu** or **RemoveMenu** functions are used to delete a menu item from a menu. If the item being deleted is a pop-up item, **DeleteMenu** deletes the associated pop-up menu, discarding the menu handle and freeing the memory used by the pop-up menu. The **RemoveMenu** function deletes a menu item, but if the item activates a pop-up menu, it does not destroy the pop-up menu or its handle, allowing the menu to be reused.

After a menu bar has been modified, the **DrawMenuBar** function must be called to redraw the menu bar. Otherwise, the modifications will not appear until Windows redraws the owner window.

16.2 Using Menus

This section explains how to perform the following tasks:

- Use a menu-template resource.
- Create a floating pop-up menu.
- Use menu-item bitmaps.
- Create owner-drawn menu items.
- Use bitmaps to display custom check marks.

16.2.1 Using a Menu-Template Resource

The developer typically includes a menu in an application by defining a menu template in the application's resource-definition file and then loading the menu at run time. This section describes how to define and load a menu-template resource.

16.2.1.1 Defining a Menu-Template Resource

A menu-template resource represents an application's menu bar and all the related pop-up menus. The **MENU** statement marks the beginning of a menu template and provides the identifier used to load the menu. The identifier must be either a unique string or a unique integer.

The **POPUP** statement defines a pop-up item. A top-level pop-up item appears in the menu bar and activates a pop-up menu when it is selected. A nested pop-up item appears in a pop-up menu and activates a cascaded pop-up menu when it is selected.

The **MENUITEM** statement defines a command item. A top-level command item appears in the menu bar and generates a command message when it is selected. A nested command item appears in a pop-up menu and also generates a command message.

To define a string for a pop-up item or command item, enclose it in quotation marks and place it immediately to the right of the **POPUP** statement. You should include an ampersand (&) in the string to specify the mnemonic for the menu item. You should also include a keyboard accelerator, if applicable, and use the "\t" escape sequence to separate the accelerator text from the menu-item text.

The command identifier for a command item must appear immediately to the right of the menu-item text string. Use a named constant as the identifier and define the constant in your application's header file.

A number of options control the appearance and behavior of pop-up and command items. You can specify these options to the right of the menu-item text string (for a pop-up item) or to the right of the menu-item identifier (for a command item). The following menu-item options can be specified:

Option	Description
CHECKED	Item has a check mark next to it. This option is not valid for a top-level pop-up menu.
GRAYED	Item is disabled and its text string appears on the menu in a dimmed (grayed) shade of the menu-text color.
INACTIVE	Item is disabled and its text string appears in the normal menu-text color.
MENUBARBREAK	Same as **MENUBREAK** except that in pop-up menus, it separates the new column from the old column with a vertical line.
MENUBREAK	Menu-bar item is placed on a new line. An item on a pop-up menu is placed in a new column with no dividing line between the columns.

You can use the bitwise OR operator to combine these options. The **INACTIVE** and **GRAYED** options cannot be used together.

Here is a resource-definition file defining a menu bar with three pop-up items: File, Edit, and Font. The File and Edit pop-up items each activates a pop-up menu containing several command items. The Font pop-up menu has two other pop-up menus (Style and Size) within it.

```
MyMenuResource MENU
BEGIN
    POPUP "&File"
    BEGIN
        MENUITEM "&Open...",            IDM_FI_OPEN
        MENUITEM "&Close\tF3",          IDM_FI_CLOSE, GRAYED
        MENUITEM "&Quit",               IDM_FI_QUIT
        MENUITEM SEPARATOR
        MENUITEM "&About Sample...",    IDM_FI_ABOUT
    END

    POPUP "&Edit"
    BEGIN
        MENUITEM "&Undo",    IDM_ED_UNDO, GRAYED
        MENUITEM SEPARATOR
        MENUITEM "&Cut",     IDM_ED_CUT
        MENUITEM "C&opy",    IDM_ED_COPY
        MENUITEM "&Paste",   IDM_ED_PASTE
        MENUITEM "C&lear",   IDM_ED_ABOUT
    END

    POPUP "Fo&nt"
    BEGIN
```

```
        POPUP "&Style"
        BEGIN
            MENUITEM "&Regular\tF5",        IDM_FNT_STY_REGULAR
            MENUITEM SEPARATOR
            MENUITEM "&Bold\tCtrl+B",        IDM_FNT_STY_BOLD
            MENUITEM "&Italic\tCtrl+I",      IDM_FNT_STY_ITALIC
            MENUITEM "&Underline\tCtrl+U",   IDM_FNT_STY_ULINE
        END

        POPUP "Si&ze"
        BEGIN
            MENUITEM "10",  IDM_FNT_SZ_10
            MENUITEM "12",  IDM_FNT_SZ_12
            MENUITEM "14",  IDM_FNT_SZ_14
        END

    END
END
```

16.2.1.2 Loading a Menu-Template Resource

You can load a menu-template resource for your application by calling the **LoadMenu** function, specifying the handle of the module that contains the resource and the menu-template's identifier. **LoadMenu** returns a menu handle that you can use to assign the menu to a window. This window becomes the menu's owner window, receiving all the messages generated by the menu.

Use the **SetMenu** function to assign a menu to a window, or specify the menu's handle in the *hmenu* parameter of the **CreateWindowEx** function when you create a window. Another way that you can assign a menu to a window is to specify a menu template when you register a window class. This identifies the menu as the class menu for the given window class. Whenever you create a window of the given class, Windows automatically assigns the given menu to the window.

You can create a class menu by including the identifier of the menu-template resource as the **lpszMenuName** member of a **WNDCLASS** structure and then passing the address of the structure to the **RegisterClass** function.

16.2.1.3 Creating a Class Menu

The following example shows how to create a class menu for an application, how to create a window that uses the class menu, and how to process menu commands in the window procedure.

```
HINSTANCE hinst;

int APIENTRY WinMain(hinstance, hPrevInstance, lpCmdLine, nCmdShow)
HINSTANCE hinstance;
```

```
HINSTANCE hPrevInstance;
LPSTR lpCmdLine;
int nCmdShow;
{
    MSG msg;         /* message              */
    WNDCLASS wc;     /* window-class data    */
    HWND hwnd;       /* handle of main window */

    /*
     * Create the window class for the main window. Specify
     * the identifier of the menu-template resource as the
     * lpszMenuName member of the WNDCLASS structure to create
     * the class menu.
     */

    wc.style = 0;
    wc.lpfnWndProc = (WNDPROC) MainWndProc;
    wc.cbClsExtra = 0;
    wc.cbWndExtra = 0;
    wc.hInstance = hinstance;
    wc.hIcon = LoadIcon(NULL, IDI_APPLICATION);
    wc.hCursor = LoadCursor(NULL, IDC_ARROW);
    wc.hbrBackground = GetStockObject(WHITE_BRUSH);
    wc.lpszMenuName =  "MyMenuResource";
    wc.lpszClassName = "MainWClass";

    if (!RegisterClass(&wc))
        return FALSE;

    hinst = hinstance;

    /*
     * Create the main window. Set the hmenu parameter to NULL so
     * that Windows uses the class menu for the window.
     */

    hwnd = CreateWindow("MainWClass", "Sample Application",
        WS_OVERLAPPEDWINDOW, CW_USEDEFAULT, CW_USEDEFAULT,
        CW_USEDEFAULT, CW_USEDEFAULT, NULL, NULL, hinstance,
        NULL);

    if (hwnd == NULL)
        return FALSE;

    /*
     * Make the window visible and send a WM_PAINT message to the
     * window procedure.
     */

    ShowWindow(hwnd, nCmdShow);
```

```
                UpdateWindow(hwnd);

                /* Start the main message loop. */

                while (GetMessage(&msg, NULL, 0, 0)) {
                    TranslateMessage(&msg);
                    DispatchMessage(&msg);
                }
                return msg.wParam;
                    UNREFERENCED_PARAMETER(hPrevInstance);
        }


        LRESULT APIENTRY MainWndProc(hwnd, uMsg, wParam, lParam)
        HWND hwnd;
        UINT uMsg;
        WPARAM wParam;
        LPARAM lParam;
        {

            switch (uMsg) {
                .
                . /* Process other window messages. */
                .

                case WM_COMMAND:

                    /* Test for the identifier of a command item. */

                    switch(LOWORD(wParam)) {
                        case IDM_FI_OPEN:
                            DoFileOpen();   /* application-defined */
                            break;

                        case IDM_FI_CLOSE:
                            DoFileClose();  /* application-defined */
                            break;

                            .
                            . /* Process other menu commands. */
                            .

                        default:
                            break;

                    }
                    return 0;


                .
                . /* Process other window messages. */
                .
```

```
        default:
            return DefWindowProc(hwnd, uMsg, wParam, lParam);
    }
    return NULL;
}
```

16.2.2 Creating a Floating Pop-up Menu

To use a floating pop-up menu in an application, pass the handle of a pop-up menu to the **TrackPopupMenu** function. An application typically calls **TrackPopupMenu** in a window procedure in response to a user-generated message, such as WM_LBUTTONDOWN or WM_KEYDOWN.

In addition to the pop-up menu handle, **TrackPopupMenu** requires that you specify the handle of the owner window, the position of the floating pop-up menu (in screen coordinates), and the mouse button the user can use to choose an item.

Specify the position by providing x- and y-coordinates along with the TPM_CENTERALIGN, TPM_LEFTALIGN, or TPM_RIGHTALIGN flag. The flag specifies the position of the menu relative to the x- and y-coordinates.

You should permit the user to choose an item from a pop-up menu by using the same mouse button used to display the menu. To do this, specify either TPM_LEFTBUTTON or TPM_RIGHTBUTTON flags to indicate which mouse button the user can use to select a menu item.

16.2.2.1 Creating a Floating Font-Attributes Menu

The example in this section contains portions of code from an application that creates and displays a floating pop-up menu that enables the user to set fonts and font attributes. The application displays the menu in the client area of its main window whenever the user clicks the left mouse button.

Here is the menu template for the pop-up menu that is provided in the application's resource-definition file.

```
PopupMenu MENU
BEGIN
  POPUP "Dummy Popup"
    BEGIN
      POPUP "Fonts"
        BEGIN
          MENUITEM "Courier",     IDM_FONT_COURIER
          MENUITEM "Times Roman", IDM_FONT_TMSRMN
          MENUITEM "Swiss",       IDM_FONT_SWISS
          MENUITEM "Helvetica",   IDM_FONT_HELV
          MENUITEM "Old English", IDM_FONT_OLDENG
        END
```

```
        POPUP "Sizes"
          BEGIN
            MENUITEM "7",  IDM_SIZE_7
            MENUITEM "8",  IDM_SIZE_8
            MENUITEM "9",  IDM_SIZE_9
            MENUITEM "10", IDM_SIZE_10
            MENUITEM "11", IDM_SIZE_11
            MENUITEM "12", IDM_SIZE_12
            MENUITEM "14", IDM_SIZE_14
          END
        POPUP "Styles"
          BEGIN
            MENUITEM "Bold",        IDM_STYLE_BOLD
            MENUITEM "Italic",      IDM_STYLE_ITALIC
            MENUITEM "Strike Out",  IDM_STYLE_SO
            MENUITEM "Superscript", IDM_STYLE_SUPER
            MENUITEM "Subscript",   IDM_STYLE_SUB
          END
      END

  END
```

The following example gives the window procedure and supporting functions used to create and display the floating pop-up menu.

```
LRESULT APIENTRY MenuWndProc(hwnd, uMsg, wParam, lParam)
HWND hwnd;
UINT uMsg;
WPARAM wParam;
LPARAM lParam;
{
    RECT rc;    /* client area            */
    POINT pt;   /* location of mouse click */

    switch (uMsg) {
        case WM_LBUTTONDOWN:

            /* Get the bounding rectangle of the client area. */

            GetClientRect(hwnd, (LPRECT) &rc);

            /* Get the client coordinates for the mouse click. */

            pt.x = LOWORD(lParam);
            pt.y = HIWORD(lParam);

            /*
             * If the mouse click took place inside the client
             * area, execute the application-defined function
             * that displays the floating pop-up menu.
```

```
                              */

                    if (PtInRect((LPRECT) &rc, pt))
                        HandlePopupMenu(hwnd, pt);
                    break;

                .
                . /* Process other window messages. */
                .

            default:
                return DefWindowProc(hwnd, uMsg, wParam, lParam);
        }
        return NULL;
}


VOID APIENTRY HandlePopupMenu(hwnd, pt)
HWND hwnd;
POINT pt;
{
    HMENU hmenu;            /* menu template            */
    HMENU hmenuTrackPopup;  /* floating pop-up menu     */

    /*
     * Load the menu template containing the pop-up menu from the
     * application's resources.
     */

    hmenu = LoadMenu(hinst, "PopupMenu");
    if (hmenu == NULL)
        return;

    /*
     * Get the first pop-up menu in the menu template. This is the
     * menu that TrackPopupMenu displays.
     */

    hmenuTrackPopup = GetSubMenu(hmenu, 0);

    /*
     * TrackPopup uses screen coordinates, so convert the
     * coordinates of the mouse click to screen coordinates.
     */

    ClientToScreen(hwnd, (LPPOINT) &pt);

    /* Draw and track the floating pop-up menu. */

    TrackPopupMenu(hmenuTrackPopup, TPM_LEFTALIGN | TPM_LEFTBUTTON,
        pt.x, pt.y, 0, hwnd, NULL);
```

```
/* Destroy the menu.*/

DestroyMenu(hmenu);
}
```

16.2.3 Using Menu-Item Bitmaps

Windows can use a bitmap instead of a text string to display a menu item. To use a bitmap, you must set the MF_BITMAP flag for the menu item and specify the handle of the bitmap that Windows should display for the menu item. This section describes how to set the MF_BITMAP flag and retrieve the handle of a bitmap.

16.2.3.1 Setting the MF_BITMAP Flag

The MF_BITMAP flag tells Windows to use a bitmap rather than a text string to display a menu item. A menu item's MF_BITMAP flag must be set at run time; you cannot set it in the resource-definition file.

You can use the **ModifyMenu**, **InsertMenu**, or **AppendMenu** function to set the MF_BITMAP flag. To convert a menu item from a text string item to a bitmap item, use **ModifyMenu**. To add a new bitmap item to a menu, use the MF_BITMAP flag with the **InsertMenu** or **AppendMenu** function.

16.2.3.2 Creating the Bitmap

When you set the MF_BITMAP flag for a menu item, you must also specify the handle of the bitmap that Windows should display for the menu item. You can provide the bitmap as a bitmap resource or create the bitmap at run time.

To provide a bitmap resource, use a resource editor, such as ImageEdit, to create a bitmap resource, and then use a resource compiler to add the bitmap to your application's executable file. At run time, use the **LoadBitmap** function to load the bitmap and obtain its handle.

To create the bitmap at run time, use GDI functions. GDI provides several ways to create a bitmap at run time, but developers typically use the following method:

- Use the **CreateCompatibleDC** function to create a device context compatible with the device context used by the application's main window.

- Use the **CreateCompatibleBitmap** function to create a bitmap compatible with the application's main window.

- Use the **SelectObject** function to select the bitmap into the compatible device context.

- Use GDI drawing functions, such as **Ellipse** and **LineTo**, to draw an image into the bitmap.

- Pass the handle of the bitmap to the **ModifyMenu**, **InsertMenu**, or **AppendMenu** function.

For more information about bitmaps, see Chapter 29, "Bitmaps."

16.2.3.3 Adding Lines and Graphs to a Menu

The following code sample shows how to create a menu that contains menu-item bitmaps. It creates two pop-up menus shown in the following illustration. The first is a Chart menu that contains three menu-item bitmaps: a pie chart, a line chart, and a bar chart. The example demonstrates how to load these bitmaps from the application's resource file, and then use the **CreatePopupMenu** and **AppendMenu** functions to create the menu and menu items.

The second pop-up menu is a Lines menu. It contains bitmaps showing the line styles provided by the predefined pen in Windows. The line-style bitmaps are created at run time by using GDI functions.

Here are the definitions of the bitmap resources in the application's resource-definition file.

```
PIE BITMAP pie.bmp
LINE BITMAP line.bmp
BAR BITMAP bar.bmp
```

Here are the relevant portions of the application's header file.

```
/* Menu-item identifiers */

#define IDM_SOLID        PS_SOLID
#define IDM_DASH         PS_DASH
#define IDM_DASHDOT      PS_DASHDOT
#define IDM_DASHDOTDOT   PS_DASHDOTDOT

#define IDM_PIE   1
#define IDM_LINE  2
#define IDM_BAR   3

/* Line-type flags */

#define SOLID        0
#define DOT          1
```

```
#define DASH        2
#define DASHDOT     3
#define DASHDOTDOT  4

/* Count of pens */

#define CPENS 5

/* Chart-type flags */

#define PIE  1
#define LINE 2
#define BAR  3

/* Function prototypes */

LRESULT APIENTRY MainWndProc(HWND, UINT, WPARAM, LPARAM);
VOID MakeChartMenu(HWND);
VOID MakeLineMenu(HWND, HPEN, HBITMAP);
```

The following example shows how menus and menu-item bitmaps are created in an application.

```
LRESULT APIENTRY MainWndProc(hwnd, uMsg, wParam, lParam)
HWND hwnd;
UINT uMsg;
WPARAM wParam;
LPARAM lParam;
{

    static HPEN hpen[CPENS];
    static HBITMAP hbmp[CPENS];
    int i;

    switch (uMsg) {
        case WM_CREATE:

            /* Create the Chart and Line menus. */

            MakeChartMenu(hwnd);
            MakeLineMenu(hwnd, hpen, hbmp);
            return 0;

            .
        . /* Process other window messages. */
            .

        case WM_DESTROY:

            for (i = 0; i < CPENS; i++) {
```

```
                        DeleteObject(hbmp[i]);
                        DeleteObject(hpen[i]);
                    }

                    PostQuitMessage(0);
                    break;

            default:
                return DefWindowProc(hwnd, uMsg, wParam, lParam);
        }
    return NULL;
}

VOID MakeChartMenu(hwnd)
HWND hwnd;                   /* handle of owner window       */
{
    HBITMAP hbmpPie;        /* handle of pie chart bitmap  */
    HBITMAP hbmpLine;       /* handle of line chart bitmap */
    HBITMAP hbmpBar;        /* handle of bar chart bitmap  */
    HMENU hmenuMain;        /* handle of main menu          */
    HMENU hmenuChart;       /* handle of chart pop-up menu */

    /*
     * Load the pie, line, and bar chart bitmaps from the
     * resource-definition file.
     */

    hbmpPie = LoadBitmap(hinst, MAKEINTRESOURCE(PIE));
    hbmpLine = LoadBitmap(hinst, MAKEINTRESOURCE(LINE));
    hbmpBar = LoadBitmap(hinst, MAKEINTRESOURCE(BAR));

    /*
     * Create the Chart pop-up menu and add it to the menu bar.
     * Append the Pie, Line, and Bar menu items to the Chart
     * pop-up menu.
     */

    hmenuMain = GetMenu(hwnd);
    hmenuChart = CreatePopupMenu();
    AppendMenu(hmenuMain, MF_STRING | MF_POPUP, (UINT) hmenuChart,
        "Chart");
    AppendMenu(hmenuChart, MF_BITMAP, IDM_PIE, (LPCTSTR) hbmpPie);
    AppendMenu(hmenuChart, MF_BITMAP, IDM_LINE,
        (LPCTSTR) hbmpLine);
    AppendMenu(hmenuChart, MF_BITMAP, IDM_BAR, (LPCTSTR) hbmpBar);

    return;
}

VOID MakeLineMenu(hwnd, phpen, phbmp)
```

```
HWND hwnd;
HPEN *phpen;
HBITMAP *phbmp;
{
    HMENU hmenuLines;       /* handle of Lines pop-up menu    */
    HMENU hmenu;            /* handle of main menu            */
    COLORREF crMenuClr;     /* menu-item background color     */
    HBRUSH hbrBackground;   /* handle of background brush     */
    HBRUSH hbrOld;          /* handle of previous brush       */
    LONG lCheckXY;          /* dimensions of check mark bitmap */
    WORD wLineX;            /* width of line bitmaps          */
    WORD wLineY;            /* height of line bitmaps         */
    HDC hdcMain;            /* handle of main window's DC     */
    HDC hdcLines;           /* handle of compatible DC        */
    HBITMAP hbmpOld;        /* handle of previous bitmap      */
    int i;                  /* loop counter                   */

    /* Create the Lines pop-up menu. Add it to the menu bar. */

    hmenu = GetMenu(hwnd);
    hmenuLines = CreatePopupMenu();
    AppendMenu(hmenu, MF_STRING | MF_POPUP,
        (UINT) hmenuLines, "&Lines");

    /* Create a brush for the menu-item background color. */

    crMenuClr = GetSysColor(COLOR_MENU);
    hbrBackground = CreateSolidBrush(crMenuClr);

    /*
     * Create a compatible device context for the line bitmaps,
     * and then select the background brush into it.
     */

    hdcMain = GetDC(hwnd);
    hdcLines = CreateCompatibleDC(hdcMain);
    hbrOld = SelectObject(hdcLines, hbrBackground);

    /*
     * Get the dimensions of the check mark bitmap. The width of
     * the line bitmaps will be five times the width of the
     * check mark bitmap.
     */

    lCheckXY = GetMenuCheckMarkDimensions();
    wLineX = LOWORD(lCheckXY) * (WORD) 5;
    wLineY = HIWORD(lCheckXY);

    /*
     * Create the bitmaps and select them, one at a time, into the
```

```
 * compatible device context. Initialize each bitmap by
 * filling it with the menu-item background color.
 */

for (i = 0; i < CPENS; i++) {
    phbmp[i] = CreateCompatibleBitmap(hdcMain, wLineX, wLineY);
    if (i == 0)
        hbmpOld = SelectObject(hdcLines, phbmp[i]);
    else
        SelectObject(hdcLines, phbmp[i]);
    ExtFloodFill(hdcLines, 0, 0, crMenuClr, FLOODFILLBORDER);
}

/* Create the pens. */

phpen[0] = CreatePen(PS_SOLID, 1, RGB(0, 0, 0));
phpen[1] = CreatePen(PS_DOT, 1, RGB(0, 0, 0));
phpen[2] = CreatePen(PS_DASH, 1, RGB(0, 0, 0));
phpen[3] = CreatePen(PS_DASHDOT, 1, RGB(0, 0, 0));
phpen[4] = CreatePen(PS_DASHDOTDOT, 1, RGB(0, 0, 0));

/*
 * Select a pen and a bitmap into the compatible device
 * context, draw a line into the bitmap, and then append
 * the bitmap as an item in the Lines menu.
 */

for (i = 0; i < CPENS; i++) {
    SelectObject(hdcLines, phbmp[i]);
    SelectObject(hdcLines, phpen[i]);
    MoveToEx(hdcLines, 0, wLineY / 2, NULL);
    LineTo(hdcLines, wLineX, wLineY / 2);
    AppendMenu(hmenuLines, MF_BITMAP, i + 1,
        (LPCTSTR) phbmp[i]);
}

/*
 * Release the main window's device context and destroy the
 * compatible device context. Also, destroy the background
 * brush.
 */

ReleaseDC(hwnd, hdcMain);
SelectObject(hdcLines, hbrOld);
DeleteObject(hbrBackground);
SelectObject(hdcLines, hbmpOld);
DeleteDC(hdcLines);

return;
}
```

16.2.4 Creating Owner-drawn Menu Items

If you need complete control over the appearance of a menu item, you can use an owner-drawn menu item on your application. This section describes the steps involved in creating and using an owner-drawn menu item.

16.2.4.1 Setting the MF_OWNERDRAW Flag

You cannot define an owner-drawn menu item on your application's resource-definition file. Instead, you must create a new menu item or modify an existing one by using the MF_OWNERDRAW menu flag.

You can use the **AppendMenu**, **InsertMenu**, or **ModifyMenu** function to specify an owner-drawn menu item. Use **AppendMenu** to add a new item to the end of the given menu. Use **InsertMenu** to place a new item onto a menu, moving the other items down. Use **ModifyMenu** to change the contents of a menu.

When you call any of these three functions, you can pass a 32-bit value as the *lpNewItem* parameter. This value can represent any information that is meaningful to your application, and that will be available to your application when the item is to be displayed. For example, the value could contain a pointer to a structure; the structure, in turn, might contain a text string and the handle of a logical font that your application will use to draw the string.

16.2.4.2 Responding to the WM_MEASUREITEM Message

Before Windows displays an owner-drawn menu item for the first time, it sends the WM_MEASUREITEM message to the window procedure of the window that owns the item's menu. This message contains a pointer to a **MEASUREITEMSTRUCT** structure that identifies the item and contains an optional 32-bit value for the item. When the window procedure receives the WM_MEASUREITEM message, it must fill the **itemWidth** and **itemHeight** members of the structure before returning from processing the message. Windows uses the information in these members when creating the bounding rectangle in which your application draws the menu item. It also uses the information to detect when the user chooses the item.

16.2.4.3 Responding to the WM_DRAWITEM Message

Whenever the item must be drawn (for example, when it is first displayed or when the user chooses it as a command), Windows sends the WM_DRAWITEM message to the window procedure of the menu's owner window. This message contains a pointer to a **DRAWITEMSTRUCT** structure. Like the **MEASUREITEMSTRUCT** structure, **DRAWITEMSTRUCT** contains information about the item and its optional 32-bit data. In addition, **DRAWITEMSTRUCT** contains flags that indicate the state of the item (such as whether it is grayed or checked) as well as a bounding rectangle and a device context that the application uses to draw the item.

In response to the WM_DRAWITEM message, your application must perform the following actions before returning from processing the message:

1. Determine the type of drawing that is necessary. To do so, check the **itemAction** member of the **DRAWITEMSTRUCT** structure.

2. Draw the menu item appropriately, using the bounding rectangle and device context obtained from the **DRAWITEMSTRUCT** structure. Your application must draw only within the bounding rectangle. For performance reasons, Windows doesn't clip portions of the image that are drawn outside the rectangle.

3. Restore all GDI objects selected for the menu item's device context.

If the menu item is selected, Windows sets the **itemAction** member of the **DRAWITEMSTRUCT** structure to ODA_SELECT and sets the ODS_SELECTED flag in the **itemState** member. This is an application's cue to redraw the menu item to indicate that it is selected.

16.2.4.4 Setting Fonts for Menu-Item Text Strings

This section contains an example from an application that uses owner-drawn menu items in a pop-up menu. The pop-up menu contains items that set the attributes of the current font, and the items are displayed using the appropriate font attribute, as shown in the following illustration.

Here is how the menu is defined in the resource-definition file. Note that the strings for the Regular, Bold, Italic, and Underline items are assigned at run time, so their strings are empty in the resource-definition file.

```
MainMenu MENU
BEGIN
    POPUP    "&Character"
    BEGIN
        MENUITEM    "",        IDM_REGULAR
        MENUITEM SEPARATOR
        MENUITEM    "",        IDM_BOLD
        MENUITEM    "",        IDM_ITALIC
        MENUITEM    "",        IDM_ULINE
    END
END
```

The application's window procedure processes the messages involved in using owner-drawn menu items. The application uses the WM_CREATE message to do the following:

- Set the MF_OWNERDRAW flag for the menu items.
- Set the text strings for the menu items.
- Obtain handles of the fonts used to draw the items.
- Obtain the text and background color values for selected menu items.

The text strings and font handles are stored in an array of application-defined MYITEM structures. The application-defined GetAFont function creates a font that corresponds to the given font attribute and returns the handle of the font. The handles are destroyed during the processing of the WM_DESTROY message.

During the processing of the WM_MEASUREITEM message, the example gets the width and height of a menu-item string and copies these values into the **MEASUREITEMSTRUCT** structure. Windows uses the width and height values to calculate the size of the pop-up menu.

During the processing of the WM_DRAWITEM message, the menu item's string is drawn with room left next to the string for the check mark bitmap. If the user selects the item, the selected text and background colors are used to draw the item.

```
LRESULT APIENTRY MainWndProc(hwnd, uMsg, wParam, lParam)
HWND hwnd;
UINT uMsg;
WPARAM wParam;
LPARAM lParam;
{

    typedef struct _MYITEM {
        HFONT hfont;
        LPSTR psz;
    } MYITEM;                 /* structure for item font and string */

    MYITEM *pmyitem;        /* pointer to item's font and string      */
    static MYITEM myitem[CITEMS];   /* array of MYITEMS               */
    static HMENU hmenu;             /* handle of main menu            */
    static COLORREF crSelText;  /* text color of selected item        */
    static COLORREF crSelBkgnd; /* background color of selected item */
    COLORREF crText;            /* text color of unselected item      */
    COLORREF crBkgnd;           /* background color unselected item   */
    LPMEASUREITEMSTRUCT lpmis;  /* points to item of data             */
    LPDRAWITEMSTRUCT lpdis;     /* points to item drawing data        */
    HDC hdc;                    /* handle of screen DC                */
    SIZE size;                  /* menu-item text extents             */
```

```
    DWORD dwCheckXY;            /* check mark dimensions      */
    WORD wCheckX;              /* check mark width           */
    int nTextX;                /* width of menu item         */
    int nTextY;                /* height of menu item        */
    int i;                     /* loop counter               */
    HFONT hfontOld;            /* handle of old font         */
    BOOL fSelected = FALSE;    /* menu-item selection flag   */

    switch (uMsg) {
        case WM_CREATE:

            /*
             * Modify the Regular, Bold, Italic, and Underline
             * menu items to make them owner-drawn items. Associate
             * a MYITEM structure with each item to contain the
             * string and font handle for each item.
             */

            hmenu = GetMenu(hwnd);
            ModifyMenu(hmenu, IDM_REGULAR, MF_BYCOMMAND |
                MF_CHECKED | MF_OWNERDRAW, IDM_REGULAR,
                (LPTSTR) &myitem[REGULAR]);
            ModifyMenu(hmenu, IDM_BOLD, MF_BYCOMMAND |
                MF_OWNERDRAW, IDM_BOLD, (LPTSTR) &myitem[BOLD]);
            ModifyMenu(hmenu, IDM_ITALIC, MF_BYCOMMAND |
                MF_OWNERDRAW, IDM_ITALIC,
                (LPTSTR) &myitem[ITALIC]);
            ModifyMenu(hmenu, IDM_ULINE, MF_BYCOMMAND |
                MF_OWNERDRAW, IDM_ULINE, (LPTSTR) &myitem[ULINE]);

            /*
             * Retrieve each item's font handle and copy it into
             * the hfont member of each item's MYITEM structure.
             * Also, copy each item's string into the structures.
             */

            myitem[REGULAR].hfont = GetAFont(REGULAR);
            myitem[REGULAR].psz = "Regular";
            myitem[BOLD].hfont = GetAFont(BOLD);
            myitem[BOLD].psz = "Bold";
            myitem[ITALIC].hfont = GetAFont(ITALIC);
            myitem[ITALIC].psz = "Italic";
            myitem[ULINE].hfont = GetAFont(ULINE);
            myitem[ULINE].psz = "Underline";

            /*
             * Retrieve the text and background colors of the
             * selected menu text.
             */
```

```
                                crSelText = GetSysColor(COLOR_HIGHLIGHTTEXT);
                                crSelBkgnd = GetSysColor(COLOR_HIGHLIGHT);

                                return 0;

                        case WM_MEASUREITEM:

                                /* Retrieve a device context for the main window. */

                                hdc = GetDC(hwnd);

                                /*
                                 * Retrieve pointers to the menu item's
                                 * MEASUREITEMSTRUCT structure and MYITEM structure.
                                 */

                                lpmis = (LPMEASUREITEMSTRUCT) lParam;
                                pmyitem = (MYITEM *) lpmis->itemData;

                                /*
                                 * Select the font associated with the item into
                                 * the main window's device context.
                                 */

                                hfontOld = SelectObject(hdc, pmyitem->hfont);

                                /*
                                 * Retrieve the width and height of the item's string,
                                 * and then copy the width and height into the
                                 * MEASUREITEMSTRUCT structure's itemWidth and
                                 * itemHeight members.
                                 */

                                GetTextExtentPoint(hdc, pmyitem->psz,
                                    lstrlen(pmyitem->psz), &size);
                                lpmis->itemWidth = size.cx;
                                lpmis->itemHeight = size.cy;

                                /*
                                 * Select the old font back into the device context,
                                 * and then release the device context.
                                 */

                                SelectObject(hdc, hfontOld);
                                ReleaseDC(hwnd, hdc);

                                return TRUE;

                                break;
```

```
case WM_DRAWITEM:

    /*
     * Get pointers to the menu item's DRAWITEMSTRUCT
     * structure and MYITEM structure.
     */

    lpdis = (LPDRAWITEMSTRUCT) lParam;
    pmyitem = (MYITEM *) lpdis->itemData;

    /*
     * If the user has selected the item, use the selected
     * text and background colors to display the item.
     */

    if (lpdis->itemState & ODS_SELECTED) {
        crText = SetTextColor(lpdis->hDC, crSelText);
        crBkgnd = SetBkColor(lpdis->hDC, crSelBkgnd);
        fSelected = TRUE;
    }

    /*
     * Remember to leave space in the menu item for the
     * check mark bitmap. Retrieve the width of the bitmap
     * and add it to the width of the menu item.
     */

    dwCheckXY = GetMenuCheckMarkDimensions();
    wCheckX = LOWORD(dwCheckXY);
    nTextX = wCheckX + lpdis->rcItem.left;
    nTextY = lpdis->rcItem.top;

    /*
     * Select the font associated with the item into the
     * item's device context, and then draw the string.
     */

    hfontOld = SelectObject(lpdis->hDC, pmyitem->hfont);
    ExtTextOut(lpdis->hDC, nTextX, nTextY, ETO_OPAQUE,
        &lpdis->rcItem, pmyitem->psz,
        lstrlen(pmyitem->psz), NULL);

    /*
     * Select the previous font back into the device
     * context.
     */

    SelectObject(lpdis->hDC, hfontOld);

    /*
```

```
                          * Return the text and background colors to their
                          * normal state (not selected).
                          */

                     if (fSelected) {
                         SetTextColor(lpdis->hDC, crText);
                         SetBkColor(lpdis->hDC, crBkgnd);
                     }

                     return TRUE;

                 .
                 . /* Process other messages. */
                 .


            case WM_DESTROY:

                /* Destroy the menu items' font handles. */

                for (i = 0; i < CITEMS; i++)
                    DeleteObject(myitem[i].hfont);

                PostQuitMessage(0);
                break;

            default:
                return DefWindowProc(hwnd, uMsg, wParam, lParam);
        }
        return NULL;
}

HFONT GetAFont(fnFont)
int fnFont;               /* font-attribute flag              */
{
    static LOGFONT lf;  /* structure for font information */

    /*
     * Get a handle to the ANSI fixed-pitch font, and copy
     * information about the font to a LOGFONT structure.
     */

    GetObject(GetStockObject(ANSI_FIXED_FONT), sizeof(LOGFONT),
        &lf);

    /* Set the font attributes, as appropriate. */

    if (fnFont == BOLD)
        lf.lfWeight = FW_BOLD;
    else
```

```
        lf.lfWeight = FW_NORMAL;

    lf.lfItalic = (fnFont == ITALIC);
    lf.lfItalic = (fnFont == ULINE);

    /* Create the font, and then return its handle. */

    return CreateFont(lf.lfHeight, lf.lfWidth,
        lf.lfEscapement, lf.lfOrientation, lf.lfWeight,
        lf.lfItalic, lf.lfUnderline, lf.lfStrikeOut, lf.lfCharSet,
        lf.lfOutPrecision, lf.lfClipPrecision, lf.lfQuality,
        lf.lfPitchAndFamily, lf.lfFaceName);
}
```

16.2.5 Using Custom Check Mark Bitmaps

A Windows video device driver provides a default check mark bitmap that
Windows displays next to a menu item that is checked. You can customize an
individual menu item by providing a pair of bitmaps to replace the default check
mark bitmap. Windows displays one bitmap when the item is checked and the
other when it is unchecked. This section describes the steps involved in creating
and using custom check mark bitmaps.

16.2.5.1 Creating Custom Check Mark Bitmaps

A custom check mark bitmap must be the same size as the default check mark
bitmap. You can retrieve the default check mark bitmap's size by calling the
GetMenuCheckMarkDimensions function. The low-order word of this
function's return value specifies the width; the high-order word specifies the
height.

Bitmap resources can be used to provide check mark bitmaps. However, a bitmap
resource is not suitable for all screen resolutions and aspect ratios, so you'll need
to use the **StretchBlt** function to size the bitmap, as appropriate. Depending on
the bitmap being sized, the result of the sizing may not be acceptable, because
stretching may distort the bitmap.

Instead of using a bitmap resource, GDI functions can be used to provide check
mark bitmaps at run time. This involves the following steps, which an application
typically performs during the WM_CREATE message:

1. Create a device context in memory that is compatible with the screen.

2. Create a bitmap that is compatible with the display.

3. Select the bitmap into the device context.

4. Draw or copy an image into the bitmap.

Call the **CreateCompatibleDC** function to create a device context that is compatible with the screen. The function's *hdc* parameter can specify either NULL or the return value from the **GetDC** function. **CreateCompatibleDC** returns the handle of the compatible device context.

Call the **CreateCompatibleBitmap** function to create an "empty" bitmap that is compatible with the screen. This function's *nWidth* and *nHeight* parameters set the size of the bitmap; they should specify the width and height information returned by the **GetMenuCheckMarkDimensions** function.

The **CreateCompatibleBitmap** function returns the handle of the bitmap. Pass this handle of the **SelectObject** function to select the bitmap into the compatible device context. Afterward, you can use the GDI drawing functions such as **Rectangle** and **Ellipse** to draw into the bitmap, or you can use functions such as **BitBlt** and **StretchBlt** to copy an image into the bitmap.

GDI provides several other ways to create bitmaps. For more information about bitmaps, see Chapter 29, "Bitmaps."

16.2.5.2 Associating Bitmaps with a Menu Item

You associate a pair of check mark bitmaps with a menu item by passing the handles of the bitmaps to the **SetMenuItemBitmaps** function. The *hbmUnchecked* parameter identifies the unchecked bitmap; the *hbmChecked* parameter identifies the checked bitmap. If you want to remove one or both check marks from a menu item, you can set the *hbmUnchecked* or *hbmChecked* parameter, or both, to NULL.

16.2.5.3 Setting the Check Mark Attribute

The **CheckMenuItem** function sets a menu item's check mark attribute to either checked or unchecked. Specify the MF_CHECKED flag to set the check mark attribute to checked, or specify MF_UNCHECKED to set it to unchecked.

16.2.5.4 Simulating Check Boxes in a Menu

This section contains an example that shows how to simulate check boxes in a pop-up menu. The example contains a Character menu whose items allow the user to set the bold, italic, and underline attributes of the current font. When a font attribute is in effect, a check mark is displayed in the check box next to the corresponding menu item; otherwise, it is displayed in an empty check box next to the item. The following illustration shows both kinds of check boxes.

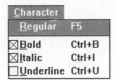

The example in this section replaces the default check mark bitmap with two bitmaps: a bitmap with a checked box and the bitmap with an empty box. The checked check box bitmap is displayed next to the Bold, Italic, or Underline menu item when the item's check mark attribute is set to MF_CHECKED. The unchecked or empty check box bitmap is displayed when the check mark attribute is set to MF_UNCHECKED.

Windows provides a predefined bitmap that contains the images used for check boxes and radio buttons (as shown in the following illustration). The example in this section isolates the checked and empty check boxes, copies them to two separate bitmaps, and then uses them as the checked and unchecked bitmaps for items in the Character menu.

Predefined Checkbox Bitmap

To retrieve the handle of the system-defined check box bitmap, the example in this section calls the **LoadBitmap** function, specifying NULL as the *hinst* parameter and OBM_CHECKBOXES as the *lpBitmapName* parameter. Because the images in the bitmap are all the same size, the example can isolate them by dividing the bitmap's width and height by the number of images in its rows and columns.

The following portion of a resource-definition file shows how the menu items in the Character menu are defined. Note that no font attributes are in effect initially, so the check mark attribute for the Regular item is set to checked and, by default, the check mark attribute of the remaining items is set to unchecked.

```
#include "men3.h"

MainMenu MENU
BEGIN
    POPUP    "&Character"
    BEGIN
        MENUITEM    "&Regular",      IDM_REGULAR, CHECKED
        MENUITEM SEPARATOR
        MENUITEM    "&Bold",         IDM_BOLD
        MENUITEM    "&Italic",       IDM_ITALIC
        MENUITEM    "&Underline",    IDM_ULINE
    END
END
```

Here is the relevant contents of the application's header file.

```
/* Menu-item identifiers */
```

```
#define IDM_REGULAR 0x1
#define IDM_BOLD    0x2
#define IDM_ITALIC  0x4
#define IDM_ULINE   0x8

/* Check mark flags */

#define CHECK   1
#define UNCHECK 2

/* Font-attribute mask */

#define ATTRIBMASK 0xe

/* Function prototypes */

LRESULT APIENTRY MainWndProc(HWND, UINT, WPARAM, LPARAM);
HBITMAP GetMyCheckBitmaps(UINT);
BYTE CheckOrUncheckMenuItem(BYTE, HMENU);
```

The following example shows the portions of the window procedure that create
the check mark bitmaps, set the check mark attribute of the Bold, Italic, and
Underline menu items, and destroy check mark bitmaps.

```
LRESULT APIENTRY MainWndProc(hwndMain, uMsg, wParam, lParam)
HWND hwndMain;
UINT uMsg;
WPARAM wParam;
LPARAM lParam;
{

    static HBITMAP hbmpCheck;   /* handle of checked bitmap   */
    static HBITMAP hbmpUncheck; /* handle of unchecked bitmap */
    static HMENU hmenu;         /* handle of main menu        */
    BYTE fbFontAttrib;          /* font-attribute flags       */

    switch (uMsg) {
        case WM_CREATE:

            /*
             * Call the application-defined GetMyCheckBitmaps
             * function to get the predefined checked and
             * unchecked check box bitmaps.
             */

            hbmpCheck = GetMyCheckBitmaps(CHECK);
            hbmpUncheck = GetMyCheckBitmaps(UNCHECK);

            /*
             * Set the checked and unchecked bitmaps for the menu
```

```
     * items.
     */

    hmenu = GetMenu(hwndMain);
    SetMenuItemBitmaps(hmenu, IDM_BOLD, MF_BYCOMMAND,
        hbmpUncheck, hbmpCheck);
    SetMenuItemBitmaps(hmenu, IDM_ITALIC, MF_BYCOMMAND,
        hbmpUncheck, hbmpCheck);
    SetMenuItemBitmaps(hmenu, IDM_ULINE, MF_BYCOMMAND,
        hbmpUncheck, hbmpCheck);

    return 0;

case WM_COMMAND:
    switch (LOWORD(wParam)) {

        /* Process the menu commands. */

        case IDM_REGULAR:
        case IDM_BOLD:
        case IDM_ITALIC:
        case IDM_ULINE:

            /*
             * CheckOrUncheckMenuItem is an application-
             * defined function that sets the menu item
             * check marks and returns the user-selected
             * font attributes.
             */

            fbFontAttrib = CheckOrUncheckMenuItem(
                (BYTE) LOWORD(wParam), hmenu);


            .
            . /* Set the font attributes. */
            .

            return 0;


        .
        . /* Process other command messages. */
        .

        default:
            break;
    }

    break;

            .
```

```
        . /* Process other window messages. */
        .

    case WM_DESTROY:

        /* Destroy the checked and unchecked bitmaps. */

        DeleteObject(hbmpCheck);
        DeleteObject(hbmpUncheck);

        PostQuitMessage(0);
        break;

    default:
        return DefWindowProc(hwndMain, uMsg, wParam, lParam);
    }
    return NULL;
}

HBITMAP GetMyCheckBitmaps(fuCheck)
UINT fuCheck;                /* CHECK or UNCHECK flag                */
{
    COLORREF crBackground;   /* background color                    */
    HBRUSH hbrBackground;    /* background brush                    */
    HBRUSH hbrTargetOld;     /* original background brush           */
    HDC hdcSource;           /* source device context               */
    HDC hdcTarget;           /* target device context               */
    HBITMAP hbmpCheckboxes;  /* handle of check box bitmap          */
    BITMAP bmCheckbox;       /* structure for bitmap data           */
    HBITMAP hbmpSourceOld;   /* handle of original source bitmap    */
    HBITMAP hbmpTargetOld;   /* handle of original target bitmap    */
    HBITMAP hbmpCheck;       /* handle of check mark bitmap         */
    RECT rc;                 /* rectangle for check box bitmap      */
    DWORD dwCheckXY;         /* dimensions of check mark bitmap     */
    WORD wBitmapX;           /* width of check mark bitmap          */
    WORD wBitmapY;           /* height of check mark bitmap         */

    /*
     * Get the menu background color and create a solid brush
     * with that color.
     */

    crBackground = GetSysColor(COLOR_MENU);
    hbrBackground = CreateSolidBrush(crBackground);

    /*
     * Create memory device contexts for the source and
     * destination bitmaps.
     */
```

```
hdcSource = CreateCompatibleDC((HDC) NULL);
hdcTarget = CreateCompatibleDC(hdcSource);

/*
 * Get the size of the Windows default check mark bitmap and
 * create a compatible bitmap of the same size.
 */

dwCheckXY = GetMenuCheckMarkDimensions();
wBitmapX = LOWORD(dwCheckXY);
wBitmapY = LOWORD(dwCheckXY);

hbmpCheck = CreateCompatibleBitmap(hdcSource, wBitmapX,
    wBitmapY);

/*
 * Select the background brush and bitmap into the target DC.
 */

hbrTargetOld = SelectObject(hdcTarget, hbrBackground);
hbmpTargetOld = SelectObject(hdcTarget, hbmpCheck);

/*
 * Use the selected brush to initialize the background color
 * of the bitmap in the target device context.
 */

PatBlt(hdcTarget, 0, 0, wBitmapX, wBitmapY, PATCOPY);

/*
 * Load the predefined check box bitmaps and select it
 * into the source DC.
 */

hbmpCheckboxes = LoadBitmap((HINSTANCE) NULL,
    (LPTSTR) OBM_CHECKBOXES);

hbmpSourceOld = SelectObject(hdcSource, hbmpCheckboxes);

/*
 * Fill a BITMAP structure with information about the
 * check box bitmaps, and then find the upper-left corner of
 * the unchecked check box or the checked check box.
 */

GetObject(hbmpCheckboxes, sizeof(BITMAP), &bmCheckbox);

if (fuCheck == UNCHECK) {
    rc.left = 0;
    rc.right = (bmCheckbox.bmWidth / 4);
```

```
        }
        else {
            rc.left = (bmCheckbox.bmWidth / 4);
            rc.right = (bmCheckbox.bmWidth / 4) * 2;
        }

        rc.top = 0;
        rc.bottom = (bmCheckbox.bmHeight / 3);

        /*
         * Copy the appropriate bitmap into the target DC. If the
         * check box bitmap is larger than the default check mark
         * bitmap, use StretchBlt to make it fit; otherwise, just
         * copy it.
         */

        if (((rc.right - rc.left) > (int) wBitmapX ||
                ((rc.bottom - rc.top) > (int) wBitmapY))
            StretchBlt(hdcTarget, 0, 0, wBitmapX, wBitmapY,
                hdcSource, rc.left, rc.top, rc.right - rc.left,
                rc.bottom - rc.top, SRCCOPY);

        else
            BitBlt(hdcTarget, 0, 0, rc.right - rc.left,
                rc.bottom - rc.top,
                hdcSource, rc.left, rc.top, SRCCOPY);

        /*
         * Select the old source and destination bitmaps into the
         * source and destination DCs, and then delete the DCs and
         * the background brush.
         */

        SelectObject(hdcSource, hbmpSourceOld);
        SelectObject(hdcTarget, hbrTargetOld);
        hbmpCheck = SelectObject(hdcTarget, hbmpTargetOld);

        DeleteObject(hbrBackground);
        DeleteObject(hdcSource);
        DeleteObject(hdcTarget);

        /* Return the handle of the new check mark bitmap. */

        return hbmpCheck;
}


BYTE CheckOrUncheckMenuItem(bMenuItemID, hmenu)
BYTE bMenuItemID;
HMENU hmenu;
```

```
{
    DWORD fdwMenu;
    static BYTE fbAttributes;

    switch (bMenuItemID) {
        case IDM_REGULAR:

            /*
             * Whenever the Regular menu item is selected, add a
             * check mark to it and then remove check marks from
             * any font-attribute menu items.
             */

            CheckMenuItem(hmenu, IDM_REGULAR, MF_BYCOMMAND |
                MF_CHECKED);

            if (fbAttributes & ATTRIBMASK) {
                CheckMenuItem(hmenu, IDM_BOLD, MF_BYCOMMAND |
                    MF_UNCHECKED);
                CheckMenuItem(hmenu, IDM_ITALIC, MF_BYCOMMAND |
                    MF_UNCHECKED);
                CheckMenuItem(hmenu, IDM_ULINE, MF_BYCOMMAND |
                    MF_UNCHECKED);
            }
            fbAttributes = IDM_REGULAR;
            return fbAttributes;

        case IDM_BOLD:
        case IDM_ITALIC:
        case IDM_ULINE:

            /*
             * Toggle the check mark for the selected menu item and
             * set the font attribute flags appropriately.
             */

            fdwMenu = GetMenuState(hmenu, (UINT) bMenuItemID,
                MF_BYCOMMAND);
            if (!(fdwMenu & MF_CHECKED)) {
                CheckMenuItem(hmenu, (UINT) bMenuItemID,
                    MF_BYCOMMAND | MF_CHECKED);
                fbAttributes |= bMenuItemID;

            } else {
                CheckMenuItem(hmenu, (UINT) bMenuItemID,
                    MF_BYCOMMAND | MF_UNCHECKED);
                fbAttributes ^= bMenuItemID;
            }

            /*
```

```
                            * If any font attributes are currently selected,
                            * remove the check mark from the Regular menu item;
                            * if no attributes are selected, add a check mark
                            * to the Regular menu item.
                            */

                           if (fbAttributes & ATTRIBMASK) {
                               CheckMenuItem(hmenu, IDM_REGULAR,
                                   MF_BYCOMMAND | MF_UNCHECKED);
                               fbAttributes &= (BYTE) ~IDM_REGULAR;

                           } else {
                               CheckMenuItem(hmenu, IDM_REGULAR,
                                   MF_BYCOMMAND | MF_CHECKED);
                               fbAttributes = IDM_REGULAR;
                           }

                           return fbAttributes;
                       }
                   }
```

16.3 Functions and Messages

Following are the Windows functions and messages used with menus.

Functions

AppendMenu
ChangeMenu
CheckMenuItem
CreateMenu
CreatePopupMenu
DeleteMenu
DestroyMenu
DrawMenuBar
EnableMenuItem
GetMenu
GetMenuCheckMarkDimensions
GetMenuItemCount
GetMenuItemID
GetMenuState
GetMenuString
GetSubMenu
GetSystemMenu
HiliteMenuItem
InsertMenu

LoadMenu
LoadMenuIndirect
ModifyMenu
RemoveMenu
SetMenu
SetMenuItemBitmaps
TrackPopupMenu

Messages

WM_COMMAND
WM_DRAWITEM
WM_ENTERIDLE
WM_ENTERMENULOOP
WM_EXITMENULOOP
WM_INITMENU
WM_INITMENUPOPUP
WM_MEASUREITEM
WM_MENUCHAR
WM_MENUSELECT
WM_NCHITTEST
WM_SYSCOMMAND

CHAPTER 17

Keyboard Accelerators

17.1 About Keyboard Accelerators

In Microsoft ® Windows ™, a *keyboard accelerator* (or, simply, accelerator) is a keystroke or combination of keystrokes that generates a WM_COMMAND or WM_SYSCOMMAND message for an application. Accelerators are closely related to menus—both provide the user with access to an application's command set. Typically, users rely on an application's menus to learn the command set and then switch over to using accelerators as they become more proficient with the application. Accelerators provide faster, more direct access to commands than menus do. At a minimum, an application should provide accelerators for the more commonly used commands. Although accelerators typically generate commands that exist as menu items, they can also generate commands that have no equivalent menu items.

17.1.1 Accelerator Tables

An *accelerator table* consists of an array of **ACCEL** structures, each defining an individual accelerator. Each **ACCEL** structure includes the following information:

- The accelerator's keystroke combination
- The accelerator's identifier
- Various flags. This includes one that specifies whether Windows is to provide visual feedback by highlighting the corresponding menu item, if any, when the accelerator is used

To process accelerator keystrokes for a given thread, the developer must call the **TranslateAccelerator** function in the message loop associated with the thread's message queue. The **TranslateAccelerator** function monitors keyboard input to the message queue, checking for key combinations that match an entry in the accelerator table. When **TranslateAccelerator** finds a match, it translates the keyboard input (that is, the WM_KEYUP and WM_KEYDOWN messages) into a WM_COMMAND or WM_SYSCOMMAND message and then sends the message to the window procedure of the specified window. The following illustration shows how accelerators are processed.

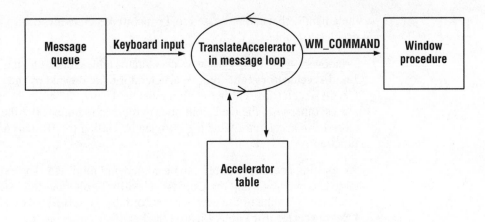

The WM_COMMAND message includes the identifier of the accelerator that caused **TranslateAccelerator** to generate the message. The window procedure examines the identifier to determine the source of the message and then processes the message accordingly.

Accelerator tables exist at two different levels in Windows. Windows maintains a single, system-wide accelerator table that applies to all applications. An application cannot modify the system accelerator table. For a description of the accelerators provided by the system accelerator table, see Section 17.1.3, "Accelerator Keystroke Assignments."

Windows also maintains accelerator tables for each application. An application can define any number of accelerator tables for use with its own windows. A unique 32-bit handle (**HACCEL**) identifies each table. However, only one accelerator table can be active at a time for a given thread. The handle of the accelerator table passed to the **TranslateAccelerator** function determines which accelerator table is active for a thread. The active accelerator table can be changed at any time by passing a different accelerator-table handle to **TranslateAccelerator**.

17.1.2 Accelerator-Table Creation

Several steps are required to create an accelerator table for an application. First, a resource compiler is used to create accelerator-table resources and to add them to the application's executable file. At run time, the **LoadAccelerators** function is used to load the accelerator table into memory and retrieve the handle of the accelerator table. This handle is passed to the **TranslateAccelerator** function to activate the accelerator table.

An accelerator table can also be created for an application at run time by passing an array of **ACCEL** structures to the **CreateAcceleratorTable** function. This method supports user-defined accelerators in the application. Like the **LoadAccelerators** function, **CreateAcceleratorTable** returns an accelerator-table handle that can be passed to **TranslateAccelerator** to activate the accelerator table.

Windows automatically destroys accelerator tables loaded by the **LoadAccelerators** function. An accelerator table created by the **CreateAcceleratorTable** function must be destroyed before an application closes; otherwise, the table continues to exist in memory after the application has closed. An accelerator table is destroyed by calling the **DestroyAcceleratorTable** function.

An existing accelerator table can be copied and modified. The existing accelerator table is copied by using the **CopyAcceleratorTable** function. After the copy is modified, a handle of the new accelerator table is retrieved by calling **CreateAcceleratorTable**. Finally, the handle is passed to the **TranslateAccelerator** function to activate the new table.

17.1.3 Accelerator Keystroke Assignments

An ASCII character code or a virtual-key code can be used to define the accelerator. An ASCII character code makes the accelerator case sensitive. The ASCII "C" character can define the accelerator as ALT+c rather than ALT + C. Case-sensitive accelerators can, however, be confusing to use. For example, the ALT+C accelerator will be generated if the CAPS LOCK key is down or if the SHIFT key is down, but not if both are down.

Typically, accelerators don't need to be case sensitive, so most applications use virtual-key codes for accelerators rather than ASCII character codes. For a list of virtual-key codes, see Appendix B, "Virtual-Key Codes."

Avoid accelerators that conflict with an application's menu mnemonics because the accelerator overrides the mnemonic, and this can confuse the user. For more information about menu mnemonics, see Chapter 16, "Menus."

If an application defines an accelerator that is also defined in the system accelerator table, the application-defined accelerator overrides the system accelerator, but only within the context of the application. Avoid this practice, however, because it prevents the system accelerator from performing its standard role in the Windows user interface. The system-wide accelerators are described in the following list:

Accelerator	Description
ALT+ESC	Switches to the next application.
ALT+F4	Closes an application or a window.
ALT+HYPHEN	Opens the System menu for a document window.
ALT+PRINT SCREEN	Copies an image in the active window onto the Clipboard.

ALT+SPACEBAR	Opens the System menu for an application window.
ALT+TAB	Switches to the next application.
CTRL+ESC	Switches to Windows Task List.
CTRL+F4	Closes the active group or document window.
F1	Starts Help if the application has Help.
PRINT SCREEN	Copies an image on the screen onto the Clipboard.
SHIFT+ALT+TAB	Switches to the previous application. The user must press and hold down ALT+SHIFT while pressing TAB.

17.1.4 Accelerators and Menus

Using an accelerator is the same as choosing a menu item: both actions cause Windows to send a WM_COMMAND or WM_SYSCOMMAND message to the corresponding window procedure. The WM_COMMAND message includes an identifier that the window procedure examines to determine the source of the message. If an accelerator generated the WM_COMMAND message, the identifier is that of the accelerator. Similarly, if a menu item generated the WM_COMMAND message, the identifier is that of the menu item. Because an accelerator provides a shortcut for choosing a command from a menu, an application usually assigns the same identifier to the accelerator and the corresponding menu item.

An application processes an accelerator WM_COMMAND message in exactly the same way as the corresponding menu item WM_COMMAND message. However, the WM_COMMAND message contains a flag that specifies whether the message originated from an accelerator or a menu item, in case accelerators need to be processed differently from their corresponding menu items. The WM_SYSCOMMAND message does not contain this flag.

The identifier determines whether an accelerator generates a WM_COMMAND or WM_SYSCOMMAND message. If the identifier has the same value as a menu item in the System menu, the accelerator generates a WM_SYSCOMMAND message. Otherwise, the accelerator generates a WM_COMMAND message.

If an accelerator has the same identifier as a menu item and the menu item is grayed or disabled, the accelerator is disabled and does not generate a WM_COMMAND or WM_SYSCOMMAND message. Also, an accelerator does not generate a command message if the corresponding window is minimized.

When the user uses an accelerator that corresponds to a menu item, the window procedure receives the WM_INITMENU and WM_INITMENUPOPUP messages as though the user had selected the menu item. For information on how to process these messages, see Chapter 16, "Menus."

An accelerator that corresponds to an item in a menu should be included in the text of the menu item. For example, the Windows Write includes accelerators in the text of the first four items in its Edit menu:

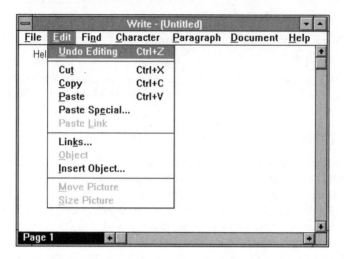

17.2 Using Keyboard Accelerators

This section explains how to perform the following tasks:

- Use an accelerator-table resource.
- Use an accelerator table created at run time.

17.2.1 Using an Accelerator-Table Resource

The most common way to add accelerator support to a Windows-based application is to include an accelerator-table resource with the application's executable file and then load the resource at run time. The steps involved in using an accelerator-table resource are as follows:

- Create an accelerator table in a resource-definition file. Then compile it and add the resulting resource to your application's executable file.
- Include a call to the **LoadAccelerators** function to load the accelerator-table resource and receive a handle of the accelerator table.
- Add the **TranslateAccelerator** function to the message loop associated with the accelerator table.
- Process the WM_COMMAND messages generated when the user uses the accelerator.

17.2.1.1 Creating the Accelerator-Table Resource

You create an accelerator-table resource by using the **ACCELERATORS** statement in your application's resource-definition file. You must assign a name or resource identifier to the accelerator table, preferably unlike that of any other resource. Windows uses this identifier to load the resource at run time.

Each accelerator that you define requires a separate entry in the accelerator table. In each entry, you define the keystroke (either an ASCII character code or virtual-key code) that generates the accelerator and the accelerator's identifier. You also need to specify whether the keystroke must be used in some combination with the ALT, SHIFT, or CTRL keys. For more information about virtual keys, see Chapter 5, "Keyboard Input."

An ASCII keystroke is specified either by enclosing the ASCII character in double quotation marks or by using the integer value of the character in combination with the ASCII flag. The following examples show how to define ASCII accelerators.

```
"A", ID_ACCEL1          ; SHIFT+A
65,  ID_ACCEL2, ASCII   ; SHIFT+A
```

A virtual-key code keystroke is specified differently depending on whether the keystroke is an alphanumeric key or a non-alphanumeric key. For an alphanumeric key, the key's letter or number, enclosed in double quotation marks, is combined with the VIRTKEY flag. For a non-alphanumeric key, the Windows virtual-key code for the specific key is combined with the VIRTKEY flag. The following examples show how to define virtual-key code accelerators.

```
"a",        ID_ACCEL3, VIRTKEY   ; A (caps-lock on) or a
VK_INSERT, ID_ACCEL4, VIRTKEY    ; INSERT key
```

The following example shows an accelerator-table resource that defines accelerators for file operations. The name of the resource is FileAccel.

```
FileAccel ACCELERATORS
BEGIN
    VK_F12, IDM_OPEN, CONTROL, VIRTKEY  ; CTRL+F12
    VK_F4,  IDM_CLOSE, ALT, VIRTKEY     ; ALT+F4
    VK_F12, IDM_SAVE, SHIFT, VIRTKEY    ; SHIFT+F12
    VK_F12, IDM_SAVEAS, VIRTKEY         ; F12
END
```

If you want the user to press the ALT, SHIFT, or CTRL keys in some combination with the accelerator keystroke, specify the ALT, SHIFT, and CONTROL flags in the accelerator's definition. Following are some examples.

```
"B",   ID_ACCEL5, ALT                        ; ALT_SHIFT+B
"I",   ID_ACCEL6, CONTROL, VIRTKEY           ; CTRL+I
VK_F5, ID_ACCEL7, CONTROL, ALT, VIRTKEY ; CTRL+ALT+F5
```

By default, when an accelerator key corresponds to a menu item, Windows
highlights the menu item. You can use the NOINVERT flag to prevent
highlighting for an individual accelerator. The following example shows how to
use the NOINVERT flag.

```
VK_DELETE, ID_ACCEL8, VIRTKEY, SHIFT, NOINVERT  ; SHIFT+DELETE
```

To define accelerators that correspond to menu items in your application, include
the accelerators in the text of the menu items. The following example shows how
to include accelerators in menu-item text in a resource-definition file.

```
FilePopup MENU
BEGIN
    POPUP   "&File"
    BEGIN
        MENUITEM    "&New..",         IDM_NEW
        MENUITEM    "&Open\tCtrl+F12", IDM_OPEN
        MENUITEM    "&Close\tAlt+F4"   IDM_CLOSE
        MENUITEM    "&Save\tShift+F12", IDM_SAVE
        MENUITEM    "Save &As...\tF12", IDM_SAVEAS
    END
END
```

17.2.1.2 Loading the Accelerator-Table Resource

An application loads an accelerator-table resource by calling the
LoadAccelerators function and specifying the instance handle of the application
whose executable file contains the resource and the name or identifier of the
resource. **LoadAccelerators** loads the specified accelerator table into memory
and returns the handle of the accelerator table.

An application can load an accelerator-table resource at any time. Usually, a
single-threaded application loads its accelerator table before entering its main
message loop. An application that uses multiple threads typically loads the
accelerator-table resource for a thread before entering the message loop for the
thread. An application or thread might also use multiple accelerator tables, each
associated with a particular window in the application. Such an application would
load the accelerator table for the window each time the user activated the window.
For more information about threads, see Chapter 43, "Processes and Threads."

17.2.1.3 Calling the TranslateAccelerator Function

To process accelerators, an application's (or thread's) message loop must contain
a call to the **TranslateAccelerator** function. **TranslateAccelerator** compares

keystrokes to an accelerator table and, if it finds a match, translates the keystrokes into a WM_COMMAND (or WM_SYSCOMMAND) message and then sends the message to a window procedure. The parameters of the **TranslateAccelerator** function include the handle of the window that is to receive the WM_COMMAND messages, the handle of the accelerator table used to translate accelerators, and a pointer to an **MSG** structure containing a message from the queue. The following example shows how to call **TranslateAccelerator** from within a message loop.

```
while (GetMessage(&msg, (HWND) NULL, 0, 0)) {

    /* Check for accelerator keystrokes. */

    if (!TranslateAccelerator(
            hwndMain,      /* handle of receiving window   */
            haccel,        /* handle of active accel. table */
            &msg)) {       /* address of message data       */
        TranslateMessage(&msg);
        DispatchMessage(&msg);
    }
}
```

17.2.1.4 Processing WM_COMMAND Messages

When an accelerator is used, the window specified in the **TranslateAccelerator** function receives a WM_COMMAND or WM_SYSCOMMAND message. The low-order word of the *wParam* parameter contains the identifier of the accelerator. The window procedure examines the identifier to determine the source of the WM_COMMAND message and process the message accordingly.

Typically, if an accelerator corresponds to a menu-item in the application, the accelerator and menu item are assigned the same identifier. If you need to know whether a given WM_COMMAND message was generated by an accelerator or by a menu item, you can examine the high-order word of the *wParam* parameter. If an accelerator generated the message, the high-order word is 1, but if a menu item generated the message, it is 0.

17.2.1.5 Destroying the Accelerator-Table Resource

Windows automatically destroys accelerator-table resources loaded by the **LoadAccelerators** function, removing the resource from memory after the application closes.

17.2.1.6 Creating Accelerators for Font Attributes

The example in this section shows how to perform the following tasks:

- Create an accelerator-table resource.

- Load the accelerator table at run time.
- Translate accelerators in a message loop.
- Process WM_COMMAND messages generated by the accelerators.

These tasks are demonstrated in the context of an application that includes a Character menu and corresponding accelerators that allow the user to select attributes of the current font.

The following portion of a resource-definition file defines the Character menu and the associated accelerator table. Note that the menu items show the accelerator keystrokes and that each accelerator has the same identifier as its associated menu item.

```
#include <windows.h>
#include "acc.h"

MainMenu MENU
BEGIN
    POPUP    "&Character"
    BEGIN
        MENUITEM    "&Regular\tF5",        IDM_REGULAR
        MENUITEM    "&Bold\tCtrl+B",       IDM_BOLD
        MENUITEM    "&Italic\tCtrl+I",     IDM_ITALIC
        MENUITEM    "&Underline\tCtrl+U",  IDM_ULINE
    END
END

FontAccel ACCELERATORS
BEGIN
    VK_F5,  IDM_REGULAR,    VIRTKEY
    "B",    IDM_BOLD,       CONTROL, VIRTKEY
    "I",    IDM_ITALIC,     CONTROL, VIRTKEY
    "U",    IDM_ULINE,      CONTROL, VIRTKEY
END
```

The following sections from the application's source file show how to implement the accelerators.

```
HWND hwndMain;      /* handle of main window          */
HANDLE hinstAcc;    /* handle of application instance */

int WINAPI WinMain(hinst, hinstPrev, lpCmdLine, nCmdShow)
HINSTANCE hinst;
HINSTANCE hinstPrev;
LPSTR lpCmdLine;
int nCmdShow;
{
    MSG msg;             /* application messages           */
```

```
    HACCEL haccel;      /* handle of accelerator table        */

    .
    . /* Perform the initialization procedure. */
    .

    /* Create a main window for this application instance. */

    hwndMain = CreateWindowEx(0L, "MainWindowClass",
        "Sample Application", WS_OVERLAPPEDWINDOW, CW_USEDEFAULT,
        CW_USEDEFAULT, CW_USEDEFAULT, CW_USEDEFAULT, NULL, NULL,
        hinst, NULL );

    /* If a window cannot be created, return "failure." */

    if (!hwndMain)
        return FALSE;

    /* Make the window visible and update its client area. */

    ShowWindow(hwndMain, nCmdShow);
    UpdateWindow(hwndMain);

    /* Load the accelerator table. */

    haccel = LoadAccelerators(hinstAcc, "FontAccel");
    if (haccel == NULL)
        HandleAccelErr(ERR_LOADING);        /* application defined */

    /*
     * Get and dispatch messages until a WM_QUIT message is
     * received.
     */

    while (GetMessage(&msg, NULL, NULL, NULL)) {

        /* Check for accelerator keystrokes. */

        if (!TranslateAccelerator(
                hwndMain,       /* handle of receiving window   */
                haccel,         /* handle of active accel. table */
                &msg)) {        /* address of message data      */
            TranslateMessage(&msg);
            DispatchMessage(&msg);
        }
    }
    return msg.wParam;
}

LRESULT APIENTRY MainWndProc(hwndMain, uMsg, wParam, lParam)
```

```
HWND hwndMain;
UINT uMsg;
WPARAM wParam;
LPARAM lParam;
{
    BYTE fbFontAttrib;          /* array of font-attribute flags  */
    static HMENU hmenu;         /* handle of main menu            */

    switch (uMsg) {
        case WM_CREATE:

            /*
             * Add a check mark to the Regular menu item to
             * indicate that it is the default.
             */

            hmenu = GetMenu(hwndMain);
            CheckMenuItem(hmenu, IDM_REGULAR, MF_BYCOMMAND |
                MF_CHECKED);
            return 0;

        case WM_COMMAND:
            switch (LOWORD(wParam)) {

                /* Process the accelerator and menu commands. */

                case IDM_REGULAR:
                case IDM_BOLD:
                case IDM_ITALIC:
                case IDM_ULINE:

                    /*
                     * GetFontAttributes is an application-defined
                     * function that sets the menu-item check marks
                     * and returns the user-selected font attributes.
                     */

                    fbFontAttrib = GetFontAttributes(
                        (BYTE) LOWORD(wParam), hmenu);

                    /*
                     * SetFontAttributes is an application-defined
                     * function that creates a font with the
                     * user-specified attributes the font with
                     * the main window's device context.
                     */

                    SetFontAttributes(fbFontAttrib);
                    break;
```

```
                    default:
                         break;
                }
                break;

                .
                . /* Process other messages. */
                .


          default:
                return DefWindowProc(hwndMain, uMsg, wParam, lParam);
     }
     return NULL;
}
```

17.2.2 Using an Accelerator Table Created at Run Time

The Win32 application programming interface (API) allows you to create
accelerator tables at run time. The steps involved in creating and using an
accelerator table at run time are as follows:

- Define the accelerators by filling an array of **ACCEL** structures and then
  create an accelerator table by passing the array to the
  CreateAcceleratorTable function.

- Activate the accelerator table and process WM_COMMAND messages
  generated by the accelerators.

- Destroy the accelerator table before the application closes.

17.2.2.1 Creating the Accelerator Table

The first step in creating an accelerator table at run time is filling an array of
ACCEL structures. Each structure in the array defines an accelerator in the table.
An accelerator's definition includes its flags, its key, and its identifier. The
ACCEL structure has the following form.

```
typedef struct tagACCEL { /* accl */
     BYTE    fVirt;
     WORD    key;
     WORD    cmd;
} ACCEL;
```

You define an accelerator's keystroke by specifying an ASCII character code or a
virtual-key code in the **key** member of the **ACCEL** structure. If you specify a
virtual-key code, you must first include the FVIRTKEY flag in the **fVirt** member;
otherwise, Windows interprets the code as an ASCII character code. You can
include the FCONTROL, FALT, or FSHIFT flag, or all three, to combine the
CTRL, ALT, or SHIFT key with the keystroke.

To create the accelerator table, pass the address of the array of **ACCEL** structures to the **CreateAcceleratorTable** function. **CreateAcceleratorTable** creates the accelerator table and returns the handle of the table.

17.2.2.2 Processing Accelerators

The process of loading and calling accelerators provided by an accelerator table created at run time is the same as processing those provided by an accelerator table resource. For more information, see Section 17.2.1.2, "Loading the Accelerator-Table Resource" through Section 17.2.1.4, "Processing WM_COMMAND Messages."

17.2.2.3 Destroying the Accelerator Table

Before an application closes, it must destroy accelerator tables created at run time. You can destroy an accelerator table and remove it from memory by passing the table's handle to the **DestroyAcceleratorTable** function.

17.2.2.4 Creating User-Editable Accelerators

This example shows how to construct a dialog box that allows the user to change the accelerator associated with a menu item. The dialog box consists of a combo box containing menu items, a combo box containing the names of keys, and check boxes for selecting the CTRL, ALT, and SHIFT keys. The following illustration shows the dialog box.

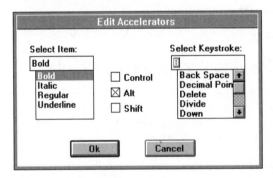

The following example shows how the dialog box is defined in the resource-definition file.

```
EdAccelBox DIALOG 5, 17, 193, 114
STYLE DS_MODALFRAME | WS_POPUP | WS_VISIBLE | WS_CAPTION
CAPTION "Edit Accelerators"
BEGIN
        COMBOBOX        IDD_MENUITEMS, 10, 22, 52, 53,
                        CBS_SIMPLE | CBS_SORT | WS_VSCROLL |
                        WS_TABSTOP
        CONTROL         "Control", IDD_CNTRL, "Button",
```

```
                                BS_AUTOCHECKBOX | WS_TABSTOP,
                                76, 35, 40, 10
        CONTROL                 "Alt", IDD_ALT, "Button",
                                BS_AUTOCHECKBOX | WS_TABSTOP,
                                76, 48, 40, 10
        CONTROL                 "Shift", IDD_SHIFT, "Button",
                                BS_AUTOCHECKBOX | WS_TABSTOP,
                                76, 61, 40, 10
        COMBOBOX                IDD_KEYSTROKES, 124, 22, 58, 58,
                                CBS_SIMPLE | CBS_SORT | WS_VSCROLL |
                                WS_TABSTOP
        PUSHBUTTON              "Ok", IDOK, 43, 92, 40, 14
        PUSHBUTTON              "Cancel", IDCANCEL, 103, 92, 40, 14
        LTEXT                   "Select Item:", 101, 10, 12, 43, 8
        LTEXT                   "Select Keystroke:", 102, 123, 12, 60, 8
END
```

The dialog box uses an array of application-defined VKEY structures, each
containing a keystroke-text string and an accelerator-text string. When the dialog
box is created, it parses the array and adds each keystroke-text string to the Select
Keystroke combo box. When the user clicks the Ok button, the dialog box looks
up the selected keystroke-text string and retrieves the corresponding accelerator-
text string. The dialog box appends the accelerator-text string to the text of the
menu item that the user selected. The following example shows the array of
VKEY structures:

```
/* VKey Lookup Support */

#define MAXKEYS 26

typedef struct _VKEYS {
    char *pKeyName;
    char *pKeyString;
} VKEYS;

VKEYS vkeys[MAXKEYS] = {
    "BkSp",     "Back Space",
    "PgUp",     "Page Up",
    "PgDn",     "Page Down",
    "End",      "End",
    "Home",     "Home",
    "Lft",      "Left",
    "Up",       "Up",
    "Rgt",      "Right",
    "Dn",       "Down",
    "Ins",      "Insert",
    "Del",      "Delete",
    "Mult",     "Multiply",
    "Add",      "Add",
```

```
    "Sub",      "Subtract",
    "DecPt",    "Decimal Point",
    "Div",      "Divide",
    "F2",       "F2",
    "F3",       "F3",
    "F5",       "F5",
    "F6",       "F6",
    "F7",       "F7",
    "F8",       "F8",
    "F9",       "F9",
    "F11",      "F11",
    "F12",      "F12"
};
```

The dialog box's initialization procedure fills the Select Item and Select Keystroke combo boxes. After the user selects a menu item and associated accelerator, the dialog box examines the controls in the dialog box to get the user's selection, updates the text of the menu item, and then creates a new accelerator table that contains the user-defined new accelerator. The following example shows the dialog-box procedure.

```
/* Global variables */

HWND hwndMain;          /* handle of main window              */
HANDLE hinstAcc;        /* handle of application instance */
HACCEL haccel;          /* handle of accelerator table      */

    .
    .
    .

/* Dialog-box procedure */

LRESULT CALLBACK EdAccelProc(hwndDlg, uMsg, wParam, lParam)
HWND hwndDlg;
UINT uMsg;
WPARAM wParam;
LPARAM lParam;
{
    int nCurSel;            /* index of list box item        */
    UINT idItem;            /* menu-item identifier          */
    UINT uItemPos;          /* menu-item position            */
    UINT i, j = 0;          /* loop counters                 */
    static UINT cItems;     /* count of items in menu        */
    char szTemp[32];        /* temporary buffer              */
    char szAccelText[32];   /* buffer for accelerator text   */
    char szKeyStroke[16];   /* buffer for keystroke text     */
    static char szItem[32]; /* buffer for menu-item text     */
    HWND hwndCtl;           /* handle of control window       */
```

```
static HMENU hmenu;        /* handle of "Character" menu      */
PCHAR pch, pch2;           /* pointers for string copying     */
WORD wVKCode;              /* accelerator virtual-key code    */
BYTE fAccelFlags;          /* fVirt flags for ACCEL structure */
LPACCEL lpaccelNew;        /* address of new accel. table     */
HACCEL haccelOld;          /* handle of old accel. table      */
int cAccelerators;         /* number of accelerators in table */
static BOOL fItemSelected = FALSE; /* item selection flag      */
static BOOL fKeySelected = FALSE;  /* key selection flag       */

switch (uMsg) {
    case WM_INITDIALOG:

        /* Get the handle of the menu-item combo box. */

        hwndCtl = GetDlgItem(hwndDlg, IDD_MENUITEMS);

        /*
         * The application's menu bar contains a "Character"
         * submenu whose items have accelerators associated
         * with them. Get the handle of the "Character"
         * submenu (its position within the main menu is 2),
         * and count the number of items it has.
         */

        hmenu = GetSubMenu(GetMenu(hwndMain), 2);
        cItems = GetMenuItemCount(hmenu);

        /*
         * Get the text of each item, strip out the '&' and
         * the accelerator text, and add the text to the
         * menu-item combo box.
         */

        for (i = 0; i < cItems; i++) {
            if (!(GetMenuString(hmenu, i, szTemp,
                    sizeof(szTemp), MF_BYPOSITION)))
                continue;
            for (pch = szTemp, pch2 = szItem;
                    *pch != '\0'; ) {

                if (*pch != '&') {
                    if (*pch == '\t') {
                        *pch = '\0';
                        *pch2 = '\0';
                    }
                    else
                        *pch2++ = *pch++;
                }
                else
```

```
                        pch++;
            }
            SendMessage(hwndCtl, CB_ADDSTRING, 0,
                (LONG) (LPSTR) szItem);
        }

        /*
         * Now fill the keystroke combo box with the list of
         * keystrokes that will be allowed for accelerators.
         * The list of keystrokes is in the application-defined
         * structure called "vkeys".
         */

        hwndCtl = GetDlgItem(hwndDlg, IDD_KEYSTROKES);
        for (i = 0; i < MAXKEYS; i++)
            SendMessage(hwndCtl, CB_ADDSTRING, 0,
                (LONG) (LPSTR) vkeys[i].pKeyString);

        return TRUE;

    case WM_COMMAND:
        switch (LOWORD(wParam)) {
            case IDD_MENUITEMS:

                /*
                 * The user must select an item from the menu-
                 * item combo box. This flag is checked during
                 * IDOK processing to be sure a selection was made.
                 */

                fItemSelected = TRUE;
                return 0;

            case IDD_KEYSTROKES:

                /*
                 * The user must select an item from the menu-
                 * item combo box. This flag is checked during
                 * IDOK processing to be sure a selection was made.
                 */

                fKeySelected = TRUE;

                return 0;

            case IDOK:

                /*
                 * If the user has not selected a menu item
                 * and a keystroke, display a reminder in a
```

```
 * message box.
 */

if (!fItemSelected || !fKeySelected) {
    MessageBox(hwndDlg,
        "Item or key not selected.", NULL,
        MB_OK);
    return 0;
}

/*
 * Determine whether the CTRL, ALT, and SHIFT
 * keys are selected. Concatenate the
 * appropriate strings to the accelerator-
 * text buffer, and set the appropriate
 * accelerator flags.
 */

szAccelText[0] = '\0';
hwndCtl = GetDlgItem(hwndDlg, IDD_CNTRL);
if (SendMessage(hwndCtl, BM_GETCHECK, 0, 0)
        == 1) {
    lstrcat(szAccelText, "Ctl+");
    fAccelFlags |= FCONTROL;
}
hwndCtl = GetDlgItem(hwndDlg, IDD_ALT);
if (SendMessage(hwndCtl, BM_GETCHECK, 0, 0)
        == 1) {
    lstrcat(szAccelText, "Alt+");
    fAccelFlags |= FALT;
}
hwndCtl = GetDlgItem(hwndDlg, IDD_SHIFT);
if (SendMessage(hwndCtl, BM_GETCHECK, 0, 0)
        == 1) {
    lstrcat(szAccelText, "Shft+");
    fAccelFlags |= FSHIFT;
}

/*
 * Get the selected keystroke, and look up the
 * accelerator text and the virtual-key code
 * for the keystroke in the vkeys structure.
 */

hwndCtl = GetDlgItem(hwndDlg, IDD_KEYSTROKES);
nCurSel = (int) SendMessage(hwndCtl,
    CB_GETCURSEL, 0, 0);
SendMessage(hwndCtl, CB_GETLBTEXT,
    nCurSel, (LONG) (LPSTR) szKeyStroke);
for (i = 0; i < MAXKEYS; i++) {
```

```
                        if(lstrcmp(vkeys[i].pKeyString,
                            szKeyStroke) == 0) {
                        lstrcpy(szKeyStroke,
                            vkeys[i].pKeyName);
                        break;
                    }
                }

                /*
                 * Concatenate the keystroke text to the
                 * "Ctl+","Alt+", or "Shft+" string.
                 */

                lstrcat(szAccelText, szKeyStroke);

                /*
                 * Determine the position in the menu of the
                 * selected menu item. Menu items in the
                 * "Character" menu have positions 0,2,3, and 4.
                 */

                if (lstrcmp(szItem, "Regular") == 0)
                    uItemPos = 0;
                else if (lstrcmp(szItem, "Bold") == 0)
                    uItemPos = 2;
                else if (lstrcmp(szItem, "Italic") == 0)
                    uItemPos = 3;
                else if (lstrcmp(szItem, "Underline") == 0)
                    uItemPos = 4;

                /*
                 * Get the string that corresponds to the
                 * selected item.
                 */

                GetMenuString(hmenu, uItemPos, szItem,
                    sizeof(szItem), MF_BYPOSITION);

                /*
                 * Append the new accelerator text to the
                 * menu-item text.
                 */

                for (pch = szItem; *pch != '\t'; pch++);
                ++pch;

                for (pch2 = szAccelText; *pch2 != '\0';
                        pch2++)
                    *pch++ = *pch2;
                *pch = '\0';
```

```
/*
 * Modify the menu item to reflect the new
 * accelerator text.
 */

idItem = GetMenuItemID(hmenu, uItemPos);
ModifyMenu(hmenu, idItem, MF_BYCOMMAND |
    MF_STRING, idItem, szItem);

/* Reset the selection flags. */

fItemSelected = FALSE;
fKeySelected = FALSE;

/* Save the current accelerator table. */

haccelOld = haccel;

/*
 * Count the number of entries in the current
 * table, allocate a buffer for the table, and
 * then copy the table into the buffer.
 */

cAccelerators = CopyAcceleratorTable(
    haccelOld, NULL, 0);
lpaccelNew = (LPACCEL) LocalAlloc(LPTR,
    cAccelerators * sizeof(ACCEL));

if (lpaccelNew != NULL)
    CopyAcceleratorTable(haccel, lpaccelNew,
        cAccelerators);

/*
 * Find the accelerator that the user modified
 * and change its flags and virtual-key code
 * as appropriate.
 */

for (i = 0; (lpaccelNew[i].cmd ==
            (WORD) idItem)
        && (i < (UINT) cAccelerators); i++) {
    lpaccelNew[i].fVirt = fAccelFlags;
    lpaccelNew[i].key = wVKCode;
}

/*
 * Create the new accelerator table, and
 * destroy the old one.
```

```
                                    */

                          DestroyAcceleratorTable(haccelOld);
                          haccel = CreateAcceleratorTable(lpaccelNew,
                              cAccelerators);

                          /* Destroy the dialog box. */

                          EndDialog(hwndDlg, TRUE);
                          return 0;

                    case IDCANCEL:
                          EndDialog(hwndDlg, TRUE);
                          return TRUE;

                    default:
                          break;
                }
            default:
                break;
        }
        return FALSE;
}
```

17.3 Functions and Messages

Following are the functions and messages used with accelerators.

Functions

CopyAcceleratorTable
CreateAcceleratorTable
DestroyAcceleratorTable
LoadAccelerators
TranslateAccelerator

Messages

WM_COMMAND
WM_INITMENU
WM_INITMENUPOPUP
WM_MENUCHAR
WM_MENUSELECT
WM_SYSCHAR
WM_SYSCOMMAND

CHAPTER 18

Dialog Boxes

18.1 About Dialog Boxes

In Microsoft ® Windows ™, a *dialog box* is a temporary window an application creates to retrieve user input. An application typically uses dialog boxes to prompt the user for additional information for commands. A dialog box usually contains one or more controls (child windows) with which the user enters text, chooses options, or directs the action of the command.

Windows provides many functions, messages, and predefined controls to help create and manage dialog boxes, thus making it easier to develop the user interface for an application. This chapter describes the dialog box functions and messages and explains how to use them create and use dialog boxes.

Windows also provides many predefined or "common" dialog boxes that support commands, such as File Open and File Print. Applications that use these commands should use the common dialog boxes to prompt for the same user input, regardless of the type of application carrying out the commands. For more information about using common dialog boxes in your applications, see Chapter 76, "Common Dialog Box Library."

18.1.1 When to Use a Dialog Box

Most applications use dialog boxes to prompt for additional information for commands that require user input. Using a dialog box is the only recommended way for an application to retrieve the input. For example, the File Open command requires the name of a file to open, so an application should use a dialog box to prompt the user for the name. In such cases, the application creates the dialog box when the user chooses the command and destroys the dialog box immediately after the user supplies the information.

Many applications also use dialog boxes to display information or options while the user works in another window. For example, word processing applications often use a dialog box with a text search command. While the application searches for the text, the dialog box remains on the screen. The user can then return to the dialog box and search for the same word again, or change the entry in the dialog box and search for a new word. Applications that use dialog boxes in this way typically create one when the user chooses a command and continue to display it for as long as the application runs or until the user explicitly closes the dialog box.

To support the different ways applications use dialog boxes, Windows provides two types of dialog box: modal and modeless. A *modal dialog box* requires the user to supply information or cancel the dialog box before allowing the application to continue. Applications use modal dialog boxes in conjunction with commands that require additional information before they can proceed. A *modeless dialog box* allows the user to supply information and return to the previous task without closing the dialog box. Modal dialog boxes are simpler to manage than modeless dialog boxes because they are created, perform their task, and are destroyed by calling a single function.

To create either a modal or modeless dialog box, an application must supply a dialog box template to describe the dialog box style and content and a dialog box procedure to carry out tasks. The *dialog box template* is a binary description of the dialog box and the controls it contains. The developer can create this template as a resource to be loaded from the application's executable file, or created in memory while the application runs. The *dialog box procedure* is an application-defined callback function that Windows calls when it has input for the dialog box or tasks for the dialog box to carry out. Although a dialog box procedure is similar to a window procedure, it does not have the same responsibilities.

An application typically creates a dialog box by using either the **DialogBox** or **CreateDialog** function. **DialogBox** creates a modal dialog box; **CreateDialog** creates a modeless dialog box. These functions load a dialog box template from the application's executable file and create a pop-up window that matches the template's specifications. There are other functions that create dialog boxes by using templates in memory and pass additional information to the dialog box procedure as the dialog box is created.

Dialog boxes usually belong to a predefined, exclusive window class. Windows uses this window class and its corresponding window procedure for both modal and modeless dialog boxes. When the function is called, it creates the window for the dialog box, as well as the windows for all controls in the dialog box, then sends selected messages to the dialog box procedure. While the dialog box is visible, the predefined window procedure manages all messages, processing some messages and passing others to the dialog box procedure so that the procedure can carry out tasks. Applications do not have direct access to the predefined window class or window procedure, but they can use the dialog box template and dialog box procedure to modify the style and behavior of a dialog box.

18.1.2 Owner Window

Most dialog boxes have an owner window (or more simply, an owner). When creating the dialog box, the application sets the owner by specifying the owner's window handle. Windows uses the owner to determine the position of the dialog box in the Z order so that a dialog box is always positioned above its owner. Also, Windows can send messages to the window procedure of the owner, notifying it of events in the dialog box.

Windows automatically hides or destroys the dialog box whenever its owner is hidden or destroyed. This means the dialog box procedure requires no special processing to detect changes to the state of the owner window.

Because the typical dialog box is used in conjunction with a command in a menu, the owner window is usually the window containing the menu. Although it is possible to create a dialog box that has no owner, it is not recommended. For example, when a modal dialog box has no owner, Windows does not disable any of the application's other windows and allows the user to continue to carry out work in the other windows, defeating the purpose of the modal dialog box.

When a modeless dialog box has no owner, Windows neither hides nor destroys the dialog box when other windows in the application are hidden or destroyed. Although this does not defeat the purpose of the modeless dialog box, it requires that the application carry out special processing to ensure the dialog box is hidden and destroyed at appropriate times.

18.1.3 Message Boxes

A message box is a special dialog box that an application can use to display messages and prompt for simple input. A message box typically contains a text message and one or more push buttons. An application creates the message box by using the **MessageBox** function, specifying the text and the number and types of buttons to display.

Although the message box is a dialog box, Windows takes complete control of the creation and management of the message box. This means the application does not provide a dialog box template and dialog box procedure. Windows creates its own template based on the text and buttons specified for the message box and supplies its own dialog box procedure.

A message box is a modal dialog box and Windows creates it by using the same internal functions that the **DialogBox** function uses. If the application specifies an owner window when calling **MessageBox**, Windows disables the owner. An application can also direct Windows to disable all top-level windows belonging to the current task by specifying the MB_TASKMODAL value when creating the dialog box.

Windows can send messages to the owner, such as the WM_CANCELMODE and WM_ENABLE, just as it does when creating a modal dialog box. The owner window should carry out any actions requested by these messages.

18.1.4 Modal Dialog Boxes

A modal dialog box should be a pop-up window having a System menu, a title bar, and a thick border; that is, the dialog box template should specify the WS_POPUP, WS_SYSMENU, WS_CAPTION, and DS_MODALFRAME styles. Although an application can designate the WS_VISIBLE style, Windows always displays a modal dialog box regardless of whether the dialog box template specifies the WS_VISIBLE style. An application must not create a modal dialog box having the WS_CHILD style. A modal dialog box with this style disables itself, preventing any subsequent input from reaching the application.

An application creates a modal dialog box by using the **DialogBox** or **DialogBoxIndirect** function. **DialogBox** requires the name or identifier of a resource containing a dialog box template; **DialogBoxIndirect** requires the handle of a memory object containing a dialog box template. The **DialogBoxParam** and **DialogBoxIndirectParam** functions also create modal dialog boxes; they are identical to the previously mentioned functions but pass a specified parameter to the dialog box procedure when the dialog box is created.

When creating the modal dialog box, Windows makes it the active window. The dialog box remains active until the dialog box procedure calls the **EndDialog** function or Windows activates a window in another application. Neither the user nor the application can make the owner window active until the modal dialog box is destroyed.

When the owner window is not already disabled, Windows automatically disables the window and any child windows belonging to it when it creates the modal dialog box. The owner window remains disabled until the dialog box is destroyed. Although a dialog box procedure could potentially enable the owner window at any time, enabling the owner defeats the purpose of the modal dialog box and is not recommended. When the dialog box procedure is destroyed, Windows enables the owner window again, but only if the modal dialog box caused the owner to be disabled.

As Windows creates the modal dialog box, it sends the WM_CANCELMODE message to the window (if any) currently capturing mouse input. An application that receives this message should release the mouse capture so that the user can move the mouse in the modal dialog box. Because Windows disables the owner window, all mouse input is lost if the owner fails to release the mouse upon receiving this message.

To process messages for the modal dialog box, Windows starts its own message loop, taking temporary control of the message queue for the entire application. When Windows retrieves a message that is not explicitly for the dialog box, it dispatches the message to the appropriate window. If it retrieves a WM_QUIT message, it posts the message back to the application message queue so that the application's main message loop can eventually retrieve the message.

Windows sends the WM_ENTERIDLE message to the owner window whenever the application message queue is empty. The application can use this message to carry out a background task while the dialog box remains on the screen. When an application uses the message in this way, the application must frequently yield control (for example, by using the **PeekMessage** function) so that the modal dialog box can receive any user input. An application can prevent the modal dialog box from sending the WM_ENTERIDLE messages by specifying the DS_NOIDLEMSG style when creating the dialog box.

An application destroys a modal dialog box by using the **EndDialog** function. In most cases, the dialog box procedure calls **EndDialog** when the user chooses the Close command from the dialog box's System menu or presses the OK or Cancel button in the dialog box. The dialog box can return a value through the **DialogBox** function (or other creation function) by specifying a value when it calls the **EndDialog** function. Windows returns this value after destroying the dialog box. Most applications use this return value to determine whether the dialog box completed its task successfully or was canceled by the user. Windows does not return control from the function that creates the dialog box until the dialog box procedure has called the **EndDialog** function.

18.1.5 Modeless Dialog Boxes

A modeless dialog box should be a pop-up window having a System menu, a title bar, and a thin border; that is, the dialog box template should specify the WS_POPUP, WS_CAPTION, WS_BORDER, and WS_SYSMENU styles. Windows does *not* automatically display the dialog box unless the template specifies the WS_VISIBLE style.

An application creates a modeless dialog box using the **CreateDialog** or **CreateDialogIndirect** function. **CreateDialog** requires the name or identifier of a resource containing a dialog box template; **CreateDialogIndirect** requires the handle of a memory object containing a dialog box template. The **CreateDialogParam** and **CreateDialogIndirectParam** functions also create modeless dialog boxes; they pass a specified parameter to the dialog box procedure when the dialog box is created.

CreateDialog and other creation functions return a window handle for the dialog box. The application and the dialog box procedure can use this handle to manage the dialog box. For example, if WS_VISIBLE is not given in the dialog box template, the application can display the dialog box by passing the window handle to the **ShowWindow** function.

A modeless dialog box neither disables the owner window nor sends messages to it. When creating the dialog box, Windows makes it the active window, but the user or the application can change the active window at any time. If the dialog box becomes inactive, it remains above the owner window in the Z order, even if the owner window is active.

The application is responsible for retrieving and dispatching input messages to the dialog box. Most applications use the main message loop for this. However, to permit the user to move to and select controls by using the keyboard, the application must call the **IsDialogMessage** function. For more information about this function, see Section 18.1.8, "Dialog Box Keyboard Interface."

A modeless dialog box cannot return a value to the application as a modal dialog box does, but the dialog box procedure can send information to the owner window by using the **SendMessage** function.

An application must destroy all modeless dialog boxes before terminating. It can destroy a modeless dialog box by using the **DestroyWindow** function. In most cases, the dialog box procedure calls **DestroyWindow** in response to user input, such as clicking the Cancel button. If the user never closes the dialog box in this way, the application must call **DestroyWindow**.

The **DestroyWindow** function invalidates the window handle for the dialog box, so any subsequent calls to functions that use the handle return error values. To prevent errors, the dialog box procedure should notify the owner that the dialog box has been destroyed. Many applications maintain a global variable containing the handle for the dialog box . When the dialog box procedure destroys the dialog box, it also sets the global variable to NULL, indicating that the dialog box is no longer valid.

The dialog box procedure must not call the **EndDialog** function to destroy a modeless dialog box.

18.1.6 Dialog Box Template

A dialog box template is binary data that describes the dialog box, defining its height, width, style, and the controls it contains. To create a dialog box, Windows either loads a dialog box template from the resources in the application's executable file or uses the template passed to it in global memory by the application. In either case, the application is responsible for supplying a template when it creates a dialog box.

A developer creates template resources by using a resource compiler or a dialog box editor. A resource compiler converts a text description into a binary resource, and a dialog box editor saves an interactively constructed dialog box as a binary resource.

Note An explanation of how to create template resources and add them to the application's executable file is beyond the scope of this book. For more information, see the documentation provided with your application development tools.

Applications that create dialog boxes without using template resources must create templates in memory and pass the templates to the **DialogBoxIndirect** or **CreateDialogIndirect** function. An application creates a memory template by allocating a global memory object and filling it with a **DLGTEMPLATE** structure and one or more **DLGITEMTEMPLATE** structures. A memory template is identical in form and content to a template resource. Many applications that use memory templates first load a template resource into memory by using the the **LoadResource** function, then modify the loaded resource to create a new memory template.

The following sections describe the styles, measurements, and other values used in a dialog box template.

18.1.6.1 Styles

Every dialog box template specifies a combination of style values that define the appearance and features of the dialog box. The style values can be window styles, such as WS_POPUP and WS_SYSMENU, and dialog box styles, such as DS_MODALFRAME. The number and type of styles for a template depends on the type and purpose of the dialog box.

Windows passes all window styles given in the template to the **CreateWindowEx** function when it creates the dialog box. Windows may pass one or more extended styles depending on the given dialog box styles. For example, when the template specifies the DS_MODALFRAME style, Windows uses the WS_EX_DLGMODALFRAME style when creating the dialog box. When the template specifies the DS_SYSMODAL style, Windows uses the WS_EX_TOPMOST style. All other dialog box styles affect how Windows manages the dialog box.

Most dialog boxes are pop-up windows that have a system menu and a title bar. Therefore, the typical template specifies the WS_POPUP, WS_SYSMENU, and WS_CAPTION styles. The template also specifies a border style: DS_MODALFRAME for modal dialog boxes, and WS_BORDER for modeless dialog boxes. A template may specify a window type other than pop-up (such as WS_OVERLAPPED) if it creates a customized window instead of a dialog box.

Windows always displays a modal dialog box regardless of whether the WS_VISIBLE style is given. When the template for a modeless dialog box specifies the WS_VISIBLE style, Windows automatically displays the dialog box when it is created. Otherwise, the application is responsible for displaying the dialog box by using the **ShowWindow** function.

The template can specify the DS_SETFOREGROUND style to force Windows to bring the dialog box to the foreground. This is especially useful for modal dialog boxes that require immediate attention from the user regardless of whether the owner window is the foreground window. This style is available in Windows NT only.

The DS_ABSALIGN style causes Windows to interpret dialog box measurements as screen coordinates; DS_SETFONT causes Windows to use a given font, instead of the system font, to draw text in the dialog box client area and in the controls in the dialog box; and DS_NOIDLEMSG prevents a modal dialog box from sending WM_ENTERIDLE messages to the owner window. These styles are described in more detail in later sections in this chapter.

The DS_SYSMODAL and DS_LOCALEDIT styles apply to applications written for Windows 3.x. Windows NT does not allow system modal dialog boxes but does ensure that dialog boxes with this style receive the WS_EX_TOPMOST style. Windows NT ignores the DS_LOCALEDIT style.

Portability Issue Windows NT does not support system modal dialog boxes. When creating modal dialog boxes, Windows NT ignores the DS_SYSMODAL style if it is given in the dialog box template. Applications should not depend on the behavior of a system modal dialog box.

18.1.6.2 Dialog Box Measurements

Every dialog box template contains measurements that specify the position, width, and height of the dialog box and the controls it contains. These measurements are device independent, so an application can use a single template to create the same dialog box for all types of display devices. This ensures that a dialog box will have the same proportions and appearance on all screens despite differing resolutions and aspect ratios between screens.

Dialog box measurements are given in dialog base units. One horizontal unit is equal to one-fourth of the average character width for the system font. One vertical unit is equal to one-eighth of the average character height for the system font. An application can retrieve the number of pixels per base unit for the current display by using the **GetDialogBaseUnits** function. An application can convert measurements from dialog base units to pixels by using the **MapDialogRect** function.

The template must specify the initial coordinates of the upper left corner of the dialog box. Usually the coordinates are relative to the upper left corner of the owner window's client area. When the template specifies the DS_ABSALIGN style or the dialog box has no owner, the position is relative to the upper left corner of the screen. Windows sets this initial position when it creates the dialog box, but permits an application to adjust the position before displaying the dialog box. For example, an application can retrieve the dimensions of the owner window, calculate a new position that centers the dialog box in the owner window, then set the position by using the **SetWindowPos** function.

The template should specify a dialog box width and height that does not exceed the width and height of the screen and ensures that all controls and are within the client area of the dialog box. Although Windows permits a dialog box to be any size, creating one that is too small or too large can prevent the user from providing input, defeating the purpose of the dialog box. Many applications use more than one dialog box when there are a large number of controls. In such cases, the initial dialog box usually contains one or more push buttons that the user can click to display the next dialog box.

18.1.6.3 Controls

The template specifies the position, width, height, style, identifier, and window class for each control in the dialog box. Windows creates each control by passing this data to the **CreateWindowEx** function. Controls are created in the order they are given in the template. The template should specify the appropriate number, type, and order of controls to ensure that the user can enter the input needed to complete the command associated with the dialog box.

For each control, the template specifies style values that define the appearance and operation of the control. Every control is a child window and therefore must have the WS_CHILD style. To ensure that the control is visible when the dialog box is displayed, each control must also have the WS_VISIBLE style. Other commonly used window styles are WS_BORDER for controls that have optional borders, WS_DISABLED for controls that should be disabled when the dialog box is initially created, and WS_TABSTOP and WS_GROUP for controls that can be accessed using the keyboard. The WS_TABSTOP and WS_GROUP styles are used in conjunction with the dialog keyboard interface described later in this chapter.

The template may also specify control style values that are specific to the control's window class. For example, a template that specifies a button control must give a button control style such as BS_PUSHBUTTON or BS_CHECKBOX. Windows passes the control styles to the control window procedure through the WM_CREATE message, allowing the procedure to adapt the appearance and operation of the control.

Windows converts the position coordinates and the width and height measurements from dialog base units to pixels, before passing these to the **CreateWindowEx** function. When Windows creates a control, it specifies the dialog box as the parent window. This means Windows always interprets the position coordinates of the control as client coordinates, relative to the upper left corner of the dialog box's client area.

The template specifies the window class for each control. A typical dialog box contains controls belonging to the predefined control window classes, such as the button and edit control window classes. In this case, the template specifies window classes by giving the corresponding predefined atom values for the classes. When a dialog box contains a control belonging a custom control window class, the template gives the name of that registered window class or the atom value currently associated with the name.

Each control in a dialog box must have a unique identifier to distinguish it from other controls. Controls send information to the dialog box procedure through

WM_COMMAND messages, so the control identifiers are essential for the procedure to determine which control sent a given message. The only exception to this rule are control identifiers for static controls. Static controls do not require unique identifiers because they send no WM_COMMAND messages.

To permit the user to close the dialog box, the template should specify at least one push button and give it the control identifier IDCANCEL. To permit the user to choose between completing or canceling the command associated with the dialog box, the template should specify two push buttons, labeled OK and Cancel. In this case, the control identifier for the OK button should be IDOK and, for the Cancel button, IDCANCEL.

A template also specifies optional text and creation data for a control. The text typically provides labels for button controls or specifies the initial content of a static text control. The creation data is one or more bytes of data that Windows passes to the control window procedure when creating the control. Creation data is useful for controls that require more information about their initial content or style than is given by other data. For example, an application can use creation data to set the initial setting and range for a scroll bar control.

18.1.6.4 System Menu

Windows gives a dialog box a System menu when the template specifies the WS_SYSMENU style. To prevent inappropriate command input, Windows automatically disables all commands in the menu except the Move and Close commands. The user can use the Move command to move the dialog box. When the user chooses the Close command, Windows sends a WM_COMMAND message to the dialog box procedure with the *wParam* parameter set to IDCANCEL. This is identical to the message sent by the Cancel button when the user chooses it. The recommended action for this message is to close the dialog box and cancel the requested command or task.

Although other menus in dialog boxes are not recommended, a dialog box template can specify a menu by supplying the identifier or the name of a menu resource. In this case, Windows loads the resource and creates the menu for the dialog box. Applications typically use menu identifiers or names in templates when using the templates to create custom windows rather than dialog boxes.

18.1.6.5 Fonts

Windows draws all text in dialog box using the system font by default. An application can direct Windows to use another font by setting the DS_SETFONT style for the dialog box and specifying a point size and typeface name. Although a dialog box template can specify a font, Windows always uses the system font for the title and menus of the dialog box; the DS_SETFONT style does not change this.

When the DS_SETFONT style is specified, the system sends a WM_SETFONT message to the dialog box procedure and to each control as it creates the control. The dialog box procedure is responsible for saving the font handle passed with the WM_SETFONT message and selecting the handle into the display device context whenever it writes text to the window. Predefined controls do this by default.

When the DS_SETFONT style is given, Windows uses the average character width of the font to calculate the position and dimensions of the dialog box. Otherwise, it uses the average character width of the system font.

18.1.6.6 Templates in Memory

A template in memory consists of a **DLGTEMPLATE** structure and related data followed by one or more **DLGITEMTEMPLATE** structures and related data. There is one **DLGITEMTEMPLATE** structure for each control in the dialog box.

The **DLGTEMPLATE** structure specifies the position, width, height, style, and number of controls in the dialog box. Additional data following the structure specifies the optional menu, class, title, and font for the dialog box. The **DLGTEMPLATE** structure has the following form.

```
typedef struct { /* dltt */
    DWORD style;
    DWORD dwExtendedStyle;
    WORD  cdit;
    WORD  x;
    WORD  y;
    WORD  cx;
    WORD  cy;
} DLGTEMPLATE;
```

The **style** member specifies the window and dialog box styles for the dialog box. Windows does not use the **dwExtendedStyle** member when creating a dialog box. An application that uses templates to create other types of windows can use this member to specify extended window styles for the other windows. The **x** and **y** members specify the dialog box position; **cx** and **cy** specify the width and height. The **cdit** member specifies the number of controls in the dialog box and is the same as the number of **DLGITEMTEMPLATE** structures in the template.

The **DLGTEMPLATE** structure is immediately followed by a 16-bit value that specifies whether the dialog box has a menu. When the value is 0x0000, the dialog box has no menu. When the value is 0xFFFF, the subsequent 16-bit value specifies the identifier of the menu resource that describes the dialog box's menu. When the initial value is neither 0x0000 nor 0xFFFF, Windows assumes it is the start of a null-terminated string specifying the name of the menu resource that describes the dialog box's menu.

The first 16-bit value following the menu identifier or name specifies the window class to which the dialog box belongs. When the value is 0x0000, Windows uses the predefined dialog box class for the dialog box. When the value is 0xFFFF, the subsequent 16-bit value is an atom value identifying a registered window class. When the initial value is neither 0x0000 nor 0xFFFF, Windows assumes it is the start of a null-terminated string identifying a registered window class.

The dialog box title immediately follows the class atom or name. The title is a null-terminated string. When the string is empty, Windows leaves the title bar for the dialog box blank. When the dialog box does not have the WS_CAPTION style, Windows sets the title to the given string but does not display it.

When the dialog box has the DS_SETFONT style, the dialog box title is immediately followed by a 16-bit value specifying the point size and by a null-terminated string specifying the typeface for the font. Windows uses this data to create a font for use when writing text in the dialog box client area and in each control. When the dialog box does not have the DS_SETFONT style, the 16-bit value and string are not part of the template.

Each **DLGITEMTEMPLATE** structure in the template contains data specifying the position, width, height, style, and identifier of the control. Additional information follows each structure, specifying the window class to which the control belongs, the initial text for the control, and any other creation data needed to create the control. A **DLGITEMTEMPLATE** structure has the following form:

```
typedef struct { /* dlit */
    DWORD style;
    DWORD dwExtendedStyle;
    WORD  x;
    WORD  y;
    WORD  cx;
    WORD  cy;
    WORD  id;
} DLGITEMTEMPLATE;
```

The **style** member specifies the control style. This member is a combination of window-style flags, such as BS_PUSHBUTTON and WS_VISIBLE. Windows does not use the **dwExtendedStyle** member to create controls for dialog boxes. Applications that use templates to create other types of windows can use this member to specify extended window styles for those controls. The **x** and **y** members specify the coordinates of the upper-left corner of the control; **cx** and **cy** specify the width and height of the control. The **id** member is the control identifier.

The control's window class is specified by an atom or name immediately following the **DLGITEMTEMPLATE** structure. When the first 16-bit value after the structure is 0xFFFF, the subsequent 16-bit value is an atom value identifying a registered window class. Otherwise, the first value is the start of a null-terminated string specifying the name of a registered window class.

The control text starts on the first 16-bit boundary after the class atom or name. This text is either two 16-bit values specifying a resource identifier or a null-terminated string specifying the initial text for the control. If this member is a resource identifier, the first 16-bit value is 0xFFFF and the second is the identifier. Resource identifiers are usually given for controls, such as static icon controls, that load and display icons or other resources rather than displaying text.

Any additional creation data required by the control follows the control text. Windows passes this data to the control as the creation parameters when it calls the **CreateWindowEx** function.

18.1.7 Dialog Box Procedure

A dialog box procedure is similar to a window procedure in that Windows sends messages to the procedure when it has information to give or tasks to carry out. Unlike a window procedure, a dialog box procedure never calls the **DefWindowProc** function. Instead, it returns the Boolean value TRUE if it processes a message or FALSE if it does not.

Every dialog box procedure has the following form:

```
BOOL APIENTRY DlgProc(hwndDlg, message, wParam, lParam)
HWND hwndDlg;
UINT message;
WPARAM wParam;
LPARAM lParam;
{
    switch (message) {

        /* Place message cases here. */

        default:
            return FALSE;
    }
}
```

The procedure parameters serve the same purpose as in a window procedure, with the *hwndDlg* parameter receiving the window handle of the dialog box.

Most dialog box procedures process the WM_INITDIALOG message and the WM_COMMAND messages sent by the controls, but process few if any other messages. If a dialog box procedure does not process a message, it must return FALSE to direct Windows to process the messages internally. The only exception to this rule is the WM_INITDIALOG message. The dialog box procedure must return TRUE to direct Windows to further process the WM_INITDIALOG message. In any case, the procedure must not call **DefWindowProc**.

18.1.7.1 The WM_INITDIALOG Message

Windows does *not* send a WM_CREATE message to the dialog box procedure. Instead it sends a WM_INITDIALOG message when it creates the dialog box and all its controls, but before it displays the dialog box. The procedure should carry out any initialization required to ensure that the dialog box displays the current settings associated with the command or task. For example, when a dialog box contains a control to show the current drive and directory, the procedure must determine the current drive and directory and set the control to that value.

The procedure can initialize controls by using functions such as **SetDlgItemText** and **CheckDlgButton**. Because controls are windows, the procedure can also manipulate them by using window-management functions such as **EnableWindow** and **SetFocus**. The procedure can retrieve the window handle for a control by using the **GetDlgItem** function.

The dialog box procedure can change the contents, state, and position of any control as needed. For example, in a dialog box that contains a list box of filenames and an Open button, the procedure can disable the Open button until the user selects a file from the list. In this example, the dialog box template specifies the WS_DISABLED style for the Open button and Windows automatically disables the button when creating it. When the dialog box procedure receives a notification message from the list box indicating that the user has selected a file, the procedure calls the **EnableWindow** function to enable the Open button.

If the application creates the dialog box by using the **DialogBoxParam**, **DialogBoxIndirectParam**, **CreateDialogParam**, or **CreateDialogIndirectParam** function, the *lParam* parameter for the WM_INITDIALOG message contains the extra parameter passed to the function. Applications typically use this extra parameter to pass the address of additional initialization information to the dialog box procedure, but the dialog box procedure must determine the meaning of the parameter. If the application uses another function to create the dialog box, Windows sets the *lParam* parameter to NULL.

Before returning from the WM_INITDIALOG message, the procedure should determine whether it should set the input focus to a given control. If the dialog box procedure returns TRUE, Windows automatically sets the input focus to the control whose window handle is in the *wParam* parameter. If the control receiving the default focus is not appropriate, it can set the focus to the appropriate control by using the **SetFocus** function. If the procedure sets the input focus, it must return FALSE to prevent Windows from setting the default focus. The control receiving the default input focus is always the first control given in the template that is visible, not disabled, and has the WS_TABSTOP style. If no such control exists, Windows sets the default input focus to the first control in the template.

18.1.7.2 The WM_COMMAND Message

A control can send a WM_COMMAND message to the dialog box procedure when the user carries out an action in the control. These messages, called notification messages, inform the procedure of user input and permit it to carry out appropriate responses.

All predefined controls, except static controls, send notification messages for selected user actions. For example, a push button sends the BN_CLICKED notification message whenever the user chooses the button. In all cases, the low word of the *wParam* parameter contains the control identifier, the high word of *wParam* contains the notification code, and the *lParam* parameter contains the control window handle.

Portability Issue In Windows NT, the placement of the notification code has moved from the *lParam* parameter to the *wParam* parameter. When porting your Windows 3.*x*–applications to Windows NT, modify the code that processes notification messages to accommodate this change in placement.

The dialog box procedure should monitor and process notification messages. In particular, the procedure must process messages having the IDOK or IDCANCEL identifiers; these messages represent a request by the user to close the dialog box. The procedure should close the dialog box by using the **EndDialog** function for modal dialog boxes and the **DestroyWindow** function for modeless dialog boxes.

Windows also sends WM_COMMAND messages to the dialog box procedure if the dialog box has a menu, such as the System menu, and the user chooses a command. In particular, Windows sends a WM_COMMAND message with the *wParam* parameter set to IDCANCEL whenever the user chooses the Close command in the dialog box's System menu. The message is nearly identical to the notification message sent by the Cancel button and should be processed in exactly the same way.

18.1.7.3 The WM_PARENTNOTIFY Message

A control sends a WM_PARENTNOTIFY message whenever the user presses a mouse button while pointing to the control. Some applications interpret this message as a signal to carry out an action related to the control, such as displaying a line of text describing to purpose of the control.

Ordinarily, Windows also sends WM_PARENTNOTIFY messages when it creates and destroys a window, but not for controls created from a dialog box template. Windows prevents these messages by specifying the WS_EX_NOPARENTNOTIFY style when creating the controls. An application cannot override this default behavior unless it creates its own controls for the dialog box.

18.1.7.4 The Control-Color Messages

Controls and Windows can send control-color messages when they want the dialog box procedure to paint the background of a control or other window by using a specific brush and colors. This can be useful when applications override the default colors used in dialog boxes and their controls. Following are the control-color messages.

WM_CTLCOLORBTN
WM_CTLCOLORDLG
WM_CTLCOLOREDIT
WM_CTLCOLORLISTBOX
WM_CTLCOLORSCROLLBAR
WM_CTLCOLORSTATIC

A control sends a control-color message to the dialog box procedure just before it paints its own background. The message allows the procedure to specify which brush to use and to set the background and foreground colors. The procedure specifies a brush by returning the brush handle. To set the background and foreground colors, the procedure uses the **SetBackgroundColor** and **SetTextColor** functions with the control's display device context. The control-color message passes a handle of the display device context to the procedure in the message's *wParam* parameter.

Windows sends a WM_CTLCOLORDLG message to the dialog box procedure if the dialog procedure does not process the WM_ERASEBKGND message. The predefined dialog box class does not have a class background brush, so this message lets the procedure define its own background without having to include the code to carry out the work.

In any case, when a dialog box procedure does not process a control-color message, Windows uses a brush with the default window color to paint the background for all controls and windows except scroll bars. An application can retrieve the default window color by passing the COLOR_WINDOW value to the **GetSysColor** function. While the background is painted, the foreground color for the display device context is set to the default text color (COLOR_WINDOWTEXT). For scroll bars, Windows uses a brush having the default scroll bar color (COLOR_SCROLLBAR). In this case, the background and foreground colors for the display device context are set to white and black, respectively.

Portability Issue   In Windows NT, the WM_CTLCOLOR message has been replaced by the set of control-color messages. When porting your Windows 3.*x*–based application to Windows NT, remember to modify the code to accommodate this change.

18.1.7.5 Default Message Processing

The window procedure for the predefined dialog box class carries out default processing for all messages that the dialog box procedure does not process. When the dialog box procedure returns FALSE for any message, the predefined window procedure checks the messages and carries out the following default actions:

Message	Default action
DM_GETDEFID	Returns the control identifier of the default push button if it exists. Otherwise, return zero.
DM_SETDEFID	Sets the control specified by the control identifier in the *wParam* parameter to the default push button.
WM_ACTIVATE	Restores the input focus to the control identified by the previously saved handle if the dialog box is activated. Otherwise, the procedure saves the handle of the control having the input focus.
WM_CHARTOITEM	Returns zero.
WM_CLOSE	Posts the BN_CLICKED notification message to the dialog box, specifying IDCANCEL as the control identifier. If the dialog box has an IDCANCEL control identifier and the control is currently disabled, the procedure sounds a warning and does not post the message.
WM_COMPAREITEM	Returns zero.
WM_ERASEBKGND	Fills the dialog box client area using the brush returned from the WM_CTLCOLORDLG message or with the default window color.
WM_GETFONT	Returns the handle of the application-defined dialog box font.
WM_INITDIALOG	Returns zero.
WM_LBUTTONDOWN	Sends a CB_SHOWDROPDOWN message to the combo box having the input focus, directing the control to hide its dropdown list box. The procedure calls the **DefWindowProc** function to complete the default action.

WM_NCDESTROY	Releases global memory allocated for edit controls in the dialog box (applies to dialog boxes in Windows 3.*x* applications that specify the DS_LOCALEDIT style) and frees any application-defined font (applies to dialog boxes that specify the DS_SETFONT style). The procedure calls the **DefWindowProc** function to complete the default action.
WM_NCLBUTTONDOWN	Sends a CB_SHOWDROPDOWN message to the combo box having the input focus, directing the control to hide its dropdown list box. The procedure calls the **DefWindowProc** function to complete the default action.
WM_NEXTDLGCTL	Sets the input focus to the next or previous control in the dialog box, or sets the focus to the control identified by the handle in the *wParam* parameter, or sets the focus to the first control in the dialog box that is visible, not disabled, and has the WS_TABSTOP style. The procedure ignores this message if the current window with the input focus is not a control.
WM_SETFOCUS	Sets the input focus to the control identified by a previously saved control window handle. If no such handle exists, the procedure sets the input focus to the first control in the dialog box template that is visible, not disabled, and has the WS_TABSTOP style. If no such control exists, the procedure sets the input focus to the first control in the template.
WM_SHOWWINDOW	Saves the handle of the control having the input focus if the dialog box is being hidden, then calls the **DefWindowProc** function to complete the default action.
WM_SYSCOMMAND	Saves the handle of the control having the input focus if the dialog box is being minimized, then calls the **DefWindowProc** function to complete the default action.
WM_VKEYTOITEM	Returns zero.

The predefined window procedure passes all other messages to the **DefWindowProc** function for default processing.

18.1.8 Dialog Box Keyboard Interface

Windows provides a special keyboard interface for dialog boxes that carries out special processing for several keys. The interface generates messages that correspond to certain buttons in the dialog box or changes the input focus from one control to another. Following are the keys used in this interface and the respective actions.

Key	Action
ALT+*mnemonic*	Moves the input focus to the first control (having the WS_TABSTOP style) after the static control containing the given mnemonic.
DOWN	Moves the input focus to the next control in the group.
ENTER	Sends a WM_COMMAND message to the dialog box procedure. The *wParam* parameter is set to IDOK or control identifier of the default push button.
ESC	Sends a WM_COMMAND message to the dialog box procedure. The *wParam* parameter is set to IDCANCEL.
LEFT	Moves the input focus to the previous control in the group.
mnemonic	Moves the input focus to the first control (having the WS_TABSTOP style) after the static control containing the given mnemonic.
RIGHT	Moves the input focus to the next control in the group.
SHIFT+TAB	Moves the input focus to the previous control that has the WS_TABSTOP style.
TAB	Moves the input focus to the next control that has the WS_TABSTOP style.
UP	Moves the input focus to the previous control in the group.

The Win32 application programming interface (API) automatically provides the keyboard interface for all modal dialog boxes. It does not provide the interface for modeless dialog boxes unless the application calls the **IsDialogMessage** function to filter messages in its main message loop. This means that the application must pass the message to **IsDialogMessage** immediately after retrieving the message from the message queue. The function processes the messages if it is for the dialog box and returns a nonzero value to indicate that the message has been processed and must not be passed to the **TranslateMessage** or **DispatchMessage** function.

Because the dialog box keyboard interface uses direction keys to move between controls in a dialog box, an application cannot use these keys to scroll the contents of any modal dialog box or any modeless dialog box for which the **IsDialogMessage** function is called. When a dialog box has scroll bars, the application must provide an alternate keyboard interface for the scroll bars. Note that the mouse interface for scrolling is available when the system includes a mouse.

18.1.8.1 The WS_TABSTOP Style

The TAB key and SHIFT+TAB keys have no effect when the controls in the dialog box do not have the WS_TABSTOP style. Windows looks for these styles as it searches for the next control in the dialog box to receive the input focus.

When the user presses TAB or SHIFT+TAB, Windows first determines whether the control having the input focus processes these keys. It sends a WM_GETDLGCODE message to the control, and if the control returns the DLGC_WANTTAB value, Windows passes the keys to the control. Otherwise, Windows uses the **GetNextDlgTabItem** function to locate the next control that is visible, not disabled, and has the WS_TABSTOP style. The search starts with the control currently having the input focus and proceeds in the order in which the controls were created—that is, the order in which they are defined in the dialog box template. When the system locates a control having the required characteristics, Windows moves the input focus to it.

An application can also use **GetNextDlgTabItem** to locate controls having the WS_TABSTOP style. The function retrieves the window handle of the next or previous control having the WS_TABSTOP style without moving the input focus.

18.1.8.2 The WS_GROUP Style

By default, Windows moves the input focus to the next or previous control whenever the user presses a direction key. As long as the current control with the input focus does not process these keys and the next or previous control is not a static control, Windows continues to move the input focus through all controls in the dialog box as the user continues to press the direction keys.

An application can use the WS_GROUP style to modify this default behavior. The style marks the beginning of a group of controls. If a control in the group has the input focus when the user begins pressing direction keys, the focus remains in the group. In general, the first control in a group must have the WS_GROUP style and all other controls in the group must *not* have this style. All controls in the group must be contiguous; that is, they must have been created consecutively with no intervening controls.

When the user presses a direction key, Windows first determines whether the current control having the input focus processes the direction keys. Windows sends a WM_GETDLGCODE message to the control and if the control returns the DLGC_WANTARROWS value, passes the key to the control. Otherwise, Windows uses the **GetNextDlgGroupItem** function to determine the next control in the group.

The **GetNextDlgGroupItem** function searches controls in the order (or reverse order) they were created. If the user presses the RIGHT or DOWN keys, **GetNextDlgGroupItem** returns the next control if that control does *not* have WS_GROUP style. Otherwise, the function reverses the order of the search and returns the first control that has the WS_GROUP style. If the user presses the LEFT or UP keys, **GetNextDlgGroupItem** returns the previous control unless the current control already has the WS_GROUP style. If the current control has this style, the function reverses the order of the search, locates the first control having the WS_GROUP style, and returns the control that immediately precedes the located control.

Once Windows has the next or previous control, it sends a WM_GETDLGCODE message to the control to determine the control type. Windows then moves the input focus to control if it is not a static control. If the control is an automatic radio button, Windows sends a BM_CLICK message to it. An application can also use the **GetNextDlgGroupItem** function to locate controls in a group.

Generally, the first control in the group combines the WS_GROUP and WS_TABSTOP styles so that the user can move from group to group by using the TAB key. If the group contains radio buttons, the application should apply the WS_TABSTOP style only to the first control in the group. Windows automatically moves the style when the user moves between controls in the group. This ensures that the input focus will always be on the most recently selected control when the user moves to the group using the TAB key.

18.1.8.3 Mnemonics

A mnemonic is a selected letter or digit in the label of a button or in the text of a static control. Windows moves the input focus to the control associated with the mnemonic whenever the user either presses the key that corresponds to the mnemonic or presses this key and the ALT key in combination. Mnemonics provide a quick way for the user to move to a given control by using the keyboard.

An application creates a mnemonic for a control by inserting the ampersand (&) immediately before the selected letter or digit in the label or text for the control. In most cases, the null-terminated string provided with the control in the dialog box template contains the ampersand. However, an application can create a mnemonic at any time by replacing a control's existing label or text by using the **SetDlgItemText** function. Only one mnemonic can be given for each control. Although it is recommended, mnemonics in a dialog box need not be unique.

When the user presses a letter or digit key, Windows first determines whether the current control having the input focus processes the key. Windows sends a WM_GETDLGCODE message to the control, and if the control returns the DLGC_WANTALLKEYS or DLG_WANTMESSAGE values, Windows passes the key to the control. Otherwise, it searches for a control whose mnemonic matches the given letter or digit. It continues to search until it locates a control or has examined all controls. During the search, it skips any static controls that have the SS_NOPREFIX style.

If Windows locates a static control and the control is not disabled, Windows moves the input focus to the first control after the static control that is visible, not disabled, and that has the WS_TABSTOP style. If Windows locates some other control that has a matching mnemonic, it moves the input focus to that control. If the control is a default push button, Windows sends a BN_CLICKED notification message to the dialog box procedure. If the control is another style of button and there is no other control in the dialog box having the same mnemonic, Windows sends the BM_CLICK message to the control.

18.1.9 Dialog Box Settings

The dialog box settings are the current selections and values for the controls in the dialog box. The dialog box procedure is responsible for initializing the controls to these settings when creating the dialog box. It is also responsible for retrieving the current settings from the controls before destroying the dialog box. The methods used to initialize and retrieve settings depend on the type of control.

18.1.9.1 Radio Buttons and Check Boxes

Dialog boxes use radio buttons and check boxes to let the user choose from a list of options. Radio buttons let the user choose from mutually exclusive options; check boxes let the user pick a combination of options.

The dialog box procedure can set the initial state of a check box by using the **CheckDlgButton** function, which sets or clears the check box. For radio buttons in a group of mutually exclusive radio buttons, the dialog box procedure can use the **CheckRadioButton** function to set the appropriate radio button and automatically clear any other radio button.

Before a dialog box terminates, the dialog box procedure can check the state of each radio button and check box by using the **IsDlgButtonChecked** function, which returns the current state of the button. A dialog box typically saves this information to initialize the buttons the next time it creates the dialog box.

18.1.9.2 Edit Controls

Many dialog boxes have edit controls that let the user supply text as input. Most dialog box procedures initialize an edit control when the dialog box first starts. For example, the dialog box procedure may place a proposed filename in the control that the user can then select, modify, or replace. The dialog box procedure can set the text in an edit control by using the **SetDlgItemText** function, which copies text from a given buffer to the edit control. When the edit control receives the input focus, it automatically selects the complete text for editing.

Because edit controls do not automatically return their text to the dialog box, the dialog box procedure must retrieve the text before it terminates. It can retrieve the text by using the **GetDlgItemText** function, which copies the edit control text to a buffer. The dialog box procedure typically saves this text to initialize the edit control later or passes it on to the parent window for processing.

Some dialog boxes use edit controls that let the user enter numbers. The dialog box procedure can retrieve a number from an edit control by using the **GetDlgItemInt** function, which retrieves the text from the edit control and converts the text to a decimal value. The user types the number in decimal digits. It can be either signed or unsigned. The dialog box procedure can display an integer by using the **SetDlgItemInt** function. **SetDlgItemInt** converts a signed or unsigned integer to a string of decimal digits.

18.1.9.3 List Boxes, Combo Boxes, and Directory Listings

Some dialog boxes display lists of names from which the user can select one or more names. To display a list of filenames, for example, a dialog box typically uses a list box and the **DlgDirList** and **DlgDirSelect** functions. The **DlgDirList** function automatically fills a list box with the filenames in the current directory. The **DlgDirSelect** function retrieves the selected filename from the list box. Together, these two functions provide a convenient way for a dialog box to display a directory listing so the user can select a file without having to type the location and name of the file.

A dialog box can also use a combo box to display a list of filenames. The **DlgDirListComboBox** function automatically fills a list box portion of the combo box with the filenames in the current directory. The **DlgDirSelectComboBox** function retrieves the selected filename from the list box portion.

18.1.9.4 Control Messages

Many controls recognize predefined messages that, when received by controls, cause them to carry out some action. For example, the BM_SETCHECK message sets the check in a check box and the EM_GETSEL message retrieves the portion of the control's text that is currently selected. The control messages give a dialog procedure greater and more flexible access to the controls than the standard functions, so they are often used when the dialog box requires complex interactions with the user.

A dialog box procedure can send a message to a control by supplying the control identifier and using the **SendDlgItemMessage** function, which is identical to the **SendMessage** function, except that it uses a control identifier instead of a window handle to identify the control that is to receive the message. A given message may require that the dialog procedure send parameters with the message and the message may have corresponding return values. The operation and requirements of each control message depends on the purpose of the message and the control that processes it.

For more information about the control messages, see Chapter 9, "Controls."

18.1.10 Custom Dialog Boxes

An application can create custom dialog boxes by using an application-defined window class for the dialog boxes instead of the predefined dialog box class. Applications typically use this method when a dialog box is their main window, but it is also useful for creating modal and modeless dialog boxes for applications that have standard overlapping windows.

The application-defined window class allows the application to define a window procedure for the dialog box and process messages before sending them to the dialog box procedure. It also lets the application define a class icon, class background brush, and a class menu for the dialog box. The application must register the window class before attempting to create a dialog box and must provide the dialog box template with the atom value or name of the window class.

Many applications create a new dialog box class by first retrieving the class information for the predefined dialog box class, and passing it to the **GetClassInfo** function, which fills a **WNDCLASS** structure with the information. The application modifies individual members of the structure, such as the class name, brush, and icon, then registers the new class by using the **RegisterWindow** function. If an application fills the **WNDCLASS** structure on its own, it must set the **cbWndExtra** member to the value DLGWINDOWEXTRA, which is the number of extra bytes Windows requires for each dialog box. If an application also uses extra bytes for each dialog box, they must be beyond the extra bytes required by Windows.

The window procedure for the custom dialog box has the same parameters and requirements as any other window procedure. Unlike other window procedures, however, the window procedure for this dialog box should call the **DefDlgProc** function instead of the **DefWindowProc** function for any messages it does not process. **DefDlgProc** carries out the same default message processing as the window procedure for the predefined dialog box, which includes calling the dialog box procedure.

An application can also create custom dialog boxes by subclassing the window procedure of the predefined dialog box. The **SetWindowLong** function lets an application set the address of the window procedure for a given window. The application may also attempt to subclass by using the **SetClassLong** function, but doing so affects all dialog boxes in the system, not just those belonging to the application.

Applications that create custom dialog boxes sometimes provide an alternate keyboard interface for the dialog boxes. For modeless dialog boxes, this may mean the application does not call the **IsDialogMessage** function and instead processes all keyboard input in the custom window procedure. In such cases, the application can use the WM_NEXTDLGCTL message to minimize the code needed to move the input focus from one control to another. This message, when passed to the **DefDlgProc** function, moves the input focus to a specified control and updates the appearance of the controls, such as moving the default push button border or setting an automatic radio button.

18.2 Using Dialog Boxes

You use dialog boxes to display information and prompt for input from the user. Your application loads and initializes the dialog box, processes user input, and destroys the dialog box when the user finishes the task. The process for handling dialog boxes varies, depending on whether the dialog box is modal or modeless. A modal dialog box requires the user to close the dialog box before activating another window in the application. However, the user can activate windows in different applications. A modeless dialog box does not require an immediate response from the user. It is similar to a main window containing controls. The following sections discuss how to use both types of dialog boxes.

18.2.1 Displaying a Message Box

The simplest form of modal dialog box is the message box. Most applications use message boxes to warn the user of errors and to prompt for directions on how to proceed after an error. You create a message box by using the **MessageBox** function, specifying the message and the number and type of buttons to display. Windows creates a modal dialog box, providing its own dialog box template and procedure. After the user closes the message box, **MessageBox** returns a value identifying the button chosen by the user to close the message box.

In the following example, the application displays a message box if the *fError* variable is TRUE. The message box displays the message describing the error. The MB_OKCANCEL style directs **MessageBox** to provide two buttons with which the user can choose how to proceed.

```
if (fError) {
    if (MessageBox(hwndDlg, SZNOTFOUND, SZDELETEITEM,
        MB_OKCANCEL)==IDOK)

        .
        . /* Prompt for a new item name and repeat the command. */
        .

    else

        .
        . /* Cancel the command. */
        .

}
```

In this example, SZNOTFOUND and SZDELETEITEM are application-defined, null-terminated strings that represent the message text and the title for the message box.

18.2.2 Creating a Modal Dialog Box

You create a modal dialog box by using the **DialogBox** function. You must specify the identifier or name of a dialog box template resource and the address of the dialog box procedure. The **DialogBox** function loads the template, displays the dialog box, and processes all user input until the user closes the dialog box.

In the following example, the application displays a modal dialog box when the user chooses a Delete Item command from an application menu. The dialog box contains an edit control (in which the user enters the name of an item) and OK and Cancel buttons. The control identifiers for these controls are ID_ITEMNAME, IDOK, and IDCANCEL, respectively.

The first part of the example consists of the statements that create the modal dialog box. These statements, in the window procedure for the application's main window, create the dialog box when the system receives a WM_COMMAND message having the IDM_DELETEITEM command identifier. The second part of the example is the dialog box procedure. The procedure retrieves the contents of the edit control and closes the dialog box upon receiving a WM_COMMAND message.

The following statements create the modal dialog box. The dialog box template is a resource in the application's executable file and has the resource identifier DLG_DELETEITEM.

```
case WM_COMMAND:
    switch (LOWORD(wParam)) {
        case IDM_DELETEITEM:
            if (DialogBox(hinst, MAKEINTRESOURCE(DLG_DELETEITEM),
                hwnd, (DLGPROC)DeleteItemProc)==IDOK)

                    .
                    . /*
                    . * Complete the command; szItemName contains
                    . * the name of the item to delete.
                    . */
                    .

                else

                    .
                    . /* Cancel the command. */
                    .

            break;
```

```
    }
    return 0L;
```

In this example, the application identifies its main window as the owner window for the dialog box. When Windows initially displays the dialog box, its position is relative to the upper left corner of the owner window's client area. The application uses the return value from **DialogBox** to determine whether to proceed with the command or cancel it. The following statements define the dialog box procedure.

```
char szItemName[80]; /* receives name of item to delete. */

BOOL CALLBACK DeleteItemProc(hwndDlg, message, wParam, lParam)
HWND hwndDlg;
UINT message;
WPARAM wParam;
LPARAM lParam;
{
    switch (message) {
        case WM_COMMAND:
            switch (LOWORD(wParam)) {
                case IDOK:
                    if (!GetDlgItemText(hwndDlg, ID_ITEMNAME,
                            szItemName, 80))
                        *szItemName=0;

                    /* Fall through. */

                case IDCANCEL:
                    EndDialog(hwndDlg, wParam);
                    return TRUE;
            }
    }
    return FALSE;
}
```

In this example, the procedure uses the **GetDlgItemText** function to retrieve the current text from the edit control identified by ID_ITEMNAME. The procedure then calls the **EndDialog** function to set the dialog box's return value to either IDOK or IDCANCEL depending on message received and to begin the process of closing the dialog box. The IDOK and IDCANCEL identifiers correspond to the OK and Cancel buttons. After the procedure calls **EndDialog**, Windows sends additional messages to the procedure to destroy the dialog box and returns the dialog box's return value back to the function that created the dialog box.

18.2.3 Creating a Modeless Dialog Box

You create a modeless dialog box by using the **CreateDialog** function, specifying the identifier or name of a dialog box template resource and the address of the dialog box procedure. **CreateDialog** loads the loads the template, creates the dialog box, and optionally displays it. Your application is responsible for retrieving and dispatching user input messages to the dialog box procedure.

In the following example, the application displays a modeless dialog box—if it is not already displayed—when the user chooses a Go To command from an application menu. The dialog box contains an edit control, a check box, and OK and Cancel buttons. The dialog box template is a resource in the application's executable file and has the resource identifier DLG_GOTO. The user enters a line number in the edit control and checks the check box to specify that the line number is relative to the current line. The control identifiers are ID_LINE, ID_ABSREL, IDOK, and IDCANCEL.

The statements in the first part of the example create the modeless dialog box. These statements, in the window procedure for the application's main window, create the dialog box when the window procedure receives a WM_COMMAND message having the IDM_GOTO command identifier, but only if the global variable *hwndGoto* does not already contain a valid handle. The second part of the example is the application's main message loop. The loop includes the **IsDialogMessage** function to ensure that the user can use the dialog box keyboard interface in this modeless dialog box. The third part of the example is the dialog box procedure. The procedure retrieves the contents of the edit control and check box when the user chooses the OK button. The procedure destroys the dialog box when the user chooses the Cancel button.

```
HWND hwndGoto = NULL;  /* window handle of dialog box */
       .
       .
       .

    case WM_COMMAND:
        switch (LOWORD(wParam)) {
            case IDM_GOTO:
                if (!IsWindow(hwndGoto)) {
                    hwndGoto = CreateDialog(hinst,
                        MAKEINTRESOURCE(DLG_GOTO),
                        hwnd, (DLGPROC) GoToProc);
                    ShowWindow(hwndGoto, SW_SHOW);
                }
                break;
        }
        return 0L;
```

In the preceding statements, the **CreateDialog** function is called only if the *hwndGoto* variable does *not* contain a valid window handle. This ensures that the application does not display two dialog boxes at the same time. To support this method of checking, the dialog procedure must set the *hwndGoto* variable to NULL when it destroys the dialog box.

The message loop for an application consists of the following statements.

```
while (GetMessage(&msg, NULL, NULL, NULL)) {
    if (!IsWindow(hwndGoto) || !IsDialogMessage(hwndGoto, &msg)) {
        TranslateMessage(&msg);
        DispatchMessage(&msg);
    }
}
```

The loop checks the validity of the window handle for the dialog box and only calls the **IsDialogMessage** function if the handle is valid. **IsDialogMessage** only processes the message if it belongs to the dialog box. Otherwise, it returns FALSE and the loop dispatches the message to the appropriate window.

The following statements define the dialog box procedure.

```
int iLine;              /* receives line number      */
BOOL fRelative;         /* receives check box status */


    .
    .
    .


BOOL CALLBACK GoToProc(hwndDlg, message, wParam, lParam)
HWND hwndDlg;
UINT message;
WPARAM wParam;
LPARAM lParam;
{
    BOOL fError;

    switch (message) {
        case WM_INITDIALOG:
            CheckDlgButton(hwndDlg, ID_ABSREL, fRelative);
            return TRUE;

        case WM_COMMAND:
            switch (LOWORD(wParam)) {
                case IDOK:
                    fRelative = IsDlgButtonChecked(hwndDlg, ID_ABSREL);
                    iLine = GetDlgItemInt(hwndDlg, ID_LINE, &fError,
                        fRelative);
                    if (fError) {
                        MessageBox(hwndDlg, SZINVALIDNUMBER,
```

```
                        SZGOTOERR, MB_OK);
                    SendDlgItemMessage(hwndDlg, ID_LINE,
                        EM_SETSEL, 0, -1L);
                } else

                    .
                    . /*
                    . * Notify the owner window to carry out the
                    . * command.
                    . */
                    .


                    return TRUE;

                case IDCANCEL:
                    DestroyWindow(hwndDlg);
                    hwndGoto = NULL;
                    return TRUE;
            }
        }
        return FALSE;
}
```

In the preceding statements, the procedure processes the WM_INITDIALOG and WM_COMMAND messages. During WM_INITDIALOG processing, the procedure initializes the check box by passing the current value of the global variable *fRelative* to the **CheckDlgButton** function. The procedure then returns TRUE to direct Windows to set the default input focus.

During WM_COMMAND processing, the procedure closes the dialog box only if the user chooses the Cancel button—that is, the button having the IDCANCEL identifier. The procedure must call the **DestroyWindow** function to close a modeless dialog box. Notice that the procedure also sets the *hwndGoto* variable to NULL to ensure that other statements that depend on this variable operate correctly.

If the user chooses the OK button, the procedure retrieves the current state of the check box and assigns it to the *fRelative* variable. It then uses the variable to retrieve the line number from the edit control. The **GetDlgItemInt** function translates the text in the edit control into a integer number. The value of *fRelative* determines whether the function interprets the number as a signed or unsigned value. If the edit control text is not a valid number, **GetDlgItemInt** sets the value of the *fError* variable to nonzero. The procedure checks this value to determine whether to display an error message or carry out the command. Notice that on an error, the dialog box procedure sends a message to the edit control, directing it to select the text in the control so that the user can easily replace it. If the **GetDlgItemInt** function does not return an error, the procedure can either carry out the requested command itself or send a message to the owner window, directing it to carry out the command.

18.2.4 Initializing a Dialog Box

You initialize the dialog box and its contents while processing the WM_INITDIALOG message. The most common task is to initialize the controls to reflect the current dialog box settings. Another common task is to center a dialog box on the screen or within its owner window. Finally, a useful task for some dialog boxes is to set the input focus to a given control rather than accept the default input focus.

In the following example, the dialog box procedure centers the dialog box and sets the input focus while processing the WM_INITDIALOG message. To center the dialog box, the procedure retrieves the window rectangles for the dialog box and the owner window and calculates a new position for the dialog box. To set the input focus, the procedure checks the *wParam* parameter to determine the identifier of the default input focus:

```
HWND hwndOwner;
RECT rc, rcDlg, rcOwner;

    case WM_INITDIALOG:
        /* Get the owner window and dialog box rectangles. */

        if ((hwndOwner = GetParent(hwndDlg)) == NULL)
            hwndOwner = GetDesktopWindow();
        GetWindowRect(hwndOwner, &rcOwner);
        GetWindowRect(hwndDlg, &rcDlg);
        CopyRect(&rc, &rcOwner);

        /*
         * Offset the owner and dialog box rectangles so that
         * right and bottom values represent the width and
         * height, and then offset the owner again to discard
         * space taken up by the dialog box.
         */

        OffsetRect(&rcDlg, -rcDlg.left, -rcDlg.top);
        OffsetRect(&rc, -rc.left, -rc.top);
        OffsetRect(&rc, -rcDlg.right, -rcDlg.bottom);

        /*
         * The new position is the sum of half the remaining
         * space and the owner's original position.
         */

        SetWindowPos(hwndDlg,
```

```
                    HWND_TOP,
                    rcOwner.left + (rc.right / 2),
                    rcOwner.top + (rc.bottom / 2),
                    0, 0,          /* ignores size arguments */
                    SWP_NOSIZE);

                if (GetDlgCtrlID((HWND) wParam) != ID_ITEMNAME) {
                    SetFocus(GetDlgItem(hwndDlg, ID_ITEMNAME));
                    return FALSE;
                }
                return TRUE;
```

In the preceding statements, the procedure uses the **GetParent** function to retrieve the owner window handle for a dialog box. The function returns the owner window handle for dialog boxes, and the parent window handle for child windows. Because an application can create a dialog box that has no owner, the procedure checks the returned handle and uses the **GetDesktopWindow** function to retrieve the desktop window handle, if necessary. After calculating the new position, the procedure uses the **SetWindowPos** function to move the dialog box, specifying the HWND_TOP value to ensure that the dialog box remains on top of the owner window.

Before setting the input focus, the procedure checks the control identifier of the default input focus. Windows passes the window handle of the default input focus in the *wParam* parameter. The **GetDlgCtrlID** function returns the control identifier for the control identified by the window handle. If the identifier does not match the correct identifier, the procedure uses the **SetFocus** function to set the input focus. The **GetDlgItem** function is required to retrieve the window handle of the desired control.

18.2.5 Creating a Template in Memory

Applications sometimes adapt or modify the content of dialog boxes depending on the current state of the data being processed. In such cases, it is not practical to provide all possible dialog box templates as resources in the application's executable file. But creating templates in memory gives the application more flexibility to adapt to any circumstances.

In the following example, the application creates a template in memory for a modal dialog box that contains a message and OK and Help buttons:

```
LRESULT DisplayMyMessage(HINSTANCE hinst, HWND hwndOwner, LPSTR lpszMessage)
{

    HGLOBAL hgbl;
    LPDLGTEMPLATE lpdt;
    LPDLGITEMTEMPLATE lpdit;
    LPWORD lpw;
```

```
LPWSTR lpwsz;
LRESULT ret;

hgbl = GlobalAlloc(GMEM_ZEROINIT, 1024);
if (!hgbl)
    return -1;

lpdt = (LPDLGTEMPLATE)GlobalLock(hgbl);

/* Define a dialog box. */

lpdt->style = WS_POPUP | WS_BORDER | WS_SYSMENU
    | DS_MODALFRAME | WS_CAPTION;
lpdt->cdit = 3; /* number of controls */
lpdt->cdit = 1;
lpdt->x  = 10;  lpdt->y  = 10;
lpdt->cx = 100; lpdt->cy = 100;

lpw = (LPWORD) (lpdt + 1);
*lpw++ = 0;   /* no menu */
*lpw++ = 0;   /* predefined dialog box class (by default) */

lpwsz = (LPWSTR) lpw;
lstrcpyW(lpwsz, L"My Message"); /* dialog box title (Unicode) */
lpw = (LPWORD) (lpwsz + lstrlenW(lpwsz) + 1);

/* Define an OK button. */

lpdit = (LPDLGITEMTEMPLATE) lpw;
lpdit->x  = 10; lpdit->y  = 10;
lpdit->cx = 40; lpdit->cy = 20;
lpdit->id = IDOK;   /* OK button identifier */
lpdit->style = WS_CHILD | WS_VISIBLE | BS_DEFPUSHBUTTON;

lpw = (LPWORD) (lpdit + 1);
*lpw++ = 0xFFFF;
*lpw++ = 0x0080;     /* button class */

lpwsz = (LPWSTR) lpw;
lstrcpyW(lpwsz, L"OK"); /* button label (Unicode) */
lpw = (LPWORD) (lpwsz + lstrlenW(lpwsz) + 1);
*lpw++ = 0;              /* no creation data */

/* Define a Help button. */

lpdit = (LPDLGITEMTEMPLATE) lpw;
lpdit->x  = 55; lpdit->y  = 10;
lpdit->cx = 40; lpdit->cy = 20;
lpdit->id = ID_HELP;    /* help button identifier */
lpdit->style = WS_CHILD | WS_VISIBLE | BS_PUSHBUTTON;
```

```
lpw = (LPWORD) (lpdit + 1);
*lpw++ = 0xFFFF;
*lpw++ = 0x0080;                    /* button class atom */
lpwsz = (LPWSTR) lpw;
lstrcpyW(lpwsz, L"Help");           /* button label (Unicode) */
lpw = (LPWORD) (lpwsz + lstrlenW(lpwsz) + 1);
*lpw++ = 0;                         /* no creation data */

/* Define a static text control. */

lpdit = (LPDLGITEMTEMPLATE) lpw;
lpdit->x  = 55; lpdit->y  = 10;
lpdit->cx = 40; lpdit->cy = 20;
lpdit->id = ID_TEXT;  /* text identifier */
lpdit->style = WS_CHILD | WS_VISIBLE | SS_LEFT;

lpw = (LPWORD) (lpdit + 1);
*lpw++ = 0xFFFF;
*lpw++ = 0x0082;                        /* static class */
for (lpwsz = (LPWSTR) lpw;
    *lpwsz++ = (WCHAR) *lpszMessage++;  /* message (Unicode) */
    );
lpw = (LPWORD) lpwsz;
*lpw++ = 0;                             /* no creation data */

GlobalUnlock(hgbl);

ret = DialogBoxIndirect(hinst, (LPDLGTEMPLATE) hgbl,
    hwndOwner, (DLGPROC) DialogProc);

GlobalFree(hgbl);

return ret;

}
```

18.3 Functions and Messages

Following are the functions and messages used to create and manage dialog boxes and controls within dialog boxes.

CreateDialog
CreateDialogIndirect
CreateDialogIndirectParam
CreateDialogParam
DefDlgProc
DialogBox

DialogBoxIndirect
DialogBoxIndirectParam
DialogBoxParam
DialogProc
EndDialog
GetDialogBaseUnits
GetDlgCtrlID
GetDlgItem
GetDlgItemInt
GetDlgItemText
GetNextDlgGroupItem
GetNextDlgTabItem
IsDialogMessage
MapDialogRect
MessageBox
MessageBoxEx
SendDlgItemMessage
SetDlgItemInt
SetDlgItemText
WM_CTLCOLORMSGBOX
WM_ENTERIDLE
WM_GETDLGCODE
WM_INITDIALOG
WM_NEXTDLGCTL

C H A P T E R   1 9

Rectangles

19.1 About Rectangles

Applications written for Microsoft ® Windows ™ use rectangles to specify rectangular areas on the screen or in a window. Rectangles are used for the cursor clipping region, the invalid portion of the client area, an area for displaying formatted text, or the scroll area. Your applications can also use rectangles to fill, frame, or invert a portion of the client area with a given brush, and to retrieve the coordinates of a window or a window's client area.

19.1.1 Rectangle Coordinates

An application must use a **RECT** structure to define a rectangle. The structure specifies the coordinates of two points: the upper left and lower right corners of the rectangle. The sides of the rectangle extend from these two points and are parallel to the x- and y-axes.

The coordinate values for a rectangle are expressed as signed integers. The coordinate value of a rectangle's right side must be greater than that of its left side. Likewise, the coordinate value of the bottom must be greater than that of the top.

Because applications can use rectangles for many different purposes, the Windows rectangle functions do not use an explicit unit of measure. Instead, all rectangle coordinates and dimensions are given in signed, logical values. The mapping mode and the function in which the rectangle is used determine the units of measure. For more information about coordinates and mapping modes, see Chapter 39, "Coordinate Spaces and Transformations."

19.1.2 Rectangle Operations

The Microsoft Win32 ™ application programming interface (API) provides several functions for working with rectangles.

The **SetRect** function creates a rectangle, the **CopyRect** function makes a copy of a given rectangle, and the **SetRectEmpty** function creates an empty rectangle. An empty rectangle is any rectangle that has zero width, zero height, or both. The **IsRectEmpty** function determines whether a given rectangle is empty. The **EqualRect** function determines whether two rectangles are identical—that is, whether they have the same coordinates.

The **InflateRect** function increases or decreases the width or height of a rectangle, or both. It can add or remove width from both ends of the rectangle; it can add or remove height from both the top and bottom of the rectangle.

The **OffsetRect** function moves a rectangle by a given amount. It moves the rectangle by adding the given x-amount, y-amount, or x- and y-amounts to the corner coordinates.

The **PtInRect** function determines whether a given point lies within a given rectangle. The point is in the rectangle if it lies on the left or top side or is completely within the rectangle. The point is not in the rectangle if it lies on the right or bottom side.

The **IntersectRect** function creates a new rectangle that is the intersection of two existing rectangles, as shown in the following figure.

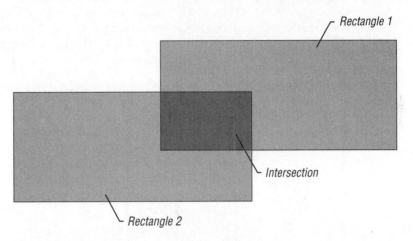

The **UnionRect** function creates a new rectangle that is the union of two existing rectangles, as shown in the following figure.

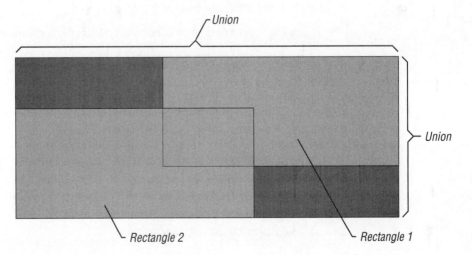

For information about functions that draw ellipses and polygons, see Chapter 34, "Filled Shapes."

19.2 Using Rectangles

The example in this section illustrates how to use the rectangle functions. It consists of the main window procedure from an application that enables the user to move and size a bitmap.

When the application starts, it draws a 32-pixel by 32-pixel bitmap in the upper left corner of the screen. The user can move the bitmap by dragging it. To size the bitmap, the user creates a target rectangle by dragging the mouse, then drags the bitmap and "drops" it on the target rectangle. The application responds by copying the bitmap into the target rectangle.

The following illustration shows the target rectangle as it is being drawn.

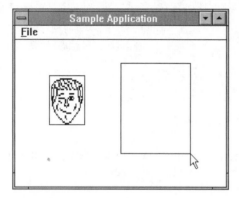

The following illustration shows the bitmap being dragged to the target rectangle.

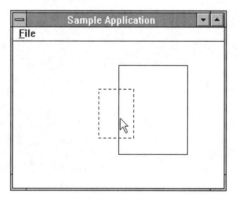

Finally, the following illustration shows the bitmap after it has been dropped on the target rectangle.

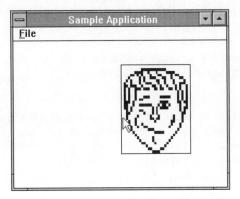

The window procedure that allows the user to move and size the bitmap is given in the following example.

```
LRESULT CALLBACK MainWndProc(hwnd, uMsg, wParam, lParam)
HWND hwnd;        /* handle of window        */
UINT uMsg;        /* message                 */
WPARAM wParam;    /* first message parameter */
LPARAM lParam;    /* second message parameter */
{
    HDC hdc;                    /* device context (DC) for window  */
    RECT rcTmp;                 /* temporary rectangle             */
    PAINTSTRUCT ps;             /* paint data for Begin/EndPaint   */
    POINT ptClientUL;           /* client area upper left corner   */
    POINT ptClientLR;           /* client area lower right corner  */
    static HDC hdcCompat;       /* DC for copying bitmap           */
    static POINT pt;            /* x and y coordinates of cursor   */
    static RECT rcBmp;          /* rectangle that encloses bitmap  */
    static RECT rcTarget;       /* rectangle to receive bitmap     */
    static RECT rcClient;       /* client-area rectangle           */
    static BOOL fDragRect;      /* TRUE if bitmap rect. is dragged  */
    static HBITMAP hbmp;        /* handle of bitmap to display     */
    static HBRUSH hbrBkgnd;     /* handle of background-color brush */
    static COLORREF crBkgnd;    /* color of client-area background  */
    static HPEN hpenDot;        /* handle of dotted pen            */

    switch (uMsg) {
        case WM_CREATE:

            /* Load the bitmap resource. */

            hbmp = LoadBitmap(hinst, MAKEINTRESOURCE(1));

            /*
```

```
                    * Create a device context (DC) to hold the bitmap.
                    * The bitmap is copied from this DC to the window's DC
                    * whenever it must be drawn.
                    */

                   hdc = GetDC(hwnd);
                   hdcCompat = CreateCompatibleDC(hdc);
                   SelectObject(hdcCompat, hbmp);

                   /*
                    * Create a brush of the same color as the background
                    * of the client area. The brush is used later to erase
                    * the old bitmap before copying the bitmap into the
                    * target rectangle.
                    */

                   crBkgnd = GetBkColor(hdc);
                   hbrBkgnd = CreateSolidBrush(crBkgnd);
                   ReleaseDC(hwnd, hdc);

                   /*
                    * Create a dotted pen. The pen is used to draw the
                    * bitmap rectangle as the user drags it.
                    */

                   hpenDot = CreatePen(PS_DOT, 1, RGB(0, 0, 0));

                   /*
                    * Set the initial rectangle for the bitmap. Note that
                    * this application supports only a 32- by 32-pixel
                    * bitmap. The rectangle is slightly larger than the
                    * bitmap.
                    */

                   SetRect(&rcBmp, 1, 1, 34, 34);
                   return 0;

               case WM_PAINT:

                   /*
                    * Draw the bitmap rectangle and copy the bitmap into
                    * it. The 32-pixel by 32-pixel bitmap is centered
                    * in the rectangle by adding 1 to the left and top
                    * coordinates of the bitmap rectangle, and subtracting
                    * 2 from the right and bottom coordinates.
                    */

                   BeginPaint(hwnd, &ps);
                   Rectangle(ps.hdc, rcBmp.left, rcBmp.top,
                       rcBmp.right, rcBmp.bottom);
```

```
            StretchBlt(ps.hdc, rcBmp.left + 1, rcBmp.top + 1,
                (rcBmp.right - rcBmp.left) - 2,
                (rcBmp.bottom - rcBmp.top) - 2, hdcCompat,
                0, 0, 32, 32, SRCCOPY);
            EndPaint(hwnd, &ps);
            break;

        case WM_MOVE:
        case WM_SIZE:

            /*
             * Convert the client coordinates of the client-area
             * rectangle to screen coordinates and save them in a
             * rectangle. The rectangle is passed to the ClipCursor
             * function during WM_LBUTTONDOWN processing.
             */

            GetClientRect(hwnd, &rcClient);
            ptClientUL.x = rcClient.left;
            ptClientUL.y = rcClient.top;
            ptClientLR.x = rcClient.right;
            ptClientLR.y = rcClient.bottom;
            ClientToScreen(hwnd, &ptClientUL);
            ClientToScreen(hwnd, &ptClientLR);
            SetRect(&rcClient, ptClientUL.x, ptClientUL.y,
                ptClientLR.x, ptClientLR.y);
            return 0;

        case WM_LBUTTONDOWN:

            /*
             * Restrict the mouse cursor to the client area. This
             * ensures that the window receives a matching
             * WM_LBUTTONUP message.
             */

            ClipCursor(&rcClient);

            /* Save the coordinates of the mouse cursor. */

            pt.x = (LONG) LOWORD(lParam);
            pt.y = (LONG) HIWORD(lParam);

            /*
             * If the user has clicked the bitmap rectangle, redraw
             * it using the dotted pen. Set the fDragRect flag to
             * indicate that the user is about to drag the
             * rectangle.
             */
```

```
            if (PtInRect(&rcBmp, pt)) {
                hdc = GetDC(hwnd);
                SelectObject(hdc, hpenDot);
                Rectangle(hdc, rcBmp.left, rcBmp.top, rcBmp.right,
                    rcBmp.bottom);
                fDragRect = TRUE;
                ReleaseDC(hwnd, hdc);
            }
            return 0;

        case WM_MOUSEMOVE:

            /*
             * Draw a target rectangle or drag the bitmap
             * rectangle, depending on the status of the fDragRect
             * flag.
             */

            if ((wParam && MK_LBUTTON)
                    && !fDragRect) {  /* draw a target rectangle */

                /*
                 * Set the mix mode so that the pen color is the
                 * inverse of the background color. The previous
                 * rectangle can then be erased by drawing
                 * another rectangle on top of it.
                 */

                hdc = GetDC(hwnd);
                SetROP2(hdc, R2_NOTXORPEN);

                /*
                 * If a previous target rectangle exists, erase
                 * it by drawing another rectangle on top of it.
                 */

                if (!IsRectEmpty(&rcTarget))
                    Rectangle(hdc, rcTarget.left, rcTarget.top,
                        rcTarget.right, rcTarget.bottom);

                /*
                 * Save the coordinates of the target rectangle.
                 * Avoid invalid rectangles by ensuring that the
                 * value of the left coordinate is greater than
                 * that of the right coordinate, and that the
                 * value of the bottom coordinate is greater than
                 * that of the top.
                 */

                if ((pt.x < (LONG) LOWORD(lParam)) &&
```

```
            (pt.y > (LONG) HIWORD(lParam)))
        SetRect(&rcTarget, pt.x, HIWORD(lParam),
            LOWORD(lParam), pt.y);

    else if ((pt.x > (LONG) LOWORD(lParam)) &&
            (pt.y > (LONG) HIWORD(lParam)))
        SetRect(&rcTarget, LOWORD(lParam),
            HIWORD(lParam), pt.x, pt.y);

    else if ((pt.x > (LONG) LOWORD(lParam)) &&
            (pt.y < (LONG) HIWORD(lParam)))
        SetRect(&rcTarget, LOWORD(lParam), pt.y,
            pt.x, HIWORD(lParam));
    else
        SetRect(&rcTarget, pt.x, pt.y, LOWORD(lParam),
            HIWORD(lParam));

    /* Draw the new target rectangle. */

    Rectangle(hdc, rcTarget.left, rcTarget.top,
        rcTarget.right, rcTarget.bottom);
    ReleaseDC(hwnd, hdc);
}
else if ((wParam && MK_LBUTTON)
        && fDragRect) { /* drag the bitmap rectangle */

    /*
     * Set the mix mode so that the pen color is the
     * inverse of the background color.
     */

    hdc = GetDC(hwnd);
    SetROP2(hdc, R2_NOTXORPEN);

    /*
     * Select the dotted pen into the DC and erase
     * the previous bitmap rectangle by drawing
     * another rectangle on top of it.
     */

    SelectObject(hdc, hpenDot);
    Rectangle(hdc, rcBmp.left, rcBmp.top,
        rcBmp.right, rcBmp.bottom);

    /*
     * Set the new coordinates of the bitmap
     * rectangle, then redraw it.
     */

    OffsetRect(&rcBmp, LOWORD(lParam) - pt.x,
```

```
                    HIWORD(lParam) - pt.y);
                Rectangle(hdc, rcBmp.left, rcBmp.top,
                    rcBmp.right, rcBmp.bottom);
                ReleaseDC(hwnd, hdc);

                /* Save the coordinates of the mouse cursor. */

                pt.x = (LONG) LOWORD(lParam);
                pt.y = (LONG) HIWORD(lParam);
            }
            return 0;

        case WM_LBUTTONUP:

            /*
             * If the bitmap rectangle and target rectangle
             * intersect, copy the bitmap into the target
             * rectangle. Otherwise, copy the bitmap into the
             * rectangle bitmap at its new location.
             */

            if (IntersectRect(&rcTmp, &rcBmp, &rcTarget)) {

                /*
                 * Erase the bitmap rectangle by filling it with
                 * the background color.
                 */

                hdc = GetDC(hwnd);
                FillRect(hdc, &rcBmp, hbrBkgnd);

                /*
                 * Redraw the target rectangle because the part
                 * that intersected with the bitmap rectangle was
                 * erased by the call to FillRect.
                 */

                Rectangle(hdc, rcTarget.left, rcTarget.top,
                    rcTarget.right, rcTarget.bottom);

                /* Copy the bitmap into the target rectangle. */

                StretchBlt(hdc, rcTarget.left + 1, rcTarget.top + 1,
                    (rcTarget.right - rcTarget.left) - 2,
                    (rcTarget.bottom - rcTarget.top) - 2, hdcCompat,
                    0, 0, 32, 32, SRCCOPY);

                /*
                 * Copy the target rectangle to the bitmap
                 * rectangle, set the coordinates of the target
```

```
                          * rectangle to 0, then reset the fDragRect flag.
                          */

                        CopyRect(&rcBmp, &rcTarget);
                        SetRectEmpty(&rcTarget);
                        ReleaseDC(hwnd, hdc);
                        fDragRect = FALSE;
                    }

                    else if (fDragRect) {

                        /*
                         * Draw the bitmap rectangle, copy the bitmap into
                         * it, and reset the fDragRect flag.
                         */

                        hdc = GetDC(hwnd);
                        Rectangle(hdc, rcBmp.left, rcBmp.top,
                            rcBmp.right, rcBmp.bottom);
                        StretchBlt(hdc, rcBmp.left + 1, rcBmp.top + 1,
                            (rcBmp.right - rcBmp.left) - 2,
                            (rcBmp.bottom - rcBmp.top) - 2, hdcCompat,
                            0, 0, 32, 32, SRCCOPY);
                        ReleaseDC(hwnd, hdc);
                        fDragRect = FALSE;
                    }

                    /* Release the mouse cursor. */

                    ClipCursor((LPRECT) NULL);
                    return 0;

            case WM_DESTROY:

                    /*
                     * Destroy the background brush, compatible bitmap,
                     * and the bitmap.
                     */

                    DeleteObject(hbrBkgnd);
                    DeleteDC(hdcCompat);
                    DeleteObject(hbmp);
                    PostQuitMessage(0);
                    break;

            default:
                    return DefWindowProc(hwnd, uMsg, wParam, lParam);
        }
        return (LRESULT) NULL;
    }
```

19.3 Functions

Following are the functions used with rectangles.

CopyRect
EqualRect
InflateRect
IntersectRect
IsRectEmpty
OffsetRect
PtInRect
SetRect
SetRectEmpty
UnionRect

CHAPTER 20

Painting and Drawing

20.1 About Painting and Drawing

Nearly all applications use the screen to display the data they manipulate. An application paints images, draws figures, and writes text so that the user can view data as it is created, edited, and printed. Microsoft ® Windows ™ provides a rich environment for painting and drawing, but, because Windows is a multitasking operating system, applications must cooperate with one another when accessing the screen.

To keep all applications functioning smoothly and cooperatively, Windows manages all output to the screen. Applications use windows as their primary output device rather than the screen itself. Windows supplies *display device contexts* (or, more simply, *display DCs*) that uniquely correspond to the windows. Applications use display DCs to direct their output to the given windows. Drawing in a window (directing output to it) prevents an application from interfering with the output of other applications and allows applications to coexist with one another while still taking full advantage of the graphics capabilities of Windows.

This chapter describes how Windows manages output to the screen and explains what applications must do to draw in a window. In particular, this chapter describes display DCs and how to prepare and use them. This chapter does not explain how to use graphics device interface (GDI) functions to generate output, nor does it explain how to print. For information on these topics, see other chapters in this book.

20.1.1 When to Draw in a Window

An application draws in a window at a variety of times: when first creating a window, when changing the size of the window, when moving the window from behind another window, when minimizing or maximizing the window, when displaying data from an opened file, and when scrolling, changing, or selecting a portion of the displayed data.

Windows manages actions such as moving and sizing a window. If an action affects the content of the window, Windows marks the affected portion of the window as ready for updating and, at the next opportunity, sends a WM_PAINT message to the window procedure corresponding to the window. The message is a signal to the application to determine what must be updated and to carry out the drawing that is necessary.

Some actions are managed by the application, such as displaying open files and selecting displayed data. For these actions, an application can mark for updating the portion of the window affected by the action, causing a WM_PAINT message to be sent at the next opportunity. If an action requires immediate feedback, the application can draw while the action takes place, without waiting for a

WM_PAINT message. For example, a typical application applies highlight to the area the user selects rather than waiting for the next WM_PAINT message.

In all cases, an application can draw in a window as soon as it is created. To draw in the window, the application must first retrieve a handle of a display DC for the window. Ideally, an application carries out most of its drawing operations during the processing of WM_PAINT messages. In this case, the application retrieves a display DC by calling the **BeginPaint** function. If an application draws at any other time, such as from within the **WinMain** function or during processing of keyboard or mouse messages, it calls the **GetDC** or **GetDCEx** function to retrieve the display DC.

20.1.2 The WM_PAINT Message

Typically, an application draws in a window in response to a WM_PAINT message. Windows sends this message to a window procedure when changes to the window have altered the content of the client area. Windows sends the message only if there are no other messages in the application message queue.

Upon receiving a WM_PAINT message, an application can call **BeginPaint** to retrieve the display DC for the client area and use it in calls to GDI functions to carry out whatever drawing operations are necessary to update the client area. After completing the drawing operations, the application calls the **EndPaint** function to release the display DC.

Before **BeginPaint** returns the display DC, Windows prepares the DC for the given window. In particular, it sets the clipping region for the DC to be equal to the intersection of the portion of the window that needs updating and the portion that is visible to the user. Only those portions of the window that have changed are redrawn. Attempts to draw outside this region are clipped and do not appear on the screen.

Windows may also send WM_NCPAINT and WM_ERASEBKGND messages to the window procedure before **BeginPaint** returns. These messages direct the application to draw the nonclient area and window background. The *nonclient area* is the part of a window that is outside of the client area. The area includes features such as the title bar, System menu (also known as the Control menu), and scroll bars. Most applications rely on the default window function, **DefWindowProc**, to draw this area and therefore pass the WM_NCPAINT message to this function. The *window background* is the color or pattern a window is filled with before other drawing operations begin. The background covers any images previously in the window or on the screen under the window. If a window belongs to a window class having a class background brush, the **DefWindowProc** function draws the window background automatically.

BeginPaint fills a **PAINTSTRUCT** structure with information such as the dimensions of the portion of the window to be updated and a flag indicating whether the window background has been drawn. The application can use this information to optimize drawing. For example, it can use the dimensions of the update region, specified by the **rcPaint** member, to limit drawing to only those portions of the window that need updating. If an application has very simple output, it can ignore the update region and draw in the entire window, relying on Windows to clip any unneeded output. Because the system discards (clips) drawing that extends outside the clipping region, only drawing that is in the update region is visible.

BeginPaint sets the update region of a window to NULL. This clears the region, preventing it from generating subsequent WM_PAINT messages. If an application processes a WM_PAINT message but does not call **BeginPaint** or otherwise clear the update region, the application continues to receive WM_PAINT messages as long as the region is not empty. In all cases, an application must clear the update region before returning from the WM_PAINT message.

After the application finishes drawing, it should call **EndPaint**. For most windows, **EndPaint** releases the display DC, making it available to other windows. **EndPaint** also shows the caret, if it was previously hidden by **BeginPaint**. **BeginPaint** hides the caret to prevent drawing operations from corrupting it.

20.1.2.1 The Update Region

The *update region* identifies the portion of a window that is out of date or invalid and in need of redrawing. Windows uses the update region to generate WM_PAINT messages for applications and to minimize the time applications spend bringing the contents of their windows up to date. Windows adds only the invalid portion of the window to the update region, requiring only that portion to be drawn.

When Windows determines that a window needs updating, it sets the dimensions of the update region to the invalid portion of the window. Setting the update region does not immediately cause the application to draw. Instead, the application continues retrieving messages from the application message queue until no messages remain. At this point, Windows checks the update region, and if the region is not empty (non-NULL), it sends a WM_PAINT message to the window procedure.

An application can use the update region to generate its WM_PAINT messages. For example, an application that loads data from open files typically sets the update region while loading so that new data is drawn during processing of the next WM_PAINT message. In general, an application should not draw at the time its data changes but route all drawing operations through the WM_PAINT message.

Invalidating and Validating the Update Region

An application invalidates a portion of a window and sets the update region by using the **InvalidateRect** or **InvalidateRgn** function. These functions add the specified rectangle or region (given in client coordinates) to the update region, combining the rectangle or region with anything Windows or the application may have previously added to the update region.

The **InvalidateRect** and **InvalidateRgn** functions do not generate WM_PAINT messages. Instead, Windows accumulates the changes made by these functions and its own changes while a window processes other messages in its message queue. By accumulating changes, a window processes all changes at once instead of updating bits and pieces one step at a time.

The **ValidateRect** and **ValidateRgn** functions validate a portion of the window by removing a specified rectangle or region from the update region. These functions are typically used when the window has updated a specific part of the screen in the update region before receiving the WM_PAINT message.

Retrieving the Update Region

The **GetUpdateRect** and **GetUpdateRgn** functions retrieve the current update region for the window. **GetUpdateRect** retrieves the smallest rectangle (in client coordinates) that encloses the entire update region. **GetUpdateRgn** retrieves the update region itself. These functions can be used to calculate the current size of the update region to determine where to carry out a drawing operation.

BeginPaint also retrieves the dimensions of the smallest rectangle enclosing the current update region, copying the dimensions to the **rcPaint** member in the **PAINTSTRUCT** structure. Because **BeginPaint** validates the update region, any call to **GetUpdateRect** and **GetUpdateRgn** immediately after a call to **BeginPaint** returns an empty update region.

Excluding the Update Region

The **ExcludeUpdateRgn** function excludes the update region from the clipping region for the display DC. This function is useful when drawing in a window other than when a WM_PAINT message is processing. It prevents drawing in the areas that will be updated during the next WM_PAINT message.

20.1.2.2 Synchronous and Asynchronous Drawing

Most drawing carried out during processing of the WM_PAINT message is asynchronous. That is, there is a delay between the time a portion of the window is invalidated and the time the WM_PAINT message is sent. During the delay, the application typically retrieves messages from the queue and carries out other tasks. The reason for the delay is that Windows generally treats drawing in a window as a low-priority operation and works as though user-input messages and

messages that may affect the position or size of a window will be processed
before a WM_PAINT message.

In some cases, it is necessary for an application to draw synchronously—that is,
draw in the window immediately after invalidating a portion of the window. A
typical application draws its main window immediately after creating the window
to signal the user that the application has started successfully. Windows
synchronously draws some control windows, such as buttons, because such
windows serve as the focus for user input. Although any window with a simple
drawing routine can be drawn synchronously, all such drawing should be done
quickly and should not interfere with the application's ability to respond to user
input.

The **UpdateWindow** and **RedrawWindow** functions allow for synchronous
drawing. **UpdateWindow** sends a WM_PAINT message directly to the window if
the update region is not empty. **RedrawWindow** also sends a WM_PAINT
message, but gives the application greater control over how to draw the window,
such as whether to draw the nonclient area and window background or whether to
send the message regardless of whether the update region is empty. These
functions send the WM_PAINT message directly to the window, regardless of the
number of other messages in the application message queue.

Any window requiring time-consuming drawing operations should be drawn
asynchronously to prevent pending messages from being blocked as the window
is drawn. Also, any application that frequently invalidates small portions of a
window should usually allow these invalid portions to consolidate into a single
asynchronous WM_PAINT message, rather than a series of synchronous
WM_PAINT messages.

20.1.3 Drawing Without the WM_PAINT Message

Although applications carry out most drawing operations as the WM_PAINT
message is processing, it is sometimes more efficient for an application to draw
directly in a window without relying on the WM_PAINT message. This can be
useful when the user needs immediate feedback, such as when selecting text and
dragging or sizing an object. In such cases, the application usually draws while
processing keyboard or mouse messages.

To draw in a window without using a WM_PAINT message, the application uses
the **GetDC** or **GetDCEx** function to retrieve a display DC for the window. With
the display DC, the application can draw in the window and avoid intruding into
other windows. When the application has finished drawing, it calls the
ReleaseDC function to release the display DC for use by other applications.

When drawing without using a WM_PAINT message, the application usually
does not invalidate the window. Instead, it draws in such a fashion that it can
easily restore the window and remove the drawing. For example, when the user

selects text or an object, the application typically draws the selection by inverting whatever is already in the window. The application can remove the selection and restore the original contents of the window by simply inverting again.

The application is responsible for carefully managing any changes it makes to the window. In particular, if an application draws a selection and an intervening WM_PAINT message occurs, the application must ensure that any drawing done during the message does not corrupt the selection. To avoid this, many applications remove the selection, carry out usual drawing operations, and then restore the selection when complete.

20.1.4 Window Coordinate System

The coordinate system for a window is based on the coordinate system of the display device. The basic unit of measure is the device unit (typically, the pixel). Points on the screen are described by x- and y-coordinate pairs. The x-coordinates increase to the right; y-coordinates increase from top to bottom. The origin (0,0) for the system depends on the type of coordinates being used.

Windows and applications specify the position of a window on the screen in *screen coordinates*. For screen coordinates, the origin is the upper-left corner of the screen. The full position of a window is often described by a **RECT** structure containing the screen coordinates of two points that define the upper-left and lower-right corners of the window.

Windows and applications specify the position of points in a window by using *client coordinates*. The origin in this case is the upper-left corner of the window or client area. Client coordinates ensure that an application can use consistent coordinate values while drawing in the window, regardless of the position of the window on the screen.

The dimensions of the client area are also described by a **RECT** structure containing client coordinates for the area. In all cases, the upper-left coordinate of the rectangle is included in the window or client area, while the lower-right coordinate is excluded. Graphics operations in a window or client area are excluded from the right and lower edges of the enclosing rectangle.

Occasionally, applications may be required to map coordinates in one window to those of another window. An application can map coordinates by using the **MapWindowPoints** function. If one of the windows is the desktop window, the function effectively converts screen coordinates to client coordinates and vice versa; the desktop window is always specified in screen coordinates.

20.1.5 Window Regions

In addition to the update region, every window has a *visible region* that defines the window portion visible to the user. The system changes the visible region for the window whenever the window changes size or whenever another window is moved such that it obscures or exposes a portion of the window. Applications cannot change the visible region directly, but Windows automatically uses the visible region to create the clipping region for any display DC retrieved for the window.

The *clipping region* determines where the system permits drawing. When the application retrieves a display DC using the **BeginPaint**, **GetDC**, or **GetDCEx** function, the system sets the clipping region for the DC to the intersection of the visible region and the update region. Applications can change the clipping region by using functions such as **SelectClipPath** and **SelectClipRgn**, to further limit drawing to a particular portion of the update area.

The WS_CLIPCHILDREN and WS_CLIPSIBLINGS styles further specify how Windows calculates the visible region for a window. If a window has one or both of these styles, the visible region excludes any child window or sibling windows (windows having the same parent window). Therefore, drawing that would otherwise intrude in these windows will always be clipped.

20.1.6 Window Background

The window background is the color or pattern used to fill the client area before a window begins drawing. The window background covers whatever was on the screen before the window was moved there, erasing existing images and preventing the application's new output from being mixed with unrelated information.

Windows paints the background for a window or gives the window the opportunity to do so by sending it a WM_ERASEBKGND message when the application calls **BeginPaint**. If an application does not process the message but passes it to the **DefWindowProc** function, Windows erases the background by filling it with the pattern in the background brush specified by the window's class. If the class has no background brush or the brush is not valid, Windows sets the **fErase** member in the **PAINTSTRUCT** structure returned by **BeginPaint**, but carries out no other action. This gives the application a second chance to draw the window background, if necessary.

If it processes the WM_ERASEBKGND message, the application should use the message's *wParam* parameter to draw the background. This parameter contains the handle of the display DC for the window. After drawing the background, the application should return a nonzero value. This ensures that **BeginPaint** does not erroneously set the **fErase** member of the **PAINTSTRUCT** structure to a nonzero value (indicating the background should be erased) when the application processes the subsequent WM_PAINT message.

An application can define a class background brush by assigning a brush handle or a system color value to the **hbrBackground** member of the **WNDCLASS** structure when registering the class with the **RegisterClass** function. The **GetStockObject** or **CreateSolidBrush** function can be used to create a brush handle; a system color value can be one of those defined for the **SetSysColors** function. (The value must be increased by one before it is assigned to the member.)

An application can process the WM_ERASEBKGND message even though a class background brush is defined. This is typical in applications that enable the user to change the window background color or pattern for a given window without affecting other windows in the class. In such cases, the application must not pass the message to **DefWindowProc**.

In Windows 3.*x*, the origin of the screen is the point of reference for drawing brushes. The pattern in a window background can become misaligned if the window is moved to a new location. To prevent misalignment when running with Windows 3.*x*, applications that use pattern brushes for the window background must use the **SetBrushOrg** and **UnrealizeObject** functions to align the brush with the window before drawing.

In Windows NT ™, it is not necessary for an application to align brushes, because the system draws the brush using the window origin as the point of reference. Given this, the user can move the window without affecting the alignment of pattern brushes.

20.1.7 Minimized Windows

Windows reduces an application's main window (overlapping style) to a minimized window when the user chooses the Minimize command from the System menu or the application calls the **ShowWindow** function and specifies a value such as SW_MINIMIZE. Minimizing a window speeds up system performance by reducing the amount of work an application must do when updating its main window.

For a typical application, Windows draws an icon, called the class icon, when the window is minimized, labeling the icon with the name of the window. The class icon, a static image that represents the application, is specified by the application when it registers the window class. The application assigns the handle of the class icon to the **hIcon** member of the **WNDCLASS** structure before calling **RegisterClass**. The application can use the **LoadIcon** function to retrieve the icon handle.

Before drawing the class icon, Windows sends a WM_ICONERASEBKGND message to the window procedure, enabling the application to prepare the background for drawing the icon and by setting the best possible background colors for the icon. This is useful for applications that combine the icon with the current background colors. If the application processes the message, it should use the display DC provided with the message to draw the background (the *wParam* parameter contains the handle of the display DC). If the application does not process the WM_ICONERASEBKGND message, it should pass the message to **DefWindowProc**; the function fills the icon area with the current desktop color and pattern. After sending WM_ICONERASEBKGND, Windows sends the WM_PAINTICON message to the window procedure. The application should immediately forward this internal message to **DefWindowProc**.

Windows does not require that a window class have a class icon. If an application sets the **hIcon** member of the **WNDCLASS** structure to NULL, a class icon is not defined. In this case, Windows sends the WM_ERASEBKGND message (instead of the WM_ICONERASEBKGND message) to a window of the class whenever the window must paint the icon background. Windows then sends a WM_PAINT message and the application draws an icon or another image representing the minimized window. In such cases, the application must determine when the window is minimized and draw accordingly. It can do so by calling the **IsIconic** function. If the function returns TRUE, the window is minimized. If an application has no class icon and fails to process the WM_ERASEBKGND and WM_PAINT messages, the area that Windows reserves for the application's icon will contain whatever was previously on the screen.

20.1.8 Window Size

Windows changes the size of a window when the user chooses System menu commands, such as Size and Maximize, or when the application calls functions, such as the **SetWindowPos** function. When a window changes size, Windows assumes that the contents of the previously exposed portion of the window are not affected and need not be redrawn. Windows invalidates only the newly exposed portion of the window, which saves time when the eventual WM_PAINT message is processed by the application. In this case, WM_PAINT message is not generated when the size of the window is reduced.

For some windows, however, any change to the size of the window invalidates the contents. For example, a clock application that adapts the face of the clock to fit neatly within its window must redraw the clock anytime the window changes size. To force Windows to invalidate the entire client area of the window when a vertical, horizontal, or both vertical and horizontal change is made, an application must specify the CS_VREDRAW or CS_HREDRAW style, or both, when registering the window class. Any window belonging to a window class having these styles is invalidated each time the user or the application changes the size of the window.

20.1.9 Nonclient Area

Windows sends a WM_NCPAINT message to the window whenever a part of the nonclient area of the window, such as the title bar, menu bar, or window frame, must be updated. Windows may also send other messages to direct a window to update a portion of its client area; for example, when a window becomes active or inactive it sends the WM_NCACTIVATE message to update its title bar. In general, processing these messages for standard windows is not recommended, because the application must be able to draw all the required parts of the nonclient area for the window. For this reason, most applications pass these messages to **DefWindowProc** for default processing.

An application that creates custom nonclient areas for its windows must process these messages. When doing so, the application must use a window DC to carry out drawing in the window. The *window DC* enables the application to draw in all portions of the window, including the nonclient area. An application retrieves a window DC by using the **GetWindowDC** or **GetDCEx** function and must release the window DC by using the **ReleaseDC** function when drawing is complete.

Windows maintains an update region for the nonclient area. When an application receives a WM_NCPAINT message, the *wParam* parameter contains the handle of a region defining the dimensions of the update region. The application can use the handle to combine the update region with the clipping region for the window DC. Windows does not automatically combine the update region when retrieving the window DC unless the application uses **GetDCEx** and specifies both the region handle and the DCX_INTERSECTRGN flag. If the application does not combine the update region, only drawing operations that would otherwise extend outside the window are clipped. The application is not responsible for clearing the update region, regardless of whether it uses the region.

If an application processes the WM_NCACTIVATE message, it must return TRUE after processing the message to direct Windows to complete the change of active window. If the window is minimized when the application receives the WM_NCACTIVATE message, it should pass the message to **DefWindowProc**. In such cases, the default function redraws the label for the icon.

20.1.10 Child Windows

A child window is a window having the WS_CHILD or WS_CHILDWINDOW style. Like other window styles, child windows receive WM_PAINT messages to prompt updating. Each child window has an update region, which either Windows or the application can set to generate eventual WM_PAINT messages.

A child window's update and visible regions are affected by the child's parent window; this is not true for windows of other styles. Windows often sets the child window's update region when it sets the parent window's update region, causing the child window to receive WM_PAINT messages when the parent window receives them. Also, Windows limits the location of the child window's visible region to within the client area of the parent window. Windows clips any portion of the child window moved outside the parent window.

Windows sets the update region for a child window whenever part of the parent window's update region includes a portion of the child window. In such cases, Windows first sends a WM_PAINT message to the parent window and then sends a message to the child window, allowing the child to restore any portions of the window that the parent may have drawn over.

Windows does not set the parent's update region when the child's is set. An application cannot generate a WM_PAINT message for the parent window by invalidating the child window. Similarly, an application cannot generate a WM_PAINT message for the child by invalidating a portion of the parent's client area that lies entirely under the child window. In such cases, neither window receives a WM_PAINT message.

An application can prevent a child window's update region from being set when the parent window's is set by specifying the WS_CLIPCHILDREN style when creating the parent window. When this style is set, Windows excludes the child windows from the parent's visible region and therefore ignores any portion of the update region that may contain the child windows. When the application paints in the parent window, any drawing that would cover the child window is clipped, making a subsequent WM_PAINT message to the child window unnecessary.

The update and visible regions of a child window are also affected by the child window's siblings. Sibling windows are any windows that have a common parent window. If sibling windows overlap, then setting the update region for one affects the update region of another, causing WM_PAINT messages to be sent to both windows. Sibling windows receive WM_PAINT messages in the reverse order of their position in the Z order. Given this, the window highest in the Z order (on the top) receives its WM_PAINT message last, and vice versa.

Sibling windows are not automatically clipped. One sibling can draw over another overlapping sibling even if the window that is drawing has a position in the Z order that is lower. An application can prevent this by specifying the WS_CLIPSIBLINGS style when creating the windows. When this style is set, Windows excludes all portions of an overlapping sibling window from a window's visible region if the overlapping sibling window has a higher position in the Z order.

Note The update and visible regions for windows that have the WS_POPUP or WS_POPUPWINDOW style are not affected by their parent windows.

20.1.11 Display Device Contexts

A display DC is a device context, created by Windows, that an application uses to paint and draw a window. Windows prepares each display DC for output to a window, setting the drawing objects, colors, and modes for the window instead of for the display device. When the application supplies the display DC in calls to GDI functions, GDI uses the information in the context to generate output in the given window without intruding on other windows or other parts of the screen.

Windows provides five kinds of display device context: common, class, parent, private, and window. The common, class, and private DCs permit drawing in the client area of a given window. The parent and window DCs permit drawing anywhere in the window. Although the parent DC also permits drawing in the parent window, it is not intended to be used in this way.

Windows supplies a common, class, parent, or private DC to a window based on the type of display DC specified in that window's class style. Windows supplies a window DC only when the application explicitly requests one; for example, by calling the **GetWindowDC** or **GetDCEx** function. In all cases, an application can determine which window a display DC currently represents by using the **WindowFromDC** function.

20.1.11.1 Display Device Context Cache

Windows maintains a cache of display DCs that it uses for common, parent, and window DCs. Windows retrieves a DC from the cache whenever an application calls the **GetDC** or **BeginPaint** function; Windows returns the DC to the cache when the application subsequently calls the **ReleaseDC** or **EndPaint** function.

In Windows 3.x, the cache contains five display DCs, but only five DCs from the cache can be active at a time. To ensure that other applications have access to these DCs, an application must release a device context immediately after using it. Failure to do so eventually causes the application to fail.

In Windows NT, there is no predetermined limit on the amount of DCs that a cache can hold; Windows NT creates a new display DC for the cache if none is available. Given this, an application designed for Windows NT can have more than five active DCs from the cache at a time. However, an application must continue to release these DCs after use. Because new display DCs for the cache are allocated in the application's heap space, failing to release the DCs eventually consumes all available heap space. Windows NT indicates this failure by returning an error when it cannot allocate space for the new DC. Other functions unrelated to the cache may also return errors.

Portability To minimize porting efforts, applications that use common DCs should be limited to no more than five and ensure that a common DC is released as soon as possible after it is used.

20.1.11.2 Display Device Context Defaults

Upon first creating a display DC, Windows assigns default values for the attributes (that is, drawing objects, colors, and modes) that comprise the DC. The following table shows the default values for the attributes of a display DC.

Attribute	Default value
Background color	Background color setting from Windows Control Panel (typically, white).
Background mode	OPAQUE.
Bitmap	None.
Brush	WHITE_BRUSH.
Brush origin	(0,0).
Clipping region	Entire window or client area with the update region clipped as appropriate. Child and pop-up windows in the client area may also be clipped.
Palette	DEFAULT_PALETTE.
Current pen position	(0,0).
Device origin	Upper-left corner of the window or the client area.
Drawing mode	R2_COPYPEN.
Font	SYSTEM_FONT (SYSTEM_FIXED_FONT for applications written to run with Windows versions 3.0 and earlier).
Intercharacter spacing	0.
Mapping mode	MM_TEXT.
Pen	BLACK_PEN.
Polygon-fill mode	ALTERNATE.
Stretch mode	BLACKONWHITE.
Text color	Text color setting from Windows Control Panel (typically, black).
Viewport extent	(1,1).
Viewport origin	(0,0).
Window extent	(1,1).
Window origin	(0,0).

An application can modify the values of the display DC attributes by using selection and attribute functions, such as **SelectObject**, **SetMapMode**, and **SetTextColor**. For example, an application can modify the default units of measure in the coordinate system by using **SetMapMode** to change the mapping mode.

Changes to the attribute values of a common, parent, or window DC are not permanent. When an application releases these DCs, the current selections, such as mapping mode and clipping region, are lost as the context is returned to the cache. Changes to a class or private DC persist indefinitely. To restore these DCs to the original defaults, an application must explicitly set each attribute.

20.1.11.3 Common Display Device Contexts

A *common DC* is used for drawing in the client area of the window. Windows provides a common DC by default for any window whose window class does not explicitly specify a display DC style. Common DCs are typically used with windows that can be drawn without extensive changes to the DC attributes. Common DCs are convenient because they do not require additional memory or system resources, but they can be inconvenient if the application must set up many attributes before using it.

Windows retrieves all common DCs from the display DC cache. An application can retrieve a common DC immediately after the window is created. Because the common DC is from the cache, the application must always release the DC as soon as possible after drawing. After the common DC is released, it is no longer valid and the application must not attempt to draw with it. To draw again, the application must retrieve a new common DC, and continue to retrieve and release a common DC each time it draws in the window. If the application retrieves the DC handle by using the **GetDC** function, it must use the **ReleaseDC** function to release the handle. Similarly, for each **BeginPaint** function, the application must use a corresponding **EndPaint** function.

When the application retrieves the DC, Windows adjusts the origin so that it aligns with the upper-left corner of the client area. It also sets the clipping region so that output to the DC is clipped to the client area. Any output that would otherwise appear outside the client area is clipped. If the application retrieves the common DC by using **BeginPaint**, Windows also includes the update region in the clipping region to further restrict the output.

When an application releases a common DC, Windows restores the default values for the attributes of the DC. An application that modifies attribute values must do so each time it retrieves a common DC. Releasing the DC releases any drawing objects the application may have selected into the DC, so the application need not release these objects before releasing the DC. In all cases, an application must never assume that the common DC retains nondefault selections after being released.

20.1.11.4 Private Display Device Contexts

A *private DC* enables an application to avoid retrieving and initializing a display DC each time the application must draw in a window. Private DCs are useful for windows that require many changes to the values of the attributes of the DC to prepare it for drawing. Private DCs reduce the time required to prepare the DC and therefore the time needed to carry out drawing in the window.

An application directs Windows to create a private DC for a window by specifying the CS_OWNDC style in the window class. Windows creates a unique private DC each time it creates a new window belonging to the class. Initially, the private DC has the same default values for attributes as a common DC, but the application can modify these at any time. Windows preserves changes to the DC for the life of the window or until the application makes additional changes.

An application can retrieve the handle of the private DC by using the **GetDC** function any time after the window is created. The application must retrieve the handle only once. Thereafter, it can keep and use the handle any number of times. Because a private DC is not part of the display DC cache, an application never needs to release the DC by using the **ReleaseDC** function.

Windows automatically adjusts the DC to reflect changes to the window, such as moving or sizing. This ensures that any overlapping windows are always properly clipped; that is, no action is required by the application to ensure clipping. However, Windows does not revise the DC to include the update region. Therefore, when processing a WM_PAINT message, the application must incorporate the update region either by calling **BeginPaint** or by retrieving the update region and intersecting it with the current clipping region. If the application does not call **BeginPaint**, it must explicitly validate the update region by using the **ValidateRect** or **ValidateRgn** function. If the application does not validate the update region, the window receives an endless series of WM_PAINT messages.

Because **BeginPaint** hides the caret if a window is showing it, an application that calls **BeginPaint** should also call the **EndPaint** function to restore the caret. **EndPaint** has no other effect on a private DC.

Although a private DC is convenient to use, it is expensive in terms of system resources, requiring 800 or more bytes to store. Private DCs are recommended when performance considerations outweigh storage costs.

Windows includes the private DC when sending the WM_ERASEBKGND message to the application. The current selections of the private DC, including mapping mode, are in effect when the application or Windows processes these messages. To avoid undesirable effects, Windows uses logical coordinates when erasing the background; for example, it uses the **GetClipBox** function to retrieve the logical coordinates of the area to erase and passes these coordinates to the **FillRect** function. Applications that process these messages can use similar techniques. Windows supplies a window DC with the WM_ICONERASEBKGND message regardless of whether the corresponding window has a private DC.

An application can use the **GetDCEx** function to force Windows to return a common DC for the window that has a private DC. This is useful for carrying out quick touch-ups to a window without changing the current values of the attributes of the private DC.

20.1.11.5 Class Display Device Contexts

By using a *class DC*, an application can use a single display DC for every window belonging to a given class. Class DCs are often used with control windows that are drawn using the same attribute values. Like private DCs, class DCs minimize the time required to prepare a DC for drawing.

Windows supplies a class DC for a window if it belongs to a window class having the CS_CLASSDC style. Windows creates the DC when creating the first window belonging to the class and then uses the same DC for all subsequently created windows in the class. Initially, the class DC has the same default values for attributes as a common DC, but the application can modify these at any time. Windows preserves all changes, except for the clipping region and device origin, until the last window in the class has been destroyed. A change made for one window applies to all windows in that class.

An application can retrieve the handle for the class DC by using the **GetDC** function any time after the first window has been created. The application can keep and use the handle without releasing it because the class DC is not part of the display DC cache. If the application creates another window in the same window class, the application must retrieve the class DC again. Retrieving the DC sets the correct device origin and clipping region for the new window. After the application retrieves the class DC for a new window in the class, the DC can no longer be used to draw in the original window without again retrieving it for that window. In general, each time it must draw in a window, an application must explicitly retrieve the class DC for the window.

Applications that use class DCs should always call **BeginPaint** when processing a WM_PAINT message. The function sets the correct device origin and clipping region for the window, and incorporates the update region. The application should also call **EndPaint** to restore the caret if **BeginPaint** hid it. **EndPaint** has no other effect on a class DC.

Windows passes the class DC when sending the WM_ERASEBKGND message to the application, permitting the current attribute values to affect any drawing carried out by the application or Windows when processing this message. Windows supplies a window DC with the WM_ICONERASEBKGND message regardless of whether the corresponding window has a class DC. As it could with a window having a private DC, an application can use **GetDCEx** to force Windows to return a common DC for the window that has a class DC.

In Windows 3.*x*, class DCs are intended to be used with windows created by a single application. This ensures that drawing objects, such as pens and brushes, selected into the class DC are created and maintained by a single application. Errors can occur if several applications attempt to create and select drawing objects into a single class DC. In particular, assumptions made about the validity of handles returned by the **SelectObject** function can be wrong. In Windows NT, using class DCs is not recommended.

20.1.11.6 Window Display Device Contexts

A window DC enables an application to draw anywhere in a window, including the nonclient area. Window DCs are typically used by applications that process the WM_NCPAINT and WM_NCACTIVATE messages for windows with custom nonclient areas. Using a window DC is not recommended for any other purpose.

An application can retrieve a window DC by using the **GetWindowDC** or **GetDCEx** function with the DCX_WINDOW option specified. The function retrieves a window DC from the display DC cache. A window that uses a window DC must release it after drawing by using the **ReleaseDC** function as soon as possible. Window DCs are always from the cache; the CS_OWNDC and CS_CLASSDC class styles do not affect the DC.

When an application retrieves a window DC, Windows sets the device origin to the upper-left corner of the window instead of the upper-left corner of the client area. It also sets the clipping region to include the entire window, not just the client area. Windows sets the current attribute values of a window DC to the same default values as a common DC. An application can change the attribute values, but Windows does not preserve any changes when the DC is released.

20.1.11.7 Parent Display Device Contexts

A *parent DC* enables an application to minimize the time necessary to set up the clipping region for a window. An application typically uses parent DCs to speed up drawing for control windows without requiring a private or class DC. For example, Windows uses parent DCs for push button and edit controls. Parent DCs are intended for use with child windows only, never with top-level or pop-up windows.

Windows supplies a parent DC for any window belonging to a window class specifying the CS_PARENTDC style. An application can retrieve the parent DC by using **GetDC** immediately after the window is created. Windows always retrieves the parent DC from the display DC cache even if the parent uses a private or class DC, so the application must release the DC by using **ReleaseDC** as soon as possible after drawing. When processing a WM_PAINT message, the application must retrieve the parent DC by using **BeginPaint** and release it by using **EndPaint**.

When a parent DC is retrieved, Windows searches the cache for the display DC previously used by the parent window. In most cases, the parent window retrieves and releases a display DC before the child window attempts to retrieve one, so the parent DC is usually in the cache. If Windows finds the display DC, Windows uses it and its corresponding clipping region, which was previously calculated for the parent DC. The time saved is in skipping the calculation required to define the clipping region. If Windows does not find the parent DC, it retrieves a common DC for the window and calculates the clipping region for the window rather than for the parent window.

Windows sets the device origin for the parent DC to the upper-left corner of the child window. Attribute values set by the parent window are not preserved for the child window; for example, the parent window cannot set the brush for its child windows. The only property preserved is the clipping region. The window is responsible for clipping its own output to the limits of the window. Because the clipping region for the parent DC is identical to the parent window, the child window can potentially draw over the entire parent window, but the parent DC must not be used in this way.

Windows ignores the CS_PARENTDC style if the parent window uses a private or class DC, if the parent window clips its child windows, or if the child window clips its child windows or sibling windows. In these cases, Windows always retrieves a common DC for the window.

20.1.12 Window Update Lock

A *window update lock* is a temporary suspension of drawing in a window. Windows uses the lock to prevent other windows from drawing over the tracking rectangle whenever the user moves or sizes a window. Applications can use the lock to prevent drawing if they carry out similar moving or sizing operations with their own windows.

An application sets and clears the window update lock by using the **LockWindowUpdate** function, specifying the window to lock. The lock applies to the given window and all of its child windows. When the lock is set, the **GetDC** and **BeginPaint** functions return a display DC whose visible region is empty. Given this, the application can continue to draw in the window, but all output is clipped. The lock continues until the application clears it by calling **LockWindowUpdate**, specifying NULL for the window. Although **LockWindowUpdate** forces a window's visible region to be empty, the function does not make the given window invisible and does not clear the WS_VISIBLE style bit.

After the lock is set, the application can use the **GetDCEx** function, with the DCX_LOCKWINDOWUPDATE value, to retrieve a display DC to draw over the locked window. This allows the application to draw a tracking rectangle when processing keyboard or mouse messages. Windows uses this method when the user moves and sizes windows. **GetDCEx** retrieves the display DC from the display DC cache, so the application must release the DC as soon as possible after drawing.

While a window update lock is set, the system creates an accumulated bounding rectangle for each locked window. When the lock is cleared, Windows uses this bounding rectangle to set the update region for the window and its child windows, forcing an eventual WM_PAINT message. If the accumulated bounding rectangle is empty (that is, if no drawing has occurred while the lock was set), the update region is not set.

20.1.13 Accumulated Bounding Rectangle

The *accumulated bounding rectangle* is the smallest rectangle enclosing the portion of a window or client area affected by recent drawing operations. An application can use this rectangle to conveniently determine the extent of changes caused by drawing operations. It is sometimes used in conjunction with **LockWindowUpdate** to determine which portion of the client area must be redrawn after the update lock is cleared.

An application starts accumulating the bounding rectangle by using the **SetBoundsRect** function, specifying the DCB_ENABLE value. Windows subsequently accumulates points for the bounding rectangle as the application uses the specified display DC. The application can retrieve the current bounding rectangle at any time by using the **GetBoundsRect** function. The application stops the accumulation by calling **SetBoundsRect** again, specifying DCB_DISABLE.

20.2 Using the WM_PAINT Message

You can use the WM_PAINT message to carry out the drawing necessary for displaying information. Because Windows sends WM_PAINT messages to your application when your window must be updated or when you explicitly request an update, you can consolidate the code for drawing in your application's window procedure. You can then use this code whenever your application must draw either new or existing information.

The following sections show a variety of ways to use the WM_PAINT message to draw in a window.

20.2.1 Drawing in the Client Area

You use the **BeginPaint** and **EndPaint** functions to prepare for and complete the drawing in the client area. **BeginPaint** returns a handle of the display DC used for drawing in the client area, and **EndPaint** ends the paint request and releases the display DC.

In the following code sample, the window procedure writes the message "Hello, Windows!" in the client area. To make sure the string is visible when the window is first created, the **WinMain** function calls the **UpdateWindow** function immediately after creating and showing the window. This causes a WM_PAINT message to be sent immediately to the window procedure.

```
LRESULT APIENTRY WndProc(hwnd, message, wParam, lParam)
HWND hwnd;
UINT message;
WPARAM wParam;
LPARAM lParam;
{
    PAINTSTRUCT ps;
    HDC hdc;

    switch (message) {
        case WM_PAINT:
            hdc = BeginPaint(hwnd, &ps);
            TextOut(hdc, 0, 0, "Hello, Windows!", 15);
            EndPaint(hwnd, &ps);
            return 0L;


            .
            .
            .


    }
}


int APIENTRY WinMain(hInstance, hPrevInstance, lpCmdLine, nCmdShow)
HINSTANCE hInstance;          /* handle of current instance   */
HINSTANCE hPrevInstance;      /* handle of previous instance  */
LPSTR lpCmdLine;              /* address of command line      */
int nCmdShow;                 /* show-window type (open/icon) */
{
    HWND hwnd;


    hwnd = CreateWindowEx( /* parameters */ );

    ShowWindow(hwnd, SW_SHOW);
```

```
    UpdateWindow(hwnd);

        .
        .
        .

    return msg.wParam;
}
```

20.2.2 Redrawing the Entire Client Area

You can have your application redraw the entire contents of the client area
whenever the window changes size by setting the CS_HREDRAW and
CS_VREDRAW styles for the window class. Applications that adjust the size of
the drawing based on the size of the window use these styles to ensure that they
start with a completely empty client area when drawing.

In the following code, the window procedure draws a five-pointed star that fits
neatly in the client area. It uses a common DC and must set the mapping mode
and window and viewport extents each time the WM_PAINT message is
processed.

```
LRESULT APIENTRY WndProc(hwnd, message, wParam, lParam)
HWND hwnd;
UINT message;
WPARAM wParam;
LPARAM lParam;
{
    PAINTSTRUCT ps;
    HDC hdc;
    RECT rc;
    POINT aptStar[6] = {50,2, 2,98, 98,33, 2,33, 98,98, 50,2};

        .
        .
        .

        case WM_PAINT:
            hdc = BeginPaint(hwnd, &ps);
            GetClientRect(hwnd, &rc);
            SetMapMode(hdc, MM_ANISOTROPIC);
            SetWindowExtEx(hdc, 100, 100, NULL);
            SetViewportExtEx(hdc, rc.right, rc.bottom, NULL);
            Polyline(hdc, aptStar, 6);
            EndPaint(hwnd, &ps);
            return 0L;

        .
        .
```

```
}

int APIENTRY WinMain(hInstance, hPrevInstance, lpCmdLine, nCmdShow)
HINSTANCE hInstance;              /* handle of current instance   */
HINSTANCE hPrevInstance;          /* handle of previous instance  */
LPSTR lpCmdLine;                  /* address of command line      */
int nCmdShow;                     /* show-window type (open/icon) */
{
    WNDCLASS wc;

        .
        .
        .

        wc.style = CS_HREDRAW | CS_VREDRAW;
        wc.lpfnWndProc = (WNDPROC) WndProc;

        .
        .
        .


        RegisterClass(&wc);

        .
        .
        .


        return msg.wParam;
}
```

20.2.3 Redrawing in the Update Region

You can limit the amount of drawing your application carries out when processing the WM_PAINT message by determining the size and location of the update region. Because Windows uses the update region when creating the clipping region for the window's display DC, you can indirectly determine the update region by examining the clipping region.

In the following code sample, the window procedure draws a triangle, a rectangle, a pentagon, and a hexagon, but only if all or a portion of each figure lies within the update region. The window procedure uses the **RectVisible** function and a 100-by-100 rectangle to determine whether a figure is within the clipping region (and therefore the update region) for the common DC retrieved by the **BeginPaint** function.

```
POINT aptTriangle[4]  = {50,2, 98,86,  2,86, 50,2},
      aptRectangle[5] = { 2,2, 98,2,  98,98,  2,98, 2,2},
      aptPentagon[6]  = {50,2, 98,35, 79,90, 21,90, 2,35, 50,2},
      aptHexagon[7]   = {50,2, 93,25, 93,75, 50,98, 7,75, 7,25, 50,2};

          .
          .
          .


    case WM_PAINT:
        hdc = BeginPaint(hwnd, &ps);
        SetRect(&rc, 0, 0, 100, 100);

        if (RectVisible(hdc, &rc))
            Polyline(hdc, aptTriangle, 4);

        SetViewportOrgEx(hdc, 100, 0, NULL);
        if (RectVisible(hdc, &rc))
            Polyline(hdc, aptRectangle, 5);

        SetViewportOrgEx(hdc, 0, 100, NULL);
        if (RectVisible(hdc, &rc))
            Polyline(hdc, aptPentagon, 6);

        SetViewportOrgEx(hdc, 100, 100, NULL);
        if (RectVisible(hdc, &rc))
            Polyline(hdc, aptHexagon, 7);
        EndPaint(hwnd, &ps);
        return 0L;

          .
          .
          .
```

In this example, the coordinates of each figure lie within the same 100-by-100 rectangle. Before drawing a figure, the window procedure uses the **SetViewportOrgEx** function to set the viewport origin to a different part of the client area. This prevents the figures from being drawn one on top of the other. Changing the viewport origin does not affect the clipping region but does affect how the coordinates of the rectangle passed to **RectVisible** are interpreted. Changing the origin also allows you to use a single rectangle to check the update region rather than individual rectangles for each figure.

20.2.4 Invalidating the Client Area

Windows is not the only source of WM_PAINT messages. The **InvalidateRect** or **InvalidateRgn** function can indirectly generate WM_PAINT messages for your windows. These functions mark all or part of a client area as invalid (that must be redrawn).

In the following code sample, the window procedure invalidates the entire client area when processing WM_CHAR messages. This allows the user to change the figure by typing a number and view the results, which are drawn as soon as there are no other messages in the application's message queue.

```
POINT aptPentagon[6] = {50,2, 98,35, 79,90, 21,90, 2,35, 50,2},
       aptHexagon[7]  = {50,2, 93,25, 93,75, 50,98, 7,75, 7,25, 50,2};
POINT *ppt = aptPentagon;
int cpt = 6;

    .
    .
    .

case WM_CHAR:
    switch (wParam) {
    case '5':
        ppt = aptPentagon;
        cpt = 6;
        break;
    case '6':
        ppt = aptHexagon;
        cpt = 7;
        break;
    }
    InvalidateRect(hwnd, NULL, TRUE);
    return 0L;

case WM_PAINT:
    hdc = BeginPaint(hwnd, &ps);
    GetClientRect(hwnd, &rc);
    SetMapMode(hdc, MM_ANISOTROPIC);
    SetWindowExtEx(hdc, 100, 100, NULL);
    SetViewportExtEx(hdc, rc.right, rc.bottom, NULL);
    Polyline(hdc, ppt, cpt);
    EndPaint(hwnd, &ps);
    return 0L;
```

In this example, the NULL argument used in **InvalidateRect** specifies the entire client area; the TRUE argument causes the background to be erased. If you do not want the application to wait until the application's message queue has no other messages, use the **UpdateWindow** function to force the WM_PAINT message to be sent immediately. If there is any invalid part of the client area, **UpdateWindow** sends the WM_PAINT message for the given window directly to the window procedure.

20.2.5 Drawing a Minimized Window

You can draw your own minimized windows rather than having Windows draw them for you. Most applications define a class icon when registering the window class for the window, and Windows draws the icon when the window is minimized. If you set the class icon to NULL, however, Windows sends a WM_PAINT message to your window procedure whenever the window is minimized, enabling the window procedure to draw in the minimized window.

In the following code sample, the window procedure draws a star in the minimized window. The procedure uses the **IsIconic** function to determine when the window is minimized. This ensures that the star is drawn only when the window is minimized.

```
POINT aptStar[6] = {50,2, 2,98, 98,33, 2,33, 98,98, 50,2};

    .
    .
    .

case WM_PAINT:
    hdc = BeginPaint(hwnd, &ps);

    /* Determine whether the window is minimized. */

    if (IsIconic(hwnd)) {
        GetClientRect(hwnd, &rc);
        SetMapMode(hdc, MM_ANISOTROPIC);
        SetWindowExtEx(hdc, 100, 100, NULL);
        SetViewportExtEx(hdc, rc.right, rc.bottom, NULL);
        Polyline(hdc, aptStar, 6);
    } else {
        TextOut(hdc, 0,0, "Hello, Windows!", 15);
    }
    EndPaint(hwnd, &ps);
    return 0L;
```

You set the class icon to NULL by setting the **hIcon** member of the **WNDCLASS** structure to NULL before calling the **RegisterClass** function for the window class.

20.2.6 Drawing a Custom Window Background

You can draw your own window background rather than having Windows draw it for you. Most applications specify a brush handle or system color value for the class background brush when registering the window class; Windows uses the brush or color to draw the background. If you set the class background brush to

NULL, however, Windows sends a WM_ERASEBKGND message to your window procedure whenever the window background must be drawn, letting you draw a custom background.

In the following code sample, the window procedure draws a large checkerboard pattern that fits neatly in the window. The procedure fills the client area with a white brush and then draws thirteen 20-by-20 rectangles using a gray brush. The display DC to use when drawing the background is in the *wParam* parameter for the message.

```
HBRUSH hbrWhite, hbrGray;

    .
    .
    .

case WM_CREATE:
    hbrWhite = GetStockObject(WHITE_BRUSH);
    hbrGray  = GetStockObject(GRAY_BRUSH);
    return 0L;

case WM_ERASEBKGND:
    hdc = (HDC) wParam;
    GetClientRect(hwnd, &rc);
    SetMapMode(hdc, MM_ANISOTROPIC);
    SetWindowExtEx(hdc, 100, 100, NULL);
    SetViewportExtEx(hdc, rc.right, rc.bottom, NULL);
    FillRect(hdc, &rc, hbrWhite);

    for (i = 0; i < 13; i++) {
        x = (i * 40) % 100;
        y = ((i * 40) / 100) * 20;
        SetRect(&rc, x, y, x + 20, y + 20);
        FillRect(hdc, &rc, hbrGray);
    }
    return 1L;
```

If the application draws its own minimized window, Windows also sends the WM_ERASEBKGND message to the window procedure to draw the background for the minimized window. You can use the same technique used with the WM_PAINT message to determine whether the window is minimized—that is, call the **IsIconic** function and check for the return value TRUE.

20.3 Using the GetDC Function

You use the **GetDC** function to carry out drawing that must occur instantly rather than when a WM_PAINT message is processing. Such drawing is usually in response to an action by the user, such as making a selection or drawing with the mouse. In such cases, the user should receive instant feedback and must not be forced to stop selecting or drawing in order for the application to display the result. The following sections show how to use **GetDC** to draw in a window.

20.3.1 Drawing with the Mouse

You can permit the user to draw lines with the mouse by having your window procedure draw while processing the WM_MOUSEMOVE message. Windows sends the WM_MOUSEMOVE message to the window procedure whenever the user moves the cursor within the window. To draw lines, the window procedure can retrieve a display DC and draw a line in the window between the current and previous cursor positions.

In the following code sample, the window procedure prepares for drawing when the user presses and holds the left mouse button (the WM_LBUTTONDOWN message). As the user moves the cursor within the window, the window procedure receives a series of WM_MOUSEMOVE messages. For each message, the window procedure draws a line connecting the previous position and the current position. To draw the line, the procedure uses **GetDC** to retrieve a display DC; then, as soon as drawing is complete and before returning from the message, the procedure uses the **ReleaseDC** function to release the display DC. As soon as the user releases the mouse button, the window procedure clears the flag, and the drawing stops (the WM_LBUTTONUP message).

```
BOOL fDraw = FALSE;
POINT ptPrevious;

    .
    .
    .

case WM_LBUTTONDOWN:
    fDraw = TRUE;
    ptPrevious.x = LOWORD(lParam);
    ptPrevious.y = HIWORD(lParam);
    return 0L;

case WM_LBUTTONUP:
    if (fDraw) {
        hdc = GetDC(hwnd);
        MoveToEx(hdc, ptPrevious.x, ptPrevious.y, NULL);
```

```
                LineTo(hdc, LOWORD(lParam), HIWORD(lParam));
                ReleaseDC(hwnd, hdc);
            }
            fDraw = FALSE;
            return 0L;

    case WM_MOUSEMOVE:
        if (fDraw) {
            hdc = GetDC(hwnd);
            MoveToEx(hdc, ptPrevious.x, ptPrevious.y, NULL);
            LineTo(hdc, ptPrevious.x = LOWORD(lParam),
                ptPrevious.y = HIWORD(lParam));
            ReleaseDC(hwnd, hdc);
        }
        return 0L;
```

An application that enables drawing, as in this example, typically records either the points or lines so that the lines can be redrawn whenever the window is updated. Drawing applications often use a memory DC and an associated bitmap to store lines that were drawn by using a mouse.

20.3.2 Drawing at Timed Intervals

You can draw at timed intervals by creating a timer with the **SetTimer** function. By using a timer to send WM_TIMER messages to the window procedure at regular intervals, an application can carry out simple animation in the client area while other applications continue running.

In the following code sample, the application bounces a star from side to side in the client area. Each time the window procedure receives a WM_TIMER message, the procedure erases the star at the current position, calculates a new position, and draws the star at the new position. The procedure starts the timer by calling **SetTimer** while processing the WM_CREATE message.

```
RECT rcCurrent = {0,0,20,20};
POINT aptStar[6] = {10,1, 1,19, 19,6, 1,6, 19,19, 10,1};
int X = 2, Y = -1, idTimer = -1;
BOOL fVisible = FALSE;
HDC hdc;

LRESULT APIENTRY WndProc(hwnd, message, wParam, lParam)
HWND hwnd;
UINT message;
WPARAM wParam;
LPARAM lParam;
{
    PAINTSTRUCT ps;
    RECT rc;
```

```
switch (message) {
    case WM_CREATE:

        /* Calculate the starting point. */

        GetClientRect(hwnd, &rc);
        OffsetRect(&rcCurrent, rc.right / 2, rc.bottom / 2);

        /* Initialize the private DC. */

        hdc = GetDC(hwnd);
        SetViewportOrgEx(hdc, rcCurrent.left,
            rcCurrent.top, NULL);
        SetROP2(hdc, R2_NOT);

        /* Start the timer. */

        SetTimer(hwnd, idTimer = 1, 10, NULL);
        return 0L;

    case WM_DESTROY:
        KillTimer(hwnd, 1);
        PostQuitMessage(0);
        return 0L;

    case WM_SIZE:
        switch (wParam) {
            case SIZE_MINIMIZED:

                /* Stop the timer if the window is minimized. */

                KillTimer(hwnd, 1);
                idTimer = -1;
                break;

            case SIZE_RESTORED:

                /*
                 * Move the star back into the client area
                 * if necessary.
                 */

                if (rcCurrent.right > (int) LOWORD(lParam))
                    rcCurrent.left =
                        (rcCurrent.right =
                            (int) LOWORD(lParam)) - 20;
                if (rcCurrent.bottom > (int) HIWORD(lParam))
                    rcCurrent.top =
                        (rcCurrent.bottom =
```

```
                                  (int) HIWORD(lParam)) - 20;

                    /* Fall through to the next case. */

                case SIZE_MAXIMIZED:

                    /* Start the timer if it had been stopped. */

                    if (idTimer == -1)
                        SetTimer(hwnd, idTimer = 1, 10, NULL);
                    break;
            }
            return 0L;

        case WM_TIMER:

            /* Hide the star if it is visible. */

            if (fVisible)
                Polyline(hdc, aptStar, 6);

            /* Bounce the star off a side if necessary. */

            GetClientRect(hwnd, &rc);
            if (rcCurrent.left + X < rc.left ||
                rcCurrent.right + X > rc.right)
                X = -X;
            if (rcCurrent.top + Y < rc.top ||
                rcCurrent.bottom + Y > rc.bottom)
                Y = -Y;

            /* Show the star in its new position. */

            OffsetRect(&rcCurrent, X, Y);
            SetViewportOrgEx(hdc, rcCurrent.left,
                rcCurrent.top, NULL);
            fVisible = Polyline(hdc, aptStar, 6);

            return 0L;

        case WM_ERASEBKGND:

            /* Erase the star. */

            fVisible = FALSE;
            return DefWindowProc(hwnd, message, wParam, lParam);

        case WM_PAINT:

            /*
```

```
                    * Show the star if it is not visible. Use BeginPaint
                    * to clear the update region.
                    */

                   BeginPaint(hwnd, &ps);
                   if (!fVisible)
                       fVisible = Polyline(hdc, aptStar, 6);
                   EndPaint(hwnd, &ps);
                   return 0L;

        }
        return DefWindowProc(hwnd, message, wParam, lParam);
}
```

This application uses a private DC to minimize the time required to prepare the DC for drawing. The window procedure retrieves and initializes the private DC when processing the WM_CREATE message, setting the binary raster operation mode to allow the star to be erased and drawn using the same call to the **Polyline** function. The window procedure also sets the viewport origin to allow the star to be drawn using the same set of points regardless of the star's position in the client area.

The application uses the WM_PAINT message to draw the star whenever the window must be updated. The window procedure draws the star only if it is not visible; that is, only if it has been erased by the WM_ERASEBKGND message. The window procedure intercepts the WM_ERASEBKGND message to set the *fVisible* variable, but passes the message to the **DefWindowProc** function so that Windows can draw the window background.

The application uses the WM_SIZE message to stop the timer when the window is minimized and to restart the timer when the minimized window is restored. The window procedure also uses the message to update the current position of the star if the size of the window has been reduced so that the star is no longer in the client area. The application keeps track of the star's current position by using the **rcCurrent** structure, which defines the bounding rectangle for the star. Keeping all corners of the rectangle in the client area keeps the star in the area. The window procedure initially centers the star in the client area when processing the WM_CREATE message.

20.4 Functions and Messages

Use the following functions and messages for painting and drawing in windows.

Functions
BeginPaint
EndPaint
ExcludeUpdateRgn

GdiFlush
GdiGetBatchLimit
GdiSetBatchLimit
GetBoundsRect
GetUpdateRect
GetUpdateRgn
GetWindowDC
InvalidateRect
InvalidateRgn
LockWindowUpdate
RedrawWindow
SetBoundsRect
SetRectRgn
UpdateWindow
ValidateRect
ValidateRgn
WindowFromDC

Messages

WM_ERASEBKGND
WM_ICONERASEBKGND
WM_NCPAINT
WM_PAINT
WM_PAINTICON

C H A P T E R   2 1

Cursors

21.1 About Cursors

A *cursor* is a small bitmap whose location on the screen is controlled by a pointing device, such as a mouse, pen, or trackball. (In the remainder of this chapter, the term *mouse* refers to any pointing device.) When the user moves the mouse, Microsoft ® Windows ™ moves the cursor accordingly. Win32 ™ cursor functions enable applications to create, load, display, move, confine, and destroy cursors.

Windows supports two kinds of cursors: standard and custom. *Standard cursors* are predefined cursors that Windows displays automatically as the user moves windows or icons, resizes windows, or pauses while a process is underway. Win32 display driver files provide 13 standard cursors, such as the arrow, hourglass, and crosshair. Windows and Windows-based applications can use these cursors. The following illustration shows these standard cursors and their identifiers.

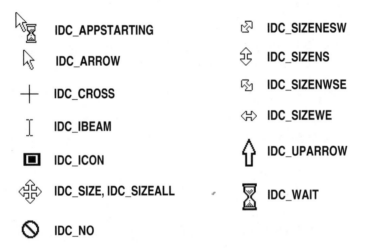

Custom cursors are designed for use in a specific application and can be any design the developer defines. The following illustration shows several custom cursors.

21.1.1 The Hot Spot

In the cursor, a pixel called the *hot spot* marks the exact screen location that is affected by a mouse event, such as clicking a mouse button. Typically, the hot spot is the focal point of the cursor. The system tracks and recognizes this point as the position of the cursor. For example, typical hot spots are the pixel at the tip of an arrow-shaped cursor and the pixel in the middle of a crosshair-shaped cursor.

When a mouse input event occurs, the Windows mouse driver translates the event into an appropriate mouse message that includes the coordinates of the hot spot. Windows sends the mouse message to the window that contains the hot spot or to the window that is capturing mouse input. For more information about mouse input, see Chapter 6, "Mouse Input."

21.1.2 The Mouse and the Cursor

If the system includes a mouse, Windows reflects the movement of the mouse by moving the cursor on the screen accordingly. As the cursor moves over different parts of windows or into different windows, Windows changes the appearance of the cursor. For example, when the cursor crosses a window border, Windows changes the cursor into a two-headed arrow.

If the system does not have a mouse, Windows displays and moves the cursor only when the user chooses certain system commands, such as those used to size or move a window. To provide the user with a method of displaying and moving the cursor when a mouse isn't available, an application can use the cursor functions to simulate mouse movement. Given this, the user can use the arrow keys to move the cursor.

21.1.3 Cursor Creation

Because standard cursors are predefined, it is not necessary to create them. To use a standard cursor, an application retrieves a cursor handle by using the **LoadCursor** function. A *cursor handle* is a unique value of the **HCURSOR** type that identifies a standard or custom cursor.

To create a custom cursor for an application, developers typically use a graphics application and include the cursor as a resource in the application's resource-definition file. At run time, an application calls **LoadCursor** to retrieve the cursor handle. Cursor resources contain data for several different display devices. **LoadCursor** automatically selects the most appropriate data for the current display device.

An application can also create a custom cursor at run time by using the **CreateCursor** function. This function creates a cursor having the specified size, design, and hot spot.

Applications should implement custom cursors as resources and use **LoadCursor** rather than create the cursor at run time. Using cursor resources avoids device dependence, simplifies localization, and enables applications to share cursor designs.

21.1.3.1 Alternative Cursor Creation

Two other functions create cursors at run time: **CreateIconFromResource** and **CreateIconIndirect**. These functions enable an application to browse through the system's resources and create icons and cursors based on resource data. **CreateIconFromResource** creates a cursor based on binary resource data from other executable files or dynamic-link libraries. It must be preceded by calls to the **LookupIconIDFromDirectory** function, as well as several resource functions. **LookupIconIDFromDirectory** identifies the most appropriate cursor data for the current display device. For more information about resource functions, see Chapter 51, "Resources."

CreateIconIndirect creates a cursor based on the contents of an **ICONINFO** structure. The **GetIconInfo** function fills this structure with hot spot coordinates and information concerning the associated bitmask and color.

21.1.4 Cursor Location and Appearance

If the system includes a mouse, Windows automatically displays a cursor and updates its position on the screen. Applications can obtain current screen coordinates of the cursor and move the cursor to any location on the screen by using the **GetCursorPos** and **SetCursorPos** functions, respectively.

Applications can also retrieve the handle of the current cursor by using the **GetCursor** function and can set the cursor by using the **SetCursor** function. After an application uses **SetCursor**, the appearance of the cursor does not change until the mouse moves, until the cursor is explicitly set to a different cursor, or until a system command is executed.

When the user moves the mouse, the system redraws the cursor at the new location as designated by the mouse. The system automatically redraws the cursor design associated with the window to which the cursor is pointing.

Applications can hide and redisplay the cursor, without changing the cursor design, by using the **ShowCursor** function. This function uses an internal counter to determine when to hide or display the cursor. An attempt to show the cursor increments the counter; an attempt to hide the cursor decrements the counter. The cursor is visible only if this counter is greater than or equal to zero.

21.1.4.1 The Window Class Cursor

When registering a window class, an application can assign it a default cursor, known as the *class cursor*. After the application registers the window class, each window of that class will have the specified class cursor.

To override the class cursor, an application can process the WM_SETCURSOR message. Applications can also replace a class cursor by using the **SetClassLong** function. This function changes the default window settings for all windows of a given class. For more information about window classes, see Chapter 3, "Window Classes."

21.1.5 Cursor Confinement

Applications can confine the cursor to a rectangular area on the screen by using the **ClipCursor** function. This can be useful when the user must respond to a certain event within the confined area of the rectangle. For example, an application might use **ClipCursor** to confine the cursor to a modal dialog box, preventing the user from interacting with other windows until the dialog box is closed.

The **GetClipCursor** function retrieves the screen coordinates of the rectangular area to which the cursor is temporarily confined. When it is necessary to confine the cursor, the application can also use this function to save the coordinates of the original area in which the cursor can move. Then, the application can restore the cursor to the original area when the new confinement is no longer necessary.

21.1.6 Cursor Destruction

When an application no longer needs a cursor it created by using the **CreateCursor** function, it should destroy the cursor. The **DestroyCursor** function destroys the cursor handle and frees any memory that it used. Applications should use this function only on cursors that were created with **CreateCursor**; it is not necessary to destroy other cursors.

21.1.7 Cursor Duplication

The **CopyCursor** function copies a cursor handle. This enables an application or dynamic-link library to retrieve the handle of a cursor owned by another module. Then, if the other module is freed, the application that copied the cursor will still be able to use the cursor design.

For information on how to add, remove, or replace cursor resources in executable files, see Chapter 51, "Resources."

21.2 Using Cursors

This section describes how to perform the following tasks:

- Create a cursor.
- Display a cursor.
- Confine a cursor.
- Use a cursor in a mousetrap.
- Use the keyboard to move the cursor.

21.2.1 Creating a Cursor

The following code sample creates two cursor handles: one for the standard hourglass cursor and one for a custom cursor included as a resource in the application's resource-definition file.

```
HINSTANCE hinst;            /* handle of current instance */
HCURSOR hCurs1, hCurs2;     /* cursor handles             */

/* Create a standard hourglass cursor. */

hCurs1 = LoadCursor(NULL, IDC_WAIT);

/* Create a custom cursor based on a resource. */

hCurs2 = LoadCursor(hinst, MAKEINTRESOURCE(240));
```

An application should implement custom cursors as resources. Rather than create the cursors at run time, use the **LoadCursor** function to avoid device dependence, to simplify localization, and to enable applications to share cursor designs.

The following example is included to illustrate how the system interprets cursor bitmasks. Use the **CreateCursor** function to create a custom cursor at run time, based on cursor bitmasks.

```
HINSTANCE hinst;            /* handle of current instance */
HCURSOR hCurs1, hCurs2;     /* cursor handles             */

HCURSOR hCurs3;             /* cursor handle              */

/* Yin cursor AND bitmask */

BYTE ANDmaskCursor[] = {0xFF, 0xFC, 0x3F, 0xFF,    /* line 1 */
                        0xFF, 0xC0, 0x1F, 0xFF,    /* line 2 */
                        0xFF, 0x00, 0x3F, 0xFF,    /* line 3 */
                        0xFE, 0x00, 0xFF, 0xFF,    /* line 4 */
```

```
                          0xF7, 0x01, 0xFF, 0xFF,    /* line 5 */
                          0xF0, 0x03, 0xFF, 0xFF,    /* line 6 */
                          0xF0, 0x03, 0xFF, 0xFF,    /* line 7 */
                          0xE0, 0x07, 0xFF, 0xFF,    /* line 8 */

                          0xC0, 0x07, 0xFF, 0xFF,    /* line 9 */
                          0xC0, 0x0F, 0xFF, 0xFF,    /* line 10 */
                          0x80, 0x0F, 0xFF, 0xFF,    /* line 11 */
                          0x80, 0x0F, 0xFF, 0xFF,    /* line 12 */

                          0x80, 0x07, 0xFF, 0xFF,    /* line 13 */
                          0x00, 0x07, 0xFF, 0xFF,    /* line 14 */
                          0x00, 0x03, 0xFF, 0xFF,    /* line 15 */
                          0x00, 0x00, 0xFF, 0xFF,    /* line 16 */

                          0x00, 0x00, 0x7F, 0xFF,    /* line 17 */
                          0x00, 0x00, 0x1F, 0xFF,    /* line 18 */
                          0x00, 0x00, 0x0F, 0xFF,    /* line 19 */
                          0x80, 0x00, 0x0F, 0xFF,    /* line 20 */

                          0x80, 0x00, 0x07, 0xFF,    /* line 21 */
                          0x80, 0x00, 0x07, 0xFF,    /* line 22 */
                          0xC0, 0x00, 0x07, 0xFF,    /* line 23 */
                          0xC0, 0x00, 0x0F, 0xFF,    /* line 24 */

                          0xE0, 0x00, 0x0F, 0xFF,    /* line 25 */
                          0xF0, 0x00, 0x1F, 0xFF,    /* line 26 */
                          0xF0, 0x00, 0x1F, 0xFF,    /* line 27 */
                          0xF8, 0x00, 0x3F, 0xFF,    /* line 28 */

                          0xFE, 0x00, 0x7F, 0xFF,    /* line 29 */
                          0xFF, 0x00, 0xFF, 0xFF,    /* line 30 */
                          0xFF, 0xC3, 0xFF, 0xFF,    /* line 31 */
                          0xFF, 0xFF, 0xFF, 0xFF};   /* line 32 */

        /* Yin cursor XOR bitmask */

BYTE XORmaskCursor[] = {0x00, 0x00, 0x00, 0x00,    /* line 1 */
                        0x00, 0x03, 0xC0, 0x00,    /* line 2 */
                        0x00, 0x3F, 0x00, 0x00,    /* line 3 */
                        0x00, 0xFE, 0x00, 0x00,    /* line 4 */

                        0x0E, 0xFC, 0x00, 0x00,    /* line 5 */
                        0x07, 0xF8, 0x00, 0x00,    /* line 6 */
                        0x07, 0xF8, 0x00, 0x00,    /* line 7 */
                        0x0F, 0xF0, 0x00, 0x00,    /* line 8 */

                        0x1F, 0xF0, 0x00, 0x00,    /* line 9 */
                        0x1F, 0xE0, 0x00, 0x00,    /* line 10 */
                        0x3F, 0xE0, 0x00, 0x00,    /* line 11 */
```

```
                              0x3F, 0xE0, 0x00, 0x00,    /* line 12 */

                              0x3F, 0xF0, 0x00, 0x00,    /* line 13 */
                              0x7F, 0xF0, 0x00, 0x00,    /* line 14 */
                              0x7F, 0xF8, 0x00, 0x00,    /* line 15 */
                              0x7F, 0xFC, 0x00, 0x00,    /* line 16 */

                              0x7F, 0xFF, 0x00, 0x00,    /* line 17 */
                              0x7F, 0xFF, 0x80, 0x00,    /* line 18 */
                              0x7F, 0xFF, 0xE0, 0x00,    /* line 19 */
                              0x3F, 0xFF, 0xE0, 0x00,    /* line 20 */

                              0x3F, 0xC7, 0xF0, 0x00,    /* line 21 */
                              0x3F, 0x83, 0xF0, 0x00,    /* line 22 */
                              0x1F, 0x83, 0xF0, 0x00,    /* line 23 */
                              0x1F, 0x83, 0xE0, 0x00,    /* line 24 */

                              0x0F, 0xC7, 0xE0, 0x00,    /* line 25 */
                              0x07, 0xFF, 0xC0, 0x00,    /* line 26 */
                              0x07, 0xFF, 0xC0, 0x00,    /* line 27 */
                              0x01, 0xFF, 0x80, 0x00,    /* line 28 */

                              0x00, 0xFF, 0x00, 0x00,    /* line 29 */
                              0x00, 0x3C, 0x00, 0x00,    /* line 30 */
                              0x00, 0x00, 0x00, 0x00,    /* line 31 */
                              0x00, 0x00, 0x00, 0x00};   /* line 32 */

/* Create a custom cursor at run time. */

hCurs3 = CreateCursor(hinst,   /* app instance */
                19,      /* horiz pos of hot spot */
                2,       /* vert pos of hot spot  */
                32,      /* cursor width          */
                32,      /* cursor height         */
                ANDmaskCursor,     /* AND bitmask */
                XORmaskCursor);    /* XOR bitmask */
```

To create the cursor, **CreateCursor** applies the following truth table to the AND
and XOR bitmasks.

AND	XOR	Display
0	0	Black
0	1	White
1	0	Screen
1	1	Reverse screen

For more information about bitmaps, see Chapter 29, "Bitmaps."

Before closing, your application must use the **DestroyCursor** function to destroy any cursors it created with **CreateCursor**. It is not necessary to destroy cursors created by other functions.

21.2.2 Displaying a Cursor

If the system includes a mouse, Windows automatically displays the class cursor (the cursor associated with the window to which the cursor is pointing). Your application can assign a class cursor while registering a window class. The following example illustrates this by assigning a cursor handle to the **hCursor** member of the **WNDCLASS** structure identified by the *wc* parameter.

```
WNDCLASS  wc;

/*
 * Fill the window class structure with parameters that describe
 * the main window.
 */

wc.style = NULL;                            /* class style(s)    */
wc.lpfnWndProc = (WNDPROC) MainWndProc; /* window procedure */
wc.cbClsExtra = 0;              /* no per-class extra data   */
wc.cbWndExtra = 0;              /* no per-window extra data  */
wc.hInstance = hinstance;       /* app that owns the class   */
wc.hIcon = LoadIcon(NULL, IDI_APPLICATION);    /* class icon */
wc.hCursor = LoadCursor(hinstance, MAKEINTRESOURCE(230));
                                            /* class cursor */
wc.hbrBackground = GetStockObject(WHITE_BRUSH);
                                        /* class background */
wc.lpszMenuName =  "GenericMenu";           /* class menu */
wc.lpszClassName = "GenericWClass";         /* class name */

/* Register the window class. */

return RegisterClass(&wc);
```

When the window class is registered, the cursor identified by 230 in the application's resource-definition file will be the default cursor for all windows based on the class.

Your application can change the design of the cursor by using the **SetCursor** function and specifying a different cursor handle. However, when the cursor moves, Windows redraws the class cursor at the new location. To prevent the class cursor from being redrawn, your application must process the WM_SETCURSOR message. Each time the cursor moves and mouse input is not captured, Windows sends this message to the window in which the cursor is moving.

You can specify different cursors for different conditions while processing WM_SETCURSOR. For example, the following code shows how to display the *hCurs3* cursor whenever the cursor moves over the icon of a minimized application.

```
case WM_SETCURSOR:

    /*
     * If the window is minimized, draw the hCurs3 cursor.
     * If the window is not minimized, draw the default
     * cursor (class cursor).
     */

    if (IsIconic(hwnd)) {
        SetCursor(hCurs3);
        break;
    }
```

When the window is not minimized, Windows displays the class cursor.

Your application can replace a class cursor by using the **SetClassLong** function. This function changes the default window settings for all windows of a given class. The following example replaces the existing class cursor with the *hCurs2* cursor.

```
/* Change the cursor for hwnd's window class. */

SetClassLong(hwnd,      /* window handle */
    GCL_HCURSOR,        /* change cursor */
    (LONG) hCurs2);     /* new cursor    */
```

For more information about window classes and mouse input, see Chapter 3, "Window Classes," and Chapter 6, "Mouse Input."

21.2.3 Confining a Cursor

The following example confines the cursor to the application's window and then restores the cursor to its previous window. The example uses the **GetClipCursor** function to record the area in which the cursor can move and the **ClipCursor** function to confine and restore the cursor.

```
RECT rcClip;            /* new ClipCursor area     */
RECT rcOldClip;         /* previous ClipCursor area */

/* Record the area in which the cursor can move. */

GetClipCursor(&rcOldClip);

/* Get the dimensions of the application's window. */
```

```
GetWindowRect(hwnd, &rcClip);

/* Confine the cursor to the application's window. */

ClipCursor(&rcClip);

    .
    . /* Process input from the confined cursor. */
    .

/* Restore the cursor to its previous area. */

ClipCursor(&rcOldClip);
```

Because there is only one cursor at a time available in the system, an application that confines the cursor must restore the cursor before relinquishing control to another window.

21.2.4 Creating a Mousetrap

The following example uses the **SetCursorPos**, **GetCursorPos**, **CreateCursor**, **LoadCursor**, and **SetCursor** functions to create a simple mousetrap. It also uses cursor and timer functions to monitor the cursor's position every 10 seconds. If the cursor position has not changed in the last 10 seconds and the application's main window is minimized, the application changes the cursor and moves it to the mousetrap icon.

Sample code for a similar mousetrap is included in Chapter 23, "Icons." It uses the **LoadCursor** and **LoadIcon** functions instead of the more device-dependent **CreateCursor** and **CreateIcon**.

```
HICON hIcon1;              /* icon handles            */
POINT ptOld;               /* previous cursor location */
HCURSOR hCurs1;            /* cursor handle           */


/*
 * The following cursor bitmasks are defined in a code example
 * that appears earlier in this chapter.
 */

/* Yin cursor AND and XOR bitmasks */

BYTE ANDmaskCursor[] = ...
BYTE XORmaskCursor[] = ...

/* Yang icon AND bitmask */
```

```
BYTE ANDmaskIcon[] = {0xFF, 0xFF, 0xFF, 0xFF,    /* line 1 */
                      0xFF, 0xFF, 0xC3, 0xFF,    /* line 2 */
                      0xFF, 0xFF, 0x00, 0xFF,    /* line 3 */
                      0xFF, 0xFE, 0x00, 0x7F,    /* line 4 */

                      0xFF, 0xFC, 0x00, 0x1F,    /* line 5 */
                      0xFF, 0xF8, 0x00, 0x0F,    /* line 6 */
                      0xFF, 0xF8, 0x00, 0x0F,    /* line 7 */
                      0xFF, 0xF0, 0x00, 0x07,    /* line 8 */

                      0xFF, 0xF0, 0x00, 0x03,    /* line 9 */
                      0xFF, 0xE0, 0x00, 0x03,    /* line 10 */
                      0xFF, 0xE0, 0x00, 0x01,    /* line 11 */
                      0xFF, 0xE0, 0x00, 0x01,    /* line 12 */

                      0xFF, 0xF0, 0x00, 0x01,    /* line 13 */
                      0xFF, 0xF0, 0x00, 0x00,    /* line 14 */
                      0xFF, 0xF8, 0x00, 0x00,    /* line 15 */
                      0xFF, 0xFC, 0x00, 0x00,    /* line 16 */

                      0xFF, 0xFF, 0x00, 0x00,    /* line 17 */
                      0xFF, 0xFF, 0x80, 0x00,    /* line 18 */
                      0xFF, 0xFF, 0xE0, 0x00,    /* line 19 */
                      0xFF, 0xFF, 0xE0, 0x01,    /* line 20 */

                      0xFF, 0xFF, 0xF0, 0x01,    /* line 21 */
                      0xFF, 0xFF, 0xF0, 0x01,    /* line 22 */
                      0xFF, 0xFF, 0xF0, 0x03,    /* line 23 */
                      0xFF, 0xFF, 0xE0, 0x03,    /* line 24 */

                      0xFF, 0xFF, 0xE0, 0x07,    /* line 25 */
                      0xFF, 0xFF, 0xC0, 0x0F,    /* line 26 */
                      0xFF, 0xFF, 0xC0, 0x0F,    /* line 27 */
                      0xFF, 0xFF, 0x80, 0x1F,    /* line 28 */

                      0xFF, 0xFF, 0x00, 0x7F,    /* line 29 */
                      0xFF, 0xFC, 0x00, 0xFF,    /* line 30 */
                      0xFF, 0xF8, 0x03, 0xFF,    /* line 31 */
                      0xFF, 0xFC, 0x3F, 0xFF};   /* line 32 */

/* Yang icon XOR bitmask */

BYTE XORmaskIcon[] = {0x00, 0x00, 0x00, 0x00,    /* line 1 */
                      0x00, 0x00, 0x00, 0x00,    /* line 2 */
                      0x00, 0x00, 0x00, 0x00,    /* line 3 */
                      0x00, 0x00, 0x00, 0x00,    /* line 4 */

                      0x00, 0x00, 0x00, 0x00,    /* line 5 */
                      0x00, 0x00, 0x00, 0x00,    /* line 6 */
                      0x00, 0x00, 0x00, 0x00,    /* line 7 */
```

```
                          0x00, 0x00, 0x38, 0x00,    /* line 8 */

                          0x00, 0x00, 0x7C, 0x00,    /* line 9 */
                          0x00, 0x00, 0x7C, 0x00,    /* line 10 */
                          0x00, 0x00, 0x7C, 0x00,    /* line 11 */
                          0x00, 0x00, 0x38, 0x00,    /* line 12 */

                          0x00, 0x00, 0x00, 0x00,    /* line 13 */
                          0x00, 0x00, 0x00, 0x00,    /* line 14 */
                          0x00, 0x00, 0x00, 0x00,    /* line 15 */
                          0x00, 0x00, 0x00, 0x00,    /* line 16 */

                          0x00, 0x00, 0x00, 0x00,    /* line 17 */
                          0x00, 0x00, 0x00, 0x00,    /* line 18 */
                          0x00, 0x00, 0x00, 0x00,    /* line 19 */
                          0x00, 0x00, 0x00, 0x00,    /* line 20 */

                          0x00, 0x00, 0x00, 0x00,    /* line 21 */
                          0x00, 0x00, 0x00, 0x00,    /* line 22 */
                          0x00, 0x00, 0x00, 0x00,    /* line 23 */
                          0x00, 0x00, 0x00, 0x00,    /* line 24 */

                          0x00, 0x00, 0x00, 0x00,    /* line 25 */
                          0x00, 0x00, 0x00, 0x00,    /* line 26 */
                          0x00, 0x00, 0x00, 0x00,    /* line 27 */
                          0x00, 0x00, 0x00, 0x00,    /* line 28 */

                          0x00, 0x00, 0x00, 0x00,    /* line 29 */
                          0x00, 0x00, 0x00, 0x00,    /* line 30 */
                          0x00, 0x00, 0x00, 0x00,    /* line 31 */
                          0x00, 0x00, 0x00, 0x00};   /* line 32 */

hIcon1 = CreateIcon(hinstance, /* handle of app instance   */
            32,           /* icon width                    */
            32,           /* icon height                   */
            1,            /* number of XOR planes          */
            1,            /* number of bits per pixel       */
            ANDmaskIcon,  /* AND bitmask                   */
            XORmaskIcon); /* XOR bitmask                   */

hCurs1 = CreateCursor(hinstance, /* handle of app instance */
            19,           /* horiz. position of hot spot   */
            2,            /* vert. position of hot spot    */
            32,           /* cursor width                  */
            32,           /* cursor height                 */
            ANDmaskCursor,           /* AND bitmask        */
            XORmaskCursor);          /* XOR bitmask        */
```

```
.   /* Fill in the window class structure. */
.

WNDCLASS  wc;

wc.hIcon = hIcon1;                          /* class icon   */
wc.hCursor = LoadCursor(NULL, IDC_ARROW); /* class cursor */


.
. /*
. * Register the window class and perform
. * other application initialization.
. */
.

/* Set a timer for the mousetrap. */

GetCursorPos(&ptOld);

SetTimer(hwnd, IDT_CURSOR, 10000, (TIMERPROC) NULL);

LONG APIENTRY MainWndProc(
    HWND hwnd,          /* window handle         */
    UINT message,       /* type of message       */
    UINT wParam,        /* additional information */
    LONG lParam)        /* additional information */
{

    HDC hdc;            /* handle of device context */
    POINT pt;           /* current cursor location  */
    RECT rc;            /* iconized window location */

    switch (message) {
        .
        . /* Process other messages. */
        .

        case WM_TIMER:

            /*
             * If the window is minimized, compare the current
             * cursor position with the one 10 seconds before.
             * If the cursor position has not changed, move the
             * cursor to the icon.
             */

            if (IsIconic(hwnd)) {
                GetCursorPos(&pt);

                if ((pt.x == ptOld.x) && (pt.y == ptOld.y)) {
```

```
                    GetWindowRect(hwnd, &rc);
                    SetCursorPos(rc.left + 20, rc.top + 4);

                        /*
                         * Note that the additional constants
                         * (20 and 4) are application-specific
                         * values to align the yin-shaped cursor
                         * and the yang-shaped icon.
                         */

                    }
                else {
                    ptOld.x = pt.x;
                    ptOld.y = pt.y;
                }
            }

            return 0;

        case WM_SETCURSOR:

            /*
             * If the window is minimized, draw hCurs1.
             * If the window is not minimized, draw the default
             * cursor (class cursor).
             */

            if (IsIconic(hwnd)) {
                SetCursor(hCurs1);
                break;
            }

        case WM_DESTROY:

            /* Destroy timer. */

            KillTimer(hwnd, IDT_CURSOR);

            PostQuitMessage(0);
            break;

                .
                . /* Process other messages. */
                .

    }           /* ends switch (message) */
```

21.2.5 Using the Keyboard to Move the Cursor

Because Windows does not require a mouse, an application should be able to simulate mouse actions with the keyboard. The following example shows how to achieve this, by using the **GetCursorPos** and **SetCursorPos** functions, and by processing input from the arrow keys.

```
HCURSOR hCurs1, hCurs2;    /* cursor handles        */

POINT pt;                  /* cursor location       */
RECT rc;                   /* client area coordinates */
static int repeat = 1;     /* repeat key counter    */


.
. /* Other declarations and initialization. */
.

switch (message) {

.
. /* Process other messages. */
.

    case WM_KEYDOWN:

        if (wParam != VK_LEFT && wParam != VK_RIGHT &&
        wParam != VK_UP && wParam != VK_DOWN) {
            break;
        }

        GetCursorPos(&pt);

        /* Convert screen coordinates to client coordinates. */

        ScreenToClient(hwnd, &pt);

        switch (wParam) {

            /*
             * Move the cursor to reflect which
             * arrow keys are pressed.
             */

            case VK_LEFT: /* left arrow */
                pt.x -= repeat;
                break;

            case VK_RIGHT: /* right arrow */
                pt.x += repeat;
```

```
                    break;

             case VK_UP: /* up arrow */
                 pt.y -= repeat;
                 break;

             case VK_DOWN: /* down arrow */
                 pt.y += repeat;
                 break;

             default:
                 return NULL;

         }

         repeat++;                /* increments repeat count */

         /* Keep the cursor in the client area. */

         GetClientRect(hwnd, &rc);

         if (pt.x >= rc.right) {
             pt.x = rc.right - 1;
         }
         else {
             if (pt.x < rc.left) {
                 pt.x = rc.left;
             }
         }

         if (pt.y >= rc.bottom) {
             pt.y = rc.bottom - 1;
         }
         else {
             if (pt.y < rc.top) {
                 pt.y = rc.top;
             }
         }

         /* Convert client coordinates to screen coordinates. */

         ClientToScreen(hwnd, &pt);
         SetCursorPos(pt.x, pt.y);
         break;

     case WM_KEYUP:

         repeat = 1;                /* clears repeat count */
         break;
```

.

.

.

```
}                       /* ends switch (message) */
```

21.3 Functions and Messages

The following functions and messages are used with cursors.

Functions

ClipCursor
CopyCursor
CreateCursor
DestroyCursor
GetClipCursor
GetCursor
GetCursorPos
LoadCursor
SetCursor
SetCursorPos
ShowCursor

Messages

WM_SETCURSOR

CHAPTER 22

Carets

22.1 About Carets

A caret is a flashing line, block, or bitmap in the client area of a window; the caret typically indicates the place at which text or graphics will be inserted. The following illustration shows some common variations in the appearance of the caret.

Underline
Vertical Line |
Solid Block
Gray Block
Bitmap

Because only one window at a time can have the keyboard focus or be active, there is only one caret in the system. Generally, each window that accepts keyboard input must create the caret when it receives the keyboard focus and destroy the caret when it loses the keyboard focus. For more information on keyboard input, see Chapter 5, "Keyboard Input."

An application written for Microsoft ® Windows ™ can create a caret, display or hide it, relocate the caret, and change its blink time.

An application uses the **CreateCaret** function to specify the parameters for a caret. Microsoft Windows forms a caret by inverting the pixel color within the rectangle specified by the caret's position, width, and height. The width and height are specified in logical units; therefore, the appearance of a caret is subject to the window's mapping mode.

After the caret is defined, an application uses the **ShowCaret** function to make the caret visible. When the caret appears, it automatically begins flashing. To display a solid caret, Windows inverts every pixel in the rectangle; to display a gray caret, Windows inverts every other pixel; to display a bitmap caret, Windows inverts only the white bits of the bitmap.

The elapsed time, in milliseconds, required to invert the caret is called the *blink time*. An application can determine the caret's blink time by using the **GetCaretBlinkTime** function. If it is necessary to define a specific blink time, use the **SetCaretBlinkTime** function to set the rate of the blink time to a specified number of milliseconds. The *flash time* is the elapsed time, in milliseconds, required to display, invert, and restore the caret's display. The flash time of a caret is twice as much as the blink time.

An application can determine the caret's position by using the **GetCaretPos** function. The position, in client coordinates, is copied to a **POINT** structure specified by a parameter in **GetCaretPos**. An application can move a caret in a window by using the **SetCaretPos** function. A window can move a caret only if it already owns the caret. **SetCaretPos** can move the caret whether it is visible or not.

An application can use the **HideCaret** function to remove the caret from the screen. This is useful when your application must redraw the screen while processing a message but must keep the caret out of the way. When the application finishes drawing, it can display the caret again by using the **ShowCaret** function. Hiding the caret does not destroy its shape or invalidate the insertion point. Hiding the caret is cumulative; that is, if the application calls **HideCaret** five times, it must also call **ShowCaret** five times before the caret will reappear.

An application can remove the caret from the screen and destroy its shape by using the **DestroyCaret** function. **DestroyCaret** destroys the caret only if the window involved in the current task owns the caret.

22.2 Using Carets

This section explains how to perform the following tasks:

- Create and display a caret.
- Hide a caret.
- Destroy a caret
- Adjust the blink time.
- Move the caret while processing keyboard input.

22.2.1 Creating and Displaying a Caret

Upon receiving the keyboard focus, the window should create and display the caret. Use the **CreateCaret** function to create a caret in the given window. Then call **SetCaretPos** to set the current position of the caret and **ShowCaret** to make the caret visible.

The system sends the WM_SETFOCUS message to the window receiving keyboard focus; therefore, an application should create and display the caret while processing this message.

```
HWND hwnd,     /* window handle                    */
int x;         /* horizontal coordinate of cursor  */
int y;         /* vertical coordinate of cursor    */
int nWidth;      /* width of cursor                */
int nHeight;     /* height of cursor               */
char *lpszChar;  /* pointer to character           */

    case WM_SETFOCUS:
```

```
/* Create a solid black caret. */

CreateCaret(hwnd, (HBITMAP) NULL, nWidth, nHeight);

/* Adjust the caret position, in client coordinates. */

SetCaretPos(x, y);

/* Display the caret. */

ShowCaret(hwnd);

break;
```

To create a caret based on a bitmap, you must specify a bitmap handle when using **CreateCaret**. You can use a graphics application to create the bitmap and a resource compiler to add the bitmap to your application's resources. Your application can then use the **LoadBitmap** function to load the bitmap handle. For example, you could replace the **CreateCaret** line in the preceding example with the following lines to create a bitmap caret.

```
/* Load the application-defined caret resource. */

hCaret = LoadBitmap(hinst, MAKEINTRESOURCE(120));

/* Create a bitmap caret. */

CreateCaret(hwnd, hCaret, 0, 0);
```

Alternatively, you can use the **CreateBitmap** or **CreateDIBitmap** function to retrieve the handle of the caret bitmap. For more information about bitmaps, see Chapter 29, "Bitmaps."

If your application specifies a bitmap handle, **CreateCaret** ignores the width and height parameters. The bitmap defines the size of the caret.

22.2.2 Hiding a Caret

Whenever your application redraws a screen while processing a message other than WM_PAINT, it must make the caret invisible by using the **HideCaret** function. When your application is finished drawing, redisplay the caret by using the **ShowCaret** function. If your application processes the WM_PAINT message, it is not necessary to hide and redisplay the caret, because this function does this automatically.

The following code sample shows how to have your application hide the caret while drawing a character on the screen and while processing the WM_CHAR message.

```
HWND hwnd,    /* window handle                 */
HDC hdc;      /* device context                */

    case WM_CHAR:

        switch (wParam) {

            case 0x08:

                .
                . /* Process a backspace. */
                .

                    break;

            case 0x09:

                .
                . /* Process a tab. */
                .

                    break;

            case 0x0D:

                .
                . /* Process a carriage return. */
                .

                    break;

            case 0x1B:

                .
                . /* Process an escape. */
                .

                    break;

            case 0x0A:

                .
                . /* Process a linefeed. */
                .

                    break;
```

```
            default:

                /* Process all other characters. */

                /* Hide the caret. */

                HideCaret(hwnd);

                /* Draw the character on the screen. */

                hdc = GetDC(hwnd);
                SelectObject(hdc,
                    GetStockObject(SYSTEM_FIXED_FONT));

                TextOut(hdc, x, y, lpszChar, 1);

                ReleaseDC(hwnd, hdc);

                /* Display the caret. */

                ShowCaret(hwnd);

        }
```

If your application calls the **HideCaret** function several times without calling **ShowCaret**, the caret will not be displayed until the application also calls **ShowCaret** the same number of times.

22.2.3 Destroying a Caret

When a window loses the keyboard focus, the system sends the WM_KILLFOCUS message to the window. Your application should destroy the caret while processing this message by using the **DestroyCaret** function. The following code shows how to destroy a caret in a window that no longer has the keyboard focus.

```
case WM_KILLFOCUS:

    /*
     * The window is losing the keyboard focus,
     * so destroy the caret.
     */

    DestroyCaret();

    break;
```

22.2.4 Adjusting the Blink Time

Because there is only one caret in the system, use caution when your application must adjust the rate of the blink time, so as not to disrupt subsequent windows that may receive the keyboard focus. If your application changes the blink time, it must restore the blink time to its original value upon losing the keyboard focus. The **GetCaretBlinkTime** function returns the current blink time, in milliseconds, and the **SetCaretBlinkTime** function sets the blink time to the specified number of milliseconds.

If you anticipate that your application will adjust the blink time, add the following line to the WM_SETFOCUS message processing:

```
uOldBlink = GetCaretBlinkTime();
```

Then, you can restore the blink time to its original rate by including the following line in the WM_KILLFOCUS message processing:

```
SetCaretBlinkTime(uOldBlink);
```

22.2.5 Processing Keyboard Input

The following code sample demonstrates how to use a caret in a simple text editor. The code updates the caret position as the user types printable characters and uses various keys to move through the client area.

```
#define TEXTMATRIX(x, y) *(pTextMatrix + (y * nWindowCharsX) + x)
HINSTANCE hinst;                /* current instance                 */
HBITMAP hCaret;                 /* caret bitmap                     */
HDC hdc;                        /* device context                   */
PAINTSTRUCT ps;                 /* client area paint info           */
static char *pTextMatrix = NULL;    /* pointer to text matrix       */
static int  nCharX,             /* width of char. in logical units  */
            nCharY,             /* height of char. in logical units */
            nWindowX,           /* width of client area             */
            nWindowY,           /* height of client area            */
            nWindowCharsX,      /* width of client area in char.s   */
            nWindowCharsY,      /* height of client area in char.s  */
            nCaretPosX,         /* x-position of caret in matrix    */
            nCaretPosY;         /* y-position of caret in matrix    */
static UINT uOldBlink;          /* holds previous blink rate        */
int x, y;       /* x and y coordinates to use in text matrix       */
TEXTMETRIC tm;                  /* font information                 */

LONG APIENTRY MainWndProc(
        HWND hwnd,              /* window handle            */
        UINT message,          /* type of message          */
        UINT wParam,           /* additional information   */
        LONG lParam)           /* additional information   */
```

```
{

switch (message) {

    case WM_CREATE:

        /*
         * Select a fixed-width system font,
         * and get the text metrics of the font.
         */

        hdc = GetDC(hwnd);
        SelectObject(hdc, GetStockObject(SYSTEM_FIXED_FONT));
        GetTextMetrics(hdc, &tm);
        ReleaseDC(hwnd, hdc);

        /* Save the avg. width and height of the characters. */

        nCharX = tm.tmAveCharWidth;
        nCharY = tm.tmHeight;

        return 0;

    case WM_SIZE:

        /*
         * Determine the width of the client area, in pixels
         * and in number of characters.
         */

        nWindowX = LOWORD(lParam);
        nWindowCharsX = max(1, nWindowX/nCharX);

        /*
         * Determine the height of the client area, in pixels
         * and in number of characters.
         */

        nWindowY = HIWORD(lParam);
        nWindowCharsY = max(1, nWindowY/nCharY);

        /* Clear the buffer that holds the text input. */

        if (pTextMatrix != NULL) {
            free(pTextMatrix);
        }

        /*
         * If there is enough memory, allocate space for the
         * text input buffer.
```

```
        */

        pTextMatrix = malloc(nWindowCharsX * nWindowCharsY);

        if (pTextMatrix == NULL) {
            ErrorHandler("Not enough memory.");
        }
        else {
            for (y = 0; y < nWindowCharsY; y++)
                for (x = 0; x < nWindowCharsX; x++)
                    TEXTMATRIX(x, y) = ' ';
        }

        /* Move the caret to the origin. */

        SetCaretPos(0, 0);

        return 0;

    case WM_KEYDOWN:
        switch (wParam) {

            case VK_HOME: /* Home */
                nCaretPosX = 0;
                break;

            case VK_END: /* End */
                nCaretPosX = nWindowCharsX - 1;
                break;

            case VK_PRIOR: /* Page Up */
                nCaretPosY = 0;
                break;

            case VK_NEXT: /* Page Down */
                nCaretPosY = nWindowCharsY -1;
                break;

            case VK_LEFT: /* Left arrow */
                nCaretPosX = max(nCaretPosX - 1, 0);
                break;

            case VK_RIGHT: /* Right arrow */
                nCaretPosX = min(nCaretPosX + 1,
                    nWindowCharsX - 1);
                break;

            case VK_UP: /* Up arrow */
                nCaretPosY = max(nCaretPosY - 1, 0);
                break;
```

```
case VK_DOWN: /* Down arrow */
    nCaretPosY = min(nCaretPosY + 1,
        nWindowCharsY - 1);
    break;

case VK_DELETE: /* Delete */

    /*
     * Move all the characters that followed the
     * deleted character (on the same line) one
     * space back (to the left) in the matrix.
     */

    for (x = nCaretPosX; x < nWindowCharsX; x++)
        TEXTMATRIX(x, nCaretPosY) =
            TEXTMATRIX(x + 1, nCaretPosY);

    /*
     * Replace the last character on the
     * line with a space.
     */

    TEXTMATRIX(nWindowCharsX - 1,
        nCaretPosY) = ' ';

    /*
     * The application will draw outside the
     * WM_PAINT message processing, so hide the
     * caret.
     */

    HideCaret(hwnd);

    /*
     * Redraw the line, adjusted for the
     * deleted character.
     */

    hdc = GetDC(hwnd);
    SelectObject(hdc,
        GetStockObject(SYSTEM_FIXED_FONT));

    TextOut(hdc,
        nCaretPosX * nCharX, nCaretPosY * nCharY,
        &TEXTMATRIX(nCaretPosX, nCaretPosY),
        nWindowCharsX - nCaretPosX);

    ReleaseDC(hwnd, hdc);
```

```
                              /* Display the caret. */

                              ShowCaret(hwnd);

                              break;
                }

                /*
                 * Adjust the caret position based on the
                 * virtual-key processing.
                 */

                SetCaretPos(nCaretPosX * nCharX, nCaretPosY * nCharY);

                return 0;

          case WM_CHAR:

                switch (wParam) {

                     case 0x08: /* Backspace */

                          /*
                           * Move the caret back one space, and then process
                           * this like the DEL key.
                           */

                          if (nCaretPosX > 0) {
                              nCaretPosX--;
                              SendMessage(hwnd, WM_KEYDOWN,
                                  VK_DELETE, 1L);
                          }
                          break;

                     case 0x09: /* Tab */

                          /*
                           * Tab stops exist every four spaces, so add
                           * spaces until the user hits the next tab stop.
                           */

                          do {
                              SendMessage(hwnd, WM_CHAR, ' ', 1L);
                          } while (nCaretPosX % 4 != 0);
                          break;


                     case 0x0D: /* Carriage return */

                          /*
```

```
               * Go to the beginning of the next line.
               * The bottom line wraps around to the top.
               */

              nCaretPosX = 0;

              if (++nCaretPosY == nWindowCharsY) {
                  nCaretPosY = 0;
              }
              break;

      case 0x1B: /* Escape */
      case 0x0A: /* Linefeed */

              /* No processing. */

              MessageBeep((UINT) -1);
              break;

      default: /* all other characters */

              /* Add the character to the text buffer. */

              TEXTMATRIX(nCaretPosX, nCaretPosY) =
                  (char) wParam;

              /*
               * The application will draw outside the
               * WM_PAINT message processing, so hide the
               * caret.
               */

              HideCaret(hwnd);

              /* Draw the character on the screen. */

              hdc = GetDC(hwnd);
              SelectObject(hdc,
                  GetStockObject(SYSTEM_FIXED_FONT));

              TextOut(hdc, nCaretPosX * nCharX,
                  nCaretPosY * nCharY,
                  &TEXTMATRIX(nCaretPosX, nCaretPosY), 1);

              ReleaseDC(hwnd, hdc);

              /* Display the caret. */

              ShowCaret(hwnd);
```

```
            /*
             * Prepare to wrap around if you reached the
             * end of the line.
             */

            if (++nCaretPosX == nWindowCharsX) {
                nCaretPosX = 0;
                if (++nCaretPosY == nWindowCharsY) {
                    nCaretPosY = 0;
                }
            }
            break;
    }

    /*
     * Adjust the caret position based on the
     * character processing.
     */

    SetCaretPos(nCaretPosX * nCharX, nCaretPosY * nCharY);

    return 0;

case WM_PAINT:

    /* Draw all the characters in the buffer, line by line. */

    hdc = BeginPaint(hwnd, &ps);

    SelectObject(hdc, GetStockObject(SYSTEM_FIXED_FONT));

    for (y = 0; y < nWindowCharsY; y++)
        TextOut(hdc, 0, y * nCharY, &TEXTMATRIX(0, y),
            nWindowCharsX);

    EndPaint(hwnd, &ps);

case WM_SETFOCUS:

    /*
     * The window has the input focus. Load the
     * application-defined caret resource.
     */

    hCaret = LoadBitmap(hinst, MAKEINTRESOURCE(120));

    /* Create the caret. */

    CreateCaret(hwnd, hCaret, 0, 0);
```

```
                        /* Adjust the caret position. */

                        SetCaretPos(nCaretPosX * nCharX, nCaretPosY * nCharY);

                        /* Display the caret. */

                        ShowCaret(hwnd);

                        break;

                    case WM_KILLFOCUS:

                        /*
                         * The window is losing the input focus,
                         * so destroy the caret.
                         */

                        DestroyCaret();

                        break;

                    default: /* passes it on if unprocessed */
                        return DefWindowProc(hwnd, message, wParam, lParam);

        }                                  /* ends switch (message)     */

            return NULL;
        }                                  /* ends main window procedure */
```

22.3 Functions

The following functions are used with carets.

CreateCaret
DestroyCaret
GetCaretBlinkTime
GetCaretPos
HideCaret
SetCaretBlinkTime
SetCaretPos
ShowCaret

CHAPTER 23

Icons

23.1 About Icons

An *icon* is a small bitmap that usually represents a minimized application, but can also illustrate a warning message or other window. If an icon represents a minimized application, the user can move the icon or size the window by using the mouse or other pointing device. Icons that do not represent minimized applications cannot be moved by the mouse. The icon functions in Microsoft ® Windows ™ enable applications to create, load, display, arrange, destroy, and retrieve information about icons.

Windows supports two kinds of icons: standard and custom. *Standard icons* are predefined icons that Windows displays in system message boxes. The Windows display driver files provide five standard icons, such as the stop sign, for use by the operating system or by any Windows-based application. The following illustration shows the standard icons and their identifiers.

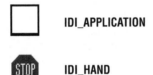 IDI_APPLICATION

  IDI_HAND

 IDI_QUESTION

 IDI_EXCLAMATION

 IDI_ASTERISK

Custom icons are designed to represent a particular application and can be any design the developer defines. Following are several custom icons.

23.1.1 The Hot Spot

In the center of an icon, one pixel called the *hot spot* is the point the system tracks and recognizes as the position of the icon. Unlike the cursor's hot spot, which can be any pixel in the cursor bitmap, the icon hot spot is always in the center of the icon bitmap.

23.1.2 Icon Creation

Standard icons are predefined by Windows, so it is not necessary to create them. To use a standard icon, an application can obtain its handle by using the **LoadIcon** function. An *icon handle* is a unique value of the **HICON** type that identifies a standard or custom icon.

To create a custom icon for an application, developers typically use a graphics application and include the icon as a resource in the application's resource-definition file. At run time, an application can call **LoadIcon** to retrieve the handle of the icon. An icon resource contains data for several different display devices. **LoadIcon** automatically selects the most appropriate data for the current display device.

An application can also create a custom icon at run time by using the **CreateIcon** function. This function creates an icon of the specified size, colors, and bit patterns.

Applications should implement custom icons as resources and should use **LoadIcon**, rather than create the icon at run time. Using icon resources avoids device dependence, simplifies localization, and enables applications to share icon shapes.

23.1.2.1 Alternative Icon Creation

Two other functions can create icons at run time: **CreateIconFromResource** and **CreateIconIndirect**. These functions enable an application to browse through the system's resources and create icons and cursors based on resource data. **CreateIconFromResource** creates an icon based on binary resource data from other executable files or dynamic-link libraries. An application must precede this function with calls to the **LookupIconIDFromDirectory** function and several of the resource functions. **LookupIconIDFromDirectory** returns the identifier of the most appropriate icon data for the current display device. For more information about the resource functions, see Chapter 51, "Resources."

CreateIconIndirect creates an icon based on the contents of an **ICONINFO** structure. The **GetIconInfo** function fills this structure with the hot spot coordinates and information about the bitmask bitmap and color bitmap for the icon.

23.1.3 Icon Display

The Win32 application programming interface (API) provides several functions that display and manipulate icons. Once an application has loaded an icon, it can use **DrawIcon** to draw the icon at a specified location in a window's client area. **ArrangeIconicWindows** arranges all of the minimized child windows in a parent window. **OpenIcon** activates and restores a minimized window to its previous size and location. **IsIconic** tests to see whether a window is minimized.

DrawIcon requires that the icon be loaded; the other functions do not. **ArrangeIconicWindows**, **OpenIcon**, and **IsIconic** operate on minimized windows, which may or may not have an icon drawn on top.

23.1.3.1 The Window Class Icon

While registering a window class, applications can assign a default icon, known as the *class icon*, to the class. After the application registers the window class, each window of that class will have that class icon when it is minimized. When the user minimizes a window, Windows uses the **DrawIcon** function to paint the class icon.

To override a class icon, an application can process the WM_PAINTICON message. Applications can also replace the class icon by using the **SetClassLong** function. This function changes the default window settings for all windows of a given class. For more information about window classes, see Chapter 3, "Window Classes."

23.1.4 Icon Destruction

When an application no longer needs an icon it created by using **CreateIcon**, it should destroy the icon. The **DestroyIcon** function destroys the icon handle and frees any memory used by the icon. Applications should use this function only for icons created with **CreateIcon**; it is not necessary to destroy other icons.

23.1.5 Icon Duplication

The **CopyIcon** function copies an icon handle. This enables an application or dynamic-link library to get its own handle for an icon owned by another module. Then, if the other module is freed, the application that copied the icon will still be able to use the icon.

For information about adding, removing, or replacing icon resources in executable files, see Chapter 51, "Resources."

23.2 Using Icons

This section describes how to perform the following tasks:

- Create an icon.
- Display an icon.
- Use an icon in a mousetrap.

- Share an icon resource.

23.2.1 Creating an Icon

To use an icon, your application must get the handle of the icon. The following example shows how to create two different icon handles: one for the standard exclamation icon and one for a custom icon included as a resource in the application's resource-definition file.

```
HICON hIcon1;   /* icon handle        */
HICON hIcon2;   /* icon handle        */

/* Create a standard question icon. */

hIcon1 = LoadIcon(NULL, IDI_QUESTION);

/* Create a custom icon based on a resource. */

hIcon2 = LoadIcon(hinst, MAKEINTRESOURCE(460));

/* Create a custom icon at run time. */
```

An application should implement custom icons as resources and should use **LoadIcon**, rather than create the icons at run time. This approach avoids device dependence, simplies localization, and enables applications to share icon bitmaps. However, the following code uses **CreateIcon** to create a custom icon at run time, based on bitmap bitmasks. It is included to illustrate how the system interprets icon bitmap bitmasks.

```
HICON hIcon3;                  /* icon handle        */

/* Yang icon AND bitmask */

BYTE ANDmaskIcon[] = {0xFF, 0xFF, 0xFF, 0xFF,    /* line 1 */
                      0xFF, 0xFF, 0xC3, 0xFF,    /* line 2 */
                      0xFF, 0xFF, 0x00, 0xFF,    /* line 3 */
                      0xFF, 0xFE, 0x00, 0x7F,    /* line 4 */

                      0xFF, 0xFC, 0x00, 0x1F,    /* line 5 */
                      0xFF, 0xF8, 0x00, 0x0F,    /* line 6 */
                      0xFF, 0xF8, 0x00, 0x0F,    /* line 7 */
                      0xFF, 0xF0, 0x00, 0x07,    /* line 8 */

                      0xFF, 0xF0, 0x00, 0x03,    /* line 9 */
                      0xFF, 0xE0, 0x00, 0x03,    /* line 10 */
                      0xFF, 0xE0, 0x00, 0x01,    /* line 11 */
                      0xFF, 0xE0, 0x00, 0x01,    /* line 12 */
```

```
                    0xFF, 0xF0, 0x00, 0x01,    /* line 13 */
                    0xFF, 0xF0, 0x00, 0x00,    /* line 14 */
                    0xFF, 0xF8, 0x00, 0x00,    /* line 15 */
                    0xFF, 0xFC, 0x00, 0x00,    /* line 16 */

                    0xFF, 0xFF, 0x00, 0x00,    /* line 17 */
                    0xFF, 0xFF, 0x80, 0x00,    /* line 18 */
                    0xFF, 0xFF, 0xE0, 0x00,    /* line 19 */
                    0xFF, 0xFF, 0xE0, 0x01,    /* line 20 */

                    0xFF, 0xFF, 0xF0, 0x01,    /* line 21 */
                    0xFF, 0xFF, 0xF0, 0x01,    /* line 22 */
                    0xFF, 0xFF, 0xF0, 0x03,    /* line 23 */
                    0xFF, 0xFF, 0xE0, 0x03,    /* line 24 */

                    0xFF, 0xFF, 0xE0, 0x07,    /* line 25 */
                    0xFF, 0xFF, 0xC0, 0x0F,    /* line 26 */
                    0xFF, 0xFF, 0xC0, 0x0F,    /* line 27 */
                    0xFF, 0xFF, 0x80, 0x1F,    /* line 28 */

                    0xFF, 0xFF, 0x00, 0x7F,    /* line 29 */
                    0xFF, 0xFC, 0x00, 0xFF,    /* line 30 */
                    0xFF, 0xF8, 0x03, 0xFF,    /* line 31 */
                    0xFF, 0xFC, 0x3F, 0xFF};   /* line 32 */

/* Yang icon XOR bitmask */

BYTE XORmaskIcon[] = {0x00, 0x00, 0x00, 0x00,    /* line 1 */
                    0x00, 0x00, 0x00, 0x00,    /* line 2 */
                    0x00, 0x00, 0x00, 0x00,    /* line 3 */
                    0x00, 0x00, 0x00, 0x00,    /* line 4 */

                    0x00, 0x00, 0x00, 0x00,    /* line 5 */
                    0x00, 0x00, 0x00, 0x00,    /* line 6 */
                    0x00, 0x00, 0x00, 0x00,    /* line 7 */
                    0x00, 0x00, 0x38, 0x00,    /* line 8 */

                    0x00, 0x00, 0x7C, 0x00,    /* line 9 */
                    0x00, 0x00, 0x7C, 0x00,    /* line 10 */
                    0x00, 0x00, 0x7C, 0x00,    /* line 11 */
                    0x00, 0x00, 0x38, 0x00,    /* line 12 */

                    0x00, 0x00, 0x00, 0x00,    /* line 13 */
                    0x00, 0x00, 0x00, 0x00,    /* line 14 */
                    0x00, 0x00, 0x00, 0x00,    /* line 15 */
                    0x00, 0x00, 0x00, 0x00,    /* line 16 */
```

```
                           0x00, 0x00, 0x00, 0x00,   /* line 17 */
                           0x00, 0x00, 0x00, 0x00,   /* line 18 */
                           0x00, 0x00, 0x00, 0x00,   /* line 19 */
                           0x00, 0x00, 0x00, 0x00,   /* line 20 */

                           0x00, 0x00, 0x00, 0x00,   /* line 21 */
                           0x00, 0x00, 0x00, 0x00,   /* line 22 */
                           0x00, 0x00, 0x00, 0x00,   /* line 23 */
                           0x00, 0x00, 0x00, 0x00,   /* line 24 */

                           0x00, 0x00, 0x00, 0x00,   /* line 25 */
                           0x00, 0x00, 0x00, 0x00,   /* line 26 */
                           0x00, 0x00, 0x00, 0x00,   /* line 27 */
                           0x00, 0x00, 0x00, 0x00,   /* line 28 */

                           0x00, 0x00, 0x00, 0x00,   /* line 29 */
                           0x00, 0x00, 0x00, 0x00,   /* line 30 */
                           0x00, 0x00, 0x00, 0x00,   /* line 31 */
                           0x00, 0x00, 0x00, 0x00};  /* line 32 */

hIcon3 = CreateIcon(hinst,      /* application instance   */
            32,                 /* icon width             */
            32,                 /* icon height            */
            1,                  /* number of XOR planes   */
            1,                  /* number of bits per pixel */
            ANDmaskIcon,        /* AND bitmask            */
            XORmaskIcon);       /* XOR bitmask            */
```

To create the icon, **CreateIcon** applies the following truth table to the AND and XOR bitmasks.

AND bitmask	XOR bitmask	Display
0	0	Black
0	1	White
1	0	Screen
1	1	Reverse screen

For information about full-color bitmaps, see Chapter 29, "Bitmaps," and Chapter 36, "Colors."

Before closing, your application must use **DestroyIcon** to destroy any icon it created by using **CreateIcon**. It is not necessary to destroy icons created by other functions.

23.2.2 Displaying an Icon

Your application can load and create icons to display in the application's client area or child windows. The following code demonstrates how to draw an icon in the client area of the window whose display context is identified by *hdc*.

```
HICON hIcon1;    /* icon handle                */
HDC hdc;         /* handle of display context */

DrawIcon(hdc, 10, 20, hIcon1);
```

Windows automatically displays the class icon—the icon associated with the window—when the window is minimized. Your application can assign a class icon while registering a window class. The following example assigns an icon handle to the **hIcon** member of the **WNDCLASS** structure identified by *wc*.

```
wc.hIcon = LoadIcon(hinstance, MAKEINTRESOURCE(430));
```

When the window class is registered, the icon identified by 430 in the application's resource-definition file will be the default icon for all windows based on the class.

Your application can replace a class icon by using **SetClassLong**. This function changes the default window settings for all windows of a given class. The following example replaces the existing class icon with the icon whose resource identifier is 480.

```
HINSTANCE hinst;           /* handle of current instance */
HWND hwnd;                 /* main window handle         */

/* Change the icon for hwnd's window class. */

SetClassLong(hwnd,          /* window handle */
    GCL_HICON,              /* changes icon  */
    (LONG) LoadIcon(hinst, MAKEINTRESOURCE(480))); /* new */
```

For more information about window classes, see Chapter 3, "Window Classes."

23.2.2.1 Managing the Icon Background

If your application assigns a class icon, Windows automatically repaints the icon's background whenever it repaints the icon. Your application can prevent Windows from painting the background by processing the WM_ICONERASEBKGND message.

If your application sets the class icon to NULL, there is no icon associated with the window class. In this situation, Windows sends the WM_ERASEBKGND message to the window whenever it paints the icon. If the window does not process this message, Windows draws part of the window's client area onto the iconic window.

23.2.3 Creating a Mousetrap

The following code sample uses **IsIconic**, **LoadIcon**, and several cursor and timer functions to create a simple mousetrap. The example uses the cursor and timer functions to monitor the location of the cursor at 10-second intervals. If the cursor location has not changed in the last 10 seconds and the application's main window is minimized, the application changes the cursor shape and moves the cursor to the icon.

```
HICON hIcon1;              /* icon handle                    */
POINT ptOld;              /* previous cursor location       */
HCURSOR hCurs1;           /* cursor handle                  */
HINSTANCE hinstance;      /* handle of current instance     */

hCurs1 = LoadCursor(hinstance, MAKEINTRESOURCE(220));


    .
    . /* Fill in the window class structure. */
    .

WNDCLASS  wc;

wc.hIcon = LoadIcon(hinstance, MAKEINTRESOURCE(470));
wc.hCursor = LoadCursor(hinstance, MAKEINTRESOURCE(240));


    .
    . /*
    . * Register the window class and perform
    . * other application initialization.
    . */
    .

/* Set a timer for the mousetrap. */

GetCursorPos(&ptOld);

SetTimer(hwnd, IDT_CURSOR, 10000, (TIMERPROC) NULL);
```

```
LONG APIENTRY MainWndProc(
    HWND hwnd,          /* window handle          */
    UINT message,       /* type of message        */
    UINT wParam,        /* additional information  */
    LONG lParam)        /* additional information  */
{

    HDC hdc;            /* device context handle  */
    POINT pt;           /* current cursor location */
    RECT rc;            /* iconized window location */

    switch (message) {

        .
        . /* Process other messages here. */
        .

        case WM_TIMER:

            /*
             * If the window is minimized, compare the current
             * cursor position with the one from 10 seconds
             * earlier. If the cursor position has not changed,
             * move the cursor to the icon.
             */

            if (IsIconic(hwnd)) {
                GetCursorPos(&pt);

                if ((pt.x == ptOld.x) && (pt.y == ptOld.y)) {
                    GetWindowRect(hwnd, &rc);
                    SetCursorPos(rc.left, rc.top);

                }
                else {

                    ptOld.x = pt.x;
                    ptOld.y = pt.y;
                }
            }

            return 0;

        case WM_SETCURSOR:

            /*
             * If the window is minimized, draw hCurs1.
             * If the window is not minimized, draw the default
             * cursor (class cursor).
             */
```

```
                        if (IsIconic(hwnd)) {
                            SetCursor(hCurs1);
                            break;
                        }

                case WM_DESTROY:

                    /* Destroy the timer. */

                    KillTimer(hwnd, IDT_CURSOR);

                    PostQuitMessage(0);
                    break;
                        .
                        . /* Process other messages here. */
                        .

                }               /* ends switch (message) */
```

A code sample for a similar mousetrap is included in Chapter 21, "Cursors." That example uses **CreateIcon** to create the class icon.

23.2.4 Sharing Icon Resources

The following code uses **CreateIconFromResource**, **LookupIconIdFromDirectory**, **DrawIcon**, and several of the resource functions to create an icon handle based on icon data from another executable file. Then, it displays the icon in a window.

```
HICON hIcon1;       /* icon handle               */
HINSTANCE hExe;     /* handle to loaded .EXE file */
HRSRC hResource;    /* handle for FindResource   */
HRSRC hMem;         /* handle for LoadResource   */
BYTE *lpResource;   /* address of resource data  */
int nID;            /* ID of resource that best
                       fits current screen       */

HDC hdc;        /* handle of display context */

/* Load the file from which to copy the icon. */

hExe = LoadLibrary("myapp.exe");

/* Find the icon directory whose identifier is 440. */

hResource = FindResource(hExe,
    MAKEINTRESOURCE(440),
    RT_GROUP_ICON);
```

```
/* Load and lock the icon directory. */

hMem = LoadResource(hExe, hResource);

lpResource = LockResource(hMem);

/*
 * Get the identifier of the icon that is most appropriate
 * for the video display.
 */

nID = LookupIconIdFromDirectory(
    (PBYTE) lpResource, TRUE);

/* Find the bits for the nID icon. */

hResource = FindResource(hExe,
    MAKEINTRESOURCE(nID),
    MAKEINTRESOURCE(RT_ICON));

/* Load and lock the icon. */

hMem = LoadResource(hExe, hResource);

lpResource = LockResource(hMem);

/* Create a handle to the icon. */

hIcon1 = CreateIconFromResource(
    (PBYTE) lpResource,
    SizeofResource(hExe, hResource),
    TRUE,
    0x00030000);

/* Draw the icon in the client area. */

DrawIcon(hdc, 10, 20, hIcon1);
```

23.3 Functions and Messages

Following are the functions and messages used with icons.

Functions

ArrangeIconicWindows
CopyIcon
CreateIcon
CreateIconFromResource
CreateIconIndirect
DestroyIcon
DrawIcon
GetIconInfo
IsIconic
LoadIcon
LookupIconIdFromDirectory
OpenIcon

Messages

WM_ICONERASEBKGND
WM_PAINTICON

CHAPTER 24

Window Properties

24.1 About Window Properties

A *window property* is any data assigned to a window by the **SetProp** function. A window property is usually a handle of the window-specific data, but it may be any 32-bit value. Each window property is identified by a string name.

Window properties are typically used to associate data with a subclassed window or a window in a multiple document interface (MDI) application. In either case, it is not convenient to use the extra bytes specified in the **CreateWindow** function or class structure for the following two reasons:

- An application might not know how many extra bytes are available or how the space is being used. By using window properties, the application can associate data with a window without accessing the extra bytes.

- An application must access the extra bytes by using offsets. Window properties, however, are accessed by their string identifiers, not by offsets.

For more information about subclassing, see Chapter 4, "Window Procedures." For more information about MDI windows, see Chapter 27, "Multiple Document Interface."

The Microsoft ® Win32 ™ application programming interface (API) provides several functions that enable applications to use window properties. The **SetProp** function assigns a window property and its string identifier to a window. The **GetProp** function retrieves the window property identified by a given string. The **RemoveProp** function destroys the association between a window and a window property but does not destroy the data itself. The **EnumProps** and **EnumPropsEx** functions enumerate all of a window's properties by using an application-defined callback function. **EnumPropsEx** includes an extra parameter for application-defined data used by the callback function.

24.2 Using Window Properties

This section illustrates how to use Win32 functions to perform the following tasks:

- Add a window property
- Retrieve a window property
- List the window properties of a given window
- Delete a window property

24.2.1 Adding a Window Property

The following example loads an icon and then a cursor and allocates memory for a buffer. The example then uses the **SetProp** function to assign the resulting icon, cursor, and memory handles as window properties for the window identified by the hwndSubclass value. The properties are identified by the strings PROP_ICON, PROP_CURSOR, and PROP_BUFFER.

```
#define BUFFER 4096

HINSTANCE hinst;        /* handle of current instance    */
HWND hwndSubclass;      /* handle of a subclassed window */
HANDLE hIcon, hCursor;
HGLOBAL hMem;
char *lpMem;
TCHAR tchPath[] = "c:\\winnt\\samples\\winprop.c";

/* Load resources. */

hIcon = LoadIcon(hinst, MAKEINTRESOURCE(400));
hCursor = LoadCursor(hinst, MAKEINTRESOURCE(220));

/* Allocate and fill a memory buffer. */

hMem = GlobalAlloc(GPTR, BUFFER);
lpMem = GlobalLock(hMem);
lstrcpy(lpMem, tchPath);
GlobalUnlock(hMem);

/* Set the window properties for hwndSubclass. */

SetProp(hwndSubclass, "PROP_ICON", hIcon);
SetProp(hwndSubclass, "PROP_CURSOR", hCursor);
SetProp(hwndSubclass, "PROP_BUFFER", hMem);
```

24.2.2 Retrieving a Window Property

A window can create handles to its window property data and use the data for any purpose. The following example uses the **GetProp** function to obtain handles to the window properties identified by PROP_ICON, PROP_CURSOR, and PROP_BUFFER. The example then displays the contents of the newly obtained memory buffer, cursor, and icon in the window's client area.

```
#define PATHLENGTH 256

HWND hwndSubclass;      /* handle of a subclassed window */
HANDLE hIconProp, hCursProp;
HGLOBAL hMemProp;
```

```
char *lpFilename;
TCHAR tchBuffer[PATHLENGTH];
int nSize;
HDC hdc;

/* Get the window properties, then use the data. */

hIconProp = (HICON) GetProp(hwndSubclass, "PROP_ICON");
TextOut(hdc, 10, 40, "PROP_ICON", 9);
DrawIcon(hdc, 90, 40, hIconProp);

hCursProp = (HCURSOR) GetProp(hwndSubclass, "PROP_CURSOR");
TextOut(hdc, 10, 85, "PROP_CURSOR", 9);
DrawIcon(hdc, 110, 85, hCursProp);

hMemProp = (HGLOBAL) GetProp(hwndSubclass, "PROP_BUFFER");
lpFilename = GlobalLock(hMemProp);
nSize = sprintf(tchBuffer,
    "Path to file: %s", lpFilename);
TextOut(hdc, 10, 10, tchBuffer, nSize);
```

24.2.3 Listing Window Properties for a Given Window

In the following example, the **EnumPropsEx** function lists the string identifiers
of the window properties for the window identified by the hwndSubclass value.
This function relies on the application-defined callback function WinPropProc to
display the strings in the window's client area.

```
EnumPropsEx(hwndSubclass, WinPropProc, NULL);

/*
 * WinPropProc is an application-defined callback function that
 * lists a window property.
 */

BOOL CALLBACK WinPropProc(
    HWND hwndSubclass,          /* handle of window with property */
    LPCSTR lpszString,          /* property string or atom        */
    HANDLE hData)               /* data handle                    */
{
    static int nProp = 1;       /* property counter               */
    TCHAR tchBuffer[BUFFER];    /* buffer for expanded string     */
    int nSize;                  /* size of string in buffer       */
    HDC hdc;                    /* device-context handle          */

    hdc = GetDC(hwndSubclass);

    /* Display the window property string in the client area. */
```

```
nSize = sprintf(tchBuffer, "WinProp %d: %s", nProp++,
    lpszString);
TextOut(hdc, 10, nProp * 20, tchBuffer, nSize);

ReleaseDC(hwndSubclass, hdc);

return TRUE;
}
```

24.2.4 Deleting a Window Property

When a window is destroyed, it must destroy any window properties it set. The following example uses the **EnumPropsEx** function and the application-defined callback function DelPropProc to destroy the properties associated with the hwndSubclass window. The callback function, which uses the **RemoveProp** function, is also shown.

```
case WM_DESTROY:

    EnumPropsEx(hwndSubclass, DelPropProc, NULL);

    PostQuitMessage(0);
    break;

        .
        .
        .


/*
 * DelPropProc is an application-defined callback function that
 * deletes a window property.
 */

BOOL CALLBACK DelPropProc(
    HWND hwndSubclass,          /* handle of window with property */
    LPCSTR lpszString,          /* property string or atom        */
    HANDLE hData)               /* data handle                    */
{
    RemoveProp(hwndSubclass, lpszString);

    return TRUE;
}
```

24.3 Functions

Following are the functions used with window properties.

EnumPropProc
EnumProps
EnumPropsEx
GetProp
RemoveProp
SetProp

C H A P T E R   2 5

Clipboard

25.1 About the Clipboard

The *clipboard* is a set of functions and messages that enable applications designed for the Microsoft ® Win32 ™ application programming interface (API) to transfer data. Because all applications have access to the clipboard, data can be easily transferred between applications or within an application.

A memory object on the clipboard can be in any data format, called a *clipboard format*. Each format is identified by an unsigned integer value. For standard (predefined) clipboard formats, this value is a constant defined by the Win32 API; for registered clipboard formats, it is the return value of the **RegisterClipboardFormat** function.

Except for registering clipboard formats, individual windows carry out most clipboard operations. Typically, a window procedure transfers information to or from the clipboard in response to the WM_COMMAND message.

The clipboard is user-driven. A window should transfer data to or from the clipboard only in response to a command from the user. A window must not use the clipboard to transfer data without the user's knowledge.

This chapter does not describe how to copy and paste linked or embedded objects. For information on these subjects, see the object linking and embedding (OLE) documentation.

25.1.1 Clipboard Formats

A window can place more than one memory object on the clipboard, each representing the same information in a different clipboard format. Users need not be aware of the clipboard formats used for an object on the clipboard.

25.1.1.1 Registered Clipboard Formats

Many applications work with data that cannot be translated into a standard clipboard format without loss of information. Such applications can register new clipboard formats by using the **RegisterClipboardFormat** function. For example, if a word processing application copied formatted text to the clipboard using a standard text format, the formatting information would be lost. The solution would be to register a new clipboard format, such as rich-text format (RTF).

If more than one application registers a clipboard format with exactly the same name, the clipboard format is registered only once. Both calls to the **RegisterClipboardFormat** function return the same value. In this way, two different applications can share data by using a *registered clipboard format*.

For a list of standard clipboard formats, see the **SetClipboardData** function.

25.1.1.2 Private and GDI Object Clipboard Formats

An application can identify a private clipboard format by defining a value in the range CF_PRIVATEFIRST through CF_PRIVATELAST. An application can use a private clipboard format for an application-defined data format that does not need to be registered with the system.

Data handles associated with private clipboard formats are not automatically freed by the system when a window empties the clipboard. Windows that use private clipboard formats should process the WM_DESTROYCLIPBOARD message to free clipboard data when the data is no longer needed.

Graphics Device Interface (GDI) object clipboard formats are similar to private clipboard formats. An application can identify a GDI object format by defining a value in the range CF_GDIOBJFIRST through CF_GDIOBJLAST. Like objects associated with standard clipboard formats for GDI objects, objects associated with GDI object formats are automatically deleted (by using the **DeleteObject** function) when the clipboard is emptied.

For more information about the WM_DESTROYCLIPBOARD message, see Section 25.1.2.3, "Clipboard Ownership."

25.1.1.3 Multiple Clipboard Formats

A window can place more than one clipboard object on the clipboard, each representing the same information in a different clipboard format. When placing information on the clipboard, the window should provide data in as many formats as possible.

Clipboard formats that contain the most information should be placed on the clipboard first, followed by less descriptive formats. A window pasting information from the clipboard typically retrieves a clipboard object in the first format it recognizes. Because clipboard formats are enumerated in the order they are placed on the clipboard, the first recognized format is also the most descriptive.

For example, suppose a user copies styled text from a word-processing document. The window containing the document might first place data on the clipboard in a registered format such as RTF. Afterwards, the window would place data on the clipboard in a less descriptive format such as text (CF_TEXT).

When the contents of the clipboard are pasted into another window, the window retrieves data in the most descriptive format it recognizes. If the window recognizes RTF, the corresponding data is pasted into the document. Otherwise, the text data is pasted into the document and the formatting information is lost.

25.1.1.4 Synthesized Clipboard Formats

Adding some formats to the clipboard implicitly creates other formats. When an application places any of the three text formats on the clipboard, the other two text formats are added implicitly. Similarly, when the application places either of the two metafile formats on the clipboard, the other metafile format is added implicitly.

When one of the implicit formats is requested by an application, the system synthesizes it by converting from an available format. For example, if an application places data on the clipboard using the CF_TEXT format, the CF_OEMTEXT and CF_UNICODETEXT clipboard formats are added implicitly. If another application requests data in the CF_UNICODETEXT clipboard format, the system synthesizes the data by converting it from the CF_TEXT format.

Synthesized clipboard formats are not added until the clipboard is closed. This enables an application to place more than one text format or both metafile formats on the clipboard.

25.1.2 Clipboard Operations

A window should use the clipboard when cutting, copying, or pasting data. A window places data on the clipboard for cut and copy operations and retrieves data from the clipboard for paste operations. The following sections describe these operations and related issues.

To place data on or retrieve data from the clipboard, a window must first open the clipboard by using the **OpenClipboard** function. Only one window can have the clipboard open at a time. When it has finished, the window must close the clipboard by calling the **CloseClipboard** function.

25.1.2.1 Cut and Copy Operations

To place information on the clipboard, a window first clears any previous clipboard contents by using the **EmptyClipboard** function. This function sends the WM_DESTROYCLIPBOARD message to the previous clipboard owner, frees resources associated with data on the clipboard, and assigns clipboard ownership to the window that has the clipboard open.

After emptying the clipboard, a window places data on the clipboard in as many clipboard formats as possible. For each format, the window calls the **SetClipboardData** function, specifying the format identifier and a global memory handle. The memory handle can be NULL, indicating that the window renders the data on request. (For more information, see Section 25.1.2.4, "Delayed Rendering.") A window should place data on the clipboard in order from the most descriptive clipboard format to the least descriptive.

25.1.2.2 Paste Operations

To retrieve paste information from the clipboard, a window first determines the clipboard format to retrieve. Typically, a window enumerates the available clipboard formats by using the **EnumClipboardFormats** function and uses the first format it recognizes. This method selects the best available format according to the priority set when the data was placed on the clipboard.

Alternatively, a window can use the **GetPriorityClipboardFormat** function. This function identifies the best available clipboard format according to a specified priority. A window that recognizes only one clipboard format can simply determine whether that format is available by using the **IsClipboardFormatAvailable** function.

After determining the clipboard format to use, a window calls the **GetClipboardData** function. This function returns the handle of a global memory object containing data in the specified format. A window can briefly lock the memory object in order to examine or copy the data. However, a window should not free the object or leave it locked for a long period of time.

25.1.2.3 Clipboard Ownership

The *clipboard owner* is the window associated with the information on the clipboard. A window becomes the clipboard owner when it places data on the clipboard—specifically, when it calls the **EmptyClipboard** function. The window remains the clipboard owner until it is closed or another window empties the clipboard.

When the clipboard is emptied, the clipboard owner receives a WM_DESTROYCLIPBOARD message. Following are some reasons why a window might process this message:

- The window delayed rendering of one or more clipboard formats. In response to the WM_DESTROYCLIPBOARD message, the window might free resources it had allocated in order to render data on request. For more information, see Section 25.1.2.4, "Delayed Rendering."

- The window placed data on the clipboard in a private clipboard format. The data for private clipboard formats is not freed by the system when the clipboard is emptied. Therefore, the clipboard owner should free the data upon receiving the WM_DESTROYCLIPBOARD message. For more information, see Section 25.1.1.2, "Private and GDI Object Clipboard Formats."

- The window placed data on the clipboard using the CF_OWNERDISPLAY clipboard format. In response to the WM_DESTROYCLIPBOARD message, the window might free resources it had used to display information in the clipboard viewer window. For more information, see Section 25.1.3.3, "Owner-Display Format."

25.1.2.4 Delayed Rendering

When placing a clipboard format on the clipboard, a window can delay rendering the data in that format until the data is needed. To do so, an application can specify NULL for the *hData* parameter of the **SetClipboardData** function. This is useful if the application supports several clipboard formats, some or all of which are time-consuming to render. By passing a NULL handle, a window renders complex clipboard formats only when and if they are needed.

If a window delays rendering a clipboard format, it must be prepared to render the format on request for as long as it is the clipboard owner. The system sends the clipboard owner a WM_RENDERFORMAT message when a request is received for a specific format that has not been rendered. Upon receiving this message, the window should call the **SetClipboardData** function to place a global memory handle on the clipboard in the requested format.

If the clipboard owner is destroyed and has delayed rendering some or all clipboard formats, it receives the WM_RENDERALLFORMATS message. Upon receiving this message, the window should place valid memory handles on the clipboard for all clipboard formats that it provides. This ensures that these formats remain available after the clipboard owner is destroyed.

An application should not open the clipboard before calling **SetClipboardData** in response to the WM_RENDERFORMAT or WM_RENDERALLFORMATS message.

Any clipboard formats that are not rendered in response to the WM_RENDERALLFORMATS message cease to be available to other applications and are no longer enumerated by the clipboard functions.

25.1.2.5 Memory and the Clipboard

A memory object that is to be placed on the clipboard should be allocated by using the **GlobalAlloc** function with the GMEM_DDESHARE and GMEM_MOVEABLE flags.

Once a memory object is placed on the clipboard, ownership of that memory handle is transferred to the system. In particular, an application should not free a memory object that has been placed on the clipboard. The exception to this rule is for private clipboard formats. A window is responsible for freeing a memory handle it has placed on the clipboard using a private clipboard format; however, it must not free the memory handle until after the clipboard has been emptied.

25.1.3 Clipboard Viewers

A *clipboard viewer* is a window that displays the current contents of the clipboard. The clipboard viewer is a convenience for the user and does not affect the data-transaction functions of the clipboard.

Typically, a clipboard viewer window can display at least the three most common formats: CF_TEXT, CF_BITMAP, and CF_METAFILEPICT. If a window does not make data available in any of these three formats, it should provide data in a display format, or use the owner-display format.

25.1.3.1 Clipboard Viewer Windows

A window adds itself to the clipboard viewer chain by calling the **SetClipboardViewer** function. The return value is the handle of the next window in the chain. Each clipboard viewer window must keep track of the next window in the clipboard viewer chain. When the contents of the clipboard change, the system sends a WM_DRAWCLIPBOARD message to the first window in the chain. After updating its display, each clipboard viewer window must pass this message on to the next window in the chain.

Before closing, a clipboard viewer window must remove itself from the clipboard viewer chain by calling the **ChangeClipboardChain** function. The system then sends a WM_CHANGECBCHAIN message to the first window in the chain.

For more information about processing the WM_DRAWCLIPBOARD and WM_CHANGECBCHAIN messages, see Section 25.2.2, "Creating a Clipboard Viewer Window."

25.1.3.2 Display Formats

A display format is a clipboard format used to display information in a clipboard viewer window. A clipboard owner that uses a private or registered clipboard format, and none of the most common standard formats, must provide data in a display format for viewing in a clipboard viewer window. The display formats are intended for viewing only and must not be pasted into a document.

The four display formats CF_DSPBITMAP, CF_DSPMETAFILEPICT, CF_DSPTEXT, and CF_DSPENHMETAFILE are rendered in the same way as the standard CF_BITMAP, CF_TEXT, CF_METAFILEPICT, and CF_ENHMETAFILE formats.

25.1.3.3 Owner-Display Format

For a clipboard owner that does not use any of the common standard clipboard formats, an alternative to providing a display format is to use the owner-display (CF_OWNERDISPLAY) clipboard format.

By using the owner-display format, a clipboard owner can avoid the overhead of rendering data in an additional format by taking direct control over painting the clipboard viewer window. The clipboard viewer window sends messages to the clipboard owner whenever a portion of the window must be repainted or when the window is scrolled or resized.

25.1.4 Clipboard Commands

A user typically carries out clipboard operations by choosing commands in an application's Edit menu. Following is a brief description of the standard clipboard commands.

Command	Description
Cut	Places a copy of the current selection on the clipboard and deletes the selection from the document. The previous contents of the clipboard are destroyed.
Copy	Places a copy of the current selection on the clipboard. The document remains unchanged. The previous contents of the clipboard are destroyed.
Paste	Replaces the current selection with the contents of the clipboard. The contents of the clipboard are not changed.
Delete	Deletes the current selection from the document. The contents of the clipboard are not changed. This command does not involve the clipboard, but it should appear with the clipboard commands on the Edit menu.

25.2 Using the Clipboard

This section explains how to perform the following tasks:

- Implement the Cut, Copy, and Paste commands.
- Create a clipboard viewer window.

25.2.1 Implementing the Cut, Copy, and Paste Commands

This section describes how standard Cut, Copy, and Paste commands are implemented in an application. The example in this section uses these methods to place data on the clipboard using a registered clipboard format, the CF_OWNERDISPLAY format, and the CF_TEXT format. The registered format is used to represent rectangular or elliptical text windows, called labels.

25.2.1.1 Selecting Data

Before information can be copied to the clipboard, the user must select specific information to be copied or cut. An application should provide a means for the user to select information within a document, and some kind of visual feedback to indicate selected data.

The following illustration shows selected data in the example application Label. In one window, an inverted rectangle indicates a selected range of text within a label; in the other window, sizing boxes indicate a label that is itself selected.

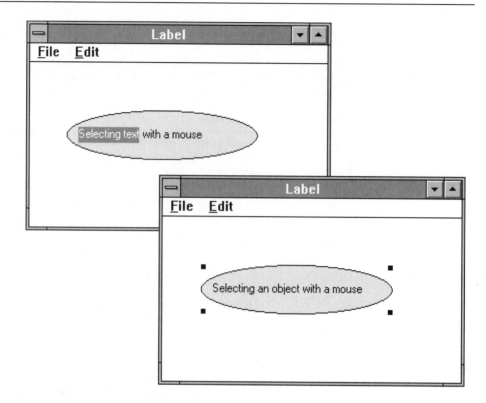

25.2.1.2 Creating an Edit Menu

The following illustration shows a typical Edit menu.

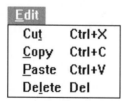

An application should load an accelerator table containing the standard keyboard accelerators for the Edit menu commands. The **TranslateAccelerator** function must be added to the applications message loop for the accelerators to take effect. For more information, see Chapter 17, "Keyboard Accelerators."

25.2.1.3 Processing the WM_INITMENUPOPUP Message

Not all clipboard commands are available to the user at any given time. An application should process the WM_INITMENUPOPUP message to enable the menu items for available commands and disable unavailable commands.

Following is the WM_INITMENUPOPUP case for the Label application.

```
case WM_INITMENUPOPUP:
    InitMenu((HMENU) wParam);
    break;
```

The InitMenu function is defined as follows.

```
void PASCAL InitMenu(HMENU hmenu)
{
    int  cMenuItems = GetMenuItemCount(hmenu);
    int  nPos;
    UINT id;
    UINT fuFlags;
    PLABELBOX pbox = (hwndSelected == NULL) ? NULL :
        (PLABELBOX) GetWindowLong(hwndSelected, 0);

    for (nPos = 0; nPos < cMenuItems; nPos++) {
        id = GetMenuItemID(hmenu, nPos);

        switch (id) {
            case IDM_CUT:
            case IDM_COPY:
            case IDM_DELETE:
                if (pbox == NULL || !pbox->fSelected)
                    fuFlags = MF_BYCOMMAND | MF_GRAYED;
                else if (pbox->fEdit)
                    fuFlags = (id != IDM_DELETE && pbox->ichSel
                            == pbox->ichCaret) ?
                        MF_BYCOMMAND | MF_GRAYED :
                        MF_BYCOMMAND | MF_ENABLED;
                else
                    fuFlags = MF_BYCOMMAND | MF_ENABLED;

                EnableMenuItem(hmenu, id, fuFlags);
                break;

            case IDM_PASTE:
                if (pbox != NULL && pbox->fEdit)
                    EnableMenuItem(hmenu, id,
                        IsClipboardFormatAvailable(CF_TEXT) ?
                            MF_BYCOMMAND | MF_ENABLED :
                            MF_BYCOMMAND | MF_GRAYED
                    );
                else
                    EnableMenuItem(hmenu, id,
                        IsClipboardFormatAvailable(
                            uLabelFormat) ?
                            MF_BYCOMMAND | MF_ENABLED :
                            MF_BYCOMMAND | MF_GRAYED
                    );
```

```
            }
        }
}
```

25.2.1.4 Processing the WM_COMMAND Message

To process menu commands, add the WM_COMMAND case to your
application's main window procedure. Following is the WM_COMMAND case
for the Label application's window procedure.

```
case WM_COMMAND:
    switch (LOWORD(wParam)) {
        case IDM_CUT:
            if (EditCopy())
                EditDelete();
            break;

        case IDM_COPY:
            EditCopy();
            break;

        case IDM_PASTE:
            EditPaste();
            break;

        case IDM_DELETE:
            EditDelete();
            break;

        case IDM_EXIT:
            DestroyWindow(hwnd);
    }
    break;
```

To carry out the Copy and Cut commands, the window procedure calls the
application-defined EditCopy function. For more information, see Section
25.2.1.5, "Copying Information to the Clipboard." To carry out the Paste
command, the window procedure calls the application-defined EditPaste function.
For more information, see Section 25.2.1.6, "Pasting Information from the
Clipboard."

25.2.1.5 Copying Information to the Clipboard

In the Label application, the application-defined EditCopy function copies the
current selection to the clipboard. This function does the following:

1. Opens the clipboard by calling the **OpenClipboard** function.

2. Empties the clipboard by calling the **EmptyClipboard** function.

3. Calls the **SetClipboardData** function once for each clipboard format the application provides.

4. Closes the clipboard by calling the **CloseClipboard** function.

Depending on the current selection, the EditCopy function either copies a range of text or copies an application-defined structure representing an entire label. The structure, call LABELBOX, is defined as follows.

```
#define BOX_ELLIPSE  0
#define BOX_RECT     1

#define CCH_MAXLABEL 80
#define CX_MARGIN    12

typedef struct tagLABELBOX {  /* box */
    RECT rcText;     /* coordinates of rectangle containing text  */
    BOOL fSelected;  /* TRUE if the label is selected             */
    BOOL fEdit;      /* TRUE if text is selected                  */
    int nType;       /* rectangular or elliptical                 */
    int ichCaret;    /* caret position                            */
    int ichSel;      /* with ichCaret, delimits selection         */
    int nXCaret;     /* window position corresponding to ichCaret */
    int nXSel;       /* window position corresponding to ichSel   */
    int cchLabel;    /* length of text in atchLabel               */
    TCHAR atchLabel[CCH_MAXLABEL];
} LABELBOX, *PLABELBOX;
```

Following is the EditCopy function.

```
BOOL PASCAL EditCopy(VOID)
{
    PLABELBOX pbox;
    LPTSTR lptstrCopy;
    HGLOBAL hglbCopy;
    int ich1, ich2, cch;

    if (hwndSelected == NULL)
        return FALSE;

    /* Open the clipboard, and empty it. */

    if (!OpenClipboard(hwndMain))
        return FALSE;
    EmptyClipboard();

    /* Get a pointer to the structure for the selected label. */

    pbox = (PLABELBOX) GetWindowLong(hwndSelected, 0);
```

```
/* If text is selected, copy it using the CF_TEXT format. */

if (pbox->fEdit) {
    if (pbox->ichSel == pbox->ichCaret) {    /* zero-length */
        CloseClipboard();                     /* selection   */
        return FALSE;
    }

    if (pbox->ichSel < pbox->ichCaret) {
        ich1 = pbox->ichSel;
        ich2 = pbox->ichCaret;
    }
    else {
        ich1 = pbox->ichCaret;
        ich2 = pbox->ichSel;
    }
    cch = ich2 - ich1;

    /* Allocate a global memory object for the text. */

    hglbCopy = GlobalAlloc(GMEM_DDESHARE,
        (cch + 1) * sizeof(TCHAR));
    if (hglbCopy == NULL) {
        CloseClipboard();
        return FALSE;
    }

    /* Lock the handle and copy the text to the buffer. */

    lptstrCopy = GlobalLock(hglbCopy);
    memcpy(lptstrCopy, &pbox->atchLabel[ich1],
        cch * sizeof(TCHAR));
    lptstrCopy[cch] = (TCHAR) 0;    /* null character */
    GlobalUnlock(hglbCopy);

    /* Place the handle on the clipboard. */

    SetClipboardData(CF_TEXT, hglbCopy);
}

/* If no text is selected, the label as a whole is copied. */

else {

    /*
     * Save a copy of the selected label as a local memory
     * object. This copy is used to render data on request.
     * It is freed in response to the WM_DESTROYCLIPBOARD
     * message.
     */
```

```
            pboxLocalClip = (PLABELBOX) LocalAlloc(
                LMEM_FIXED,
                sizeof(LABELBOX)
            );
            if (pboxLocalClip == NULL) {
                CloseClipboard();
                return FALSE;
            }
            memcpy(pboxLocalClip, pbox, sizeof(LABELBOX));
            pboxLocalClip->fSelected = FALSE;
            pboxLocalClip->fEdit = FALSE;

            /*
             * Place a registered clipboard format, the owner-display
             * format, and the CF_TEXT format on the clipboard using
             * delayed rendering.
             */

            SetClipboardData(uLabelFormat, NULL);
            SetClipboardData(CF_OWNERDISPLAY, NULL);
            SetClipboardData(CF_TEXT, NULL);
        }

        /* Close the clipboard. */

        CloseClipboard();

        return TRUE;
}
```

25.2.1.6 Pasting Information from the Clipboard

In the Label application, the application-defined EditPaste function pastes the contents of the clipboard. This function does the following:

1. Opens the clipboard by calling the **OpenClipboard** function.

2. Determines which of the available clipboard formats to retrieve.

3. Retrieves the handle of the data in the selected format by calling the **GetClipboardData** function.

4. Inserts a copy of the data into the document.

   The handle returned by **GetClipboardData** is still owned by the clipboard, so an application must not free it or leave it locked.

5. Closes the clipboard by calling the **CloseClipboard** function.

If a label is selected and contains an insertion point, the EditPaste function inserts the text from the clipboard at the insertion point. If there is no selection or if a

label is selected, the function creates a new label, using the application-defined
LABELBOX structure on the clipboard. The LABELBOX structure is placed on
the clipboard by using a registered clipboard format.

Following is the EditPaste function.

```
VOID PASCAL EditPaste(VOID)
{
    PLABELBOX pbox;
    HGLOBAL   hglb;
    LPTSTR    lptstr;
    PLABELBOX pboxCopy;
    int cx, cy;
    HWND hwnd;

    pbox = hwndSelected == NULL ? NULL :
        (PLABELBOX) GetWindowLong(hwndSelected, 0);

    /*
     * If the application is in edit mode,
     * get the clipboard text.
     */

    if (pbox != NULL && pbox->fEdit) {
        if (!IsClipboardFormatAvailable(CF_TEXT))
            return;
        if (!OpenClipboard(hwndMain))
            return;

        hglb = GetClipboardData(CF_TEXT);
        if (hglb != NULL) {
            lptstr = GlobalLock(hglb);
            if (lptstr != NULL) {

                /*
                 * Call the application-defined ReplaceSelection
                 * function to insert the text and repaint the
                 * window.
                 */

                ReplaceSelection(hwndSelected, pbox, lptstr);
                GlobalUnlock(hglb);
            }
        }
        CloseClipboard();

        return;
    }

    /*
```

```
 * If the application is not in edit mode,
 * create a label window.
 */

if (!IsClipboardFormatAvailable(uLabelFormat))
    return;
if (!OpenClipboard(hwndMain))
    return;

hglb = GetClipboardData(uLabelFormat);
if (hglb != NULL) {
    pboxCopy = GlobalLock(hglb);
    if (pboxCopy != NULL) {
        cx = pboxCopy->rcText.right + CX_MARGIN;
        cy = pboxCopy->rcText.top * 2 + cyText;

        hwnd = CreateWindowEx(
            WS_EX_NOPARENTNOTIFY | WS_EX_TRANSPARENT,
            atchClassChild, NULL, WS_CHILD, 0, 0, cx, cy,
            hwndMain, NULL, hinst, NULL
        );
        if (hwnd != NULL) {
            pbox = (PLABELBOX) GetWindowLong(hwnd, 0);
            memcpy(pbox, pboxCopy, sizeof(LABELBOX));
            ShowWindow(hwnd, SW_SHOWNORMAL);
            SetFocus(hwnd);
        }
        GlobalUnlock(hglb);
    }
}
CloseClipboard();
}
```

25.2.1.7 Registering a Clipboard Format

To register a clipboard format, add a call to the **RegisterClipboardFormat** function to your application's instance initialization function, as follows.

```
/* Register a clipboard format. */

LoadString(hinstCurrent, IDS_FORMATNAME, atchTemp,
    sizeof(atchTemp));
uLabelFormat = RegisterClipboardFormat(atchTemp);
if (uLabelFormat == 0)
    return FALSE;
```

25.2.1.8 Processing the WM_RENDERFORMAT and WM_RENDERALLFORMATS Messages

If a window passes a NULL handle to the **SetClipboardData** function, it must process the WM_RENDERFORMAT and WM_RENDERALLFORMATS messages to render data on request.

The WM_RENDERFORMAT message is sent to the clipboard owner if it delayed rendering a specific format and an application requested data in that format. The WM_RENDERALLFORMATS message is sent to the clipboard owner before it is destroyed if it has delayed rendering one or more clipboard formats.

To render a clipboard format, the window procedure must place a data handle on the clipboard by using the **SetClipboardData** function. It must not open the clipboard before calling **SetClipboardData**.

The Label application processes the WM_RENDERFORMAT and WM_RENDERALLFORMATS messages as follows.

```
case WM_RENDERFORMAT:
    RenderFormat((UINT) wParam);
    break;

case WM_RENDERALLFORMATS:
    RenderFormat(uLabelFormat);
    RenderFormat(CF_TEXT);
    break;
```

In both cases, the window procedure calls the application-defined RenderFormat function, defined as follows.

```
void PASCAL RenderFormat(UINT uFormat)
{
    HGLOBAL hglb;
    PLABELBOX pbox;
    LPTSTR  lptstr;
    int cch;

    if (pboxLocalClip == NULL)
        return;

    if (uFormat == CF_TEXT) {

        /* Allocate a buffer for the text. */

        cch = pboxLocalClip->cchLabel;
        hglb = GlobalAlloc(GMEM_DDESHARE,
            (cch + 1) * sizeof(TCHAR));
        if (hglb == NULL)
```

```
            return;

        /* Copy the text from pboxLocalClip. */

        lptstr = GlobalLock(hglb);
        memcpy(lptstr, pboxLocalClip->atchLabel,
            cch * sizeof(TCHAR));
        lptstr[cch] = (TCHAR) 0;
        GlobalUnlock(hglb);

        /* Place the handle on the clipboard. */

        SetClipboardData(CF_TEXT, hglb);
    }
    else if (uFormat == uLabelFormat) {
        hglb = GlobalAlloc(GMEM_DDESHARE, sizeof(LABELBOX));
        if (hglb == NULL)
            return;
        pbox = GlobalLock(hglb);
        memcpy(pbox, pboxLocalClip, sizeof(LABELBOX));
        GlobalUnlock(hglb);

        SetClipboardData(uLabelFormat, hglb);
    }
}
```

25.2.1.9 Processing the WM_DESTROYCLIPBOARD Message

A window can process the WM_DESTROYCLIPBOARD message in order to free any resources it set aside to support delayed rendering. For example, the Label application, when copying a label to the clipboard, allocates a local memory object. It then frees this object in response to the WM_DESTROYCLIPBOARD message, as follows.

```
case WM_DESTROYCLIPBOARD:
    if (pboxLocalClip != NULL) {
        LocalFree(pboxLocalClip);
        pboxLocalClip = NULL;
    }
    break;
```

25.2.1.10 Using the Owner-Display Clipboard Format

If a window places information on the clipboard by using the CF_OWNERDISPLAY clipboard format, it must do the following:

- Process the WM_PAINTCLIPBOARD message. This message is sent to the clipboard owner when a portion of the clipboard viewer window must be repainted.

- Process the WM_SIZECLIPBOARD message. This message is sent to the clipboard owner when the clipboard viewer has been resized or its contents have changed.

  Typically, a window responds to this message by setting the scroll positions and ranges for the clipboard viewer window. In response to this message, the Label application also updates a **SIZE** structure for the clipboard viewer window.

- Process the WM_HSCROLLCLIPBOARD and WM_VSCROLLCLIPBOARD messages. These messages are sent to the clipboard owner when a scroll bar event occurs in the clipboard-viewer window.

- Process the WM_ASKCBFORMATNAME message. The clipboard viewer sends this message to an application to retrieve the name of the owner-display format.

The window procedure for the Label application processes these messages, as follows.

```
LRESULT CALLBACK MainWindowProc(hwnd, msg, wParam, lParam)
HWND hwnd;
UINT msg;
WPARAM wParam;
LPARAM lParam;
{
    static RECT rcViewer;

    RECT rc;
    LPRECT lprc;
    LPPAINTSTRUCT lpps;



        .
        .
        .


    switch (msg) {
        .
        .
        .


        case WM_PAINTCLIPBOARD:

            /* Determine the dimensions of the label. */

            SetRect(&rc, 0, 0,
```

```
                pboxLocalClip->rcText.right + CX_MARGIN,
                pboxLocalClip->rcText.top * 2 + cyText
        );

        /* Center the image in the viewer window. */

        if (rc.right < rcViewer.right) {
            rc.left = (rcViewer.right - rc.right) / 2;
            rc.right += rc.left;
        }
        if (rc.bottom < rcViewer.bottom) {
            rc.top = (rcViewer.bottom - rc.bottom) / 2;
            rc.bottom += rc.top;
        }

        /*
         * Paint the image, using the specified PAINTSTRUCT
         * structure, by calling the application-defined
         * PaintLabel function.
         */

        lpps = (LPPAINTSTRUCT) GlobalLock((HGLOBAL) lParam);
        PaintLabel(lpps, pboxLocalClip, &rc);
        GlobalUnlock((HGLOBAL) lParam);
        break;

    case WM_SIZECLIPBOARD:

        /*
         * Save the dimensions of the window in a static
         * RECT structure.
         */

        lprc = (LPRECT) GlobalLock((HGLOBAL) lParam);
        memcpy(&rcViewer, lprc, sizeof(RECT));
        GlobalUnlock((HGLOBAL) lParam);

        /*
         * Set the scroll ranges to zero (thus eliminating
         * the need to process the WM_HSCROLLCLIPBOARD and
         * WM_VSCROLLCLIPBOARD messages).
         */

        SetScrollRange((HWND) wParam, SB_HORZ, 0, 0, TRUE);
        SetScrollRange((HWND) wParam, SB_VERT, 0, 0, TRUE);

        break;

    case WM_ASKCBFORMATNAME:
        LoadString(hinst, IDS_OWNERDISPLAY,
```

```
                    (LPSTR) lParam, wParam);
                break;



                .
                .
                .


        default:
            return DefWindowProc(hwnd, msg, wParam, lParam);
    }
    return 0;
}
```

25.2.2 Creating a Clipboard Viewer Window

A clipboard viewer window displays the current contents of the clipboard, and receives messages when the clipboard contents change. To create a clipboard viewer window, your application must do the following:

- Add the window to the clipboard viewer chain.
- Process the WM_CHANGECBCHAIN message.
- Process the WM_DRAWCLIPBOARD message.
- Remove the window from the clipboard viewer chain before it is destroyed.

25.2.2.1 Adding a Window to the Clipboard Viewer Chain

A window adds itself to the clipboard viewer chain by calling the **SetClipboardViewer** function. The return value is the handle of the next window in the chain. A window must keep track of this value—for example, by saving it in a static variable named *hwndNextViewer*.

The following example adds a window to the clipboard viewer chain in response to the WM_CREATE message.

```
case WM_CREATE:

    /* Add the window to the clipboard viewer chain. */

    hwndNextViewer = SetClipboardViewer(hwnd);
    break;
```

25.2.2.2 Processing the WM_CHANGECBCHAIN Message

A clipboard viewer window receives the WM_CHANGECBCHAIN message when another window is removing itself from the clipboard viewer chain. If the window being removed is the next window in the chain, the window receiving the message must unlink the next window from the chain. Otherwise, this message should be passed to the next window in the chain.

The following example shows the processing of the WM_CHANGECBCHAIN message.

```
case WM_CHANGECBCHAIN:

    /* If the next window is closing, repair the chain. */

    if ((HWND) wParam == hwndNextViewer)
        hwndNextViewer = (HWND) lParam;

    /* Otherwise, pass the message to the next link. */

    else if (hwndNextViewer != NULL)
        SendMessage(hwndNextViewer, uMsg, wParam, lParam);

    break;
```

25.2.2.3 Removing a Window from the Clipboard Viewer Chain

To remove itself from the clipboard viewer chain, a window calls the **ChangeClipboardChain** function. The following example removes a window from the clipboard viewer chain in response to the WM_DESTROY message.

```
case WM_DESTROY:
    ChangeClipboardChain(hwnd, hwndNextViewer);
    PostQuitMessage(0);
    break;
```

25.2.2.4 Processing the WM_DRAWCLIPBOARD Message

The WM_DRAWCLIPBOARD message notifies a clipboard viewer window that the contents of the clipboard have changed. A window should do the following when processing the WM_DRAWCLIPBOARD message:

1. Determine which of the available clipboard formats to display.
2. Retrieve the clipboard data and display it in the window. Or, if the clipboard format is CF_OWNERDISPLAY, send a WM_PAINTCLIPBOARD message to the clipboard owner.
3. Send the message to the next window in the clipboard viewer chain.

For an example of processing the WM_DRAWCLIPBOARD message, see the listing in Section 25.2.2.5, "Example of a Clipboard Viewer."

25.2.2.5 Example of a Clipboard Viewer

The following example shows a simple clipboard viewer application.

```
HINSTANCE hinst;
UINT uFormat = (UINT)(-1);
BOOL fAuto = TRUE;

LRESULT APIENTRY MainWndProc(hwnd, uMsg, wParam, lParam)
HWND hwnd;
UINT uMsg;
WPARAM wParam;
LPARAM lParam;
{
    static HWND hwndNextViewer;

    HDC hdc;
    HDC hdcMem;
    PAINTSTRUCT ps;
    LPPAINTSTRUCT lpps;
    RECT rc;
    LPRECT lprc;
    HGLOBAL hglb;
    LPSTR lpstr;
    HBITMAP hbm;
    HENHMETAFILE hemf;
    HWND hwndOwner;

    switch (uMsg) {
        case WM_PAINT:
            hdc = BeginPaint(hwnd, &ps);

            /* Branch depending on the clipboard format. */

            switch (uFormat) {
                case CF_OWNERDISPLAY:
                    hwndOwner = GetClipboardOwner();
                    hglb = GlobalAlloc(GMEM_DDESHARE,
                        sizeof(PAINTSTRUCT));
                    lpps = GlobalLock(hglb);
                    memcpy(lpps, &ps, sizeof(PAINTSTRUCT));
                    GlobalUnlock(hglb);

                    SendMessage(hwndOwner, WM_PAINTCLIPBOARD,
                        (WPARAM) hwnd, (LPARAM) hglb);

                    GlobalFree(hglb);
                    break;

                case CF_BITMAP:
```

```
        hdcMem = CreateCompatibleDC(hdc);
        if (hdcMem != NULL) {
            if (OpenClipboard(hwnd)) {
                hbm = (HBITMAP)
                    GetClipboardData(uFormat);
                SelectObject(hdcMem, hbm);
                GetClientRect(hwnd, &rc);

                BitBlt(hdc, 0, 0, rc.right, rc.bottom,
                    hdcMem, 0, 0, SRCCOPY);
                CloseClipboard();
            }
            DeleteDC(hdcMem);
        }
        break;

    case CF_TEXT:
        if (OpenClipboard(hwnd)) {
            hglb = GetClipboardData(uFormat);
            lpstr = GlobalLock(hglb);

            GetClientRect(hwnd, &rc);
            DrawText(hdc, lpstr, -1, &rc, DT_LEFT);

            GlobalUnlock(hglb);
            CloseClipboard();
        }
        break;

    case CF_ENHMETAFILE:
        if (OpenClipboard(hwnd)) {
            hemf = GetClipboardData(uFormat);
            GetClientRect(hwnd, &rc);
            PlayEnhMetaFile(hdc, hemf, &rc);
            CloseClipboard();
        }
        break;

    case 0:
        GetClientRect(hwnd, &rc);
        DrawText(hdc, "The clipboard is empty.", -1,
            &rc, DT_CENTER | DT_SINGLELINE |
            DT_VCENTER);
        break;

    default:
        GetClientRect(hwnd, &rc);
        DrawText(hdc, "Unable to display format.", -1,
            &rc, DT_CENTER | DT_SINGLELINE |
            DT_VCENTER);
```

```
        }
        EndPaint(hwnd, &ps);
        break;

case WM_SIZE:
    if (uFormat == CF_OWNERDISPLAY) {
        hwndOwner = GetClipboardOwner();
        hglb = GlobalAlloc(GMEM_DDESHARE, sizeof(RECT));
        lprc = GlobalLock(hglb);
        GetClientRect(hwnd, lprc);
        GlobalUnlock(hglb);

        SendMessage(hwndOwner, WM_SIZECLIPBOARD,
            (WPARAM) hwnd, (LPARAM) hglb);

        GlobalFree(hglb);
    }
    break;

case WM_CREATE:

    /* Add the window to the clipboard viewer chain. */

    hwndNextViewer = SetClipboardViewer(hwnd);
    break;

case WM_CHANGECBCHAIN:

    /* If the next window is closing, repair the chain. */

    if ((HWND) wParam == hwndNextViewer)
        hwndNextViewer = (HWND) lParam;

    /* Otherwise, pass the message to the next link. */

    else if (hwndNextViewer != NULL)
        SendMessage(hwndNextViewer, uMsg, wParam, lParam);

    break;

case WM_DESTROY:
    ChangeClipboardChain(hwnd, hwndNextViewer);
    PostQuitMessage(0);
    break;

case WM_DRAWCLIPBOARD: /* clipboard contents changed. */

    /* Update the window by using Auto clipboard format. */

    SetAutoView(hwnd);
```

```
                        /* Pass the message to the next window in viewer chain. */

                        SendMessage(hwndNextViewer, uMsg, wParam, lParam);
                        break;

                case WM_INITMENUPOPUP:
                        if (!HIWORD(lParam))
                                InitMenu(hwnd, (HMENU) wParam);
                        break;

                case WM_COMMAND:
                        switch (LOWORD(wParam)) {
                                case IDM_EXIT:
                                        DestroyWindow(hwnd);
                                        break;

                                case IDM_AUTO:
                                        SetAutoView(hwnd);
                                        break;

                                default:
                                        fAuto = FALSE;
                                        uFormat = LOWORD(wParam);
                                        InvalidateRect(hwnd, NULL, TRUE);
                        }
                        break;

                default:
                        return DefWindowProc(hwnd, uMsg, wParam, lParam);
        }
        return (LRESULT) NULL;
}


void PASCAL SetAutoView(HWND hwnd)
{
        static UINT auPriorityList[] = {
                CF_OWNERDISPLAY,
                CF_TEXT,
                CF_ENHMETAFILE,
                CF_BITMAP
        };

        uFormat = GetPriorityClipboardFormat(auPriorityList, 4);
        fAuto = TRUE;

        InvalidateRect(hwnd, NULL, TRUE);
        UpdateWindow(hwnd);
}
```

```
void PASCAL InitMenu(HWND hwnd, HMENU hmenu)
{
    UINT uFormat;
    char szFormatName[80];
    LPCSTR lpFormatName;
    UINT fuFlags;
    UINT idMenuItem;

    /*
     * If a menu is not the display menu, no initialization is necessary. */
     */

    if (GetMenuItemID(hmenu, 0) != IDM_AUTO)
        return;

    /* Delete all menu items except the first. */

    while (GetMenuItemCount(hmenu) > 1)
        DeleteMenu(hmenu, 1, MF_BYPOSITION);

    /* Check or uncheck the Auto menu item. */

    fuFlags = fAuto ? MF_BYCOMMAND | MF_CHECKED :
        MF_BYCOMMAND | MF_UNCHECKED;
    CheckMenuItem(hmenu, IDM_AUTO, fuFlags);

    /* If there are no clipboard formats, return. */

    if (CountClipboardFormats() == 0)
        return;

    /* Open the clipboard. */

    if (!OpenClipboard(hwnd))
        return;

    /* Add a separator and then a menu item for each format. */

    AppendMenu(hmenu, MF_SEPARATOR, 0, NULL);
    uFormat = EnumClipboardFormats(0);

    while (uFormat) {

        /*
         * Call an application-defined function to get the name
         * of the clipboard format.
         */
```

```
        lpFormatName = GetPredefinedClipboardFormatName(uFormat);

        /* For registered formats, get the registered name. */

        if (lpFormatName == NULL) {
            if (GetClipboardFormatName(uFormat, szFormatName,
                    sizeof(szFormatName)))
                lpFormatName = szFormatName;
            else
                lpFormatName = "(unknown)";
        }

        /*
         * Add a menu item for the format. For displayable
         * formats, use the format ID for the menu ID.
         */

        if (IsDisplayableFormat(uFormat)) {
            fuFlags = MF_STRING;
            idMenuItem = uFormat;
        }
        else {
            fuFlags = MF_STRING | MF_GRAYED;
            idMenuItem = 0;
        }
        AppendMenu(hmenu, fuFlags, idMenuItem, lpFormatName);

        uFormat = EnumClipboardFormats(uFormat);
    }
    CloseClipboard();

}


BOOL PASCAL IsDisplayableFormat(UINT uFormat)
{
    switch (uFormat) {
        case CF_OWNERDISPLAY:
        case CF_TEXT:
        case CF_ENHMETAFILE:
        case CF_BITMAP:
            return TRUE;
    }
    return FALSE;
}
```

25.3 Functions and Messages

Following are the functions and messages used with the clipboard.

Functions

ChangeClipboardChain
CloseClipboard
CountClipboardFormats
EmptyClipboard
EnumClipboardFormats
GetClipboardData
GetClipboardFormatName
GetClipboardOwner
GetClipboardViewer
GetOpenClipboardWindow
GetPriorityClipboardFormat
IsClipboardFormatAvailable
OpenClipboard
RegisterClipboardFormat
SetClipboardData
SetClipboardViewer

Messages

WM_ASKCBFORMATNAME
WM_CHANGECBCHAIN
WM_COPY
WM_CUT
WM_DESTROYCLIPBOARD
WM_DRAWCLIPBOARD
WM_HSCROLLCLIPBOARD
WM_PAINTCLIPBOARD
WM_PASTE
WM_RENDERALLFORMATS
WM_RENDERFORMAT
WM_SIZECLIPBOARD
WM_VSCROLLCLIPBOARD

CHAPTER 26

Dynamic Data Exchange

26.1 About Dynamic Data Exchange

The Microsoft ® Windows ™ operating system provides several methods for transferring data between applications. One way to transfer data is to use the Windows dynamic data exchange (DDE) protocol. The DDE protocol is a set of messages and guidelines. It sends messages between applications that share data and uses shared memory to exchange data between applications. Applications can use the DDE protocol for one-time data transfers and for continuous exchanges in which applications send updates to one another as new data becomes available.

Windows also includes the Dynamic Data Exchange Management Library (DDEML). The DDEML is a dynamic-link library (DLL) that applications running with Windows can use to share data. The DDEML provides an application programming interface (API) that simplifies the task of adding DDE capability to a Windows-based application. Instead of sending, posting, and processing DDE messages directly, an application uses the DDEML functions to manage DDE conversations. (A DDE conversation is the interaction between client and server applications.)

The DDEML also provides a facility for managing the strings and data that DDE applications share. Instead of using atoms and pointers to shared memory objects, DDE applications create and exchange string handles, which identify strings, and data handles, which identify memory objects. The DDEML also makes it possible for a server application to register the service names it supports. The names are broadcast to other applications in the system, which can then use the names to connect to the server. Moreover, the DDEML ensures compatibility among DDE applications by forcing them to implement the DDE protocol in a consistent manner.

Existing applications that use the message-based DDE protocol are fully compatible with those that use the DDEML. That is, an application that uses message-based DDE can establish conversations and perform transactions with applications that use the DDEML. Because of the many advantages of the DDEML, new applications should use it rather than the DDE messages. To use the API elements of the DDE management library, you must include the DDEML.H header file in your source files, link with DDEML.LIB, and ensure that DDEML.DLL is in the system's path.

This chapter provides guidelines for implementing dynamic data exchange for applications that cannot use the DDEML. For more information about the DDEML, see Chapter 77, "Dynamic Data Exchange Management Library."

26.1.1 Dynamic Data Exchange Protocol

Because Windows has a message-based architecture, passing messages is the most appropriate method for automatically transferring information between applications. However, Windows messages contain only two parameters (*wParam* and *lParam*) for passing data. As a result, these parameters must refer indirectly to other pieces of data when more than a few words of information pass between applications. The DDE protocol defines exactly how applications should use the *wParam* and *lParam* parameters to pass larger pieces of data by means of global atoms and shared memory handles. The DDE protocol has specific rules for allocating and deleting global atoms and shared memory objects.

A global atom is a reference to a character string. In the DDE protocol, atoms identify the applications exchanging data, the nature of the data being exchanged, and the data items themselves. For more information about atoms, see Chapter 61, "Atoms." A shared memory handle is a handle to a memory object allocated by **GlobalAlloc**, using the GMEM_DDESHARE flag. In the DDE protocol, shared memory objects store data items passed between applications, protocol options, and remote command execution strings.

26.1.2 Uses for Windows Dynamic Data Exchange

DDE is most appropriate for data exchanges that do not require ongoing user interaction. Usually, an application provides a method for the user to establish the link between the applications exchanging data. Once that link is established, however, the applications exchange data without further user involvement.

DDE can be used to implement a broad range of application features—for example:

- Linking to real-time data, such as to stock market updates, scientific instruments, or process control.

- Creating compound documents, such as a word processing document that includes a chart produced by a graphics application. Using DDE, the chart will change when the source data is changed, while the rest of the document remains the same.

- Performing data queries between applications, such as a spreadsheet querying a database application for accounts past due.

26.1.3 Dynamic Data Exchange from the User's Point of View

The following example illustrates illustrates how two DDE applications can cooperate, as seen from the user's point of view.

A spreadsheet user wants to use Microsoft ® Excel to track the price of a particular stock on the New York Stock Exchange. The user has a Windows-based application called Quote that in turn has access to NYSE data. The DDE conversation between Microsoft Excel and Quote takes place as follows:

- The user initiates the conversation by supplying the name of the application (Quote) that will supply the data and the particular topic of interest (NYSE). The resulting DDE conversation is used to request quotes on specific stocks.

- Microsoft Excel broadcasts the application and topic names to all DDE applications currently running in the system. Quote responds, establishing a conversation with Microsoft Excel about the NYSE topic.

- The user can then create a spreadsheet formula in a cell that requests that the spreadsheet be automatically updated whenever a particular stock quotation changes. For example, the user could request an automatic update whenever a change occurs in the selling price of ZAXX stock by specifying the following Microsoft Excel formula:

  ```
  ='Quote'|'NYSE'!ZAXX
  ```

- The user can terminate the automatic updating of the ZAXX stock quotation at any time. Other data links that were established separately (such as for quotations for other stocks) still will remain active under the same NYSE conversation.

- The user can also terminate the entire conversation between Microsoft Excel and Quote on the NYSE topic, so that no specific data links on that topic can be established without initiating a new conversation.

26.1.4 Dynamic Data Exchange Concepts

The following sections explain the important concepts and terminology that are key to understanding dynamic data exchange.

26.1.4.1 Client, Server, and Conversation

Two applications participating in dynamic data exchange are said to be engaged in a DDE *conversation*. The application that initiates the conversation is the *client application*; the application that responds to the client is the *server application*. An application can engage in several conversations at the same time, acting as the client in some and as the server in others.

A DDE conversation takes place between two windows, one for each of the participating applications. A window may be the main window of the application; a window associated with a specific document, as in a multiple document interface (MDI) application; or a hidden (invisible) window whose only purpose is to process DDE messages.

Since a DDE conversation is identified by the pair of handles of the windows engaged in the conversation, no window should be engaged in more than one conversation with another window. Either the client application or the server application must provide a different window for each of its conversations with a particular server or client application.

An application can ensure a pair of client and server windows is never involved in more than one conversation by creating a hidden window for each conversation. The sole purpose of this window is to process DDE messages.

26.1.4.2 Application, Topic, and Item Names

The DDE protocol identifies the units of data passed between the client and server with a three-level hierarchy of application, topic, and item names.

Each DDE conversation is uniquely defined by the application name and topic. At the beginning of a DDE conversation, the client and server determine the application name and topic. The application name is usually the name of the server application. For example, when Microsoft Excel acts as the server in a conversation, the application name is Excel.

The DDE topic is a general classification of data within which multiple data items may be "discussed" (exchanged) during the conversation. For applications that operate on file-based documents, the topic is usually a filename. For other applications, the topic is an application-specific name.

Because the client and server window handles together identify a DDE conversation, the application name and topic that define a conversation cannot be changed during the course of the conversation.

A DDE data item is information related to the conversation topic exchanged between the applications. Values for the data item can be passed from the server to the client, or from the client to the server. Data can be passed with any of the standard clipboard formats or with a registered clipboard format. A special, registered format named Link identifies an item in a DDE conversation. For more information about clipboard formats, see Chapter 25, "Clipboard."

26.1.4.3 The System Topic

Applications should support the System topic at all times. This topic provides a context for information that may be of general interest to another application.

Data-item values must be rendered in the CF_TEXT clipboard format. Individual elements of item values for a System topic must be delimited by tab characters. The following table suggests some items for the System topic.

Item	Description
Formats	Tab-delimited list of clipboard formats the application can render. Typically, the CF_ formats are listed with the "CF_" portion of the names removed (for example, CF_TEXT is listed as "TEXT").
Help	Text that briefly explains how to use the DDE server.

ReturnMessage	Supporting detail for the most recently used WM_DDE_ACK message. This item is useful when more than eight bits of application-specific return data are required.
Status	Indication of the current status of the application. When a server receives a WM_DDE_REQUEST message for this System-topic item, it should respond by posting a WM_DDE_DATA message with a string containing either Busy or Ready, as appropriate.
SysItems	List of System-topic items the application supports.
TopicItemList	Similar to the SysItems item, except that TopicItemList should be supported for each topic other than the System topic. This allows browsing of the items supported under any topic. If the items cannot be enumerated, this item should contain only "TopicItemList".
Topics	List of topics the application supports at the current time; this list can vary from moment to moment.

26.1.4.4 Permanent Data Links

Once a DDE conversation has begun, the client can establish one or more permanent data links with the server. A data link is a communications mechanism by which the server notifies the client whenever the value of a given data item changes. The data link is permanent in the sense that this notification process continues until the data link or the DDE conversation itself is terminated.

There are two kinds of permanent DDE data links: warm and hot. In a warm data link, the server notifies the client that the value of the data item has changed, but the server does not send the data value to the client until the client requests it. In a hot data link, the server immediately sends the changed data value to the client.

Applications that support warm or hot data links typically provide a Copy or Paste Link command in their Edit menu to enable the user to establish links between applications. For more information, see Section 26.2.3.2, "Initiating a Data Link with the Paste Link Command."

26.1.4.5 Atoms and Shared Memory Objects

Certain arguments of DDE messages are global atoms or shared memory objects. Applications using these arguments must follow explicit rules about when to allocate and delete them. In all cases, the message sender must delete any atom or shared memory object that the intended receiver will not receive because of an error condition, such as failure of the **PostMessage** function.

DDE uses shared memory objects for three purposes:

- To carry a data-item value to be exchanged. This is an item referenced by the *hData* parameter in the WM_DDE_DATA and WM_DDE_POKE messages.

- To carry options in a message. This is an item referenced by the *hOptions* parameter in a WM_DDE_ADVISE message.

- To carry a command execution string. This is an item referenced by the *hCommands* parameter in the WM_DDE_EXECUTE message and its corresponding WM_DDE_ACK message.

An application that receives a DDE shared memory object must treat it as read only. The application must not use the object as a mutual read-write area for the free exchange of data.

As it does with a DDE atom, an application should free a shared memory object to manage memory effectively. The application should also lock and unlock memory objects.

26.1.5 Dynamic Data Exchange Messages

Because DDE is a message-based protocol, it employs no special Windows functions or libraries. All DDE transactions are conducted by passing certain defined DDE messages between the client and server windows.

There are nine DDE messages; the symbolic constants for these messages are defined in the Microsoft ® Win32 ™ Software Development Kit (SDK) header file DDE.H. Certain structures for the various DDE messages are also defined in DDE.H.

The following table summarizes the nine DDE messages.

Message	Description
WM_DDE_ACK	Acknowledges receiving or not receiving a message.
WM_DDE_ADVISE	Requests the server application to supply an update or notification for a data item whenever it changes. This establishes a permanent data link.
WM_DDE_DATA	Sends a data-item value to the client application.
WM_DDE_EXECUTE	Sends a string to the server application, which is expected to process the string as a series of commands.
WM_DDE_INITIATE	Initiates a conversation between the client and server applications.
WM_DDE_POKE	Sends a data-item value to the server application.
WM_DDE_REQUEST	Requests the server application to provide the value of a data item.
WM_DDE_TERMINATE	Terminates a conversation.
WM_DDE_UNADVISE	Terminates a permanent data link.

An application calls the **SendMessage** function to issue the WM_DDE_INITIATE message or a WM_DDE_ACK message sent in response to WM_DDE_INITIATE. All other messages are sent by the **PostMessage** function. The first parameter of these calls is the handle of the receiving window. The second parameter contains the message to be sent; the third parameter identifies the sending window; and the fourth parameter contains the message-specific arguments.

26.1.6 Dynamic Data Exchange Message Flow

A typical DDE conversation consists of the following events:

1. The client application initiates the conversation, and the server application responds.

2. The applications exchange data by any or all of the following methods:

   ▪ The server application sends data to the client at the client's request.

   ▪ The client application sends unsolicited data to the server application.

   ▪ The client application requests the server application to notify the client whenever a data item changes (warm data link).

   ▪ The client application requests the server application to send data whenever the data changes (hot data link).

   ▪ The server application carries out a command at the client's request.

3. Either the client or server application terminates the conversation.

An application window that processes requests from a client or server must process them strictly in the order they are received.

A client can establish conversations with more than one server; a server can have conversations with more than one client. When handling messages from more than one source, a client or server must process the messages of a given conversation synchronously, but need not process all messages synchronously. In other words, it can shift from one conversation to another as needed.

If an application is unable to process an incoming request because it is waiting for a DDE response, it must prevent deadlock by posting a WM_DDE_ACK message with the **fBusy** member of the **DDEACK** structure set to 1. An application can also send a busy WM_DDE_ACK message if, for any reason, it cannot process an incoming request within a reasonable amount of time.

An application should be able to handle the failure of a client or server to respond to a message within a certain time. Since the length of the time-out interval may vary depending on the nature of the application and the configuration of the user's system (including whether it is connected to a network), the application should provide a way for the user to specify the interval.

26.1.7 Parameter-Packing Functions

The *lParam* parameter of many DDE messages contains two pieces of data. For example, the *lParam* of the WM_DDE_DATA message contains a data handle and an atom. In previous versions of Windows, an application could use the **MAKELONG** macro to prepare an *lParam* parameter, and the **LOWORD** and **HIWORD** macros to remove the low-order and high-order values from *lParam*. Because a Win32 data handle is a 32-bit value, a Win32 application must use the **PackDDElParam** function to pack the handle and atom into an *lParam* parameter, and the **UnpackDDElParam** function to remove the values. DDE applications must use **PackDDElParam** and **UnpackDDElParam** for all messages posted during a DDE conversation.

The Win32 API also includes the **ReuseDDElParam** and **FreeDDElParam** functions. **ReuseDDElParam** allows a DDE application to reuse a packed *lParam* parameter, helping reduce the number of memory reallocations the application must perform during a conversation. An application can use the **FreeDDElParam** to free the memory associated with a data handle received during a DDE conversation.

26.2 Using Dynamic Data Exchange

The section describes how to perform the following tasks:

- Initiate a DDE conversation.
- Transfer a single data item.
- Establish a permanent data link.
- Carry out commands in a server application.
- Terminate a DDE conversation.

26.2.1 Initiating a Conversation

To initiate a DDE conversation, the client sends a WM_DDE_INITIATE message. Usually, the client broadcasts this message by calling the **SendMessage** function, with –1 as the first parameter. If the application already has the window handle of the server application, it can send the message directly to that window. The client prepares atoms for the application name and topic name by calling the **GlobalAddAtom** function. The client can request conversations with any potential server application and for any potential topic by supplying NULL (wildcard) atoms for the application and topic.

The following example illustrates how the client initiates a conversation, where both the application and topic are specified.

```
/* Global variable */

static BOOL fInInitiate = FALSE;
    char *szApplication;
    char *szTopic;
    atomApplication = *szApplication == 0 ?
        NULL : GlobalAddAtom((LPSTR) szApplication);
    atomTopic = *szTopic == 0 ?
        NULL : GlobalAddAtom((LPSTR) szTopic);

    fInInitiate = TRUE;
    SendMessage((HWND) -1,          /* broadcasts message        */
        WM_DDE_INITIATE,            /* initiates conversation    */
        (WPARAM) hwndClientDDE,     /* handle of client DDE window */
        MAKELONG(atomApplication,   /* application-name atom      */
            atomTopic));            /* topic-name atom           */
    fInInitiate = FALSE;
    if (atomApplication != NULL)
        GlobalDeleteAtom(atomApplication);
    if (atomTopic != NULL)
        GlobalDeleteAtom(atomTopic);
```

Note that if your application uses NULL atoms, you need not use the
GlobalAddAtom and **GlobalDeleteAtom** functions. In this example, the client
application creates two global atoms containing the name of the server and the
name of the topic, respectively.

The client application sends a WM_DDE_INITIATE message with these two
atoms in the *lParam* parameter of the message. In the call to the **SendMessage**
function, the special window handle –1 directs Windows to send this message to
all other active applications. **SendMessage** does not return to the client
application until all applications that receive the message have, in turn, returned
control to Windows. This means that all WM_DDE_ACK messages sent in reply
by the server applications are guaranteed to have been processed by the client by
the time the **SendMessage** call has returned.

After **SendMessage** returns, the client application deletes the global atoms.

Server applications respond according to the logic illustrated in the following
diagram.

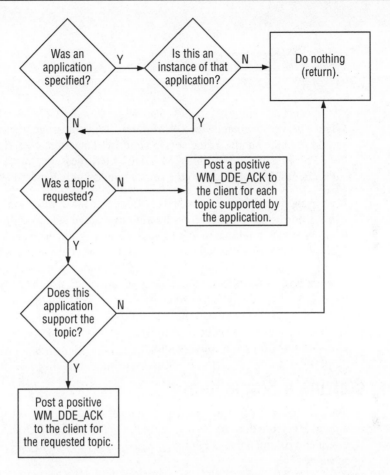

To acknowledge one or more topics, the server must create atoms for each conversation (requiring duplicate application-name atoms if there are multiple topics) and send a WM_DDE_ACK message for each conversation, as illustrated in the following example.

```
if ((atomApplication = GlobalAddAtom("Server")) != 0) {
    if ((atomTopic = GlobalAddAtom(szTopic)) != 0) {
        SendMessage(hwndClientDDE,
            WM_DDE_ACK,
            (WPARAM) hwndServerDDE,
            MAKELONG(atomApplication, atomTopic));
        GlobalDeleteAtom(atomApplication);
    }

    GlobalDeleteAtom(atomTopic);
}

if ((atomApplication == 0) || (atomTopic == 0)) {
```

```
    .
    . /* error handling */
    .

}
```

When a server responds with a WM_DDE_ACK message, the client application should save the handle of the server window. The client receiving the handle as the *wParam* parameter of the WM_DDE_ACK message, then sends all subsequent DDE messages to the server window this handle identifies.

If your client application uses NULL atoms for the application name or topic name, you should expect the application to receive acknowledgments from more than one server application. Multiple acknowledgements can also come from multiple instances of a DDE server, even if your client application does not use NULL atoms. A server should always use a unique window for each conversation. The window procedure in the client application can use the handle of the server window (provided as the *lParam* parameter of WM_DDE_INITIATE) to track the status of multiple conversations. This allows a single client window to process several conversations without needing to terminate and reconnect with a new client window for each conversation.

26.2.2 Transferring a Single Item

Once a DDE conversation has been established, the client can retrieve the value of a data item from the server by issuing the WM_DDE_REQUEST message, or the client can submit a data-item value to the server by issuing the WM_DDE_POKE message.

26.2.2.1 Retrieving an Item from the Server

To retrieve an item from the server, the client sends the server a WM_DDE_REQUEST message specifying the item and format to retrieve, as shown in the following example.

```
if ((atomItem = GlobalAddAtom(szItemName)) != 0) {
    if (!PostMessage(hwndServerDDE,
            WM_DDE_REQUEST,
            (WPARAM) hwndClientDDE,
            PackDDElParam(WM_DDE_REQUEST, CF_TEXT, atomItem)))
        GlobalDeleteAtom(atomItem);
}

if (atomItem == 0) {

    .
    . /* error handling */
```

}

In this example, the client specifies the clipboard format CF_TEXT as the preferred format for the requested data item.

The receiver (server) of the WM_DDE_REQUEST message typically must delete the item atom, but if the **PostMessage** call itself fails, the client must delete the atom.

If the server has access to the requested item and can render it in the requested format, the server copies the item value as a shared memory object and sends the client a WM_DDE_DATA message, as illustrated in the following example.

```
/*
 * Allocate the size of the DDE data header, plus the data: a
 * string,<CR><LF><NULL>. The byte for the string's terminating
 * null character is counted by DDEDATA.Value[1].
 */

if (!(hData = GlobalAlloc(GMEM_MOVEABLE | GMEM_DDESHARE,
        (LONG) sizeof(DDEDATA) + lstrlen(szItemValue) + 2)))
    return;

if (!(lpData = (DDEDATA FAR*) GlobalLock(hData))) {
    GlobalFree(hData);
    return;

}
    .
    .
    .


lpData->cfFormat = CF_TEXT;
lstrcpy((LPSTR) lpData->Value, (LPSTR) szItemValue);

/* Each line of CF_TEXT data is terminated by CR/LF. */

lstrcat((LPSTR) lpData->Value, (LPSTR) "\r\n");
GlobalUnlock(hData);
if ((atomItem = GlobalAddAtom((LPSTR) szItemName)) != 0) {
    lParam = PackDDElParam(WM_DDE_ACK, (UINT) hData, atomItem);
    if (!PostMessage(hwndClientDDE,
            WM_DDE_DATA,
            (WPARAM) hwndServerDDE,
            lParam)) {
        GlobalFree(hData);
        GlobalDeleteAtom(atomItem);
        FreeDDElParam(WM_DDE_ACK, lParam);
```

```
    }
}

if (atomItem == 0) {

    .
    . /* error handling */
    .

}
```

In this example, the server application allocates a memory object to contain the data item. The memory is allocated with the GMEM_DDESHARE option, so that the server and client applications can share the memory. After allocating the memory object, the server application locks the object so it can obtain the object's address. The data object is initialized as a **DDEDATA** structure.

The server application then sets the **cfFormat** member of the structure to CF_TEXT to inform the client application that the data is in text format. In response, the client copies the value of the requested data into the **Value** member of the **DDEDATA** structure.

After the server has filled the data object, the server unlocks the data and creates a global atom containing the name of the data item.

Finally, the server issues the WM_DDE_DATA message by calling the **PostMessage** function. The handle of the data object and the atom containing the item name are packed into the *lParam* parameter of the message by the **PackDDElParam** function.

If **PostMessage** fails, the server must use the **FreeDDElParam** function to free the packed *lParam* parameter. The server must also free the packed *lParam* parameter for the WM_DDE_REQUEST message it received.

If the server cannot satisfy the request, it sends the client a negative WM_DDE_ACK message, as shown in the following example.

```
/* negative acknowledgment */

PostMessage(hwndClientDDE,
    WM_DDE_ACK,
    (WPARAM) hwndServerDDE,
    PackDDElParam(WM_DDE_ACK, 0, atomItem));
```

Upon receiving a WM_DDE_DATA message, the client processes the data-item value as appropriate. Then, if the **fAckReq** member specified in the WM_DDE_DATA message is 1, the client must send the server a positive WM_DDE_ACK message, as shown in the following example.

```
UnpackDDElParam(WM_DDE_DATA, lParam, (PUINT) &hData,
    (PUINT) &atomItem);
if (!(lpDDEData = (DDEDATA FAR*) GlobalLock(hData))
        || (lpDDEData->cfFormat != CF_TEXT)) {
    PostMessage(hwndServerDDE,
        WM_DDE_ACK,
        (WPARAM) hwndClientDDE,
        PackDDElParam(WM_DDE_ACK, 0, atomItem)); /* negative ACK */
}

/* Copy data from lpDDEData here.*/

if (lpDDEData->fAckReq) {
    PostMessage(hwndServerDDE,
        WM_DDE_ACK,
        (WPARAM) hwndClientDDE,
        PackDDElParam(WM_DDE_ACK, 0x8000,
            atomItem)); /* positive ACK */
}

bRelease = lpDDEData->fRelease;
GlobalUnlock(hData);
if (bRelease)
    GlobalFree(hData);
```

In this example, the client examines the format of the data. If the format is not
CF_TEXT (or if the client cannot lock the memory for the data), the client sends a
negative WM_DDE_ACK message to indicate that it cannot process the data. If
the client cannot lock a data handle because the handle contains the **fAckReq**
member, the client should not send a negative WM_DDE_ACK message. Instead,
the client should terminate the conversation.

If a client sends a negative acknowledgement in response to a WM_DDE_DATA
message, the server is responsible for freeing the memory (but not the *lParam*
parameter) referenced by the WM_DDE_DATA message associated with the
negative acknowledgement.

If it can process the data, the client examines the **fAckReq** member of the
DDEDATA structure to determine whether the server requested that it be
informed that the client received and processed the data successfully. If the server
did request this information, the client sends the server a positive
WM_DDE_ACK message.

Because unlocking data invalidates the pointer to the data, the client saves the
value of the **fRelease** member before unlocking the data object. After saving the
value, the client then examines it to determine whether the server application
requested the client to free the memory containing the data; the client acts
accordingly.

Upon receiving a negative WM_DDE_ACK message, the client can ask for the same item value again, specifying a different clipboard format. Typically, a client will first ask for the most complex format it can support, then step down if necessary through progressively simpler formats until it finds one the server can provide.

If the server supports the Formats item of the System topic, the client can determine once what clipboard formats the server supports, instead of determining them each time the client requests an item. For more information about the System topic, see Section 26.1.4.3, "The System Topic."

26.2.2.2 Submitting an Item to the Server

The client may send an item value to the server by using the WM_DDE_POKE message. The client renders the item to be sent and sends the WM_DDE_POKE message, as illustrated in the following example.

```
if (!(hPokeData = GlobalAlloc(GMEM_MOVEABLE | GMEM_DDESHARE,
        (LONG) sizeof(DDEPOKE) + lstrlen(szValue) + 2)))
    return;

if (!(lpPokeData = (DDEPOKE FAR*) GlobalLock(hPokeData))) {
    GlobalFree(hPokeData);
    return;
}

lpPokeData->fRelease = TRUE;
lpPokeData->cfFormat = CF_TEXT;
lstrcpy((LPSTR) lpPokeData->Value, (LPSTR) szValue);

/* Each line of CF_TEXT data is terminated by CR/LF. */

lstrcat((LPSTR) lpPokeData->Value, (LPSTR) "\r\n");
GlobalUnlock(hPokeData);
if ((atomItem = GlobalAddAtom((LPSTR) szItem)) != 0) {


        .
        .
        .

    if (!PostMessage(hwndServerDDE,
            WM_DDE_POKE,
            (WPARAM) hwndClientDDE,
            PackDDElParam(WM_DDE_POKE, (UINT) hPokeData,
                atomItem))) {
        GlobalDeleteAtom(atomItem);
        GlobalFree(hPokeData);
    }
}
```

```
        if (atomItem == 0) {


            .
            . /* error handling */
            .


        }
```

Note that sending data by using a WM_DDE_POKE message is essentially the same as sending it by using a WM_DDE_DATA message, except that WM_DDE_POKE is sent from the client to the server.

If the server is able to accept the data-item value in the format rendered by the client, the server processes the item value as appropriate and sends the client a positive WM_DDE_ACK message. If it is unable to process the item value, because of its format or for other reasons, the server sends the client a negative WM_DDE_ACK message.

```
UnpackDDElParam(WM_DDE_POKE, lParam, (PUINT) &hPokeData,
        (PUINT) &atomItem);
GlobalGetAtomName(atomItem, szItemName, ITEM_NAME_MAX_SIZE);
if (!(lpPokeData = (DDEPOKE FAR*) GlobalLock(hPokeData))
        || lpPokeData->cfFormat != CF_TEXT
        || !IsItemSupportedByServer(szItemName)) {
    PostMessage(hwndClientDDE,
        WM_DDE_ACK,
        (WPARAM) hwndServerDDE,
        PackDDElParam(WM_DDE_ACK, 0, atomItem)); /* negative ACK */
}

lstrcpy(szItemValue, lpPokeData->Value); /* copies value */
bRelease = lpPokeData->fRelease;
GlobalUnlock(hPokeData);
if (bRelease) {
    GlobalFree(hPokeData);
}

PostMessage(hwndClientDDE,
    WM_DDE_ACK,
    (WPARAM) hwndServerDDE,
    PackDDElParam(WM_DDE_ACK,
        0x8000, atomItem));    /* positive ACK */
```

In this example, the server calls the **GlobalGetAtomName** function to retrieve the name of the item the client sent. The server then determines whether it supports the item and whether the item is rendered in the correct format (that is, CF_TEXT). If the item is not supported and not rendered in the correct format, or if the server cannot lock the memory for the data, the server sends a negative acknowledgment back to the client application. Note that in this case, sending a negative acknowledgement is correct because WM_DDE_POKE messages are always assumed to have the **fAckReq** member set. The server should ignore the member.

If a server sends a negative acknowledgement in response to a WM_DDE_POKE message, the client is responsible for freeing the memory (but not the *lParam* parameter) referenced by the WM_DDE_POKE message associated with the negative acknowledgement.

26.2.3 Establishing a Permanent Data Link

A client application can use DDE to establish a link to an item in a server application. Once such a link is established, the server sends periodic updates of the linked item to the client, typically, whenever the value of the item changes. Thus, a permanent data stream is established between the two applications; this data stream remains in place until it is explicitly disconnected.

26.2.3.1 Initiating a Data Link

The client initiates a data link by posting a WM_DDE_ADVISE message, as shown in the following example.

```
if (!(hOptions = GlobalAlloc(GMEM_MOVEABLE | GMEM_DDESHARE,
        sizeof(DDEADVISE))))
    return;
if (!(lpOptions = (DDEADVISE FAR*) GlobalLock(hOptions))) {
    GlobalFree(hOptions);
    return;
}

lpOptions->cfFormat = CF_TEXT;
lpOptions->fAckReq = TRUE;
lpOptions->fDeferUpd = FALSE;
GlobalUnlock(hOptions);
if ((atomItem = GlobalAddAtom(szItemName)) != 0) {
    if (!(PostMessage(hwndServerDDE,
            WM_DDE_ADVISE,
            (WPARAM) hwndClientDDE,
            PackDDElParam(WM_DDE_ADVISE, (UINT) hOptions,
                atomItem)))) {
        GlobalDeleteAtom(atomItem);
        GlobalFree(hOptions);
        FreeDDElParam(WM_DDE_ADVISE, lParam);
    }
}

if (atomItem == 0) {
```

```
        .
        . /* error handling */
        .
}
```

In this example, the client application sets the **fDeferUpd** member of the WM_DDE_ADVISE message to FALSE. This directs the server application to send the data to the client whenever the data changes.

If the server has access to the item and can render it in the requested format, the server notes the new link (recalling the flags specified in the *hOptions* parameter) and sends the client a positive WM_DDE_ACK message. From then on, until the client issues a matching WM_DDE_UNADVISE message, the server sends the new data to the client every time the value of the item changes in the server application.

If the server is unable to service the WM_DDE_ADVISE request, it sends the client a negative WM_DDE_ACK message.

The WM_DDE_ADVISE message establishes the format of the data to be exchanged during the link. If the client attempts to establish another link with the same item but is using a different data format, the server can choose to either reject the second data format or attempt to support it. If a warm link has been established for any data item, the server can support only one data format at a time. This is because the WM_DDE_DATA message for a warm link has a NULL data handle, which otherwise contains the format information. Thus, a server must reject all warm links for an item already linked, and it must reject all links for an item that has any warm links.

Another interpretation may be that the server changes the format and the hot/warm state of a link when a second link is requested for the same data item.

In general, client applications should not attempt to establish more than one link at a time for a data item.

26.2.3.2 Initiating a Data Link with the Paste Link Command

Applications that support hot or warm data links typically support a registered clipboard format named Link. When associated with the application's Copy and Paste Link commands, this clipboard format enables the user to establish DDE conversations between applications simply by copying a data item in the server application and pasting it into the client application.

A server application supports the Link clipboard format by placing in the clipboard a string containing the application, topic, and item names when the user chooses the Copy command from the Edit menu. Following is the standard Link format:

application\0*topic*\0*item*\0\0

A single null character separates the names, and two null characters terminate the entire string.

Both the client and server applications must register the Link clipboard format, as shown:

```
cfLink = RegisterClipboardFormat("Link");
```

A client application supports the Link clipboard format by means of a Paste Link command on its Edit menu. When the user chooses this command, the client application parses the application, topic, and item names from the Link-format clipboard data. Using these names, the client application initiates a conversation for the application and topic, if such a conversation does not already exist. The client application then sends a WM_DDE_ADVISE message to the server application, specifying the item name contained in the Link-format clipboard data.

Following is an example of a client application's response when the user chooses the Paste Link command.

```
void DoPasteLink(hwndClientDDE)
HWND hwndClientDDE;
{
    HANDLE hData;
    LPSTR lpData;
    HWND hwndServerDDE;
    CHAR szApplication[APP_MAX_SIZE + 1];
    CHAR szTopic[TOPIC_MAX_SIZE + 1];
    CHAR szItem[ITEM_MAX_SIZE + 1];
    int nBufLen;

    if (OpenClipboard(hwndClientDDE)) {
        if (!(hData = GetClipboardData(cfLink)) ||
                !(lpData = GlobalLock(hData))) {
            CloseClipboard();
            return;
        }

        /* Parse the clipboard data. */

        if ((nBufLen = lstrlen(lpData)) >= APP_MAX_SIZE) {
            CloseClipboard();
            GlobalUnlock(hData);
            return;
        }
        lstrcpy(szApplication, lpData);
```

```
                    lpData += (nBufLen + 1); /* skips over null */
                    if ((nBufLen = lstrlen(lpData)) >= TOPIC_MAX_SIZE) {
                        CloseClipboard();
                        GlobalUnlock(hData);
                        return;
                    }
                    lstrcpy(szTopic, lpData);
                    lpData += (nBufLen + 1); /* skips over null */
                    if ((nBufLen = lstrlen(lpData)) >= ITEM_MAX_SIZE) {
                        CloseClipboard();
                        GlobalUnlock(hData);
                        return;
                    }
                    lstrcpy(szItem, lpData);
                    GlobalUnlock(hData);
                    CloseClipboard();

                    if (hwndServerDDE =
                            FindServerGivenAppTopic(szApplication, szTopic)) {

                        /* App/topic conversation is already started. */

                        if (DoesAdviseAlreadyExist(hwndServerDDE, szItem))
                            MessageBox(hwndMain,
                                "Advisory already established",
                                "Client", MB_ICONEXCLAMATION | MB_OK);
                        else
                            SendAdvise(hwndClientDDE, hwndServerDDE, szItem);
                    }
                    else {

                        /* Client must initiate a new conversation first. */

                        SendInitiate(szApplication, szTopic);
                        if (hwndServerDDE =
                                FindServerGivenAppTopic(szApplication,
                                    szTopic))
                            SendAdvise(hwndClientDDE, hwndServerDDE, szItem);
                    }
                }
            return;
        }
```

In this example, the client application opens the clipboard and determines whether it contains data in the Link format (that is, cfLink) it had previously registered. If not, or if it cannot lock the data in the clipboard, the client returns.

After the client application retrieves a pointer to the clipboard data, it parses the data to extract the application, topic, and item names.

The client application determines whether a conversation on the topic already exists between it and the server application. If a conversation does exist, the client application checks whether a link already exists for the data item. If such a link exists, the client displays a message box to the user; otherwise, it calls its own SendAdvise function to send a WM_DDE_ADVISE message to the server for the item.

If a conversation on the topic does not already exist between client and the server, the client first calls its own SendInitiate function to broadcast the WM_DDE_INITIATE message to request a conversation and, second, calls its own FindServerGivenAppTopic function to establish the conversation with the window that responds on behalf of the server application. Once the conversation has begun, the client application calls SendAdvise to request the link.

26.2.3.3 Notifying the Client that Data Has Changed

When the client establishes a link by using the WM_DDE_ADVISE message, with the **fDeferUpd** member not set (that is, equal to zero), the client has requested the server send the data item each time the item's value changes. In such cases, the server renders the new value of the data item in the previously specified format and sends the client a WM_DDE_DATA message, as shown in the following example.

```
/*
 * Allocate the size of a DDE data header, plus data (a string),
 * plus a <CR><LF><NULL>
 */

if (!(hData = GlobalAlloc(GMEM_MOVEABLE | GMEM_DDESHARE,
        sizeof(DDEDATA) + lstrlen(szItemValue) + 3)))
    return;
if (!(lpData = (DDEDATA FAR*) GlobalLock(hData))) {
    GlobalFree(hData);
    return;
}

lpData->fAckReq = bAckRequest;  /* as specified in original    */
                                /* WM_DDE_ADVISE message       */
lpData->cfFormat = CF_TEXT;
lstrcpy(lpData->Value, szItemValue); /* copies value to be sent */
lstrcat(lpData->Value, "\r\n"); /* CR/LF for CF_TEXT format    */
GlobalUnlock(hData);
if ((atomItem = GlobalAddAtom(szItemName)) != 0) {
    if (!PostMessage(hwndClientDDE,
            WM_DDE_DATA,
            (WPARAM) hwndServerDDE,
            PackDDElParam(WM_DDE_DATA, (UINT) hData, atomItem))) {
        GlobalFree(hData);
        GlobalDeleteAtom(atomItem);
```

```
                    FreeDDElParam(WM_DDE_DATA, lParam);
        }
    }

    if (atomItem == 0) {

        .
        . /* error handling */
        .

    }
```

In this example, the client processes the item value as appropriate. If the **fAckReq** flag for the item is set, the client sends the server a positive WM_DDE_ACK message.

When the client establishes the link, with the **fDeferUpd** member set (that is, equal to 1), the client has requested that only a notification, not the data itself, be sent each time the data changes. In such cases, when the item value changes, the server does not render the value but simply sends the client a WM_DDE_DATA message with a null data handle, as illustrated in the following example.

```
if (bDeferUpd) {        /* checking whether the flag was originally */
                        /* set in the WM_DDE_ADVISE message         */
    if ((atomItem = GlobalAddAtom(szItemName)) != 0) {
        if (!PostMessage(hwndClientDDE,
            WM_DDE_DATA,
            (WPARAM) hwndServerDDE,
            PackDDElParam(WM_DDE_DATA, 0,
                atomItem))) {                    /* NULL data */
            GlobalDeleteAtom(atomItem);
            FreeDDElParam(WM_DDE_DATA, lParam);
        }
    }
}

if (atomItem == 0) {

    .
    . /* error handling */
    .

}
```

As necessary, the client can request the latest value of the data item by issuing a normal WM_DDE_REQUEST message, or it can simply ignore the notice from the server that the data has changed. In either case, if **fAckReq** is equal to 1, the client is expected to send a positive WM_DDE_ACK message to the server.

26.2.3.4 Terminating a Data Link

If the client requests that a specific data link be terminated, the client sends the server a WM_DDE_UNADVISE message, as shown in the following example.

```
if ((atomItem = GlobalAddAtom(szItemName)) != 0) {
    if (!PostMessage(hwndServerDDE,
            WM_DDE_UNADVISE,
            (WPARAM) hwndClientDDE,
            PackDDElParam(WM_DDE_UNADVISE, 0, atomItem))) {
        GlobalDeleteAtom(atomItem);
        FreeDDElParam(WM_DDE_UNADVISE, lParam);
    }
}

if (atomItem == 0) {

    .
    . /* error handling */
    .

}
```

The server checks whether the client currently has a link to the specific item in this conversation. If a link exists, the server sends the client a positive WM_DDE_ACK message; the server is then no longer required to send updates about the item. If no link exists, the server sends the client a negative WM_DDE_ACK message.

The WM_DDE_UNADVISE message specifies a data format. A format of zero informs the server to stop all links for the specified item, even if several hot links are established and each uses a different format.

To terminate all links for a conversation, the client sends the server a WM_DDE_UNADVISE message with a null item atom. The server determines whether the conversation has at least one link currently established. If a link exists, the server sends the client a positive WM_DDE_ACK message; the server then no longer has to send any updates in the conversation. If no link exists, the server sends the client a negative WM_DDE_ACK message.

26.2.4 Carrying Out Commands in a Server Application

A Windows-based application can use the WM_DDE_EXECUTE message to cause a certain command or series of commands to be carried out in another application. To do this, the client sends the server a WM_DDE_EXECUTE message containing a handle of a command string, as shown in the following example.

```
if (!(hCommand = GlobalAlloc(GMEM_MOVEABLE | GMEM_DDESHARE,
        sizeof(szCommandString) + 1)))
    return;
if (!(lpCommand = GlobalLock(hCommand))) {
    GlobalFree(hCommand);
    return;
}

lstrcpy(lpCommand, szCommandString);
GlobalUnlock(hCommand);
if (!PostMessage(hwndServerDDE,
        WM_DDE_EXECUTE,
        (WPARAM) hwndClientDDE,
        PackDDElParam(WM_DDE_EXECUTE, 0, (UINT) hCommand))) {
    GlobalFree(hCommand);
    FreeDDElParam(WM_DDE_EXECUTE, lParam);
}
```

In this example, the server attempts to carry out the specified command string. If it succeeds, the server sends the client a positive WM_DDE_ACK message; otherwise, it sends a negative WM_DDE_ACK message. This WM_DDE_ACK message reuses the *hCommand* handle passed in the original WM_DDE_EXECUTE message.

If the client's command execution string requests that the server terminate, the server should respond by sending a positive WM_DDE_ACK message and then post a WM_DDE_TERMINATE message before terminating. All other commands sent with a WM_DDE_EXECUTE message should be executed synchronously; that is, the server should send a WM_DDE_ACK message only after successfully completing the command.

26.2.5 Terminating a Conversation

Either the client or the server can issue a WM_DDE_TERMINATE message to terminate a conversation at any time. Similarly, both the client and server applications should be prepared to receive this message at any time. An application must terminate all of its conversations before shutting down.

In the following example, the application terminating the conversation posts a WM_DDE_TERMINATE message.

```
PostMessage(hwndServerDDE, WM_DDE_TERMINATE,
    PackDDElParam(WM_DDE_TERMINATE, (UINT) hwndClientDDE, 0), 0);
```

This informs the other application that the sending application will send no further messages and the recipient can close its window. The recipient is expected in all cases to respond promptly by sending a WM_DDE_TERMINATE message. The recipient must not send a negative, busy, or positive WM_DDE_ACK message.

After an application has sent the WM_DDE_TERMINATE message to the partner in a DDE conversation, it must not respond to any messages from that partner, since the partner might already have destroyed the window to which the response would be sent.

If a DDE application receives a DDE message other than WM_DDE_TERMINATE after it has posted a WM_DDE_TERMINATE message, it should free all objects associated with the received messages except the data handles for WM_DDE_DATA or WM_DDE_POKE messages that do *not* have the **fRelease** member set.

When an application is about to terminate, it should end all active DDE conversations before completing processing of the WM_DESTROY message. However, if an application does not end its active DDE conversations, the system will properly terminate any DDE conversations associated with a window when the window is destroyed. The following example shows how a server application terminates all DDE conversations.

```
void TerminateConversations(hwndServerDDE)
HWND hwndServerDDE;
{
    HWND hwndClientDDE;

    /* Terminate each active conversation. */

    while (hwndClientDDE = GetNextLink(hwndClientDDE)) {
        SendTerminate(hwndServerDDE, hwndClientDDE);
    }
    return;
}


BOOL AtLeastOneLinkActive(VOID)
{
    return TRUE;
}


HWND GetNextLink(hwndDummy)
    HWND hwndDummy;
{
    return (HWND) 1;
}


VOID SendTerminate(HWND hwndServerDDE, HWND hwndClientDDE)
{
    return;
}
```

26.3 Functions and Messages

Following are the functions and messages used with DDE.

Functions

DdeSetQualityOfService
FreeDDElParam
PackDDElParam
ReuseDDElParam
UnpackDDElParam

Messages

WM_DDE_ACK
WM_DDE_ADVISE
WM_DDE_DATA
WM_DDE_EXECUTE
WM_DDE_INITIATE
WM_DDE_POKE
WM_DDE_REQUEST
WM_DDE_TERMINATE
WM_DDE_UNADVISE

CHAPTER 27

Multiple Document Interface

27.1 About the Multiple Document Interface

The multiple document interface (MDI) is a specification that defines the standard user interface for applications written for Microsoft ® Windows ™. An MDI application enables the user to work with more than one document at the same time. Each document is displayed in a separate child window within the client area of the application's main window. Typical MDI applications include word processing applications that allow the user to work with multiple text documents, and spreadsheet applications that allow the user to work with multiple charts and spreadsheets.

Windows provides extensive support for MDI applications. This chapter describes the structure of an MDI application and how to take advantage of the built-in MDI support found in the Win32 application program interface (API).

27.1.1 Frame, Client, and Child Windows

An MDI application has three kinds of windows: a frame window, a client window, as well as a number of child windows. The *frame window* is like the main window of the application: it has a sizing border, a title bar, a System menu, a Minimize button, and a Maximize button. The application must register a window class for the frame window and provide a window procedure to support it.

An MDI application does not display output in the client area of the frame window. Instead, it displays the MDI client window. An *MDI client window* is a special type of child window belonging to the preregistered window class MDICLIENT. The client window is a child of the frame window; it serves as the background for child windows. It also provides support for creating and manipulating child windows. For example, an MDI application can create, activate, or maximize child windows by sending messages to the MDI client window.

When the user opens or creates a document, the client window creates a child window for the document. The client window is the parent window of all MDI child windows in a given application. Each child window has a sizing border, a title bar, a System menu (also known as the Control menu), a Minimize button, and a Maximize button. Because a child window is clipped, it is confined to the client window and cannot appear outside it.

An MDI application can support more than one kind of document. For example, a typical spreadsheet application enables the user to work with both charts and spreadsheets. For each type of document that it supports, an MDI application must register a child window class and provide a window procedure to support the windows belonging to that class. For more information about window classes, see

Chapter 3, "Window Classes." For more information about window procedures, see Chapter 4, "Window Procedures."

Following is a typical MDI application. It is named Multipad.

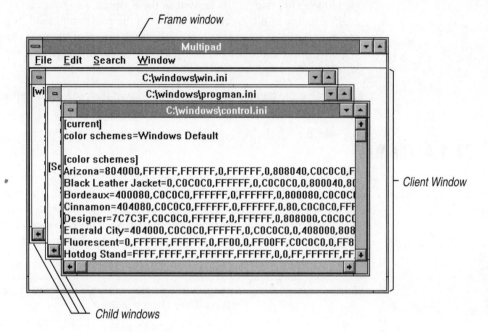

27.1.2 **Child Window Creation**

To create a child window, an MDI application either calls the **CreateMDIWindow** function or sends the WM_MDICREATE message to the MDI client window. A thread in an MDI application can use **CreateMDIWindow** to create a child window in a different thread. The WM_MDICREATE message is used only in the context of the same thread.

To destroy a child window, an MDI application sends a WM_MDIDESTROY message to the MDI client window.

27.1.3 **Child Window Activation**

Any number of child windows can appear in the client window at any one time, but only one can be active. The active child window is positioned in front of all other child windows, and its border is highlighted.

The user can activate an inactive child window by clicking it. An MDI application activates a child window by sending a WM_MDIACTIVATE message to the MDI client window. As the client window processes this message, it sends a

WM_MDIACTIVATE message to the window procedure of the child window to be activated and to the window procedure of the child window being deactivated.

Windows keeps track of each child window's position in the stack of overlapping windows. This stacking is known as the Z order. The user can activate the next child window in the Z order by choosing the Next command from the System menu in the active window. An application activates the next (or previous) child window in the Z order by sending a WM_MDINEXT message to the client window.

To retrieve the handle of the active child window, the MDI application sends a WM_MDIGETACTIVE message to the client window.

27.1.4 Menus

The frame window of an MDI application should include a menu bar with a Window menu item and its corresponding pop-up menu. The Window pop-up menu should include command items that arrange the child windows within the client window or that close all child windows. The Window menu of a typical MDI application might include the items in the following table.

Menu item	Purpose
Tile	Arranges child windows in a tile format so that each appears in its entirety in the client window.
Cascade	Arranges child windows in a cascade format. The child windows overlap one another, but the title bar of each is visible.
Arrange Icons	Arranges the icons of minimized child windows along the bottom of the client window.
Close All	Closes all child windows.

Whenever a child window is created, Windows automatically appends a new menu item to the Window menu. The text of the menu item is the same as the text on the menu bar of the new child window. By choosing the menu item, the user can activate the corresponding child window. When a child window is destroyed, Windows automatically removes the corresponding menu item from the Window menu.

Windows can add up to ten menu items to the Window menu. When the tenth child window is created, Windows adds the More Windows item to the Window menu. Choosing this item causes the Select Window dialog box to appear. The dialog box contains a list box with the titles of all MDI child windows currently available. The user can activate a child window by choosing its title from the list box.

If your MDI application supports several types of child windows, tailor the menu bar to reflect the operations associated with the active window. To do this, provide separate menu resources for each type of child window the application supports. When a new type of child window is activated, the application should send a WM_MDISETMENU message to the client window, passing to it the handle of the corresponding menu.

When no child window exists, the menu bar should contain only items used to create or open a document.

When the user is navigating through an MDI application's menus by using cursor keys, the keys behave differently than when the user is navigating through a typical application's menus. In an MDI application, control passes from the application's System menu to the System menu of the active child window, and then to the first item on the menu bar.

27.1.5 Accelerators

To receive and process accelerator keys for its child windows, an MDI application must include the **TranslateMDISysAccel** function in its message loop. The loop must call **TranslateMDISysAccel** before calling the **TranslateAccelerator** or **DispatchMessage** function.

Accelerator keys on the System menu for an MDI child window are different from those for a non–MDI child window. In an MDI child window, the ALT+ – (minus) key combination opens the System menu, the CTRL+F4 key combination closes the active child window, and the CTRL+F6 key combination activates the next child window.

27.1.6 Child Window Size and Arrangement

An MDI application controls the size and position of its child windows by sending messages to the MDI client window. To maximize the active child window, the application sends the WM_MDIMAXIMIZE message to the client window. When a child window is maximized, its client area completely fills the MDI client window. In addition, Windows automatically hides the child window's title bar, and adds the child window's System menu icon and restore icon to the MDI application's menu bar. The application can restore the client window to its original (pre-maximized) size and position by sending the client window a WM_MDIRESTORE message.

An MDI application can arrange its child windows in either a cascade or tile format. When the child windows are cascaded, the windows appear in a stack. The window on the bottom of the stack occupies the upper-left corner of the screen, and the remaining windows are offset vertically and horizontally so that the left border and title bar of each child window is visible. To arrange child windows in the cascade format, an MDI application sends the WM_MDICASCADE message. Typically, the application sends this message when the user chooses the Cascade command from the Window menu.

When the child windows are tiled, Windows displays each child window in its entirety—overlapping none of the windows. All of the windows are sized, as necessary, to fit within the client window. To arrange child windows in the tile format, an MDI application sends a WM_MDITILE message to the client window. Typically, the application sends this message when the user chooses the Tile command from the Window menu.

An MDI application should provide a different icon for each type of child window it supports. The application specifies an icon when registering the child window class. Windows automatically displays a child window's icon in the lower portion of the client window when the child window is minimized. An MDI application directs Windows to arrange child window icons by sending a WM_MDIICONARRANGE message to the client window. Typically, the application sends this message when the user chooses the Arrange Icons command from the Window menu.

27.1.7 Icon Title Windows

Because MDI child windows may be minimized, an MDI application must avoid manipulating icon title windows as if they were normal MDI child windows. Icon title windows appear when the application enumerates child windows of the MDI client window. Icon title windows differ from other child windows, however, in that they are owned by an MDI child window.

To determine whether a child window is an icon title window, use the **GetWindow** function with the GW_OWNER index. Non-title windows return NULL. Note that this test is insufficient for top-level windows, because menus and dialog boxes are owned windows.

27.1.8 Child Window Data

Because the number of child windows varies depending on how many documents the user opens, an MDI application must be able to associate data (for example, the name of the current file) with each child window. There are two ways to do this:

- Store child window data in the window structure.
- Use window properties.

27.1.8.1 Data in the Window Structure

When an MDI application registers a window class, it may reserve extra space in the window structure for application data specific to this particular class of windows. To store and retrieve data in this extra space, the application uses the **GetWindowWord**, **SetWindowWord**, **GetWindowLong**, and **SetWindowLong** functions.

To maintain a large amount of data for a child window, an application can allocate memory for a data structure and then store the handle of the memory containing the structure in the extra space associated with the child window.

27.1.8.2 Window Properties

An MDI application can also store per-document data by using window properties. (Per-document data is data specific to the type of document contained in a particular child window.) Properties are different from extra space in the window structure in that you need not allocate extra space when registering the window class. A window can have any number of properties. Also, where offsets are used to access the extra space in window structures, properties are referred to by string names. For more information about window properties, see Chapter 24, "Window Properties."

27.2 Using the Multiple Document Interface

This section explains how to perform the following tasks:

- Register frame and child window classes.
- Create frame and client windows.
- Write the main message loop.
- Write the frame window procedure.
- Write the child window procedure.
- Create a child window.

To illustrate these tasks, this section includes sample code from Multipad, a typical MDI application.

27.2.1 Registering Child and Frame Window Classes

A typical MDI application must register two window classes: one for its frame window and one for its child windows. If an application supports more than one type of document (for example, a spreadsheet and a chart), it must register a window class for each type.

The class structure for the frame window is similar to the class structure for the main window in non–MDI applications. The class structure for the MDI child windows differs slightly from the structure for child windows in non–MDI applications as follows:

- The class structure should have an icon, because the user can minimize an MDI child window as if it were a normal application window.

- The menu name should be NULL, because an MDI child window cannot have its own menu.
- The class structure should reserve extra space in the window structure. With this space, the application can associate data, such as a filename, with a particular child window.

The following code shows how Multipad registers its frame and child window classes.

```
BOOL APIENTRY InitializeApplication()
{
    WNDCLASS wc;

    /* Register the frame window class. */

    wc.style          = 0;
    wc.lpfnWndProc    = (WNDPROC) MPFrameWndProc;
    wc.cbClsExtra     = 0;
    wc.cbWndExtra     = 0;
    wc.hInstance      = hInst;
    wc.hIcon          = LoadIcon(hInst, IDMULTIPAD);
    wc.hCursor        = LoadCursor((HANDLE) NULL, IDC_ARROW);
    wc.hbrBackground  = (HBRUSH) (COLOR_APPWORKSPACE + 1);
    wc.lpszMenuName   = IDMULTIPAD;
    wc.lpszClassName  = szFrame;

    if (!RegisterClass (&wc) )
        return FALSE;

    /* Register the MDI child window class. */

    wc.lpfnWndProc    = (WNDPROC) MPMDIChildWndProc;
    wc.hIcon          = LoadIcon(hInst, IDNOTE);
    wc.lpszMenuName   = (LPCTSTR) NULL;
    wc.cbWndExtra     = CBWNDEXTRA;
    wc.lpszClassName  = szChild;

    if (!RegisterClass(&wc))
        return FALSE;

    return TRUE;
}
```

27.2.2 Creating Frame and Child Windows

After registering its window classes, an MDI application can create its windows. First, it creates its frame window by using the **CreateWindow** or **CreateWindowEx** function. After creating its frame window, the application creates its client window, again by using **CreateWindow** or **CreateWindowEx**. The application should specify MDICLIENT as the client window's class name; MDICLIENT is a preregistered window class defined by Windows. The *lpvParam* parameter of **CreateWindow** or **CreateWindowEx** should point to a **CLIENTCREATESTRUCT** structure. This structure contains the members described in the following table.

Member	Description
hWindowMenu	Identifies the Window menu used for controlling MDI child windows. As child windows are created, the application adds their titles to the Window menu as menu items. The user can then activate a child window by choosing its title from the Window menu.
idFirstChild	Specifies the identifier of the first MDI child window. The first MDI child window created is assigned this identifier. Additional windows are created with incremented window identifiers. When a child window is destroyed, Windows immediately reassigns the window identifiers to keep their range contiguous.

When a child window's title is added to the Window menu, Windows assigns an identifier to the child window. When the user chooses a child window's title, the frame window receives a WM_COMMAND message with the identifier in the *wParam* parameter. You should specify a value for the **idFirstChild** member that does not conflict with menu-item identifiers in the frame window's menu.

Multipad's frame window procedure creates the MDI client window while processing the WM_CREATE message. The following example shows how the client window is created.

```
. /* Process other messages here. */
.
case WM_CREATE:
    {
    CLIENTCREATESTRUCT ccs;

    /*
     * Retrieve the handle of the Window menu and assign the
     * first child window identifier.
     */

    ccs.hWindowMenu = GetSubMenu(GetMenu(hwnd), WINDOWMENU);
    ccs.idFirstChild = IDM_WINDOWCHILD;

    /* Create the MDI client window. */

    hwndMDIClient = CreateWindow( "MDICLIENT", (LPCTSTR) NULL,
        WS_CHILD | WS_CLIPCHILDREN | WS_VSCROLL | WS_HSCROLL,
```

```
                    0, 0, 0, 0, hwnd, (HMENU) 0xCAC, hInst, (LPSTR) &ccs);

        ShowWindow(hwndMDIClient, SW_SHOW);

        }
        break;
    }
    .
    . /* Process other messages here. */
    .
```

Titles of child windows are added to the bottom of the Window menu. If the application adds strings to the Window menu by using the **AppendMenu** function, these strings can be overwritten by the titles of the child windows when the Window menu is repainted. (The Window menu is repainted whenever a child window is created or destroyed.) An MDI application that adds strings to its Window menu should use the **InsertMenu** function and verify that the titles of child windows have not overwritten these new strings.

Use the WS_CLIPCHILDREN style to create the MDI client window to prevent the window from painting over its child windows.

27.2.3 Writing the Main Message Loop

The main message loop of an MDI application is similar to that of a non–MDI application handling accelerator keys. The difference is that the MDI message loop calls the **TranslateMDISysAccel** function before checking for application-defined accelerator keys or before dispatching the message.

The following example shows the message loop of a typical MDI application.

```
while (GetMessage(&msg, (HWND) NULL, 0, 0)) {
    if (!TranslateMDISysAccel(hwndMDIClient, &msg) &&
            !TranslateAccelerator(hwndFrame, hAccel, &msg)){
        TranslateMessage(&msg);
        DispatchMessage(&msg);
    }
}
```

The **TranslateMDISysAccel** function translates WM_KEYDOWN messages into WM_SYSCOMMAND messages and sends them to the active MDI child window. If the message is not an MDI accelerator message, the function returns FALSE, in which case the application uses the **TranslateAccelerator** function to determine whether any of the application-defined accelerator keys were pressed. If not, the loop dispatches the message to the appropriate window procedure.

27.2.4 Writing the Frame Window Procedure

The window procedure for an MDI frame window is similar to that of a non–MDI application's main window. The difference is that a frame window procedure passes all messages it does not handle to the **DefFrameProc** function rather than to the **DefWindowProc** function. In addition, the frame window procedure must also pass some messages that it does handle, including those listed in the following table.

Message	Response
WM_COMMAND	Activates the MDI child window that the user chooses. This message is sent when the user chooses an MDI child window from the Window menu of the MDI frame window. The window identifier accompanying this message identifies the MDI child window to be activated.
WM_MENUCHAR	Opens the System menu of the active MDI child window when the user presses the ALT+ – (minus) key combination.
WM_SETFOCUS	Passes the keyboard focus to the MDI client window, which in turn passes it to the active MDI child window.
WM_SIZE	Resizes the MDI client window to fit in the new frame window's client area. If the frame window procedure sizes the MDI client window to a different size, it should not pass the message to the **DefWindowProc** function.

The frame window procedure in Multipad is called MPFrameWndProc. The handling of other messages by MPFrameWndProc is similar to that of non–MDI applications. WM_COMMAND messages in Multipad are handled by the locally defined CommandHandler function. For command messages Multipad does not handle, CommandHandler calls the **DefFrameProc** function. If Multipad doesn't use **DefFrameProc** by default, the user can't activate a child window from the Window menu, because the WM_COMMAND message sent by choosing the window's menu item (command) would be lost.

27.2.5 Writing the Child Window Procedure

Like the frame window procedure, an MDI child window procedure uses a special function for processing messages by default. All messages that the child window procedure does not handle must be passed to the **DefMDIChildProc** function rather than to the **DefWindowProc** function. In addition, some window-management messages must be passed to **DefMDIChildProc**, even if the application handles the message, in order for MDI to function correctly. Following are the messages the application must pass to **DefMDIChildProc**.

Message	Response
WM_CHILDACTIVATE	Performs activation processing when MDI child windows are sized, moved, or displayed. This message must be passed.
WM_GETMINMAXINFO	Calculates the size of a maximized MDI child window, based on the current size of the MDI client window.
WM_MENUCHAR	Passes the message to the MDI frame window.
WM_MOVE	Recalculates MDI client scroll bars if they are present.
WM_SETFOCUS	Activates the child window if it is not the active MDI child window.
WM_SIZE	Performs operations necessary for changing the size of a window, especially for maximizing or restoring an MDI child window. Failing to pass this message to the **DefMDIChildProc** function produces highly undesirable results.
WM_SYSCOMMAND	Handles System menu commands: SC_NEXTWINDOW, SC_PREVWINDOW, SC_MOVE, SC_SIZE, and SC_MAXIMIZE.

27.2.6 Creating a Child Window

To create an MDI child window, an application can either call the **CreateMDIWindow** function or send a WM_MDICREATE message to the MDI client window. (The application must not use the **CreateWindow** function to create MDI child windows.) A single-threaded MDI application can use either method to create a child window. A thread in a multithreaded MDI application must use the **CreateMDIWindow** function to create a child window in a different thread.

The *lParam* parameter of a WM_MDICREATE message is a far pointer to an **MDICREATESTRUCT** structure. The structure includes four dimension members: **x** and **y**, which indicate the horizontal and vertical positions of the window, and **cx** and **cy**, which indicate the horizontal and vertical extents of the window. Any of these members may be assigned explicitly by the application, or they may be set to CW_USEDEFAULT, in which case Windows selects a position, size, or both, according to a cascading algorithm. In any case, all four members must be initialized. Multipad uses CW_USEDEFAULT for all dimensions.

The last member of the **MDICREATESTRUCT** structure is the **style** member, which may contain style bits for the window. To create an MDI child window that can have any combination of window styles, specify the MDIS_ALLCHILDSTYLES window style. When this style is not specified, an MDI child window has the WS_MINIMIZE, WS_MAXIMIZE, WS_HSCROLL, and WS_VSCROLL styles as default settings.

Multipad creates its MDI child windows by using its locally defined AddFile function (located in the source file MPFILE.C). The AddFile function sets the title of the child window by assigning the **szTitle** member of the window's **MDICREATESTRUCT** structure to either the name of the file being edited or to "Untitled." The **szClass** member is set to the name of the MDI child window class registered in Multipad's InitializeApplication function. The **hOwner** member is set to the application's instance handle.

The following code sample shows the AddFile function in Multipad.

```
HWND APIENTRY AddFile(pName)
CHAR * pName;
{
    HWND hwnd;
    CHAR sz[160];
    MDICREATESTRUCT mcs;

    if (!pName) {

        /*
         * If the pName parameter is NULL, load the "Untitled"
         * string from the STRINGTABLE resource and set the szTitle
         * member of MDICREATESTRUCT.
         */

        LoadString(hInst, IDS_UNTITLED, sz, sizeof(sz));
        mcs.szTitle = (LPCTSTR) sz;
    }
    else

        /*
         * Title the window with the full path and filename,
         * obtained by calling the OpenFile function with the
         * OF_PARSE flag, which is called before AddFile().
         */

        mcs.szTitle = of.szPathName;

    mcs.szClass = szChild;
    mcs.hOwner  = hInst;

    /* Use the default size for the child window. */

    mcs.x = mcs.cx = CW_USEDEFAULT;
    mcs.y = mcs.cy = CW_USEDEFAULT;

    /*
     * Give the child window the default style. The styleDefault
     * variable is defined in MULTIPAD.C.
```

```
    */

    mcs.style = styleDefault;

    /* Tell the MDI client window to create the child window. */

    hwnd = (HWND) SendMessage (hwndMDIClient, WM_MDICREATE, 0,
        (LONG) (LPMDICREATESTRUCT) &mcs);

    /*
     * If the file is found, read its contents into the child
     * window's client area.
     */

    if (pName) {
        if (!LoadFile(hwnd, pName)) {

            /* Cannot load the file; close the window. */

            SendMessage(hwndMDIClient, WM_MDIDESTROY,
                (DWORD) hwnd, 0L);
        }
    }
    return hwnd;
}
```

The pointer passed in the *lParam* parameter of the WM_MDICREATE message is passed to the **CreateWindow** function and appears as the first member in the **CREATESTRUCT** structure, passed in the WM_CREATE message. In Multipad, the child window initializes itself during WM_CREATE message processing by initializing document variables in its extra data and by creating the edit control's child window.

27.3 Functions and Messages

The following functions and messages are used in MDI applications.

Functions

CreateMDIWindow
DefFrameProc
DefMDIChildProc
TranslateMDISysAccel

Messages

WM_MDIACTIVATE
WM_MDICASCADE
WM_MDICREATE
WM_MDIDESTROY
WM_MDIGETACTIVE
WM_MDIICONARRANGE
WM_MDIMAXIMIZE
WM_MDINEXT
WM_MDIREFRESHMENU
WM_MDIRESTORE
WM_MDISETMENU
WM_MDITILE

PART 2

Graphics Device Interface

C H A P T E R 2 8

Device Contexts

28.1 About Device Contexts

One of the chief features of the Microsoft ® Win32 ™ application programming interface (API) is device independence. Applications written for Microsoft ® Windows ™ can draw and print output on a variety of devices. The software that supports this device independence is contained in two dynamic-link libraries. The first library is referred to as the graphics device interface (GDI); the second library is referred to as a device driver. The name of the second depends on the device where the application draws output. For example, if the application draws output in the client area of its window on a VGA display, this library is VGA.DLL; if the application prints output on an Epson ® FX-80 printer, this library is EPSON9.DLL.

An application must inform GDI to load a particular device driver; and, once the driver is loaded, prepare the device for drawing operations (such as selecting a line color and width, a brush pattern and color, a font typeface, a clipping region, and so on). These tasks are accomplished by creating and maintaining a device context. A *device context* is a structure that defines a set of graphic objects and their associated attributes, and the graphic modes that affect output. The *graphic objects* include a pen for line drawing, a brush for painting and filling, a bitmap for copying or scrolling parts of the screen, a palette for defining the set of available colors, a region for clipping and other operations, and a path for painting and drawing operations. Unlike most of the Win32 structures, an application never has direct access to the device context; instead, it operates on the structure indirectly by calling various functions.

28.1.1 Graphic Objects

The pen, brush, bitmap, palette, region, and path associated with a device context are referred to as the device context's graphic objects. Following are the attributes associated with each of these objects.

Graphic object	Associated attributes
Bitmap	Size, in bytes; dimensions, in pixels; color-format; compression scheme; and so on
Brush	Style, color, pattern, and origin
Palette	Colors and size (or number of colors)
Font	Typeface name, width, height, weight, character set, and so on
Path	Shape
Pen	Style, width, and color
Region	Location and dimensions

When an application creates a device context, Windows automatically stores a set of default objects in it. (There is, however, no default bitmap or path.) An application can examine the attributes of the default objects by calling the **GetCurrentObject** and **GetObject** functions. The application can change these defaults by creating a new object and selecting it into the device context. An object is selected into a device context by calling the **SelectObject** function. For more information about operations with graphic objects, see Section 28.1.4.1, "Operations on Graphic Objects."

28.1.2 Graphic Modes

Windows supports five graphic modes that allow an application to specify how colors are mixed, where output appears, how the output is scaled, and so on. These modes, stored in a device context, are described in the following table.

Mode	Description
Background mode	Defines how background colors are mixed with existing window or screen colors for bitmap and text operations.
Drawing mode	Defines how foreground colors are mixed with existing window or screen colors for pen, brush, bitmap, and text operations.
Mapping mode	Defines how graphics output is mapped from logical (or world) space onto the window, screen, or printer paper.
Polygon-fill mode	Defines how the brush pattern is used to fill the interior of complex regions.
Stretching mode	Defines how bitmap colors are mixed with existing window or screen colors when the bitmap is compressed (or scaled down).

As it does with graphic objects, Windows initializes a device context with default graphic modes. An application can retrieve and examine these default modes by calling the following functions.

Graphic mode	Function
Background mode	**GetBkMode**
Drawing mode	**GetROP2**
Mapping mode	**GetMapMode**
Polygon-fill mode	**GetPolyFillMode**
Stretching mode	**GetStretchBltMode**

An application can change the default modes by calling one of the following functions.

Graphic mode	Function
Background mode	**SetBkMode**
Drawing mode	**SetROP2**
Mapping mode	**SetMapMode**
Polygon-fill mode	**SetPolyFillMode**
Stretching mode	**SetStretchBltMode**

28.1.3 Device Context Types

Windows provides four types of device contexts: display, printer, memory (or compatible), and information. Each type serves a specific purpose, as described in the following table.

Device context	Purpose
Display	Supports drawing operations on a video display.
Printer	Supports drawing operations on a printer or plotter.
Memory	Supports drawing operations on a bitmap.
Information	Supports the retrieval of device data.

28.1.3.1 Display Device Contexts

Windows provides three types of device contexts for video displays: class, common and private. Class and private device contexts are used in applications that perform numerous drawing operations such as CAD applications, desktop-publishing applications, drawing and painting applications, and so on. Common device contexts are used in applications that perform infrequent drawing operations.

An application obtains a display device context by calling either the **BeginPaint** or **GetDC** function and identifying the window in which the corresponding output will appear. (The type of device context Windows returns is dependent on how the application registered its window class.) Typically, an application should obtain a display device context only when it must draw in the client area. When the application is finished drawing, it must release the device context by calling the **EndPaint** or **ReleaseDC** functions.

Class Device Contexts

Class device contexts are supported strictly for compatibility with previous versions of Windows. When writing a Win32 application, avoid using the class device context. Use a private device context instead.

Common Device Contexts

Common device contexts are display device contexts maintained in a special cache by the window management component of the Win32 API. An application obtains a handle identifying one of the available common device contexts by calling the **GetDC**, **GetDCEx**, or **BeginPaint** function. Before returning this device context handle, Windows initializes a common device context with default objects, attributes, and modes. Any drawing operations performed by the application use these defaults unless one of the GDI functions is called to select a new object, change the attributes of an existing object, or select a new mode.

Because only a limited number of common device contexts exist in the window manager's heap, an application should release these device contexts after it has finished drawing. An application releases a common device context by calling the **ReleaseDC** or **EndPaint** function. When the application releases a common device context, any changes to the default data are lost.

Private Device Contexts

Private device contexts are display device contexts that, unlike common device contexts, retain any changes to the default data—even after an application calls the **ReleaseDC** or **EndPaint** function. Private device contexts are not part of the window manager's cache and therefore need not be released after use. The window manager automatically removes a private device context after the last window of that class has been destroyed.

An application creates a private device context by first specifying the CS_OWNDC window-class style when it initializes the **style** member of the **WNDCLASS** structure and calls the **RegisterClass** function. (For more information about window classes, see Chapter 3, "Window Classes.") After creating a window with the CS_OWNDC style, an application can call the **GetDC**, **GetDCEx**, or **BeginPaint** function once to obtain a handle identifying a private device context. The application can continue using this handle (and the associated device context) until it deletes the window created with this class. Any changes to graphic objects and their attributes, or graphic modes are retained by Windows until the window is deleted.

28.1.3.2 Printer Device Contexts

Windows provides a single type of printer device context that can be used when printing on a dot-matrix printer, ink-jet printer, laser printer, or plotter. An application creates a printer device context by calling the **CreateDC** function and supplying the appropriate arguments (the name of the printer driver, the name of the printer, the file or device name for the physical output medium, and other initialization data). When an application has finished printing, it deletes the printer device context by calling the **DeleteDC** function. An application must delete (rather than release) a printer device context, because the **ReleaseDC** function fails when an application attempts to use it to release a printer device context.

28.1.3.3 Memory Device Contexts

Windows supports a memory device context that stores bitmapped images for a particular device. An application creates a memory device context by calling the **CreateCompatibleDC** function and supplying a handle that identifies a device context for a particular device. When Windows processes this call, it creates a bitmap having a color format compatible with the original device. Because the bitmap is compatible with the given device, a memory device context is also sometimes referred to as a *compatible* device context.

The original bitmap in a memory device context is simply a placeholder. Its dimensions are one pixel by one pixel. Before an application can begin drawing, it must select a bitmap with the appropriate width and height into the device context by calling the **SelectObject** function. Once the new bitmap is selected into the memory device context, an application can begin using the device context to store images. For more information about bitmaps and bitmap operations, see Chapter 29, "Bitmaps."

28.1.3.4 Information Device Contexts

Windows supports an information device context used to retrieve default device data. For example, an application can call the **CreateIC** function to create an information device context for a particular model of printer and then call the **GetCurrentObject** and **GetObject** functions to retrieve the default pen or brush attributes. Because Windows can retrieve device information without creating the structures normally associated with the other types of device contexts, an information device context involves far less overhead and is created significantly faster than any of the other types. After an application finishes retrieving data by using an information device context, it must call the **DeleteDC** function.

28.1.4 Device Context Operations

An application can perform the following operations on a device context:

- Enumerate existing graphic objects.
- Select new graphic objects.
- Delete existing graphic objects.
- Save the current graphic objects, their attributes, and the graphic modes.
- Restore previously saved graphic objects, their attributes, and the graphic modes.

In addition, an application can use a device context to determine how graphics output is translated, cancel lengthy drawing operations (begun by a thread in a multithreaded application), or reset a printer to a particular state.

28.1.4.1 Operations on Graphic Objects

Once an application creates a display or printer device context, it can begin drawing on the associated device or, in the case of the memory device context, it can begin drawing on the bitmap stored in memory. However, before drawing begins and sometimes while drawing is in progress, it is often necessary to replace the default objects with new objects.

An application can examine a default object's attributes by calling the **GetCurrentObject** and **GetObject** functions. The **GetCurrentObject** function returns a handle identifying the current pen, brush, palette, bitmap, or font, and the **GetObject** function initializes a structure containing that object's attributes.

Some printers provide resident pens, brushes, and fonts that can be used to improve drawing speed in an application. Two functions can be used to enumerate these objects: **EnumObjects** and **EnumFonts**. If the application must enumerate resident pens or brushes, it can call the **EnumObjects** function to examine the corresponding attributes. If the application must enumerate resident fonts, it can call the **EnumFonts** function (which can also enumerate GDI fonts).

Once an application determines that a default object needs replacing, it creates a new object by calling one of the following creation functions.

Graphic object	Function
Bitmap	**CreateBitmap**, **CreateBitmapIndirect**, **CreateCompatibleBitmap**, **CreateDiscardableBitmap**, **CreateDIBitmap**
Brush	**CreateBrushIndirect**, **CreateDIBPatternBrush**, **CreateDIBPatternBrushPt**, **CreateHatchBrush**, **CreatePatternBrush**, **CreateSolidBrush**
Color Palette	**CreatePalette**
Font	**CreateFont**, **CreateFontIndirect**
Pen	**CreatePen**, **CreatePenIndirect**, **ExtCreatePen**
Region	**CreateEllipticRgn**, **CreateEllipticRgnIndirect**, **CreatePolygonRgn**, **CreatePolyPolygonRgn**, **CreateRectRgn**, **CreateRectRgnIndirect**, **CreateRoundRectRgn**

Each of the functions returns a handle identifying a new object. After an application retrieves a handle, it must call the **SelectObject** function to replace the default object. However, the application should save the handle identifying the default object and use this handle to replace the new object when it is no longer needed. When the application finishes drawing with the new object, it must restore the default object by calling the **SelectObject** function and delete the new object by calling the **DeleteObject** function. Not deleting objects causes serious performance problems.

28.1.4.2 Cancellation of Drawing Operations

When complex drawing applications perform lengthy graphic operations, they consume valuable system resources. By taking advantage of Win32 multitasking features, an application can use threads and the **CancelDC** function to manage these operations. For example, if the graphic operation performed by thread A is consuming needed resources, thread B can call the **CancelDC** function to halt that operation.

28.1.4.3 Retrieving Device Data

Windows supports two functions, **GetDeviceCaps** and **DeviceCapabilitiesEx**, that applications can use to retrieve device data using a device context. **GetDeviceCaps** retrieves general device data for the following devices:

- Raster displays
- Dot-matrix printers
- Ink-jet printers
- Laser printers
- Vector plotters
- Raster cameras

The data includes the supported capabilities of the device, including device resolution (for video displays), color format (for video displays and color printers), number of graphic objects, raster capabilities, curve drawing, line drawing, polygon drawing, and text drawing. An application retrieves this data by supplying a handle identifying the appropriate device context as well as an index specifying the type of data the function retrieves.

The **DeviceCapabilitiesEx** function retrieves data specific to printers, including the number of available paper bins, the duplex capabilities of the printer, the resolutions supported by the printer, the maximum and minimum supported paper size, and so on. An application retrieves this data by supplying a handle identifying the appropriate printer device context as well as an index specifying the type of data that the function should retrieve.

28.1.4.4 Saving, Restoring, and Resetting a Device Context

Windows supports three functions that an application can use to save, restore, and reset a device context: **SaveDC**, **RestoreDC**, and **ResetDC**. The **SaveDC** function records on a special GDI stack the current device context's graphic objects and their attributes, and graphic modes. A drawing application can call this function before a user begins drawing and save the application's original state —providing a "clean slate" for the user. To return to this original state, the application calls the **RestoreDC** function.

The **ResetDC** function is provided to reset printer device context data. An application calls this function to reset the paper orientation, paper size, output scaling factor, number of copies to be printed, paper source (or bin), duplex mode, and so on. Typically, an application calls this function after a user has changed one of the printer options and Windows has issued a WM_DEVMODECHANGE message.

28.2 Using the Device Context Functions

This section contains examples that demonstrate how an application can perform the following tasks:

- Obtain a display device context.
- Create a printer device context.
- Retrieve the capabilities of a printer.
- Retrieve graphic-object attributes.
- Select a new graphic object.

28.2.1 Obtaining a Private Display Device Context

An application performing numerous drawing operations in the client area of its window must use a private display device context. To create this type of device context, the application must specify the CS_OWNDC constant for the style member of the **WNDCLASS** structure when registering the window class. After registering the window class, the application obtains a handle identifying a private display device context by calling the **GetDC** function.

The following example shows how to create a private display device context.

```
#include <windows.h> /* required for all Windows-based applications */
#include <stdio.h>
#include <string.h>  /* strtok                                      */
#include "dc.h"       /* specific to this program                   */


/* Function prototypes */

BOOL InitApplication(HINSTANCE);
long FAR PASCAL MainWndProc(HWND, UINT, UINT, LONG);


/* Global variables */

HINSTANCE hinst;                /* handle of current instance       */
```

```
        HDC hdc;                          /* display device context handle    */
                 .
                 .
                 .


        BOOL InitApplication(HINSTANCE hinstance)
        {
            WNDCLASS  wc;

            /*
             * Fill in the window class structure with parameters describing
             * the main window.
             */

            wc.style = CS_OWNDC;                    /* Private-DC constant */
            wc.lpfnWndProc = (WNDPROC) MainWndProc;

            wc.cbClsExtra = 0;
            wc.cbWndExtra = 0;
            wc.hInstance = hinstance;

            wc.hIcon = LoadIcon((HINSTANCE) NULL,
                MAKEINTRESOURCE(IDI_APPLICATION));

            wc.hCursor = LoadCursor((HINSTANCE) NULL,
                MAKEINTRESOURCE(IDC_ARROW));

            wc.hbrBackground = GetStockObject(WHITE_BRUSH);
            wc.lpszMenuName =  "GenericMenu";
            wc.lpszClassName = "GenericWClass";

            /* Register the window class and return the resultant code. */

            return RegisterClass(&wc);
        }

        LRESULT APIENTRY MainWndProc(
                HWND hwnd,                /* window handle          */
                UINT message,             /* type of message        */
                WPARAM wParam,            /* additional information */
                LPARAM lParam)            /* additional information */
        {

        PAINTSTRUCT ps;               /* paint structure          */

            /* Retrieve a handle identifying the private display DC.*/

            hdc = GetDC(hwnd);

            switch (message) {
```

```
case WM_PAINT:
        BeginPaint(hwnd, &ps);

    .
    . /* Perform drawing and painting using private DC. */
    .
```

28.2.2 Creating a Printer Device Context

An application can create a printer device context in one of two ways:

- Calling the **PrintDlg** function to display a common dialog box that allows the user to specify printer options; then creating a printer device context by using those options.

- Creating a printer device context by using the default printer data from the WIN.INI file.

This section contains code demonstrating the latter method.

To use the default printer, retrieve and parse the appropriate string from the WIN.INI file. This string is retrieved by calling the **GetProfileString** function and specifying the appropriate section and entry names. In the case of the default printer, this data is stored in the [windows] section and identified by the entry named device. The sixth line in the following excerpt from a WIN.INI file shows an entry for a Kodak ® Diconix ™ printer.

```
[windows]
    load=
    run=
    Beep=yes
    Spooler=yes
    NullPort=None
    device=Diconix,winspool,LPT1:
    CoolSwitch=1
    BorderWidth=3
    KeyboardSpeed=31
    InitialKeyboardIndicators=2
    CursorBlinkRate=530
    DoubleClickSpeed=686
    Programs=com exe bat pif cmd
    Documents=
    DeviceNotSelectedTimeout=15
    TransmissionRetryTimeout=45
    swapdisk=
    NetWarn=1
    fPromptOnVerbose=FALSE
    fPromptOnWarning=FALSE
    fPromptOnError=TRUE
```

```
fPrintVerbose=FALSE
fPrintFileLine=FALSE
shell=
ScreenSaveTimeOut=300
ScreenSaveActive=0
DebugOptions=2048
```

The following example shows how a printer device context was created by using
the data from WIN.INI.

```
HDC hdcPrint;               /* printer device context handle    */
char szDevString[120];      /* array that receives WIN.INI data */
char *szPrinter, *szDriver; /* pointers to printer and driver names */
char *szPort;               /* pointer to port name             */

    .
    .
    .

/*
 * Retrieve the printer, printer-driver, and
 * output-port names from WIN.INI.
 */

GetProfileString("windows", "device", ",,,",
    szDevString, 120);

/*
 * Parse the string of names, setting ptrs
 * as required. If the string contains the
 * required names, use them to create a
 * device context.
 */

if ((szPrinter = strtok(szDevString,
        (const char *) ","))
      && (szDriver = strtok ((char *) NULL,
        (const char *) ", "))
      && (szPort = strtok ((char *) NULL,
        (const char *) ", ")))
    hdcPrint = CreateDC(szDriver, szPrinter,
        szPort, NULL);
/*
 * Print a test page that contains the string
 * "PRINTER TEST" in the upper left corner.
 */

Escape(hdcPrint, STARTDOC, 8, "Test-Doc", NULL);
TextOut(hdcPrint, 50, 50, "PRINTER TEST", 12);
Escape(hdcPrint, NEWFRAME, 0, NULL, NULL);
```

```
Escape(hdcPrint, ENDDOC, 0, NULL, NULL);


/* Delete the printer DC. */

DeleteDC(hdcPrint);
```

28.2.3 Retrieving the Capabilities of a Printer

Not every output device supports the entire set of Win32 graphics functions. For example, because of hardware limitations, most vector plotters do not support bit-block transfers. An application can determine whether a device supports a particular Win32 graphics function by calling the **GetDeviceCaps** function, specifying the appropriate index, and examining the return value.

The following example shows how an application tests a printer to determine whether it supports bit-block transfers.

```
/*
 * Examine the raster capabilities of the device
 * identified by hdcPrint to verify that it supports
 * the BitBlt function.
 */

if ((GetDeviceCaps(hdcPrint, RASTERCAPS)
        & RC_BITBLT) == 0) {
    DeleteDC(hdcPrint);
    break;
}
else


.
. /* Print the bitmap using the printer DC. */
.
```

28.2.4 Retrieving Graphic-Object Attributes and Selecting New Graphic Objects

An application can retrieve the attributes for a pen, brush, palette, font, or bitmap by calling the **GetCurrentObject** and **GetObject** functions. The **GetCurrentObject** function returns a handle identifying the object currently selected into the device context; the **GetObject** function returns a structure that describes the object's attributes.

The following example shows how an application can retrieve the current brush attributes and use the retrieved data to determine whether it is necessary to select a new brush.

```
HDC hdc;                      /* display device context handle    */
HBRUSH hbrushNew, hbrushOld;  /* brush handles                    */
HBRUSH hbrush;                /* brush handle                     */
LOGBRUSH lb;                  /* logical-brush structure          */

    /*
     * Retrieve a handle identifying the current brush.
     */

    hbrush = GetCurrentObject(hdc, OBJ_BRUSH);

    /*
     * Retrieve a LOGBRUSH structure that contains the
     * current brush attributes.
     */

    GetObject(hbrush, sizeof(LOGBRUSH), &lb);

    /*
     * If the current brush is not a solid-black brush,
     * replace it with the solid-black stock brush.
     */

    if ((lb.lbStyle != BS_SOLID)
            || (lb.lbColor != 0x000000)) {
        hbrushNew = GetStockObject(BLACK_BRUSH);
        hbrushOld = SelectObject(hdc, hbrushNew);
    }


    .
    . /* Perform painting operations with the white brush. */
    .


    /*
     * After completing the last painting operation
     * with the new brush, the application should
     * select the original brush back into the
     * device context and delete the new brush.
     */

    SelectObject(hdc, hbrushOld);
    DeleteObject(hbrushNew);
```

Note that the application saved the original brush handle when calling the **SelectObject** function the first time. This handle is saved so that the original brush can be selected back into the device context after the last painting operation has been completed with the new brush. After the original brush is selected back into the device context, the new brush is deleted—freeing memory in the GDI heap.

28.3 Functions and Message

Following are the functions and the message used with device contexts.

Functions

CancelDC
CreateCompatibleDC
CreateDC
CreateIC
DeleteDC
DeleteObject
DeviceCapabilitiesEx
EnumObjects
EnumObjectsProc
GetCurrentObject
GetDC
GetDCEx
GetDCOrg
GetDeviceCaps
GetGraphicsMode
GetObject
GetObjectType
ReleaseDC
ResetDC
RestoreDC
SaveDC
SelectObject
SetGraphicsMode

Message

WM_DEVMODECHANGE

C H A P T E R   2 9

Bitmaps

29.1 About Bitmaps

A bitmap is a powerful graphics object used to create, manipulate (scale, scroll, rotate, and paint), and store images as files on a disk.

A bitmap is one of seven objects that can be selected into a device context. The other six objects are the pen, brush, font, region, logical palette, and drawing surface. (For more information about device contexts and related objects, see Chapter 28, "Device Contexts.")

In Microsoft ® Windows ™, Control Panel is an example of an application that uses bitmaps. When a user selects wallpaper for the desktop, the user actually selects a bitmap, which Windows uses to paint the desktop background.

The following illustration shows a desktop painted with a red-brick wallpaper pattern:

Windows creates this pattern by repeatedly drawing a 32- by 32-pixel pattern on the desktop. This pattern is stored as a bitmap in the file REDBRICK.BMP.

From the user's point of view, a bitmap is a rectangle of pixels that form a visual image. However, from the developer's perspective, a *bitmap* is a collection of structures that specify or contain the following elements:

- A header that describes the resolution of the device on which the rectangle of pixels was created, the dimensions of the rectangle, the size of the array of bits, and so on.
- A logical palette.

- An array of bits that define the relationship between pixels in the bitmapped image and entries in the logical palette.

The next illustration shows the developer's perspective of the bitmap found in the file REDBRICK.BMP. It shows a palette array, a 32- by 32-pixel rectangle, and the index array that maps colors from the palette to pixels in the rectangle.

Palette-index

```
row 0, scanline 31   00 00 00 00 00 00 00 00 00 00 00 00 00 00 00 00
row 1, scanline 30   00 00 00 00 00 00 00 00 09 00 00 00 00 00 00 00
row 2, scanline 29   11 11 01 19 11 01 10 10 09 09 01 09 11 11 01 90
        .
        .
        .
row 31, scanline 0   99 99 99 99 99 99 99 99 99 99 99 99 99 99 99 90
```

Pixel rectangle

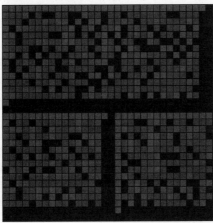

Color-palette

0 Black
1 Dark red
2 Dark green
3 Dark yellow
4 Dark bule
5 Dark magenta
6 Dark cyan
7 Dark gray
8 Light gray
9 Light red
A Light green
B Light yellow
C Light blue
D Light magenta
E Light cyan
F White

In the preceding example, the rectangle of pixels was created on a VGA display device using a palette of 16 colors. A 16-color palette requires 4-bit indices; therefore, the array that maps palette colors to pixel colors is composed of 4-bit indices as well. (For more information about logical color-palettes, see Chapter 36, "Colors.")

It is important to note that Windows maps indices to pixels beginning with the bottom scan line of the rectangular region and ending with the top scan line. (A *scan line* is a single row of adjacent *pixels* on a video display.) In the preceding example, the first row of the array (row 0) corresponds to the bottom row of pixels, scan line 31.

29.1.1 Bitmap Types

There are two types of bitmaps: device-dependent (DDBs) and device-independent (DIBs). DDBs were common in early (pre-3.0) versions of Windows. In fact, they were the only bitmaps available to developers. However, as display technology improved and as the variety of display devices increased among Windows users, certain inherent problems surfaced. For example, there was no method of storing (or retrieving) the resolution of the display type on which a bitmap was created, so a drawing application could not quickly determine whether a bitmap was suitable for the type of video display device on which the application was running. To solve this problem, Microsoft created DIBs.

29.1.1.1 Device-Independent Bitmaps

A DIB contains the following color and dimension information:

- The color format of the device on which the rectangular image was created.

- The resolution of the device on which the rectangular image was created.

- The palette for the device on which the image was created.

- An array of bits that maps red, green, blue (RGB) triplets to pixels in the rectangular image.

- A data-compression identifier that indicates the data compression scheme (if any) used to reduce the size of the array of bits.

This information is stored in a **BITMAPINFO** structure consisting of a **BITMAPINFOHEADER** structure followed by two or more **RGBQUAD** structures. The **BITMAPINFOHEADER** specifies the dimensions of the pixel rectangle, describes the device's color technology, and identifies the compression schemes used to reduce the bitmap's size. The **RGBQUAD** structures identify the colors that appear in the pixel rectangle.

The color format is specified in terms of a count of color planes and color bits. The count of color planes is always 1; the count of color bits is 1 for monochrome bitmaps, 4 for VGA bitmaps, and 8, 16, 24, or 32 for bitmaps on other color devices. An application retrieves the number of color bits a particular display (or printer) uses by calling the **GetDeviceCaps** function, specifying BITSPIXEL as the second argument.

The resolution of a display device is specified in pixels per meter. An application can retrieve the horizontal resolution for a video display, or printer, by following a three-step process:

1. Call the **GetDeviceCaps** function, specifying HORZRES as the second argument.

2. Call **GetDeviceCaps** a second time, specifying HORZSIZE as the second argument.

3. Divide the first return value by the second return value.

The application can retrieve the vertical resolution by using the same three-step process with different parameters: VERTRES in place of HORZRES, and VERTSIZE in place of HORZSIZE.

The palette is represented by an array of **RGBQUAD** structures that specify the red, green, and blue intensity components for each color in a display device's color palette. Each color index in the palette array maps to a specific pixel in the rectangular region associated with the bitmap. The size of this array, in bits, is equivalent to the width of the rectangle, in pixels, multiplied by the height of the rectangle, in pixels, multiplied by the count of color bits for the device. An application can retrieve the size of the device's palette by calling the **GetDeviceCaps** function, specifying the NUMCOLORS constant as the second argument.

Windows supports the compression of the palette array for 8-bit-per-pixel and 4-bit-per-pixel DIBs. These arrays can be compressed by using the run-length encoding (RLE) scheme. The RLE scheme uses 2-byte values, the first byte specifying the number of consecutive pixels that use a color index and the second byte specifying the index. For more information about bitmap compression, see the description of the **BITMAPINFOHEADER** structure.

An application can create a DIB by initializing the required structures and calling the **CreateDIBitmap** function. Then it can initialize the array of indices by calling the **SetDIBits** function. To determine whether a device supports this function, call the **GetDeviceCaps** function, specifying RC_DI_BITMAP as the RASTERCAPS flag.

An application can use a DIB to set pixels on the display device by calling the **SetDIBitsToDevice** or the **BitBlt** function. To determine whether a device supports the **SetDIBitsToDevice** function, call the **GetDeviceCaps** function, specifying RC_DIBTODEV as the RASTERCAPS flag.

An application that simply needs to display a preexisting DIB can use the **SetDIBitsToDevice** function. For example, a spreadsheet application can open existing charts and display them in a window by using the **SetDIBitsToDevice** function. To repeatedly redraw a bitmap in a window, however, the application should use the **BitBlt** function. For example, a multimedia application that combines animated graphics with sound would benefit from calling the **BitBlt** function because it executes faster than **SetDIBitsToDevice**.

29.1.1.2 Device-Dependent Bitmaps

Device-dependent bitmaps are supported *only* for compatibility with applications written for Windows versions earlier than 3.0. A developer writing a new application or porting an application written for a previous version of Windows to the Win32 platform should use DIBs.

DDBs are described by using a single structure, the **BITMAP** structure. The members of this structure specify the width and height of a rectangular region, in pixels; the width of the array that maps entries from the device palette to pixels; and the device's color format, in terms of color planes and bits per pixel. An application can retrieve the color format of a device by calling the **GetDeviceCaps** function and specifying the appropriate constants.

There are two types of DDBs: discardable and nondiscardable. A discardable DDB is a bitmap that Windows discards if the bitmap is not selected into a DC *and* if system memory is low. The **CreateDiscardableBitmap** function creates discardable bitmaps. The **CreateBitmap**, **CreateCompatibleBitmap**, and **CreateBitmapIndirect** functions create nondiscardable bitmaps.

29.1.2 Bitmaps, Device Contexts, and Drawing Surfaces

A *device context* (DC) is a data structure defining the graphics objects, their associated attributes, and the graphics modes affecting output on a device. An application creates a DC by calling the **CreateDC** function; it retrieves a window manager device context by calling the **GetDC** function.

29.1.2.1 The Drawing Surface

Before returning a handle that identifies that DC, the window manager selects a drawing surface into the DC. If the application called the **CreateDC** function to create a device context for a VGA display, the dimensions of this drawing surface are 640- by 480-pixels. If the application called the **GetDC** function, the dimensions reflect the size of the client area.

When an application passes the handle returned by **CreateDC** or **GetDC** to one of the graphics device interface (GDI) drawing functions, the requested output appears on the drawing surface selected into the device context.

29.1.2.2 Compatible Device Contexts

To enable applications to place output in memory rather than sending it to an actual device, Windows provides a special device context for bitmap operations called a *compatible device context*. A compatible DC enables Windows to treat a portion of memory as a virtual device. It is an array of bits in memory that an application can use to temporarily store the color data for bitmaps created on a normal drawing surface.

An application creates a compatible DC by calling the **CreateCompatibleDC** function and receives a handle that identifies a normal device context. Windows creates a temporary 1-bit placeholder for the array. Before performing drawing operations using the compatible DC handle, the application must increase the size of this array. To do this, the application can call the **CreateBitmap**, **CreateBitmapIndirect**, or **CreateCompatibleBitmap** function to create a bitmap of the appropriate dimensions and then call the **SelectObject** function to select the bitmap into the DC. After the bitmap is selected into the compatible DC, Windows replaces the single-bit array with an array large enough to store color information for the specified rectangle of pixels.

When an application passes the handle returned by **CreateCompatibleDC** to one of the GDI drawing functions, the requested output does *not* appear on a device's drawing surface. Instead, Windows stores the color information for the resultant line, curve, text or region in the array of bits. The application can copy the image stored in memory back onto a drawing surface by calling the **BitBlt** function, identifying the compatible DC as the source device context and a window or screen DC as the target device context.

29.1.3 Bitmap Rotation

Windows provides a function to copy a bitmap into a parallelogram; this function, **PlgBlt**, performs a bit-block transfer from a rectangle in a source device context into a parallelogram in a destination device context. In order to rotate the bitmap, an application must provide the coordinates, in world units, to be used for the corners of the parallelogram. (For more information about rotation and world units see Chapter 39, "Coordinate Spaces and Transformations.")

29.1.4 Bitmap Scaling

Windows also provides a function to scale a bitmap; this function, **StretchBlt**, performs a bit-block transfer from a rectangle in a source device context into a rectangle in a destination device context. However, unlike the **BitBlt** function, which duplicates the source rectangle dimensions in the destination rectangle, **StretchBlt** allows an application to specify the dimensions of both the source and the destination rectangles. When the destination bitmap is smaller than the source bitmap, Windows combines rows or columns of color data (or both) in the bitmap before rendering the corresponding image on the display device. Windows combines the color data according to the specified stretch mode, which the application defines by calling the **SetStretchBltMode** function. When the destination bitmap is larger than the source bitmap, Windows scales or magnifies each pixel in the resultant image accordingly.

The following illustration shows the client area of an application that captures the entire contents of the desktop and then stores the corresponding color data in a bitmap. The window on the left displays the original bitmap; the window on the right displays the bitmap after it was scaled to twice its original size.

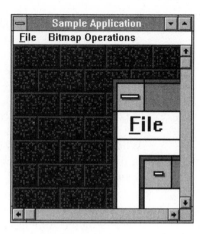

29.1.5 Bitmaps as Brushes

Windows provides a number of functions that use the brush currently selected into a device context to perform bitmap operations. For example, the **PatBlt** function replicates the brush in a rectangular region within a window, and the **FloodFill** function replicates the brush inside an area in a window bounded by the specified color (unlike **PatBlt**, **FloodFill** does fill nonrectangular shapes).

The **PatBlt** function name (an abbreviation for pattern block transfer) implies that the function simply replicates the brush (or pattern) until it fills a specified rectangle. However, the function is actually much more powerful. Before replicating the brush, it combines the color data for the pattern with the color data for the existing pixels on the video display by using a raster operation (ROP). An ROP is a bitwise operation that is applied to the bits of color data for the replicated brush and the bits of color data for the target rectangle on the display device. There are 256 ROPs in Windows; however, the **PatBlt** function recognizes only those that require a pattern and a destination (not those that require a source). The following table identifies the five most common ROPs.

ROP	Description
PATCOPY	Copies the pattern to the destination bitmap.
PATINVERT	Combines the destination bitmap with the pattern by using the Boolean OR operator.
DSTINVERT	Inverts the destination bitmap.
BLACKNESS	Turns all output to binary zeroes.
WHITENESS	Turns all output to binary ones.

The **FloodFill** function replicates the brush within a region bounded by a specified color. However, unlike the **PatBlt** function, **FloodFill** does not combine the color data for the brush with the color data for the pixels on the display; it simply sets the color of all pixels within the enclosed region on the display to the color of the brush that is currently selected into the device context.

The following illustration shows the result of calling the **FloodFill** function in the Windows Paintbrush application to paint the interior of a nonrectangular region. The window on the left shows the region before **FloodFill** was called; the window on the right shows the region after the call was made.

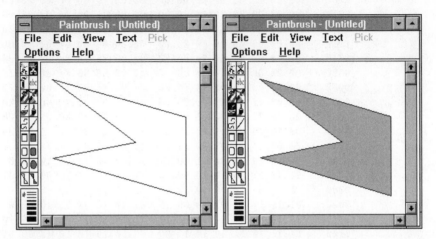

29.1.6 Bitmap Storage

Bitmaps should be saved in a file that uses the established Windows format and assigned a name with the three-character .BMP extension. The Windows format is shown in the following illustration.

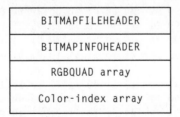

The members of the **BITMAPFILEHEADER** structure identify the file; specify the size of the file, in bytes; and specify the offset from the first byte in the header to the first byte of bitmap data. The members of the **BITMAPINFOHEADER** structure specify the bitmap's width and height, in pixels; the color format (count of color planes and color bits per pixel) of the display device on which the bitmap was created; whether the bitmap data was compressed before storage and the type of compression used; the number of bytes of bitmap data; the resolution of the display device on which the bitmap was created; and the number of colors represented in the data. The **RGBQUAD** structures specify the RGB intensity values for each of the colors in the device's palette. The color-index array maps indices values from the **RGBQUAD** array to pixels in a rectangular region on the display.

The following hexadecimal output shows the contents of the file REDBRICK.BMP.

```
0000    42 4d 76 02 00 00 00 00    00 00 76 00 00 00 28 00
0010    00 00 20 00 00 00 20 00    00 00 01 00 04 00 00 00
0020    00 00 00 00 00 00 00 00    00 00 00 00 00 00 00 00
0030    00 00 00 00 00 00 00 00    00 00 00 00 80 00 00 80
0040    00 00 00 80 80 00 80 00    00 00 80 00 80 00 80 80
0050    00 00 80 80 80 00 c0 c0    c0 00 00 00 ff 00 00 ff
0060    00 00 00 ff ff 00 ff 00    00 00 ff 00 ff 00 ff ff
0070    00 00 ff ff ff 00 00 00    00 00 00 00 00 00 00 00
0080    00 00 00 00 00 00 00 00    00 00 00 00 00 00 09 00
0090    00 00 00 00 00 00 11 11    01 19 11 01 10 10 09 09
00a0    01 09 11 11 01 90 11 01    19 09 09 91 11 10 09 11
00b0    09 11 19 10 90 11 19 01    19 19 10 10 11 10 09 01
00c0    91 10 91 09 10 10 90 99    11 11 11 11 19 00 09 01
00d0    91 01 01 19 00 99 11 10    11 91 99 11 09 90 09 91
00e0    01 11 11 11 91 10 09 19    01 00 11 90 91 10 09 01
00f0    11 99 10 01 11 11 91 11    11 19 10 11 99 10 09 10
0100    01 11 11 11 19 10 11 09    09 10 19 10 10 10 09 01
0110    11 19 00 01 10 19 10 11    11 01 99 01 11 90 09 19
0120    11 91 11 91 01 11 19 10    99 00 01 19 09 10 09 19
0130    10 91 11 01 11 11 91 01    91 19 11 00 99 90 09 01
0140    01 99 19 01 91 10 19 91    91 09 11 99 11 10 09 91
0150    11 10 11 91 99 10 90 11    01 11 11 19 11 90 09 11
0160    00 19 10 11 01 11 99 99    99 99 99 99 99 99 09 99
0170    99 99 99 99 99 99 00 00    00 00 00 00 00 00 00 00
0180    00 00 00 00 00 00 90 00    00 00 00 00 00 00 00 00
0190    00 00 00 00 00 00 99 11    11 11 19 10 19 19 11 09
01a0    10 90 91 90 91 00 91 19    19 09 01 10 09 01 11 11
01b0    91 11 11 11 10 00 91 11    01 19 10 11 10 01 01 11
01c0    90 11 11 11 91 00 99 09    19 10 11 90 09 90 91 01
01d0    19 09 91 11 01 00 90 10    19 11 00 11 11 00 10 11
01e0    01 10 11 19 11 00 90 19    10 91 01 90 19 99 00 11
01f0    91 01 11 01 91 00 99 09    09 01 10 11 91 01 10 91
0200    99 11 10 90 91 00 91 11    00 10 11 01 10 19 19 09
0210    10 00 99 01 01 00 91 01    19 91 19 91 11 09 10 11
0220    00 91 00 10 90 00 99 01    11 10 09 10 10 19 09 01
0230    91 90 11 09 11 00 90 99    11 11 11 90 19 01 19 01
0240    91 01 01 19 09 00 91 10    11 91 99 09 09 90 11 91
0250    01 19 11 11 91 00 91 19    01 00 11 00 91 10 11 01
0260    11 11 10 01 11 00 99 99    99 99 99 99 99 99 99 99
0270    99 99 99 99 99 90
```

The following table shows the data bytes associated with the structures in a bitmap file.

Structure	Corresponding bytes
BITMAPFILEHEADER	0x00 – 0x0D
BITMAPINFOHEADER	0x0E – 0x31
RGBQUAD array	0x32 – 0x75
Color-index array	0x76 – 0x275

29.2 Using Bitmaps

This section explains how to perform the following tasks:

- Capture an image
- Scale an image
- Store an image permanently

29.2.1 Capturing an Image

You can use a bitmap to capture an image, and you can store the captured image in memory, display it at a different location in your application's window, or display it in another window.

In some cases, you may want your application to capture images and store them only temporarily. For example, when you scale or "zoom" a picture created in a drawing application, the application must temporarily save the normal view of the image and display the zoomed view. Later, when the user selects the normal view, the application must replace the zoomed image with a copy of the normal view that it temporarily saved.

If your application must store an image temporarily, you must create a DC that is compatible with the current window DC. You do this by calling the **CreateCompatibleDC** function. After you create a compatible DC, you create a bitmap with the appropriate dimensions by calling the **CreateCompatibleBitmap** function and then select it into this device context by calling the **SelectObject** function.

After the compatible device context is created and the appropriate bitmap has been selected into it, you can capture the image. Windows provides the **BitBlt** function to capture images. This function performs a bit block transfer—that is, it copies data from a source bitmap into a destination bitmap. Because it copies data from bitmaps, you'd expect that two arguments to this function would be bitmap handles; however, this is not the case. Instead, the **BitBlt** function receives handles that identify two device contexts and copies the bitmap data from a bitmap selected into the source DC *into* a bitmap selected into the target DC. In this case, the target DC is the compatible DC, so when the **BitBlt** function completes the transfer, the image has been stored in memory. To redisplay the image, call the **BitBlt** function a second time, specifying the compatible device context as the source DC and a window (or printer) device context as the target DC.

The following example code, from an application that captures an image of the entire desktop, creates a compatible device context and a bitmap with the appropriate dimensions, selects the bitmap into the compatible DC, and then copies the image using the **BitBlt** function.

```
/*
 * Create a normal DC and a memory DC for the entire screen. The
 * normal DC provides a "snapshot" of the screen contents. The
 * memory DC keeps a copy of this "snapshot" in the associated
 * bitmap.
 */

hdcScreen = CreateDC("DISPLAY", NULL, NULL, NULL);
hdcCompatible = CreateCompatibleDC(hdcScreen);

/* Create a compatible bitmap for hdcScreen. */

hbmScreen = CreateCompatibleBitmap(hdcScreen,
                GetDeviceCaps(hdcScreen, HORZRES),
                GetDeviceCaps(hdcScreen, VERTRES));

if (hbmScreen == 0)
    errhandler("hbmScreen", hwnd);

/* Select the bitmaps into the compatible DC. */

if (!SelectObject(hdcCompatible, hbmScreen))
    errhandler("Compatible Bitmap Selection", hwnd);

        /* Hide the application window. */

        ShowWindow(hwnd, SW_HIDE);

        /*
         * Copy color data for the entire display into a
         * bitmap that is selected into a compatible DC.
         */

        if (!BitBlt(hdcCompatible,
              0,0,
              bmp.bmWidth, bmp.bmHeight,
              hdcScreen,
              0,0,
```

```
                    SRCCOPY))

          errhandler("Screen to Compat Blt Failed", hwnd);

          /* Redraw the application window. */

          ShowWindow(hwnd, SW_SHOW);
```

29.2.2 Scaling an Image

Some applications scale images—that is, they display zoomed or reduced views of an image. For example, a drawing application may provide a zoom feature that enables the user to view and edit a drawing on a pixel-by-pixel basis.

Applications scale images by calling the **StretchBlt** function. Like the **BitBlt** function, **StretchBlt** copies bitmap data from a bitmap in a source DC into a bitmap in a target DC. However, unlike the **BitBlt** function, **StretchBlt** scales the image based on the specified dimensions of the source and target rectangles. If the source rectangle is larger than the target rectangle, the resultant image will appear to have shrunk; if the source rectangle is smaller than the target rectangle, the resultant image will appear to have expanded.

If the target rectangle is smaller than the source rectangle, **StretchBlt** removes color data from the image according to a specified stretch mode as shown in the following table.

Stretch Mode	Method
BLACKONWHITE	Performs a logical AND operation on the color data for the eliminated pixels and the color data for the remaining pixels.
WHITEONBLACK	Performs a logical OR operation on the color data for the eliminated pixels and the color data for the remaining pixels.
COLORONCOLOR	Eliminates the color data of the deleted pixels completely.
HALFTONE	Approximates the original (source) color data in the destination.

You set the stretch-mode by calling the **SetStretchBltMode** function.

The following example code is taken from an application that displays an image either at its original size or a twice the original size. (This application uses the default stretch mode.).

```
          hdcScaled = CreateCompatibleDC(hdcScreen);

          hbmScaled = CreateCompatibleBitmap(hdcScreen,
                      GetDeviceCaps(hdcScreen, HORZRES) * 2,
                      GetDeviceCaps(hdcScreen, VERTRES) * 2);
```

```
            if (hbmScaled == 0)
                errhandler("hbmScaled", hwnd);

            /* Select the bitmaps into the compatible DC. */

            if (!SelectObject(hdcScaled, hbmScaled))
                errhandler("Scaled Bitmap Selection", hwnd);

        case WM_COMMAND: /* message: command from application menu */
            switch(wParam) {

                case IDM_SCALEX1:
                    if (fBlt){
                        fScaled = FALSE;
                        hdcWin = GetDC(hwnd);
                        BitBlt(hdcWin,
                            0,0,
                            bmp.bmWidth, bmp.bmHeight,
                            hdcCompatible,
                            0,0,
                            SRCCOPY);
                        ReleaseDC(hwnd, hdcWin);
                    }
                    break;

                case IDM_SCALEX2:
                    if (fBlt){
                        fScaled = TRUE;
                        StretchBlt(hdcScaled,
                            0, 0,
                            bmp.bmWidth * 2, bmp.bmHeight * 2,
                            hdcCompatible,
                            0, 0,
                            bmp.bmWidth, bmp.bmHeight,
                            SRCCOPY);

                        hdcWin = GetDC(hwnd);
                        BitBlt(hdcWin,
                            0,0,
                            bmp.bmWidth, bmp.bmHeight,
                            hdcScaled,
                            0,0,
                            SRCCOPY);
                        ReleaseDC(hwnd, hdcWin);
                    }
                    break;
```

29.2.3 Storing an Image

Many applications store images permanently as files. For example, drawing applications store pictures, spreadsheet applications store charts, CAD applications store drawings, and so on.

If you are writing an application that will store a bitmapped image in a file, you should use the Windows file format described in Section 29.1.6, "Bitmap Storage." In order to store a bitmap in this format, you must initialize a **BITMAPINFO** structure (consisting of a **BITMAPFILEHEADER** structure and an array of **RGBQUAD** structures), as well as an array of palette indices.

The following example code defines a function that allocates memory for and initializes members within a **BITMAPINFOHEADER** data structure.

```
PBITMAPINFO CreateBitmapInfoStruct(HWND hwnd, HBITMAP hBmp) {
    BITMAP bmp;
    PBITMAPINFO pbmi;
    WORD    cClrBits;

    /* Retrieve the bitmap's color format, width, and height. */

    if (!GetObject(hBmp, sizeof(BITMAP), (LPSTR)&bmp))
        errhandler("GetObject", hwnd);


    /* Convert the color format to a count of bits. */

    cClrBits = (WORD)(bmp.bmPlanes * bmp.bmBitsPixel);

    if (cClrBits == 1)
        cClrBits = 1;
    else if (cClrBits <= 4)
        cClrBits = 4;
    else if (cClrBits <= 8)
        cClrBits = 8;
    else if (cClrBits <= 16)
        cClrBits = 16;
    else if (cClrBits <= 24)
        cClrBits = 24;
    else
        cClrBits = 32;

    /*
     * Allocate memory for the BITMAPINFO structure. (This structure
     * contains a BITMAPINFOHEADER structure and an array of RGBQUAD
     * data structures.)
     */
```

```
        if (cClrBits != 24)
            pbmi = (PBITMAPINFO) LocalAlloc(LPTR,
                        sizeof(BITMAPINFOHEADER) +
                        sizeof(RGBQUAD) * cClrBits);

        /*
         * There is no RGBQUAD array for the 24-bit-per-pixel format.
         */

        else
            pbmi = (PBITMAPINFO) LocalAlloc(LPTR,
                        sizeof(BITMAPINFOHEADER));



        /* Initialize the fields in the BITMAPINFO structure. */

        pbmi->bmiHeader.biSize = sizeof(BITMAPINFOHEADER);
        pbmi->bmiHeader.biWidth = bmp.bmWidth;
        pbmi->bmiHeader.biHeight = bmp.bmHeight;
        pbmi->bmiHeader.biPlanes = bmp.bmPlanes;
        pbmi->bmiHeader.biBitCount = bmp.bmBitsPixel;


        /* If the bitmap is not compressed, set the BI_RGB flag. */

        pbmi->bmiHeader.biCompression = BI_RGB;

        /*
         * Compute the number of bytes in the array of color
         * indices and store the result in biSizeImage.
         */

        pbmi->bmiHeader.biSizeImage = (pbmi->bmiHeader.biWidth + 7) /8
                                        * pbmi->bmiHeader.biHeight
                                        * cClrBits;

        /*
         * Set biClrImportant to 0, indicating that all of the
         * device colors are important.
         */

        pbmi->bmiHeader.biClrImportant = 0;

        return pbmi;

    }
```

The following example code defines a function that initializes the remaining structures, retrieves the array of palette indices, opens the file, copies the data, and closes the file.

```
void CreateBMPFile(HWND hwnd, LPTSTR pszFile, PBITMAPINFO pbi,
                HBITMAP hBMP, HDC hDC)
{

        HANDLE hf;                      /* file handle                   */
        BITMAPFILEHEADER hdr;           /* bitmap file-header            */
        PBITMAPINFOHEADER pbih;         /* bitmap info-header            */
        HANDLE hmem;                    /* memory handle                 */
        LPBYTE lpBits;                  /* memory pointer                */
        DWORD dwTotal;                  /* total count of bytes          */
        DWORD cb;                       /* incremental count of bytes    */
        BYTE *hp;                       /* byte pointer                  */
        DWORD dwTmp;


        pbih = (PBITMAPINFOHEADER) pbi;

        lpBits = (LPBYTE) GlobalAlloc(GMEM_FIXED, pbih->biSizeImage);
        if (!lpBits)
            errhandler("GlobalAlloc", hwnd);

        /*
         * Retrieve the color table (RGBQUAD array) and the bits
         * (array of palette indices) from the DIB.
         */

        if (!GetDIBits(hDC, hBMP, 0, (WORD) pbih->biHeight,
                    lpBits, pbi, DIB_RGB_COLORS))
            errhandler("GetDIBits", hwnd);

        /* Create the .BMP file. */

        hf = CreateFile(pszFile,
                    GENERIC_READ | GENERIC_WRITE,
                    (DWORD) 0,
                    (LPSECURITY_ATTRIBUTES) NULL,
                    CREATE_ALWAYS,
                    FILE_ATTRIBUTE_NORMAL,
                    (HANDLE) NULL);

        if (hf == INVALID_HANDLE_VALUE)
            errhandler("CreateFile", hwnd);

        hdr.bfType = 0x4d42;            /* 0x42 = "B"  0x4d = "M" */

        /* Compute the size of the entire file. */
```

```
hdr.bfSize = (DWORD) (sizeof(BITMAPFILEHEADER) +
            pbih->biSize + pbih->biClrImportant
            * sizeof(RGBQUAD) + pbih->biSizeImage);

hdr.bfReserved1 = 0;
hdr.bfReserved2 = 0;

/* Compute the offset to the array of color indices. */

hdr.bfOffBits = (DWORD) sizeof(BITMAPFILEHEADER) +
            pbih->biSize + pbih->biClrImportant
            * sizeof (RGBQUAD);

/* Copy the BITMAPFILEHEADER into the .BMP file. */

if (!WriteFile(hf, (LPVOID) &hdr, sizeof(BITMAPFILEHEADER),
    (LPDWORD) &dwTmp, (LPOVERLAPPED) NULL))
    errhandler("WriteFile", hwnd);

/* Copy the BITMAPINFOHEADER and RGBQUAD array into the file. */

if (!WriteFile(hf, (LPVOID) pbih, sizeof(BITMAPINFOHEADER)
            + pbih->biClrImportant * sizeof (RGBQUAD),
            (LPDWORD) &dwTmp, (LPOVERLAPPED) NULL))
    errhandler("WriteFile", hwnd);

/* Copy the array of color indices into the .BMP file. */

dwTotal = cb = pbih->biSizeImage;
hp = lpBits;
while (cb > MAXWRITE)  {
        if (!WriteFile(hf, (LPSTR) hp, (int) MAXWRITE,
                    (LPDWORD) &dwTmp, (LPOVERLAPPED) NULL))
            errhandler("WriteFile", hwnd);
        cb-= MAXWRITE;
        hp += MAXWRITE;
}
if (!WriteFile(hf, (LPSTR) hp, (int) cb,
    (LPDWORD) &dwTmp, (LPOVERLAPPED) NULL))
        errhandler("WriteFile", hwnd);

/* Close the .BMP file. */

if (!CloseHandle(hf))
        errhandler("CloseHandle", hwnd);

/* Unlock and free memory. */

GlobalUnlock(hmem);
```

```
        GlobalFree(hmem);
    }
```

29.3 Functions

Following are the functions used with bitmaps.

BitBlt
CreateBitmap
CreateBitmapIndirect
CreateCompatibleBitmap
CreateDiscardableBitmap
CreateDIBitmap
CreateDIBSection
ExtFloodFill
FloodFill
GetBitmapBits
GetBitmapDimensionEx
GetDIBits
GetPixel
GetStretchBltMode
LoadBitmap
MaskBlt
PatBlt
PlgBlt
SetBitmapBits
SetBitmapDimensionEx
SetDIBits
SetDIBitsToDevice
SetPixel
SetPixelV
StretchBlt
StretchDIBits
SetStretchBltMode

CHAPTER 30

Brushes

30.1 About Brushes

A *brush* is a graphics tool that an application written for Microsoft ® Windows ™ uses to paint the interior of polygons, ellipses, and paths. Drawing applications use brushes to paint shapes; word processing applications use brushes to paint rules; computer-aided design (CAD) applications use brushes to paint the interiors of cross-section views; and spreadsheet applications use brushes to paint the sections of pie charts and the bars in bar graphs.

There are two types of brushes: logical and physical. A *logical brush* is a description of the ideal bitmap that an application would use to paint shapes. A *physical brush* is the actual bitmap that a device driver creates based on an application's logical-brush definition. For more information about bitmaps, see Chapter 29, "Bitmaps."

When an application calls one of the functions that create a brush, it retrieves a handle that identifies a logical brush. When the application passes this handle to the **SelectObject** function, the device driver for the corresponding display or printer creates the physical brush.

30.1.1 Brush Origin

When an application calls a drawing function to paint a shape, Windows positions a brush at the start of the paint operation and maps a pixel in the brush bitmap to the window origin of the client area. (The *window origin* is the upper-left corner of the window's client area.) The coordinates of the pixel that Windows maps are called the *brush origin*. The default brush origin is located in the upper-left corner of the brush bitmap, at the coordinates (0,0). Windows then copies the brush across the client area, forming a pattern that is as tall as the bitmap. The copy operation continues, row by row, until the entire client area is filled. However, the brush pattern is visible *only* within the boundaries of the specified shape.

There are instances when the default brush origin should not be used. For example, it may be necessary for an application to use the same brush to paint the backgrounds of its parent and child windows *and* blend a child window's background with that of the parent window. To do this, the application should reset the brush origin by calling the **SetBrushOrgEx** function and shifting the origin the required number of pixels. (An application can retrieve the current brush origin by calling the **GetBrushOrgEx** function.)

The following illustration shows a five-pointed star filled by using an application-defined brush. The illustration shows a zoomed image of the brush, as well as the location to which it was mapped at the beginning of the paint operation.

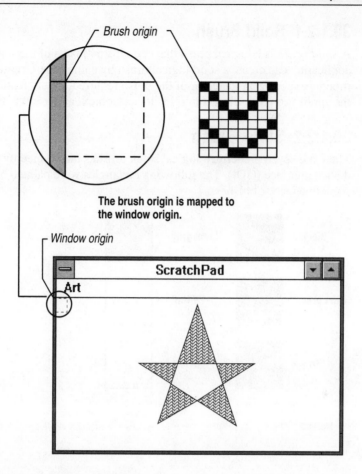

The brush origin is mapped to
the window origin.

30.1.2 Logical Brush Types

There are four types of logical brushes (solid, stock, hatch, and pattern) as shown
in the following illustration.

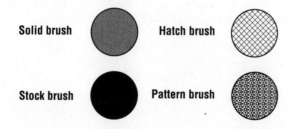

The stock and hatch types each have several predefined brushes, as described in
Section 30.1.2.3, "Hatch Brush."

30.1.2.1 Solid Brush

A *solid brush* is a logical brush that contains 64 pixels of the same color. An application can create a solid logical brush by calling the **CreateSolidBrush** function, specifying the color of the brush required. After creating the solid brush, the application can select it into its device context and use it to paint filled shapes.

30.1.2.2 Stock Brush

There are seven predefined logical stock brushes maintained by the graphics device interface (GDI). The following rectangles were painted by using the seven predefined stock brushes.

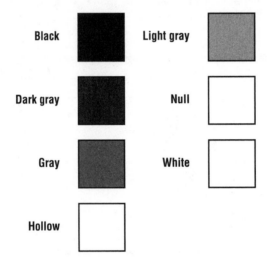

An application can retrieve a handle identifying one of the seven stock brushes by calling the **GetStockObject** function, specifying the brush type.

30.1.2.3 Hatch Brush

There are six predefined logical hatch brushes maintained by GDI. The following rectangles were painted by using the six predefined hatch brushes.

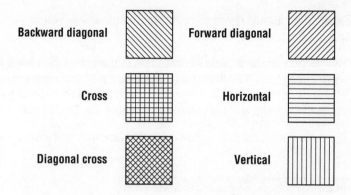

An application can create a hatch brush by calling the **CreateHatchBrush** function, specifying one of the six hatch styles.

30.1.2.4 Pattern Brush

A pattern (or custom) brush is created from an application-defined bitmap or device-independent bitmap (DIB). The following rectangles were painted by using different pattern brushes.

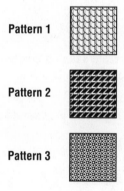

To create a logical pattern brush, an application must first create a bitmap. After creating the bitmap, the application can create the logical pattern brush by calling the **CreatePatternBrush** or **CreateDIBPatternBrush** function, supplying a handle that identifies the bitmap (or DIB). The brushes that appear in the preceding illustration were created from monochrome bitmaps. For a description of bitmaps, DIBs, and the functions that create them, see Chapter 29, "Bitmaps."

30.2 Using Brushes

You can use a brush to paint the interior of virtually any shape by using a GDI function. This includes the interiors of rectangles, ellipses, polygons, and paths.

Depending on the requirements of your application, you can use a solid brush of a specified color, a stock brush, a hatch brush, or a pattern brush.

This section contains code samples that demonstrate the creation of a custom brush dialog box. The dialog box contains a grid that represents the bitmap Windows uses as a brush. A user can use this grid to create a pattern-brush bitmap and then view the custom pattern by clicking the Test Pattern button.

The following illustration shows a pattern created by using the Custom Brush dialog box.

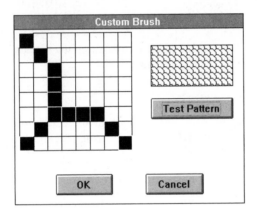

To display a dialog box, you must first create a dialog box template. The following dialog box template defines the Custom Brush dialog box.

```
CustBrush DIALOG 6, 18, 160, 118
STYLE WS_DLGFRAME | WS_POPUP | WS_VISIBLE | WS_CAPTION
CAPTION "Custom Brush"
FONT 8, "MS Sans Serif"
BEGIN
    CONTROL        "", IDD_GRID, "Static", SS_BLACKFRAME |
                   WS_CHILD, 3, 2, 83, 79
    CONTROL        "", IDD_RECT, "Static", SS_BLACKFRAME |
                   WS_CHILD, 96, 11, 57, 28
    PUSHBUTTON     "Test Pattern", IDD_PAINTRECT, 96, 47, 57, 14
    PUSHBUTTON     "OK", IDD_OK, 29, 98, 40, 14
    PUSHBUTTON     "Cancel", IDD_CANCEL, 92, 98, 40, 14
END
```

The Custom Brush dialog box contains five controls: a bitmap-grid window, a pattern-viewing window, and three push buttons, labeled Test Pattern, OK and Cancel. The Test Pattern push button enables the user to view the pattern. The dialog box template specifies the overall dimensions of the dialog box window, assigns a value to each control, specifies the location of each control, and so forth. (For more information about creating dialog box templates, see Chapter 18, "Dialog Boxes.")

The control values in the dialog box template are constants that have been defined as follows in the application's header file.

```
#define IDD_GRID  120
#define IDD_RECT  121
#define IDD_PAINTRECT 122
#define IDD_OK   123
#define IDD_CANCEL 124
```

After you create a dialog box template and include it in the application's resource-definition file, you must write a dialog procedure. This procedure processes messages that Windows sends to the dialog box. The following excerpt from an application's source code shows the dialog box procedure for the Custom Brush dialog box and the two application-defined functions it calls.

```
int APIENTRY BrushDlgProc(HWND hdlg, WORD message, LONG wParam,
                          LONG lParam)
{
    static HWND hwndGrid;        /* grid-window control     */
    static HWND hwndBrush;       /* pattern-brush control   */
    static RECT rctGrid;         /* grid-window rectangle   */
    static RECT rctBrush;        /* pattern-brush rectangle */
    static UINT bBrushBits[8];   /* bitmap bits             */
    static RECT rect[64];        /* grid-cell array         */
    static HBITMAP hbm;          /* bitmap handle           */
    HBRUSH hbrush;               /* current brush           */
    HBRUSH hbrushOld;            /* default brush           */
    HRGN hrgnCell;               /* test-region handle      */
    HDC hdc;                     /* DC handle               */
    int x, y, deltaX, deltaY;    /* drawing coordinates     */
    POINTS ptlHit;               /* mouse coordinates       */
    int i;                       /* count variable          */

    switch (message)
        {
        case WM_INITDIALOG:

            /*
             * Retrieve a window handle for the grid-window and
             * pattern-brush controls
             */

            hwndGrid = GetDlgItem(hdlg, IDD_GRID);
            hwndBrush = GetDlgItem(hdlg, IDD_RECT);

            /* Initialize the array of bits that define the
             * custom brush pattern with the value 1 to produce a
             * solid white brush).
             */
```

```
            for (i=0; i<8; i++)
                bBrushBits[i] = 0xFF;

            /*
             * Retrieve dimensions for the grid-window and pattern-brush
             * controls.
             */

            GetClientRect(hwndGrid, &rctGrid);
            GetClientRect(hwndBrush, &rctBrush);

            /* Determine the width and height of a single cell. */

            deltaX = (rctGrid.right - rctGrid.left)/8;
            deltaY = (rctGrid.bottom - rctGrid.top)/8;

            /* Initialize the array of cell rectangles. */

            for (y=rctGrid.top, i=0; y < rctGrid.bottom; y += deltaY){
                for (x=rctGrid.left; x < (rctGrid.right - 8) && i < 64;
                        x += deltaX, i++) {
                    rect[i].left = x; rect[i].top = y;
                    rect[i].right = x + deltaX;
                    rect[i].bottom = y + deltaY;
                }
            }
            return FALSE;


        case WM_PAINT:


            /* Draw the grid. */

            hdc = GetDC(hwndGrid);

            for (i=rctGrid.left; i<rctGrid.right;
                    i+=(rctGrid.right - rctGrid.left)/8){
                MoveToEx(hdc, i, rctGrid.top, NULL);
                LineTo(hdc, i, rctGrid.bottom);
            }
            for (i=rctGrid.top; i<rctGrid.bottom;
                    i+=(rctGrid.bottom - rctGrid.top)/8){
                MoveToEx(hdc, rctGrid.left, i, NULL);
                LineTo(hdc, rctGrid.right, i);
            }
            ReleaseDC(hwndGrid, hdc);
            return FALSE;
```

```
case WM_LBUTTONDOWN:

    /* Store the mouse coordinates in a POINT structure. */

    ptlHit = MAKEPOINTS((POINTS FAR *)lParam);

    /*
     * Create a rectangular region with dimensions and
     * coordinates that correspond to those of the grid
     * window.
     */

    hrgnCell = CreateRectRgn(rctGrid.left, rctGrid.top,
             rctGrid.right, rctGrid.bottom);

    /* Retrieve a window DC for the grid window. */

    hdc = GetDC(hwndGrid);

    /* Select the region into the DC. */

    SelectObject(hdc, hrgnCell);

    /* Test for a button click in the grid-window rectangle. */

    if (PtInRegion(hrgnCell, ptlHit.x, ptlHit.y)){

        /*
         * A button click occurred in the grid-window rectangle;
         * isolate the cell in which it occurred.
         */

        for(i=0; i<64; i++){
            DeleteObject(hrgnCell);

            hrgnCell = CreateRectRgn(rect[i].left, rect[i].top,
                     rect[i].right, rect[i].bottom);

            if (PtInRegion(hrgnCell, ptlHit.x, ptlHit.y)){
                InvertRgn(hdc, hrgnCell);

                /* Set the appropriate brush bits. */

                if (i % 8 == 0)
                    bBrushBits[i/8] = bBrushBits[i/8] ^ 0x80;
                else if (i % 8 == 1)
                    bBrushBits[i/8] = bBrushBits[i/8] ^ 0x40;
                else if (i % 8 == 2)
                    bBrushBits[i/8] = bBrushBits[i/8] ^ 0x20;
                else if (i % 8 == 3)
```

```
                    bBrushBits[i/8] = bBrushBits[i/8] ^ 0x10;
            else if (i % 8 == 4)
                    bBrushBits[i/8] = bBrushBits[i/8] ^ 0x08;
            else if (i % 8 == 5)
                    bBrushBits[i/8] = bBrushBits[i/8] ^ 0x04;
            else if (i % 8 == 6)
                    bBrushBits[i/8] = bBrushBits[i/8] ^ 0x02;
            else if (i % 8 == 7)
                    bBrushBits[i/8] = bBrushBits[i/8] ^ 0x01;

            /* Exit the "for" loop after the bit is set. */

                break;
            } /* end if */

        } /* end for */

    } /* end if */

    /* Release the DC for the control. */

    ReleaseDC(hwndGrid, hdc);
    return TRUE;


case WM_COMMAND:
    switch (wParam){
        case IDD_PAINTRECT:

            hdc = GetDC(hwndBrush);

            /* Create a monochrome bitmap. */

            hbm = CreateBitmap(8, 8, 1, 1,
                    (LPBYTE)bBrushBits);

            /* Select the custom brush into the DC. */

            hbrush = CreatePatternBrush(hbm);

            hbrushOld = SelectObject(hdc, hbrush);

            /* Use the custom brush to fill the rectangle. */

            Rectangle(hdc, rctBrush.left, rctBrush.top,
                    rctBrush.right, rctBrush.bottom);

            /* Clean up memory. */
            SelectObject(hdc, hbrushOld);
            DeleteObject(hbrush);
```

```
                        DeleteObject(hbm);

                        ReleaseDC(hwndBrush, hdc);
                     return TRUE;

                case IDD_OK:

                case IDD_CANCEL:
                        EndDialog(hdlg, TRUE);
                        return TRUE;

            } /* end switch */
            break;
        default:
            return FALSE;
        }
}


int GetStrLngth(LPTSTR cArray)
{
    int i = 0;

    while (cArray[i++] != 0);
    return i-1;

}

DWORD RetrieveWidth(LPTSTR cArray, int iLength)
{
    int i, iTmp;
    double dVal, dCount;

    dVal = 0.0;
    dCount = (double)(iLength-1);
    for (i=0; i<iLength; i++){
        iTmp = cArray[i] - 0x30;
        dVal = dVal + (((double)iTmp) * pow(10.0, dCount--));
    }

    return (DWORD)dVal;
}
```

The dialog box procedure for the Custom Brush dialog box processes four messages, as described in the following table.

Message	Action
WM_INITDIALOG	Retrieves a window handle and dimensions for the grid-window and pattern-brush controls, computes the dimensions of a single cell in the grid-window control, and initializes an array of grid-cell coordinates.
WM_PAINT	Draws the grid pattern in the grid-window control.
WM_LBUTTONDOWN	Determines whether the cursor is within the grid-window control when the user presses the left mouse button. If so, the dialog box procedure inverts the appropriate grid cell and records the state of that cell in an array of bits that is used to create the bitmap for the custom brush.
WM_COMMAND	Processes input for the three push button controls. If the user presses the Test Pattern button, the dialog box procedure paints the Test Pattern control with the new custom brush pattern. If the user presses the OK or Cancel button, the dialog box procedure performs actions accordingly.

For more information about messages and message processing, see Chapter 2, "Messages and Message Queues."

After you write the dialog box procedure, export it in the module-definition file, include the function definition for the procedure in the application's header file, and then call the dialog box procedure at the appropriate point in the application.

The following excerpt from the module-definition file shows how the dialog box procedure for the Custom Brush is exported.

```
; Export all functions that are called by a Windows routine.

EXPORTS
        MainWndProc   @1    ; name of window processing function
        BrushDlgProc  @2    ; name of custom-brush processing function
```

The following excerpt from the application's header file shows the function definition for the dialog box procedure and the two functions it calls.

```
int APIENTRY BrushDlgProc(HWND hdlg, WORD message, LONG wParam,
            LONG lParam);
int GetStrLngth(LPTSTR cArray);
DWORD RetrieveWidth(LPTSTR cArray, int iLength);
```

Finally, the following code shows how the dialog box procedure is called from the application's source-code file. In this example, the dialog box procedure is called when the user chooses an option from the application's menu.

```
switch (message) {
    case WM_CREATE:
```

```
                    break;
            case WM_COMMAND: /* message: command from application menu */
                switch(wParam) {

                    case IDM_CUSTOMBRUSH:
                            DialogBox((HANDLE)GetModuleHandle(NULL),
                            (LPTSTR)"CustBrush", hWnd,
                            (DLGPROC)BrushDlgProc);
                        break;
```

30.3 Functions

Following are the functions that can be used with brushes.

CreateBrushIndirect
CreateDIBPatternBrush
CreateDIBPatternBrushPt
CreateHatchBrush
CreatePatternBrush
CreateSolidBrush
GetBrushOrgEx
GetStockObject
SetBrushOrgEx

CHAPTER 31

Pens

31.1 About Pens

A pen is a graphics tools that an application for Microsoft ® Windows ™ uses to draw lines and curves. Drawing applications use pens to draw freehand lines, straight lines, and curves. Computer-aided design (CAD) applications use pens to draw visible lines, hidden lines, section lines, center lines, and so on. Word processing and desktop publishing applications use pens to draw borders and rules. Spreadsheet applications use pens to designate trends in graphs and to outline bar graphs and pie charts.

There are two types of pens: cosmetic and geometric. A *cosmetic pen* is used with applications requiring lines of fixed width and lines that are quickly drawn. A CAD application, for example, uses a cosmetic pen to generate hidden, section, center, and dimension lines that are between .015 and .022 inches wide—regardless of the scale factor. A *geometric pen* is used with applications requiring scalable lines, lines with unique end or join styles, and lines that are wider than a single pixel. A spreadsheet application, for example, uses a geometric pen to define each of the bars in a bar graph as a wide line.

31.1.1 Cosmetic Pens

The dimensions of a cosmetic pen are specified in device units. Therefore, lines drawn with a cosmetic pen always have a fixed width. Lines drawn with a cosmetic pen are generally drawn three to ten times faster than lines drawn with a geometric pen. Cosmetic pens have three attributes: width, style, and color. For more information about these attributes, see Section 31.1.3, "Pen Attributes."

To create a cosmetic pen, an application uses the **CreatePen**, **CreatePenIndirect**, or **ExtCreatePen** function. To retrieve one of the three *stock* cosmetic pens managed by window manager, the application uses the **GetStockObject** function.

After a pen is created (or a handle identifying one of the stock pens is obtained), the pen is selected into the application's device context by calling the **SelectObject** function. From this point on, the application uses this pen for any line-drawing operations in its client area.

31.1.2 Geometric Pens

The dimensions of a geometric pen are specified in logical units. Therefore, lines drawn with a geometric pen can be scaled—that is, they may appear wider or narrower, depending on the current world transformation. For more information about the world transformation, see Chapter 39, "Coordinate Spaces and Transformations."

In addition to the three attributes shared with cosmetic pens (width, style, and color), geometric pens possess the following four attributes: pattern, optional hatch, end style, and join style. For more information about these attributes, see Section 31.1.3, "Pen Attributes."

To create a geometric pen, an application uses the **ExtCreatePen** function. As with cosmetic pens, the **SelectObject** function selects a geometric pen into the application's device context.

31.1.3 Pen Attributes

There are seven pen attributes that define the type of pen and its characteristics: width, style, color, pattern, hatch, end style, and join style. Both cosmetic and geometric pens have the width, style, and color attributes. Only geometric pens have the pattern, hatch, end style, and join style attributes. The pattern and optional hatch attribute are usually associated with a brush, but can also be used with geometric pens.

31.1.3.1 Width

The width attribute specifies a cosmetic pen width in device units. When used with a geometric pen, however, it specifies the pen's width in logical units. For more information about device units, see Chapter 39, "Coordinate Spaces and Transformations."

Currently, Windows limits the width of cosmetic pens to a single pixel; however, future versions may remove this limitation.

31.1.3.2 Style

The style attribute specifies the line pattern that appears when a particular cosmetic or geometric pen is used. There are eight predefined pen styles. The following illustration shows the seven of these styles that are defined by Windows.

Solid	————————————————————
Dash	- -
Dot	··
Dash-Dot	– · – · – · – · – · – · – · – · – · – · –
Dash-Dot-Dot	– · · – · · – · · – · · – · · – · · – · · –
Null	
Inside-frame	————————————————————

The inside-frame style is identical to the solid style for cosmetic pens. However, it operates differently when used with a geometric pen. If the geometric pen is wider than a single pixel and a drawing function uses the pen to draw a border around a filled object, Windows draws the border *inside* the object's frame. By using the inside-frame style, an application can ensure that an object appears entirely within the specified dimensions, regardless of the geometric pen width.

In addition to the seven styles defined by Windows, there is an eighth style that is user (or application) defined. A user-defined style generates lines with a customized series of dashes and dots.

Use the **CreatePen**, **CreatePenIndirect**, or **ExtCreatePen** function to create a pen that has the Windows-defined styles. Use the **ExtCreatePen** function to create a pen that has a user-defined style.

31.1.3.3 Color

The color attribute specifies the pen's color. An application can create a cosmetic pen with a unique color by storing the red, green, blue (RGB) triplet that specifies the desired color in a **COLORREF** structure and passing this structure's address to the **CreatePen**, **CreatePenIndirect**, or **ExtCreatePen** function. (The stock pens are limited to black, white, and invisible.) For more information about RGB triplets and color, see Chapter 36, "Colors."

31.1.3.4 Pattern

The pattern attribute specifies the pattern of a geometric pen.

The following illustration shows lines drawn with different geometric pens. Each pen was created using a different pattern attribute.

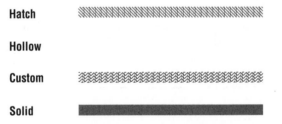

Hatch	
Hollow	
Custom	
Solid	

The first line in the previous illustration is drawn using one of the six available hatch patterns; for more information about hatch patterns, see Section 31.1.3.5, "Hatch." The next line is drawn using the hollow pattern, identical to the null pattern. The third line is drawn using a custom pattern created from an 8- by 8-pixel bitmap. (For more information about bitmaps and their creation, see Chapter 29, "Bitmaps.") The last line is drawn using a solid pattern. Creating a brush and passing its handle to the **ExtCreatePen** function creates a pattern.

31.1.3.5 Hatch

The hatch attribute specifies the hatch type of a geometric pen with the hatch pattern attribute. There are six patterns available. The following illustration shows lines drawn using different hatch patterns.

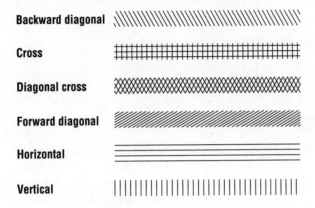

Backward diagonal

Cross

Diagonal cross

Forward diagonal

Horizontal

Vertical

31.1.3.6 End Cap

The *end cap* attribute specifies the shape of a geometric pen: round, square, or flat. The following illustration shows parallel lines drawn using each type of end cap.

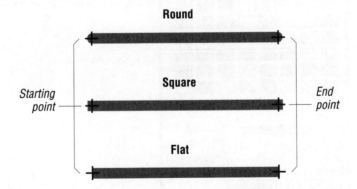

Round

Starting
point

Square

End
point

Flat

The round and square end caps extend past the starting and ending points of a line drawn with a geometric pen; the flat end cap does not.

31.1.3.7 Join

The *join* attribute specifies how the ends of two geometric lines are joined: beveled, mitered, or round. The following illustration shows pairs of connected lines drawn using each type of join.

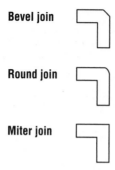

Bevel join

Round join

Miter join

31.2 Using Pens

This section contains example code that demonstrates how to create and use a simple pen selection dialog box. The dialog box is a modified Color common dialog box that enables the user to select a pen color, width, style, and join. For more information about the Color common dialog box, see Chapter 76, "Common Dialog Box Library."

The following illustration shows the modified dialog box.

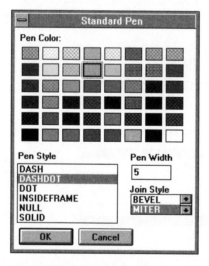

31.2.1 Modifying the Dialog Box Template

To modify the Color common dialog box, it is necessary to modify the dialog box template stored in the file COLOR.DLG. The modifications include changing the coordinates of the custom-colors box and custom-colors button (so that they are drawn outside the dialog box window and are therefore invisible) and adding three new controls. Two of these new controls are list boxes that enable the user to select a style and a join. The third control is an edit box in which the user can specify a pen width (in the range 1 through 99). The following excerpt from the application's resource file shows part of the modified dialog box template.

```
DLGINCLUDE RCDATA DISCARDABLE
BEGIN
     "colordlg.h\0"
END


CHOOSECOLOR DIALOG 2, 0, 298, 184
STYLE DS_MODALFRAME | WS_POPUP | WS_CAPTION | WS_SYSMENU
CAPTION "Standard Pen"
FONT 8, "Helv"
BEGIN
     LTEXT         "Pen Color:", -1, 4, 4, 140, 9
     CONTROL       "", COLOR_BOX1, "Static", SS_SIMPLE | WS_GROUP |
                   WS_TABSTOP, 4, 14, 140, 86
     LTEXT         "&Custom Colors:", -1, 4, 806, 140, 9
     CONTROL       "", COLOR_CUSTOM1, "Static", SS_SIMPLE | WS_GROUP |
                   WS_TABSTOP, 4, 816, 140, 28
     PUSHBUTTON    "&Define Custom Colors...", COLOR_MIX, 4, 850, 140, 14,
                   WS_GROUP
     DEFPUSHBUTTON "OK", IDOK, 4, 166, 44, 14, WS_GROUP
     PUSHBUTTON    "Cancel", IDCANCEL, 52, 166, 44, 14, WS_GROUP
     PUSHBUTTON    "&Help", 1038, 100, 166, 44, 14, WS_GROUP
     CONTROL       "", COLOR_RAINBOW, "Static", SS_BLACKFRAME, 152, 4, 118,
                   116
     CONTROL       "", COLOR_LUMSCROLL, "Static", SS_SIMPLE, 280, 4, 8, 116
     CONTROL       "", COLOR_CURRENT, "Static", SS_BLACKFRAME, 152, 124,
                   40, 26
     RTEXT         "Color|", -1, 152, 151, 20, 9
     LTEXT         "S&olid", -1, 172, 151, 20, 9
     PUSHBUTTON    "&o", COLOR_SOLID, 300, 200, 4, 14, WS_GROUP
     RTEXT         "&Hue:", COLOR_HUEACCEL, 194, 126, 20, 9
     EDITTEXT      COLOR_HUE, 216, 124, 18, 12, WS_GROUP
     RTEXT         "&Sat:", COLOR_SATACCEL, 194, 140, 20, 9
     EDITTEXT      COLOR_SAT, 216, 138, 18, 12, WS_GROUP
     RTEXT         "&Lum:", COLOR_LUMACCEL, 194, 154, 20, 9
     EDITTEXT      COLOR_LUM, 216, 152, 18, 12, WS_GROUP
     RTEXT         "&Red:", COLOR_REDACCEL, 243, 126, 24, 9
     EDITTEXT      COLOR_RED, 269, 124, 18, 12, WS_GROUP
     RTEXT         "&Green:", COLOR_GREENACCEL, 243, 140, 24, 9
     EDITTEXT      COLOR_GREEN, 269, 138, 18, 12, WS_GROUP
     RTEXT         "Bl&ue:", COLOR_BLUEACCEL, 243, 154, 24, 9
     EDITTEXT      COLOR_BLUE, 269, 152, 18, 12, WS_GROUP
     PUSHBUTTON    "&Add to Custom Colors", COLOR_ADD, 152, 166, 142, 14,
                   WS_GROUP
     LISTBOX       101, 3, 113, 80, 52, LBS_SORT | WS_VSCROLL | WS_TABSTOP
     LTEXT         "Pen Style", 102, 3, 102, 57, 10
     LTEXT         "Pen Width", 103, 93, 103, 37, 8
```

```
    EDITTEXT        104, 94, 113, 32, 12, ES_AUTOHSCROLL
    LTEXT           "Join Style", 105, 93, 129, 40, 8
    LISTBOX         106, 94, 138, 48, 24, LBS_SORT | WS_VSCROLL | WS_TABSTOP
END
```

31.2.2 Processing Dialog Box Input

After the dialog box template is modified, it is necessary to provide a callback function that initializes the new controls in the dialog box and processes the corresponding input. The following excerpt from the application's source file shows the callback function.

```
DWORD dwPenStyle;
DWORD dwJoinStyle;
DWORD dwWidth;

UINT FAR PASCAL SetPenAttr(HWND hwndDlg, UINT uMsg, UINT wParam,
                           LONG lParam)
{
    static HWND hwndLineStyles;
    static HWND hwndJoinStyles;
    static HWND hwndWidth;
    DWORD adwPenStyle[] = {
                            PS_DASH,
                            PS_DASHDOT,
                            PS_DOT,
                            PS_INSIDEFRAME,
                            PS_NULL,
                            PS_SOLID
                          };
    DWORD adwJoinStyle[] = {
                            PS_JOIN_BEVEL,
                            PS_JOIN_MITER,
                            PS_JOIN_ROUND
                          };
    CHAR  chWidth[3];
    int iCount;
    int  index;

    switch(uMsg){

        case WM_INITDIALOG:

            /* Initialize each custom control with the required data. */

            hwndLineStyles = GetDlgItem(hwndDlg, IDD_PEN_STYLE);

            /* Use the PenStyle constants as indices. */
```

```
            SendMessage(hwndLineStyles, LB_ADDSTRING, 0,
                      (LONG) "DASH");
            SendMessage(hwndLineStyles, LB_ADDSTRING, 0,
                      (LONG) "DASHDOT");
            SendMessage(hwndLineStyles, LB_ADDSTRING, 0,
                      (LONG) "DOT");
            SendMessage(hwndLineStyles, LB_ADDSTRING, 0,
                      (LONG) "INSIDEFRAME");
            SendMessage(hwndLineStyles, LB_ADDSTRING, 0,
                      (LONG) "NULL");
            SendMessage(hwndLineStyles, LB_ADDSTRING, 0,
                      (LONG) "SOLID");

            hwndJoinStyles = GetDlgItem(hwndDlg, IDD_JOIN_STYLE);

            /* Use the JoinStyle constants as indices. */

            SendMessage(hwndJoinStyles, LB_ADDSTRING, PS_JOIN_BEVEL,
                      (LONG) "BEVEL");
            SendMessage(hwndJoinStyles, LB_ADDSTRING, PS_JOIN_MITER,
                      (LONG) "MITER");
            SendMessage(hwndJoinStyles, LB_ADDSTRING, PS_JOIN_ROUND,
                      (LONG) "ROUND");

            hwndWidth = GetDlgItem(hwndDlg, IDD_PEN_WIDTH);
            SetWindowText(hwndWidth, (LPTSTR)"1");

        return TRUE;

        case WM_COMMAND:

            /* Retrieve the requested pen style. */

            index = SendMessage(hwndLineStyles, LB_GETCURSEL, 0, 0L);
            dwPenStyle = adwPenStyle[index];

            /* Retrieve the requested join style. */

            index = SendMessage(hwndJoinStyles, LB_GETCURSEL, 0, 0L);
            dwJoinStyle = adwJoinStyle[index];

            /* Retrieve the requested width. */

            GetDlgItemText(hwndDlg, IDD_PEN_WIDTH, chWidth, 3);
            dwWidth = RetrieveWidth(chWidth, GetStrLngth(chWidth));

        return FALSE;
    }
    return FALSE;
```

```
    UNREFERENCED_PARAMETER(wParam);
    UNREFERENCED_PARAMETER(lParam);
    UNREFERENCED_PARAMETER(iCount);
}
```

You must register the callback function with the common dialog box procedure by initializing the appropriate members of a **CHOOSECOLOR** structure, which is passed to the **ChooseColor** function. The following excerpt from the application's source file shows how this can be done.

```
static CHOOSECOLOR cc; /* structure required for Color dialog box */
static COLORREF clr;
static COLORREF aclrCust[256];

                /*
                 * Initialize the necessary CHOOSECOLOR
                 * members.
                 */

                cc.lStructSize = sizeof(CHOOSECOLOR);
                cc.hwndOwner = hwnd;
                cc.hInstance = (HWND)hInst;
                cc.rgbResult = clr;
                cc.lpCustColors = aclrCust;
                cc.Flags =  CC_ENABLEHOOK | CC_ENABLETEMPLATE;
                cc.lpfnHook = (LPCCHOOKPROC)SetPenAttr;
                cc.lpTemplateName = "CHOOSECOLOR";
```

After the **ChooseColor** function executes, the **rgbResult** member of the **CHOOSECOLOR** structure contains the user-requested color, the *dwPenStyle* parameter specifies the requested pen style, the *dwJoinStyle* parameter specifies the requested join, and the *dwWidth* parameter specifies the requested width. These values are passed to the **ExtCreatePen** function and used to create a geometric pen, which is selected into a device context and used for various line-drawing operations.

```
if (ChooseColor(&cc)){

    hdc = GetDC(hwnd);

    /* Initialize the pen's "brush." */

    logbrush.lbStyle = BS_SOLID;
    logbrush.lbColor = cc.rgbResult;
    logbrush.lbHatch = 0;

    /* Create a pen and select it into the DC. */

    hpenOld = SelectObject(hdc,
```

```
ExtCreatePen(PS_GEOMETRIC | dwPenStyle
             | dwJoinStyle, dwWidth,
             &logbrush, (DWORD) NULL,
             (LPDWORD) NULL));

/* Perform drawing operations. */

MoveToEx(hdc, 100, 100, NULL);
LineTo(hdc, 100, 200);
LineTo(hdc, 200, 200);
LineTo(hdc, 200, 100);
LineTo(hdc, 100, 100);

ReleaseDC(hwnd, hdc);
}
```

For more information about customizing common dialog boxes, see Chapter 76, "Common Dialog Box Library."

31.3 Functions

Following are the functions that support the pen interface.

CreatePen
CreatePenIndirect
ExtCreatePen
GetStockObject

C H A P T E R   3 2

Regions

32.1 About Regions

In Microsoft ® Windows ™, a *region* is a rectangle, polygon, or ellipse (or a combination of two or more of these shapes) that can be filled, painted, inverted, framed, and used to perform hit testing (testing for the cursor location).

Following are three types of regions that have been filled and framed.

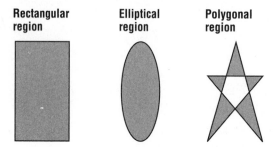

Rectangular region   Elliptical region   Polygonal region

32.1.1 Region Creation and Selection

An application creates a region by calling a function associated with a specific shape. The following table shows the function(s) associated with each of the standard shapes.

Shape	Function
Rectangular region	**CreateRectRgn**, **CreateRectRgnIndirect**
Rectangular region with rounded corners	**CreateRoundRectRgn**
Elliptical region	**CreateEllipticRgn**, **CreateEllipticRgnIndirect**
Polygonal region	**CreatePolygonRgn**, **CreatePolygonRgnIndirect**

Each region-creation function returns a handle that identifies the new region. An application can use this handle of select the region into a device context by calling the **SelectObject** function and supplying this handle as the second argument. After a region is selected into a device context, an application can perform various operations on it.

32.1.2 Region Operations

Applications can combine regions, compare them, paint or invert their interiors, draw a frame around them, retrieve their dimensions, and test to see whether the cursor lies within their boundaries.

32.1.2.1 Combining

An application combines two regions by calling the **CombineRgn** function. Using this function, an application can combine the intersecting parts of two regions, all but the intersecting parts of two regions, the two original regions in their entirety, and so on. Following are the five region combinations.

Value	Description
RGN_AND	The intersecting parts of two original regions define a new region.
RGN_COPY	A copy of the first (of the two original regions) defines a new region.
RGN_DIFF	The part of the first region that does not intersect the second defines a new region.
RGN_OR	The two original regions define a new region.
RGN_XOR	Those parts of the two original regions that do not overlap define a new region.

The following illustration shows the five possible combinations of a square and a circular region resulting from a call to the **CombineRgn** function.

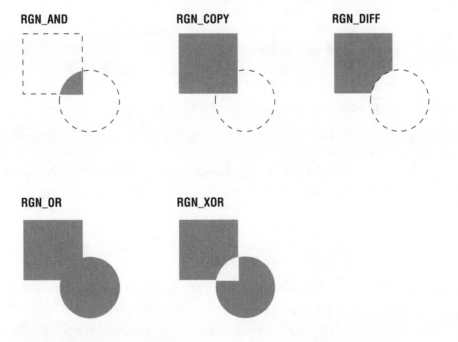

32.1.2.2 Comparing

An application compares two regions to determine whether or not they are identical by calling the **EqualRgn** function. **EqualRgn** considers two regions identical if they are equal in size and shape.

32.1.2.3 Filling

An application fills the interior of a region by calling the **FillRgn** function and supplying a handle that identifies a specific brush. When an application calls **FillRgn**, Windows fills the region with the brush by using the current fill mode for the specified device context. There are two fill modes: alternate and winding. The application can set the fill mode for a device context by calling the **SetPolyFillMode** function. An application can retrieve the current fill mode for a device context by calling the **GetPolyFillMode** function.

The following illustration shows two identical regions: one filled using alternate mode, the other filled using winding mode.

Alternate mode   **Winding mode**

Alternate Mode

To determine which pixels Windows highlights when alternate mode is specified, perform the following test:

1. Select a pixel within the region's interior.

2. Draw an imaginary ray, in the positive x-direction, from that pixel towards infinity.

3. Each time the ray intersects a boundary line, increment a count value.

Windows highlights the pixel if the count value is an odd number.

Winding Mode

To determine which pixels Windows highlights when winding mode is specified, perform the following test:

1. Determine the direction in which each boundary line is drawn.

2. Select a pixel within the region's interior.

3. Draw an imaginary ray, in the positive x-direction, from the pixel toward infinity.

4. Each time the ray intersects a boundary line with a positive y-component, increment a count value; each time the ray intersects a boundary line with a negative y-component, decrement the count value.

Windows highlights the pixel if the count value is nonzero.

32.1.2.4 Painting

An application fills the interior of a region by using the brush currently selected into a device context by the **PaintRgn** function. This function uses the current polygon fill modes (alternate and winding).

32.1.2.5 Inverting

An application inverts the colors that appear within a region by calling the **InvertRgn** function. On monochrome displays, the **InvertRgn** function makes white pixels black and black pixels white. On color screens, this inversion is dependent on the type of technology used to generate the colors for the screen.

32.1.2.6 Framing

An application draws a border around a region by calling the **FrameRgn** function and specifying the border width and brush pattern that Windows uses when drawing the frame.

32.1.2.7 Retrieving a Bounding Rectangle

An application retrieves the dimensions of a region's bounding rectangle by calling the **GetRgnBox** function. If the region is rectangular, **GetRgnBox** returns the dimensions of the region. If the region is elliptical, the function returns the dimensions of the smallest rectangle that can be drawn around the ellipse. The long sides of the rectangle are the same length as the ellipse's major axis; the short sides of the rectangle are the same length as the ellipse's minor axis. If the region is polygonal, **GetRgnBox** returns the dimensions of the smallest rectangle that can be drawn around the entire polygon.

32.1.2.8 Moving

An application moves a region by calling the **OffsetRgn** function. The given offsets along the x-axis and y-axis determine the number of logical units to move left or right and up or down.

32.1.2.9 Hit Testing

An application performs hit testing on regions to determine the coordinates of the current cursor position. It then passes these coordinates—as well as a handle identifying the region—to the **PtInRegion** function. The cursor coordinates can be retrieved by processing the various mouse messages such as WM_LBUTTONDOWN, WM_LBUTTONUP, WM_RBUTTONDOWN, WM_RBUTTONUP. The **PtInRegion** return value indicates whether the cursor position is within the given region.

32.2 Using Regions

The examples in this section show how applications can manipulate regions to perform the following tasks:

- Define a clipping region.
- Clip output.
- Perform hit testing.

32.2.1 Using Regions to Clip Output

This section contains a single example that demonstrates how you can use regions to enable the user to define how a part of the client area output can appear. Regions used for this purpose are called clipping regions.

The example for this section is taken from a Windows-based application that enables a user to capture the entire desktop as a bitmap and then isolate and save a part of this image as a .BMP file. The following illustration shows the application's window and client area immediately after the user has captured the desktop contents.

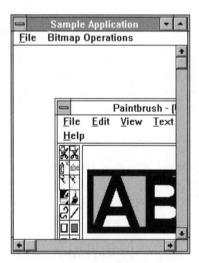

By selecting the Define Clip Region option from the application's menu, the user is able to select a clipping region by clicking the left mouse button and dragging the mouse. As the user drags the mouse, the application draws a rectangle that corresponds to the new clipping region. The following illustration shows the application's window, client area, and the rectangle created by the user.

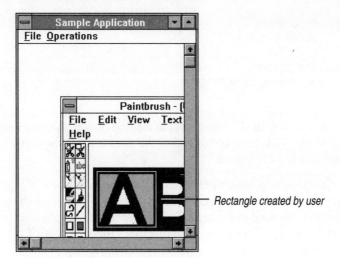

Rectangle created by user

By selecting the Clip option, the user is able to redraw the isolated part of the image within the boundaries of the specified rectangle. The following illustration shows the application's window, the client area, and the clipped output.

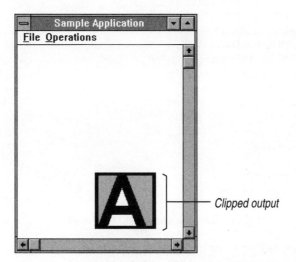

Clipped output

32.2.1.1 Defining the Clipping Region

When the user selects the Define Clip Region option, Windows issues a WM_COMMAND message. The *wParam* parameter of this message contains an application-defined constant, IDM_DEFINE, that indicates that the user selected this option from the menu. The application processes this input by setting a Boolean flag, fDefineRegion, as shown in the following code.

```
case WM_COMMAND:
    switch (wParam) {

case IDM_DEFINE:
    fDefineRegion = TRUE;
break;
```

After selecting the Define Clipping Region option, the user can begin drawing the rectangle by clicking and dragging the mouse while the cursor is in the application's client area.

When the user presses the left button, Windows issues a WM_LBUTTONDOWN message. The *lParam* parameter of this message contains the cursor coordinates, which correspond to the upper left corner of a rectangle used to define the clipping region. The application processes the WM_LBUTTONDOWN message as follows:

```
/* These variables are required for clipping. */

static POINT ptUpperLeft;
static POINT ptLowerRight;
static POINT aptRect[5];
static POINT ptTmp;
static POINTS ptsTmp;
static BOOL fDefineRegion;
static BOOL fRegionExists;
static HRGN hrgn;
static RECT rctTmp;
int i;

switch (message) {

case WM_LBUTTONDOWN:
    if (fDefineRegion) {

        /* Retrieve the new upper left corner. */

        ptsTmp = MAKEPOINTS(lParam);
        ptUpperLeft.x = (LONG) ptsTmp.x;
        ptUpperLeft.y = (LONG) ptsTmp.y;
    }

    if (fRegionExists) {

        /* Erase the previous rectangle. */

        hdc = GetDC(hwnd);
        SetROP2(hdc, R2_NOTXORPEN);
```

```
        if (!Polyline(hdc, (CONST POINT *) aptRect, 5))
            errhandler("Polyline Failed", hwnd);
        ReleaseDC(hwnd, hdc);

        /* Clear the rectangle coordinates. */

        for (i = 0; i < 4; i++) {
                aptRect[i].x = 0;
                aptRect[i].y = 0;
        }

        /* Clear the temporary point structure. */

        ptTmp.x = 0;
        ptTmp.y = 0;

        /* Clear the lower right coordinates. */

        ptLowerRight.x = 0;
        ptLowerRight.y = 0;

        /* Reset the flag. */

        fRegionExists = FALSE;
        fDefineRegion = TRUE;

        /* Retrieve the new upper left corner. */

        ptsTmp = MAKEPOINTS(lParam);
        ptUpperLeft.x = (LONG) ptsTmp.x;
        ptUpperLeft.y = (LONG) ptsTmp.y;
    }
break;
```

As the user drags the mouse, Windows issues WM_MOUSEMOVE messages and
stores the new cursor coordinates in the *lParam* parameter. Each time the
application receives a new WM_MOUSEMOVE message, it erases the previous
rectangle (if one exists) and draws the new rectangle by calling the **Polyline**
function and passing the coordinates of the four corners of the rectangle. The
application performs these tasks as shown in the following example.

```
/* These variables are required for clipping. */

static POINT ptUpperLeft;
static POINT ptLowerRight;
static POINT aptRect[5];
static POINT ptTmp;
static POINTS ptsTmp;
static BOOL fDefineRegion;
```

```
          static BOOL fRegionExists;
          static HRGN hrgn;
          static RECT rctTmp;
          int i;

          switch (message) {

          case WM_MOUSEMOVE:

              if (wParam & MK_LBUTTON && fDefineRegion) {

                  /* Get a window DC. */

                  hdc = GetDC(hwnd);

                  if (!SetROP2(hdc, R2_NOTXORPEN))
                      errhandler("SetROP2 Failed", hwnd);


                  /*
                   * If previous mouse movement occurred, store the original
                   * lower right corner coordinates in a temporary structure.
                   */

                  if (ptLowerRight.x) {
                      ptTmp.x = ptLowerRight.x;
                      ptTmp.y = ptLowerRight.y;
                  }

                  /*
                   * Get the new coordinates of the clipping region's lower
                   * right corner.
                   */

                  ptsTmp = MAKEPOINTS(lParam);
                  ptLowerRight.x = (LONG) ptsTmp.x;
                  ptLowerRight.y = (LONG) ptsTmp.y;


                  /*
                   * If previous mouse movement occurred, erase the original
                   * rectangle.
                   */

                  if (ptTmp.x) {
                      aptRect[0].x = ptUpperLeft.x;
                      aptRect[0].y = ptUpperLeft.y;
                      aptRect[1].x = ptTmp.x;
                      aptRect[1].y = ptUpperLeft.y;
                      aptRect[2].x = ptTmp.x;
```

```
                    aptRect[2].y = ptTmp.y;
                    aptRect[3].x = ptUpperLeft.x;
                    aptRect[3].y = ptTmp.y;
                    aptRect[4].x = aptRect[0].x;
                    aptRect[4].y = aptRect[0].y;

                    if (!Polyline(hdc, (CONST POINT *) aptRect, 5))
                        errhandler("Polyline Failed", hwnd);
                }

                aptRect[0].x = ptUpperLeft.x;
                aptRect[0].y = ptUpperLeft.y;
                aptRect[1].x = ptLowerRight.x;
                aptRect[1].y = ptUpperLeft.y;
                aptRect[2].x = ptLowerRight.x;
                aptRect[2].y = ptLowerRight.y;
                aptRect[3].x = ptUpperLeft.x;
                aptRect[3].y = ptLowerRight.y;
                aptRect[4].x = aptRect[0].x;
                aptRect[4].y = aptRect[0].y;

                if (!Polyline(hdc, (CONST POINT *) aptRect, 5))
                    errhandler("Polyline Failed", hwnd);

                ReleaseDC(hwnd, hdc);
            }
        break;
```

32.2.1.2 Clipping Output

After the user chooses the Clip option from the menu, the application uses the coordinates of the rectangle the user created to define a clipping region. After defining the clipping region and selecting it into the application's device context, the application redraws the bitmapped image. The application performs these tasks as shown in the following example.

```
/* These variables are required for clipping. */

static POINT ptUpperLeft;
static POINT ptLowerRight;
static POINT aptRect[5];
static POINT ptTmp;
static POINTS ptsTmp;
static BOOL fDefineRegion;
static BOOL fRegionExists;
static HRGN hrgn;
static RECT rctTmp;
int i;
```

```
case WM_COMMAND:
    switch (wParam) {

case IDM_CLIP:

    hdc = GetDC(hwnd);

    /*
     * Retrieve the application's client rectangle and paint
     * with the default (white) brush.
     */

    GetClientRect(hwnd, &rctTmp);
    FillRect(hdc, &rctTmp, GetStockObject(WHITE_BRUSH));

    /* Use the rectangle coordinates to define a clipping region. */

    hrgn = CreateRectRgn(aptRect[0].x, aptRect[0].y,
        aptRect[2].x, aptRect[2].y);
    SelectClipRgn(hdc, hrgn);

    /* Transfer (draw) the bitmap into the clipped rectangle. */

    BitBlt(hdc,
        0, 0,
        bmp.bmWidth, bmp.bmHeight,
        hdcCompatible,
        0, 0,
        SRCCOPY);

    ReleaseDC(hwnd, hdc);
break;
```

32.2.2 Using Regions to Perform Hit Testing

The example in Chapter 30, "Brushes," uses regions to simulate a "zoomed" view of an 8- by 8-pixel monochrome bitmap. By clicking on the pixels in this bitmap, the user creates a custom brush suitable for drawing operations. This example shows how to use the **PtInRegion** function to perform hit testing and the **InvertRgn** function to invert the colors in a region.

32.3 Functions

Following are the functions used with regions.

CombineRgn
CreateEllipticRgn
CreateEllipticRgnIndirect
CreatePolygonRgn
CreatePolyPolygonRgn
CreateRectRgn
CreateRectRgnIndirect
CreateRoundRectRgn
EqualRgn
ExtCreateRegion
FillRgn
FrameRgn
GetPolyFillMode
GetRgnBox
GetRegionData
InvertRgn
OffsetRgn
PaintRgn
PtInRegion
RectInRegion
SetPolyFillMode

C H A P T E R   3 3

Lines and Curves

33.1 About Lines and Curves

All types of applications written for Microsoft ® Windows ™ use lines and curves to draw graphics output on raster devices. Computer-aided design (CAD) and drawing applications use lines and curves to outline objects, specify the centers of objects, the dimensions of objects, and so on. Spreadsheet applications use lines and curves to draw grids, charts, and graphs. Word processing applications use lines to create rules and borders on a page of text.

33.1.1 Lines

A *line* is a set of highlighted pixels on a raster display (or a set of dots on a printed page) identified by two points: a starting point and an ending point. In Windows, the pixel located at the starting point is always included in the line, and the pixel located at the ending point is always excluded (these lines are sometimes called inclusive-exclusive).

When an application calls one of the Windows line-drawing functions, the graphics device interface (GDI), or in some cases a device driver, determines which pixels should be highlighted. *GDI* is a dynamic-link library that processes graphics function calls from a Windows-based application and passes those calls to a device driver. A *device driver* is a dynamic-link library that receives input from GDI, converts the input to device commands, and passes these commands to the appropriate device. GDI uses a digital differential analyzer (DDA) to determine the set of pixels that define a line. A *DDA* determines the set of pixels by examining each point on the line and identifying those pixels on the display surface (or dots on a printed page) that correspond to these points. The following illustration shows a line, its starting point, its ending point, and the pixels highlighted by using a simple DDA.

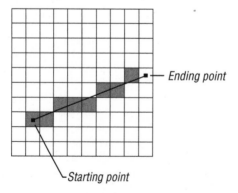

Ending point

Starting point

The simplest and most common DDA is the Bresenham, or incremental DDA. A modified version of this algorithm draws lines in Windows versions 3.*x*. The incremental DDA is noted for its simplicity, but it is also noted for its inaccuracy;

because it rounds off to the nearest integer value, it sometimes fails to represent the original line requested by the application. The DDA used by the new GDI does *not* round off to the nearest integer. As a result, it produces output that is sometimes much closer in appearance to the original line requested by the application.

Note If an application requires line output that cannot be achieved with the new Win32 DDA, it can draw its own lines by calling the **LineDDA** function and supplying a private DDA. However, the **LineDDA** function draws lines much slower than the Windows line-drawing functions; do *not* use this function within an application if speed is a primary concern.

An application can use the new Win32 DDA to draw single lines and multiple, connected line segments. An application can draw a single line by calling the **LineTo** function. This function draws a line from a device context's current position to a specified ending point. An application can draw a series of connected line segments by calling the **Polyline** function, supplying an array of points that specify the ending point of each line segment. An application can draw multiple, disjointed series of connected line segments by calling the **PolyPolyline** function, supplying the required ending points.

The following illustration shows line output created by calling the **LineTo**, **Polyline**, and **PolyPolyline** functions.

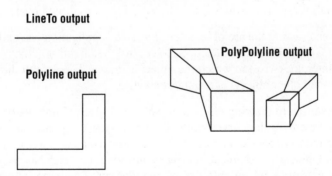

33.1.2 Curves

A *regular curve* is a set of highlighted pixels on a raster display (or dots on a printed page) that define the perimeter (or part of the perimeter) of a conic section. An *irregular curve* is a set of pixels that define a curve that does not fit the perimeter of a conic section. In Windows, the ending point is excluded from a curve just as it is excluded from a line.

When an application calls one of the Windows curve-drawing functions, GDI breaks the curve into a number of extremely small, discrete line segments. After determining the ending points for each of these line segments, GDI determines which pixels (or dots) define each line by applying its DDA.

An application can draw an ellipse or part of an ellipse by calling the **Arc** function. This function draws the curve within the perimeter of an invisible rectangle called a bounding rectangle. The size of the ellipse is specified by two invisible radials extending from the center of the rectangle to the sides of the rectangle. The following illustration shows an arc (part of an ellipse) drawn using the **Arc** function.

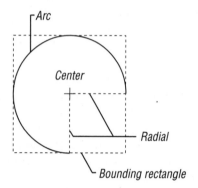

When calling the **Arc** function, an application specifies the coordinates of the bounding rectangle and radials. The preceding illustration shows the rectangle and radials with dashed lines while the actual arc was drawn using a solid line.

When drawing the arc of another object, the application can call the **SetArcDirect** and **GetArcDirection** functions to control the direction (clockwise, counterclockwise) in which the object is drawn. The default direction for drawing arcs and other objects is counterclockwise.

In addition to drawing ellipses or parts of ellipses, Windows-based applications can draw irregular curves called Bézier splines. Originally, the term spline referred to a tool used by draftsmen to draw irregular curves. With the development of graphical interfaces, however, the term has come to refer to the curve itself. A *Bézier spline* is an irregular curve with the following characteristics: The curvature of the spline is defined by four control points (*p1*, *p2*, *p3*, and *p4*). The control points *p1* and *p4* define the starting and ending points of the curve; the control points *p2* and *p3* define the shape of the curve by marking points where the curve reverses orientation. The following illustration shows two Bézier splines, their starting and ending points, and control points.

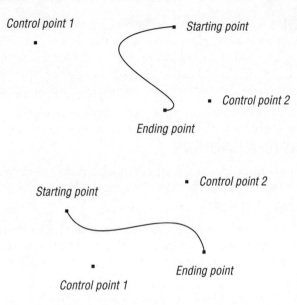

An application can draw irregular curves by calling the **PolyBezier** function, supplying the appropriate control points.

33.1.3 Combined Lines and Curves

In addition to drawing lines *or* curves, Windows-based applications can draw combinations of line and curve output by calling a single function. For example, an application can draw the outline of a pie chart by calling the **AngleArc** function, as shown in the following illustration.

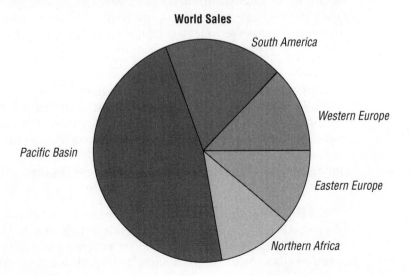

The **AngleArc** function draws an arc along a circle's perimeter and draws a line connecting the starting point of the arc to the circle's center. The pie chart in the preceding illustration was created by calling the **AngleArc** function five consecutive times. In addition to using the **AngleArc** function, a Windows-based application could also combine line and irregular curve output by using the **PolyDraw** function.

33.1.4 Line and Curve Attributes

A device context contains attributes that affect line and curve output. These attributes include current position, brush style, brush color, pen style, pen color, transformation, and so on.

The default current position for any device context is located at the point (0,0) in logical (or world) space. You can set these coordinates to a new position by calling the **MoveToEx** function and passing a new set of coordinates.

Note Windows provides two sets of line- and curve-drawing functions: the first set retains the current position in a device context; the second set alters the position. You can identify the functions that alter the current position by examining the function name. If the function name ends with the preposition "To", the function sets the current position to the ending point of the last line drawn (**LineTo**, **ArcTo**, **PolylineTo**, or **PolyBezierTo**). If the function name does not end with this preposition, it leaves the current position intact (**Arc**, **Polyline**, **PolyBezier**).

The default brush is a solid white brush. An application can create a new brush by calling the **CreateBrushIndirect** function. After creating a brush, your application can select it into its device context by calling the **SelectObject** function. Windows provides a complete set of functions to create, select, and alter the brush in your application's device context. For more information about these functions and about brushes in general, see Chapter 30, "Brushes."

The default pen is a cosmetic, solid black pen that is one pixel wide. The application can create a pen by using the **ExtCreatePen** function. After creating a pen, your application can select it into its device context by calling the **SelectObject** function. Windows provides a complete set of functions to create, select, and alter the pen in your application's device context. For more information about these functions and about pens in general, see Chapter 31, "Pens."

The default transformation is the unity transformation (specified by the identity matrix). An application can specify a new transformation by calling the **SetWorldTransform** function. Windows provides a complete set of functions to transform lines and curves by altering their width, location, and general appearance. For more information about these functions, see Chapter 39, "Coordinate Spaces and Transformations."

33.2 Using Lines and Curves

You can use the line and curve functions to draw virtually any shape or object in the client area of the application window. This section contains two code samples that illustrate how these functions might be used.

33.2.1 Drawing Markers

You can use the line functions to draw markers. A marker is a symbol centered over a point. Drawing applications use markers to designate starting points, ending points, and control points. Spreadsheet applications use markers to designate points of interest on a chart or graph. The following illustration shows a screen from a drawing application that uses markers to designate the ending points and control points for a Bézier spline.

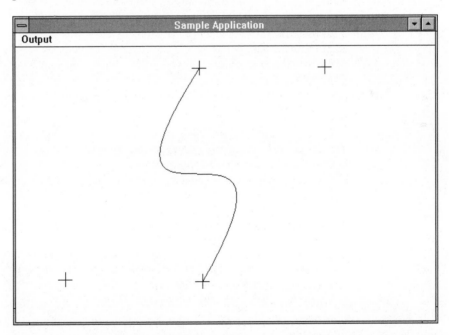

In the following code sample, the application-defined Marker function creates a marker by using the **MoveToEx** and **LineTo** functions. These functions draw two intersecting lines, 20 pixels in length, centered over the cursor coordinates.

```
void Marker(LONG x, LONG y, HWND hwnd)
{
    HDC hdc;

    hdc = GetDC(hwnd);
        MoveToEx(hdc, (int) x - 10, (int) y, (LPPOINT) NULL);
        LineTo(hdc, (int) x + 10, (int) y);
        MoveToEx(hdc, (int) x, (int) y - 10, (LPPOINT) NULL);
        LineTo(hdc, (int) x, (int) y + 10);
    ReleaseDC(hwnd, hdc);
}
```

Windows stores the coordinates of the cursor in the *lParam* parameter of the
WM_LBUTTONDOWN message when the user presses the left mouse button.
The following code demonstrates how an application gets these coordinates,
determines whether they lie within its client area, and passes them to the Marker
function to draw the marker.

```
/* Line- and arc-drawing variables */

static BOOL bCollectPoints;
static POINT ptMouseDown[32];
static int index;
POINTS ptTmp;
RECT rc;

    case WM_LBUTTONDOWN:


        if (bCollectPoints && index < 32){

            /* Create the region from the client area. */

            GetClientRect(hwnd, &rc);
            hrgn = CreateRectRgn(rc.left, rc.top,
                rc.right, rc.bottom);

            ptTmp = MAKEPOINTS((POINTS FAR *) lParam);
            ptMouseDown[index].x = (LONG) ptTmp.x;
            ptMouseDown[index].y = (LONG) ptTmp.y;

            /* Test for a hit in the client rectangle. */

            if (PtInRegion(hrgn, ptMouseDown[index].x,
                    ptMouseDown[index].y)) {


                /* If a hit occurs, record the mouse coordinates. */
```

```
                        Marker(ptMouseDown[index].x, ptMouseDown[index].y,
                            hwnd);
                        index++;
                }
        }
        break;
```

33.2.2 Drawing a Pie Chart

You can use the line and curve functions to draw a pie chart. The primary function used to draw pie charts is the **AngleArc** function, which requires you to supply the coordinates of the center of the pie, the radius of the pie, a start angle, and a sweep angle. Following is a dialog box that the user can use to enter these values.

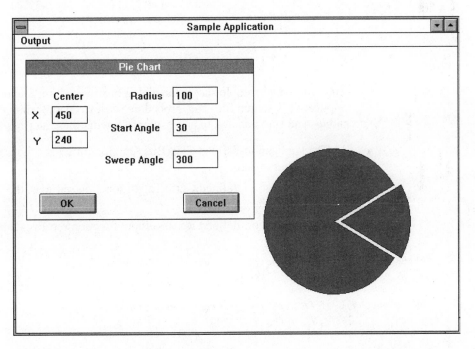

LEFT

The following example shows the dialog box template found in the application's resource script (.RC) file. This template specifies characteristics of the preceding dialog box (its height, the controls it contains, and its style).

```
AngleArc DIALOG 6, 18, 160, 100
STYLE WS_DLGFRAME | WS_POPUP | WS_VISIBLE | WS_CAPTION
CAPTION "Pie Chart"
FONT 8, "MS Sans Serif"
BEGIN
    EDITTEXT        IDD_X, 18, 22, 25, 12, ES_AUTOHSCROLL
    LTEXT           "X", 102, 4, 24, 9, 8
    EDITTEXT        IDD_Y, 18, 39, 25, 12, ES_AUTOHSCROLL
    LTEXT           "Y", 104, 5, 42, 12, 8
    LTEXT           "Center", 105, 19, 11, 23, 8
    EDITTEXT        IDD_RADIUS, 103, 9, 32, 12, ES_AUTOHSCROLL
    EDITTEXT        IDD_STARTANGLE, 103, 31, 32, 12, ES_AUTOHSCROLL
    EDITTEXT        IDD_SWEEPANGLE, 103, 53, 32, 12, ES_AUTOHSCROLL
    LTEXT           "Radius", 109, 73, 11, 25, 8
    LTEXT           "Start Angle", 110, 59, 33, 42, 8
    LTEXT           "Sweep Angle", 111, 55, 55, 43, 8
    PUSHBUTTON      "OK", IDD_OK, 9, 82, 40, 14
    PUSHBUTTON      "Cancel", IDD_CANCEL, 110, 82, 40, 14
END
```

The following example shows the dialog box procedure, found in the
application's source file. This procedure retrieves data (center coordinates, arc
radius, and start and sweep angles) by following these steps:

1. The application-defined ClearBits function initializes the array receiving the
   user-input to zero.

2. The application-defined GetStrLngth function retrieves the length of the string
   entered by the user.

3. The application-defined RetrieveInput function retrieves the value entered by
   the user.

```
BOOL CALLBACK ArcDlgProc(HWND hdlg, UINT uMsg, WPARAM wParam,
                    LPARAM lParam)
{
    CHAR chInput[4];    /* receives control-window input   */
    int cch;            /* array-size and count variable   */

    switch (uMsg) {
        case WM_INITDIALOG:
            return FALSE;

        case WM_COMMAND:
            switch (wParam){


                /*
                 * If the user pressed the OK button, retrieve the
                 * data that was entered in the various AngleArc
```

```
 * controls.
 */

case IDD_OK:

    /*
     * Retrieve the x-coordinate of the arc's
     * center.
     */

    ClearBits(chInput, sizeof(chInput));
    GetDlgItemText(hdlg, IDD_X, chInput,
        sizeof(chInput));
    cch = GetStrLngth(chInput);
    nX = (int)RetrieveInput(chInput, cch);

    /*
     * Retrieve the y-coordinate of the arc's
     * center.
     */

    ClearBits(chInput, sizeof(chInput));
    GetDlgItemText(hdlg, IDD_Y, chInput,
        sizeof(chInput));
    cch = GetStrLngth(chInput);
    nY = (int)RetrieveInput(chInput, cch);

    /* Retrieve the radius of the arc. */

    ClearBits(chInput, sizeof(chInput));
    GetDlgItemText(hdlg, IDD_RADIUS, chInput,
        sizeof(chInput));
    cch = GetStrLngth(chInput);
    dwRadius = (DWORD) RetrieveInput(chInput, cch);

    /* Retrieve the start angle. */

    ClearBits(chInput, sizeof(chInput));
    GetDlgItemText(hdlg, IDD_STARTANGLE, chInput,
        sizeof(chInput));
    cch = GetStrLngth(chInput);
    xStartAngle = (float) RetrieveInput(chInput, cch);

    /* Retrieve the sweep angle. */

    ClearBits(chInput, sizeof(chInput));
    GetDlgItemText(hdlg, IDD_SWEEPANGLE, chInput,
        sizeof(chInput));
    cch = GetStrLngth(chInput);
```

```
                            xSweepAngle = (float) RetrieveInput(chInput, cch);

                            EndDialog(hdlg, FALSE);
                            return TRUE;

                    /*
                     * If user presses the CANCEL button, close the
                     * dialog box.
                     */

                    case IDD_CANCEL:
                            EndDialog(hdlg, FALSE);
                            return TRUE;
                } /* end switch (wParam) */

                break;

        default:
            return FALSE;
    } /* end switch (message) */

    UNREFERENCED_PARAMETER(lParam);
}


void ClearBits(LPTSTR cArray, int iLength)
{
    int i;

    for (i = 0; i < iLength; i++)
        cArray[i] = 0;
}

int GetStrLngth(LPTSTR cArray)
{
    int i = 0;

    while (cArray[i++] != 0);
        return i - 1;
}


DWORD RetrieveInput(LPTSTR cArray, int iLength)
{
    int i, iTmp;
    double dVal, dCount;

    dVal = 0.0;
    dCount = (double) (iLength - 1);
```

```
/* Convert ASCII input to a floating-point value. */

for (i = 0; i < iLength; i++) {
    iTmp = cArray[i] - 0x30;
    dVal = dVal + (((double)iTmp) * pow(10.0, dCount--));
}

return (DWORD) dVal;
}
```

To draw each section of the pie chart, pass the values entered by the user to the **AngleArc** function. To fill the pie chart using the current brush, embed the call to the **AngleArc** function in a path bracket. The following example shows the defined path bracket and the **AngleArc** function call.

```
int nX;
int nY;
DWORD dwRadius;
float xStartAngle;
float xSweepAngle;

    case (IDM_ANGLEARC):

        DialogBox((HINSTANCE) GetModuleHandle (NULL),
                (LPTSTR) "AngleArc",
                hwnd, (DLGPROC) ArcDlgProc);

    hdc = GetDC(hwnd);
        BeginPath(hdc);
            SelectObject(hdc,
                GetStockObject(GRAY_BRUSH));
            MoveToEx(hdc, nX, nY, (LPPOINT) NULL);
            AngleArc(hdc, nX, nY, dwRadius,
                xStartAngle, xSweepAngle);
            LineTo(hdc, nX, nY);
        EndPath(hdc);
    StrokeAndFillPath(hdc);
    ReleaseDC(hwnd, hdc);
    break;
```

33.3 Functions

Following are the functions used with lines and curves.

AngleArc
Arc
ArcTo
GetArcDirection

LineDDA
LineDDAProc
LineTo
MoveToEx
PolyBezier
PolyBezierTo
PolyDraw
Polyline
PolylineTo
PolyPolyline
SetArcDirection

CHAPTER 34

Filled Shapes

34.1 About Filled Shapes

Filled shapes are geometric shapes that are outlined by using the current pen and filled by using the current brush. There are five filled shapes: ellipse, chord, pie, polygon, and rectangle. An application written for Microsoft ® Windows ™ uses filled shapes in a variety of ways. Spreadsheet applications, for example, use filled shapes to construct charts and graphs; drawing and painting applications use filled shapes to allow the user to draw figures and illustrations.

34.1.1 Ellipse

An *ellipse* is a closed curve defined by two fixed points (*f1* and *f2*) such that the sum of the distances (*d1* + *d2*) from any point on the curve to the two fixed points is constant. The following illustration shows an ellipse drawn by using the **Ellipse** function.

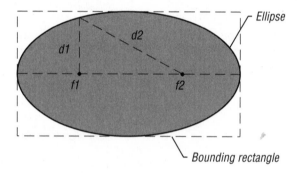

When calling the **Ellipse** function, an application supplies the coordinates of the upper-left and lower-right corners of the ellipse's bounding rectangle. A *bounding rectangle* is the smallest rectangle completely surrounding the ellipse. When Windows draws the ellipse, it excludes the right and lower sides if no world transformations are set. Therefore, for any rectangle measuring *x* units wide by *y* units high, the associated ellipse measures *x*–1 units wide by *y*–1 units high. If the application set a world transformation by calling the **SetWorldTransform** or **ModifyWorldTransform** function, Windows includes the right and lower sides.

34.1.2 Chord

A *chord* is a region bounded by the intersection of an ellipse and a line segment called a secant. The following illustration shows a chord drawn by using the **Chord** function.

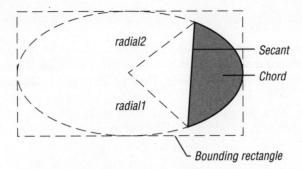

When calling the **Chord** function, an application supplies the coordinates of the upper-left and lower-right corners of the ellipse's bounding rectangle, as well as the coordinates of two points defining two radials. A *radial* is a line drawn from the center of an ellipse's bounding rectangle to a point on the ellipse.

When Windows draws the curved part of the chord, it does so by using the current arc direction for the specified device context. The default arc direction is counterclockwise. You can have your application reset the arc direction by calling the **SetArcDirection** function.

34.1.3 Pie

A *pie* is a region bounded by the intersection of an ellipse curve and two radials. The following illustration shows a pie drawn by using the **Pie** function.

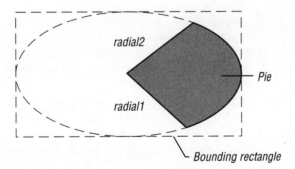

When calling the **Pie** function, an application supplies the coordinates of the upper-left and lower-right corners of the ellipse's bounding rectangle, as well as the coordinates of two points defining two radials.

When Windows draws the curved part of the pie, it uses the current arc direction for the given device context. The default arc direction is counterclockwise. An application can reset the arc direction by calling the **SetArcDirection** function.

34.1.4 Polygon

A *polygon* is a filled shape with straight sides. The sides of a polygon are drawn by using the current pen. When Windows fills a polygon, it uses the current brush and the current polygon fill mode. The two fill modes—alternate (the default) and winding—determine whether regions within a complex polygon are filled or left unpainted. An application can select either mode by calling the **SetPolyFillMode** function. For more information about polygon fill modes, see Chapter 32, "Regions."

The following illustration shows a polygon drawn by using the **Polygon** function.

In addition to drawing a single polygon with the **Polygon** function, an application can draw multiple polygons by using the **PolyPolygon** function.

34.1.5 Rectangle

A rectangle is a four-sided polygon whose opposing sides are parallel and equal in length. Although an application can draw a rectangle by calling the **Polygon** function, supplying the coordinates of each corner, Windows provides a simpler method: the **Rectangle** function. This function requires only the coordinates for the upper-left and the lower-right corners. When an application calls the **Rectangle** function, Windows draws the rectangle, excluding the right and lower sides if no world transformation is set for the given device context.

If a world transformation has been set by using the **SetWorldTransform** or the **ModifyWorldTransform** functions, Windows includes the right and lower edges.

In addition to drawing a normal rectangle, the Win32 application programming interface (API) provides a function that applications can use to draw rectangles with rounded corners. This function, **RoundRect**, requires that the application supply the coordinates of the lower-left and upper-right corners, as well as the width and height of the ellipse used to round each corner.

The Win32 API also provides three functions that applications can use to manipulate rectangles as described in the following table.

Function	Description
FillRect	Repaints the interior of a rectangle.
FrameRect	Redraws the sides of a rectangle.
InvertRect	Inverts the colors that appear within the interior of a rectangle.

34.2 Using Filled Shapes

This section contains a code sample that illustrates how to use filled shape functions. The example uses the main window procedure from an application that enables the user to draw ellipses, rectangles, and rectangles with rounded corners.

The user draws a filled shape by selecting a particular shape from the menu, positioning the cursor at the upper-left corner of the shape (or the shape's bounding rectangle in the case of an ellipse), and then dragging the mouse until the desired dimensions are obtained.

The following illustration shows three filled shapes drawn using the code that follows.

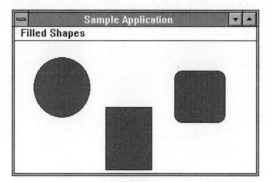

To enable the user to draw filled shapes, include the following code in your application.

```
LRESULT APIENTRY MainWndProc(hwnd, uMsg, wParam, lParam)
HWND hwnd;        /* handle of window          */
UINT uMsg;        /* message                   */
WPARAM wParam;    /* first message parameter   */
LPARAM lParam;    /* second message parameter  */
{
  HDC hdc;                        /* handle of device context (DC)   */
  PAINTSTRUCT ps;                 /* paint data for Begin/EndPaint   */
  POINT ptClientUL;               /* client area upper-left corner   */
```

```
POINT ptClientLR;          /* client area lower-right corner    */
static HDC hdcCompat;      /* handle of DC for copying bitmap    */
static POINT pt;           /* x- and y-coordinates of cursor     */
static RECT rcTarget;      /* rectangle to receive filled shape  */
static RECT rcClient;      /* client area rectangle              */
static BOOL fSizeEllipse;  /* TRUE if ellipse is being sized     */
static BOOL fDrawEllipse;  /* TRUE if ellipse is being drawn     */
static BOOL fDrawRectangle; /* TRUE if rectangle is being drawn   */
static BOOL fSizeRectangle; /* TRUE if rectangle is being sized   */
static BOOL fSizeRoundRect; /* TRUE if rounded rect. is being sized */
static BOOL fDrawRoundRect; /* TRUE if rounded rect. is being drawn */
static int nEllipseWidth;  /* ellipse width for round corners    */
static int nEllipseHeight; /* ellipse height for round corners   */

  switch (uMsg) {

      case WM_COMMAND:
          switch (wParam) {

              /*
               * Set the appropriate flag to indicate which
               * filled shape the user is drawing.
               */

              case IDM_ELLIPSE:
                  fSizeEllipse = TRUE;
              break;

              case IDM_RECTANGLE:
                  fSizeRectangle = TRUE;
              break;

              case IDM_ROUNDRECT:
                  fSizeRoundRect = TRUE;
              break;

              default:
                  return DefWindowProc(hwnd, uMsg, wParam, lParam);
          }
          break;


      case WM_CREATE:

          nEllipseWidth = 20;
          nEllipseHeight = 20;

          return 0;

      case WM_PAINT:
```

```
        BeginPaint(hwnd, &ps);

        /*
         * Because the default brush is white, select
         * a different brush into the device context
         * to demonstrate the painting of filled shapes.
         */

        SelectObject(ps.hdc, GetStockObject(GRAY_BRUSH));

        /*
         * If one of the filled shape "draw" flags is TRUE,
         * draw the corresponding shape.
         */

        if (fDrawEllipse) { /* draws ellipse */
            Ellipse(ps.hdc, rcTarget.left, rcTarget.top,
                rcTarget.right, rcTarget.bottom);
                fDrawEllipse = FALSE;
                rcTarget.left = rcTarget.right = 0;
                rcTarget.top = rcTarget.bottom = 0;
                }

        if (fDrawRectangle) { /* Draws rectangle */
            Rectangle(ps.hdc, rcTarget.left, rcTarget.top,
                rcTarget.right, rcTarget.bottom);
                fDrawRectangle = FALSE;
                rcTarget.left = rcTarget.right = 0;
                rcTarget.top = rcTarget.bottom = 0;
                }

        if (fDrawRoundRect) { /* Draws rounded rectangle */
            RoundRect(ps.hdc, rcTarget.left, rcTarget.top,
                rcTarget.right, rcTarget.bottom,
                nEllipseWidth, nEllipseHeight);
                fDrawRectangle = FALSE;
                rcTarget.left = rcTarget.right = 0;
                rcTarget.top = rcTarget.bottom = 0;
                }

        EndPaint(hwnd, &ps);
        break;

    case WM_SIZE:

        /*
         * Convert the client coordinates of the client area
         * rectangle to screen coordinates and save them in a
```

```
 * rectangle. The rectangle is passed to the ClipCursor
 * function during WM_LBUTTONDOWN processing.
 */

GetClientRect(hwnd, &rcClient);
ptClientUL.x = rcClient.left;
ptClientUL.y = rcClient.top;
ptClientLR.x = rcClient.right;
ptClientLR.y = rcClient.bottom;
ClientToScreen(hwnd, &ptClientUL);
ClientToScreen(hwnd, &ptClientLR);
SetRect(&rcClient, ptClientUL.x, ptClientUL.y,
    ptClientLR.x, ptClientLR.y);
return 0;

case WM_LBUTTONDOWN:

    /*
     * Restrict the cursor to the client area.
     * This ensures that the window receives a matching
     * WM_LBUTTONUP message.
     */

    ClipCursor(&rcClient);

    /* Save the coordinates of the cursor. */

    pt.x = (LONG) LOWORD(lParam);
    pt.y = (LONG) HIWORD(lParam);

    /*
     * If the user chooses one of the filled shapes,
     * set the appropriate flag to indicate that the
     * shape is being sized.
     */

    if (fDrawEllipse)
        fSizeEllipse = TRUE;

    return 0;

case WM_MOUSEMOVE:

    /*
     *
     * If one of the "size" flags is set, draw
     * the target rectangle as the user drags
     * the mouse.
     */
```

```
if ((wParam && MK_LBUTTON)
        && (fSizeEllipse || fSizeRectangle
        || fSizeRoundRect)) {  /* draws target rect. */

    /*
     * Set the mixing mode so that the pen color is the
     * inverse of the background color. The previous
     * rectangle can then be erased by drawing
     * another rectangle on top of it.
     */

    hdc = GetDC(hwnd);
    SetROP2(hdc, R2_NOTXORPEN);

    /*
     * If a previous target rectangle exists, erase
     * it by drawing another rectangle on top.
     */

    if (!IsRectEmpty(&rcTarget))
        Rectangle(hdc, rcTarget.left, rcTarget.top,
            rcTarget.right, rcTarget.bottom);

    /*
     * Save the coordinates of the target rectangle.
     * Avoid invalid rectangles by ensuring that the
     * value of the left coordinate is greater than
     * that of the right, and that the value of the
     * bottom coordinate is greater than that of
     * the top.
     */

    if ((pt.x < (LONG) LOWORD(lParam)) &&
            (pt.y > (LONG) HIWORD(lParam)))
        SetRect(&rcTarget, pt.x, HIWORD(lParam),
            LOWORD(lParam), pt.y);

    else if ((pt.x > (LONG) LOWORD(lParam)) &&
            (pt.y > (LONG) HIWORD(lParam)))
        SetRect(&rcTarget, LOWORD(lParam),
            HIWORD(lParam), pt.x, pt.y);

    else if ((pt.x > (LONG) LOWORD(lParam)) &&
            (pt.y < (LONG) HIWORD(lParam)))
        SetRect(&rcTarget, LOWORD(lParam), pt.y,
            pt.x, HIWORD(lParam));
    else
        SetRect(&rcTarget, pt.x, pt.y, LOWORD(lParam),
            HIWORD(lParam));
```

```
                      /* Draw the new target rectangle. */

                      Rectangle(hdc, rcTarget.left, rcTarget.top,
                          rcTarget.right, rcTarget.bottom);
                      ReleaseDC(hwnd, hdc);
                  }
              return 0;

          case WM_LBUTTONUP:

              /*
               * If one of the "size" flags is TRUE, reset
               * it to FALSE, and then set the corresponding "draw" flag.
               * Invalidate the appropriate rectangle and issue
               * a WM_PAINT message.
               */

              if (fSizeEllipse) {
                  fSizeEllipse = FALSE;
                  fDrawEllipse = TRUE;
                  }

              if (fSizeRectangle) {
                  fSizeRectangle = FALSE;
                  fDrawRectangle = TRUE;
                  }

              if (fSizeRoundRect) {
                  fSizeRoundRect = FALSE;
                  fDrawRoundRect = TRUE;
                  }

              if (fDrawEllipse || fDrawRectangle || fDrawRoundRect) {
                  InvalidateRect(hwnd, &rcTarget, TRUE);
                  UpdateWindow(hwnd);
                  }

              /* Release the cursor. */

              ClipCursor((LPRECT) NULL);
              return 0;

          case WM_DESTROY:

              /*
               * Destroy the background brush, compatible bitmap,
               * and bitmap.
               */

              DeleteDC(hdcCompat);
```

```
                PostQuitMessage(0);
                break;

        default:
                return DefWindowProc(hwnd, uMsg, wParam, lParam);
        }
    return (LRESULT) NULL;
}
```

34.3 Functions

The following functions are used with filled shapes.

Chord
Ellipse
FillRect
FrameRect
InvertRect
Pie
Polygon
PolyPolygon
Rectangle
RoundRect

C H A P T E R 3 5

Fonts and Text

35.1 About Fonts

Fonts are used to draw text on video displays and other output devices. Microsoft ® Windows ™ provides a set of functions that developers can use to install, select, and query different fonts.

To a person trained in the mechanics of manuscript composition or familiar with standard typography, some of the typographic terms used in Windows may be unusual. Most of the differences between standard typography and Windows reflect changes in technology. The original typographic terms were based on hot-metal composition, whereas the terms used in Windows, which appear as member names for the font and text output structures, reflect a new technology based on laser-printer output and composition performed on a personal computer using desktop publishing software.

35.1.1 Fonts

In Windows, a *font* is a collection of characters and symbols that share a common design. The three major elements of this design are referred to as typeface, style, and size.

Typeface

The term *typeface* refers to specific characteristics of characters and symbols in the font such as the width of the thick and thin strokes that compose the characters and the presence or absence of serifs. A *serif* is the short cross line at the ends of an unconnected stroke. A font or typeface without serifs is usually called a sans-serif font.

Style

The term *style* refers to the weight and slant of a font. Font weights can range from thin to black. The following list identifies possible weights for Windows fonts (beginning with the lightest and ending with the heaviest).

Thin
Extralight
Light
Normal
Medium
Semibold
Bold
Extrabold
Heavy

Three terms categorize the slant of a Windows font: roman, oblique, and italic.

The characters in a *roman* font are upright. The characters in an *oblique* font are artificially slanted. The slant is achieved by performing a shear transformation on the characters from a roman font. The characters in an *italic* font are truly slanted and appear as they were designed. For more information on shearing, see Chapter 39, "Coordinate Spaces and Transformations."

Size

In Windows, the *size* of a font is an imprecise value. It can generally be determined by measuring the distance from the bottom of a lowercase "g" to the top of an adjacent uppercase "M," as shown in the following illustration.

A font's size is specified in units called points. A point is .013837 of an inch. Following the point system devised by Pierre Simon Fournier, it is common practice to approximate a point as 1/72 inch.

The following illustration shows characters drawn using two different fonts. The first font, from the Century Gothic ® typeface, measures 20 points and the second font, from the Bookman Old Style ® typeface, measures 20 points. One distinguishing characteristic of the two typefaces is the stroke width: The vertical and horizontal strokes of the Century typeface are of equal width while the vertical strokes of the Bookman typeface are wider than the horizontal strokes. Another distinguishing characteristic is the absence or presence of serifs: the Century typeface does not contain serifs while the Bookman typeface does.

Century Gothic, 20-point type

Bookman Old Style, 20-point type

35.1.2 Font Families

Windows organizes fonts by family; a *family* is a set of fonts having common stroke width and serif characteristics. Windows categorizes families with five family names. A sixth name ("Dontcare") allows an application to use the default font. The following table describes the font-family names.

Font-family name	Description
Decorative	Specifies a novelty font. An example is Old English.
Dontcare	Specifies a generic family name. This name is used when information about a font does not exist or does not matter.
Modern	Specifies a font that is fixed-pitch with or without serifs. Fixed-pitch fonts are usually modern; examples include Pica, Elite, and Courier New ®.
Roman	Specifies a font that is variable pitch, with serifs. An example is Times New Roman.
Script	Specifies a font that is designed to look like handwriting; examples include Script and Cursive.
Swiss	Specifies a font that is fixed-pitch, without serifs. An example is Arial.

These family names correspond to constants found in the WINGDI.H file: FF_DECORATIVE, FF_DONTCARE, FF_MODERN, FF_ROMAN, FF_SCRIPT, and FF_SWISS. An application uses these constants when it creates a font, selects a font, or retrieves information about a font.

Fonts within a family are distinguished by size (10 point, 24 point, etc.) and style (regular, italic, etc.).

35.1.3 Raster, Vector, and TrueType Fonts

Windows-based applications can use three different kinds of font technologies to display and print text: raster, vector, and TrueType. The differences between these fonts reflect the way that the *glyph* for each character or symbol is stored in the respective font-resource file. In raster fonts, a glyph is a bitmap that Windows uses to draw a character or symbol in the font. In vector fonts, a glyph is a collection of line endpoints that define the line segments Windows uses to draw a character or symbol in the font. In TrueType fonts, a glyph is a collection of line and curve commands as well as a collection of hints. Windows uses the line and curve commands to define the outline of the bitmap for a character or symbol in the TrueType font. Windows uses the hints to adjust the length of the lines and shapes of the curves used to draw the character or symbol. These hints and the respective adjustments are based on the amount of scaling used to reduce or increase the size of the bitmap.

Because the bitmaps for each glyph in a raster font are designed for a specific resolution of device, raster fonts are generally considered to be device dependent. Vector fonts, on the other hand, are not device dependent, because each glyph is stored as a collection of scalable lines. However, vector fonts are generally drawn more slowly than raster or TrueType fonts. TrueType fonts provide both relatively fast drawing speed and true device independence. By using the hints associated with a glyph, a developer can scale the characters from a TrueType font up or down and still maintain their original shape.

As previously mentioned, the glyphs for a font are stored in a font-resource file. A font-resource file is actually a Windows library that contains only data—there is no code. For raster and vector fonts, this data is divided into two parts: a header describing the font's metrics and the glyph data. A font-resource file for a raster or vector font is identified by the .FON filename extension. For TrueType fonts, there are two files for each font: the first file contains a relatively short header and the second contains the actual font data. The first file is identified by a .FOT extension and the second is identified by a .TTF extension.

35.1.4 Character Sets Used by Fonts

All fonts use a character set. A character set contains punctuation marks, numerals, uppercase and lowercase letters, and all other printable characters. Each element of a character set is identified by a number.

Most character sets used in Windows are supersets of the U.S. ASCII character set, which defines characters for the 96 numeric values from 32 through 127. There are five major groups of character sets:

- Windows
- Unicode ™
- OEM (original equipment manufacturer)
- Symbol
- Vendor-specific

Windows Character Set

The Windows character set is the most commonly used character set in Windows programming. It is essentially equivalent to the ANSI character set. The blank character is the first character in the Windows character set. It has a hexadecimal value of 0x20 (decimal 32). The last character in the Windows character set has a hexadecimal value of 0xFF (decimal 255).

Many fonts specify a default character. Whenever a request is made for a character that is not in the font, Windows provides this default character. Many fonts using the Windows character set specify the period (.) as the default character. TrueType fonts typically use an open box as the default character.

Fonts use a break character called a quad to separate words and justify text. Most fonts using the Windows character set specify that the blank character will serve as the break character.

Windows version 3.1 added 24 characters to the Windows code page, as shown in the following table.

Character	Name	Windows character code
,	base line single quote	130
å	florin	131
„	base line double quote	132
…	ellipsis	133
†	dagger	134
‡	double dagger	135
•	circumflex	136
‰	permille	137
Š	S Hacek	138
‹	left single guillemet	139
Œ	OE ligature	140
'	left single quote	145
'	right single quote	146
"	left double quote	147
"	right double quote	148
•	bullet	149
–	en dash	150
—	em dash	151
•	tilde	152
œ	trademark ligature	153
š	s Hacek	154
›	right single guillemet	155
œ	oe ligature	156
Ÿ	Y Dieresis	159

It should be noted that the characters for left and right single quote were first added to the character set for the release of Windows version 3.0.

Unicode Character Set

The Windows ANSI character uses 8 bits to represent each character; therefore, the maximum number of characters that can be expressed using 8 bits is 256 (2^8). This is usually sufficient for Western languages, including the diacritical marks used in French, German, Spanish, and other languages. However, Eastern languages employ thousands of separate characters, which cannot be encoded by using a single-byte coding scheme. With the proliferation of computer commerce, double-byte coding schemes were developed so that characters could be represented in 8-bit, 16-bit, 24-bit, or 32-bit sequences. This requires complicated passing algorithms; even so, using different code sets could yield entirely different results on two different computers.

To address the problem of multiple coding schemes, the Unicode standard for data representation was developed. A 16-bit character coding scheme, Unicode can represent 65,536 (2^{16}) characters, which is enough to include all languages in computer commerce today, as well as punctuation marks, mathematical symbols, and room for future expansion. Unicode establishes a unique code for every character to ensure that character translation is always accurate.

OEM Character Set

The OEM character set is typically used in full-screen MS-DOS ® sessions for screen display. Characters 32 through 127 are usually the same in the OEM, U.S. ASCII, and Windows character sets. The other characters in the OEM character set (0 through 31 and 128 through 255) correspond to the characters that can be displayed in a full-screen MS-DOS session. These characters are generally different from the Windows characters.

Symbol Character Set

The Symbol character set contains special characters typically used to represent mathematical and scientific formulas.

Vendor-Specific Character Sets

Many printers and other output devices provide fonts based on character sets that differ from the Windows and OEM sets—for example, the Extended Binary Coded Decimal Interchange Code (EBCDIC) character set. To use one of these character sets, the printer driver translates from the Windows character set to the vendor-specific character set.

35.1.5 Font Installation and Deletion

A font must already be resident on a given device or installed in the Windows font table in order for an application to draw text using glyphs from that font. The Windows font table is an internal array that identifies all nondevice fonts that are available to a Windows-based application. An application can retrieve the names of fonts currently installed on a device and stored in the internal font table by calling the **EnumFonts** or **ChooseFont** function.

An application can install a font by calling one of the two font installation functions: **AddFontResource** or **AddFontModule**. The **AddFontResource** function loads a font that is stored in a font-resource file. The **AddFontModule** function loads a font that is stored as a resource in a Windows executable file or a dynamic-link library (DLL). Because fonts are typically stored in font-resource files, applications call the **AddFontResource** function in most cases; however, there are some instances where an application stores a font resource for a unique font as part of the executable file or as part of a DLL. In these cases, the application must call **AddFontModule** to extract the font resource and install it.

In the case of TrueType fonts, an additional step is sometimes necessary before the font can be installed in the font table. Some font manufacturers ship only the TrueType font-data files (identified by the .TTF extension). Before Windows can load these fonts, it requires a corresponding header file (identified by the .FOT extension). To create this header file, an application must call the **CreateScalableFontResource** function and pass the name of the font-data file as the third parameter. When this header file is created, an application can install the font by calling the **AddFontResource** function and passing the name of the new header file.

When an application finishes using an installed font, it must remove that font by calling either the **RemoveFontResource** function (for fonts installed with the **AddFontResource** function) or the **RemoveFontModule** function (for fonts installed by calling the **AddFontModule** function).

Whenever an application calls the functions that add and delete font resources, it should also call the **SendMessage** function and send a WM_FONTCHANGE message to all top-level windows in the system. This message notifies other applications that the internal font table has been altered by an application that added or removed a font.

35.1.6 Font Creation and Selection

Previous versions of Windows required that the application developer provide source code and a dialog box template to support an interface that displayed the available fonts from which the user could choose. The new Font common dialog box simplifies the creation and selection process. By initializing the **CHOOSEFONT** structure and calling the **ChooseFont** function, an application can support the same font-selection interface that previously required many lines of code. (For more information about the Font common dialog box, see Chapter 76, "Common Dialog Box Library.") The following illustration shows the dialog box displayed when an application calls the **ChooseFont** function.

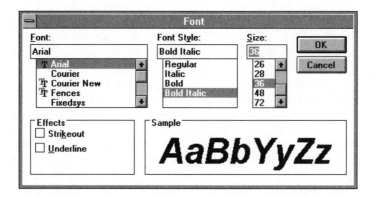

Selection by the User

Most font creation and selection operations involve the user. For example, word processing applications let the user select unique fonts for headings, footnotes, and body text. After the user selects a font by using the Font dialog box and presses the OK button, the **ChooseFont** function initializes the members of a **LOGFONT** structure with the attributes of the requested font. To use this font for text-output operations, an application must first create a logical font and then select that font into its device context. A *logical font* is an application-supplied description of an ideal font. A developer can create a logical font by calling the **CreateFont** or the **CreateFontIndirect** functions. In this case, the application would call **CreateFontIndirect** and supply a pointer to the **LOGFONT** structure initialized by **ChooseFont**. In general, it is more efficient to call **CreateFontIndirect** because **CreateFont** requires 4 parameters while **CreateFontIndirect** requires only 1, a pointer to **LOGFONT**.

Before an application can actually begin drawing text with a logical font, it must find the closest match from the fonts stored internally on the device and the fonts whose resources have been loaded into the operating system. The fonts stored on the device or in the operating system are called *physical fonts*. The process of finding the physical font that most closely matches a specified logical font is referred to as *font mapping*. This process occurs when an application calls the **SelectObject** function and supplies a handle identifying a logical font. Font mapping is performed by using an internal algorithm that compares the attributes of the requested logical font against the attributes of available physical fonts. When the font mapper algorithm completes its search and determines the closest possible match, the **SelectObject** function returns and the application can begin drawing text with the new font.

The **SetMapperFlags** function specifies whether or not the font mapper algorithm searches only for physical fonts with aspect ratios that match the physical device. The *aspect ratio* for a device is the ratio formed by the width and the height of a pixel on that device.

35.1.6.1 Special Font Selection Considerations

Although most font selection operations involve the user, there are some instances where this is not true. For example, a developer may want to use a unique font in an application to draw text in a control window. To select an appropriate font, the application must be able to determine what fonts are available, create a logical font that describes one of these available fonts, and then select that font into the appropriate device context.

An application can enumerate the available fonts by using the **EnumFontFamilies** function. This can be useful when an application must determine which fonts are available from a given family. (The **EnumFonts** function is an obsolete version of the **EnumFontFamilies** function.)

Once an application has enumerated the available fonts and located an appropriate match, it should use the values returned by the font enumeration function to initialize the members of a **LOGFONT** structure and call the **CreateFontIndirect** function, passing a pointer to the initialized **LOGFONT** structure. If the **CreateFontIndirect** function is successful, the application can select the logical font by calling the **SelectObject** function.

35.1.7 Embedded Fonts

Embedding a font is the technique of bundling a document and the fonts it contains into a file for transmission to another computer. Embedding a font guarantees that a font specified in a transmitted file will be present on the computer receiving the file. Not all fonts can be moved from computer to computer, however, since most fonts are licensed to only one computer at a time. In Windows, only TrueType fonts can be embedded.

Applications should embed a font in a document only when requested by a user. An application cannot be distributed along with documents that contain embedded fonts, nor can an application itself contain an embedded font. Whenever an application distributes a font, in any format, the proprietary rights of the owner of the font must be acknowledged.

It may be a violation of a font vendor's proprietary rights and/or user license agreement to embed any fonts where embedding is not permitted or to fail to observe the following guidelines on embedding fonts. A font's license may give only read-write permission for a font to be installed and used on the destination computer; or it may give read-only permission. Read-only permission allows a document to be viewed and printed (but not modified) by the destination computer; documents with read-only embedded fonts are themselves read-only. Read-only embedded fonts may not be unbundled from the document and installed on the destination computer.

An application can determine the license status, and thus whether or not a font can be embedded in a document, by calling the **GetOutlineTextMetrics** function and examining the **otmfsType** member of the **OUTLINETEXTMETRIC** structure. If bit 1 of **otmfsType** is set, embedding is not permitted for the font. If bit 1 is clear, the font can be embedded. If bit 2 is set, the embedding is read-only.

To determine if a font can be embedded, an application can use the **GetFontData** function to read the font file. Setting the *dwTable* and *dwOffset* parameters of **GetFontData** to 0L and the *cbData* parameter to –1L ensures that the application reads the entire font file from the beginning.

After an application retrieves the font data, it can store the data with the document by using any applicable format. Most applications build a font directory in the document, listing the embedded fonts and whether the embedding is read-write or read-only. An application can use the **otmpStyleName** and **otmFamilyName** members of the **OUTLINETEXTMETRIC** structure to identify the font.

If the read-only bit is set for the embedded font, applications must encrypt the font data before storing it with the document. The encryption method need not be complicated; for example, using the XOR operator to combine the font data with an application-specified constant is adequate and fast.

35.2 About Text Output

Text output is the most common type of graphic output found within the client area of Windows-based applications. It is used by Windows-based applications in different ways. Word processing and desktop publishing applications create documents with formatted text; spreadsheet applications use text, numbers, and symbols to specify formulas, label columns, and list values; database applications create records and display queries with text, and CAD applications use text to label objects and display dimensions.

The Win32 application programming interface (API) provides a complete set of functions to format and draw text in an application's client area and on a page of printer paper. These functions can be divided into two categories: those that format the text (or prepare it for output) and those that actually draw the text. The formatting functions align text, set the intercharacter spacing, set the text and text-background colors, and justify text. The drawing functions draw individual characters (or symbols) or entire strings of text.

35.2.1 Formatting Text

The formatting functions can be divided into three categories: those that retrieve or set the text-formatting attributes for a device context, those that retrieve character widths, and those that retrieve string widths and heights.

35.2.1.1 Text-Formatting Attributes

An application can use six functions to set the text-formatting attributes for a device context: **SetBKColor**, **SetBKMode**, **SetTextAlign**, **SetTextCharacterExtra**, **SetTextColor**, and **SetTextJustification**. These functions affect the text alignment, the intercharacter spacing, the text justification, and text and background colors. In addition to these six functions, six other functions can be used to retrieve the current text formatting attributes for any device context: **GetBkColor**, **GetBkMode**, **GetTextAlign**, **GetTextCharacterExtra**, **GetTextColor**, and **GetTextExtentPoint**.

Text Alignment

Applications can use the **SetTextAlign** function to specify how Windows should position the characters in a string of text when they call one of the drawing functions. This function can be used to position headings, page numbers, callouts, and so on. Windows positions a string of text by aligning a reference point on an imaginary rectangle that surrounds the string, with the current cursor position or with a point passed as an argument to one of the text drawing functions. The **SetTextAlign** function lets the application specify the location of this reference point. The list below identifies the possible reference point locations.

Location	Description
left/bottom	The reference point is located at the bottom-left corner of the rectangle.
left/base line	The reference point is located at the intersection of the character-cell base line and the left edge of the rectangle.
left/top	The reference point is located at the top-left corner of the rectangle.
center/bottom	The reference point is located at the center of the bottom of the rectangle.
center/base line	The reference point is located at the intersection of the character-cell base line and the center of the rectangle.
center/top	The reference point is located at the center of the top of the rectangle.
right/bottom	The reference point is located at the bottom-right corner of the rectangle.
right/base line	The reference point is located at the intersection of the character-cell base line and the right edge of the rectangle.
right/top	The reference point is located at the top-right corner of the rectangle.

(For a description of the character-cell base line, see Section 35.1, "About Fonts.")

The following illustration shows a string of text drawn by calling the **TextOut** function. Before drawing the text, the **SetTextAlign** function was called to relocate the reference point at each one of the nine possible locations.

Text-alignment demonstration.

Text-alignment demonstration.

Text-alignment demonstration.

Text-alignment demonstration.

Text-alignment demonstration.

Text-alignment demonstration.

Text-alignment demonstration.

Text-alignment demonstration.

Text-alignment demonstration.

The default text alignment for a device context is the upper left corner of the imaginary rectangle that surrounds the text. An application can retrieve the current text alignment setting for any device context by calling the **GetTextAlign** function.

Intercharacter Spacing

Applications can use the **SetTextCharacterExtra** function to alter the intercharacter spacing for all text output operations in a given device context. The following illustration shows a string of text drawn twice by calling the **TextOut** function. Before drawing the text the second time, the **SetTextCharacterExtra** function was called to increment the intercharacter spacing.

Experiments in Typography

Experiments in Typography

The default intercharacter spacing value for any device context is zero. An application can retrieve the current intercharacter spacing value for a device context by calling the **GetTextCharacterExtra** function.

Text Justification

Applications can use the **GetTextExtentPoint** and **SetTextJustification** functions to justify a line of text. Text justification is a common operation in any desktop publishing and in most word processing applications. The **GetTextExtentPoint** function computes the width and height of a string of text. After the width is computed, the application can call the **SetTextJustification** function to distribute extra spacing between each of the words in a line of text. The following illustration shows a paragraph of text printed twice: in the first paragraph, the text was not justified; in the second paragraph, the text was justified by calling the **GetTextExtentPoint** and **SetTextJustification** functions.

GDI transforms the width, height, and depth parameters, once by using the destination display context and once by using the source display context. If the resulting extents do not match, GDI uses the StretchBit function to compress or stretch the source bitmap as necessary. — *Unjustified text*

GDI transforms the width, height, and depth parameters, once by using the destination display context and once by using the source display context. If the resulting extents do not match, GDI uses the StretchBit function to compress or stretch the source bitmap as necessary. — *Justified text*

Text and Background Color

Applications can use the **SetTextColor** function to set the color of text drawn in the client-area of their windows, as well as the color of text drawn on a color printer. An application can use the **SetBkColor** function to set the color that appears behind each character and the **SetBkMode** function to specify how Windows should blend the selected background color with the current color(s) on the video display.

The default text color for a display device context is black; the default background color is white; and the default background mode is opaque. An application can retrieve the current text color for a device context by calling the **GetTextColor** function. An application can retrieve the current background color for a device context by calling the **GetBkColor** function and the current background mode by calling the **GetBkMode** function.

35.2.1.2 Character Widths

Applications need to retrieve character-width data when they fit strings of text to page or column widths as they prepare to alter the appearance of a string of text, and so forth. There are four functions that an application can use to retrieve character-width data. Two of these functions retrieve the character-advance width and two of these functions retrieve actual character-width data.

An application can use the **GetCharWidth** and **GetCharWidthFloat** functions to retrieve the advance width for individual characters or symbols in a string of text. The *advance width* is the distance that the cursor on a video display or the print-head on a printer must advance before printing the next character in a string of text. The **GetCharWidth** function returns the advance width as an integer value. If greater precision is required, an application can use the **GetCharWidthFloat** function to retrieve fractional advance-width values.

An application can retrieve actual character-width data by using the **GetCharABCWidths** and **GetCharABCWidthsFloat** functions. To retrieve character widths for characters in a string of text that will be printed using a TrueType font, an application can call the **GetCharABCWidths** function; however, for any other font, the application should call the **GetCharABCWidthsFloat** function. (For more information about TrueType fonts, see Section 35.1, "About Fonts"). The following illustration shows the three components of the *ABC width*:

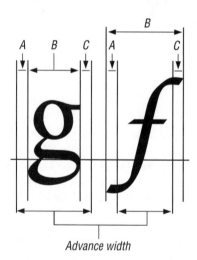

Advance width

The "A" spacing is the width to add to the current position before placing the character. The "B" spacing is the width of the character itself. The "C" spacing is the white space to the right of the character. The total advance width is determined by calculating the sum of A+B+C. The *character cell* is an imaginary rectangle that surrounds each character or symbol in a Windows font. Because characters can overhang or underhang the character cell, either or both of the A and C increments can be a negative number.

35.2.1.3 String Widths and Heights

In addition to retrieving character-width data for individual characters, applications also need to compute the width and height of entire strings. Two functions retrieve string-width and height measurements: **GetTextExtentPoint**, and **GetTabbedTextExtent**. If the string does not contain tab characters, an application can use the **GetTextExtentPoint** function to retrieve the width and height of a specified string. If the string contains tab characters, an application should call the **GetTabbedTextExtent** function.

Windows also supports a special function that applications can use for word-wrapping operations called **GetTextExtentExPoint**. This function returns the number of characters from a specified string that fit within a given space.

Font Ascenders and Descenders

Some applications determine the line spacing between text lines of different sizes by using a font's maximum ascender and descender. An application can retrieve these values by calling the **GetTextMetrics** function and then checking the **tmAscent** and **tmDescent** members of the **TEXTMETRIC** or **NEWTEXTMETRIC** structure. (The **TEXTMETRIC** structure is returned for raster fonts; the **NEWTEXTMETRIC** structure is returned for TrueType fonts).

The maximum ascent and descent are different from the typographic ascent and descent; in TrueType fonts, the typographic ascent and descent are typically the top of the "f" glyph and bottom of the "g" glyph. An application can retrieve the typographic ascender and descender for a TrueType font by calling the **GetOutlineTextMetrics** function and checking the values in the **otmMacAscent** and **otmMacDescent** members of the **OUTLINETEXTMETRIC** structure. It is important to note that TrueType font metrics do not correspond exactly to the metrics for Windows raster fonts, because TrueType font metrics have been designed by Apple Computer, Inc. for consistency across a variety of display and output devices.

The following figure shows the difference between the vertical text metric values returned in the **NEWTEXTMETRIC** and **OUTLINETEXTMETRIC** structures. (The names beginning with *otm* are members of the **OUTLINETEXTMETRIC** structure.)

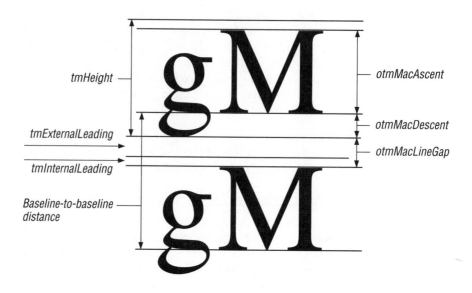

Font Dimensions

An application can retrieve the physical dimensions of a TrueType font by calling the **GetOutlineTextMetrics** function. An application can retrieve the physical dimensions of any other font by calling the **GetTextMetrics** function. To determine the dimensions of an output device, an application can call the **GetDeviceCaps** function. **GetDeviceCaps** returns both physical and logical dimensions.

A logical inch is a measure Windows uses to present legible fonts on the screen and is approximately 30 to 40 percent larger than a physical inch. The use of logical inches precludes an exact match between the output of the screen and printer. Developers should be aware that the text on a screen is not simply a scaled version of the text that will appear on the page, particularly if graphics are incorporated into the text.

35.2.2 Drawing Text

After an application selects the appropriate font, sets the required text-formatting options, and computes the necessary character width and height values for a string of text, it can begin drawing characters and symbols by calling any of the four text-output functions. Two of these functions, **DrawText** and **TabbedTextOut**, are part of Window Manager and the remaining two functions are part of GDI. When an application calls one of these functions, the operating system passes the call to the graphics engine, which in turn passes the call to the appropriate device driver. At the device driver level, all of these calls are supported by one or more calls to the driver's own **ExtTextOut** or **TextOut** function. An application will achieve the fastest execution by calling the **ExtTextOut** function, which is quickly converted into an **ExtTextOut** call for the device. However, there are instances when an application should call one of the other three functions; for example, to draw multiple lines of text within the borders of a specified rectangular region, it is more efficient to call the **DrawText** function. To create a multicolumn table with justified columns of text, it is more efficient to call the **TabbedTextOut** function.

35.3 Using the Font and Text-Output Functions

This section describes how you can use the font and text-output functions to draw normal text, draw text from different fonts on the same line, rotate lines of text, display the font-selection common dialog-box, enumerate fonts, and so on.

35.3.1 Using a Stock Font to Draw Text

Windows provides six stock fonts. A *stock font* is a logical font that an application can obtain by calling the **GetStockObject** function and passing a value that identifies the requested font. The following list contains the six values that you can specify to obtain a stock font.

Value	Meaning
ANSI_FIXED_FONT	Specifies a fixed-pitch font based on the Windows character set. A Courier font is typically used.
ANSI_VAR_FONT	Specifies a variable-pitch font based on the Windows character set. MS Sans Serif is typically used.
DEVICE_DEFAULT_FONT	Specifies the preferred font for the given device. This is typically the System font for display devices; however, for some dot-matrix printers this is a font that is resident on the device. (Printing with this font is usually faster than printing with a downloaded, bitmapped font).
OEM_FIXED_FONT	Specifies a fixed-pitch font based on an OEM character set. For IBM ® computers and compatibles, the OEM font is based on the IBM PC character set.
SYSTEM_FONT	Specifies the System font. This is a variable-pitch font based on the Windows character set, and is used by the operating system to display window titles, menu names, and text in dialog boxes. The System font is always available. Other fonts are available only if they have been installed.

SYSTEM_FIXED_FONT   Specifies a fixed-pitch font compatible with the System font in Windows versions earlier than 3.0.

The following example retrieves a handle of the Windows variable stock font, selects it into a device context, and then writes a string using that font:

```
HFONT hfnt, hOldFont;

    hfnt = GetStockObject(ANSI_VAR_FONT);
    if (hOldFont = SelectObject(hdc, hfnt)) {
        TextOut(hdc, 10, 50, "Sample ANSI_VAR_FONT text.", 26);
        SelectObject(hdc, hOldFont);
    }
```

If other stock fonts are not available, **GetStockObject** returns a handle to the System font (SYSTEM_FONT). You should use stock fonts only if the mapping mode for your application's device context is MM_TEXT.

35.3.2 Creating a Logical Font

You can use the Font common dialog box to display available fonts. The **ChooseFont** dialog box is displayed after an application initializes the members of a **CHOOSEFONT** structure and calls the **ChooseFont** function. After the user chooses one of the available fonts and presses the OK button, the **ChooseFont** function initializes a **LOGFONT** structure with the relevant data. Your application can then call the **CreateLogFont** function and create a logical font based on the user's request. The following example demonstrates how this is done.

```
HFONT FAR PASCAL MyCreateFont( void )
{

CHOOSEFONT cf;
LOGFONT lf;
HFONT hfont;

    /* Initialize members of the CHOOSEFONT structure. */

    cf.lStructSize = sizeof(CHOOSEFONT);
    cf.hwndOwner = (HWND)NULL;
    cf.hDC = (HDC)NULL;
    cf.lpLogFont = &lf;
    cf.iPointSize = 0;
    cf.Flags = CF_SCREENFONTS;
    cf.rgbColors = RGB(0,0,0);
    cf.lCustData = 0L;
    cf.lpfnHook = (LPCFHOOKPROC)NULL;
    cf.lpTemplateName = (LPSTR)NULL;
```

```
        cf.hInstance = (HINSTANCE) NULL;
        cf.lpszStyle = (LPSTR)NULL;
        cf.nFontType = SCREEN_FONTTYPE;
        cf.nSizeMin = 0;
        cf.nSizeMax = 0;

        /* Display the CHOOSEFONT common-dialog box. */

        ChooseFont(&cf);

        /* Create a logical font based on the user's   */
        /* selection and return a handle identifying   */
        /* that font. */

        hfont = CreateFontIndirect(cf.lpLogFont);
        return (hfont);
}
```

35.3.3 Enumerating the Installed Fonts

In some instances, an application must be able to enumerate the available fonts and select the one most appropriate for a particular operation. An application can enumerate the available fonts by calling the **EnumFonts** or **EnumFontFamilies** function. These functions send information about the available fonts to a callback function that the application supplies. The callback function receives information in **LOGFONT** and **NEWTEXTMETRIC** structures. (The **NEWTEXTMETRIC** structure contains information about a TrueType font. When the callback function receives information about a non-TrueType font, the information is contained in a **TEXTMETRIC** structure.) By using this information, an application can limit the user's choices to only those fonts that are available.

The **EnumFontFamilies** function is similar to the **EnumFonts** function but includes some extra functionality. **EnumFontFamilies** allows an application to take advantage of styles available with TrueType fonts. New and upgraded applications should use **EnumFontFamilies** instead of **EnumFonts**.

In previous versions of Windows, the only style attributes were weight and italic; any other styles were specified in the family name for the font. For example, when an application used the **EnumFonts** function to query the available Courier fonts, **EnumFonts** might return information for Courier, Courier Bold, Courier Bold Italic, and Courier Italic. It would not return information about any other Courier fonts that might be installed, because any other Courier fonts would typically have a different family name.

TrueType fonts are organized around a family name (for example, Courier New) and style names (for example, italic, bold, and extra-bold). The

EnumFontFamilies function enumerates all the styles associated with a given family name, not simply the bold and italic attributes; when the system includes a TrueType font called Courier New Extra-Bold, **EnumFontFamilies** lists it with the other Courier New fonts. The capabilities of **EnumFontFamilies** are helpful for fonts with many or unusual styles and for fonts that cross international borders.

If an application does not supply a typeface name, the **EnumFonts** and **EnumFontFamilies** functions supply information about one font in each available family. To enumerate all the fonts in a device context, the application can specify NULL for the typeface name, compile a list of the available typefaces, and then list each font in each typeface.

The following example uses the **EnumFontFamilies** function to retrieve the number of available raster, vector, and TrueType font families.

```
UINT uAlignPrev;
int aFontCount[] = { 0, 0, 0 };
char szCount[8];

EnumFontFamilies(hdc, (LPCTSTR) NULL,
    (FONTENUMPROC) EnumFamCallBack, (LPARAM) aFontCount);

uAlignPrev = SetTextAlign(hdc, TA_UPDATECP);

MoveToEx(hdc, 10, 50, (LPPOINT)NULL);
TextOut(hdc, 0, 0, "Number of raster fonts: ", 24);
itoa(aFontCount[0], szCount, 10);
TextOut(hdc, 0, 0, szCount, strlen(szCount));

MoveToEx(hdc, 10, 75, (LPPOINT)NULL);
TextOut(hdc, 0, 0, "Number of vector fonts: ", 24);
itoa(aFontCount[1], szCount, 10);
TextOut(hdc, 0, 0, szCount, strlen(szCount));

MoveToEx(hdc, 10, 100, (LPPOINT)NULL);
TextOut(hdc, 0, 0, "Number of TrueType fonts: ", 26);
itoa(aFontCount[2], szCount, 10);
TextOut(hdc, 0, 0, szCount, strlen(szCount));

SetTextAlign(hdc, uAlignPrev);
    .
    .
    .

BOOL FAR PASCAL EnumFamCallBack(lplf, lpntm, FontType, aFontCount)
LPLOGFONT lplf;
LPNEWTEXTMETRIC lpntm;
DWORD FontType;
```

```
LPVOID aFontCount;
{
    int far * aiFontCount = (int far *) aFontCount;

    /*
     * Record the number of raster, TrueType, and vector
     * fonts in the font-count array.
     */

    if (FontType & RASTER_FONTTYPE)
        aiFontCount[0]++;
    else if (FontType & TRUETYPE_FONTTYPE)
        aiFontCount[2]++;
    else
        aiFontCount[1]++;

    if (aiFontCount[0] || aiFontCount[1] || aiFontCount[2])
        return TRUE;
    else
        return FALSE;

    UNREFERENCED_PARAMETER( lplf );
    UNREFERENCED_PARAMETER( lpntm );
}
```

This example uses two masks, RASTER_FONTTYPE and TRUETYPE_FONTTYPE, to determine the type of font being enumerated. If the RASTER_FONTTYPE bit is set, the font is a raster font. If the TRUETYPE_FONTTYPE bit is set, the font is a TrueType font. If neither bit is set, the font is a vector font. A third mask, DEVICE_FONTTYPE, is set when a device (for example, a laser printer) supports downloading TrueType fonts; it is zero if the device is a display adapter, dot-matrix printer, or other raster device. An application can also use the DEVICE_FONTTYPE mask to distinguish GDI-supplied raster fonts from device-supplied fonts. Windows can simulate bold, italic, underline, and strikeout attributes for GDI-supplied raster fonts, but not for device-supplied fonts.

An application can also check bits 1 and 2 in the **tmPitchAndFamily** member of the **NEWTEXTMETRIC** structure to identify a TrueType font. If bit 1 is 0 and bit 2 is 1, the font is a TrueType font.

Vector fonts are categorized as OEM_CHARSET instead of ANSI_CHARSET. Some applications identify vector fonts by using this information, checking the **tmCharSet** member of the **NEWTEXTMETRIC** structure. This categorization usually prevents the font mapper from choosing vector fonts unless they are specifically requested. (Most applications no longer use vector fonts, because their strokes are single lines and they take longer to draw than TrueType fonts, which offer many of the same scaling and rotation features that required vector fonts in earlier versions of Windows.)

35.3.4 Checking the Text Capabilities of a Device

You can use the **EnumFonts** and **EnumFontFamilies** functions to enumerate the fonts that are available in a printer-compatible memory device context. You can also use the **GetDeviceCaps** function to retrieve information about the text capabilities of a device. By calling the **GetDeviceCaps** function with the NUMFONTS index, you can determine the minimum number of fonts supported by a printer. (An individual printer may support more fonts than specified in the return value from **GetDeviceCaps** with the NUMFONTS index.) By using the TEXTCAPS index, you can identify many of the text capabilities of the specified device.

35.3.5 Setting the Text Alignment

You can query and set the text alignment for a device context by using the **GetTextAlign** and **SetTextAlign** functions. The text-alignment settings determine how text is positioned relative to a given location. Text can be aligned to the right or left of the position or centered over it; it can also be aligned above or below the point.

The following example shows a method for determining which horizontal alignment flag is set:

```
switch ((TA_LEFT | TA_RIGHT | TA_CENTER) & GetTextAlign(hdc))
{
case TA_LEFT:
    .
    .
    .

case TA_RIGHT:
    .
    .
    .

case TA_CENTER:
    .
    .
    .

}
```

You can also use the **SetTextAlign** function to update the current position when a text-output function is called. For instance, the following example uses the **SetTextAlign** function to update the current position when the **TextOut** function is called. In this example, the *cArial* parameter is an integer that specifies the number of Arial fonts.

```
UINT uAlignPrev;
char szCount[8];

uAlignPrev = SetTextAlign(hdc, TA_UPDATECP);
MoveToEx(hdc, 10, 50, (LPPOINT) NULL);
TextOut(hdc, 0, 0, "Number of Arial fonts: ", 23);
itoa(cArial, szCount, 10);

TextOut(hdc, 0, 0, (LPSTR) szCount, strlen(szCount));
SetTextAlign(hdc, uAlignPrev);
```

35.3.6 Drawing Text From Different Fonts on the Same Line

Different type styles within a font family can have different widths. For example, bold and italic styles of a family are always wider than the roman style for a given point size. When you display or print several type styles on a single line, you must keep track of the width of the line to avoid having characters displayed or printed on top of one another.

You can use two functions to retrieve the width (or extent) of text in the current font. The **GetTabbedTextExtent** function computes the width and height of a character string. If the string contains one or more tab characters, the width of the string is based upon a specified array of tab-stop positions. The **GetTextExtent** function computes the width and height of a line of text.

When necessary, Windows synthesizes a font by changing the character bitmaps. To synthesize a character in a bold font, Windows draws the character twice: once at the starting point, and again one pixel to the right of the starting point. To synthesize a character in an italic font, Windows draws two rows of pixels at the bottom of the character cell, moves the starting point one pixel to the right, draws the next two rows, and continues until the character has been drawn. By shifting pixels, each character appears to be sheared to the right. The amount of shear is a function of the height of the character.

One way to write a line of text that contains multiple fonts is to use the **GetTextExtent** function after each call to **TextOut** and add the length to a current position. The following example writes the line "This is a sample string." using bold characters for "This is a", switches to italic characters for "sample", then returns to bold characters for "string." After printing all the strings, it restores the system default characters.

```
int XIncrement;
int YStart;
TEXTMETRIC tm;
HFONT hfntDefault, hfntItalic, hfntBold;
SIZE sz;
LPSTR lpszString1 = "This is a ";
LPSTR lpszString2 = "sample ";
```

```
LPSTR lpszString3 = "string.";

/* Create a bold and an italic logical font. */

hfntItalic = MyCreateFont();
hfntBold = MyCreateFont();


/* Select the bold font and draw the first string        */
/* beginning at the specified point (XIncrement, YStart). */

XIncrement = 10;
YStart = 50;
hfntDefault = SelectObject(hdc, hfntBold);
TextOut(hdc, XIncrement, YStart, lpszString1,
        lstrlen(lpszString1));

/*
 * Compute the length of the first string and add
 * this value to the x-increment that is used for the
 * text-output operation.
 */

GetTextExtentPoint(hdc, lpszString1,
                   lstrlen(lpszString1), &sz);
XIncrement += sz.cx;

/*
 * Retrieve the overhang value from the TEXTMETRIC
 * structure and subtract it from the x-increment.
 * (This is only necessary for non-TrueType raster
 * fonts.)
 */

GetTextMetrics(hdc, &tm);
XIncrement -= tm.tmOverhang;

/*
 * Select an italic font and draw the second string
 * beginning at the point (XIncrement, YStart).
 */

hfntBold = SelectObject(hdc, hfntItalic);
GetTextMetrics(hdc, &tm);
XIncrement -= tm.tmOverhang;
TextOut(hdc, XIncrement, YStart, lpszString2,
        lstrlen(lpszString2));

/*
 * Compute the length of the second string and add
```

```
 * this value to the x-increment that is used for the
 * text-output operation.
 */

GetTextExtentPoint(hdc, lpszString2, lstrlen(lpszString2), &sz);
XIncrement += sz.cx;

/*
 * Re-select the bold font and draw the third string
 * beginning at the point (XIncrement, YStart).
 */

SelectObject(hdc, hfntBold);
TextOut(hdc, XIncrement - tm.tmOverhang, YStart, lpszString3,
             lstrlen(lpszString3));

/* Re-select the original font. */

SelectObject(hdc, hfntDefault);

/* Delete the bold and italic fonts. */

DeleteObject(hfntItalic);
DeleteObject(hfntBold);
```

In this example, the **GetTextExtentPoint** function initializes the members of a **SIZE** structure with the length and height of the specified string. The **GetTextMetrics** function retrieves the overhang for the current font. Because the overhang is zero if the font is a TrueType font, the overhang value does not change the string placement. For raster fonts, however, it is important to use the overhang value.

The overhang is subtracted from the bold string once, to bring subsequent characters closer to the end of the string if the font is a raster font. Because overhang affects both the beginning and end of the italic string in a raster font, the glyphs start at the right of the specified location and end at the left of the endpoint of the last character cell. (The **GetTextExtent** function retrieves the extent of the character cells, not the extent of the glyphs.) To account for the overhang in the raster italic string, the example subtracts the overhang before placing the string and subtracts it again before placing subsequent characters.

The **SetTextJustification** function adds extra space to the break characters in a line of text. You can use the **GetTextExtent** function to determine the extent of a string, then subtract that extent from the total amount of space the line should occupy, and use the **SetTextJustification** function to distribute the extra space among the break characters in the string. The **SetTextCharacterExtra** function adds extra space to every character cell in the selected font, including the break character. (You can use the **GetTextCharacterExtra** function to determine the current amount of extra space being added to the character cells; the default setting is zero.)

You can place characters with greater precision by using the **GetCharWidth** or **GetCharABCWidths** function to retrieve the widths of individual characters in a font. The **GetCharABCWidths** function is more accurate than the **GetCharWidth** function, but only when it is used with TrueType fonts; when you use **GetCharABCWidths** with non-TrueType fonts, it retrieves the same information as **GetCharWidth**.

ABC spacing also allows an application to perform very accurate text alignment. For example, when the application right aligns a raster roman font without using ABC spacing, the advance width is calculated as the character width. This means the white space to the right of the glyph in the bitmap is aligned, not the glyph itself. By using ABC widths, applications have more flexibility in the placement and removal of white space when aligning text, because they have information that allows them to finely control intercharacter spacing.

35.3.7 Rotating Lines of Text

You can rotate TrueType fonts at any angle. This is useful for labeling charts and other illustrations. The following example rotates a string in 10-degree increments around the center of the client area by changing the value of the **lfEscapement** and **lfOrientation** members of the **LOGFONT** structure used to create the font.

```
RECT rc;
int angle;
HFONT hfnt, hfntPrev;
LPSTR lpszRotate = "String to be rotated.";

/* Allocate memory for a LOGFONT structure. */

PLOGFONT plf = (PLOGFONT) LocalAlloc(LPTR, sizeof(LOGFONT));


/* Specify a font typeface name and weight. */

lstrcpy(plf->lfFaceName, "Arial");
plf->lfWeight = FW_NORMAL;

/* Retrieve the client-rectangle dimensions. */

GetClientRect(hwnd, &rc);

/*
 * Set the background mode to transparent for the
 * text-output operation.
 */
```

```
SetBkMode(hdc, TRANSPARENT);

/*
 * Draw the string 36 times, rotating 10 degrees
 * counter-clockwise each time.
 */

for (angle = 0; angle < 3600; angle += 100) {
    plf->lfEscapement = angle;
    hfnt = CreateFontIndirect(plf);
    hfntPrev = SelectObject(hdc, hfnt);
    TextOut(hdc, rc.right / 2, rc.bottom / 2,
        lpszRotate, lstrlen(lpszRotate));
    SelectObject(hdc, hfntPrev);
    DeleteObject(hfnt);
}

/* Reset the background mode to its default. */

SetBkMode(hdc, OPAQUE);

/* Free the memory allocated for the LOGFONT structure. */

LocalFree((LOCALHANDLE) plf);
```

35.3.8 **Retrieving Character Outlines**

You can use the **GetGlyphOutline** function to retrieve the outline of a glyph from a TrueType font. The glyph outline returned by the **GetGlyphOutline** function is for a grid-fitted glyph. (A grid-fitted glyph has been modified so that its bitmap image conforms as closely as possible to the original design of the glyph.) If your application requires an unmodified glyph outline, request the glyph outline for a character in a font whose size is equal to the font's em units. (To create a font with this size, set the **lfHeight** member of the **LOGFONT** structure to the negative of the value of the **ntmSizeEM** member of the **NEWTEXTMETRIC** structure.)

GetGlyphOutline returns the outline as a bitmap or as a series of polylines and splines. When an application retrieves a glyph outline as a series of polylines and splines, the information is returned in a **TTPOLYGONHEADER** structure followed by as many **TTPOLYCURVE** structures as required to describe the glyph. All points are returned as **POINTFX** structures and represent absolute positions, not relative moves. The starting point given by the **pfxStart** member of the **TTPOLYGONHEADER** structure is the point where the outline for a contour begins. The **TTPOLYCURVE** structures that follow can be either polyline records or spline records.

To render a TrueType character outline in Windows, you must use both the polyline and the spline records. Windows can render both polylines and splines easily. Each polyline and spline record contains as many sequential points as possible, to minimize the number of records returned.

The starting point given in the **TTPOLYGONHEADER** structure is always on the outline of the glyph. The specified point serves as both the starting and ending points for the contour.

35.3.8.1 Polyline Records

Polyline records are a series of points; lines drawn between the points describe the outline of the character. A polyline record begins with the last point in the previous record (or, for the first record in the contour, the starting point). Each point in the record is on the glyph outline and can be connected simply by using straight lines.

35.3.8.2 Spline Records

Spline records represent the quadratic curves (that is, quadratic b-splines) used by TrueType. A spline record begins with the last point in the previous record (or for the first record in the contour, with the starting point). For the first spline record, the starting point and the last point in the record are on the glyph outline. For all other spline records, only the last point is on the glyph outline. All other points in the spline records are off the glyph outline and must be rendered as the control points of b-splines.

The last spline or polyline record in a contour always ends with the contour's starting point. This arrangement ensures that every contour is closed.

Because b-splines require three points (one point off the glyph outline between two points that are on the outline), you must perform some calculations when a spline record contains more than one off-curve point.

For example, if a spline record contains three points (A, B, and C) and it is not the first record, points A and B are off the glyph outline. To interpret point A, use the current position (which is always on the glyph outline) and the point on the glyph outline between points A and B. To find the midpoint (M) between A and B, you can perform the following calculation.

$$M = A + (B - A)/2$$

The midpoint between consecutive off-outline points in a spline record is a point on the glyph outline, according to the definition of the spline format used in TrueType fonts.

If the current position is designated by P, the two quadratic splines defined by this spline record are (P, A, M) and (M, B, C).

35.3.9 Using Portable TrueType Metrics

Applications that use the TrueType text metrics can achieve a high degree of printer and document portability; even applications that must maintain compatibility with earlier versions of Windows can use the TrueType metrics.

Design widths overcome most of the problems of device-dependent text introduced by physical devices. Design widths are a kind of logical width. Independent of any rasterization problems or scaling transformations, each glyph has a logical width and height. Composed to a logical page, each character in a string has a place that is independent of the physical device widths. Although a logical width implies that widths can be scaled linearly at all point sizes, this is not necessarily true for either nonportable or most TrueType fonts. At smaller point sizes, some glyphs are made wider relative to their height for better readability.

The characters in TrueType core fonts are designed against a 2048 by 2048 grid. The design width is the width of a character in these grid units. (TrueType supports any integer grid size up to 16,384 by 16,384; grid sizes that are integer powers of 2 scale faster than other grid sizes.)

The font outline is designed in notional units. The em square is the notional grid against which the font outline is fitted. (You can use the **otmEMSquare** member of **OUTLINETEXTMETRIC** and the **ntmSizeEM** member of **NEWTEXTMETRIC** to retrieve the size of the em square in notional units.) When a font is created that has a point size (in device units) equal to the size of its em square, the ABC widths for this font are the desired design widths. For example, assume the size of an em square is 1000 and the ABC widths of a character in the font are 150, 400, and 150. A character in this font that is 10 device units high would have ABC widths of 1.5, 4, and 1.5, respectively. Since the MM_TEXT mapping mode is most commonly used with fonts (and MM_TEXT is equivalent to device units), this is a simple calculation.

Because of the high resolution of TrueType design widths, applications that use them must take into account the large numeric values that can be created.

35.3.9.1 Device vs. Design Units

An application can retrieve font metrics for a physical font only after the font has been selected into a device context. When a font is selected into a device context, it is scaled for the device. The font metrics specific to the device are known as device units.

Portable metrics in fonts are known as design units. To apply to a given device, design units must be converted to device units. Use the following formula to convert design units to device units.

DeviceUnits = (DesignUnits/unitsPerEm) * (PointSize/72) * DeviceResolution

The variables in this formula have the following meanings.

Variable	Description
DeviceUnits	Specifies the *DesignUnits* font metric converted to device units. This value is in the same units as the value given for *DeviceResolution*.
DesignUnits	Specifies the font metric to be converted to device units. This value can be any font metric, including the width of a character or the ascender value for an entire font.
unitsPerEm	Specifies the em square size for the font.
PointSize	Specifies size of the font, in points. (One point equals 1/72 of an inch.)
DeviceResolution	Specifies number of device units (pixels) per inch. Typical values might be 300 for a laser printer or 96 for a VGA screen.

This formula should not be used to convert device units back to design units. Device units are always rounded to the nearest pixel. The propagated round-off error can become very large, especially when an application is working with screen sizes.

To request design units, you should create a logical font whose height is specified as *–unitsPerEm*. Your applications can retrieve the value for *unitsPerEm* by calling the **EnumFontFamilies** function and checking the **ntmSizeEM** member of the **NEWTEXTMETRIC** structure.

35.3.9.2 Metrics for Portable Documents

The following table specifies the most important font metrics for applications that require portable documents and the functions that allow an application to retrieve them.

Function	Metric	Use
EnumFontFamilies	**ntmSizeEM**	Retrieval of design metrics; conversion to device metrics
GetCharABCWidths	**ABCWidths**	Accurate placement of characters at the start and end of margins, picture boundaries, and other text breaks
GetCharWidth	**AdvanceWidths**	Placement of characters on a line
GetOutlineTextMetrics	**otmfsType**	Font-embedding bits
	otmsCharSlopeRise	Y-component for slope of cursor for italic fonts

otmsCharSlopeRun	X-component for slope of cursor for italic fonts
otmAscent	Line spacing
otmDescent	Line spacing
otmLineGap	Line spacing
otmpFamilyName	Font identification
otmpStyleName	Font identification
otmpFullName	Font identification (typically, family and style name)

The **otmsCharSlopeRise**, **otmsCharSlopeRun**, **otmAscent**, **otmDescent**, and **otmLineGap** members of the **OUTLINETEXTMETRIC** structure are scaled or transformed to correspond to the current device mode and physical height (as given in the **tmHeight** member of the **NEWTEXTMETRIC** structure).

Font identification is important in those instances when an application must select the same font—for example, when a document is reopened or moved to a different operating system. The font mapper always selects the correct font when an application requests a font by full name. The family and style names provide input to the standard font dialog box, which ensures that the selection bars are properly placed.

The **otmsCharSlopeRise** and **otmsCharSlopeRun** values are used to produce a close approximation of the main italic angle of the font. For typical roman fonts, **otmsCharSlopeRise** is 1 and **otmsCharSlopeRun** is 0. For italic fonts, the values attempt to approximate the sine and cosine of the main italic angle of the font (in counterclockwise degrees past vertical); note that the italic angle for upright fonts is 0. Because these values are not expressed in design units, they should not be converted into device units.

The character placement and line spacing metrics enable an application to compute device-independent line breaks that are portable across screens, printers, typesetters, and even platforms.

Device-independent page layout requires the following seven basic steps:

1. Normalize all design metrics to a common ultra-high resolution (UHR) value (for example, 65,536 DPI); this prevents round-off errors.
2. Compute line breaks based on UHR metrics and physical page width; this yields a starting point and an ending point of a line within the text stream.
3. Compute the device page width in device units (for example, pixels).
4. Fit each line of text into the device page width, using the line breaks computed in step 2.

5. Compute page breaks by using UHR metrics and the physical page length; this yields the number of lines per page.

6. Compute the line heights in device units.

7. Fit the lines of text onto the page, using the lines per page from step 5 and the line heights from step 6.

If all applications adopt these techniques, developers can virtually guarantee that documents moved from one application to another will retain their original appearance and format.

35.3.10 Using PANOSE Numbers

TrueType font files include PANOSE numbers, which applications can use to choose a font that closely matches their specifications. The PANOSE system classifies faces by 10 different attributes. For more information about these attributes, see the **PANOSE** structure. A **PANOSE** structure is part of the **OUTLINETEXTMETRIC** structure (whose values are filled in by calling the **GetOutlineTextMetrics** function).

The PANOSE attributes are rated individually on a scale. The resulting values are concatenated to produce a number. Given this number for a font and a mathematical metric to measure distances in the PANOSE space, an application can determine the nearest neighbors.

35.3.11 Creating Customized Fonts

Windows keeps a operating system font table containing all the fonts that applications can use. Windows chooses a font from this table when an application calls the **CreateFont** or **CreateFontIndirect** function. There can be up to 253 entries in the table.

A font resource is a group of individual fonts representing characters in a given character set that have various combinations of heights, widths, and pitches. You can load font resources and add the fonts in each resource to the operating system font table by using the **AddFontResource** function. To remove a font resource from the font table, you can use the **RemoveFontResource** function.

After you add a font resource to the operating system font table, you can use the individual fonts in the resource. In other words, the **CreateFont** function takes the fonts into account when it tries to match a physical font to the specified logical font. (Fonts in the table are never directly accessible to an application. They are available only through the **CreateFontIndirect** and **CreateFont** functions, which return the handles of the fonts, not their memory addresses.)

Whenever your application adds or removes a font resource, it should inform all other applications of the change by sending a WM_FONTCHANGE message to them. Use the following call to the **SendMessage** function to send the message to all windows.

```
SendMessage(HWND_BROADCAST, WM_FONTCHANGE, 0, 0);
```

You can use the **GetProfileString** function to search the [Fonts] section of the WIN.INI file for the list of fonts that the user has used Control Panel to install.

35.3.11.1 Creating Font Resources

A font resource file is an empty Windows dynamic-link library; it contains no code or data, but it does contain resources. You can create font resources by creating font files and adding them as resources to a font resource file. To create a font resource file, your application should follow these steps:

1. Create the font files.
2. Create a resource-definition file for the font.
3. Create a dummy code module.
4. Create a module-definition file that describes the fonts and the devices that use the fonts.
5. Compile and link the source files.

You can add a font file to an empty library, along with such resources as icons, cursors, and menus, by using resource compiler.

Note   A complete explanation of how to create a font resource file is beyond the scope of this book. For more information on this topic, see the documentation provided with your application development tools.

35.3.11.2 Installing and Using an Embedded Font

You must separate an embedded font from the containing document and install it in the user's operating system before Windows can use it. Although the exact procedure for separating the font from the document depends on the method used to embed it, your application should always perform these steps:

1. Resolve name conflicts before installing the font.
2. Write the font data to a file, decoding read-only fonts as necessary.
3. Use the **CreateScalableFontResource** function to create a font resource file for the unembedded font.

Only a TrueType font can be embedded in Windows.

Your application should avoid installing a font with the same name as a font that is already on the system. To determine whether there are duplicate style names, an application can compare the information returned by **EnumFontFamilies** against the family name and style name stored with the embedded font.

Read-Write Permission

Embedded fonts that have read-write permission (and that therefore can be permanently installed on the user's system) should be written to a file that has the .TTF filename extension.

Most applications put the files for embedded fonts that have read-write permission into either the SYSTEM subdirectory of the user's Windows directory or into the application's working directory. Files for read-only embedded fonts are typically put into a temporary directory.

Before installing an embedded font, you must use the **CreateScalableFontResource** function to create a font resource file. Because Windows cannot directly interpret the native TrueType font file format, it requires a file that mimics the standard .FON file (called a .FOT file) to make internal bookkeeping and enumeration easier. The **CreateScalableFontResource** function produces a .FOT file that points to the TrueType font file. Once this .FOT file is produced, Windows applications can use TrueType fonts transparently by using the **AddFontResource** and **RemoveFontResource** functions. You can also use the **CreateScalableFontResource** function to install special fonts for logos, icons, and other graphics. Font resource files for read-only fonts should use a different extension (for example, .FOR) and should be hidden from other applications in the system by specifying 1 for the first parameter of **CreateScalableFontResource**.

Your application should offer users the option of permanently installing embedded fonts that have read-write permission. To permanently install a font, applications should concatenate the family and style names and then use the **WriteProfileString** function to insert this string along with the .FOT file name in the [Fonts] section of the WIN.INI file. A typical font entry in the [Fonts] section looks like the following example.

```
Times New Roman Bold (TrueType)=TIMESBD.FOT
```

Read-Only Permission

Embedded fonts with read-only permission should not use the .TTF extension and should avoid the .FOT and .FON extensions. A typical filename extension for read-only embedded fonts is .TTR. Files for read-only embedded fonts must be removed from the operating system and from both physical and logical memory as soon as the containing document is closed, so their names do not need to be meaningful except to the application.

If a document contains one or more read-only embedded fonts, the user must not be permitted to edit the document. If the user is allowed to edit the document in any way, your application must first strip away and delete the read-only embedded fonts. As mentioned earlier, read-only embedded fonts must be removed from the operating system and memory immediately when the document in which they are bundled is closed.

To delete read-only embedded fonts, your application should follow these steps:

1. Call the **RemoveFontResource** function for each font to be deleted.
2. Delete the font resource file for each font.
3. Delete each TrueType font file for each font.

When an application creates a file for a read-only embedded font and specifies 1 for the first parameter of the **CreateScalableFontResource** function, the **EnumFonts** and **EnumFontFamilies** functions will not enumerate this font. Hiding read-only embedded fonts in this manner makes it unlikely that another application can use them, even though Windows resources are theoretically available to all processes in Windows. The **RemoveFontResource** function does not delete a font currently in use. If your application uses a read-only embedded font installed by another application, it can be difficult for the installing application to delete the font. In this case, your application should delete the resource file and the TrueType font file when the user closes the document containing the read-only fonts.

It is very important that applications delete the TrueType font file for read-only embedded fonts. If the delete operation fails when the user closes the document, the application should periodically attempt to delete the file as the application runs, when it closes, and the next time it starts.

In some cases, an application is unable to delete a TrueType font file for a read-only embedded font because of external events (such as a system failure). There is no legal liability for events that are out of the control of the application.

35.4 Font and Text Functions

The following list identifies the font and text functions:

AddFontModule
AddFontResource
CreateFont
CreateFontIndirect
CreateScalableFontResource
DrawText
EnumFontFamilies
EnumFontFamProc
EnumFonts
EnumFontsProc

ExtCreateFontIndirect
ExtTextOut
GetAspectRatioFilter
GetAspectRatioFilterEx
GetCharABCWidths
GetCharABCWidthsFloat
GetCharWidth
GetCharWidthFloat
GetFontData
GetGlyphOutline
GetKerningPairs
GetOutlineTextMetrics
GetRasterizerCaps
GetTabbedTextExtent
GetTextAlign
GetTextCharacterExtra
GetTextColor
GetTextExtent
GetTextExtentExPoint
GetTextExtentPoint
GetTextFace
GetTextMetrics
MulDiv
PolyTextOut
RemoveFontModule
RemoveFontResource
SetMapperFlags
SetTextAlign
SetTextCharacterExtra
SetTextColor
SetTextJustification
TabbedTextOut
TextOut

CHAPTER 36

Colors

36.1 About Color

Color functions, messages, and structures enable applications written for
Microsoft ® Windows ™ to take advantage of recent improvements in display-
adapter and printer technology. Colors are used by Windows-based applications
in a variety of ways. Word-processing applications display and print text by using
a variety of foreground and background colors, spreadsheet applications display
and print charts and graphs that have been outlined and filled with a variety of pen
and brush colors, and image-editing applications display and print bitmapped
pictures by using a rich set of colors that give the images a realistic appearance.
This chapter focuses on the use of colors on video displays.

36.1.1 Colors and Light

Light is a form of electromagnetic radiation consisting of millions of small
particles called photons. Although light consists of particles, it is analyzed as a
wave form. It can be divided into three color groups, each characterized by a
specific wavelength. The first group with the shortest wavelength is blue, the
second with medium wavelength is green, and the third group with the longest
wavelength is red. The RGB **format** uses these groups (red,green, and blue) to
identify a color.

Three different elements characterize human perception of color: hue, luminosity,
and saturation. Each of these elements loosely corresponds to one of the physical
characteristics of light: hue corresponds to wavelength, luminosity corresponds to
intensity, and saturation corresponds to purity. The **HLS format** uses these
elements (hue, luminosity, and saturation) to identify a color.

The HLS format is supported in the Color common dialog box, shown in the
following illustration. The Color common dialog box enables users to specify an
HLS triplet that identifies a specific color.

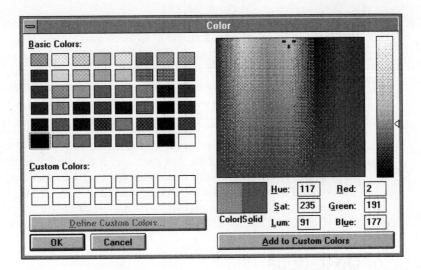

Note Although colors can be specified in the Color common dialog box by using the HLS format Windows stores colors internally by using the RGB format.

For more information about the Color common dialog box, see Chapter 76, "Common Dialog Box Library.")

36.1.2 Colors and Video Display Technology

The 8514, Video Graphics Adapter (VGA), and super-VGA video adapters are significant improvements over the early video displays such as the Color Graphics Adapter (CGA) and the Enhanced Graphics Adapter (EGA). The CGA is capable of producing a maximum of 4 colors with a resolution of 320 by 200 pixels. The EGA is capable of producing a maximum of 16 simultaneous colors from an array of 64 total available colors with a resolution of 640 by 350 pixels. The more recent VGA is capable of producing 16 simultaneous colors from an array of 262,144 colors with a resolution of 640 by 480 pixels. The 8514 and super VGA displays offer resolutions and color capabilities beyond that of the standard VGA. Some super VGA displays are capable of displaying over 16 million colors at a resolution of 1024 by 768 pixels. The improvements in color capabilities and resolution have finally made it possible to display realistic bitmapped images in the client area of an application's window without dithering or mixing colors to produce shades.

A color video display is normally a raster device that treats the display surface as a coordinate space and draws lines, curves, text, and filled objects by repeatedly scanning rows of picture elements called pixels from left to right and from top to bottom. A pixel becomes visible when one or more electron guns in the back of the display fire an electron beam onto a phosphor coating on the back of the display surface. When struck by the electron beam, the phosphor emits visible light. In the simplest case, a single pixel is created by combining the light produced by three electron guns. When the beam of each gun strikes the phosphor coating, it generates red, green, or blue light of varying intensity. When viewed by the human eye, the three dots produced by the three guns appear to merge and form a single color. The point at which the three dots merge is a pixel.

Color video technology is often called an *additive technology* because the color of each pixel on a display is specified by *adding* the intensity values for each of the primaries: red, green, and blue. For example, if the minimum intensity on a given display was specified as 0 and maximum intensity was specified as 255, a white pixel would be identified by the RGB triplet (255, 255, 255), a black pixel would be identified by the RGB triplet (0, 0, 0), and a cyan pixel would be identified by the RGB triplet (0, 255, 255).

36.1.3 Color Operations

Most of the 8514 and super VGA display adapters impose a limit on the number of colors that can appear simultaneously on the screen. This limit is a function of the resolution of the display and the amount of memory on the adapter card. For example, an adapter with 512 kilobytes (K) of video memory could display as many as 256 colors simultaneously on a display with a resolution of 640 by 480 pixels. If the display resolution were increased to 1024 by 768 pixels, the memory limitations of the adapter card would prevent the simultaneous display of 256 colors—instead, only 16 different colors could appear at the same time. This problem is fairly common on a number of displays—only a subset of the total number of colors can appear simultaneously. The array which identifies this subset is called the system palette. Windows adds entries from another palette, the logical palette, to the system palette when an application realizes its logical palette. The two palettes are described in the following sections.

36.1.3.1 System Palette

The *system palette* is an array identifying a subset of the total number of colors that can appear simultaneously on a display. It is shared by all Windows-based applications. Windows provides a set of palette-manager functions that are used to alter the colors in the system palette. These functions are designed for applications that require realistic colors when displaying bitmapped images.The code supporting these functions is part of a dynamic-link library (DLL) called the display driver. A *display driver* is a Windows DLL that converts graphics device interface (GDI) function calls to corresponding device commands. Not all display drivers support the palette-manager functions. For example, standard VGA display drivers do not support the palette-manager functions, super-VGA display drivers do. You can determine whether or not a device supports a system palette by calling the **GetDeviceCaps** function and specifying the RASTERCAPS constant. If a device supports a system palette, you can retrieve the system palette size by calling the **GetDeviceCaps** function and specifying the NUMCOLORS constant as the second argument.

The palette-manager functions are powerful but potentially problematic; by altering colors in the system palette can could also change the colors in every window on the desktop. In order to prevent this from happening, Windows provides the following:

- An object called a logical palette that is associated with each application's device context. For more information about the logical palette, see Section 36.1.3.2, "Logical Palette."
- A set of messages that informs an application that changes have been made to the system palette.
- A set of functions used to create, alter, and remove a logical palette.

36.1.3.2 Logical Palette

A *logical palette* is an array of colors that an application can use when drawing graphics output using the device context. Each device context has a default logical palette containing 20 entries. Of these 20 entries, 16 of the colors correspond to the colors found on a standard VGA display while the remaining 4 correspond to unique colors used by Window Manager. The following table shows the default logical palette and the RGB triplets found in each entry:

Index value	Red	Green	Blue
0	0x00	0x00	0x00
1	0x80	0x00	0x00
2	0x00	0x80	0x00
3	0x80	0x80	0x00
4	0x00	0x00	0x80
5	0x80	0x00	0x80
6	0x00	0x80	0x80
7	0xC0	0xC0	0xC0
8	0xC0	0xDC	0xC0
9	0xA6	0xCA	0xF0
10	0xFF	0xFB	0xF0
11	0xA0	0xA0	0xA4
12	0x80	0x80	0x80
13	0xFF	0x00	0x00
14	0x00	0xFF	0x00
15	0xFF	0xFF	0x00

16	0x00	0x00	0xFF
17	0xFF	0x00	0xFF
18	0x00	0xFF	0xFF
19	0xFF	0xFF	0xFF

The 16 standard VGA colors are found at locations 0–7 and locations 12–19; the nonstandard colors are found at locations 8–11.

36.1.3.3 Custom Logical Palette

If an application creates or displays bitmapped images, it may be necessary to use more than the 20 default colors. It may also be necessary to replace the 20 default colors with colors that are better suited to the image that is created or displayed. Before creating a custom logical palette, an application must determine the number of colors that are supported by the device. This is done by calling the **GetDeviceCaps** function and passing the NUMCOLORS constant as the second argument.

The colors requested in the logical palette are mapped to the system palette when the application's window is the active window on the desktop *and* when the application realizes its logical palette by calling the **RealizePalette** function. If an application replaces the entire system palette with new colors, it must call the **SetSystemPaletteUse** function before to realizing its logical palette.

In order to prevent one application from altering the colors in other application's windows, three messages are supported by window manager. If the currently active application realizes a custom palette by calling the **RealizePalette** function, Windows sends the WM_PALETTEISCHANGING message to all top-level and overlapped windows, indicating the system palette is about to change. If the function executes successfully, Windows sends the WM_PALETTECHANGED message to the windows, indicating the system palette has changed. When one of the top-level or overlapped windows is about to be activated, Windows sends the WM_QUERYNEWPALETTE message. Upon receiving this message, the corresponding application must call the **RealizePalette** function to realize its own logical palette.

To create a custom logical palette, an application first needs to create a **LOGPALETTE** structure, call the **CreatePalette** function, and pass a pointer to the structure. An application can select a logical palette into the application device context by calling the **SelectPalette** function. However, before you can draw in the client area of your application's window by using the colors specified in the custom logical palette, you'll need to call the **RealizePalette** function. If your application's window is currently the active window, the colors requested in your logical palette are stored in the system palette, and you can begin drawing. If the application's window is not the active window, the colors requested in the custom logical palette may not be matched to the system palette. Whether or not a match occurs depends on such things as the size of the system palette, the size of the custom palette, the size of the logical palette associated with the active window, and the colors specified in both logical palettes.

Once a logical palette is created, an application can change or update its colors by calling the **AnimatePalette** or **SetPaletteEntries** function. If the application's window is active, the application can update the colors on the screen immediately by calling the **AnimatePalette** function. To update the logical-palette colors but continue displaying the current colors for a period of time, it can call the **SetPaletteEntries** function to alter the logical palette and then later call the **RealizePalette** function when it is appropriate to actually update the image on the screen.

36.1.3.4 Colored Pens, Brushes, and Text

Applications can use the palette manager and the Color common dialog box to let a user select a custom color. The dialog box is displayed by calling the **ChooseColor** function, which returns an RGB triplet for the requested color. To retrieve the logical-palette index for the closest color in the logical palette, call the **GetNearestPaletteIndex** function. Use this index to create a pen, brush, or text output with the closest match to the requested color.

When creating color pens, brushes, and text, it is actually faster to use an RGB triplet (instead of a Palette index) to set the colors of objects in a device context. Once the **ChooseColor** function returns an RGB triplet, determine the closest match by calling the **GetNearestColor** function. Use the triplet returned by **GetNearestColor** to create a colored pen by calling the **CreatePenIndirect** function, create a colored brush by calling the **CreateBrushIndirect** function, or create colored text by calling the **SetTextColor** function.

36.2 Using Color

This section contains sample code demonstrating common tasks performed with the color and palette manager functions.

36.2.1 Creating a Colored Pen

You can use the Color common dialog box to let the user choose pen, brush, and text colors. This dialog box is displayed by initializing a **CHOOSECOLOR** structure and calling the **ChooseColor** function. Upon executing successfully, the **ChooseColor** function stores an RGB triplet corresponding to the user's selection in the **rgbResult** member of the **CHOOSECOLOR** structure. You can use this member to specify a pen, brush, or text color by calling the **CreatePenIndirect**, **CreateBrushIndirect**, or **SetTextColor** function and copying the RGB data from this member to the appropriate argument.

In the following example, the data contained in the **rgbResult** member is copied into the **lopnColor** member of a **LOGPEN** structure and is used to create a new pen.

```
case IDM_PENCOLOR:

    /* Retrieve the default logical palette entries. */

    iRet = GetPaletteEntries(hpal, 0, 20, ape);

    /* Set the custom color controls to white. */

    for (i = 0; i < 16; i++)
        aclrCust[i] = RGB(255, 255, 255);

    /* Initialize clr to black. */

    clr = RGB(0, 0, 0);

    /* Set all structure members to zero. */

    memset(&cc, 0, sizeof(CHOOSECOLOR));

    /* Initialize the necessary CHOOSECOLOR members. */

    cc.lStructSize = sizeof(CHOOSECOLOR);
    cc.hwndOwner = hWnd;
    cc.rgbResult = clr;
    cc.lpCustColors = aclrCust;
    cc.Flags = CC_PREVENTFULLOPEN;

    if (ChooseColor(&cc)) {

        /* Initialize the LOGPEN structure. */

        lp.lopnStyle = PS_SOLID;
        lp.lopnWidth.x = 1;
        lp.lopnColor = cc.rgbResult;

        /* Select the new pen and draw. */

        hdc = GetDC(hWnd);
        hpenOld = SelectObject(hdc, CreatePenIndirect(&lp));
        MoveToEx(hdc, 100, 100, NULL);
        LineTo(hdc, 100, 200);
        /*    . */
        /*    . */
        /*    . */
        ReleaseDC(hWnd, hdc);
    }
```

```
break;
```

36.3 Functions and Messages

Following are the functions and messages that support the use of color in a Win32 application.

Functions

AnimatePalette
CreateHalftonePalette
CreatePalette
GetColorAdjustment
GetNearestColor
GetNearestPaletteIndex
GetPaletteEntries
GetSystemPaletteEntries
GetSystemPaletteUse
RealizePalette
ResizePalette
SelectPalette
SetColorAdjustment
SetPaletteEntries
SetSystemPaletteUse
UpdateColors

Messages

WM_PALETTECHANGED
WM_PALETTEISCHANGING
WM_QUERYNEWPALETTE
WM_SYSCOLORCHANGE

C H A P T E R   3 7

Paths

37.1 About Paths

A *path* is one or more figures (or shapes) that are filled, outlined, or both filled and outlined. Applications written for Microsoft ® Windows ™ use paths in many ways. Paths are used in drawing and painting applications. Computer-aided design (CAD) applications use paths to create unique clipping regions, to draw outlines of irregular shapes, and to fill the interiors of irregular shapes. An *irregular shape* is a shape composed of Bézier curves *and* straight lines. (A *regular* shape is an ellipse, a circle, a rectangle, or a polygon.)

A path is one of the objects associated with a device context (DC). However, unlike the default objects (the pen, the brush, and the font) that are part of any new DC, there is no default path. For more information about device contexts, see Chapter 28, "Device Contexts."

To create a path and select it into a device context, it is first necessary to define the points that describe it. This is done by calling the **BeginPath** function, specifying the appropriate drawing functions, and then by calling the **EndPath** function. This combination of functions (**BeginPath**, drawing functions, and **EndPath**) constitute a *path bracket*. The following functions can be used in a path bracket:

AngleArc	**LineTo**	**Polyline**
Arc	**MoveToEx**	**PolylineTo**
ArcTo	**Pie**	**PolyPolygon**
Chord	**PolyBezier**	**PolyPolyline**
CloseFigure	**PolyBezierTo**	**Rectangle**
Ellipse	**PolyDraw**	**RoundRect**
ExtTextOut	**Polygon**	**TextOut**

When an application calls the **EndPath** function, Windows selects the associated path into the specified DC. (If another path had previously been selected into the DC, Windows deletes that path without saving it.) After Windows selects the path into the DC, an application can operate on the path in one of the following ways:

- Draw the outline of the path (using the current pen).
- Paint the interior of the path (using the current brush).
- Draw the outline *and* fill the interior of the path.
- Modify the path (by converting curves to line segments).
- Convert the path into a clip path.
- Convert the path into a region.
- Flatten the path by converting each curve in the path into a series of line segments.

- Retrieve the coordinates of the lines and curves that compose a path.

37.1.1 Outlined and Filled Paths

An application can draw the outline of a path by calling the **StrokePath** function; it can fill the interior of a path by calling the **FillPath** function; and it can both outline and fill the path by calling the **StrokeAndFillPath** function.

Whenever an application fills a path, Windows uses the device context's current fill mode. An application can retrieve this mode by calling the **GetPolyFillMode** function and, it can set a new fill mode by calling the **SetPolyFillMode** function. For a description of the two fill modes, see Chapter 32, "Regions."

The following illustration shows the cross-section of an object created by a computer-aided design (CAD) application using paths that were both outlined and filled.

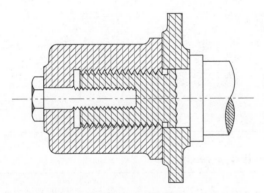

37.1.2 Transformations of Paths

Paths are defined by using logical units and current transformations. (If the **SetWorldTransform** function has been called, the logical units are world units; if this function has not been called, the logical units are page units.) An application can use world transformations to scale, rotate, shear, translate, and reflect the lines and Bézier curves which define a path.

Note A world transformation within a path bracket only affects those lines and curves drawn *after* the transformation was set. It will have no affect on those lines and curves that were drawn before setting the transformation. For a description of world transformation, see Chapter 39, "Coordinate Spaces and Transformations."

An application can also use the **SetWorldTransform** function to outline the shape of the pen used to outline a path if the pen is a geometric pen. For a description of geometric pens, see Chapter 31, "Pens."

37.1.3 Clip Paths

An application can use clipping and paths to create special graphic effects. The following illustration shows a string of text drawn by using a large Arial font.

The next illustration shows the result of selecting the text as a clip path and drawing radial lines for a circle whose center is located above and left of the string.

Note Before GDI adds text created with a bitmapped font to a path, it converts the font to an outline or vector font.

An application creates a clip path by generating a path bracket and then by calling the **SelectClipPath** function. After a clip path is selected into a DC, output only appears within the borders of the path.

In addition to creating special graphic effects, clip paths are also useful in applications that save images as enhanced metafiles. By using a clip path, an application is able to ensure device independence because the units used to specify a path are logical units (as opposed to device units that are used to specify a region).

37.1.4 Conversion of Paths to Regions

An application can convert a path into a region by calling the **PathToRegion** function. Like the **SelectClipPath** function, **PathToRegion** is useful in the creation of special graphic effects. For example, there are no functions that allow an application to offset a path; however, there is a function that enables an application to offset a region (**OffsetRgn**). Using **PathToRegion**, an application can create the effect of animating a complex shape by creating a path that defines the shape, converting the path into a region (by calling **PathToRegion**), and then repeatedly painting, moving, and erasing the region (by calling functions such as **FillRgn**, **OffsetRgn**, **FillRgn**).

37.1.5 Curved Paths

An application can flatten the curves in a path by calling the **FlattenPath** function. This function is especially useful in applications that fit text onto the contour of a path which contains curves. To fit the text, the application must perform the following steps:

1. Create the path where the text appears.

2. Call the **FlattenPath** function to convert the curves in a path into line segments.

3. Call the **GetPath** function to retrieve these line segments.

4. Calculate the length of each line and the width of each character in the string.

5. Use the line-width and character-width data to position each character along the curve.

37.2 Using Paths

This section contains a code sample that enables the user to select a font of a particular point size (by using the Choose Font dialog box), select a clip path (by using text drawn with this font), and then view the result of clipping to the text.

This code was used to create the illustrations that appear in Section 37.1.3, "Clip Paths."

```
CHOOSEFONT cf;          /* common dialog box font structure          */
LOGFONT lf;             /* logical font structure                    */
HFONT hfont;            /* new logical font handle                   */
HFONT hfontOld;         /* original logical font handle              */
HDC hdc;                /* display DC handle                         */
int nXStart, nYStart;   /* drawing coordinates                       */
RECT rc;                /* rectangle structure for painting window   */
SIZE sz;                /* size structure that receives text extents */
double aflSin[90];      /* sine of 0-90 degrees in 1 degree increments   */
double aflCos[90];      /* cosine of 0-90 degrees in 1 degree increments */
double flRadius,a;      /* radius of circle                          */
int iMode;              /* clipping mode                             */
HRGN hrgn;              /* clip region handle                        */

LRESULT APIENTRY MainWndProc(
    HWND hwnd,              /* window handle             */
    UINT message,          /* type of message           */
    WPARAM wParam,         /* additional information    */
    LPARAM lParam)         /* additional information    */
```

```
{

    PAINTSTRUCT ps;

    switch (message) {

        case WM_PAINT:
            hdc = BeginPaint(hwnd, &ps);
            EndPaint(hwnd, &ps);
            break;

        case WM_COMMAND: /* message: command from application menu */
            switch (wParam) {

                case IDM_VANISH: /* erases client area */
                    hdc = GetDC(hwnd);
                    GetClientRect(hwnd, &rc);
                    FillRect(hdc, &rc, GetStockObject(WHITE_BRUSH));
                    ReleaseDC(hwnd, hdc);
                    break;

                case IDM_AND: /* sets clip mode to RGN_AND */
                    iMode = RGN_AND;
                    break;

                case IDM_COPY: /* sets clip mode to RGN_COPY */
                    iMode = RGN_COPY;
                    break;

                case IDM_DIFF: /* sets clip mode to RGN_DIFF */
                    iMode = RGN_DIFF;
                    break;

                case IDM_OR: /* sets clip mode to RGN_OR */
                    iMode = RGN_OR;
                    break;

                case IDM_XOR: /* sets clip mode to RGN_XOR */
                    iMode = RGN_XOR;
                    break;

                case IDM_CLIP_PATH:

                    /* Retrieve a cached DC for the window. */

                    hdc = GetDC(hwnd);

                    /*
```

```
* Use the font requested by the user in the
* Choose Font dialog box to create a logical font, and then
* select that font into the device context.
*/

hfont = CreateFontIndirect(cf.lpLogFont);
hfontOld = SelectObject(hdc, hfont);

/*
* Retrieve the dimensions of the rectangle
* that surrounds the text.
*/

GetTextExtentPoint(hdc, "Clip Path", 9, &sz);

/*
* Set a clipping region using the rectangle that
* surrounds the text.
*/

hrgn = CreateRectRgn(nXStart, nYStart,
    nXStart + sz.cx,
    nYStart + sz.cy);

SelectClipRgn(hdc, hrgn);

/*
* Create a clip path using text drawn with
* the user's requested font.
*/

BeginPath(hdc);
    TextOut(hdc, nXStart, nYStart, "Clip Path", 9);
EndPath(hdc);
SelectClipPath(hdc, iMode);

/* Compute the sine of 0, 1, 2, ... 90 degrees. */
for (i = 0; i < 90; i++) {
    aflSin[i] = sin( (((double)i) / 180.0) * 3.14159);
    }

/* Compute the cosine of 0, 1, 2, ... 90 degrees. */
for (i = 0; i < 90; i++) {
    aflCos[i] = cos( (((double)i) / 180.0) * 3.14159);
    }

/* Set the radius value. */

flRadius = (double)(2 * sz.cx);
```

```
/*
 * Draw the 90 rays extending from the
 * radius to the edge of the circle.
 */

for (i = 0; i < 90; i++) {
    MoveToEx(hdc, nXStart, nYStart, (LPPOINT) NULL);
    LineTo(hdc, nXStart + ((int) (flRadius * aflCos[i])),
            nYStart + ((int) (flRadius * aflSin[i])));
    }

/* Reselect the original font into the DC. */

 SelectObject(hdc, hfontOld);

/* Delete the user's font. */

 DeleteObject(hfont);

/* Release the DC. */

ReleaseDC(hwnd, hdc);

break;


case IDM_FONT:

    /* Initialize necessary members. */

    cf.lStructSize = sizeof (CHOOSEFONT);
    cf.hwndOwner = hwnd;
    cf.lpLogFont = &lf;
    cf.Flags = CF_SCREENFONTS | CF_EFFECTS;
    cf.rgbColors = RGB(0, 255, 255);
    cf.nFontType = SCREEN_FONTTYPE;

    /*
     * Display the Font dialog box, allow the user to
     * choose a font, and render text in the
     * window with that selection.
     */

    if (ChooseFont(&cf)) {
        hdc = GetDC(hwnd);
        hfont = CreateFontIndirect(cf.lpLogFont);
        hfontOld = SelectObject(hdc, hfont);
        crOld = SetTextColor(hdc, cf.rgbColors);
        TextOut(hdc, nXStart, nYStart,
            "Clip Path", 9);
```

```
                        SetTextColor(hdc, crOld);
                        SelectObject(hdc, hfontOld);
                        DeleteObject(hfont);
                        ReleaseDC(hwnd, hdc);
                }

                break;

            default:
                return DefWindowProc(hwnd, message, wParam, lParam);
        }
        break;

    case WM_DESTROY: /* message: window being destroyed    */
        PostQuitMessage(0);
        break;

    default: /* passes it on if unprocessed          */
        return DefWindowProc(hwnd, message, wParam, lParam);
    }
    return 0;
}
```

37.3 Functions

Use the following functions to create, alter, or draw paths.

AbortPath
BeginPath
CloseFigure
EndPath
FillPath
FlattenPath
GetMiterLimit
GetPath
PathToRegion
SelectClipPath
SetMiterLimit
StrokeAndFillPath
StrokePath
WidenPath

C H A P T E R   3 8

Clipping

38.1 About Clipping

Clipping is the process of limiting output to a region or path within the client area of an application's window. Clipping is used by applications written for Microsoft ® Windows ™ in a variety of ways. Word processing and spreadsheet applications clip keyboard input to keep it from appearing in the margins of a page or spreadsheet. Computer-aided design (CAD) and drawing applications clip graphics output to keep it from overwriting the edges of a drawing or picture.

A *clipping region* is a region with edges that are either straight lines or curves. A *clip path* is a region with edges that are straight lines, Bézier curves, or combinations of both. For more information about regions, see Chapter 32, "Regions." For more information about paths, see Chapter 37, "Paths."

38.1.1 Clipping Regions

A clipping region is one of the graphic objects that an application can select into a device context (DC). It is typically rectangular. Some device contexts provide a predefined or default clipping region while others do not. For example, if you obtain a device context handle from the **BeginPaint** function, the DC contains a predefined, rectangular clipping region that corresponds to the invalid rectangle that requires repainting. However, if you obtain a device context handle by calling the **CreateDC** or **GetDC** function, the DC does not contain a default clipping region. For more information about device contexts returned by the **BeginPaint** function, see Chapter 20, "Painting and Drawing." For more information about device contexts returned by the **CreateDC** and **GetDC** functions, see Chapter 28, "Device Contexts."

Applications can perform a variety of operations on clipping regions. Some of these operations require a handle identifying the region and some do not. For example, an application can perform the following operations directly on a device context's clipping region:

- Determine whether graphics output appears within the region's borders by passing coordinates of the corresponding line, arc, bitmap, text, or filled shape to the **PtVisible** function.

- Determine whether part of the client area intersects a region by calling the **RectVisible** function.

- Move the existing region by a specified offset by calling the **OffsetClipRgn** function.

- Exclude a rectangular part of the client area from the current clipping region by calling the **ExcludeClipRect** function.

- Combine a rectangular part of the client area with the current clipping region by calling the **IntersectClipRect** function.

After obtaining a handle identifying the region, an application can perform any operation that is common with regions; for example:

- Combining a copy of the current clipping region with a second region by calling the **CombineRgn** function.

- Compare a copy of the current clipping region to a second region by calling the **EqualRgn** function.

- Determine whether a point lies within the interior of a copy of the current clipping region by calling the **PtInRegion** function.

38.1.2 Clip Paths

Like a clipping region, a clip path is another graphics object an application can select into a device context. Unlike a clipping region, a clip path is always created by an application and it is used for clipping to one or more irregular shapes. For example, an application can use the lines and curves that form the outlines of characters in a string of text to define a clip path.

To create a clip path, it's first necessary to create a path that describes the required irregular shape. Paths are created by calling the appropriate GDI drawing functions after calling the **BeginPath** function and before calling the **EndPath** function. This collection of functions is called a path bracket. For more information about paths and path brackets, see Chapter 37, "Paths."

After the path is created, it can be converted to a clip path by calling the **SelectClipPath** function, identifying a device context, and specifying a usage mode. The usage mode determines how Windows combines the new clip path with the device context's original clipping region. The following table describes the usage modes.

Mode	Description
RGN_AND	The clip path includes the intersection (overlapping areas) of the device context's clipping region and the current path.
RGN_COPY	The clip path is the current path.
RGN_DIFF	The clip path includes the device context's clipping region with any intersecting parts of the current path excluded.
RGN_OR	The clip path includes the union (combined areas) of the device context's clipping region and the current path.
RGN_XOR	The clip path includes the union of the device context's clipping region and the current path but excludes the intersection.

38.2 Using Clipping

This section contains a code example that demonstrates how an application can generate a clip path consisting of the characters "ABC" drawn by using a font specified by the user.

The following illustration shows the string of text drawn in the usual fashion by using a brush with the current text color.

The next illustration shows the string of text selected as a clip path and filled by drawing horizontal and vertical lines.

```
CHOOSEFONT cf;        /* common dialog box font structure        */
LOGFONT lf;           /* logical font structure                  */
HFONT hfont;          /* new logical font handle                 */
HFONT hfontOld;       /* original logical font handle            */
HDC hdc;              /* display DC handle                       */
int nXStart, nYStart; /* drawing coordinates                     */
RECT rc;              /* rectangle structure for painting window */
SIZE sz;              /* size structure that receives text extents */

    /* Retrieve a cached DC for the window. */

    hdc = GetDC(hwnd);

    /* Erase the current window contents. */

    GetClientRect(hwnd, &rc);
    FillRect(hdc, &rc, GetStockObject(WHITE_BRUSH));

    /*
     * Use the font requested by the user in the
     * Font dialog box to create a logical font, and
     * then select that font into the DC.
     */

    hfont = CreateFontIndirect(cf.lpLogFont);
    hfontOld = SelectObject(hdc, hfont);
```

```
/*
 * Create a clip path using text drawn with
 * the user's requested font.
 */

BeginPath(hdc);
    TextOut(hdc, nXStart, nYStart, "ABC", 3);
EndPath(hdc);
SelectClipPath(hdc, RGN_DIFF);

/*
 * Retrieve the dimensions of the rectangle
 *that surrounds the text.
 */

GetTextExtentPoint(hdc, "ABC", 3, &sz);

/*
 *Draw horizontal lines through the clip
 * path.
 */

for (i = nYStart + 1; i < (nYStart + sz.cy); i+=3) {
    MoveToEx(hdc, nXStart, i, (LPPOINT) NULL);
    LineTo(hdc, (nXStart + sz.cx), i);
}

/* Draw vertical lines through the clip path. */

for (i = nXStart + 1; i < (nXStart + sz.cx); i+=3){
    MoveToEx(hdc, i, nYStart, (LPPOINT) NULL);
    LineTo(hdc, i, (nYStart + sz.cy));
}

/* Reselect the original font into the DC. */

SelectObject(hdc, hfontOld);

/* Delete the user's font. */

DeleteObject(hfont);

/* Release the DC. */

ReleaseDC(hwnd, hdc);
```

For an example that demonstrates how an application creates a rectangular clipping region, see Chapter 32, "Regions."

38.3 Functions

Following are the functions used with clipping:

ExcludeClipRect
ExtSelectClipRgn
GetClipBox
GetClipRgn
GetMetaRgn
IntersectClipRect
OffsetClipRgn
PtVisible
RectVisible
SelectClipPath
SelectClipRgn
SetMetaRgn

CHAPTER 39

Coordinate Spaces and Transformations

39.1 About Coordinate Spaces and Transformations

Applications written for Microsoft ® Windows ™ use coordinate spaces and transformations to scale, rotate, translate, shear, and reflect graphics output. For example, desktop publishing applications use coordinate spaces and transformations to "zoom" parts of a page or to display adjacent pages in a window; computer-aided design (CAD) applications use them to rotate objects, scale drawings, or to create perspective views; and spreadsheet applications use them to move and size graphs.

The following illustrations show successive views of an object created in a drawing application. The first illustration shows the object as it appears in the original drawing; the five remaining illustrations show the effects of applying various transformations.

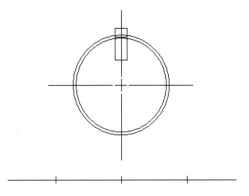

Original View

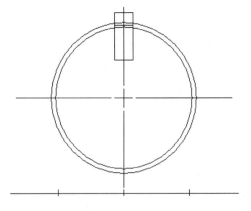

Scaled View

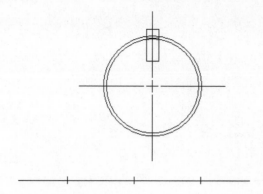

Translated View

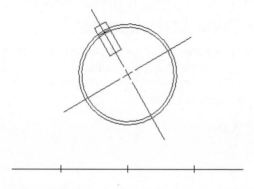

Rotated View

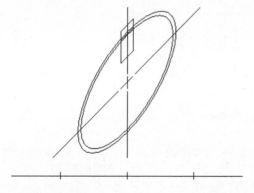

Sheared View

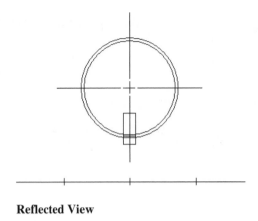

Reflected View

39.1.1 Transformation of Coordinate Spaces

A *coordinate space* is a planar space based on the Cartesian coordinate system. This system provides a means of specifying the location of each point on a plane. It requires two axes that are perpendicular *and* equal in length. The following illustration shows a coordinate space.

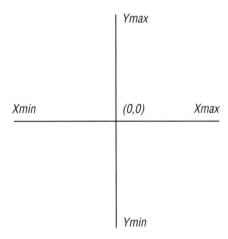

The Win32 application programming interface (API) uses four coordinate spaces: world, page, device, and physical device. Applications use world space to rotate, shear, or reflect graphics output. World space measures 2^{32} units high by 2^{32} units wide. Page space (referred to as logical space in earlier versions of Windows) also measures 2^{32} units high by 2^{32} units wide. Device space measures 2^{27} units high by 2^{27} units wide. Page space works with device space to provide applications with device-independent units, such as millimeters and inches. The Win32 API refers to both world space and page space as logical space. The final coordinate space, physical device, usually refers to the client area of the application's window; however, it can also include the entire desktop, a complete window (including the frame, title bar, and menu bar), or a page of printer or plotter paper. Physical device dimensions vary according to the dimensions set by the display, printer, or plotter technology.

To depict output on a physical device, Windows copies (or maps) a rectangular region from one coordinate space into the next coordinate space until finally the output appears in its entirety on the physical device. Mapping begins in the application's world space if the application has called the **SetWorldTransform** function; otherwise, mapping occurs in page space. As Windows copies each point within the rectangular region from one space into another, it applies an algorithm called a transformation. A *transformation* alters (or transforms) the size, orientation, and shape of objects that are copied from one coordinate space into another. Although a transformation affects an object as a whole, it is applied to each point, or to each line, in the object.

The following illustration shows a typical transformation performed by using the **SetWorldTransform** function.

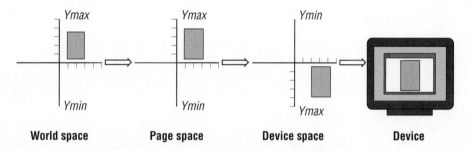

| World space | Page space | Device space | Device |

39.1.2 World-Space to Page-Space Transformations

World-space to page-space transformations are new to Windows. They support translation and scaling that were available in previous versions of Windows. In addition, they support rotation, shear, and reflection capabilities. The following sections describe these transformations, illustrate their effects, and provide the algorithms used to achieve them.

39.1.2.1 Translation

Some applications translate (or shift) objects drawn in the client area. If your application features this capability, use the **SetWorldTransform** function to set the appropriate world-space to page-space transformation. This function receives a pointer to an **XFORM** structure containing the appropriate values. The **eDx** and **eDy** members of **XFORM** specify the horizontal and vertical translation components, respectively.

When *translation* occurs, each point in an object is shifted vertically, horizontally, or both, by a specified amount. The following illustration shows a 20- by 20-unit rectangle that was translated to the right by 10 units when copied from world coordinate space to page coordinate space.

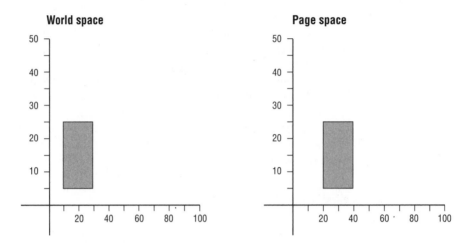

In the preceding illustration, the x-coordinate of each point in the rectangle is 10 units greater than the original x-coordinate.

Horizontal translation can be represented by the following algorithm.

```
x' = x + Dx
```

Where *x'* is the new x-coordinate, *x* is the original x-coordinate, and *Dx* is the horizontal distance moved.

Vertical translation can be represented by the following algorithm.

```
y' = y + Dy
```

Where *y'* is the new y-coordinate, *y* is the original y-coordinate, and *Dy* is the vertical distance moved.

The horizontal and vertical translation transformations can be combined into a single operation by using a 3-by-3 matrix.

```
                |1    0    0|
|x' y' 1| = |x y 1| * |0    1    0|
                |Dx   Dy   1|
```

(The rules of matrix multiplication state that the number of rows in one matrix must equal the number of columns in the other. The integer 1 in the matrix |x y 1| is a placeholder that was added to meet this requirement.)

The 3-by-3 matrix that produced the illustrated translation transformation contains the following values.

```
|1   0   0|
|0   1   0|
|10  0   1|
```

39.1.2.2 Scaling

Most CAD and drawing applications provide features that scale output created by the user. If your application features scaling (or "zoom") capabilities, use the **SetWorldTransform** function to set the appropriate world-space to page-space transformation. This function receives a pointer to an **XFORM** structure containing the appropriate values. The **eM11** and **eM22** members of **XFORM** specify the horizontal and vertical scaling components, respectively.

When *scaling* occurs, the vertical and horizontal lines (or vectors) that constitute an object are stretched or compressed with respect to the x-axis or the y-axis. The following illustration shows a 20- by 20-unit rectangle scaled vertically to twice its original height when copied from world coordinate space to page coordinate space.

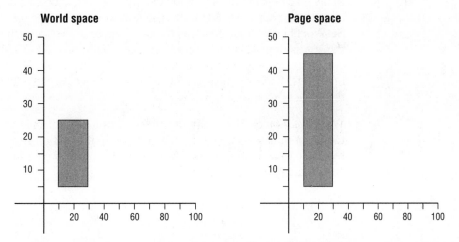

In the preceding illustration, the vertical lines that define the original rectangle's side measure 20 units, while the vertical lines that define the scaled rectangle's sides measure 40 units.

Vertical scaling can be represented by the following algorithm.

```
y' = y * Dy
```

Where *y'* is the new length, *y* is the original length, and *Dy* is the vertical scaling factor.

Horizontal scaling can be represented by the following algorithm.

```
x' = x * Dx
```

Where x' is the new length, x is the original length, and Dx is the horizontal scaling factor.

The vertical and horizontal scaling transformations can be combined into a single operation by using a 2-by-2 matrix.

```
|x' y' |  =  |Dx   0|  *  |x y|
             |0   Dy|
```

The 2-by-2 matrix that produced the illustrated scaling transformation contains the following values.

```
|1    0|
|0    2|
```

39.1.2.3 Rotation

Many CAD applications provide features that rotate objects drawn in the client area. If your application features rotation capabilities, use the **SetWorldTransform** function to set the appropriate world-space to page-space transformation. This function receives a pointer to an **XFORM** structure containing the appropriate values. The **eM11**, **eM12**, **eM21**, and **eM22** members of **XFORM** specify, respectively, the cosine, sine, negative cosine, and cosine of the angle of rotation.

When *rotation* occurs, the points that constitute an object are rotated with respect to the coordinate-space origin. The following illustration shows a 20- by 20-unit rectangle rotated 30 degrees when copied from world coordinate space to page coordinate space.

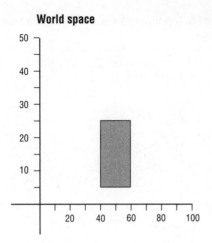

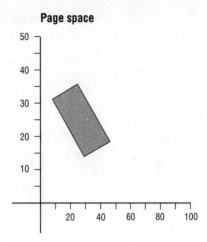

In the preceding illustration, each point in the rectangle was rotated 30 degrees with respect to the coordinate-space origin.

The following algorithm computes the new x-coordinate (*x'*) for a point (*x,y*) that is rotated by angle *A* with respect to the coordinate-space origin.

```
x' = (x * cos A) - (y * sin A)
```

The following algorithm computes the y-coordinate (*y'*) for a point (*x,y*) that is rotated by the angle *A* with respect to the origin.

```
y' = (x * sin A) - (y * cos A)
```

The two rotation transformations can be combined in a 2-by-2 matrix as follows.

```
|x' y'| == |x y| * | cos A    sin A|
                   |-sin A    cos A|
```

The 2-by-2 matrix that produced the rotation contained the following values.

```
| .8660    .5000|
|-.5000    .8660|
```

The Rotation Algorithm Derivation

Rotation algorithms are based on trigonometry's addition theorem stating that the trigonometric function of a sum of two angles (*A1* and *A2*) can be expressed in terms of the trigonometric functions of the two angles.

```
sin(A1 + A2) = (sin A1 * cos A2) + (cos A1 * sin A2)
cos(A1 + A2) = (cos A1 * cos A2) - (sin A1 * sin A2)
```

The following illustration shows a point *p* rotated counterclockwise to a new position *p'*. In addition, it shows two triangles formed by a line drawn from the coordinate-space origin to each point and a line drawn from each point through the x-axis.

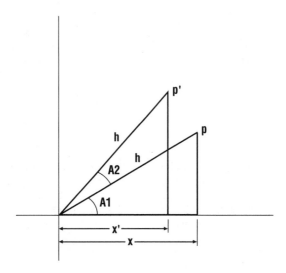

Using trigonometry, the x-coordinate of point p can be obtained by multiplying the length of the hypotenuse h by the cosine of $A1$.

```
x = h * cos A1
```

The y-coordinate of point p can be obtained by multiplying the length of the hypotenuse h by the sine of $A1$.

```
y = h * sin A1
```

Likewise, the x-coordinate of point p' can be obtained by multiplying the length of the hypotenuse h by the cosine of $(A1 + A2)$.

```
x' = h * cos (A1 + A2)
```

Finally, the y-coordinate of point p' can be obtained by multiplying the length of the hypotenuse h by the sine of $(A1 + A2)$.

```
y' = h * sin (A1 + A2)
```

Using the addition theorem, the preceding algorithms become the following.

```
x' = (h * cos A1 * cos A2) - (h * sin A1 * sin A2)
y' = (h * cos A1 * sin A2) - (h * sin A1 * cos A2)
```

The rotation algorithms for a given point rotated by angle *A2* can be obtained by substituting *x* for each occurrence of (*h* * cos *A1*) and substituting *y* for each occurrence of (*h* * sin *A1*).

```
x' = (x * cos A2) - (y * sin A2)
y' = (x * sin A2) - (y * cos A2)
```

39.1.2.4 Shear

Some applications provide features that shear objects drawn in the client area. If your application features shear capabilities, use the **SetWorldTransform** function to set appropriate values in the world-space to page-space transformation. This function receives a pointer to an **XFORM** structure containing the appropriate values. The **eM12** and **eM21** members of **XFORM** specify the horizontal and vertical proportionality constants, respectively.

There are two components of the *shear* transformation: The first alters the vertical lines in an object; the second alters the horizontal lines. The following example shows a 20- by 20-unit rectangle sheared horizontally when copied from world-space to page-space.

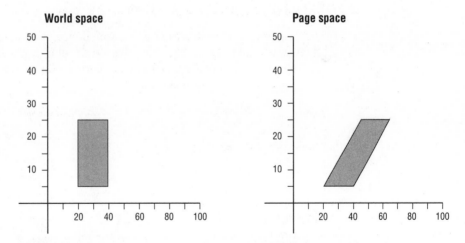

A horizontal shear can be represented by the following algorithm.

```
x' = x + (Sx * y)
```

Where *x* is the original x-coordinate, *Sx* is the proportionality constant, and *x'* is the result of the shear transformation.

A vertical shear can be represented by the following algorithm.

```
y' = y + (Sy * x)
```

Where *y* is the original y-coordinate, *Sy* is the proportionality constant, and *y'* is the result of the shear transformation.

The horizontal-shear and vertical-shear transformations can be combined into a single operation using a 2-by-2 matrix.

```
|x' y'| == |x y| * |  1    Sx|
                   |  Sy    1|
```

The 2-by-2 matrix that produced the shear contains the following values.

```
|1    1|
|0    1|
```

39.1.2.5 Reflection

Some applications provide features that reflect (or mirror) objects drawn in the client area. If your application features reflection capabilities, use the **SetWorldTransform** function to set the appropriate values in the world-space to page-space transformation. This function receives a pointer to an **XFORM** structure containing the appropriate values. The **eM11** and **eM22** members of **XFORM** specify the horizontal and vertical reflection components, respectively.

The *reflection* transformation creates a "mirror" image of an object with respect to either the x-axis or the y-axis. The following illustration shows a 20- by 20-unit rectangle reflected horizontally and vertically upon being copied from world coordinate space to page coordinate space.

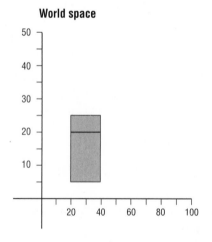
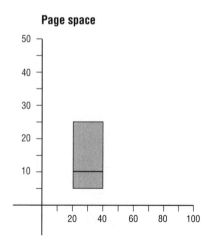

Reflection

Horizontal reflection can be represented by the following algorithm.

```
x' = x * Rx
```

Where x is the x-coordinate, Rx is negative one (-1), and x' is the result of the reflection.

Vertical reflection is represented by the following algorithm.

```
y' = y * Ry
```

Where y is the y-coordinate, Ry is negative one (-1), and y' is the result of the reflection.

The horizontal-reflection and vertical-reflection operations can be combined into a single operation using a 2-by-2 matrix.

```
|x' y'| == |x y| * |Rx    0|
                   |0    Ry|
```

The 2-by-2 matrix that produced the illustrated reflection contains the following values.

```
|-1    0|
|0     1|
```

39.1.2.6 Combined World-to-Page Space Transformations

You can combine the five world-to-page transformations into a single 3-by-3 matrix. Use these combined transformations to alter output associated with a particular device context by calling the **SetWorldTransform** function and supplying the elements for this matrix. When an application calls the **SetWorldTransform** function, it stores the elements of the 3-by-3 matrix in an **XFORM** structure. The members of this structure correspond to the first two columns of a 3-by-3 matrix; the last column of the matrix is not required, because its values are constant.

You can retrieve the elements of the current world transformation matrix by calling the **GetWorldTransform** function and supplying a pointer to an **XFORM** structure.

39.1.3 Page-Space to Device-Space Transformations

The page-space to device-space transformation was part of the original Windows interface. This transformation determines the mapping mode for all graphics output associated with a particular device context. A *mapping mode* is a scaling transformation that specifies the size of the units used for drawing operations. In some cases, the mapping mode alters the orientation of the x-axis and the y-axis in device space. The mapping modes are described in the following table.

Mapping mode	Description
MM_ANISOTROPIC	Each unit in page space is mapped to an application-specified unit in device space. The axis may or may not be equally scaled (for example, a circle drawn in world space may appear to be an ellipse when depicted on a given device). The orientation of the axis is also specified by the application.
MM_HIENGLISH	Each unit in page space is mapped to 0.001 inch in device space. Increasing values of x occur as you move to the right; increasing values of y occur as you move up.
MM_HIMETRIC	Each unit in page space is mapped to 0.01 millimeter in device space. Increasing values of x occur as you move to the right; increasing values of y occur as you move up.
MM_ISOTROPIC	Each unit in page space is mapped to an application-defined unit in device space. The axes are always equally scaled. The orientation of the axes may be specified by the application.
MM_LOENGLISH	Each unit in page space is mapped to 0.01 inch in device space. Increasing values of x occur as you move to the right; increasing values of y occur as you move up.
MM_LOMETRIC	Each unit in page space is mapped to 0.1 millimeter in device space. Increasing values of x occur as you move to the right; increasing values of y occur as you move up.
MM_TEXT	Each unit in page space is mapped to one pixel. Increasing values of x occur as you move to the right; increasing values of y occur as you move down.
MM_TWIPS	Each unit in page space is mapped to one twentieth of a printer's point (1/1440 inch). Increasing values of x occur as you move to the right; increasing values of y occur as you move down.

You set a mapping mode by calling the **SetMapMode** function. You retrieve the current mapping mode for a device context by calling the **GetMapMode** function.

Unlike the world-space to page-space transformations that use a 3-by-3 matrix, the page-space to device-space transformations use the width and height ratios of two rectangles: the rectangle in page space is called a *window* and the rectangle in device space is called a *viewport*. The transformation occurs when Windows *maps* the window origin to the viewport origin and the window extents to the viewport extents, as shown in the following figure.

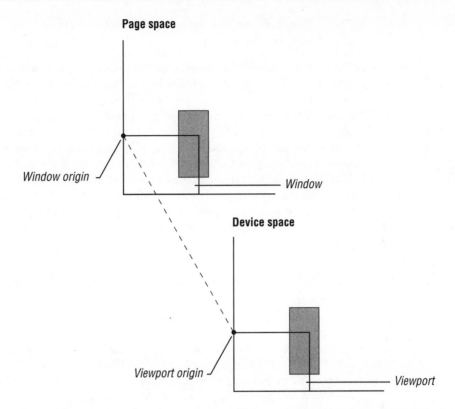

For the six predefined mapping modes (MM_HIENGLISH, MM_LOENGLISH, MM_HIMETRIC, MM_LOMETRIC, MM_TEXT, and MM_TWIPS), the width and height of these rectangles are set by Windows when you call **SetMapMode**. They cannot be changed. The other two mapping modes (MM_ISOTROPIC and MM_ANISOTROPIC) require that you specify the width and height of these rectangles. This is done by calling **SetMapMode** to set the appropriate mode and then calling **SetViewportExtEx** and **SetWindowExtEx** to specify the width and height of each rectangle.

39.1.3.1 Predefined Mapping Modes

Of the six predefined mapping modes, one is device dependent (MM_TEXT), while the remaining five (MM_HIENGLISH, MM_LOENGLISH, MM_HIMETRIC, MM_LOMETRIC, and MM_TWIPS) are device independent.

The device-dependent mapping mode is provided for text-output operations that use device-specific fonts. *Device-specific fonts* are fonts created for a device with a specific aspect ratio. The *aspect ratio* of a device is the ratio formed by the width and height of a single pixel. You can retrieve a device's aspect ratio and the total number of device-specific fonts by calling the **GetDeviceCaps** function. You can limit the user's selection of fonts to only device-specific fonts by calling the

ChooseFont function and setting the CF_PRINTERFONTS or CF_SCREENFONTS constants.

The device-independent mapping modes are provided for non-text drawing operations. If your application displays geometric shapes (circles, squares, polygons, and so on), choose one of the device-independent mapping modes. For example, if you are writing code to provide charting capabilities for a spreadsheet application and want to can guarantee that the diameter of each pie chart is 2 inches, you can choose the MM_LOENGLISH mapping mode and call the appropriate functions to draw and fill the charts. By specifying MM_LOENGLISH, you guarantee that the diameter of the charts are consistent on any display or printer. (If you were to choose MM_TEXT instead of MM_LOENGLISH, a chart that appears circular on a VGA display would appear elliptical on an EGA display and would appear very small on a 300 dpi laser printer.)

39.1.3.2 Application-Defined Mapping Modes

The two application-defined mapping modes (MM_ISOTROPIC and MM_ANISOTROPIC) are provided for application-specific mapping modes. The MM_ISOTROPIC mode guarantees that logical units in the x-direction and in the y-direction are equal, while the MM_ANISOTROPIC mode allows the units to differ. A CAD or drawing application can benefit from the MM_ISOTROPIC mapping mode but may need to specify logical units that correspond to the increments on an engineer's scale (1/64 inch). These units would be difficult to obtain with the predefined mapping modes (MM_HIENGLISH or MM_HIMETRIC); however, they can easily be obtained by selecting the MM_ISOTROPIC mode, setting the window extents to the width and height of the display (expressed in units of 1/64 inch) and setting the viewport width and height to the width and height of the display in pixels.

39.1.4 Device-Space to Physical-Device Transformation

The device-space to physical-device transformation is unique in several respects: It is limited to translation and is controlled by the window manager component of Windows. The sole purpose of this transformation is to ensure that the origin of device space is mapped to the proper point on the physical device. There are no functions to set this transformation, nor are there any functions to retrieve related data.

39.1.5 Default Transformations

Whenever an application creates a device context and immediately begins calling GDI drawing or output functions, it takes advantage of the default page-space to device-space, and device-space to client-area transformations. (World-to-page space transformation cannot happen until the application calls the **SetWorldTransform** function.)

The default page-space to device-space transformation results in a one-to-one mapping; that is, a given point in page space maps to the same point in device space. As previously mentioned, this transformation is not specified by a matrix. Instead, it is obtained by dividing the width of the viewport by the width of the window and the height of the viewport by the height of the window. In the default case, the viewport dimensions are 1-pixel by 1-pixel and the window dimensions are 1-page unit by 1-page unit.

The device-space to physical-device (client area, desktop, or printer paper) transformation *always* results in a one-to-one mapping; that is, one unit in device space is always equivalent to one unit in the client area, on the desktop, or on a page. The sole purpose of this transformation is translation; it ensures that output appears correctly in an application's window no matter where that window is moved on the desktop.

The one unique aspect of the default transformation is the orientation of the y-axis in device space and the application's window. In the default case, the positive y-axis extends downward and the negative y-axis extends upward.

39.2 Using Coordinates Spaces and Transformations

This section contains an example that demonstrates the following tasks.

- Drawing graphics with predefined units
- Centering graphics in the application's client area
- Scaling graphics output to half its original size
- Translating graphics output 3/4 of an inch to the right
- Rotating graphics 30 degrees
- Shearing graphics output along the x-axis
- Reflecting graphics output about an imaginary horizontal axis drawn through its midpoint

The following example was used to create the illustrations that appear earlier in this chapter.

```
void TransformAndDraw(int iTransform, HWND hWnd)
{

HDC hDC;
XFORM xForm;
RECT rect;

/* Retrieve a DC handle for the application's window. */
```

```
hDC = GetDC(hWnd);


/*
 * Set the mapping mode to LOENGLISH. This moves the
 * client-area origin from the upper-left corner of the
 * window to the lower-left corner (this also reorients
 * the y-axis so that drawing operations occur in a true
 * Cartesian space). It guarantees portability so that
 * the object drawn retains its dimensions on any
 * display running Windows.
 */

SetMapMode(hDC, MM_LOENGLISH);

/*
 * Set the appropriate world transformation (based on the
 * user's menu selection).
 */

switch (iTransform) {
        case SCALE: /* Scale to 1/2 of the original size. */
            xForm.eM11 = (FLOAT) 0.5;
            xForm.eM12 = (FLOAT) 0.0;
            xForm.eM21 = (FLOAT) 0.0;
            xForm.eM22 = (FLOAT) 0.5;
            xForm.eDx  = (FLOAT) 0.0;
            xForm.eDy  = (FLOAT) 0.0;
            SetWorldTransform(hDC, &xForm);
            break;

        case TRANSLATE: /* Translate right by 3/4 inch. */
            xForm.eM11 = (FLOAT) 1.0;
            xForm.eM12 = (FLOAT) 0.0;
            xForm.eM21 = (FLOAT) 0.0;
            xForm.eM22 = (FLOAT) 1.0;
            xForm.eDx  = (FLOAT) 75.0;
            xForm.eDy  = (FLOAT) 0.0;
            SetWorldTransform(hDC, &xForm);
            break;

        case ROTATE: /* Rotate 30 degrees counterclockwise. */
            xForm.eM11 = (FLOAT) 0.8660;
            xForm.eM12 = (FLOAT) 0.5000;
            xForm.eM21 = (FLOAT) -0.5000;
            xForm.eM22 = (FLOAT) 0.8660;
            xForm.eDx  = (FLOAT) 0.0;
            xForm.eDy  = (FLOAT) 0.0;
            SetWorldTransform(hDC, &xForm);
```

```
                 break;

          case SHEAR: /* Shear along the x-axis with a      */
                        /* proportionality constant of 1.0. */
               xForm.eM11 = (FLOAT) 1.0;
               xForm.eM12 = (FLOAT) 1.0;
               xForm.eM21 = (FLOAT) 0.0;
               xForm.eM22 = (FLOAT) 1.0;
               xForm.eDx  = (FLOAT) 0.0;
               xForm.eDy  = (FLOAT) 0.0;
               SetWorldTransform(hDC, &xForm);
               break;

          case REFLECT: /* Reflect about a horizontal axis. */
               xForm.eM11 = (FLOAT) 1.0;
               xForm.eM12 = (FLOAT) 0.0;
               xForm.eM21 = (FLOAT) 0.0;
               xForm.eM22 = (FLOAT) -1.0;
               xForm.eDx  = (FLOAT) 0.0;
               xForm.eDy  = (FLOAT) 0.0;
               SetWorldTransform(hDC, &xForm);
               break;

          case NORMAL: /* Set the unity transformation. */
               xForm.eM11 = (FLOAT) 1.0;
               xForm.eM12 = (FLOAT) 0.0;
               xForm.eM21 = (FLOAT) 0.0;
               xForm.eM22 = (FLOAT) 1.0;
               xForm.eDx  = (FLOAT) 0.0;
               xForm.eDy  = (FLOAT) 0.0;
               SetWorldTransform(hDC, &xForm);
               break;

     }

/* Find the midpoint of the client area. */

GetClientRect(hWnd, (LPRECT) &rect);
DPtoLP(hDC, (LPPOINT) &rect, 2);

/* Select a hollow brush. */

SelectObject(hDC, GetStockObject(HOLLOW_BRUSH));


/* Draw the exterior circle. */

Ellipse(hDC, (rect.right / 2 - 100), (rect.bottom / 2 + 100),
    (rect.right / 2 + 100), (rect.bottom / 2 - 100));
```

```
/* Draw the interior circle. */

Ellipse(hDC, (rect.right / 2 -94), (rect.bottom / 2 + 94),
    (rect.right / 2 + 94), (rect.bottom / 2 - 94));

/* Draw the key. */

Rectangle(hDC, (rect.right / 2 - 13), (rect.bottom / 2 + 113),
    (rect.right / 2 + 13), (rect.bottom / 2 + 50));
Rectangle(hDC, (rect.right / 2 - 13), (rect.bottom / 2 + 96),
    (rect.right / 2 + 13), (rect.bottom / 2 + 50));


/* Draw the horizontal lines. */


MoveToEx(hDC, (rect.right / 2 - 150), (rect.bottom / 2 + 0), NULL);
LineTo(hDC, (rect.right / 2 - 16), (rect.bottom / 2 + 0));

MoveToEx(hDC, (rect.right / 2 - 13), (rect.bottom / 2 + 0), NULL);
LineTo(hDC, (rect.right / 2 + 13), (rect.bottom / 2 + 0));

MoveToEx(hDC, (rect.right / 2 + 16), (rect.bottom / 2 + 0), NULL);
LineTo(hDC, (rect.right / 2 + 150), (rect.bottom / 2 + 0));


/* Draw the vertical lines. */

MoveToEx(hDC, (rect.right / 2 + 0), (rect.bottom / 2 - 150), NULL);
LineTo(hDC, (rect.right / 2 + 0), (rect.bottom / 2 - 16));

MoveToEx(hDC, (rect.right / 2 + 0), (rect.bottom / 2 - 13), NULL);
LineTo(hDC, (rect.right / 2 + 0), (rect.bottom / 2 + 13));

MoveToEx(hDC, (rect.right / 2 + 0), (rect.bottom / 2 + 16), NULL);
LineTo(hDC, (rect.right / 2 + 0), (rect.bottom / 2 + 150));

ReleaseDC(hWnd, hDC);

}
```

39.3 Functions

Following are the functions used with coordinate spaces and transformations.

ClientToScreen
CombineTransform
DPtoLP
GetCurrentPositionEx
GetMapMode
GetViewportExtEx
GetViewportOrgEx
GetWindowExtEx
GetWindowOrgEx
GetWorldTransform
LPtoDP
ModifyWorldTransform
OffsetViewportOrgEx
OffsetWindowOrgEx
ScaleViewportExtEx
ScaleWindowExtEx
ScreenToClient
SetMapMode
SetViewportExtEx
SetViewportOrgEx
SetWindowExtEx
SetWindowOrgEx
SetWorldTransform

C H A P T E R   4 0

Metafiles

40.1 About Metafiles

Applications written for Microsoft ® Windows ™ use two graphics tools to store pictures: metafiles and bitmaps. For information about bitmaps, see Chapter 29, "Bitmaps." This chapter describes metafiles.

A *metafile* is a collection of structures that store a picture in a device-independent format. Device independence is the one feature that sets metafiles apart from bitmaps: Unlike a bitmap, a metafile guarantees device independence. For example, when an application creates a picture measuring 2 by 2 inches on a VGA display and stores that picture in a metafile, the picture maintains its original dimensions when printed on a 300 dpi laser printer or copied over a network and displayed in another application that is running on an 8514/A video display. There is a drawback to metafiles, however: they are generally drawn more slowly than bitmaps. Therefore, if an application requires fast drawing and device independence is not an issue, it should use bitmaps instead of metafiles.

Internally, a metafile is an array of variable-length structures called *metafile records.* The first records in the metafile specify general information such as the resolution of the device on which the picture was created, the dimensions of the picture, and so on. The remaining records, which constitute the bulk of any metafile, correspond to the graphics device interface (GDI) functions required to draw the picture. These records are stored in the metafile after a special metafile device context (DC) is created. This DC is then used for all drawing operations required to create the picture. When Windows processes a GDI function associated with a metafile DC, it converts the function into the appropriate data and stores this data in a record appended to the metafile.

After a picture is complete and the last record is stored in the metafile, the metafile can be passed to another application by means of the clipboard, embedded within another file, stored on disk, or played repeatedly. A metafile is *played* when its records are converted to device commands and processed by the appropriate device.

There are two types of metafiles: enhanced and Windows. An *enhanced metafile* is used in applications written using the Win32 application programming interface (API). The enhanced format consists of a header, a table of handles to GDI objects, a private palette, and an array of metafile records. Enhanced metafiles provide true device independence. (You can think of the picture stored in an enhanced metafile as a "snapshot" of the video display taken at a particular moment. This "snapshot" maintains its dimensions no matter where it appears: on a printer, a plotter, or the desktop, or in the client area of any Win32 application.)

A *Windows metafile* is used for applications written using the Windows version 3.*x* application programming interface (API). The Windows format consists of a header and an array of metafile records. Windows-format metafiles are limited in their capabilities and should rarely be used—the Windows-metafile API is supported to maintain backward compatibility with applications that were written to run with Windows version 3.*x*.

40.1.1 Enhanced-Format Metafiles

A developer can use enhanced metafiles to store a picture created by using the Win32 GDI functions (including new path and transformation functions). Because the enhanced metafile format is standardized for the Win32 application programming interface (API), pictures that are stored in this format can be copied from one Win32 application to another; and, because the pictures are truly device independent, they are guaranteed to maintain their shape and proportion on any output device.

40.1.1.1 Enhanced Metafile Records

An *enhanced metafile* is an array of records. A metafile record is a variable-length **ENHMETARECORD** structure. This structure identifies the record type, specifies the record length, and contains additional data that is dependent on the record type.

The first record in an enhanced metafile is always the enhanced-metafile header. The header specifies the following information:

- Size of the metafile, in bytes
- Dimensions of the picture frame, in device units
- Dimensions of the picture frame, in .01-millimeter units
- Number of records in the metafile
- Offset to an optional text description
- Size of the optional palette
- Resolution of the original device, in pixels
- Resolution of the original device, in millimeters

An optional text description can follow the header record. The text description describes the picture and the author's name. The optional palette specifies the colors used to create the enhanced metafile. The remaining records identify the GDI functions used to create the picture. The following hexadecimal output corresponds to a record generated for a call to the **SetMapMode** function.

```
00000011 0000000C 00000004
```

The value 0x00000011 specifies the record type (corresponds to the EMR_SETMAPMODE constant defined in the file WINGDI.H). The value 0x0000000C specifies the length of the record, in bytes. The value 0x00000004 identifies the mapping mode (corresponds to the MM_LOENGLISH constant defined in the file WINGDI.H).

40.1.1.2 Enhanced Metafile Operations

A developer creates an enhanced metafile by using the **CreateEnhMetaFile** function and supplying the appropriate arguments. The Win32 API uses these arguments to maintain picture dimensions, to determine whether the metafile should be stored on a disk or in memory, and so on.

To maintain picture dimensions across output devices, the Win32 API requires the resolution of the reference device. This *reference device* is the device on which the picture first appeared, and the *reference DC* is the device context (DC) associated with the reference device. When calling the **CreateEnhMetaFile** function, the application must supply a handle that identifies this DC. The application can get this handle by calling the **GetDC** or **CreateDC** function.

Most applications store pictures permanently and therefore create an enhanced metafile that is stored on a disk; however, there are some instances when this is not necessary. For example, a word processing application that provides chart-drawing capabilities could store a user-defined chart in memory as an enhanced metafile and then copy the enhanced metafile bits from memory into the user's document file. An application that requires a metafile that is stored permanently on a disk must supply the filename when it calls the **CreateEnhMetaFile** function. If the developer does not supply a filename, Windows automatically treats the metafile as a temporary file and stores it in memory.

The developer can add an optional text description to a metafile containing information about the picture and the author. An application can display these strings in the File Open dialog box to provide the user with information about metafile contents that will help in selecting the appropriate file. If an application includes the text description, the application must supply a pointer to the string when it calls the **CreateEnhMetaFile** function.

When the **CreateEnhMetaFile** function is successful, it returns a handle that identifies a special metafile device context. A metafile DC is unique in that it is associated with a file rather than with an output device. When Windows processes a GDI function that received a handle to a metafile DC, it converts the GDI function into an enhanced-metafile record and appends the record to the end of the enhanced metafile.

After a picture is complete and the last record is appended to the enhanced metafile, the application can close the file by calling the **CloseEnhMetaFile** function. This function closes and deletes the special metafile DC and returns a handle identifying the enhanced metafile. The application can use this handle to accomplish the following tasks:

▪ Display the picture stored in the enhanced metafile

- Create copies of the enhanced metafile
- Enumerate, edit, or copy the individual records in the enhanced metafile
- Retrieve the optional description that is stored in the enhanced metafile
- Retrieve a copy of the enhanced-metafile header
- Retrieve a binary version of the enhanced metafile
- Enumerate the colors in the optional palette
- Convert an enhanced-format metafile into a Windows-format metafile

Some applications create temporary backup (or duplicate) copies of a file before enabling the user to alter the original. An application can create a backup copy of an enhanced metafile by calling the **CopyEnhMetaFile** function, supplying a handle that identifies the enhanced metafile, and supplying a pointer to the name of the new file.

Most drawing, illustration, and computer-aided design (CAD) applications require a means of editing a picture stored in an enhanced metafile. Although editing an enhanced metafile is a complex task, a developer can use the **EnumEnhMetaFile** function in combination with other Win32 functions to provide this capability in your application. The **EnumEnhMetaFile** function and its associated callback function enable the application to process individual records in an enhanced metafile.

Some applications display the text description of an enhanced metafile with the corresponding filename in the File Open dialog box. An application can determine whether this string exists in an enhanced metafile by retrieving the metafile header and examining one of its members. The **GetEnhMetaFileHeader** function can retrieve the metafile header. If the string exists, the application retrieves it by calling the **GetEnhMetaFileDescription** function.

Some applications retrieve the contents of a metafile by calling the **GetEnhMetaFileBits** function; however, before retrieving the contents, the application must specify the size of the file. To get the size, the application can use the **GetEnhMetaFileHeader** function and examine the appropriate member.

To achieve consistent colors when a picture is displayed on various output devices, an application can call the **CreatePalette** function and store a logical palette in an enhanced metafile. Other applications that display the picture stored in the enhanced metafile retrieve this palette and call the **RealizePalette** function before displaying the picture. To determine whether a palette is stored in an enhanced metafile, an application can retrieve the metafile header and examine the appropriate member. If a palette exists, the application can call the **GetEnhMetaFilePaletteEntries** function to retrieve the logical palette.

40.1.2 Windows-Format Metafiles

The Win32 API supports the Windows metafile format to maintain compatibility with applications written for Windows version 3.*x*. Following are the limitations of this format:

- A Windows-format metafile is application and device dependent. Changes in the application's mapping modes or the device resolution affect the appearance of metafiles created in this format.

- A Windows-format metafile does not contain a comprehensive header that describes the original picture dimensions, the resolution of the device on which the picture was created, an optional text description, or an optional palette.

- A Windows-format metafile does not support the new curve, path, and transformation functions.

- Some Windows-format metafile records cannot be scaled.

- The metafile device context associated with a Windows-format metafile cannot be queried (that is, an application cannot retrieve device-resolution data, font metrics, and so on).

To convert a Windows-format metafile to an enhanced-format metafile, an application can call the **GetMetaFileBitsEx** function to retrieve the data from the Windows-format metafile and then call the **SetWinMetaFileBits** function to convert this data into an enhanced-format metafile.

A developer writing a Win32 application should avoid using the Windows-format functions and use the enhanced-format functions instead.

40.2 Using Metafiles

This section explains how to perform the following tasks:

- Create an enhanced metafile to be stored on a disk
- Display a picture and store it in an enhanced metafile
- Open an enhanced metafile and play back its contents
- Edit an enhanced metafile

40.2.1 Creating an Enhanced Metafile

This section contains an example that demonstrates the creation of an enhanced metafile that is stored on a disk, using a filename specified by the user.

The example uses a device context for the application window as the reference DC. (Windows stores the resolution data for this device in the enhanced-metafile's header.) The application retrieves a handle identifying this DC by calling the **GetDC** function.

The example uses the dimensions of the application's client area to define the dimensions of the picture frame. Using the rectangle dimensions returned by the **GetClientRect** function, the application converts the device units to .01-millimeter units and passes the converted values to the **CreateEnhMetaFile** function.

The example displays a Save As common dialog box that enables the user to specify the filename of the new enhanced metafile. The system appends the three-character .EMF extension to this filename and passes the name to the **CreateEnhMetaFile** function.

The example also embeds a text description of the picture in the enhanced-metafile header. This description is specified as a resource in the string table of the application's resource file. However, in a working application, this string would be retrieved from a custom control in a common dialog box or from a separate dialog box displayed solely for this purpose.

```
/* Obtain a handle to a reference DC. */

hdcRef = GetDC(hWnd);

/*
 * Determine the picture frame dimensions.
 * iWidthMM is the display width in millimeters.
 * iHeightMM is the display height in millimeters.
 * iWidthPels is the display width in pixels.
 * iHeightPels is the display height in pixels
 */

iWidthMM = GetDeviceCaps(hdcRef, HORZSIZE);
iHeightMM = GetDeviceCaps(hdcRef, VERTSIZE);
iWidthPels = GetDeviceCaps(hdcRef, HORZRES);
iHeightPels = GetDeviceCaps(hdcRef, VERTRES);

/*
 * Use iWidthMM, iWidthPels, iHeightMM, and
 * iHeightPels to determine the number of
 * .01-millimeter units per pixel in the x-
 *  and y-directions.
 */


iMMPerPelX = (iWidthMM * 100)/iWidthPels;
iMMPerPelY = (iHeightMM * 100)/iHeightPels;
```

```
/*
 * Retrieve the coordinates of the client
 * rectangle, in pixels.
 */

GetClientRect(hWnd, &rect);

/* Convert client coordinates to .01-mm units. */

rect.left = rect.left * iMMPerPelX;
rect.top = rect.top * iMMPerPelY;
rect.right = rect.right * iMMPerPelX;
rect.bottom = rect.bottom * iMMPerPelY;

/* Load the filename filter from the string table. */

LoadString(hInst, IDS_FILTERSTRING,
    (LPSTR)szFilter, sizeof(szFilter));

/*
 * Replace the '%' separators that are embedded
 * between the strings in the string-table entry
 * with '\0'.
 */

for (i=0; szFilter[i]!='\0'; i++)
    if (szFilter[i] == '%')
            szFilter[i] = '\0';

/* Load the dialog title string from the table. */

LoadString(hInst, IDS_TITLESTRING,
    (LPSTR)szTitle, sizeof(szTitle));


/* Initialize the OPENFILENAME members. */

szFile[0] = '\0';

Ofn.lStructSize = sizeof(OPENFILENAME);
Ofn.hwndOwner = hWnd;
Ofn.lpstrFilter = szFilter;
Ofn.lpstrFile= szFile;
Ofn.nMaxFile = sizeof(szFile);
Ofn.lpstrFileTitle = szFileTitle;
Ofn.nMaxFileTitle = sizeof(szFileTitle);
Ofn.lpstrInitialDir = (LPSTR)NULL;
Ofn.Flags = OFN_SHOWHELP | OFN_OVERWRITEPROMPT;
```

```
Ofn.lpstrTitle = szTitle;

/*
 * Display the Filename common dialog box. The
 * filename specified by the user is passed
 * to the CreateEnhMetaFile function and used to
 * store the metafile on disk.
 */

GetSaveFileName(&Ofn);

/* Load the description from the string table. */

LoadString(hInst, IDS_DESCRIPTIONSTRING,
     (LPSTR)szDescription, sizeof(szDescription));

/*
 * Replace the '%' string separators that are
 * embedded between strings in the string-table
 * entry with '\0'.
 */

for (i=0; szDescription[i]!='\0'; i++)
    if (szDescription[i] == '%')
           szDescription[i] = '\0';

/* Create the metafile DC. */

hdcMeta = CreateEnhMetaFile(hdcRef,
          (LPTSTR) Ofn.lpstrFile,
          &rect, (LPSTR)szDescription);

if (!hdcMeta)
    errhandler("CreateEnhMetaFile", hWnd);

/* Release the reference DC. */

ReleaseDC(hWnd, hdcRef);
```

40.2.2 Displaying a Picture and Storing It in an Enhanced Metafile

This section contains a code sample demonstrating the creation of a picture and the process of storing the corresponding records in a metafile. The code draws a picture to the display or stores it in a metafile. If a display DC handle is given, it draws a picture to the screen using various GDI functions. If an enhanced metafile DC is given, it stores the same picture in the enhanced metafile.

```
void DrawOrStore(HWND hwnd, HDC hdcMeta, HDC hdcDisplay)
{
```

```
RECT rect;
HDC hDC;
int fnMapModeOld;
HBRUSH hbrOld;

/* Draw it to the display DC or store it in the metafile DC. */

if (hdcMeta)
    hDC = hdcMeta;
else
    hDC = hdcDisplay;

/* Set the mapping mode in the DC. */

fnMapModeOld = SetMapMode(hDC, MM_LOENGLISH);

/* Find the midpoint of the client area. */

GetClientRect(hwnd, (LPRECT)&rect);
DPtoLP(hDC, (LPPOINT)&rect, 2);

/* Select a gray brush. */

hbrOld = SelectObject(hDC, GetStockObject(GRAY_BRUSH));

/* Draw an circle with an one inch raduis. */

Ellipse(hDC, (rect.right/2 - 100), (rect.bottom/2 + 100),
        (rect.right/2 + 100), (rect.bottom/2 - 100));

    .
    . /* Perform remaining drawing and clean-up operations. */
    .

}
```

40.2.3 Opening an Enhanced Metafile and Displaying Its Contents

This section contains a code sample demonstrating how an application opens an enhanced metafile stored on disk and displays the associated picture in the client area.

The example uses the Open common dialog box to enable the user to select an enhanced metafile from a list of existing files. It then passes the name of the selected file to the **GetEnhMetaFile** function, which returns a handle identifying the file. This handle is passed to the **PlayEnhMetaFile** function in order to display the picture.

```
LoadString(hInst, IDS_FILTERSTRING,
    (LPSTR)szFilter, sizeof(szFilter));

/*
 * Replace occurrences of '%' string separator
 * with '\0'.
 */

for (i=0; szFilter[i]!='\0'; i++)
    if (szFilter[i] == '%')
            szFilter[i] = '\0';

LoadString(hInst, IDS_DEFEXTSTRING,
    (LPSTR)szDefExt, sizeof(szFilter));


/*
 * Use the OpenFilename common dialog box
 * to obtain the desired filename.
 */

szFile[0] = '\0';
Ofn.lStructSize = sizeof(OPENFILENAME);
Ofn.hwndOwner = hWnd;
Ofn.lpstrFilter = szFilter;
Ofn.lpstrCustomFilter = (LPSTR)NULL;
Ofn.nMaxCustFilter = 0L;
Ofn.nFilterIndex = 1L;
Ofn.lpstrFile = szFile;
Ofn.nMaxFile = sizeof(szFile);
Ofn.lpstrFileTitle = szFileTitle;
Ofn.nMaxFileTitle = sizeof(szFileTitle);
Ofn.lpstrInitialDir = (LPSTR) NULL;
Ofn.lpstrTitle = (LPSTR)NULL;
Ofn.Flags = OFN_SHOWHELP | OFN_PATHMUSTEXIST | OFN_FILEMUSTEXIST;
Ofn.nFileOffset = 0;
Ofn.nFileExtension = 0;
Ofn.lpstrDefExt = szDefExt;

GetOpenFileName(&Ofn);

/* Open the metafile. */

hemf = GetEnhMetaFile(Ofn.lpstrFile);

/* Retrieve a handle to a window DC. */

hDC = GetDC(hWnd);

/* Retrieve the client rectangle dimensions. */
```

```
GetClientRect(hWnd, &rct);

/* Draw the picture. */

PlayEnhMetaFile(hDC, hemf, &rct);

/* Release the metafile handle. */

DeleteEnhMetaFile(hemf);

/* Release the window DC. */

ReleaseDC(hWnd, hDC);
```

40.2.4 Editing an Enhanced Metafile

To edit a picture stored in an enhanced metafile, an application must perform the following tasks:

1. Use hit-testing to capture the cursor coordinates and retrieve the position of the object (line, arc, rectangle, ellipse, polygon, or irregular shape) that the user wants to alter.

2. Convert these coordinates to logical (or world) units.

3. Call the **EnumEnhMetaFile** function and examine each metafile record.

4. Determine whether a given record corresponds to a GDI drawing function.

5. If it does, determine whether the coordinates stored in the record correspond to the line, arc, ellipse, or other graphics element that intersects the coordinates specified by the user.

6. Upon finding the record that corresponds to the output that the user wants to alter, erase the object on the screen that corresponds to the original record.

7. Delete the corresponding record from the metafile, saving a pointer to its location.

8. Permit the user to redraw or replace the object.

9. Convert the GDI functions used to draw the new object into one or more enhanced-metafile records.

10. Store these records in the enhanced metafile.

40.3 Functions

Following are the functions used with enhanced format metafiles.

CloseEnhMetaFile
CopyEnhMetaFile
CreateEnhMetaFile
DeleteEnhMetaFile
EnhMetaFileProc
EnumEnhMetaFile
GdiComment
GetEnhMetaFile
GetEnhMetaFileBits
GetEnhMetaFileDescription
GetEnhMetaFileHeader
GetEnhMetaFilePaletteEntries
GetWinMetaFileBits
PlayEnhMetaFile
PlayEnhMetaFileRecord
SetEnhMetaFileBits
SetWinMetaFileBits

The following functions are provided for compatibility with Windows-format metafiles:

CloseMetaFile
CopyMetaFile
CreateMetaFile
DeleteMetaFile
EnumMetaFile
EnumMetaFileProc
GetMetaFile
GetMetaFileBitsEx
PlayMetaFile
PlayMetaFileRecord
SetMetaFileBitsEx

C H A P T E R   4 1

Printing and Print Spooler

41.1 About Printing

Microsoft ® Windows ™ provides a complete set of functions that allow applications to print on a variety of devices: laser printers, vector plotters, raster printers, and fax machines. One of the chief features of these functions is their support of device independence; instead of issuing device-specific commands to draw output on a particular printer or plotter, an application calls high-level functions from the graphics device interface (GDI). For example, to print a bitmapped image, an application would call the **BitBlt** function, supplying the coordinates for the bitmap as well as handles identifying the source and destination device contexts. The **BitBlt** function call would then be converted to raw device commands by a printer device driver. The *device driver* is a Windows dynamic-link library (DLL) that supports the Windows device-driver interface (DDI). A device driver generates raw device commands when it processes the DDI function calls made by the graphics engine. The *graphics engine* is a Windows DLL that converts print-processor output into device-driver function calls. These commands are processed by the printer when it prints the image. The syntax, number, and type of these commands vary from device to device.

41.1.1 Default Printing Interface

In addition to GDI and the device driver, the default in the Win32 API printing interface consists of several other components that process output before it arrives at the printer. These components are the print spooler, the print processor, the graphics engine, and the monitor.

41.1.1.1 Print Spooler

The primary component of the printing interface is the print spooler. The *print spooler* is a Windows executable file that manages the printing process. This includes retrieving the location of the correct printer driver, loading that driver, converting high-level-function calls to journal records, storing those journal records on disk as a print job, and so on.

The spooler is loaded at startup and continues to run until the operating system is shut down. Windows Print Manager provides a graphic interface that the user or system administrator can use to access and configure the spooler; however, if Print Manager is disabled or shut down, the spooler continues to run.

Applications that print create a printer device context (DC). When an application creates a printer DC, the spooler performs necessary tasks such as determining the location of the required printer driver, then loading the appropriate printer driver. It also determines the data type used to record the print job. The supported data types include: journal records, ASCII text, and PostScript. A *print job* is a document stored internally (by using one of the supported data types) that may contain one or more pages of output. It may consist of multiple forms; for example, a job may consist of one envelope and three pages of A4 paper. A print job is defined (or bracketed) by two functions: **StartDoc** and **EndDoc**.

The default data type for a print job is the journal record. A *journal record* is a compact data structure used to store text-output commands, raster-graphics commands, and so on. When an application calls the **StartDoc** function, the spooler creates a journal file and a data file, and begins storing journal records in the journal file. Each time the application calls one of the GDI drawing functions, one or more new journal records are created and stored in the journal file. The journal and data files are created in an operating-system directory. The spooler uses the journal file to store journal records, and uses the data file to record the type of form, the print-job data type, the target printer, and so on. These files are deleted by the spooler when the job has successfully printed.

41.1.1.2 Print Processor

The spooler monitors the current print jobs and the target printer to determine the appropriate time to print a job. Once the spooler determines that a job should be printed, it calls the print processor. The *print processor* is a Windows DLL that reads and converts journal records into DDI calls.

41.1.1.3 Graphics Engine

The graphics engine converts the print processor output into device-driver function calls. The device driver, in turn, processes these calls and converts them into raw device commands that the device can process.

41.1.1.4 Monitor

Once a device driver has converted an entire journal file into raw device commands, the file of converted commands is passed back to the spooler. The spooler sends these low-level commands to a monitor. A *monitor* is a Windows DLL that passes the raw device commands over the network, through a parallel port, or through a serial port and to the device.

41.1.2 Printer Device Contexts

Just as an application requires a display DC before it can begin drawing in the client area of a window, it needs a special printer DC before it can begin sending output to a printer. A printer DC is similar to a display DC in that it is an internal data structure that defines a set of graphic objects and their associated attributes, and the graphic modes that affect output. The graphic objects include a pen (for line drawing), a brush (for painting and filling), and a font (for text output).

Unlike a display DC, printer DCs are not owned by the window manager component and cannot be obtained by calling the **GetDC** function. Instead, an application must call the **CreateDC** or **PrintDlg** function. When an application calls the **CreateDC** function, it must supply a driver and port name. This data is stored in one of the operating system initialization (.INI) files. It can be retrieved by calling the **EnumPrinters** function.

When an application calls the **PrintDlg** function and sets the PD_RETURNDC constant in the **Flags** member of the **PRINTDLG** structure, Windows automatically returns a handle identifying the user's selected printer device context. For an example of code that demonstrates this task, see Section 41.2.2, "Displaying a Print Dialog Box and Retrieving a Printer Device Context."

41.1.3 Printer Escapes

Windows version 3.*x* supported as many as 64 special functions called printer escapes that applications used to access special device features. An application calls these functions by specifying one of 64 predefined constants as the second argument to the **Escape** function. For example, one of these application printing on a PostScript printer could draw a PostScript graphics object called a path by calling the **Escape** function and supplying the BEGIN_PATH and END_PATH constants. Improvements to GDI in the Win32 API have made many of these escapes obsolete. As a case in point, the Win32 version of GDI supports a complete set of path functions that applications can use to draw paths on any device; thus, these new functions render the previous printer escapes obsolete.

Of the 64 original printer escapes, only 11 are supported in the Win32 API. However, of these 11, only 2 (QUERYESCSUPPORT and PASSTHROUGH) should be called by applications developed for the Win32 API. The remaining 9 are supported strictly for compatibility with applications written for Windows 3.*x*.

Following are the 11 supported escapes:

- ABORTDOC
- ENDDOC
- GETPHYSPAGESIZE
- GETPRINTINGOFFSET
- GETSCALINGFACTOR
- NEWFRAME
- NEXTBAND
- PASSTHROUGH
- QUERYESCSUPPORT
- SETABORTPROC

In addition to supporting the original **Escape** function, the Win32 API supports a new extended escape function **ExtEscape**. This function allows applications to access capabilities of a particular device not directly available through GDI.

41.1.4 WYSIWYG Display and Output

Most applications attempt to support what you see is what you get (WYSIWYG) output. This means that text drawn with a 10-point Helvetica Bold font in the application's window should have a similar appearance when it is printed. Obtaining true WYSIWYG output is virtually impossible and even undesirable in most cases. This is due, in part, to the differences in video and printer technologies; a pixel on a screen is generally larger than a dot on a common laser printer. Viewing distances are different as well; a computer user typically sits about two feet away from the screen, but a reader's eyes are usually one foot or less from the printed page.

To compensate for legibility differences between screens and the printed page, Windows supports a unit called the logical inch that is always specified in pixels. For a video display, the logical inch is always greater than the physical inch, to compensate for the longer viewing distance and the (generally) coarser resolution. For printers, the logical inch is always equal to the physical inch.

To obtain WYSIWYG effects when drawing text, applications can use the **CreateFont** function to specify the typeface name and point size of an ideal (or logical) font, then call the **SelectObject** function to identify the display or printer DC. When the application calls the **SelectObject** function, Windows selects a physical font that is the closest possible match to the specified logical font. When Windows selects the display font, it chooses a physical font that is larger than the actual point size. From the user's perspective, however, it appears to be very close to the correct height. When Windows selects the font for the printer, it chooses a physical font that is actually the requested point size. For more information about fonts and text output, see Chapter 35, "Fonts and Text."

To obtain WYSIWYG effects when drawing bitmapped graphics, applications can retrieve the width and height, in logical inches, of the screen and the printed page. Using these values, the application can create horizontal and vertical scaling factors to maintain the proportion of bitmapped images when they are drawn on a printer. For an example that demonstrates this process, see Section 41.2.4, "Printing a Document." For more information about bitmaps and bitmap output, see Chapter 29, "Bitmaps."

41.2 Using the Printing Functions

This section contains code examples that demonstrate how to print text and graphics. The code was taken from an application that allows a user to open and display a 16-color bitmapped image stored as a .BMP file. The following illustration shows the application's window after the user opened the file WINLOGO.BMP.

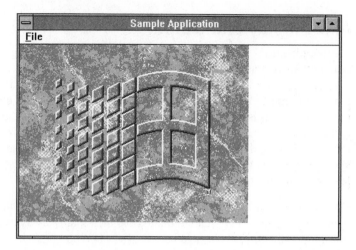

In addition to displaying the bitmapped image, the application allows the user to configure the printer and then print the image, as well as a string of text specifying the location of the file which contained the image. The application prints the text at the top of the page and the image in the center of the page.

41.2.1 Opening and Displaying a .BMP File

In the sample application, a user is able to open a .BMP file that contains a bitmapped image and display that image in the client area of the application's window. The user selects the file to be opened when the application displays the Open dialog box. (For more information about the Open dialog box, see Chapter 76, "Common Dialog Box Library.")

After the user selects a file and closes the dialog box, the file and path names are stored in members of the **OPENFILENAME** structure. The application uses this data to open the appropriate file and retrieve the bitmap header and data. The following example shows the code required to retrieve this data:

```
/* Retrieve a handle identifying the file. */

hfbm = CreateFile(ofn.lpstrFile, GENERIC_READ,
        FILE_SHARE_READ, (LPSECURITY_ATTRIBUTES) NULL,
        OPEN_EXISTING, FILE_ATTRIBUTE_READONLY,
        (HANDLE) NULL);

/* Retrieve the BITMAPFILEHEADER structure. */

ReadFile(hfbm, &bmfh, sizeof(BITMAPFILEHEADER),
    &dwRead, (LPOVERLAPPED)NULL);

/* Retrieve the BITMAPFILEHEADER structure. */
```

```
ReadFile(hfbm, &bmih, sizeof(BITMAPINFOHEADER),
    &dwRead, (LPOVERLAPPED)NULL);

/* Allocate memory for the BITMAPINFO structure. */

hmem1 = GlobalAlloc(GHND,
    sizeof(BITMAPINFOHEADER) +
    ((1<<bmih.biBitCount) * sizeof(RGBQUAD)));

lpbmi = GlobalLock(hmem1);

/*
 * Load BITMAPINFOHEADER into the BITMAPINFO
 * structure.
 */

lpbmi->bmiHeader.biSize = bmih.biSize;
lpbmi->bmiHeader.biWidth = bmih.biWidth;
lpbmi->bmiHeader.biHeight = bmih.biHeight;
lpbmi->bmiHeader.biPlanes = bmih.biPlanes;
lpbmi->bmiHeader.biBitCount = bmih.biBitCount;
lpbmi->bmiHeader.biCompression = bmih.biCompression;
lpbmi->bmiHeader.biSizeImage = bmih.biSizeImage;
lpbmi->bmiHeader.biXPelsPerMeter = bmih.biXPelsPerMeter;
lpbmi->bmiHeader.biYPelsPerMeter = bmih.biYPelsPerMeter;
lpbmi->bmiHeader.biClrUsed = bmih.biClrUsed;
lpbmi->bmiHeader.biClrImportant = bmih.biClrImportant;

/*
 * Retrieve the color table.
 * 1 << bmih.biBitCount == 2 ^ bmih.biBitCount
 */

ReadFile(hfbm, lpbmi->bmiColors,
    ((1<<bmih.biBitCount) * sizeof(RGBQUAD)),
    &dwRead, (LPOVERLAPPED) NULL);

/*
 * Allocate memory for the required number of
 * bytes.
 */

hmem2 = GlobalAlloc(GHND,
    (bmfh.bfSize - bmfh.bfOffBits));

lpvBits = GlobalLock(hmem2);

/* Retrieve the bitmap data. */

ReadFile(hfbm, lpvBits,
```

```
        (bmfh.bfSize - bmfh.bfOffBits),
        &dwRead, (LPOVERLAPPED) NULL);

    /*
     * Create a bitmap from the data stored in the
     * .BMP file.
     */

    hbm = CreateDIBitmap(hdc, &bmih,
        CBM_INIT, lpvBits,
        lpbmi, DIB_RGB_COLORS);

    /*
     * Unlock the global memory objects and
     * close the .BMP file.
     */

    GlobalUnlock(hmem1);
    GlobalUnlock(hmem2);
    CloseHandle(hfbm);

    /* Set the fDisplayBitmap flag. */

    if (hbm)
        fDisplayBitmap = TRUE;
    else
        TextOut(hdc, 100, 100, "LoadBitmap Failed", 17);

    /* Paint the window (and draw the bitmap). */

    GetClientRect(hwnd, &rect);
    InvalidateRect(hwnd, &rect, TRUE);
    UpdateWindow(hwnd);
```

Once the bitmap data is retrieved, the bitmapped image can be drawn in the application's client area. The following example shows the code required to draw the bitmap.

```
case WM_PAINT:
    BeginPaint(hwnd, &ps);
        if (fDisplayBitmap) {
            hdcMem = CreateCompatibleDC(hdc);
            SelectObject(hdcMem, hbm);
            GetObject(hbm, sizeof(BITMAP), (LPSTR) &bm);
            BitBlt(hdc, 0, 0, bmih.biWidth, bmih.biHeight,
                hdcMem, 0, 0, SRCCOPY);
            DeleteDC(hdcMem);
        }
    EndPaint(hwnd, &ps);
    break;
```

41.2.2 Displaying a Print Dialog Box and Retrieving a Printer Device Context

The first step in printing involves setting up the printer and obtaining a printer device context. In the sample application, the File menu contains two options: Print and Print Setup. By selecting either option, the user can configure the printer. When the user selects the Print Setup option, the Print Setup dialog box is displayed and the user can select a printer, a page orientation, a paper size, and so on. When the user selects the Print option, the Print dialog box is displayed and the user can select a range of pages, a print quality, a number of copies, and so on. The user can also display the Print Setup dialog box by clicking the Setup push button. The following illustration shows the Print dialog box that appears when the user selects the Print option.

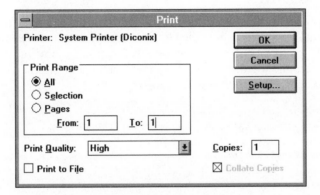

The Print and the Print Setup dialog boxes are both displayed by initializing the members of a **PRINTDLG** structure and calling the **PrintDlg** function. (For more information about displaying the Print Setup dialog box, see Chapter 76, "Common Dialog Box Library.") In addition to retrieving user-specified data, the **PrintDlg** function can be used to obtain a printer device context by setting the **Flags** member of **PRINTDLG** to PD_RETURNDC. The following example code shows how this can be done.

```
/* Initialize the PRINTDLG members. */

pd.lStructSize = sizeof(PRINTDLG);
pd.hDevMode = (HANDLE) NULL;
pd.hDevNames = (HANDLE) NULL;
pd.Flags = PD_RETURNDC;
pd.hwndOwner = hwnd;
pd.hDC = (HDC) NULL;
pd.nFromPage = 1;
pd.nToPage = 1;
pd.nMinPage = 0;
```

```
pd.nMaxPage = 0;
pd.nCopies = 1;
pd.hInstance = (HANDLE) NULL;
pd.lCustData = 0L;
pd.lpfnPrintHook = (LPPRINTHOOKPROC) NULL;
pd.lpfnSetupHook = (LPSETUPHOOKPROC) NULL;
pd.lpPrintTemplateName = (LPSTR) NULL;
pd.lpSetupTemplateName = (LPSTR)  NULL;
pd.hPrintTemplate = (HANDLE) NULL;
pd.hSetupTemplate = (HANDLE) NULL;

/* Display the PRINT dialog box. */

PrintDlg(&pd);
```

41.2.3 Preparing to Print

The following code sample determines whether the selected printer is capable of printing bitmaps by calling the **GetDeviceCaps** function and specifying the RASTERCAPS flag. By examining this function's return value, the application can determine whether it should print a document or inform the user that the device does not support raster output.

```
/*
 * Examine the raster capabilities of the device
 * identified by pd.hDC to verify that it supports
 * the BitBlt function.
 */

if (!(GetDeviceCaps(pd.hDC, RASTERCAPS)
    & RC_BITBLT)) {
    DeleteDC(pd.hDC);
    MessageBox(hwnd,
        "Printer cannot display bitmaps.",
        "Device Error",
        MB_OK);
    break;
}
```

After the sample application determines that the selected printer is capable of printing bitmaps, it follows these steps:

1. Sets a Boolean flag that the application's abort procedure can examine to determine whether to allow printing to continue.

2. Registers the application's print-job abort function.

3. Displays a modeless Cancel dialog box.

4. Disables the application's window while the dialog box is displayed.

```
/*
 * Set the flag used by the AbortPrintJob
 * dialog procedure.
 */

bPrint = TRUE;


/*
 * Register the application's AbortProc
 * function with GDI.
 */

SetAbortProc(pd.hDC, AbortProc);

/* Display the modeless Cancel dialog box. */

hdlgCancel = CreateDialog(hinst, (LPTSTR) "AbortDlg",
    hwnd, (DLGPROC) AbortPrintJob);

/* Disable the application's window. */

EnableWindow(hwnd, FALSE);
```

Once the application registers its abort procedure with Windows, GDI calls the procedure repeatedly during the printing process to determine whether to cancel a job. In the current version of the Win32 API, GDI calls this function approximately every 2 seconds until the entire job has been spooled.

If the user does choose to cancel the job, GDI notifies the spooler that it should delete the corresponding journal file from the print queue and reset the printer to its default state.

41.2.3.1 The Abort Procedure

Any application written for Windows that supports printing should provide an abort procedure and a modeless dialog that allow a user to cancel a print job. The abort procedure for the sample application contains a message loop that retrieves messages for the modeless dialog box.

```
BOOL CALLBACK AbortProc(HDC hdc, int nCode)
{
    MSG msg;

    /*
     * Retrieve and remove messages from the thread's message
     * queue.
     */
```

```
while (PeekMessage((LPMSG) &msg, (HWND) NULL,
        0, 0, PM_REMOVE)) {

    /* Process any messages for the Cancel dialog box. */

    if (!IsDialogMessage(hdlgCancel, (LPMSG) &msg)) {
        TranslateMessage((LPMSG) &msg);
        DispatchMessage((LPMSG) &msg);
    }
}

/*
 * Return the global bPrint flag (which is set to FALSE
 * if the user presses the Cancel button).
 */

return bPrint;

}
```

This procedure must be exported in the application's module-definition file.

41.2.3.2 The Cancel Dialog Box

The Cancel dialog box typically contains a single push button that allows the user to cancel a print job. The following template for the Cancel dialog box was taken from the application's resource file.

```
AbortDlg DIALOG LOADONCALL MOVEABLE DISCARDABLE 33, 32, 160, 70

CAPTION "Sample Printing App"

STYLE WS_BORDER | WS_CAPTION | WS_DLGFRAME | WS_VISIBLE |
    WS_POPUP | WS_SYSMENU

BEGIN

    CONTROL "Now Printing: ", IDD_TEXT, "static",
        SS_CENTER | WS_CHILD, 0, 10, 160, 8

    CONTROL "", IDD_FILE, "static",
        SS_CENTER | WS_CHILD, 0, 25, 160, 8

    CONTROL "Cancel", IDD_CANCEL, "button",
        BS_DEFPUSHBUTTON | WS_TABSTOP | WS_CHILD,
        60, 45, 45, 15

END
```

The example code that follows shows the dialog box procedure for the sample application.

```
LRESULT CALLBACK AbortPrintJob(
        HWND hwndDlg,               /* window handle of dialog box   */
        UINT message,               /* type of message              */
        WPARAM wParam,              /* message-specific information  */
        LPARAM lParam)              /* message-specific information  */
{
    switch (message) {
        case WM_INITDIALOG: /* message: initialize dialog box  */

            /* Initialize the static text control. */

            SetDlgItemText(hwndDlg, IDD_FILE, ofn.lpstrFile);

            return TRUE;


        case WM_COMMAND: /* message: received a command */

            /* User pressed "Cancel" button--stop print job. */

            MessageBox(hwndDlg, "Incoming", "WM_COMMAND", MB_OK);

            bPrint = FALSE;

            return TRUE;

        default:
            return FALSE;               /* didn't process a message   */

    }
        UNREFERENCED_PARAMETER(lParam);
        UNREFERENCED_PARAMETER(wParam);
        UNREFERENCED_PARAMETER(message);
}
```

41.2.4 Printing a Document

Once the application initializes the necessary variables, registers its abort procedure, and displays its modeless Cancel dialog box, it can start the print job by calling the **StartDoc** function.

After the application begins a print job, it can define individual pages in the document by calling the **StartPage** and **EndPage** functions and embedding the appropriate GDI drawing function calls within this bracket. After the application has defined the last page, it can close the document and end the print job by calling the **EndDoc** function.

The following example shows the code required to print a string of text and a bitmapped image. The string of text, centered at the top of the page, identifies the path and file name for the file that contains the bitmapped image. The bitmapped image, centered vertically and horizontally on the page, is drawn while maintaining the same proportions used to draw the image in the application's client area.

```
/*
 * Initialize the members of a DOCINFO
 * structure.
 */

di.cbSize = sizeof(DOCINFO);
di.lpszDocName = "Bitmap Printing Test";
di.lpszOutput = (LPTSTR) NULL;

/*
 * Begin a print job by calling the StartDoc
 * function.
 */

nError = StartDoc(pd.hDC, &di);
if (nError == SP_ERROR) {
    errhandler("StartDoc", hwnd);
    goto Error;
    }

/*
 * Inform the driver that the application is
 * about to begin sending data.
 */

nError = StartPage(pd.hDC);
if (nError <= 0) {
    errhandler("StartPage", hwnd);
    goto Error;
    }

/*
 * Retrieve the number of pixels-per-logical-inch
 * in the horizontal and vertical directions
 * for the display upon which the bitmap
 * was created.
 */

fLogPelsX1 = (float) GetDeviceCaps(hdc, LOGPIXELSX);
fLogPelsY1 = (float) GetDeviceCaps(hdc, LOGPIXELSY);
```

```
/*
 * Retrieve the number of pixels-per-logical-inch
 * in the horizontal and vertical directions
 * for the printer upon which the bitmap
 * will be printed.
 */

fLogPelsX2 = (float) GetDeviceCaps(pd.hDC, LOGPIXELSX);
fLogPelsY2 = (float) GetDeviceCaps(pd.hDC, LOGPIXELSY);

/*
 * Determine the scaling factors required to
 * print the bitmap and retain its original
 * proportions.
 */

if (fLogPelsX1 > fLogPelsX2)
    fScaleX = (fLogPelsX1 / fLogPelsX2);
else
    fScaleX = (fLogPelsX2 / fLogPelsX1);

if (fLogPelsY1 > fLogPelsY2)
    fScaleY = (fLogPelsY1 / fLogPelsY2);
else
    fScaleY = (fLogPelsY2 / fLogPelsY1);

/*
 * Compute the coordinate of the upper left
 * corner of the centered bitmap.
 */

cWidthPels = GetDeviceCaps(pd.hDC, HORZRES);
xLeft = ((cWidthPels / 2) -
            ((int) (((float) bmih.biWidth) * fScaleX)) / 2);
cHeightPels = GetDeviceCaps(pd.hDC, VERTRES);
yTop = ((cHeightPels / 2) -
            ((int) (((float) bmih.biHeight) * fScaleY)) / 2);

/*
 * Create a memory DC that is compatible with
 * the printer and select the bitmap (which
 * the user requested) into this DC.
 */

hdcMem = CreateCompatibleDC(pd.hDC);

if (!SelectObject(hdcMem, hbm))
    errhandler("SelectObject Failed", hwnd);
```

```
/*
 * Use the StretchBlt function to scale the
 * bitmap and maintain its original proportions
 * (that is, if the bitmap was square when it
 * appeared in the application's client area,
 * it should also appear square on the page).
 */


if (!StretchBlt(pd.hDC, xLeft, yTop,
        (int) ((float) bmih.biWidth * fScaleX),
        (int) ((float) bmih.biHeight * fScaleY),
        hdcMem, 0, 0,
        bmih.biWidth, bmih.biHeight,
        SRCCOPY))
    errhandler("StretchBlt Failed", hwnd);


/* Delete the memory DC. */

DeleteDC(hdcMem);

/*
 * Retrieve the width of the string that
 * specifies the full path and filename for the
 * file that contains the bitmap.
 */

GetTextExtentPoint(pd.hDC, ofn.lpstrFile,
    ofn.nFileExtension + 3,
    &szMetric);

/*
 * Compute the starting point for the
 * text-output operation. The string will
 * be centered horizontally and positioned
 * three-lines down from the top of the page.
 */

xLeft = ((cWidthPels / 2) - (szMetric.cx / 2));
yTop = (szMetric.cy * 3);
```

```
        /*
         * Print the path and filename for the bitmap,
         * centered at the top of the page.
         */

        TextOut(pd.hDC, xLeft, yTop, ofn.lpstrFile,
            ofn.nFileExtension + 3);

        /*
         * Determine whether the user has pressed
         * the Cancel button in the AbortPrintJob
         * dialog box; if the button has been pressed,
         * call the AbortDoc function. Otherwise, inform
         * the spooler that the page is complete.
         */

        nError = EndPage(pd.hDC);

        if (nError <= 0) {
            errhandler("EndPage", hwnd);
            goto Error;
        }

    /* Inform the driver that the document has ended. */

        nError = EndDoc(pd.hDC);
        if (nError <= 0) {
            errhandler("EndDoc", hwnd);
        }

Error:

    /* Enable the application's window. */

    EnableWindow(hwnd, TRUE);

    /* Remove the AbortPrintJob dialog box. */

    DestroyWindow(hdlgCancel);

    /* Delete the printer DC. */

    DeleteDC(pd.hDC);
```

Because the pixels on a screen typically have different dimensions than the dots on a printer, it is necessary to scale bitmapped images to obtain WYSIWYG output. This is done by first obtaining horizontal and vertical scaling factors, then applying these factors to the width and height values passed to the bitmap drawing function **StretchBlt**. In the sample application, these scaling factors were obtained by retrieving the horizontal and vertical logical-pixel count for the two devices. Once the scaling factors were obtained, they were used to adjust the bitmap width and height.

To center the bitmap on the page, the application first computed the width and height of the scaled bitmap. (The bitmap was scaled in order to maintain the original proportions of the image.) These values were divided by two and then subtracted from half of the width and height of the page. The results define the coordinates of the upper left corner of the bitmap.

To center the text at the top of the page, the application retrieved the width and height of the string specifying the path names and filenames by calling the **GetTextExtentPoint** function. Once these values were obtained, the application used the height to position the string three lines down the page and the width to position the string horizontally centered on the page.

The following illustration shows a representation of the page that appeared when the application printed the bitmapped image in the file WINLOGO.BMP. This illustration also depicts the variables used to position the text and to position and scale the bitmap.

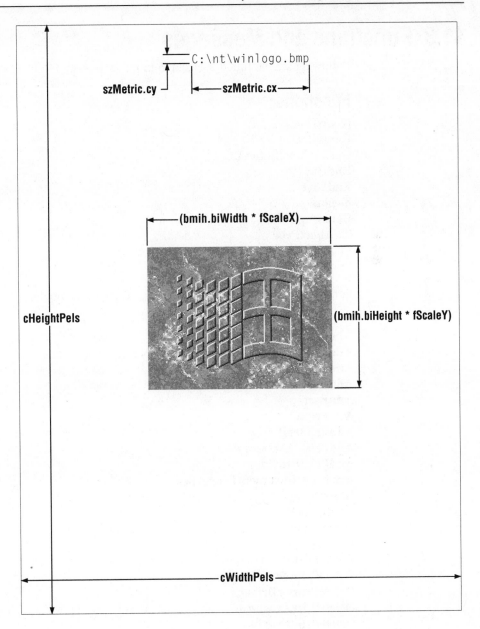

41.3 Functions and Messages

Following are the functions used to print.

Functions

AbortDoc
CancelDC
DeviceCapabilitiesEx
EndDoc
EndPage
Escape
ExtEscape
SetAbortProc
StartDoc
StartPage

Following are the functions used to access the print spooler.

AbortPrinter
AbortProc
AddForm
AddJob
AddMonitor
AddPort
AddPrinter
AddPrinterDriver
AddPrintProcessor
AddPrintProvidor
AdvancedDocumentProperties
ClosePrinter
ConfigurePort
DeleteForm
DeleteMonitor
DeletePort
DeletePrinter
DeletePrinterDriver
DeletePrintProcessor
DeletePrintProvidor
DocumentProperties
EndDocPrinter
EndPagePrinter
EnumForms
EnumJobs
EnumMonitors
EnumPorts

EnumPrinterDrivers
EnumPrinters
EnumPrintProcessors
GetForm
GetJob
GetPrinter
GetPrinterData
GetPrinterDriver
GetPrinterDriverDirectory
GetPrintProcessorDirectory
OpenPrinter
PrinterProperties
ReadPrinter
ScheduleJob
SetForm
SetJob
SetPrinter
SetPrinterData
StartDocPrinter
StartPagePrinter
WritePrinter

Messages

WM_SPOOLERSTATUS

Comprehensive Index

Key

A

B

G

General window styles, described V1 13
GenerateConsoleCtrlEvent function V2 350
Generic access rights, overview of V2 134
Generic data types, using V2 253–254
Generic function prototype V2 248–249
GENERIC_MAPPING structure V2 134, 135
Geometric pens V1 634–635
GetAce function V2 133
GetACP function V2 243
GetActiveWindow function V1 21, 83
GetArcDirection function V1 662
GetAsyncKeyState function V1 88
GetAtomName function V2 412
GetBkMode function V1 699
GetBoundsRect function V1 441
GetBrushOrgEx function V1 620
GetCapture function V1 105
GetCaretBlinkTime function V1 474, 479
GetCaretPos function V1 474
GetCharABCWidths function V1 700, 712, 716
GetCharABCWidthsFloat function V1 700
GetCharWidth function V1 700, 712, 716
GetCharWidthFloat function V1 700
GetClassInfo function V1 58, 74
GetClassLong function V1 58, 63
GetClassName function V1 59
GetClassWord function V1 63
GetClientRect function V1 26, 777
GetClipboardData function V1 512
GetClipBox function V1 437
GetClipCursor function V1 459, 464
GetCommandLine function V2 58, 253
GetCommMask function V2 510
GetCommModemStatus function V2 511
GetCommProperties function V2 506
GetCommState function V2 505
GetCommTimeouts function V2 508
GetComputerName function V2 490, 492
GetConsoleCP function V2 348
GetConsoleCursorInfo function V2 334, 337
GetConsoleMode function V2 334, 340, 341, 344
GetConsoleOutputCP function V2 348
GetConsoleScreenBufferInfo function
    cursor position, determining V2 338
    example of using V2 360
    overview V2 334
    text attributes, determining V2 338
    window rectangle, determining V2 335
GetCPInfo function V2 244

GetCurrentDirectory function V2 82, 91
GetCurrentObject function V1 588, 589, 595
GetCurrentProcess function V2 33
GetCurrentProcessId function V2 33
GetCurrentThread function V2 33
GetCurrentThreadId function V1 50, V2 33
GetCurrentTime function V2 404
GetCursorPos function V1 458, 465, 470
GetDC function
    cache of display device contexts V1 434
    class display device contexts V1 438
    clipping region V1 429
    common display device contexts V1 436, 587
    drawing at timed intervals V1 450–453
    drawing with the mouse V1 449–450
    drawing without using a WM_PAINT message V1 427
    obtaining a display device context V1 586
    parent display device contexts V1 439–440
    private display device contexts V1 437, 587
    reference device context V1 774
    window update locks V1 440
GetDCEx function
    clipping region V1 429
    common display device contexts V1 587
    drawing without using a WM_PAINT message V1 427
    locked window, drawing over V1 441
    private display device contexts V1 438, 587
    window display device context V1 439
GetDeviceCaps function
    aspect ratio, retrieving V1 763
    color bits, retrieving the number of V1 602
    color format, retrieving V1 604
    custom logical palette V1 728
    dimensions of output devices, retrieving V1 702
    display device data, retrieving V1 280
    fonts supported by a printer, determining V1 708
    overview V1 590
    printer capabilities, retrieving V1 595
    system palette V1 726–727
GetDialogBaseUnits function V1 380
GetDiskFreeSpace function V2 83
GetDlgCtrlID function V1 151, 404
GetDlgItem function V1 386, 404
GetDlgItemInt function V1 207, 395, 402
GetDlgItemText function V1 202, 394, 399
GetDoubleClickTime function V1 107
GetDriveType function V2 83
GetEnhMetaFile function V1 780
GetEnhMetaFileBits function V1 775
GetEnhMetaFileDescription function V1 775
GetEnhMetaFileHeader function V1 775